neXus

THE WORLD HOUSE CHURCH MOVEMENT READER

D1237076

neXus

THE WORLD HOUSE CHURCH MOVEMENT READER

EDITOR RAD ZDERO

WILLIAM CAREY
LIBRARY

BIBLE VERSIONS QUOTED THROUGHOUT THIS BOOK

ESV—The Holy Bible, English Standard Version. Copyright © 2001 by Crossway Bibles, a division of Good News Publishers. All rights reserved.

KJV—The Holy Bible, King James Version. Copyright © 1977, 1984, Thomas Nelson Inc., Publishers.

LB—The Living Bible, © 1971, owned by assignment by Illinois Regional Bank N.A. (as trustee), Tyndale House Publishers, Inc., Wheaton, IL 60189.

The Message—The Message: The Bible in Contemporary Language. Copyright © by Eugene H. Peterson, 1993, 1994, 1995. Used by permission of NavPress Publishing Group.

NASB—New American Standard Bible translation. Copyright © 1960, 1962, 1963, 1968, 1971, 1972, 1973, 1975, 1977, 1995, by The Lockman Foundation. All rights reserved.

NEB—The New English Bible © The Delegates of the Oxford University Press and The Syndics of the Cambridge University Press, 1961, 1970.

NIV—Scripture taken from the HOLY BIBLE, NEW INTERNATIONAL VERSION ® Copyright © 1973, 1978, 1984 by International Bible Society. Used by permission of Zondervan Publishing House. All Rights Reserved.

NLT—The Holy Bible, New Living Translation, copyright © 1996. Used by permission of Tyndale House Publishers, Inc., Wheaton, IL, 60189. All rights reserved.

RSV—The Revised Standard Version of the Bible, copyright © 1946, 1952, 1971, 1973 by the Division of Christian Education of the National Council of the Churches of Christ in the USA.

TEV—Today's English Version, the Good News Bible, Old Testament copyright © American Bible Society 1976, New Testament copyright © American Bible Society 1966, 1971, 1976.

TNIV—Holy Bible, Today's New International Version ® TNIV ® Copyright © 2001, 2005 by International Bible Society ®. All rights reserved worldwide.

LIBRARY OF CONGRESS CATALOGING IN PUBLICATION DATA

Main entry under title: *NEXUS: The World House Church Movement Reader* / edited by Zdero, Radovan (Rad), 1969—
Includes Bibliographical References and Indexes
1. Missions.   2. Evangelism.   3. Biblical Studies.   4. Church History.
ISBN: 9780878084593
Printed in the United States of America

DISCLAIMER

Though all contributing authors fully endorse the general theme of this book, individual authors do not necessarily endorse the chapters written by others or their ministries.

FOREWORD

As the body of Christ grows from the infant to the toddler stage, it is seeking direction for its journey forward. It has gradually stepped around the barrier of old wineskins and has come to view different infrastructures.

Our view is often limited. Old paradigms are blinders, making it impossible to see peripherally. To describe it another way, we now "see through a glass darkly."

As we step forward, we must see the emerging Last Days wineskin for Christ's *ekklesia*. It does not yet exist. Should the Lord tarry, perhaps it will arise in the last half of this century. Can we set our vision to pioneer its lifestyle?

Consider this definition, the theme of my forthcoming, yet untitled, book: *Christ's Basic Body is a community selected and baptized by the Holy Spirit. They are led by the embodied Christ, who edifies and reveals His presence and power through them.*

We must understand the body of Christ is not defined by a meeting place (whether in a house or elsewhere), but by her participation as the Bride serving her Husband. It must be positioned wherever He places her to reveal His Presence and Power. If an assembly of Christians is not a participant in Christ's present task—declaring the Kingdom to specific groups—it is an anomaly!

The most sacred body on the face of the earth is the authentic *ekklesia*. It will be intimately associated with the indwelling Christ, exposing unbelievers and the ungifted to Him, causing them to cry out, "God is certainly among you!"

It will share its message by observation of its body life, clothed with love and performing edification ministry. It will be a friend of "winebibbers and sinners," not a monastic community withdrawn from the society that surrounds it.

Let us not stop our journey to focus on structure when we should be seeking the final expression that will bring back the King! This book is an awesome collection of writings to assist in our search for what will emerge.

Ralph Neighbour, D.Min.
Author of Where Do We Go From Here?
Touch Outreach Ministries (www.touchusa.org)

WELCOME TO THE *NEXUS* !

Dear reader, this is your point of connection—your nexus—to today's world house church movement! The book you hold in your hand is not merely meant to satisfy your curiosity about what God is accomplishing in various places around the globe through other people. Yes, it will help you discover how God is building himself an army of ordinary folks to accomplish great exploits for his kingdom. But, it is also meant to stir you up so that you will actually go forth and become part of this revolutionary force of grassroots, living, breathing Christianity. The *Nexus* was deliberately designed with your training and learning in mind, with study questions at the end of each chapter that will provoke you to pray, think, feel, and act!

THE WINDS OF CHANGE ARE BLOWING THROUGH THE CHURCH

The church of Jesus Christ has always adapted itself to new circumstances and contexts. But, today's changes are happening on a massive scale unseen in history. A fresh Christianity is on the rise all around the world. God is bringing back the power and simplicity of grassroots, New Testament-style Christianity to the earth. This is not driven by human genius or plans, but rather by the Spirit of God blowing through the church, cleansing it, shaking it, changing it, stretching it, and preparing it to better deal with the persecution, poverty, unity, and revival of the years ahead. The Lord himself is raising up the world house church movement.

Recently, unprecedented numbers of people have come to faith in Christ and then launched out to plant new communities of faith, repeating the process over and over again. This phenomenon is sweeping across many parts of the globe. Consider the following. Northern India has seen 4,000 churches planted in just a decade. Latin America witnessed two Baptist unions surmount persecution to grow from 235 to 3,200 churches in a mere eight years. China saw 160,000 new Chinese believers baptized in a single year. Ethiopia underwent a decade of persecution by Marxist authorities, under whose harsh watch a Pentecostal denomination grew from 5,000 to 50,000 believers through underground house groups. Cuba's petrol crisis catalyzed the growth of between 6,000 and 10,000 multiplying house churches from 1992 to 2000. Cambodia saw the start of 220 house churches with 10,000 new believers from 1992 to 2001. The USA witnessed Dove Christian Fellowship grow in 20 years from three cell groups totaling 25 people to 80 cell group and house church networks spread across five continents and encompassing over 20,000 people. In less than a decade, the USA-based Church Multiplication Associates started 1,000 churches that meet in homes, offices, and just about anywhere.

What is happening in all these diverse places? The answer: *saturation church planting through simple, inexpensive, reproducible, and missional congregations of 'house churches'*. Research on mission work around the globe has discovered that the most rapidly growing church planting and evangelistic strategies today utilize home-based and house-sized churches.

WHAT'S THE DIFFERENCE BETWEEN SMALL GROUPS, CELL GROUPS, AND HOUSE CHURCHES?

The question that now naturally arises is: What's the difference between small groups, cell groups, and the main topic of this book, namely, house churches? Many believers today participate in 'small groups', such as Bible study groups, prayer groups, accountability groups, affinity groups, etc. However, 'small groups' are often utilized differently in various types of churches, which will be broadly classified here for the purpose of discussion as traditional churches, cell churches, and house church networks. Small groups in all three styles of churches usually meet in homes and encourage the participation of believers. But, that's where the similarities end. While we must clearly recognize and celebrate the hand of God in all manner of churches, there are important differences between traditional churches, cell churches, and house churches that should be understood. On one end of the spectrum, for instance, is the *traditional church* that only infrequently uses small groups (often misnamed 'cell groups')—this can be described as a 'church *WITH* small groups.' Further along the spectrum is the *cell church* that places an equal or greater emphasis on its mission-minded small groups (properly called 'cell groups') compared to its weekly large group services—this can be described as a 'church *OF* small groups.' However, the *house church network* sees each house church as a fully fledged, autonomous, church in itself—this can be explained by the principle that 'church *IS* small groups' (see diagram).

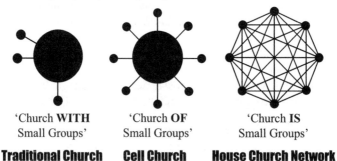

'Church **WITH** Small Groups'	'Church **OF** Small Groups'	'Church **IS** Small Groups'
Traditional Church	**Cell Church**	**House Church Network**

WHAT IS A HOUSE CHURCH?

Let us describe the 'house church' in more detail, drawing out points of contrast with small groups and cell groups where necessary. Though exceptions and variations appear even in this book, the following description is generally reflective of the world house church movement today.

Firstly, house churches are an attempt to get back to early grassroots Christianity by following the New Testament pattern. The term 'house church' is just a convenient label that involves a much broader effort to see the pattern and power, the simplicity and strategy, of the early church fully restored. This involves far more than seeing small groups of believers meeting in living rooms and around kitchen tables for prayer and Bible study. House churches, rather, intentionally wish to implement sweeping changes to both church function and form back to a more streamlined New Testament blueprint, so that more people can be effectively reached for Christ. House churches, therefore, are part of a 'restoration' of biblical church life for the sake of biblical mission. Traditional churches, on the other hand, use small groups as an optional 'enhancement' program for an otherwise traditional church system that includes church buildings, hierarchical leadership systems, preplanned worship services, and expensive programs. Cell churches, though sharing the same passion for biblical mission and church renewal as the house church movement, still retain some traditional organizational features.

Secondly, house churches are fully functioning churches in and of themselves. Consequently, they engage in a full range of activities like the Lord's Supper, baptisms, burials, marriages, money management, church discipline, and charting their own course. They gather in homes for interactive meetings that involve worship and prayer, Bible discovery and discussion, mentoring and evangelism, mutual ministry and encouragement, as well as food and fun. Each house church is commonly facilitated by a co-equal team of unpaid leaders. Traditional churches, however, often do not fully release their small groups to be the church in many of these matters. Cell churches often go much further than their traditional counterparts in empowering cell group members for ministry inside and outside the cell.

Thirdly, house churches are self-governing with regard to their own internal affairs. This means that decision-making responsibility rests with the group itself by consensus of all its members. Thus, a house church does not require permission for its activities from a formal paid minister or even other house churches, nor is it part of a highly centralized church system. As such, these groups more easily adapt to persecution, growth, and change. Both traditional small groups and even cell groups, though, in many matters must seek permission or guidance from a formal pastor, a zone leader, a church board, or some other vertical chain of command.

Fourthly, house church meetings are open to the leading of the Spirit of God. These meetings allow everyone's spiritual gifts to be used, since they are participatory, interactive, spontaneous, and Spirit-led (1 Cor 14:26, Col 3:16). Jesus is the Master of Ceremonies who leads each member and directs the meeting. There are no one-man shows or a few active people performing for a crowd of spectators. Everyone can become involved. Traditional small groups and cell groups, in contrast, often have a preplanned agenda for meetings, though cell groups by design wish to allow the Spirit to lead them in making a positive impact on non-believers.

Fifthly, house churches are formed with the intention of growth through the multiplication of new house churches. These simple faith communities desire to be active, reproducing, neighborhood mission outposts which see people come to Christ, grow in faith, get trained, and launch out as ambassadors of hope to repeat the process in unreached areas by planting other house churches. This is a deliberate strategy on the part of today's house church movement. Many traditional church and cell church planting approaches, however, use an initial 'home group' as a vehicle for the birth of a larger centralized congregation equipped with a building, paid senior pastor, and programmed Sunday morning worship service.

Sixthly, house churches form cohesive networks with one another as peers and partners in a 'decentralized' way. Isolated house churches tend not to be healthy and do not survive for too long. Vibrant house churches, however, unite together into networks for mutual encouragement, accountability, resourcing, and training. As such, there are three strands that often connect autonomous house churches together into clusters, namely, (a) mobile 'circuit riders' that travel from group-to-group and place-to-place, (b) house church leaders' meetings that are held on a regular basis, and (c) city-wide or regional events that happen occasionally such as conferences and celebrations. However, this is done less formally than with cell churches, in which cell groups are but one part of a larger church system that has a leadership structure that is fixed, multi-layered, and 'centralized'.

THE BOOK IN YOUR HAND

Do you want to reach people with an approach to church life and church planting that is biblical, simple, inexpensive, reproducible, and a training ground for launching new leaders? Do you want to start a vibrant network of multiplying house churches right where you live? If so, this book is for you.

The contributing authors are practitioners, leaders, and academics from all over the world with many years of involvement in the 'revitalization' of the Body of Christ. Their collective wisdom is provided in six main parts:

Part 1. God's Passion for the World
Part 2. The New Testament Origins of House Churches
Part 3. House Church and Small Group Movements through the Ages
Part 4. House Church Movements on the World Scene Today
Part 5. Practical Lessons in Starting a House Church Network
Part 6. Strategic Directions for Launching House Church Movements

It is with the compelling hope of seeing many, new, vibrant, house church movements launched which reach, heal, and transform the nations for Jesus Christ, that this work is offered. Once again, welcome to the *Nexus*! Let's be about our Master's business!

Rad Zdero (Editor)
Toronto, Canada
May 2007

CONTENTS

PART 3. HOUSE CHURCH AND SMALL GROUP MOVEMENTS THROUGH THE AGES

PART 4. HOUSES CHURCH MOVEMENTS ON THE WORLD SCENE TODAY

PART 5. PRACTICAL LESSONS IN STARTING A HOUSE CHURCH NETWORK

PART 6. STRATEGIC DIRECTIONS FOR LAUNCHING HOUSE CHURCH MOVEMENTS

PART 1

GOD'S PASSION
FOR
THE WORLD

Chapter 1

THE GREAT COMMISSION: BASIC VISION, BASIC TASKS, AND BASIC CHANGES

VICTOR CHOUDHRIE

Victor Choudhrie is a well respected and accomplished former cancer surgeon. He received his training in India and is a fellow of the Royal College of Surgeons in the U.K., the American College of Surgeons, and the International College of Surgeons. In 1992, he and his wife Bindu began a full-time church planting ministry that has resulted in thousands of house churches planted in India and around the world. [Adapted from Victor Choudhrie (2005), Greet the Ekklesia in Your House. Used by permission of the author. Email: vchoudhrie@gmail.com].

INTRODUCTION

Jesus Christ's passion for the world is so vast that he willingly died to bridge the gap between God and humanity. He is looking for a people like himself, a people who will dare to 'stand in the gap'. The Lord Jesus, in his Great Commission to the church, told his followers to go out into the world and make disciples of all nations. Sadly, a Christian believer or Christian church that is not passionately and practically seeking to fulfill the Great Commission is, in effect, neutered because it has lost both the desire and the DNA to reproduce and multiply. We are out of sync with God's vision if our vision is limited only to the welfare of our family, our church, or our city. These are only platforms for launching out into the world to make disciples of all nations. The Great Commission should be the signature tune of every believer and church. In the following, we will explore the basic vision, the basic tasks, and the basic changes needed to accomplish the Great Commission.

THE BASIC VISION OF THE GREAT COMMISSION

What is the Great Commission?

The Great Commission is the homework assignment that Jesus gave to his church just prior to his return to the heavenly realm. Linked with it are compassion, challenge, and command. It comes from Jesus' heart of compassion—he desires that none should perish and that all should be reconciled back to God! It is a challenge because Jesus has a vision to see the whole world reached—there is no endeavor grander in scope for us to imagine! It is also a command because Jesus asked us to do it—there is no way for us, with Christ as our Lord, to avoid this duty!

The Great Commission was stated by Jesus in several different ways, at several different times, and to several different groups of disciples. He wanted to drive home the point.

In the Gospel of Matthew, Jesus says:

> All authority has been given to Me in heaven and on earth. Go therefore and make disciples of all the nations, baptizing them in the name of the Father and the Son and the Holy Spirit, teaching them to observe all that I commanded you; and lo, I am with you always, even to the end of the age.[1]

In the Gospel of Mark, Jesus says:

> Go into all the world and preach the gospel to all creation. He who has believed and has been baptized shall be saved; but he who has disbelieved shall be condemned.[2]

In the Gospel of Luke, Jesus says:

> Thus it is written, that the Christ would suffer and rise again from the dead the third day, and that repentance for forgiveness of sins would be proclaimed in His name to all the nations, beginning from Jerusalem. You are witnesses of these things.[3]

In the Gospel of John, Jesus says:

> Peace be with you; as the Father has sent Me, I also send you...Receive the Holy Spirit. If you forgive the sins of any, their sins have been forgiven them; if you retain the sins of any, they have been retained.[4]

In the book of Acts, Jesus says:

> But you will receive power when the Holy Spirit has come upon you; and you shall be My witnesses both in Jerusalem, and in all Judea and Samaria, and even to the remotest part of the earth.[5]

World Evangelization

World evangelization is the goal, the crux of the business, and the essence of the mission that Jesus gave to the church. We must pursue this with apostolic and prophetic zeal. We must prioritize this agenda over all others. There are millions of villages and cities in the world. Every person must be

---

[1] Matt 28:18-20 (NASB)
[2] Mark 16:15-16 (NASB)
[3] Luke 24:46-48 (NASB)
[4] John 20:21-23 (NASB)
[5] Acts 1:8 (NASB)

confronted with the gospel, until they accept or reject it. We cannot say that the whole world has been evangelized until every human habitation has its own witnessing church, its own spiritual lifeline, its own lighthouse of hope.

When the Lord Jesus went to Samaria, he spoke to a woman at a well and told her things about herself and the kingdom of God that deeply impressed her. Not many days later, many of her friends and neighbors throughout the region believed. We are told, "And from that city many of the Samaritans believed in Him because of the word of the woman who testified...and many more believed because of His word."[6]

The Jerusalem church after Pentecost was so successful that it had filled the entire city with its teaching about Jesus. It is reported that the religious authorities confronted the apostles, saying, "We gave you strict orders not to continue teaching in this name, and behold, you have filled Jerusalem with your teaching."[7]

When Philip went to Samaria and preached the gospel and healed all those who came to him, we are told that there was great rejoicing in the entire city. The record tells us that "...Philip went down to the city of Samaria and began proclaiming Christ to them. And the multitudes with one accord were giving attention to what was said by Philip, as they heard and saw the signs which he was performing...And there was much rejoicing in that city."[8]

Through his work in Ephesus for two years, Paul performed signs and wonders, disputed and persuaded, until all who dwelt in Asia heard the gospel. The Scripture says that "...this took place for two years, so that all who lived in Asia heard the word of the Lord, both Jews and Greeks."[9]

Paul claimed to have fully preached the gospel from Jerusalem to Illyricum and that there was no place left unreached. He writes that he did so "in the power of signs and wonders, in the power of the Spirit; so that from Jerusalem and round about as far as Illyricum I have fully preached the gospel of Christ."[10] Actually, he planted only a few regional churches, but through a 'cluster effect' eventually the whole region would be saturated with churches.

These are the appropriate models for us today.

World Discipleship
When Jesus saw the multitude, he was filled with compassion. He did not go away and forget about them. We are not to be just evangelists who preach and then vanish. We are also to be shepherds who take care of the sheep. We

---

[6] John 4:39,41 (NASB)
[7] Acts 5:28 (NASB)
[8] Acts 8:5-7,8 (NASB)
[9] Acts 19:10 (NASB)
[10] Rom 15:19 (NASB)

must disciple people into maturity, so that they too can be prepared to be sent into the world to accomplish the Great Commission.

But, what are the marks of a true disciple?

First, a disciple obeys the Master. Naturally, disciples obey their Master, otherwise, they are not true disciples. When the Lord called Peter, John, and the other fishermen, they left their boats full of fish and followed him.[11] When he told them to go to Jerusalem, Judea, Samaria, and to the ends of the earth as his witnesses, they obeyed him unto death.[12] To qualify as true disciples, we must obey our Master's command to go and make disciples of the people of other faiths or no faith. Jesus said, "And why do you call me 'Lord, Lord,' and do not do what I say?"[13]

Second, a disciple is one who makes other disciples. It does not matter how religious we are, how wonderful our worship service is, or how wonderful our church programs are, if there is no fruit in our lives in 'spiritually reproducing' other disciples, we must question how far along we really are. One of the marks of a disciple is that they make new disciples. Jesus said, "By this is my father glorified, that you bear much fruit, and so prove to be My disciples."[14]

Third, a disciple is willing to make sacrifices. Nobody can serve two masters, the world and the Lord, at the same time. We cannot be true disciples if anything is more important to us than the Lord—whether that be family, friends, career, money, television, hobbies, and even our own lives. Jesus said, "If anyone comes to Me, and does not hate his own father and mother and wife and children and brothers and sisters, yes, and even his own life, he cannot be My disciple."[15]

Fourth, a disciple loves others well. If there is strife and lack of love for others, then we are missing something vital. In the church, it is very important to be of one heart and mind. Lack of love among Christians is sometimes a great obstacle to people coming to Christ. Loving and caring relationships for others, especially the family of believers, proves we are Jesus' followers. Jesus said, "By this all men will know that you are My disciples, if you have love for one another."[16]

THE BASIC TASKS OF THE GREAT COMMISSION

Preaching

Our God is the God of the whole creation. Jesus shed his blood to reconcile the whole creation, not just human beings. Therefore, we must proclaim the good news to the whole creation. Preaching must be accompanied with signs

---

[11] Luke 5:4-11
[12] Acts 1:8
[13] Luke 6:46 (NASB)
[14] John 15:8 (NASB)
[15] Luke 14:26 (NASB)
[16] John 13:35 (NASB)

and wonders and expulsion of demons, demonstrating that God rules both the spiritual and physical realm. This must be done wherever Christ has not been named. Preaching and healing like our Master Jesus must be instant, spontaneous, and extemporaneous. It should be dialogical in character with room for enquiry.[17]

Spiritual Warfare

The church is the army of the Lord of Hosts. To bind and loose in the name of Jesus is the most powerful evangelistic weapon on earth, causing immediate meltdown of the gates of Hell and its angels.[18] It is also the most underutilized weapon, resulting in a church with no firepower.[19] Jesus came to destroy the works of the devil. He seated his church beside him to shoot missiles of the manifold wisdom of God at the prince of the power of the air. We must bind the bully, break the gates of Hell, and release the captives. Only then will the boundaries be breached, new territories opened up, and the apostolic agenda of reaching, multiplying, filling the earth, and blessing every family accomplished.[20]

Strategy for Making Disciples

Disciple-making is a process and not a series of haphazard events. It needs a well-planned, goal-oriented, and time-bound strategy for reaching the unreached. Making disciples of all nations, tribes, and tongues is a deliberate act that comes through praying and preparing. Strategy is not something made annually at a conference, but it should be part of our daily thinking. Jesus taught us to lift up our eyes and see the harvest now.[21]

Community Repentance and Mass Baptism

John the Baptist immediately baptized all those who repented. Jesus baptized more than John, since he is not only a personal savior but also the Lord of nations. Christianity is not just a personal faith, but a community of the faithful, the Body of Christ, wherein all members repent, die to the world, and acknowledge the Lordship of Jesus. When Jonah preached in Nineveh, the king and all the subjects put on sackcloth and ashes, fasted, and repented. Ezra did the same with those who had returned from the Diaspora. Thousands of Jews received baptism at Pentecost in Jerusalem. Even today in some Christian traditions, during the Lent period, people corporately go through a process of repentance, prayer, fasting, and rejuvenation. Individual baptism is rare in the New Testament. Household or community baptism is the general rule.[22] Repentance and baptism are linked in the New

---

[17] Mk 16:15-20; Acts 19:8-11; Rom 15:20; 1 Cor 14:26; Col 1:19,20; 2 Tim 4:2
[18] Zech 14:12
[19] 1 Thess 1:5; 2 Tim 3:5
[20] Gen 1:28; Matt 12:29,16:19; Acts 1:8; Eph 2:2, 6:10-18; 1 John 3:8
[21] John 4:35; Rom 15:20; Philip 3:13-14
[22] Acts 2:37-39,41, 10:44-48, 16:14-16,30-33

Testament.[23] Christian baptism in the early first century church was without delay upon confession of faith and was never a priestly function—any believer could do it.

Breaking Bread

Jesus said that when we gather in his name, we are to remember him in his fellowship meal.[24] Whenever believers come together, eating a communal meal is a central act of worship. This is to be repeated as often as the church comes together. One can also think of breaking bread as the breaking of Christ's body, the church, into many smaller pieces which are multiplied to reach the masses. Breaking bread in the first century church was never a priestly function, because the Lord's Supper was not a religious ritual. Any believer can 'serve' the Lord's Supper.

Equipping

The aim of the church is to make every member of the Body of Christ a fisherman. We should all learn to share whatever we have learned from faithful people and share it with others. The members of the household of God should be equipped for different ministries based on their calling and giftedness, by the five-fold ministries of apostles, prophets, evangelists, shepherds, and teachers.[25] Believers should be equipped to function as priests and kings to reign on the earth now and bring in the righteous kingdom of God to their families, workplaces, neighborhoods, cities, nations, etc. Believers should be equipped in sound doctrine so that they can exhort and challenge those who contradict. Many Christians cannot handle objections raised by skeptics or practitioners of the world's religions and cults. A truly equipped person should be able to deftly handle all their questions and quickly bring them to repentance and baptism.[26]

Sending

We should lay hands on those called believers to send them out two by two to find 'persons of peace' and to plant new churches. Like the demon-infested Gadarene and the sinful Samaritan woman, once delivered, believers can start witnessing immediately to their friends and family and neighbors about the generosity of God in their lives. The testimony of the freshly redeemed is very powerful and opens doors, which can later be entered by others to complete the task. The ultimate function of the apostolic church is to make every believer a 'fisher of men'. Jesus' church is specifically designed and mandated to reach the ends of the earth and make disciples of all nations.[27]

---

[23] Mark 16:16

[24] Acts 20:7; 1 Cor 11:20,24-26, 10:16,17

[25] Eph 4:11-16

[26] 1 Cor 14:26-31; Eph 2:19,20, 4:11,12; 2 Tim 2:2; Rev 5:10

[27] Matt 4:19; Luke 10:19; Acts 1:8, 13:1-3

THE BASIC CHANGES AND THE GREAT COMMISSION

Change has a Cost

In order to accomplish, or at least pursue, the Great Commission, the church needs to be ready and willing to make shifts in its thinking and methodology to become more strategic and biblical. Jesus told people to count the cost. There is always some cost associated with change. When a Jew became a follower of Jesus in the first century, he would often leave the temple, the sabbath, the circumcision, and the sacrifices. He would start fellowshipping in homes, saturate the city with the gospel, and suffer persecution. This is exactly the situation of the early church in Jerusalem after Pentecost. Similarly, today, when a person of another faith or no faith becomes a Christian, there is often a price tag associated with switching allegiances—losing family, friends, community, and sometimes physical life. In the church—or anywhere for that matter—change is often resisted because of the threat of losing control and because of the strangeness of something new. But change, just like in the healthy human body, is a good sign of growth and, therefore, inevitable. If the church navigates changes well, it has the potential of exploding into the world. If it does not, there is always the danger of implosion. One way or the other, there will be a cost.

The Purpose of Systems

Systems are set up to accomplish a specific purpose. If, for instance, the primary purpose of a church is 'worship' through music and song, then a special worship building, a special worship day, a special worship leader or team, a special worship funding stream, and a special worship organizing committee must be put in place. However, none of these items is to be found in the New Testament because that is not the primary mandate that Jesus gave to the church. His primary mandate was the Great Commission—making disciples of all nations. If the real purpose of the church is the fulfillment of the Great Commission, then specific systems must be set up to accomplish this mission.

Strategic Systems

To make this strategy actionable, we need a large number of those especially skilled in evangelism, warfare prayer, disciple-making, church planting, lucid communication, team building, networking, and empowering of ordinary people. Ultimately, success depends on the quality and the quantity of ordinary believers that are adequately equipped. We need to develop administrative systems in the form of translocal apostolic teams that start new churches and ministries, as well as local eldership teams that manage the citywide church. We need to develop financial systems to support translocal apostolic teams and the needy among us. We also need to give up on egos, logos, and titles, and switch from event and celebrity to being highly purpose driven. This process involves learning from those in the actual harvest fields of the world, who genuinely and spontaneously resonate a faith, character, and commitment necessary for such change. All this requires a radical upgrading of the church and the implementation of more strategic systems.

Biblical Systems

The word 'church' to many believers and non-believers often conjures up images of a building, a Sunday service, professional clergy, tithes, pulpits, pews, programming, etc. However, the church, in reality, does not require most of the traditional paraphernalia it has accumulated over the years to accomplish its mission. The blueprint of the New Testament church is in many ways radically different than what we have been doing—it was much more streamlined. This is not about semantics, but about a complete change in form and function. The early Christians were the only people who had no temples, priests, or sacrifices, quietly meeting in small groups in homes and yet growing and multiplying exponentially. They had streamlined churches and streamlined systems. The only real resources the early church had were the Holy Spirit and people. Therefore, we need a more Scripture-based and Spirit-driven approach that actively engages senders,[28] sent ones,[29] equippers,[30] intercessors,[31] encouragers,[32] financers,[33] shelter givers,[34] and helpers,[35] to saturate the neighborhoods, the cities, and the nations with simple, inexpensive, multiplying, home-based, and house-sized churches.

CONCLUSIONS

The Great Commission is the homework assignment that Jesus left for us, the church. If we are to engage it fully we must understand the basic vision before us, undertake the basic tasks at hand, and undergo the basic changes required. Are we willing and able to do so?

STUDY QUESTIONS

1. Describe the basic vision of the Great Commission.
2. Describe the basic tasks of the Great Commission.
3. Do you agree or disagree with the basic changes suggested that the church needs to undergo in order to be better equipped for accomplishing the Great Commission? Explain.

---

[28] Acts 13:1-3; Rom 10:14,15
[29] Luke 10:1-11; Acts 13:1-3
[30] Eph 4:11,12
[31] Eph 6:18; 1 Tim 2:8
[32] Acts 4:36; Rom 16:3-16
[33] Luke 8:1-3; Acts 11:29,30; 2 Cor 9:6-15
[34] Acts 16:14-15; 3 John 1:6-8
[35] John 14:16; Rom 16:2; Heb 13:6

Chapter 2

THE PROMISES OF GOD AND SPIRITUAL GENERATIONS

ROSS RAINS

Ross Rains is the founding facilitator of Pathfinders Fellowships (www.pathfindersfellowships.com), a house church network for ordinary people that focuses on fellowships built around seeker evangelism and discipleship. He also tentmakes as the president of BBL Canada (www.bblforum.com), which mentors Christian CEOs in the marketplace to build business for the glory of God and to extend their business as ministry. Ross served as President of The Navigators of Canada for 13 years, being on Navigator staff for 26 years in total. He also holds an M.Div. degree (Central Baptist Seminary, Toronto, Canada). Ross and his wife Sandy are the parents of four and make their home in London, Canada. Ross's mission is to help Christians to be fruitful and multiply spiritual generations. [Used by permission of the author. Email: ross@pathfindersfellowships.com].

INTRODUCTION

God's passion is to bless the nations through Jesus. He desires that his followers be fruitful and multiply. God is committed to blessing his people in every generation and on behalf of future generations. Such lasting fruitfulness is rooted in God's promises. This chapter provides an overview of the place that the promises of God play in helping Christ's followers to lay the foundations of spiritual generations. As the spiritual descendants of Abraham, believers in Christ have inherited a plan and promises that are as big as the world. Kingdom living and missional activity flow from these belief-centered promises. The historical flow of God's generational promises starts with Abraham and Sarah around 2000 BC. They are personalized in the Psalms, picked up by prophets such as Isaiah, then fulfilled in Christ, freshly inaugurated at Pentecost, and then propelled into the church age by the work of the apostles. God's promises bring us a spiritual heritage, a general calling, and a focusing purpose to the life of the ordinary believer. These enable us to believe God in our daily lives, to extend the kingdom and to *be church* where we live and work. This enables the birthing of subsequent spiritual generations.

PROMISE THEOLOGIES

First, the promises of God provide believers with a framework for conscious discipleship, an earnest following after Christ. The God of the Bible is *Missio Dei*, the sending, going God! The one who sends his Son into the world to live, to love, and to impact lives for the kingdom.

Second, these promises bring theological context to the *purpose-driven* era in which Evangelicals talk much about mission. Yet, as few as 1 to 2% are actually actively identifying with Christ and leading others to faith.[1]

Third, the promises provide specific perspectives and motivators for mission-minded believers who want to believe God for his full will and work through their daily lives, as they live out Christ in the home, the marketplace, or the campus.

Historically, the study of the promises of God has been captured in various schools of thought. *Covenant theology*, simply expressed, adheres to a works view of the Old Testament and a grace view of the New Testament. *Dispensational theology* systematizes several eras of unfolding promises through biblical history. *'Name it and claim it' theology* has been known to take Scriptures out of context to believe God for extraordinary things. From the systematic to the spontaneous, the promises of God have had diverse applications over the centuries, more focused on theological formulas and personal freedoms, than spiritual generations.

So, what are the fundamentals of the promises as they relate to the ordinary man and woman? There are promises that relate to protection and provision, but it is the promises of God for people, spiritual generations, that this chapter examines.

THE PROMISE-MAKER GOD

God Reveals His Purposes in History

God created a universe for the display of his splendor and glory, and put mankind in the unparalleled role of vice-regent of the creation, to rule, steward, and make fruitful.[2] It was to be a heaven on earth, with man obeying God and believing him. God was king and the kingdom of God, the rule of God in the hearts of humanity, was fully in operation in the pre-Fall garden.

When the first man and woman rejected the rule of the Creator-King in their hearts, through disobedience, a fracture occurred in the relationship with God and curse entered into creation. The condition of sin created a labyrinth out of which humankind could not work itself. The operative word is 'work'. It took an act of mercy and grace, on the part of the Creator, to provide a full redemption through the cross and resurrection of Christ. Only by *believing* in this provision, can people be made right with God.[3]

The promises of God for spiritual generations rests on this fundamental truth that the people of God in every generation are to *believe God* for his work in reaching others. Just as salvation does not come about by the will

---

[1] Lorne Sanny (1982), "The Key to World Evangelism", *Discipleship Journal*, Issue 7, January/February.
[2] Gen 1:26
[3] Eph 2:8.9

and capacity of man, so too, the movement of mission is not works-dependent, but belief-dependent.

The substance of the belief is found in the declared promises of God which endure for every generation. The worldwide missionary movement is a *believing movement*, not merely a doing movement. Works of love, service, and proclamation of the gospel are part of the outworking of faith in the promises. The content of belief is the 'promise framework' God makes clear in the Scriptures.

God Expresses His Purposes Through Promises

There is a clear direction in the flow of biblical history which reflects the heart and purposes of God. God expresses his purposes through promises. Just as a father promises a child a good thing for which to look forward, so it is with the people of God. God asks his people only to believe the good things he has promised. The Bible teaches that God is the great promise keeper from eternity past and that his purposes in creation have been revealed in the Scriptures. "The words of the LORD are flawless, like silver refined in a furnace of clay, purified seven times."[4] God has carefully woven promises into the Scriptures that form the basis of the covenants.

God Calls Out a Kingdom People in Every Generation

God is always at work, revealing himself in each generation. It is the account of God's disclosures to Abraham which most clearly inaugurates the idea of spiritual generations. God begins to disclose his purposes by making promises to Abraham. God promised to accomplish three outcomes through Abraham's life. He would be the father of a great nation, namely, Israel.[5] A seed, the Messiah, would come through his family line.[6] And finally, spiritual descendants would follow in every generation after him.[7] The first two have been accomplished. The third is ongoing in each generation, and every believer can be involved.

THE PROMISE-DRIVEN BELIEVER

The Promises of God Meet People in Their Life Context

Forty centuries ago, Abraham was a farmer from Ur of the Chaldees, present day Iraq. He was not a Jew, but an immigrant, commanded by God to move from all that was familiar, to receive what God had purposed, to believe what God had said, and to achieve the outworking of those promises.

There is a rough hewn texture to the promises of God, in that, though rooted in the eternal purposes of God, they are earthly and realistic for the ordinary man and woman. They are simple. There is a progression not only in purpose, but they accommodate the learning style and weaknesses of

---

[4] Ps 12:6 (NIV)
[5] Gen 12:2
[6] Gal 3:16-18
[7] Gal 3:8-9

people. Abraham had the promises of God come to him in three distinct revelations.[8] There was a progression in what was revealed by God. This seems to perfectly match the progression in Abraham's responsiveness.

In the last century, Dawson Trotman, founder of the worldwide evangelism and discipleship organization called The Navigators, was a pacesetter for recovery of a focus on the promises of God:

> In November [1931]...[Daws] found God renewing to him many previous promises for his life work. His conviction was deepening that the Word was far more than an inspired record: it was the living, present voice of God. With due respect to dispensationalists, he still did not feel Scripture should be apportioned to certain peoples for certain times exclusively. In the margin above Jeremiah he wrote, "Is it possible that God wrote this whole Book to one small people, or did He, knowing the end from the beginning write to others herein." And beside Isaiah 58:12 "Given many times when praying about my life work." Why should Christians who claim God's promise of peace from Isaiah 26:3 or forgiveness of sins from Isaiah 1:18 consider the promise in Isaiah 58:12 off limits? Even Isaiah 58:11 "And the Lord shall guide thee continually..." was commonly claimed and quoted. Telling later of God's promises to him from Isaiah for his life work, he explained with a light touch, "Some say the Book of Isaiah is for the Jews. Well it's full of promises, and as I looked around, I didn't see the Jews claiming them—somebody should be using them!"[9]

THE PROMISE-KEEPING CHRIST

God's Promises Find their Fulfillment in Christ

God was thinking of Christ when he said to Abraham, "All peoples on earth will be blessed through you."[10] And, "Through your offspring all nations on earth will be blessed."[11] God was thinking of the cross and of justification through faith in Christ. The apostle Paul reveals the truth of these promises and how they involve believers in every generation.[12]

Christ was the embodiment of the promises of God. The prophecies of the Old Testament were one expression of the flow of God's promises. Over 300 prophecies point to the birth, life, work, and resurrection of the coming

---

[8] Gen 12:1-3, 15:1-5, 17:7
[9] Betty Skinner (1974), *Daws*, Zondervan, p.63. By permission of NavPress.com
[10] Gen 12:3 (NIV)
[11] Gen 22:18 (NIV)
[12] Gal 3:6-9

Messiah. Promises on this level provided intersecting vectors by which later generations could recognize the true Messiah. The Great Commission[13] is Christ's sanction and extension of the promises given to Abraham for the calling out of a kingdom people in every generation. It is God's commitment to reaching people in fulfillment of the promise given to Abraham. Thus, all of God's promises are made true through Christ.[14]

The book of Revelation also captures the fulfillment in Christ of the promises and plan God gave to Abraham. The redeemed of the Lord sing a new song to express their love and appreciation of Christ:

> You are worthy to take the scroll and to open its seals, because you were slain, and with your blood you purchased men for God *from every tribe and language and people and nation.* You have made them to be a kingdom and priests to serve our God, and they will reign on the earth.[15]

The promises of God give certainty about the ultimate ends God has for the future, to call out spiritual generations from every tribe, language and people. The ultimate purposes of God are revealed in the Bible. The movement of the promises into the future is not about a linear progression from the present forward, as in the Latin word *futurum.* The promises have to do with the Latin *adventus,* from which the word advent, *to come,* is derived.[16] The promises come to us from eternity. From the ultimate to the penultimate, from last things to the *second to last.* God's people are in the penultimate stage where the promises point to the ultimate purposes of God for generations of people. This is God's plan and promise, and Christ is going to fulfill it—with or without obedience from his people. God has spoken, and what God blesses no one can curse. Nothing can be done to stop Jesus Christ from discipling the nations and reaping a harvest that will bring an eternally new song to his praise and to his glory. *It is inevitable!*

RECEIVING THE PROMISES

There is a flow to biblical history and the promises of God. It is not so much that the believer is to claim the promises of God, because the promises already *claim* him or her, in Christ. It is only for the believer to *believe* that what God has said will come to pass, shall indeed come to pass.

Paul reminds the Galatians of the importance of *believing*: "Understand, then, that those who *believe* are children of Abraham. The Scripture foresaw that God would justify the Gentiles *by faith,* and announced the gospel in advance to Abraham."[17]

---

[13] Matt 28:18-20
[14] 2 Cor 1:20
[15] Rev 5:9-10 (NIV, emphasis added)
[16] Ray Anderson (1992), *Minding God's Business,* Fuller Seminary Press.
[17] Gal 3:7-8 (NIV, emphasis added)

In Christ, a person is justified, made righteous, and the very righteousness of Christ is theirs forever. This grounds us to expect that God will bless us because we are positioned in Christ alone and not because of works. Grasping this would free believers to expect with confidence the blessing of God in daily life and ministry. Believing God's promises leads to a buoyant faith.

Justification paves the way for every other blessing, for "those who have faith are blessed along with Abraham, the man of faith."[18] Justification by faith in Christ is the basis upon which God blesses us in every area of our lives, just as he blessed Abraham: "Abraham was now old and well advanced in years, and *the Lord had blessed him in every way.*"[19] Abraham had only to believe that God desired to *bless him* and *make him a blessing.* This is the gospel and the Great Commission summarized and integrated in and through one life.

The promises to Abraham flowed to his son Isaac, and then to Jacob, the grandson. They were not pristine, otherworldly encounters, but connections from the heart of God to individual persons in the rugged circumstances of their own personal lives and journeys. Right after Abraham received his calling, he tried to help God by conceiving a son through Hagar, the maidservant. Later, he lied to Abimelech about Sarah being his sister, not wife. Then he faced the test of obeying God with the life of Isaac and the surrender at Mount Moriah. Later Sarah died. All of these 'man-ward' struggles could not thwart God's promise. And so it was with Isaac. He repeated the exact lie of Abraham in regard to his wife, Rebekah. Regardless, Isaac planted crops and reaped one hundred-fold that year. Generational sin could not thwart the promises of God:

> The LORD appeared to Isaac and said, "Do not go down to Egypt; live in the land where I tell you to live. Stay in this land for a while, and I will be with you and will bless you. For to you and your descendants I will give all these lands and will confirm the oath I swore to your father Abraham. I will make your descendants as numerous as the stars in the sky and will give them all these lands, and through your offspring all nations on earth will be blessed, because Abraham obeyed me and kept my requirements, my commands, my decrees and my laws." So Isaac stayed in Gerar.[20]

Jacob, born with strife at hand, would grow up in the natural man to become a deceiver, stealing the birthright from his brother Esau. So strong

---

[18] Gal 3:9 (NIV)
[19] Gen 24:1 (The Message, emphasis added)
[20] Gen 26:2-6 (NIV)

was the blessing from the aging Isaac, that the promises would still flow through to the one who received the formal blessing, apart from any merit:

> Jacob left Beersheba and set out for Haran. When he reached a certain place, he stopped for the night because the sun had set. Taking one of the stones there, he put it under his head and lay down to sleep. He had a dream in which he saw a stairway resting on the earth, with its top reaching to heaven, and the angels of God were ascending and descending on it. There above it stood the LORD, and he said: "I am the LORD, the God of your father Abraham and the God of Isaac. I will give you and your descendants the land on which you are lying. Your descendants will be like the dust of the earth, and you will spread out to the west and to the east, to the north and to the south. All peoples on earth will be blessed through you and your offspring. I am with you and will watch over you wherever you go, and I will bring you back to this land. I will not leave you until I have done what I have promised you."[21]

The promises of God are not diminished by man's reluctance, sin, or detours. Once received, they can be believed and can make a prince out of a deceiver as one wrestles with God and context for the outworking of the blessing. Jacob illustrates this, as he wrestled the angel in the night, after which he was renamed Israel, which means "prince with God."[22]

BELIEVING THE PROMISES

Consider Abraham. "Abraham believed the Lord, and he credited it to him as righteousness."[23] Moreover, "those who believe are children of Abraham. The Scripture foresaw that God would justify the Gentiles by faith and announced the gospel in advance to Abraham: 'All nations will be blessed through you.' So those who have faith are blessed along with Abraham, the man of faith."[24] Even in the face of seemingly great odds, he trusted God's word to him:

> Against all hope, Abraham in hope believed and so became the father of many nations, just as it had been said to him, "So shall your offspring be." Without weakening in his faith, he faced the fact that his body was as good as dead—since he was about a hundred years old—and that Sarah's womb was also dead. Yet he did not waver through unbelief regarding the promise of God, but was

---

[21] Gen 28:10-15 (NIV)
[22] Gen 32:24-30
[23] Gen 15:6 (NIV)
[24] Gal 3:7-9 (NIV); cf. Gen 18:18, 22:18

strengthened in his faith and gave glory to God, being fully persuaded that God had power to do what he had promised. This is why "it was credited to him as righteousness." The words "it was credited to him" were written not for him alone, but also for us, to whom God will credit righteousness—for us who believe in him who raised Jesus our Lord from the dead.[25]

Doug Sparks, pioneer missionary with The Navigators to Asia advocated applied faith in the promises of God. He saw three things in this passage which Paul draws from Genesis 15:4–6, in which we see *the process of faith*.[26] First, Abraham *heard* God. "The word of the Lord came to him". God took him outside and said to him, "Look at the heavens and count the stars—if indeed you can count them. So shall your offspring be." Second, Abraham *saw* what God meant. He saw the reality and the truth of it. He looked up into the skies and saw the countless stars. Third, Abraham *believed*, and God rewarded his faith. Abraham "believed the Lord, and the Lord credited it to him as righteousness." Abraham heard, he saw, he believed, and God credited it to him as righteousness. Believers are children of Abraham by faith because they belong to Christ. Abraham had only to believe that God would bless him and make him a blessing to others. Thirteen centuries later, the Scripture conveys a tribute to Sarah, the woman of faith, and inspires those who emulate her to stretch their faith and initiative:

> Sing, O barren woman, you who never bore a child; burst into song, shout for joy, you who were never in labor; because more are the children of the desolate woman than of her who has a husband," says the LORD. "Enlarge the place of your tent, stretch your tent curtains wide, do not hold back; lengthen your cords, strengthen your stakes. For you will spread out to the right and to the left; your descendants will dispossess nations and settle in their desolate cities.[27]

Later, there is a union of Spirit and promise, foreshadowing the life and work of Christ to come, and of those who follow in his steps:

> The Spirit of the Sovereign LORD is on me, because the LORD has anointed me to preach good news to the poor. He has sent me to bind up the brokenhearted, to proclaim freedom for the captives and release from darkness for the prisoners, to proclaim the year of the LORD's favor and the

---

[25] Rom 4:18-24 (NIV)

[26] Doug Sparks (1983), "Get the Big Picture", *Discipleship Journal*, Issue 17, September/October.

[27] Isa 54:1-3 (NIV)

day of vengeance of our God, to comfort all who mourn, and provide for those who grieve in Zion—to bestow on them a crown of beauty instead of ashes, the oil of gladness instead of mourning, and a garment of praise instead of a spirit of despair. They will be called oaks of righteousness, a planting of the LORD for the display of his splendor. They will rebuild the ancient ruins and restore the place long devastated; they will renew the ruined cities that have been devastated for generations.[28]

Even the Law before this, as well as the Psalmist, would underscore that to receive and believe the promises are the great need and mission of every generation.[29]

PRACTICAL APPLICATION IN LIVING OUT THE PROMISES

Generational thinking is rooted in the promises of God. But, what might standing in the flow of the promises of God look like practically?

First, we must immerse ourselves in the Scriptures, meditating on them with open hearts. We should prayerfully discern if the Holy Spirit is making emphasis on certain promises to us. This includes the desire for 'spiritual generations'. The gospel is entrusted to the people of God and is a legacy to be passed on from one generation to the next. Spiritual generations are a standard by which one can measure fruitfulness and stewardship in participating in God's unfolding plan for the human race.

Second, the promises are not so much to be claimed, as they are to be *believed*. The promises are already there in Scripture, but they must be found and trusted. When God makes a promise to us through the Scriptures and the Spirit, we can know that it will indeed be fulfilled, as we respond in faithful obedience. This gives us hope to believe God for fruitful lives.

Third, we should recognize that each of us has a unique faith contribution[30] to make in extending God's kingdom. From traveling leaders to local leaders, from those in the public eye to those behind the scenes, from extraordinary miracles to ordinary acts of kindness. God wants to bless the lives of all believers and to make them a blessing in the lives of others.

Fourth, we can delight in the fact that God works through our lives usually one person at a time. Believing God's promises can start simply by praying in faith for the outworking of God's blessing in another person's life—perhaps a non-believing family member, friend, neighbor, workmate, or classmate. We can then 'show and tell' the gospel by loving them in word and deed. We can also help disciple those who come to faith by encouraging them to join us as active participants in a local fellowship of believers.

---

[28] Isa 61:1-4 (NIV)
[29] Deut 6:1-9; Ps 78:1-8
[30] 1 Cor 12:1-12; James 2:22

Fifth, local and translocal Christian leaders who are motivated by specific promises should share them often with others and leave a legacy of such promises in the culture of each Christian fellowship and network to which they are connected. This can propel others to continuously step out in faith and believe God.

CONCLUSIONS

The promises flowed from an Abraham to an Isaac and on to a Jacob, impacting Joseph and beyond. In the Gospels, Jesus would work closely with three, Peter, James, and John.[31] Then, he worked with his 12 disciple recruits as a whole[32] and also the 70.[33] In the Epistles, we read that Paul infers a flow of the gospel from himself to Timothy to "faithful men who will be able to teach others also."[34]

The key to spiritual generations is imparting the legacy of the promises of God to the next generation. The promises to Abraham are still efficacious for today's believers, as they point to Christ and his worldwide mission to bear witness of God's love and offer of salvation. The worldwide Christian movement is about essentials, the essential primacy of Christ among his people whenever and however they gather. The dominant essential is Christ's headship, present and dynamic, where his promises are believed by faith and affirmed by works and words of the gospel undertaken with the hope of a harvest of new spiritual generations. The replicating DNA of the promises of God brings blessing to new people.

Whether it is households such as the children and grandchildren of Abraham and Sarah, the affinity group of fishermen that Jesus attracted, or the promise of nations that can be touched by a single person, the promises are true and flow forward from the God who cannot lie. These promises can enable one ordinary promise-believing person to influence spiritual generations, "The least of you will become a thousand, the smallest a mighty nation. I am the LORD; in its time I will do this swiftly."[35] The core of the promises of God remains, "I will bless you ... and you will be a blessing."[36]

STUDY QUESTIONS

1. God's first word to Abraham in Genesis 15:1-5 was "Do not be afraid". This is an encouragement that the people of God often need. The 12 disciples frequently heard it from Jesus, and later the apostle Paul mentioned the inner fears that harassed him (2 Cor 7:5). As we are

---

[31] Matt 17:1
[32] Matt 10:1
[33] Luke 10:1
[34] 2 Tim 2:2 (NASB)
[35] Isa 60:22 (NIV)
[36] Gen 12:2 (NIV)

involved in bearing witness to Christ and making disciples of him wherever we are, what fears are likely to attack us?

2. How do the words of Jesus in John 8:56 help us understand Abraham?

3. What can we learn from Romans 4:18–25 about how to follow Abraham's example of faith?

4. How should we interpret and apply promises that God gave to a different people at a different time?

5. What do these Scriptures lead us to expect from God?

6. What implications do these passages have on how we live missionally and reproduce simple 'house church' fellowships?

Chapter 3

THE NEED FOR WORLD REVIVAL

NATE KRUPP

Nate Krupp has been calling the church to be all that God would have it be for over 40 years. He was led to Christ in 1957 by two converted Jews while an engineering student at Purdue University. He and his wife, Joanne, pioneered Lay Evangelism, Inc., have served with Youth With A Mission (YWAM), are professors with Christian Leadership University, and oversee the work of Preparing the Way Publishers. They have had a house-church understanding since 1966. Nate has written over 20 books on evangelism, prayer, Bible study, and the church [This article is adapted from Nate Krupp (1988), The Church Triumphant at the End of the Age, Preparing the Way Publishers. Used by permission of the author. Email: kruppnj@open.org].

INTRODUCTION

What do you think about when you hear the word, *revival*? For some, it brings back negative feelings of some frightening hell-and-brimstone message at a camp meeting where sinners were exhorted to come forward and repent. For others, it stirs up the excitement of days gone by when God came by his Spirit and changed the course of a nation. So, what is revival? What does it have to do with us today in the 21st century?

WHAT IS 'REVIVAL'?

The words *revive, revived*, and *reviving* occur 30 times in the New American Standard translation of the English Bible. In all of these cases, the basic meaning of the Hebrew words, *chayah* and *michayah*, and the Greek words, *anathallo* and *anazao*, is "to live", "to live again", and "to come to life." The English word *revival* is derived from the Latin words *re*, meaning "again", and *vivo*, meaning "to live." Thus, *revival* literally means "to live again." Revival, in the context of Christianity, can be defined as occurring when the Holy Spirit moves upon a person, local church, community, nation, or the whole world in an extraordinary way which results in Christians being greatly awakened and drawn closer to God, in multitudes of new people being brought to Christ, in the social climate of that area being greatly changed for the good, and in many new Christian workers being thrust forth into the harvest. A further explanation of revival is given by two respected men of God of recent history, one an English Methodist leader, Dr. A. Skevington Wood, and the other an English Baptist leader, Charles Spurgeon.

Characteristics of Holy Spirit Revival [1]

- An intensified awareness of God
- An acute sensitivity to sin.
- A jealous concern for the truth.
- An absorbing concentration on prayer.
- An enhanced standard of conduct.
- A strengthened loyalty to the church.
- An exciting realization of unity.
- An augmented zeal in evangelism.
- A passion for social justice.

Genuine Revival [2]

- An uncommon eagerness to hear the word of God, and an unusual readiness to speak and be spoken to about the interests of the soul.
- An unusual sense of sin and personal unworthiness, together with a readiness to unite in prayer for pardon and holiness.
- A singularly cordial appreciation of the atoning sacrifice of Christ, and a joyful acceptance of the personal Savior.
- Personal consecration and covenanting with God in the Spirit of grace, accompanied by reformation of life and manner.
- Great delight in secret and social prayer, and in all the ordinances of God.
- An uncommon sense of the nearness of God, with joy in the Holy Ghost, and abounding with thanksgiving and praise.
- Increased fervor of love and deepened sense of unity among Christians.
- An extraordinary concern for the salvation of others, and boldness in testifying to the grace of God in his Son.

REVIVALS IN THE OLD TESTAMENT

There were times recorded throughout the Bible when God met with and renewed his people in extraordinary ways. In the Old Testament we find times when God worked on behalf of his people bringing renewal. Since this was not yet the age of the Holy Spirit, which began on the Day of Pentecost, they were not times of revival, in the strictest sense of the word. But, in another sense, they were, for they were times when God refreshed his people in an unusual way. The following are some striking examples in which God used certain individuals to bring about his grand purposes.

---

[1] A. Skevington Wood, "Characteristics of Holy Spirit Revival", *Convention Herald*, Salem, OH, USA, April 1981, p.4.

[2] Charles Spurgeon, "Genuine Revival", *Herald of His Coming*, May 1983.

Samuel the Prophet[3]

Israel had been under constant threat of foreign aggression by the Philistines for many years. A major Philistine invasion loomed ominously. The prophet Samuel responded to the crisis and urged the people to return to God with heartfelt repentance and commitment. The entire nation was called to assemble at Mizpah. On that day they fasted and confessed that they had sinned against the Lord. Samuel sacrificed a burnt offering and fervently interceded, crying out to God on Israel's behalf. The Philistines drew near to engage Israel in battle, but God supernaturally threw them into a panic and they were routed before the Israelites. So the foreign aggressor was subdued and cities that had been captured from Israel were restored.

King Solomon[4]

The historic dedication of the temple took place under Solomon's leadership. All the men of Israel were summoned and came together for the festival. The entire assembly gathered before the ark, and so many sheep and cattle were sacrificed that they could not be recorded. A vast group of musicians and singers joined in unison as with one voice to give praise and thanks to God. Then the glory of the Lord fell upon the Temple. Sometime later, God appeared to King Solomon at night and gave him the famous covenant promise: "[If] My people who are called by My name humble themselves and pray, and seek My face and turn from their wicked ways, then I will hear from heaven, will forgive their sin, and will heal their land."[5]

King Asa[6]

In the midst of zealous national reform, King Asa assembled the nation in the capital city, Jerusalem. Thousands of animal sacrifices were offered up, and the people made a covenant to seek God wholeheartedly. They ministered to God with much joyful worship. As a result God gave them rest on every side from their enemies.

King Jehoshaphat[7]

A vast army from Edom was coming against Judah. Disaster and debacle were imminent. King Jehoshaphat resolved to inquire of the Lord and proclaimed a fast for all Judah. People came from every town to seek God. The king fervently led in prayer and the men of Judah with their wives and children stood before the Lord. The prophetic word came forth. Then the people fell down and worshipped. Many then stood up and praised the Lord with a very loud voice. Because of the time of prayer and fasting, God gave them a miraculous, overwhelming victory in battle and rest on every side.

---

[3] 1 Sam 7:4-10
[4] 2 Chron 5-7
[5] 2 Chron 7:14 (NASB)
[6] 2 Chron 15:8-15
[7] 2 Chron 20:1-19

King Hezekiah[8]

King Hezekiah sent word to all Israel and Judah to come to Jerusalem to celebrate the Passover which had been neglected for many years. Some people mocked and ridiculed, but others humbled themselves and came. A very large crowd assembled in the capital. Sacrifices were offered and leaders prayed. There was much worship and joyful celebration. Sweeping national reforms followed.

King Josiah[9]

Idolatry had been prevalent for many years. Finally, the book of the Law was found. King Josiah called all the people of Jerusalem and Judah to gather together. God's word was read from a large platform. The people made a covenant to seek God. As a result, the nation followed God for a generation.

Ezra the Priest[10]

The nation was deep in sin through disobedience and unfaithfulness. But God had prepared Ezra to be his agent in the revival process. All the men were commanded to come to the capital, Jerusalem. The people gathered, and the leaders prayed, wept, confessed, and prostrated themselves before God. This gathering took place in the rain. The people committed themselves to change their ways. Because of the repentance and consecration, God allowed them to remain in the land.

Nehemiah[11]

After Nehemiah was used by God to rebuild the physical city walls of Jerusalem, a spiritual rebuilding was also needed. The entire nation assembled in Jerusalem. Ezra read God's word aloud from sunrise to noon. The people worshipped God and prostrated themselves. Leaders explained the word, and the people wept. Then the people went away with great rejoicing to celebrate because of their new understanding of God's requirements for their lives. This national gathering led to national reforms and the reinstitution of godly traditions.

Jonah the Prophet[12]

The prophet Jonah had publicly declared in the foreign city-state of Nineveh its imminent destruction by God. The people of the city believed Jonah, and a national fast was called. The entire population, from the greatest to the least, put on sackcloth and ashes. For days, not a single person or beast ate or drank. They called upon God earnestly and turned from their evil ways. God had compassion on the city and national judgment was averted.

---

[8] 2 Chron 30:1-27
[9] 2 Chron 34
[10] Ezra 10:1-17
[11] Neh 8
[12] Jonah 3

REVIVALS IN THE NEW TESTAMENT

Pentecost[13]

The initial dramatic outpouring of the Spirit of God upon those 120 gathered believers in the upper room also resulted in a mass conversion to Christ of 3000 people. After this initial outpouring, Peter and John were put into prison for preaching to the crowds and healing a lame man. When released, they returned to their fellow believers and told them what had happened. They all went to prayer, in desperate need of God's help, and the Holy Spirit came in a mighty way, shaking the building they were in and freshly filling all of them again just like on Pentecost. This resulted in unity, generosity, powerful witnessing, and abundant grace.

Philip the Evangelist visits Samaria[14]

After many of the Jerusalem believers were scattered because of a citywide persecution Philip (a mere 'table waiter' for the church) went to Samaria. He began to proclaim Christ to the people and was used by God to heal the sick and cast out demons. Multitudes were affected, and there was much rejoicing in the city. The apostles Peter and John heard about these events, visited the city, laid hands on people, and saw many receive a powerful baptism of the Holy Spirit.

The Need for Revival in the Churches[15]

By about AD 90, much of the church in Asia Minor was in need of revival. The majority of the churches that the apostle John wrote to in the book of Revelation were called to repent. The Lord Jesus Christ said that they needed to humble themselves, seek God earnestly, cast off false teachings, stop committing immoral acts, and catch the flame of passion for God once again. They needed to experience revival.

REVIVALS IN CHURCH HISTORY

Not only do we see mighty revivals in the Bible, but we also see them throughout church history, in various times and places and in a variety of ways. The intensity of some was of short duration, whereas others lasted much longer and had more far-reaching effects. Only a few are listed below for illustrative purposes, showing that they have occurred in various places and at different times.

The Montanists (2nd Century)

Under the leadership of Montanus of Phrygia (Asia Minor), the movement was characterized by an increased use of the spiritual gifts (especially prophecy), church discipline, and passion for God. The group was criticized by the more established segments of the church.

---

[13] Acts 2:1-47, 4:23-35
[14] Acts 8:5-17
[15] Rev 2 and 3

The Priscillianists (4th Century)

Priscillian, a Spanish nobleman of great oratorical ability, began a network of 'brotherhoods' that spread throughout Spain, Portugal, and France. These were small groups that met in homes for Bible study and prayer where both men and women could participate. They were criticized by some in the established church, but supported by a good number of priests and bishops. Priscillian was eventually excommunicated and executed.

The Celtic Missionary Movement (5th Century)

Patrick came from Scotland to the Irish people. He began one of the most vigorous church planting movements in history. Thousands were baptized in their newfound faith in Christ in Ireland alone. For over 200 years, missionaries were sent out from Ireland and Scotland to all parts of the British Isles and Europe.

The Waldenses (12th Century)

This movement, gaining its name from Peter Waldo, desired to recover a strict adherence to the Scriptures and to revive apostolic practices. Though first appearing in France, it spread rapidly through its strategy of sending missionaries two by two to Spain, Italy, Germany, Austria, and Bohemia. It was said that one-third of all Christendom had attended the Waldensian meetings.

The Franciscans (13th Century)

Francis first heard the call to forsake all and follow Christ at the age of 27. He began a movement that sent out traveling apostolic teams two by two, who called people to repentance, prayed for the sick, and helped the poor. Some historians believe that God used the Franciscans to save the medieval church from complete collapse.

The First Great Awakening (18th Century)

One of the main figures of the spiritual revival in Britain (and in colonial America) at this time was John Wesley. Under his leadership, the Methodist movement started thousands of small groups for discipleship and sent out circuit riders who preached in the open air. At Wesley's death in 1791, there were about 10,000 home cell groups with over 100,000 Methodists on either side of the Atlantic.

The Welsh Revival (Early 20th Century)

After several years of local awakenings and prayer meetings, 1904 witnessed a spark of revival that saw many taverns become bankrupt, crime decrease significantly, and 100,000 people added to the churches by 1906. Evan Roberts, one of the key figures, emphasized confession of all sin, repentance, restitution, surrender to the Holy Spirit, obedience to God, and public profession of Christ.

Church Planting Movements (Late 20th Century)[16]

All around the world, there are rapidly multiplying movements of house churches that are bringing in hundreds of thousands of new believers into the kingdom. The Chinese have seen the growth of the church from 1-2 million believers in 1949 to 80-100 million believers by the year 2000 through house churches. Cambodia saw the influx of 10,000 new believers through the intentional planting of house-based congregations that saw 220 groups start during 1992 to 2001. In Ethiopia, a decade of Marxist oppression in the 1980s could not stop the growth of one denomination from 5,000 to 50,000 members via underground house fellowships. These are but a few of the church planting movements of recent years.

THE COMING WORLD REVIVAL

The World's Need

Who can deny the need for a mighty spiritual awakening today? We are surrounded by evil and need of every kind—war, military and political tyranny, terrorism, violence, famine, oppression of the poor, situational ethics, immorality, homosexuality, AIDS, pornography, abortion, idolatry, false religion, materialism, gambling, drug abuse, injustice, humanism, self-centeredness, ecological destruction, and the possibility of nuclear war. The world is approaching the point of total financial, moral, physical, and spiritual bankruptcy.

The Church's Need

The church of Jesus Christ is God's agency on earth. We are Christ's body—his heart, mouth, hands, and feet. We should be fulfilling the Great Commission to go and make disciples of all nations. We should be fighting against evil and meeting human need. But the church is all too often so involved in its own life, problems, and self-survival to even be aware of world need, let alone be ready or able to do much about it. People are looking for moral and spiritual answers. Some are turning to the church and finding answers, but some are turning to the church and not finding answers. Some are turning elsewhere—the cults, the occult, false religion, humanism—and finding false hope.

How will we, the church of Jesus Christ, ever get the gospel to every person, in every nation, in this generation? What can cause the church to become that effective, life-changing, nation-shaking, hell-defeating agency that we read about in the book of Acts? There is hope for the church and for the world. There is one hope—a mighty spiritual awakening. Nothing can turn the tide of the world's evil and need, and the church's impotency and disobedience, but a heaven-sent, God-ordained, Christ-exalting, Holy Spirit-

---

[16] David Garrison (2004), *Church Planting Movements*, Wigtake Resources; Rad Zdero (2004), *The Global House Church Movement*, William Carey Library.

breathed, mighty, worldwide revival. We are at a point in history where it is either world revival or world destruction!

This writer believes and prays for a last, great, worldwide outpouring of the Holy Spirit that will result in an awakened, purified, empowered church. It will result in a church completely restored to the Christianity of the New Testament. It will result in unity coming to the Body of Christ. It will result in the worldwide persecution of believers. But, it will also result in the fulfillment of the Great Commission and the return of King Jesus to reign upon the earth![17]

Encouraging Trends in the Church

There are many encouraging trends happening among God's people. Citywide evangelistic crusades. Interdenominational Bible study and prayer meetings. Nationwide gatherings of leaders. Pastors coming together in an area for prayer. Worldwide congresses on prayer, evangelism, and social action. Church planting movements that involve cross-pollination between different Christian groups. God is doing much to unite his Body. There are, in fact, so many situations in the Body of Christ worldwide where unity is developing that an entire book could be written just giving these examples. All of this can help the church become of 'one mind' and prepare it for revival.[18]

What about the Laodicean Church?

There are those who teach that the seven churches in the book of Revelation represent seven chronological periods in church history, with the final church period just before Jesus returns being one where the church is lukewarm—the Laodicean church period. This teaching leaves little room for revival and, in fact, gives us a picture of the church barely making it to the end of the age. It is this writer's view that, though there may be some validity to the lukewarmness that does exist in many parts of the church today, the Scripture does not explicitly state that these seven churches represent seven different church ages.

Simultaneous Trends in the Last Days

This author suggests that there will actually be five trends taking place simultaneously in the last days. First, world conditions will continue to get worse, with seemingly no solutions.[19] Second, in order to try to solve these problems, a world government will develop, which will become political, economic, and religious in nature, and will be anti-Christ.[20] Many nominal Christians will become part of this system.[21] Third, because men and nations

---

[17] Matt 24:14

[18] Acts 1:14, 2:1-4

[19] Mt 24:6-7,12; Lk 21:25-26; 1 Tim 4:1-3; 2 Tim 3:1-7,13; 2 Pet 3:3-4; Jude 18

[20] Rev 13

[21] Matt 24:10-12; Luke 21:16; 2 Thess 2:3

will continue in their sin and rebellion against God, divine judgment will continue to fall, accelerating into a great shaking of society.[22] Every system of man will crumble. Only the kingdom of God will remain. Fourth, Israel will continue to be restored to her land[23] and come to know her Messiah.[24] Fifth, the true church will experience revival, restoration, unity, harvest, and persecution.[25]

CONCLUSIONS

We have seen that revival has occurred in the Old Testament, the New Testament, and throughout church history. It is even happening around the world today in various places under different circumstances. It is a common way for God to bring people to himself and accomplish his purposes on the earth. The possibility of a worldwide revival in the last days can empower the church to brave persecution, forge unity, and fulfill the Great Commission of Christ to go and make disciples of all nations.

STUDY QUESTIONS

1. Do you or your network of house churches need revival? If so, stop right now for a few moments and pray, asking God to begin to stir you up.
2. How can the prospect of revival change your way of following Christ?
3. How can the prospect of persecution change your way of following Christ personally?
4. How can house churches spark revival and defend against persecution?

---

[22] Heb 12:25-29
[23] Isa 43:5-7, 56:8; Jer 31:8-11, 33:10-13
[24] Zech 12:10-13; Rom 11
[25] Matt 24:9,14; John 17:14-21

PART 2

THE NEW TESTAMENT
ORIGINS OF
HOUSE CHURCHES

Chapter 4

A SURVEY OF THE NEW TESTAMENT HOUSE CHURCHES

DEL BIRKEY

Del Birkey, D.Min. (Bethany Theological Seminary, USA), served in pastoral, evangelistic, and teaching ministries in churches and as a visiting seminary professor. He is the author of The House Church: A Model for Renewing the Church (1988) (scheduled for rerelease in 2007) and The Fall of Patriarchy: Its Broken Legacy Judged by Jesus and the Apostolic House Church Communities (2005). [Adapted and used by permission of the author. Email: delbirkey@birkey.com].

BEGINNINGS AND CHARACTERISTICS
OF THE EARLY HOUSE CHURCHES

Floyd Filson first drew attention to the contemporary failure of scholarship to understand the household concept of the New Testament times. His seminal article, "The Significance of the Early House Churches," bristles with insight. Filson is surely correct when he affirms, "the New Testament church would be better understood if more attention were paid to the actual physical conditions under which the first Christians met and lived. In particular, the importance and function of the house church should be carefully considered."[1] The house churches of the New Testament not only furnish numerous insights into the functioning of early Christianity; they serve as a sociological model as well. Their existence and the data we possess on them point up the practical role they played in being a base of revitalization for the renewed people of God.

If you had asked another for directions to a church in any important city of the first-century world, you would have been directed to somebody's private home! This is significant. The beginning of these churches is an exciting story to trace. Indeed, Roland Allen wrote that, "in little more than ten years Paul established the church in four provinces of the Empire, Galatia, Macedonia, Achaia, and Asia. Before AD 47, there were no churches in these provinces. In AD 57, Paul could speak as if his work there was done, and could plan extensive tours into the far West without anxiety lest the churches that he had founded might perish in his absence for want of his guidance and support."[2]

---

[1] Floyd V. Filson (1939), "The Significance of the Early House Churches," *Journal of Biblical Literature 58*, pp.105–106.

[2] Roland Allen (1927), *Missionary Methods: St. Paul's or Ours* (London), 3, cited by F.F. Bruce (1977), *Paul, Apostle of the Heart Set Free*, Eerdmans, p.18.

The following account of the beginnings and characteristics of those early house churches follows roughly the chronology of that incredible time.

THE HOUSEHOLD STRATEGY OF JESUS

Jesus modeled in his own ministry an important "house of peace" strategy to his disciples, which involved finding a household that was sympathetic to him and his message. He would then preach, teach, and heal all those connected with that household (e.g. friends, family, neighbors), which often impacted an entire village or region (e.g. Capernaum, Samaria, Bethany).[3] A more comprehensive scholarly analysis of this is developed elsewhere.[4] To emphasize this approach to his disciples, he used it to practically train them. He sent them out two by two to preach from village to village. They were to find a 'house of peace' that was responsive to the kingdom message and build a spiritual base of operations from that household in order to reach that area. He gave them detailed instructions for this hands-on assignment:

> After this the Lord appointed seventy-two others and sent them two by two ahead of him to every town and place where he was about to go. He told them, "The harvest is plentiful, but the workers are few. Ask the Lord of the harvest, therefore, to send out workers into his harvest field. Go! I am sending you out like lambs among wolves. Do not take a purse or bag or sandals; and do not greet anyone on the road. *When you enter a house, first say, 'Peace to this house.'* If the head of the house loves peace, your peace will rest on that house; if not, it will return to you. Stay there, eating and drinking whatever they give you, for workers deserve their wages. *Do not move around from house to house.* When you enter a town and are welcomed, eat what is set before you. Heal the sick who are there and tell them, 'The kingdom of God has come near to you.' But when you enter a town and are not welcomed, go into its streets and say, 'Even the dust of your town we wipe from our feet as a warning to you. Yet be sure of this: The kingdom of God has come near.'"[5]

There are several important insights here regarding Jesus' household strategy. First, Jesus organized his disciples into small teams, possibly for the sake of mutual accountability and support during their mission. Second, they were to fully rely on God's ability to meet all their physical needs, while they stayed focused on looking for a house of peace. Third, if they did

---

[3] Mark 1:29-34, 2:1-2; John 4:4-42, 11:1-46, 12:1-11
[4] Roger Gehring (2004), *House Church and Mission: The Importance of Household Structures in Early Christianity*, Hendrickson Publishers, pp.28-48.
[5] Luke 10:1-11 (TNIV, emphasis added)

indeed find such a person, they were to enjoy the hospitality of the host and understand this as God's provision for them. Fourth, they were to remain in that home and build a base of operations there, reaching out to the friends, family, and neighbors connected to that household. Fifth, they were never to spend an undue amount of time in an area that resisted their message, but they were to move on in search of a more receptive audience and household.

THE HOUSE CHURCHES IN JERUSALEM

In the face of many difficulties, the first church was established in Jerusalem. Although all its members were Jewish, they were not all of the same type.[6] The common folk were the "people of the land." They kept their practices down to the minimal law-standards. Peter was probably typical of this type. There was also the more scrupulous kind, usually with Pharisaic and priestly backgrounds, represented by James. Finally, the Hellenist Jews were represented in the Jerusalem church by Stephen and Philip.

Differences within the mother church clearly existed. For instance, in that famous occasion in Syrian Antioch, Paul boldly confronted Peter. Paul "opposed him to his face"—evidently publicly—"because he was clearly in the wrong!"[7] Peter was wrong in that he found Paul's company too inclusive and sought a more restricted fellowship. He apparently did not want to make things too awkward for some of his friends back at the Jerusalem fellowship, particularly James, the Lord's brother.

Since the Acts informs us that the church numbered several thousand at its rebirth, it could not meet as a whole in one place. In fact, the references to small groupings are precisely what we would expect. They broke bread "in their homes"[8] and did not stop teaching "at home."[9] The mention of a prayer meeting in the home of Mary, Mark's mother,[10] is further evidence that when they wanted to meet together, no place was suitable except the homes of the members.

It is noteworthy that this prayer meeting was apparently not a meeting of the whole Jerusalem church, therefore, but rather only one of the other house churches. Evidence to this phenomenon mounts when, as F.F. Bruce points out, Peter and James apparently did not belong to the same household church. "If Peter belonged to the group which met in the home of Mary...he knew that James and 'the brethren' (whoever they were) met somewhere else (Acts 12:17)."[11] Bruce goes on to comment that then, as now, we should

---

[6] R. H. Longenecker (1968), "Early Jewish Christianity at Jerusalem," Trinity Evangelical Divinity School.
[7] Gal 2:11–13 (NEB)
[8] Acts 2:46
[9] Acts 5:42
[10] Acts 12:12
[11] F.F. Bruce, "Lessons from the Early Church," in *In God's Community*, D.J. Ellis and W. Ward Gasque (eds.) (1978), Wheaton, p.154.

expect some of these small church groups to attract the more cautiously conservative while others the more adventuresome liberal.

The famous "upper room" comes into our purview here. It was in this "large upper room" of an unknown disciple's home that the first celebration of the Lord's Supper was held.[12] Most likely, this is the same large room in Jerusalem where the original group of 120 gathered to wait for the day of Pentecost.[13]

THE HOUSE CHURCH AT PHILIPPI

The town of Philippi has the unique distinction of having the first house church in Europe. Following the dramatic "Macedonian call"[14] Luke simply recorded that after Paul and Silas came out of prison, they went to Lydia's house. There they met their fellow Christians and spoke words of encouragement to them.[15] Lydia was a successful businesswoman from nearby Thyatira. The Lord opened her mind to respond to Paul's message. She and the members of her household were baptized.[16] Indeed, it is not difficult to see why Lydia was the first person to turn to the Lord in Europe. She was a hospitable person and invited Paul and his companions into her home. She said, "If you consider me a believer in the Lord, come and stay at my home." Luke notes that "she persuaded us", and the first church of Europe was born!

THE HOUSE CHURCHES AT CORINTH

When Paul sent greetings to the Roman believers from Corinth, he included Gaius, saying, "My host Gaius, in whose house the church meets, sends you his greetings."[17] This homeowner was probably the same person as Titius Justus, who put his house at Paul's disposal so that he might carry on the work that he started in the synagogue next door. His full name would then be Gaius Titius Justus, marking him out as a Roman citizen.[18]

This house apparently became the first meeting place for the Corinthian church, as well as for Paul's headquarters.[19] Evidently during Paul's stay in Corinth he lived with Priscilla and Aquila, as he worked part-time for them in their tent making business.[20] He never had more loyal friends and helpers than this amazing couple.

---

[12] Mark 14:13–16
[13] Acts 1:15, 2:1–2
[14] Acts 16:6–10
[15] Acts 16:14
[16] Acts 16:15
[17] Rom 16:23 (TEV)
[18] E. J. Goodspeed (1950), "Gaius Titius Justus," *Journal of Biblical Literature* 69, p.382.
[19] Acts 18:7, 11
[20] Acts 18:1–4

The church at Corinth is perhaps not only the most problematic but also the most colorful. The Lord had told Paul in a vision that he "has many people in this city."[21] This "many people" aggregate no doubt met in different places throughout the city.

One of those places is strongly intimated in Paul's warm response to the "household of Stephanas."[22] They were the first household to become Christians in the province of Achaia. Paul mentions that he personally baptized only them among the Corinthian converts.[23] Stephanas and his house church[24] devoted themselves in a unique way to *diakonia*, for they "addicted themselves to the ministry of the saints."[25]

The probability here is that "they"—the whole household as a ministering unit—dramatically reflected their unique giftedness in serving the saints which met together in other churches. They "laid themselves out to serve God's people",[26] a service that suggests both their strengths and possessions were used for others, not unlike that quality found in the earlier believers at Jerusalem.[27] In other words, the service extended from the local church to churches elsewhere in need.

Barclay reminds us that in the early church such willing and spontaneous service was the beginning of a more official leadership position. In such cases, a person's life and servant attitude marked him or her out as one whom all must respect.[28] In the same way, Paul urges the believers to "follow the leadership of such people as these."[29]

There may have been a third house church at Corinth. "Chloe's people," who are mentioned in the beginning of the letter to the Corinthians,[30] were the ones from whom Paul learned about the rival schools at Corinth. Presumably, "Chloe's household" was part of a well-to-do house church— Chloe was the household head and owner of the house.[31]

The internal evidence of the Corinthian correspondence reveals a "weaker brother" syndrome, the presence of problematic "men of knowledge" ("super-apostles"), as well as a four-sided schism.[32] If we caricatured the latter four groups, the Paulists would represent the

---

[21] Acts 18:9–10

[22] 1 Cor 16:5

[23] 1 Cor 1:15–18

[24] K. Hess, "Serve, Deacon, Worship," in *The New International Dictionary of New Testament Theology*, Colin Brown (ed.) (1971), Zondervan, Vol. 3, p.547.

[25] 1 Cor 16:15 (KJV)

[26] 1 Cor 16:5 (NEB)

[27] Acts 2:44

[28] W. Barclay (1975), *The Letters to the Corinthians*, Westminster, pp.166–167.

[29] 1 Cor 16:16 (TEV)

[30] 1 Cor 1:11

[31] F.F. Bruce (1977), *Paul, Apostle of the Heart Set Free*, Eerdmans, p.258.

[32] 1 Cor 1:14f

traditionalists, those who played upon the fact that Paul was there first. Peter's people characterize the renewalists, who hark back to the very beginning. Since Peter was an original apostle, a chief builder of Christ's church, they assumed he was the one to rally around. The Apollos assembly could be called the biblicists, followers of Apollos, the "seminarian" Bible teacher. After all, he was an expert in Greek! The Christ group apparently imagined itself to be the most spiritual of the church groups in Corinth. Distinctions that the others made are important, they thought, but the simple, basic thing was just to walk with Jesus!

Given these realities, it is a reasonable supposition that each rallying group found each other's company congenial, and therefore met together in separate houses. Filson points to the deep doctrinal differences which divided one group from another in Corinth, suggesting that the proneness to division which we see in apostolic churches was not unconnected with the division of the Christians of a particular city into house churches.[33]

THE HOUSE CHURCH AT EPHESUS

The first church at Ephesus centered on the most celebrated couple in the New Testament, Priscilla and Aquila. Aquila had probably been born in poverty and slavery, somehow gaining freedom and arriving in Rome. There, he worked at an honest trade as a canvas maker. Fortunately for him, one day he met a most unusual woman who became his wife. The name Prisca (a formal Roman name) suggests she was from one of the wealthy and noble Roman families. Together they developed their thriving business, Priscilla evidently providing wise expertise. Her leadership abilities are suggested in the fact that her name usually appears before her husband's.

Then one day they experienced God's sovereign grace in their lives. They became Christians and, as middle-class folk, they faced new problems. These problems were so serious that for whatever reasons they and other believers were expelled from Rome by the Edict of Claudius.[34] So Priscilla and Aquila went to Corinth, where they sold sailcloth for the tall ships in the port nearby. They also sold their skills and wares as merchants in the tent making industry. Sometime later, however, they moved to Ephesus, presumably to establish a business there also. Not long after arriving in town, this gracious couple invited the believers there into their house on the Lord's Day. The church began using their living room for the meeting place on a regular basis. Not long afterward, Paul, who also left Corinth with them, wrote back to the Corinthian believers with these warm words: "Aquila and Priscilla greet you warmly in the Lord, and so does the church that meets in their home."[35]

---

[33] Floyd V. Filson (1939), "The Significance of the Early House Churches", *Journal of Biblical Literature 58*, p.110.
[34] Acts 18:2
[35] 1 Cor. 16:19

Paul's ministry at Ephesus was stormy with adversaries, and it was probably during this time that Priscilla and Aquila "risked their necks" for his life.[36] Obviously, they were a sharing couple. When they shared their home or their faith, there was the risk of being rejected. Evidently they almost lost their lives in high-risk sharing with Paul and others. Hostile authorities were after Paul, especially since the howling uproar in Ephesus over Christianity's challenge to the silversmiths' business of making shrines of Artemis.[37] One could hardly shelter Paul and his people in those days without losing status in the business community. Furthermore, to have a church in one's home every Sunday might be acceptable to some, but what about all those slaves coming into the group? The stakes were high, but Priscilla and Aquila were more than willing to pay the price.

Indeed, Paul's own unique understanding of the gospel may well have been fostered here in the house church that enjoyed the hospitality of Priscilla and Aquila. After all, it was there that Priscilla and Aquila befriended the brilliant scholar, Apollos. He did not understand the fullness of Christianity, so they took him into their home and shared with him the way of God more accurately.[38]

THE HETEROGENEOUS HOUSE CHURCHES OF ROME

A Decentralized System of House Churches

Where did Paul go, and Peter as well, when they visited Rome? Clearly not to St. Paul's or St. Peter's, for in AD 60 of course there was no Christian basilica on Vatican Hill or by the Ostian Way. Actually, Paul was not in a position to "go" anywhere when he first arrived in Rome, since he remained under house arrest for several years. Most likely his rented flat became the locus for a small household church during his custody, one among others already existing in the great city.

There was not one centrally administered "church" in Rome, based on the evidence of Paul's letter and on the probability of the situation there. He does not use his usual form of greeting that would be designated "to the church of God which is in Rome." Rather, he addresses the letter "to all in Rome who are loved by God and called to be saints."[39] Scholars have debated over the fact that "in Rome" is omitted in one reading, as well as verse 15, together with the personal greetings to 26 individuals by name in chapter 16. In spite of the arguments that direct the final chapter to Ephesus, there is insufficient evidence to detach chapter 16 from the letter to the Romans. It may be, however, that Romans was circulated in several forms.[40]

---

[36] Rom 16:4 (RSV)

[37] Acts 19

[38] Acts 18:24–26

[39] Rom 1:7

[40] W. Barclay (1975), *The Letter to the Romans*, Westminster, pp.9–10; also F.F. Bruce (1977), *Paul, Apostle of the Heart Set Free*, Eerdmans, pp.386–388.

Robert Banks points to Paul's characteristic way of referring to the "churches" of a particular area,[41] suggesting that the idea of a unified provincial or national church is foreign to Paul's thinking. He concludes that *ekklesia* cannot refer to a group of people scattered throughout a locality unless they all do, in fact, actually gather together. Thus, it is not possible for him to describe all the Christians in Rome as a "church."[42]

For the Roman churches, the word *community* is not totally appropriate, since they existed in plurality. Since Paul found the Roman Christians decentralized, we can conclude that he did little to centralize them. Indeed, a century later Justin Martyr remarked that the Roman Christians did not all meet together "in the very same place," but that he gathered his disciples together "above one Martin, at the Timothian Baths."[43] Ignatius and Hermas provide similar evidence that the church was still decentralized and was not yet organized under the administrative authority of a single bishop. Therefore Hermas could write, "In this city you yourself shall read it aloud with the elders who stand at the head of the church."[44]

Priscilla and Aquila

Nevertheless, Paul did expect his letter to reach "all" the Christians there. It is not necessary, however, to assume that Paul had in mind a single occasion when all would together hear it read. Perhaps as Bruce suggests, Phoebe carried it from one house church to another.[45] The most well known home church in Rome was the gathering of believers meeting in the newly established home of Priscilla and Aquila. Most likely they were the co-pastors of the fellowship. Having lived and worked in Corinth and Ephesus, they had returned again to their beloved Rome, where they probably had first become believers. Paul writes to the fellowship there, requesting them to "greet Priscilla and Aquila, my fellow workers in Christ Jesus...not only I but all the churches of the Gentiles are grateful to them. Greet also the church that meets at their house."[46]

Although Aquila was a Jew,[47] Priscilla's birthplace may well have been Rome, particularly in view of Paul's preference for Prisca. Barclay pieces together the romance of their story. There is in Rome today a church of St. Prisca, as well as a cemetery of Priscilla, the cemetery being the burying place of the ancient Acilian family. Furthermore, in four of the six

---

[41] Cf. Gal 1:2, 22; 1 Cor 16:1; 16:19; 2 Cor 8: 1.

[42] Robert Banks (1980), *Paul's Idea of Community*, Eerdmans, pp.37,40.

[43] F.F. Bruce, "Lessons from the Early Church," in *In God's Community*, D. J. Ellis and W. Ward Gasque (eds.) (1978), Wheaton, p.155.

[44] "The Shepherd of Hermas," trans. by G. Snyder, in *The Apostolic Fathers Contemporary Translations*, Jack Sparks (ed.) (1978), Thomas Nelson, p.167.

[45] F.F. Bruce (1977), *Paul, Apostle of the Heart Set Free*, Eerdmans, p.384.

[46] Rom 16:4–5

[47] Acts 18:2

references to this couple, Priscilla is named before her husband. The implication is that Priscilla is not a freedwoman, but rather a great lady—a member by birth of the Acilian family. It may be that at some meeting of the Christians this great Roman lady met Aquila, the humble Jewish tentmaker, that the two fell in love, that Christianity destroyed the barriers of race and rank and wealth and birth, and that these two, the Roman aristocrat and the Jewish artisan, were joined forever in Christian love and Christian service.[48]

Due credit should be given this unusual Christian couple. Kasemann remarks that we can regard this couple as among the earliest Christian missionaries in the Diaspora. They had begun their work independently of Paul and then continued it in association with him.[49] Wherever we find them, we also find a center of Christian fellowship and ministry. Even a cursory reading of the New Testament highlights the remarkable emphasis and the high priority the earliest church placed on hospitality. The power and vitality of Christian hospitality obviously played a primary role in gathering together the first Christians into assemblies.

A Company of Friends and Households

Twenty-four more names in Romans 16 follow those of this famed couple. These names represent a company of friends and acquaintances that Paul had no doubt met in other places. In view of the ease of travel throughout the Roman world, Bruce is probably right in assuming that many of the folks that Paul met on his journeys became resident in Rome. It is also natural that he should send personal greetings to them, as well as to others of whom he had heard.

The significance of the friendship list in Romans 16 lies in its clustering phenomenon, yielding obvious groupings of earlier household churches. Together with the house church in Priscilla and Aquila's home, four other household churches are singled out. These include those "who belong to the household of Aristobulus"[50] and those "in the household of Narcissus."[51] Another cluster centers around five names together with their "brethren", followed by five other believers with "all the saints with them."[52] Banks raises the possibility that two kinds of house churches may be seen in Rome, where guild life was strong and often concentrated in certain districts. The suggestion that a domestic work grouping may lie behind several clusters should be taken into account as well.[53]

---

[48] William Barclay (1975), *The Letter to the Romans*, Westminster, pp.210–211.
[49] Ernst Kasemann (1980), *Commentary on Romans*, Geoffrey W. Bromiley (trans., ed.), Eerdmans, p.413.
[50] Rom 16:10
[51] Rom 16:11
[52] Rom 16:14-15
[53] Robert Banks (1980), *Paul's Idea of Community*, Eerdmans, p.40.

The sociological clues found underneath this list of names imply a broad racial diversity, including Peris, a Persian; Rufus, an African; and Urbanes and others, Roman Gentiles. Social Christian unity is implied by the side-by-side presence of common slave names with prominent imperial names.

There is also a strong current of gender equality. Six of the 26 are women, and the first-named Phoebe is not only a deacon but a *prostatis*, a woman beneficiary and as one presiding, alluding to the probability of elder or pastoral leadership. Junia is considered a fellow apostle, and Priscilla's credentials have been discussed above.

Moreover, positive ecumenical mobility is implied. Priscilla and Aquila labored among the empire's cities. Paul recognizes by name a wide amalgamation of believers from various parts of the empire. These now find themselves "churched" in one of the house churches of Rome.

The Hebrew House Church

To these growing clusters of home-centered churches in Rome could be added another significant group. It is reasonable conjecture that the epistle to the Hebrews was addressed to a house church. Since the churches in Rome were cosmopolitan, some of the Christian Jews may have still counted themselves as adherents of one of the synagogues. They would soon no longer be able to maintain a foot in both camps. This was perhaps the situation of the group addressed in the epistle to the Hebrews, having come to faith in Christ not long before the Romans document was written.

An advocate of the Roman destination of Hebrews was Adolph Harnack, who believed that it was sent to a house church in that city by someone well acquainted with the addressees. Also, William Manson suggests that a small conservative enclave within the Roman church clung to the more conservative principles of traditional Judaism. He believes Hebrews was addressed particularly to them.[54] Apollos may have been its author, or even Priscilla.

Bruce puts this fascinating query into perspective by noting the fact that Hebrews was well known in Rome, particularly by Clement. Nonconformist Jewish elements existed in the Christian community of Rome. Their Hellenistic orientation implies that the recipients of the Hebrews tractate were second-generation believers who derived their knowledge of the Old Testament ritual system from reading the Septuagint. "Perhaps they formed a 'house church' within the wider fellowship of a city church, and were tending to neglect the bonds of fellowship that bound them to other Christians outside their own inner circle."[55]

Archaeological Remains

A final comment regarding the Roman house churches. It is widely believed

---

[54] Summarized by F. F. Bruce (1964), *The Epistle to the Hebrews: The English Text with Introduction, Exposition and Notes*, Eerdmans, p.xxxv.
[55] F.F. Bruce (1964), *The Epistle to the Hebrews*, Eerdmans, p.xxx.

by many scholars that Rome's St. Clement basilica is built upon the remains of an earlier church that dates to about the fourth century. More significant are the remains of a structure on a yet lower level, dating back to the first century. Protestants and Catholics alike, point to the probability of this original structure being the first-century home of Clement of Rome. In his exceptional work, however, Graydon F. Snyder asserts that as yet no function for this lowest building has been determined. He feels certain that it is not a house. Rather, he supposes a private residence was later built next to the original "public" building. This was later yet transformed into a Mithraic school, therefore making the religious use of the most ancient residence Mithraic rather than Christian.[56] Even though uncertainty remains concerning a proper interpretation of the data, nevertheless, the account suggests how an early home or center of Christian interest would grow in esteem and eventually be regarded as a sacred site.

THE HOUSE CHURCHES AT COLOSSAE

The apostle Paul, in his unusual letter to Philemon, writes, "To Philemon our beloved brother and fellow worker, and to Apphia our sister, and to Archippus our fellow soldier, and to the church in your house."[57] The first person addressed in the letter would most naturally be the head of the house. Apphia was probably his wife and Archippus their son.[58] It is traditionally supposed that Philemon was a member of the Colossian fellowship. Philemon's home, therefore, was the meeting place for one of the early household churches in Colossae. Somehow Philemon had been converted to Christianity through Paul's ministry.[59] His slave Onesimus robbed him and absconded to Rome, where he came in contact with Paul. Through his influence he became a believer. Although we cannot know how or why Onesimus visited Paul, Minear suggests that they may have been imprisoned in the same place.[60]

The brief personal letter is an exquisite sociological model reflecting the power of the gospel in effecting forgiveness and in its insistence on equality in Christ's body. Onesimus is returning no longer as a slave but a dear brother,[61] implying an incongruity for a Christian master to "own" a brother in Christ. Paul's strategy, armed with the revolutionary gospel, challenged the issue on principle from within, which would in time lead to the abolishment of the outward system of slavery itself.

---

[56] Graydon F. Snyder (1985), *Ante Pacem: Archaeological Evidence of Church Life Before Constantine*, Mercer University Press, p.76.
[57] Philem 1:1-2 (NASB)
[58] F.F. Bruce (1977), *Paul, Apostle of the Heart Set Free*, Eerdmans, p.405.
[59] Philem 1:19
[60] Donald Guthrie (1966), *New Testament Introduction: The Pauline Epistles*, InterVarsity Press, p.247.
[61] Philem 1:16

Bruce brings the situation into focus by remarking that Onesimus was now in good standing as a church member, and that he was probably attached to one of the house churches of Rome. Therefore he naturally received from the Colossian church the same welcome as that given any other visiting Christian, especially one armed with a letter of recommendation from an apostle.[62] The Colossian house church must have excitedly prepared for a most heartwarming experience. They had just received word from the apostle:

> Our dear brother Tychicus, who is a faithful worker and fellow servant in the Lord's work, will give you all the news about me. That is why I am sending him to you, to cheer you up by telling you how all of us are getting along. With him goes Onesimus, the dear and faithful brother, who belongs to your group.[63]

The church fellowship in Philemon's house was evidently not the only house church regularly gathering together in Colossae. Some of "the saints and faithful brethren in Christ at Colossae" evidently met together in another house fellowship.[64] Paul's greetings to the believers in that city also include best wishes to "Nympha and the church in her house."[65] It is likely this second house fellowship was planted by Epaphras.[66] He was the evangelist of the Lycas Valley and was an informant to Paul regarding the churches of that region. Paul had apparently not yet visited the house churches at Colossae when he wrote his letter,[67] but he wanted to and may have had the opportunity at a later time.[68]

THE CHURCH AT LAODICEA

When Paul sent his letter to the Colossian church from his prison hall in Rome, he also wanted it to be read in the house church at nearby Laodicea, about ten miles away. He wrote:

> My own greetings to the Christians in Laodicea, and to Nympha and the congregation who meet in her house. When you have had this letter read in your church [i.e., the house fellowship associated with Philemon], see that the Laodiceans have it read in their church too; and see that you in turn read the letter to Laodicea.[69]

---

[62] F. F. Bruce (1957), *Commentary on the Epistles to the Ephesians and the Colossians: The English Text with Introduction, Exposition and Notes*, Eerdmans, p.302
[63] Col 4:7–9 (TEV)
[64] Col 1:2 (RSV)
[65] Col 4:15
[66] Col 1:7, 4:12–13
[67] Col 2:1
[68] Philem 1:22
[69] Col 4:15–16

Because of slight ambiguity here, some believe the house church associated with Nympha was actually at Laodicea. Although this is a viable interpretation, it is an unlikely one. By inference, the church at Laodicea can represent other New Testament churches not technically designated a "church in your home." Its close affiliation in Paul's letter with the house churches at Colossae corroborate the ideal of its home setting.

Similarly, there were no doubt house churches "scattered throughout Pontus, Galatia, Cappodocia, Asia and Bithynia" to which Peter wrote.[70] And likewise, the seven churches of Asia Minor were also house churches, as was the church at Ephesus where Timothy later ministered. Lacking evidence to the contrary, we can assume all the others were of the same structure. Furthermore, the same home environment existed in the earliest church at Thessalonica, the church at Crete where Titus evidently ministered[71] and all other churches mentioned or implied within the New Testament documents—the model that continued for 300 years.

We know little about the letter to the Laodicean church that Paul mentions was probably written by him, but lost.[72] No evidence exists that Paul visited the church.[73] However, John's reference to that church in his Apocalypse contains a profoundly serious warning to the church's growing spiritual tepidity.[74] He admonishes them to repent from being lukewarm, a condition to which the fellowship apparently succumbed.

THE UPSTAIRS APARTMENT CHURCH AT TROAS

When Paul and his friends arrived at Troas, they were joined by another companion, the author of the travel diary that is incorporated into the published edition of Acts. Luke's joining the traveling party is unobtrusively indicated by a sudden switch from the third person to the first person plural—from *they to we*.[75] There in Troas was a small community of believers probably formed during Paul's distracted and interrupted evangelization of the city and its neighborhood a year or two before.[76]

The gathered church met in somebody's third-floor apartment.[77] Paul and his companions enjoyed the fellowship of these early Christians, especially during the Sunday evening before their departure. They met then to break bread, and Paul went on dialoguing with them until midnight. Luke remembered the occasion quite vividly, since a young man of the community—Eutychus by name—was overcome by drowsiness while sitting

---

[70] 1 Pet 1:1

[71] Titus 1:5f

[72] D. Guthrie (1966), *New Testament Introduction*, InterVarsity Press, p.175.

[73] Robert H. Mounce (1977), *The Book of Revelation*, Eerdmans, p.124.

[74] Rev 3:14–22

[75] Acts 20:5

[76] F.F. Bruce (1977), *Paul, Apostle of the Heart Set Free*, Eerdmans, p.340.

[77] Acts 20:5-12

on a window ledge. The long-winded, late-night preacher apparently did not notice the sinking struggle the young man was having. Apparently, due to the fumes from the "many lamps" in the room, he fell and was picked up as dead. But after Paul performed a miraculous resuscitation, possibly in conjunction with a form of artificial respiration, it was a great relief to find Eutychus alive and well.

Several things about this house church episode are noteworthy. Ralph P. Martin significantly points out that "at Troas we see how the 'breaking of bread' service of Acts 2:42, 46 still persists in a Greco-Roman setting but as part of a structure that will later become 'fixed' and provide the two-part sequence of the Christian *sunaxis* or gathering for Sunday worship. The 'liturgy of the Word' and the 'liturgy of the upper room' are visible in their embryonic forms in the simple house celebration in Troas."[78]

Another illuminating and instructive facet of the gathering in Troas, centers on the fact that Paul did not "preach" to the believers there as commonly assumed. English translations are generally careless here and therefore only add to the confusion. For example, the Jerusalem Bible says Paul "preached a sermon."[79] The earlier edition of the New International Version says that Paul "preached," but later editions read that Paul simply "spoke" to them. The Greek text, in fact, says that Paul dialogued with them *(dialegomai)*. That is, he "conducted a discussion" giving us a clear and vital glimpse into the original and appropriate pattern of communications used in the New Testament house churches of the gathered believers.

THE THESSALONIANS AND HOUSE CHURCHES

Other textual clues suggest that the churches to which Paul sent his letters were always house churches. In writing to the Thessalonians, for example, he obviously felt it appropriate to use an extraordinarily strong word to make sure the believers there would get his message. He finished the letter with a charge: "I adjure you by the Lord that this letter be read to all the brethren."[80] What could his motive have been for such surprising language at the ending of an overall cordial letter? It implies that since the basic unit was the house church, it surely must be shared with all of the house churches so that one group could not be allowed to monopolize it, as Floyd Filson suggests.

A CHOSEN LADY AND HER CHILDREN'S HOUSE CHURCHES

John addressed his second tiny letter[81] to "the chosen lady and her children." More than mere metaphor of a church community, it probably refers to an actual Christian woman with leadership gifts and "children". This can mean

---

[78] Ralph P. Martin (1982), *The Worship of God*, Eerdmans, p.203.
[79] Acts 20:7
[80] 1 Thess 5:27 (RSV)
[81] 2 John

John met some of her children who are "hers" (just as the "children" in John's First Epistle are "his children" by faith in Christ). Other NT house churches were formed by women and evidently this woman was also the leader of a church in her home. Her "elect sister" could have been a co-elder, but it is more likely a reference to another house church nearby where she served as leader.

A Late House Church Infiltrated by Arrogant Leadership

John's tiny third letter[82] is his final word on three significant church members at the end of the New Testament canon. The letter is addressed to yet another house church fellowship in which there appears to be several different house groups of Christians. The larger group is led by one Diotrephes, a leader who wanted to be "head of everything", perhaps over the other house churches in the area. The smaller house churches, one led by Gaius and, apparently, another by Demetrius, remained faithful to the apostolic elder. Gaius was probably the person whom John had carry his letter to the fellowship of churches, and was known for his faithfulness, truthfulness, and hospitality. Obviously, Diotrephes was a domineering and contrary hegemonic church member. John probably sent a letter to the house church through this self-acclaimed leader—but it was lost—perhaps destroyed by Diotrephes himself in personal opposition to the elder apostle. In the end, he is a harbinger of what was soon to become a dark reality among the church fathers, who instituted Diotrephes-esqe positions of patriarchal leadership in the post-apostolic churches of the second and third centuries.[83]

Summary Ramifications of the Apostolic House Churches

In summarizing the household concept in the New Testament documents, Filson's research laid a needed foundation upon which others have built. The following ramifications of the house church phenomenon in the New Testament enrich our understanding of the apostolic church. Indeed, the New Testament house church provides us an authentic "Missiological Model."[84]

Distinctive Fellowship and Worship

The church in the home provided the most dynamic setting for the distinctively unique Christian fellowship and worship. The household structure provided a natural setting and enabled Christians to gather together for worship and fellowship from the earliest days. "It was the hospitality of

---

[82] 3 John

[83] Del Birkey (2005), *The Fall of Patriarchy: Its Broken Legacy Judged by Jesus & the Apostolic House Church Communities*, Fenestra, Ch. 6: "The Post-Apostolic Fathers & Ecclesiastical Patriarchy," pp.167–223.

[84] Del Birkey (1991), "The House Church: A Missiological Model," *Missiology: An International Review*, January, pp.69–80.

these homes which made possible the Christian worship, common meals, and courage-sustaining fellowship of the group. The Christian movement really rooted in these homes."[85]

These small fellowships were not dependent on conforming to temple or synagogue worship, nor on buildings they had erected. Archaeological evidence suggests the average size household could accommodate about 30 to 35 comfortably.[86] Although there is no extant church building built prior to Constantine, there are homes that were restructured for Christian assemblies. Graydon F. Snyder finds it amazing that we do not have more remains of such house churches, adding that indeed, we may have remains of such but cannot recognize them.

The one edifice unquestionably pre-Constantinian is the church at Dura-Europos. It is an ancient city on the modern Syrian desert, established as one of the Selucid fortresses. Strengthened by the Romans and occupied later by the Persians, the city was later abandoned to the ravages of the desert. Of special interest are the 1930–31 archaeological excavations on the site. These digs yielded the ruins of an early house church. Snyder affirms that these remains are "one of a kind" and are the most important discovery of pre-Constantinian church practice and architecture. Nevertheless, he is skeptical regarding the earliest private house being an early house church since it elicits no history as such.[87]

The isometric drawings of the house church in Dura-Europos portray a "photograph" of a *domus ecclesiae* as it was in the year AD 256. Before it was adapted for a Christian meeting place, the house consisted of eight rooms and a courtyard. Somewhere between AD 232 and 256, the house was altered for use as a gathering place for Christians, adding a baptistery and wall paintings. The house was well hidden in a cluster of other similar houses. Its appearance remained that of a private house even after its alterations into a Christian church meeting place. After all, the Christians in the third century had every reason not to make their meeting place conspicuous.

Experiencing the Household of God

The house church contributed to the experiential understanding of the church's essence. The family-household basis must have had an overwhelming effect on the earliest believers' understanding of the church as family, the very "household of God."[88] Ultimately, as someone has said, every home should be a church, for a church is where Jesus dwells. This

---

[85] Floyd V. Filson (1939), "The Significance of the Early House Churches," *Journal of Biblical Literature 58*, p.109.

[86] Robert Banks (1980), *Paul's Idea of Community*, Eerdmans, pp.41–42.

[87] Graydon F. Snyder (1985), *Ante Pacem: Archaeological Evidence of Church Life Before Constantine*, Mercer University, pp.68-69.

[88] Eph 2:18–9, 3:14–15, 5:1, 6:23

goes far to explain why there is so much emphasis in the New Testament on family life and interpersonal relationships. The need for making faith work in daily home life was surely intensified by the dynamic house church structure. It must be understood that the New Testament ideas of Christian education are built upon a "Hebrew model"[89] of the Old Testament, which placed the responsibility in the locus of home life.[90]

Cultural Relevance

The house church was a culturally relevant model, providing a decentralized freedom for creative expression within the varying cultural settings. For Paul, "church" does not refer to a group of people scattered throughout a locality unless they all do in fact actually gather together. He does, however, occasionally group churches together by referring to the province in which they exist, as "the churches of Galatia," where he uses the plural form.[91] When he refers to the "church" of a given locality, he infers that the house churches of the city gathered together from time to time as part of the larger fellowship of the city *ekklesia*.[92]

Small, home-centered gatherings were a generally accepted phenomenon in the context of the ancient world. This cultural mood was an impetus for each small group to move with creative freedom in a particular direction according to its own appreciations. This was, no doubt, a positive factor in the development of the early church. In Corinth, like-minded folks may have gathered in the houses in which Paul, Cephas, or Apollos had stayed during their visits to that city.

Social Integration

The house church nurtured a healthy social integration of the earliest Christians. The apostolic church was evidently a healthy cross-section of society reflecting a broad social mixture, from wealthy land-home owner to common slave. Houses large enough to gather in as a church must have been owned by persons of some means. Not necessarily rich, they at least must not have been one of the dispossessed proletariat as those like Gaius, Erastus, Crispus, and Stephanas.

The implications of the healthy integrated amalgamation of the early Christian society have been unexplored. The New Testament evidences a strong stance on the equality of minority groups, particularly the place of women. And, a commonly observed penchant of Eastern people for the practice of hospitality in their homes served as a leveling force. A hierarchy of position would seem out of place in the warm and personal surroundings of a first-century Christian home.

---

[89] Del Birkey (1984), "*A Hebrew Model,*" Bethany Theological Seminary.

[90] cf. Deut 6:1–9

[91] Gal 1:2

[92] F.F. Bruce (1957), *Commentary on the Epistle to the Colossians*, Eerdmans, p.310; see also 1 Cor 14:23

Leadership Development

The house church positively influenced the development of the church's leaders. The hosts of the churches became the natural leaders of the church. They were most likely persons of sufficient education and practical administrative ability. Filson notes that many of the hosts of the earliest Gentile churches were "God-fearers." They had already demonstrated their initiative by leaving their ancestral situations and aligning with the synagogue. Rather than inheriting leadership, the house church structure imparted, through the hosts, actual leadership which in turn determined the form of church life.[93] At the end of the first century, John, the aging apostle, penned his final words to the church fellowships in Asia Minor. Nearly 70 years had passed since he walked with Jesus. Clement of Alexandria later wrote that John "would go away when invited to the neighboring districts of the Gentiles, here to appoint presbyters, there to form new churches, and there to put into the office of the ministry some one of those who were indicated by the Spirit."[94]

John's third epistle[95] is a brief but poignant glimpse into a house church situation, one of the last apostolic and canonical admonitions to a New Testament church. In it he introduces us to the infamous Diotrephes, whose essential character was manifested in his haughty attitude. John has permanently indebted us to him for introducing this ungentlemanly person to us. The pithy account serves as a forewarning of a common problem in church leadership. Diotrephes was a "would-be leader" in the house church. He wanted "to be head of everything!" Here, then, we have the final open window on house churches at the end of the first century. It reveals the common and unending riddle of deviate and eccentric church leaders. In the final analysis, the scene John depicts only strengthens the thesis being argued. The house churches were eminently suited to the training of future leadership-leaders who would be able to provide the guidance needed in the post-apostolic days. The small church communities had been admonished, encouraged, and trained to confront those who were seeking leadership positions apart from being called by the Spirit. The dynamic of the small group at work here went far to ensure post-apostolic "succession" of suitable leadership.

Corporate Solidarity

The household church strengthened the concept of corporate solidarity in Christian conversion. Conversion in the New Testament was not an exclusively individualistic experience. It was often a decision taken by the

---

[93] Floyd V. Filson (1939), "The Significance of the Early House Churches," *Journal of Biblical Literature 58*, p.112; see also 1 Cor 16:16

[94] Eusebius 111, 23.6, cited by J. Stott (1964), *The Epistles of John*, Eerdmans, p.40.

[95] 3 John

whole household. Sociologically, each society is composed of a variety of subgroups or homogeneous units. Societies have differing procedures for making group decisions, as for instance, by the consensus of a group of leaders. Thus, we need to discern the pattern of response to the gospel most fitting for that particular culture. References to the household conversions of Cornelius, Lydia, Crispus, and the Philippian jailer provide an alternative to contemporary thinking concerning conversion.[96] Here is yet another positive characteristic of the first-century house church which much of the Western, twentieth-century church has lost. Attention needs to be given to conversion as a complex experience. Speaking on this theme, Orlando Costas reminds us that conversion is not only a distinct moment and continuum process, but a missional commitment as well. It is a socio-ecclesial reality. It does not take place in a vacuum, but rather within particular social contexts.[97]

Missionary Strategy

The household as church afforded the basic solution to the problem of early missionary strategy. A paramount point needs to be made in this context regarding Paul's missionary strategy. Simply put, it was a strategy of households. He needed a meeting place for a center of operation, as well as for gathering the new believers. It is reasonable to assume that when Paul began missionary work in a city, his primary objective was to win a household first. This then became the nucleus as well as the center for the advancement of the gospel in that area. Church growth analyst Donald McGavran enlightens this matter further by saying that the first common obstacle to multiplying churches never appeared in the early church, i.e., the cost of building buildings. The house church overcame the obstacle of introversion by exposing a new section of society in each new house church. He adds, "The physical fact of the house church should be taken into consideration in any assessment of the causes of the growth of the early church."[98]

Christian Hospitality

The house churches were the embodiment of biblical and Christian hospitality. One wonders how the first churches would have succeeded if the generous attitude of hospitality had not been among their comrades. In his *Social Aspects of Early Christianity*, A.J. Malherbe speaks to this issue by charging that the theological implications of hospitality as practiced by the early church still await our attention.[99] He points out that hospitality was

---

[96] Acts 10:1–2, 16: 13–15, 31-34, 18:18

[97] Orlando Costas, "Conversion as a Complex Experience," in *Down to Earth: Studies in Christianity and Culture*, John R.W. Stott and Robert Coote (eds.) (1980), Eerdmans, pp.183-187.

[98] D. McGavran (1970), *Understanding Church Growth*, Eerdmans, pp.192–193.

[99] Abraham J. Malherbe (1977), *Social Aspects of Early Christianity*, Louisiana State University Press, p.67.

regarded as a virtue since classical times by pagans as well as Jews. Its high priority in the New Testament only serves to show how the first Christians believed they should excel in this virtue to the degree of transforming it into a distinctly Christian principle.

In this way, the household character of a church would be retained as it became larger and existed among other groups of its kind. Malherbe is right that the early Christians believed that they had been called to a higher quality of life than could be expected of their society. They thus took measures to safeguard it in their house church communities. Their enthusiastic practice of hospitality quietly became the very protection of their life together.

Luke is especially interested in depicting Jesus as both enjoying and teaching hospitality.[100] In his Acts, the practice of hospitality is frequently reported. Other narratives assume it. The first beachhead in Europe was afforded Paul by a woman's generous and insistent provision of hospitality.[101] Philemon is urged to "prepare a guest room."[102] John's last two tiny epistles show that hospitality was still basic to church life and was going strong at the end of the first century.[103] The pastoral epistles cite hospitality as a duty of elders,[104] as well as of widows on the lower end of the social situation.[105]

Furthermore, Paul, like Peter, calls hospitality a spiritual gift.[106] Peter commended the believers to "practice hospitality" to one another without grumbling.[107] J.B. Phillips gets to the essence by phrasing it, "Be hospitable to each other without secretly wishing you hadn't got to be!" Further, the writer of Hebrews counsels, "Remember to show hospitality. There are some who, by so doing, have entertained angels without knowing it."[108]

Hospitality is affirmed in the gospels, particularly in conjunction with the sending out of apostles and other heralds. What is striking is that these earliest missionaries were to assume the hospitality of the people to whom they were to proclaim their message.[109] The very success of their heralding depended on the early believer's hospitality.

In "Early Christian Hospitality: A Factor in the Gospel Transmission," R.W. Riddle points to early Christian hospitality as one of the most charming features of the earliest church. By interrogating the extracanonical

---

[100] Luke 14:7f
[101] Acts 16:14–15
[102] Philem 1:22
[103] 2 and 3 John
[104] Titus 1:8
[105] 1 Tim 5:10
[106] Rom 12:13
[107] 1 Pet 4:9 (RSV)
[108] Heb 13:2 (NEB)
[109] Matt 10:5–42; Mark 6:7–11; Luke 9:2–5, 10:1–16

writings of the New Testament period, Riddle shows that the patristic sources add support to the extraordinary commonality of early Christian hospitality:

> These examples of hospitality suggest that the custom may account for a notable phenomenon of those days: the acceptance of the traveling preacher's message by entire households...that the primitive churches were house-churches is a detail of this, and an aspect of early Christian hospitality...This brings the student directly to the social processes in Christianity's expansion. One of them was early Christian hospitality. In it one sees an ultimate medium of Christianity's growth. Observing early Christian hospitality, venturing to look into the early Christian household, one sees a very charming, as it was a very effective, aspect of early Christian life.[110]

CONCLUSIONS

In summary, an overview of the New Testament regarding the house church phenomenon leads one to concur with Filson and others, that the apostolic church can never be properly understood without always bearing in mind the distinctive contribution the house churches made. The house church as a model provided Paul with his most demonstrative theological model for the church as "the household of God," along with his ultimate figure of the church as Christ's body. The house church in reality, therefore, did provide the paramount sociological model whose ramifications were everywhere to be seen.[111]

STUDY QUESTIONS

1. Why is it important to consider both the size and location of the early churches in order to properly understand the rest of the New Testament?

2. What were the advantages afforded by the house churches to the early Christian movement?

3. Why do you suppose that house churches were able to thrive in many contexts in the New Testament era, both in Jewish and Gentile culture, among the rich and the poor, during times of peace and persecution, etc?

---

[110] Donald W. Riddle (1938), "Early Christian Hospitality: A Factor in the Gospel Transmission," *Journal of Biblical Literature* 57, pp.152–154. See also J. B. Jordan (1981), "God's Hospitality and Holistic Evangelism," *The Journal of Christian Reconstruction* 17, pp.87–113.

[111] Derek Tidball (1984), *The Social Context of the New Testament: A Sociological Analysis*, Zondervan, p.86.

Chapter 5

THE NATURE AND FUNCTION OF THE EARLY HOUSE CHURCHES

RAD ZDERO

Rad Zdero earned his Ph.D. degree in Mechanical Engineering from Queen's University (Kingston, ON, Canada) and is the manager of a hospital-based orthopaedic research lab. He has participated in, led, and started house churches and cell groups since 1985. He is currently part of HouseChurch.Ca (www.housechurch.ca), which is a church planting team developing a network of house churches in the greater Toronto area and beyond. He is the author of The Global House Church Movement (2004). Email: rzdero@yahoo.ca.

INTRODUCTION

A survey of the New Testament record reveals that the early Christians organized themselves primarily into small house-sized units and, thus, could properly be considered a house church movement.[1] This fact has been recognized by scholars for many years[2] and is echoed by other writers and practitioners in the field.[3] But, what were these house churches like? What exactly did Christians do when they met together? How did they contribute to one another's lives day to day? Were there essentials commonly found in most or all house churches in the first century? In the following, the open format of church meetings will be examined followed by a detailed look at the mystical, intellectual, spectacular, symbolic, relational, evangelistic, material, temporal, and sociological elements that characterized the early house churches of the New Testament era.

---

[1] Acts 2:46, 5:42, 8:3, 10:1-48, 12:12, 16:14-15,29-34, 18:8, 20:6-8,20; Rom 16:3-5; 1 Cor 16:15,19; Col 4:15-16; Philem 1:2; 2 John 1:10

[2] Roger Gehring (2004), *House Church and Mission: The Importance of Household Structures in Early Christianity*, Hendrickson Publishers; Robert Banks (1994), *Paul's Idea of Community*, Hendrickson Publishers; Del Birkey (1988), *The House Church: A Model for Renewing the Church*, Herald Press; F.V. Filson (1939), "The Significance of the Early House Churches", *J. Biblical Literature*, 58:105-112.

[3] Rad Zdero (2004), *The Global House Church Movement*, William Carey Library; Steve Atkerson (ed.) (2003), *Ekklesia: To the Roots of Biblical Church Life*, New Testament Restoration Foundation, (www.ntrf.org); Robert Fitts (2001), *The Church in the House*, Preparing the Way Publishers; Wolfgang Simson (1998), *Houses that Change the World*, Paternoster Publishing.

THE OPEN FORMAT OF CHURCH MEETINGS

What were first century house church meetings like? Were they liturgical, charismatic, evangelistic, or teaching-centered? Fortunately, we do have clear guidelines as to the format and purpose of church gatherings. There are several important passages that outline the four primary characteristics that describe the open format of meetings, namely that they were participatory, interactive, spontaneous, and Spirit-led.

Participatory

Every-member contribution to the group was a prominent feature in an early church meeting. Rather than a religious service being run by a few active participants for a group of rather passive onlookers, everyone had the opportunity and the responsibility of using their God-given capacities and skills. Everyone was encouraged to participate and bring to the 'spiritual table' whatever contribution they could. During a very lengthy discussion on various aspects of church meetings, the apostle Paul describes their equal opportunity format as follows:

> What then shall we say, brothers? When you come together, *everyone* has a hymn, or a word of instruction, a revelation, a tongue or an interpretation. All of these must be done for the strengthening of the church.[4]

Interactive

Mutual learning took place among attendees in the early church meetings. Relationships and communication were not primarily between a leader and the church membership, but between each and every person. Everyone had something to learn from everyone else during church get-togethers. This is indicated by the term 'one another' in the following passages:

> Speak to *one another* with psalms, hymns and spiritual songs. Sing and make music in your heart to the Lord, always giving thanks to God the Father for everything, in the name of our Lord Jesus Christ.[5]

> Let the word of Christ dwell in you richly as you teach and admonish *one another* with all wisdom, and as you sing psalms, hymns and spiritual songs with gratitude in your hearts to God.[6]

> Let us not give up meeting together, as some are in the habit of doing, but let us encourage *one another*, and all the more as you see the Day approaching.[7]

---

[4] 1 Cor 14:26 (NIV, emphasis added)
[5] Eph 5:19-20 (NIV, emphasis added)
[6] Col 3:16 (NIV, emphasis added)
[7] Heb 10:25 (NIV, emphasis added)

Spontaneous

There was a somewhat informal atmosphere which permeated first century church meetings. A high degree of planning and programming is absent from the instructions given by the apostles to the churches in this regard. So unceremonious were the meetings that cautions sometimes were voiced by the apostles to ensure that chaos would not reign, so that God's purposes could be accomplished without disruption. This was especially necessary when multiple messages in tongues or prophetic words from several individuals were vying for expression at the same time. In these cases, Paul advised that everyone should speak in turn so that all these messages could be tabled for consideration by the assembled church:

> If anyone speaks in a tongue, it should be by two or at the most three, and each in turn, and let one interpret…And let two or three prophets speak, and let the others pass judgment…For you can all prophesy one by one, so that all may learn and all may be exhorted; and the spirits of prophets are subject to prophets; *for God is not a God of confusion but of peace*, as in all the churches of the saints.[8]

Spirit-led

God's Spirit empowered and guided believers in the full expression of their particular spiritual gift(s) for the benefit of others. Paul gives a fairly exhaustive list of the gifts that had a place in the life of the church in general which would surely have been activated during church meeting times:

> But to *each one is given the manifestation of the Spirit* for the common good. For to one is given the word of wisdom…to another the word of knowledge…to another faith…to another gifts of healing…to another the effecting of miracles…to another prophecy…to another the distinguishing of spirits…to another various kinds of tongues…to another the interpretation of tongues.[9]

Consequently, we can see that early church meetings were 'spiritual potlucks' in which everyone brought something for the benefit of others. New Testament-style church meetings afforded each person the opportunity to exercise their spiritual gifts by sharing an experience, teaching, prophecy, song, etc. There were no one-man shows, one-way communication, or formal ceremonies. Rather, meetings were occasions where everyone's spiritual capacities found expression. Such meetings would have been difficult to facilitate in a large group setting, but they were a natural outcome in the smaller more intimate context of the early house-sized churches.

---

[8] 1 Cor 14:27,29,31-33 (NASB, emphasis added)
[9] 1 Cor 12:7-10 (NASB, emphasis added)

MYSTICAL ELEMENTS: PRAYER, PRAISE, AND SINGING

Prayer, praise, and singing punctuated first century gatherings and are here categorized as 'mystical' elements. Possible definitions of these three terms are that prayer is the communication of a desire to receive something from God, praise is giving to God recognition and thanks, and singing is some combination of prayer and praise expressed melodically.

Prayer, by far, was the most common form of communication to God in New Testament era churches. Believers prayed for each other, for the apostles, for those in government authority, in times of illness, during periods of persecution, when a fellow Christian was slipping into sin, for clarity during decision-making, and for a myriad of other reasons.[10] There are even several places in the Scriptures where the words of a prayer are recorded.[11]

Interestingly, in comparison to prayer (mentioned about 90 times from Acts to Revelation), there was much less said about, and few examples given of, either praise (mentioned about 40 times) or singing (mentioned about 12 times), apart from a few passing remarks. It is probable that this relative emphasis in the early church writings on prayer in comparison to praise and singing characterized house church meetings. When Christians gathered there was a great deal of spontaneity, freedom, and opportunity for everyone to engage in prayer, praise, and singing.

INTELLECTUAL ELEMENTS: THE TEACHINGS OF THE APOSTLES

Early church gatherings were also forums for the intellectual development of members. The apostle Paul was especially keen on seeing people in his churches develop an increased understanding of the things of God with their minds. He puts such an emphasis on this throughout his letters that some might accuse the apostle of being too much of a rationalist, which may stem partially from his previous training as a Pharisee.[12]

This tendency of Paul's and, presumably, of the communities he founded, is seen by the frequency of his references to rational activity. He uses a significant number of terms and ideas to get his point across to his audience like consider, convince, discern, grasp, instruct, judge, know, knowledge, learn, meaning, mind, persuade, reasonable, remind, teach, test, think, thoughts, truth, understanding, and wisdom.[13]

---

[10] Acts 1:24-26, 2:42, 4:24-31, 16:25; Eph 6:18-20; Philip 4:6-7; Col 4:2-4; 1 Thess 2:8, 5:17-18; 2 Thess 3:1-4; 1 Tim 2:1-4; Heb 13:18; James 5:13; 1 John 5:16; Jude 1:20

[11] Acts 1:24-25, 4:24-31 7:59-60

[12] Acts 23:6, 26:5,24-25; Philip 3:4-6

[13] Acts 26:24-25; Rom 12:2, 14:5, 16:19; 1 Cor 1:10, 2:12,15, 4:6,11, 14:20,29, 15:34; 2 Cor 10:5, 11:3; Gal 3:2; Eph 4:22-24, 5:15; Philip 1:9, 2:5, 3:15, 4:8; Col 1:9-10, 3:2,10, 4:5; 1 Thess 5:21; 1 Tim 2:11, 5:4; 2 Tim 3:7; Titus 3:14; Heb 5:11-6:2

What concrete forms did this take in believers' meetings? There was some combination of learning from those who had a clear ability to teach while at the same time honoring the principle of mutual instruction. The apostles encouraged 'teachers', those who were knowledgeable and had an obvious strength in communicating, to make use of this talent for the benefit of others.[14] The early church believed that God had gifted certain individuals with a strong teaching ability to aid the Body of Christ.[15] This may have included local elders, local Christians who were not functioning as elders, and those called to travel from church to church.[16] Even so, the apostles Paul, Peter, and John all showed concern about the very real possibility that false teachers could eventually infiltrate churches and not hold true to apostolic instruction.[17] As such, all learning was to be firmly based not on people's own whims and ideas but, rather, on the teachings of the apostles—whether by word of mouth or in written form—and the scriptures.[18]

What was the format for such instruction? Was it lecture-style with one person delivering a one-way message to a crowd of quiet listeners? As demonstrated earlier, local churches knew they were to "teach and admonish one another with all wisdom"[19] and that "everyone has...a word of instruction"[20] during meetings. This interactive teaching method was even employed by visiting apostles. A clear example of this happened when the apostle Paul visited a house church in the city of Troas:

> On the first day of the week we came together to break bread. Paul *spoke* to the people and, because he intended to leave the next day, kept on *talking* until midnight. There were many lamps in the upstairs room where we were meeting...Paul *talked* on and on...After *talking* until daylight, he left.[21]

The Greek root word used for *spoke* and *talked* in this passage is *dialegomai*, from which comes the word 'dialogue', and quite literally means to have a conversation or debate. The Greek words used for the two instances of *talking* are *logon* and *homileo*, meaning talk, converse, or reason. However, altogether different Greek words in the New Testament are used for instances of one-way communication or 'preaching' (Greek = *kerusso* and *euangello*), which was reserved for communicating the message of Christ to non-Christians who had not heard it before.

---

[14] Rom 12:6-7; 1 Tim 5:17; Heb 5:11

[15] 1 Cor 12:28-29; Eph 4:11-12

[16] Acts 13:1, 15:36-41, 18:24-28; 1 Tim 5:17; 2 John 1:7-11

[17] 1 Tim 6:3-5; 2 Tim 4:3; Titus 1:10-11; 2 Pet 2:1-3; 2 John 1:9-11

[18] Rom 15:4; 1 Cor 15:3-5; 1 Thess 4:1-2; 2 Thess 3:14-15; 1 Tim 4:13, 5:7; 2 Tim 2:2, 3:16; 2 Pet 3:15-16

[19] Col 3:16 (NIV)

[20] 1 Cor 14:26 (NIV)

[21] Acts 20:7-12 (NIV, emphasis added)

Thus, Paul's teaching in this case was a lengthy two-way discussion—not a monologue—with questions and answers and ideas being formulated as the evening unfolded, albeit with Paul probably making the dominant contribution. This kind of interactive discussion and learning was a natural and common method employed in the early house churches.

SPECTACULAR ELEMENTS: PROPHECY, MIRACLES, AND OTHERS

A more dramatic set of occurrences was also present in early church meetings, presently classified together as 'spectacular' elements. These contributions from members of a local house church went beyond the ordinary and humanly explainable. When these aspects presented themselves, it was clear that people were simply the vehicles and conduits for these expressions and not their originators.

Regarding the particular spectacular elements that could be present in a given meeting,[22] the list includes prophecy (an intuitive knowledge or inner prompting to speak God's mind), tongues (speaking and interpreting a divinely given non-human language), healings (power over the physical effects of disease and accident), miraculous works (exorcisms of demons, nature miracles, etc.), and discernment of spirits (detecting whether a message originates with God, demons, or humans). Some explicit examples of their use during a meeting include the sensitivity of some prophets in discerning God's call on Barnabas and Paul to an apostolic ministry and the resuscitation at the hands of Paul of a young man who had fallen down dead during a late night gathering.[23]

These spiritual gifts were to be released during church meetings for the mutual benefit of all present.[24] Paul takes pains to convince his readers to view everyone's gift as having an important role in the life of the church by comparing Christ to a head and the church to a body, the former giving direction to the latter to benefit every part of the body.[25] Although he argues for the uniqueness and significance of everyone's contribution, to Paul some of these spectacular gifts were more inherently beneficial and intelligible to the church and curious visitors and should be strongly encouraged, especially prophecy.[26]

Paul also emphasizes that these God-given capacities were distributed differently among people, such that not everyone would have the same type or number of these spectacular abilities.[27] Consequently, we can expect the expression of these gifts in the first century church to have varied from

---

[22] Acts 15:32-33; 1 Cor 12:7-10, 28-30; 1 Thess 5:19-22; James 5:14-16; 1 John 4:1-3
[23] Acts 13:1-3, 20:7-12
[24] 1 Cor 14:26; 1 Thess 5:19-20
[25] 1 Cor 12:12-27
[26] 1 Cor 14:1-6,22
[27] 1 Cor 12:4-7, 28-30

locality to locality and perhaps even meeting to meeting. Lastly, none of these dramatic gifts were to be suppressed, except as dictated by a sense of balance and appropriateness. Their allure seems to have been somewhat problematic for the Corinthians, forcing Paul to emphasize that things were to be done in an orderly manner so that church meetings would not become chaotic and unproductive.[28]

SYMBOLIC ELEMENTS: THE LORD'S SUPPER AND BAPTISM

In the early church there were two symbolic acts used to signify milestone moments in the life of Christ and, hence, in the life of the follower of Christ, namely the Lord's Supper and Baptism.

The Lord's Supper

With its bread and wine, this was modeled by Christ and practiced by the ancient church around a full meal.[29] It is not entirely certain, though, whether this occurred every single time believers met corporately—although, apparently it was a very frequent practice—or even whether more overtly 'spiritual' elements like prayer, prophecy, teaching, etc., occurred during the meal. In either case, the Lord's Supper would have evoked several key ideas and vivid images. First and foremost, it was a reminder that Jesus came into the world to lay his life down willingly as a sacrifice—his broken body and spilt blood represented by the bread and wine—which somehow remedied the darkness and sin in the world. Being first patterned by Christ in the setting of a Passover meal, it also carried his disciples back to the story of God's rescue of the Israelites out of Egyptian slavery, both by instructing the angel of death to 'pass over' their homes and by leading them to 'pass over' the desert from Egypt to the Promised Land.[30] Thus, for the early church, Jesus was now rescuing them from a more sinister type of evil, that of spiritual slavery. Lastly, in the cultural framework of the first century, the fact that the Lord's Supper was indeed a full-scale community meal was a sign of mutual acceptance into an intimate and unique friendship not shared by others.[31] Those who had voluntarily forged a family bond in Christ now shared this 'community table' with each other.

Who was authorized to facilitate the Lord's Supper? The Scriptures are curiously silent about this issue, perhaps indicating that this was not a point of concern for the early church. The only example we have of anyone specifically administering it was that of Jesus himself during the last supper he shared with his 12 disciples. It would be difficult to make a case from this one-time event, though, that those in leadership always must have physically initiated the Lord's Supper during church meetings. Even so, we might

---

[28] 1 Cor 14:27-33,40
[29] Luke 22:14-20; 1 Cor 11:17-34
[30] Exodus 12:1-40
[31] Matt 9:10-11, Luke 15:1-2, 1 Cor 5:9-11

reasonably infer that local leaders—being responsible for managing the overall affairs of the church—may have been at least present, although not always physically involved, during such an activity to ensure that things were done appropriately.

Baptism

This was the other major symbolic act prevalent in the early church. Christ's personal baptism at the hands of John the Baptist and his last instructions to the apostles to make and baptize disciples served as the primary model and mandate for the early Christian community.[32] Consequently, right from the birth of the church at Pentecost, new members were baptized in water as an outward sign of their inward allegiance to Christ.

The baptisms recorded in the New Testament were performed both privately and publicly, in small and large groups, were reserved for believers only, and seemed to occur very soon after the first indications of genuine faith in Christ.[33] As such, it is quite conceivable that non-Christian friends who visited a church meeting and came to faith were baptized during the meeting itself; however, no explicit report of such an event survives.

Who was qualified to facilitate baptism? It seemed to have been customarily done by the apostles as they gained new converts from their preaching forays, but no explicit scriptural instruction is given on this matter. We are, in fact, given some indication that perhaps any believer could legitimately baptize a new convert.

For example, we are told that Philip baptized an Ethiopian man privately along the roadside as well as a large number of others.[34] Philip was neither one of the 12 apostles nor was he a recognized apostolic worker or a local church elder. Rather he was simply in charge of addressing some material needs of the Jerusalem church.[35]

Similarly, John the Baptist was not commissioned by any authoritative individual or religious body to engage in his baptisms. Yet, Jesus recognized the legitimacy of the Baptist's activities not only by being baptized by him, but also by showing support for John's baptisms during a debate with the Pharisees.[36] As such, similar to the Lord's Supper, it may be that those in

---

[32] Matt 3:13-17, 28:18-20

[33] Acts 2:36-41, 8:4-17, 8:34-39, 9:17-19, 10:44-48, 16:13-15, 16:29-34, 18:7-8, 1 Cor 1:14-16. Those arguing for infant baptism find support in some instances where it is recorded that a household was saved and baptized (Acts 11:11-17, 16:15, 16:31-34, 18:8; 1 Cor 1:16, 16:15), presumably including any infants. However, at best, these are arguments from silence based on vague passages, since no infants are ever mentioned explicitly on these occasions. The overwhelming scriptural evidence supports voluntary believer's baptism.

[34] Acts 8:4-13, 34-39

[35] Acts 6:1-6

[36] Matt 21:23-27

local leadership were present, although not always directly involved, during baptisms.

RELATIONAL ELEMENTS: 'ONE ANOTHER' AND 'EACH OTHER'

Jesus once made the statement that the world would know that Christians were indeed his disciples by the mutual love they demonstrated.[37] His followers were to be about the business of building a community together, living the common life, and engaging in mutual life-on-life ministry.

The early church took this seriously enough that the writers of the New Testament made sure it was replete with dozens of 'one another' and 'each other' statements, encouraging followers of Christ to consider the many ways they could practically and mutually show love. Although not elements solely restricted to church meetings, the force behind their sentiment was certainly felt during house church get-togethers and would have been a distinguishing hallmark immediately noted by the observant visitor. The 'one another' and 'each other' passages touch on themes of mutual acceptance, admonition, agreement, building up, compassion, concern, confession, devotion, encouragement, fellowship, forgiveness, greeting, harmony, honor, hospitality, humility, instruction, kindness, love, peaceability, prayer, service, submission, and tolerance.[38]

The apostles also gave directives concerning things *not* to do to 'one another' and 'each other' such as deceiving, envying, grumbling against, judging, provoking, and slandering.[39] These items were not meant merely to be part of a litany of ideals to be aspired to and discussed theoretically but, rather, were to characterize interactions between believers on a day-to-day level.

The apostles were certainly keenly aware of the practical need for such constant reminders because New Testament home churches were by nature small and intimate clusters of people and, as such, held great potential for tension and division. Conversely, the apostles knew that forging deep, authentic, and mutually transforming friendships could only occur in such intimate gatherings. This may have been another reason why their practice was to pattern the early Christian communities using a house church model.

EVANGELISTIC ELEMENTS: WHEN NON-CHRISTIANS VISIT

Most of the evangelistic activities of the first Christians were customarily done in the public eye, whereas private house-to-house patterns were reserved for believers. Evangelism, however, was not strictly limited to the

---

[37] John 13:35

[38] Rom 12:10, 12:16, 15:7, 15:14, 16:16; 1 Cor 1:10, 12:25, 16:20; 2 Cor 13:12; Gal 5:13; Eph 4:2, 4:32, 5:21; Philip 4:2; Col 3:13, 3:16; 1 Thess 3:12, 4:9,18, 5:11,13,15,25; 2 Thess 1:3; Heb 3:13, 10:24, 13:1; James 4:11, 5:16; 1 Pet 1:22, 3:8, 4:7-11, 5:5,14; 1 John 1:7, 3:11,23, 4:7,12; 2 John 1:5

[39] Gal 5:26; Col 3:9; James 4:11, 5:9

public forum, but also wove its way into the house churches whenever curious friends and neighbors visited.

For example, in giving the Corinthian Christians instructions about church gatherings, Paul encourages them to be aware of the opportunity that exists to intelligently communicate the message of Christ when visitors come.[40] Specifically, he counsels them to avoid the use of the gift of tongues—usually unintelligible unless there is someone who can interpret the message—in favor of prophecy as a more meaningful tool in this regard, convincing the seeker to surrender their life to Christ. That such things actually took place from time to time may be inferred from the very fact that Paul brings the issue to light. Evidently, when this occurred it must have been a profoundly moving experience for all involved as the visitor encounters God for the first time in the presence of all.

Although not a church gathering as such, another similar example, spelled out in some detail, is that of the apostle Peter visiting the home of Cornelius, the Roman officer whose prayers God had heard.[41] Cornelius, being a man of some position and local influence, invited a house full of friends in anticipation of the apostle's visit. Before Peter even reached the end of his message, the Holy Spirit fell on the hearers, and they began speaking in tongues and praising God. After this, they were all baptized in water. Peter stayed for a few days at the new house church's request, instructing them as to the next steps. Because Cornelius' relational circle experienced such a dramatic encounter with God, it is quite probable that they became particularly keen on the need to invite others from their familial and social networks into future house gatherings, hoping to see other conversions take place.

MATERIAL ELEMENTS: SHARING THE WEALTH

As in any era, the New Testament Christians were faced with the challenges of dealing deftly with material needs and financial decisions. The general principle endorsed by Christ and the apostles was that of a lifestyle of generosity that gave of itself, not under compulsion, but voluntarily and gladly.[42]

On what did early believers focus their financial generosity? Certainly, as a house church movement, they would not have spent finances on any church buildings or expensive programs. The early church gave money almost exclusively to two groups of people, namely the poor among them and traveling apostolic workers, whereas local church leaders did not receive financial support as discussed elsewhere.[43]

---

[40] 1 Cor 14:22-25
[41] Acts 10:1-48
[42] Mark 12:41-44; 2 Cor 9:6-8
[43] Rad Zdero (2004), *The Global House Church Movement*, William Carey Library, pp.39-48.

Local Poverty Relief

This was something close to the heart of first century believers, since many of them were faced with very real material needs of their own. For example, in the early days after Pentecost, the Jerusalem church was faced with the problem of addressing the needs of the burgeoning Christian community, now suddenly numbering over 3,000 members. This mass of people was from all over the Mediterranean world and had decided to settle in Jerusalem to be with their new spiritual family. The apostles now had to deal with the consequences of their successful preaching. The solution to the situation was a pooling of everyone's resources into a common pot, possibly collected by both apostles and elders. It seemed to work well.[44] Additionally, some of the Pauline churches evidently had local widows, without any surviving family, who were being taken care of by their Christian community.[45]

Universal Poverty Relief

Local believers, however, were not only concerned with their own situation, but they took notice of the plight of their brothers and sisters in other parts of the world. For example, years after Pentecost the situation for the Jerusalem church did not see much improvement, this time due to a famine, which was known to happen in that part of the world from time to time. Consequently, the apostles Peter, James, and John made an arrangement with the apostles Paul and Barnabas to undertake a fundraising project among some of the Gentile churches to relieve the suffering of the church in Jerusalem. Paul went on to specifically request that the Corinthians and Galatians set aside weekly amounts, depending on their own financial situation, on a regular basis until he came, so that no collections would need to be made at the last moment. It was the local house church elders who accepted contributions every week, passing the sum to Paul and Barnabas when they arrived.[46]

Apostolic Funding

The support of traveling apostolic leaders and teams was a funding focus of the early church, in addition to addressing local and universal poverty issues. The first example is that of Jesus himself, who was functionally a mobile kingdom worker for about three years. Christ was supported by a group of women who followed him with the express intention of caring for his material needs, while it was Judas who managed their donations since he was the group's treasurer.[47] Other sources of assistance came in the form of the frequent offers of hospitality he accepted as he traveled the countryside preaching, teaching, and healing.[48]

---

[44] Acts 2:43-45, 4:32-35

[45] 1 Tim 5:3,9,16

[46] Acts 11:27-30, Rom 15:25-28, 1 Cor 16:1-4, 2 Cor 9:1-15, Gal 2:1,9-10

[47] Matt 27:55-56; John 12:4-6, 13:29

[48] Matt 8:14-15, 9:9-10; Luke 7:36, 10:38-42, 19:2-6

In a similar fashion, Jesus trained his disciples to become traveling apostolic workers by sending seventy of them out in pairs to preach from town to town as a practical hands-on exercise. They were instructed to accept the hospitality of anyone who offered it and who was open to their message of the kingdom.[49]

Once the church was established at Pentecost, the apostles would look to the example of Jesus in garnering support for their own itinerant responsibilities. Most of the apostles—like Peter, Jesus' brothers, and others—did accept such material assistance as they traveled. However, Paul and Barnabas, although recognizing it was their right to expect it, were most often content working for a living to meet their own needs and those of their traveling companions. Their motivation seems to have been to avert any accusations from rivals or enemies that they were ministering solely for the money. On occasion, though, they gratefully accepted such support from churches that especially wanted to help them.[50]

Lastly, it is probable that support for apostolic workers was collected beforehand by local house church elders for a planned visit, given spontaneously when their visit to a house church was brief or unannounced, and regularly on an ongoing basis for apostolic workers who had to remain local for some time to set things in order.

TEMPORAL ELEMENTS: DAY, TIME, AND LENGTH OF MEETINGS

Another topic of interest is the temporal characteristics of the early Christian communities. In other words, what habits did they have when it came to choosing the day, time, and length of their gatherings?

Regarding the choice of day and time, there was in some cases a preference to meet on the first day of the week, i.e. Sunday, to commemorate the resurrection of Christ by breaking bread together.[51] Paul, however, took pains to ensure that communities to which he was connected were not becoming too rigidly attached to any particular day of the week as being more sacred than any other.[52] Accordingly, it is reported that the early church felt free to meet on any day of the week, morning and evening, as circumstances dictated.[53]

Regarding the length of time for a given church meeting, there was no clear apostolic practice. Meetings could be open ended and very long, as was the case when Paul visited a house church for an all night discussion session that lasted until daybreak.[54] Similarly, when Herod arrested the apostle Peter, believers in Jerusalem met with their respective home churches and

---

[49] Luke 10:1-11
[50] Acts 20:33-34; 1 Cor 9:1-18; Philip 4:14-19
[51] Luke 24:1-7; Acts 20:7-11; 1 Cor 16:2
[52] Rom 14:4-6, Gal 4:8-11, Col 2:16-17
[53] Acts 1:12-14, 2:46-47, 5:42, 6:1, 16:5; Heb 3:13
[54] Acts 20:7-11

spent all night praying for his release.[55] The general rule for meeting duration seems to have been the particular need of the moment.

SOCIOLOGICAL ELEMENTS: THE SIZE OF HOUSE CHURCHES

The size of any group will affect the individual relationships between members, overall group dynamics, and the learning process. Consequently, another important matter to understand is the sociological factor of group size in first century house churches. Though there were some larger meetings in Jerusalem's Temple for a temporary transitional time in the case of Jewish-Christians, as well as synagogues and lecture halls for evangelistic or training endeavors, these did not compete with the dominant house-to-house pattern of the first century.

Although there are some direct statements in the New Testament about the size of these house fellowships, there were certainly no apostolic directives. The following clues are worth considering.

The small band of 12 disciples gathered around Jesus may serve as a model in this regard.[56] Although not technically a house church after the manner of the Pauline churches, Christ's discipleship circle would have at least implicitly and naturally served as a prototype for the faith communities that the apostles founded. As a small group, Christ and his disciples gathered together in a home with a large upper room to celebrate the Passover together.[57] This intimate setting was ideal for the type of intense interaction they had, which involved foot washing, sharing a meal, taking part in the Lord's Supper in anticipation of Jesus' impending arrest and death, hymn singing, and heart rending conversations about denial and betrayal.[58]

Another clue is found in the account relating events just prior to Pentecost.[59] The group included between 12 and perhaps 120 disciples at any one time in the large upper room of a Jerusalem home, where they were in continual prayer. However, strictly speaking, this gathering was organized based on unusual directions given by Christ at the time of his ascension in which the disciples were to await the Spirit's power (i.e. specific timeframe for a specific purpose). Thus, this scenario is limited in the information it can provide on the more normative practice of house-sized church meetings.

A further insight comes from Peter's visit to the home of Cornelius the Roman officer. We are told that there was a large gathering of people assembled in the house to hear the message Peter was about to bring.[60] Since the listeners all became followers of Christ that day, we can assume that this large gathering continued to meet together as a newly formed house church.

---

[55] Acts 12:11-17
[56] Mark 3:13-19
[57] Mark 14:13-15
[58] Mark 14:17-26, John 13:1-38
[59] Acts 1:13-15
[60] Acts 10:19-27

Although the scriptural information we have used only provides an initial understanding there is, fortunately, archaeological evidence that indicates the physical size of the average home. This becomes important since the early church was primarily a house church movement. First century houses were able to accommodate on average 20 to 40 individuals.[61] Thus, a very large church would have been one that was filled to the brim with perhaps as many as three-dozen people. Many household churches were probably significantly smaller than this and, hence, were more reminiscent of Jesus' first discipleship circle of 12.

This small group dynamic helped maintain a kind of up-close-and-personal family atmosphere in local house churches, where everyone knew each other and had the opportunity to interact on a more intimate level. Consequently, apostolic directives to the churches—open and interactive meetings, mutual accountability, the Lord's Supper as a full meal, relationships, etc.—make much practical sense in the context of these house-sized units.

CONCLUSIONS

This article has briefly described the various elements that characterized the early house churches. The first Christian communities were not one dimensional, but rather sought to incorporate multiple elements to provide a holistic environment both for the spiritual growth of their members and for their missional outreach to society at large.

STUDY QUESTIONS

1. When people went to church in the first century, what could they expect meetings to be like?
2. Which elements helped build mutual fellowship in the early house churches?
3. Which factors were useful in the missional outreach of the early house churches?

---

[61] Roger Gehring, Ibid, p.290.

Chapter 6

CORPORATE FUNCTIONING THROUGH PERSONAL GIFTEDNESS IN THE EARLY HOUSE CHURCHES

DEL BIRKEY

Del Birkey, D.Min. (Bethany Theological Seminary, USA), served in pastoral, evangelistic, and teaching ministries in churches and as a visiting seminary professor. He is the author of The House Church: A Model for Renewing the Church (1988) (scheduled for rerelease in 2007) and The Fall of Patriarchy: Its Broken Legacy Judged by Jesus and the Apostolic House Church Communities (2005). [Adapted and used by permission of the author. Email: delbirkey@birkey.com].

INTRODUCTION

As the first century house churches spread throughout the Mediterranean, their ability to grow new disciples of Christ in both quality and quantity was largely dependent on the discovery, the development, and the use of spiritual gifts, individually as believers and corporately as churches. Both Paul and Peter provided basic introductory data on the theme of giftedness.[1] Their orientation to spiritual gifts suggests that believers had a responsibility to grasp giftedness as personal stewardship in servanthood.

BASIC THEMES IN GIFTEDNESS

Paul and the Gifts

In Paul's introduction to the Corinthians, he asserted that giftedness was something that they ought not be ignorant about.[2] His use of the word *pneumatikon*, or "spiritual things," implied that he considered spiritual gifts to be part of a broader field of influence in which the *pneuma*, or Spirit, worked within the believer. His more usual term for giftedness was *charis*, or grace, which showed itself outwardly through the servant ministry of each believer. Paul's second introductory proposition asserted that giftedness derived from the diversification within the Trinity.[3] The varieties of gifts came from the Holy Spirit. On the other hand, the purpose of serving the Son unified the varieties of services inspired by the Holy Spirit. Furthermore, the power that energized the workings of the gifts came from the Father.

---

[1] 1 Cor 12:1–7; 1 Pet 4:9–11
[2] 1 Cor 12:1–3
[3] 1 Cor 12:4–6

Paul's third proposition was that the Holy Spirit gave gifts for a special purpose.[4] Gifts were for the common good of the church. Actually, the pneumatic or spiritual found their earthly form and responsibility in the *charismata* or tangible gifts. It followed, therefore, that a *charisma* was a specific concrete form of grace in giftedness. Only their use in the service of the community could validate them.[5]

Peter and the Gifts

Peter added several pertinent introductory facts concerning spiritual gifts. Outstanding was his contention that giftedness was primarily a matter of hospitality.[6] He argued that the Holy Spirit gave gifts to each believer to serve others. To put them to use was to "administer them as good stewards." A steward or *oikonomos* was a household manager, usually a domestic official recruited from among slaves. Peter inferred, therefore, that if one belonged to God's household as a steward, it was for administering God's *oikonomia* of grace through one's spiritual gifts. Basic to Peter's argument was that hospitality—the only gift he mentions—was a kind of generic gift upon which the whole gamut of giftedness rested. This was extraordinarily significant in that hospitality was a basic gift in the earliest churches of the New Testament. It provided a practical working solution for the multiplication of house churches within the Roman Empire. Another unique contribution of Peter's theology of giftedness was his twofold understanding of their scope. He implied a category of *speaking gifts* that concentrated on words, asserting that those who ministered through speaking should utter them carefully as God's very words. Peter also implied a category of *serving gifts* that concentrated on works, asserting that those who ministered through serving works should do so with God's strength.

DEVELOPING THE GIFTEDNESS THEME

In developing the theme of giftedness to the Ephesian church, Paul unfolded his theology of spiritual gifts around several fundamental facts, as he amplified more fully the source of the gifts and the environment in which they functioned.

Charismatic Grace

First, he insisted that gifts were enveloped in charismatic grace.[7] Giftedness came from the grace-bounty of the Godhead, but was manifest in Christ's descent and ascension. As a result of his ascension, Christ's gift was the Holy Spirit poured forth at Pentecost. This historic, salvific event culminated in bringing gifts to believers. Theologically speaking, Paul was saying that grace, or *charis,* transformed itself into grace-gifts, or *charismata.*

---

[4] 1 Cor 12:7
[5] E. Kasemann (1980), *Commentary on Romans,* Eerdmans, pp.333–334.
[6] 1 Pet 4:9–11
[7] Eph 4:7–10

In Paul's theology of giftedness, therefore, sovereign grace came from the Father who, in turn, concentrated that grace in Christ and his work as saving grace. God in turn poured out saving grace to all in Christ's body in the form of service grace. Therefore, Paul is asserting that every believer is a grace-gifted "charismatic" who functions by the empowering Spirit, to fulfill the edification and ministry of the entire local body.

Contextualization

The second fundamental in Paul's theology of giftedness was that gifts were to be contextualized in the Body of Christ.[8] The words Body of Christ and head sharpened the importance of 'imaging.'[9] The impact of image of the church cannot be overestimated. Minear's treatise on images of the church lists nearly one hundred images, most of them rightly relegated to minor importance. He believes that the witness of the New Testament revealed that every congregation was all too prone to blindness. It did not always see itself as it was or as it was meant to be. The images acted as a cure for this blindness, requiring a rebirth of imagination for deeper self-perception.[10]

The major images of the church blended into a significant single metaphor of the body. Whatever image a church cultivated, it was unlikely to have a balanced self-perception unless it was conscious of being 'the Body of Christ'. More than a mere metaphor of social and psychological value, the church as body was a statement about the humanity of that relationship between Christ and his people.

Organismic Growth

In his third fundamental, Paul maintained that the Holy Spirit divinely proportioned the gifts in the body for organismic growth.[11] The principle of personification reminded the New Testament believers that there was no real distinction between the gift of teaching and gifted teachers. In other words, sometimes gifts may be personified as/in leadership persons for the purpose of building up and supporting the ministry-work of the whole group.

In this context, therefore, *pastor-teachers* referred to one leadership gift given to the same person, i.e., "teaching pastors". The same may also apply to *apostles and prophets*, since the occurrence in Ephesians 2:20 and the parallel text in 3:5 have a single definite article controlling both referents as one-and-the-same personification. This Greek rule unquestionably stands since a century-and-half ago. This suggests that apostle and prophet more correctly referred to the same person. In this case, *apostle* would likely refer to their oral witness and *prophet* to their literary deposit in the New Testament Scriptures. This was a select group in the early church that

---

[8] Eph 4:12
[9] Eph 4:15
[10] Paul S. Minear (1960), *Images of the Church in the New Testament*, Westminster, p.250.
[11] Eph 4:11–16

combined in one person this double function.[12]

Paul goes on to declare expressly that the gifts of the Spirit were for the purpose of building up the body.[13] Pastor-teachers, therefore, were to help the gifted saints get on with their ministering through giftedness. The text asserts that the immediate purpose of the gifts was to shape up the saints so they could do their work of ministry. The final purpose was to build up the body.

Furthermore, Paul said spiritual gifts helped one to grow up in Christ's body.[14] The goal of maturity was spiritual adulthood developed through knowledge and manifested in Christ-likeness. The failure of maturity, on the contrary, was evidenced in instability and lack of discernment. The sign of maturity was unadulterated communication among the members of the body—a transparency of character reflected in always "speaking the truth in love." The implication here was that personal failure to mature meant failure to minister, since the knowledge and discernment necessary to grasp personal giftedness was lacking.

Moreover, "truthing" in love suggested a high degree of integrity in talk. This, in turn, implied that believers could not avoid conflict. To work through conflict successfully, in turn, required a high degree of maturity, a growing up that occurred when one took personal giftedness and Christ-likeness seriously.

Finally, in his gift theology to the Ephesians, Paul made a summary assertion. Gifts, he said, provided the possibility of a healthy prognosis of the body's life.[15] The real concern of the body's head was the health of the body.[16] Every member was "joined," a term Paul coined implying making decisions in harmony. The body was actually formed by the extension of a single original cell, growing until all the cell parts share the original life. So it was understood to be in Christ's body, the church. Paul was saying that when each part does its work, health will result. However, when one part failed to minister properly, the body suffered ill health.

FOCUS ON CORPORATE GIFTEDNESS

In his extended correspondence to the Corinthians, Paul focused on corporate giftedness. He did this to develop a healthy optimism for each one's interdependent functioning in the Body of Christ.[17] After once again articulating the body analogy, he maintained that God arranged the body's parts as he wished.[18]

---

[12] Ralph Martin (1979), *The Family and the Fellowship,* Eerdmans, p.74.
[13] Eph 4:12
[14] Eph 4:13–15
[15] Eph 4:16
[16] cf. Eph 5:26–27
[17] 1 Cor 12–14
[18] 1 Cor 12:12–24a

In Christ's body there were two crippling gift-complexes. The *inferiority complex* alluded to the problem of depreciating the gifts, a "charisphobia" which arose out of fear or envy. The *superiority complex* alluded to the problem of discriminating among the gifts, a "charismania." This latter problem came from exalting certain gifts as spiritual status symbols or from allowing celebrities to project their assumed gifts on others.[19] Either way, these complexes crippled and needed to be overcome so cooperative inter-functioning could develop as God planned.

To carry the argument a step further, Paul said that God adjusted the body for the parts found wanting.[20] He has combined the whole body with deference to the parts lacking apparent importance, so there will be no discord or division. As is true of the human body, he suggests, so there was in the Body of Christ a discernible body language that pleases the body. It is a high quality of body language that communicates health both in suffering and in rejoicing. The body's consciousness, in which each member was aware of being in harmony with the whole, did not come about by mere commands. Rather, Paul infers, it was a phenomenon that existed by spontaneous relating together and by personally affirming one's interdependent membership in Christ's body, the church.

Finally, the apostle declared that God appointed the body's gifts as needed.[21] His rhetorical questions "are all . . . do all?" elicit a resounding "No!" God sovereignly decided on a gift-mix for each local house church, bestowing on each congregation that particular amalgam of gifts to fulfill the ministry appropriate to it. Rather than multi-gifted persons, God's plan was for a multi-gifted body, with each local house church gifted well enough to carry out its intended goals in servanthood.

DISCOVERING AND DISCERNING SPIRITUAL GIFTS

Although the biblical writers did not explicitly exhort the early believers to discover spiritual gifts,[22] nevertheless, the necessity was implicit in the doctrine of giftedness. In assessing the possibilities for personal giftedness, good answers for the right questions can contribute to their discovery and heighten discernment.

Motive

The first is the question of motive. Why should a Christian "eagerly desire" spiritual gifts? In the two places Paul addresses this issue,[23] all major English translations render *zaloute* as imperative, as a command to "eagerly

---

[19] C. Peter Wagner (1979), *Your Spiritual Gifts*, Regal, pp.52,56.
[20] 1 Cor 12:24b–27
[21] 1 Cor 12:28–31
[22] Gene Getz (176), *Building Up One Another*, Victor, p.9; see also Gene Getz (1974), *Sharpening the Focus of the Church*, Moody.
[23] 1 Cor 12:31, 14:1

desire" spiritual gifts. However, one can also translate it as an indicative, as a rebuke for being jealous of the gifts of others. This translation would read, "You are eagerly desiring," that is, in a negative manner.

Some maintain that Paul would hardly encourage striving for the greater gifts after he had just admonished them to be content with the gifts sovereignly distributed by the Spirit.[24] That the indicative may well be the better translation is strengthened by 1 Cor 14:20, where Paul characterized the Corinthians as people who strove after gifts.[25] Whatever the apostle intended, the problem served as a caution regarding misdirected zeal in spiritual gifts. Motive remained all-important.

Self-Analysis

A second question concerned the issue of self-analysis. A disciplined diagnosis of oneself was needed,[26] a self-analysis given according to the measure of faith one had. In essence, the apostle stated that Christians must think soberly about how they think about themselves. This was a major prerequisite on the way to reaching a sane estimate of one's own gift potential. This methodology also provided a safeguard against the vulnerability of failure in giftedness and the blight of envy.[27]

Interdependence

A third question regarded one's interdependent membership, or lack of it. Paul assumed that every Christian would become committed to a disciplined community in order to incarnate personal accountability through interdependent relationships.[28] Gifts were living things. They were organismic in function. Gifts were member things—they were congregational in scope. Christ's church was the "gift-evoking, gift-bearing" community that worked out its life-ministry as "the company of the committed." Paul seemed to be saying that every believer must think and act organismically or suffer the lonely incongruity of independency.[29]

Discovery and Discernment

A final question concerned how and where to begin in discovering and discerning spiritual gifts. At the periphery of this question was the issue of differentiating between spiritual gifts and natural talents. They are not the same. Two extremes tend to polarize their relatedness, however. The one is the inheritive view that perceives the gifts as mere natural capacities. This

---

[24] Michael Grifftths (1978), *Grace-Gifts: Developing What God Has Given the Church*, Eerdmans, p.75.

[25] Arnold Bittlinger (1967), *Gifts and Graces,* Herbert Klassen (trans.), Hodder and Stoughton, p.73.

[26] Rom 12:3

[27] Elizabeth O'Connor (1971), *Eighth Day of Creation*, Word, pp.40, 48-49.

[28] Rom 12:4–6

[29] cf. Col 2: 19

nearly destroys the bond existing between gifts and talents. On the other extreme is the enthusiastic view that perceives gifts as mysterious, supernatural, and sensational. It ignores the fact that Paul made no sharp distinction among the gifts, between those that are quite mundane and those that are obviously supernatural. Furthermore, we need to guard against Platonic ideas that create a Gnostic-like false dualism between the material and the spiritual.

Gifts in the New Testament were both ordinary and extraordinary, just what one might expect from the Creator of all life. The Holy Spirit is the Spirit of creation as well as recreation. Did Paul lose all he had gained through years of development and training of his natural abilities? On the contrary, Paul recognized that God had called him even before his birth.[30] When Saul became Paul, the Spirit enhanced his natural abilities and redirected them. We all know the rest of Paul's story. He then used all his finely trained abilities solely for the glory of God. His attitude, however, was that all his earthly and intellectual attainments were rubbish in comparison to what he had gained in knowing Jesus as Lord.[31] His mental abilities in philosophy, apologetics, and worldly acumen were all heightened in their transformation into spiritual gifts. Furthermore, the Holy Spirit entrusted him with new gifts as well, such as miracles, healings, and discernment.

Therefore, the Creator gave his chosen people a kind of genetic giftedness, a conditioning in preparation for their kingdom work. The key to the transformation of a talent into a gift was in one's attitude. A natural talent, if recognized as from God and dedicated to the Lord in ministry in some special way, may become a gift of the Spirit with supernatural expression.[32]

Nonetheless, since one cannot clone a spiritual gift, some identifiable differences between natural talents and spiritual gifts remain clear. Everyone had natural talents at birth by virtue of being created in God's image. But God gave gifts to believers in their second birth. Talents operated through common grace in all societies, motivating toward artistic achievement and appreciation of beauty, and were primarily for one's own enjoyment. Gifts operated through special grace in Christ's body, communicating God's love and truth, motivating toward obedience to God's will. They were not for one's own enjoyment, but for service to others in building up Christ's body.

We gain further insight on the dilemma of discovering one's gifts by evaluating the quality of personal dedication. Giftedness was rooted in a decisive dedication to sacrificial living and renewed thinking.[33] In this way,

---

[30] Gal 1:15–16

[31] Philip 3:4–10

[32] David R. Mains (1971), *Full Circle: The Creative Church for Today's Society*, Word, p.62.

[33] Rom 12:1–2

the early believers might discern God's will, since giftedness harmonized with God's will. It is unfortunate that many ignore the gift context of these forceful verses. Paul, however, had spiritual gifts in mind. In essence he said that commitment of this quality will aid one to discover God's will in personal giftedness.

Moreover, *discover* implies that one received gifts according to the grace given. *Develop* implies that one received gifts according to the faith given. Inherent was the idea of acting. One must use all the resources at one's disposal to "kindle afresh the gift of God".[34] Dormant gifts in the Body of Christ were, indeed, a distressing phenomenon. "Do not quench the Spirit," was the apostle's corrective.[35]

Warnings about Gifts

In summarizing the doctrine of giftedness, a final perturbing question demands an answer. Why should every member of Christ's body take one's giftedness seriously? The answer is clear. It is not the *presence* of spiritual gifts but the *proper use* of them that validates them in our servanthood. Therefore, Paul warns, "Do not neglect the spiritual gift within you."[36]

The first of the warning exhortations in Hebrews has to do with the use of spiritual gifts. The disconcerting rhetorical question is forthright: "How shall we escape if we neglect so great a salvation?"[37] Easily overlooked is what follows. The salvation in view was not only characterized by miraculous signs that attested the apostolic proclamation, but, surprisingly, also by "gifts of the Holy Spirit according to His own will."[38] When we deny our gifts, writes Elizabeth O'Connor, "We blaspheme against the Holy Spirit whose action is to call forth gifts."[39]

A final question is appropriate. When will the believer's giftedness be complete? The answer is unequivocal: at the time when one's kingdom work is finished, when the Master returns for gift accounting from his gifted servants. This is certainly clear in the Lord's parable of the talents.[40] Our gifts are on loan! There will be a reckoning day! The one-talented person needed as much courage in his or her stewardship of giftedness as the ten-talented person. And the reason is simple: "It is required of stewards that they be found trustworthy."[41]

This matter calls for alert diligence in our giftedness. Gift-bestowing presupposes gift-accounting by us. The Lord assured us that he would do

---

[34] 2 Tim 1:6 (NASB)

[35] 1 Thess 5:19 (NASB)

[36] 1 Tim 4: 14–16 (NASB)

[37] Heb 2:3 (NASB)

[38] Heb 2:4 (NASB)

[39] Elizabeth O'Connor, Ibid., p.16.

[40] Matt 24:14–30

[41] 1 Cor 4:2 (NRSV)

this according to the fair principle of proportions. For "much is required from those to whom much is given, for their responsibility is greater."[42]

CONCLUSIONS

These practical teachings and implications of the gifts of the Spirit motivated those earliest house church fellowships to energetic ministry. Clearly, the house churches were recipients of generous apostolic teaching concerning giftedness. Their success in personally appropriating their own gifts and corporately functioning as Christ's body is a matter of biblical and redemptive history.

STUDY QUESTIONS

1. What is the difference between 'serving gifts' and 'speaking gifts'? What are some specific examples used in the first century churches?
2. What was the purpose of the gifts as the early church understood them? What was the end result?
3. What was the connection between 'quenching the Spirit' and spiritual gifts?

---

[42] Luke 12:48 (LB)

Chapter 7

LOCAL LEADERSHIP IN THE EARLY HOUSE CHURCHES

RAD ZDERO

Rad Zdero earned his Ph.D. degree in Mechanical Engineering from Queen's University (Kingston, ON, Canada) and is the manager of a hospital-based orthopaedic research lab. He has participated in, led, and started house churches and cell groups since 1985. He is currently part of HouseChurch.Ca (www.housechurch.ca), which is a church planting team developing a network of house churches in the greater Toronto area and beyond. He is the author of The Global House Church Movement (2004). Email: rzdero@yahoo.ca.

INTRODUCTION

The New Testament documents present a vibrant and growing Christian church that spread quickly across the vastness of the Roman world. Both the Scriptures[1] and scholars[2] demonstrate that this faith found tangible expression primarily in the form of multiplying house-based congregations. The health and long-term sustainability of these early house churches would have been of paramount importance to the participants themselves. Yet, the founders of these communities of faith, primarily apostolic traveling leaders like Paul, Barnabas, Timothy, Titus, Silas, and Peter, would have recognized that their absence necessitated the emergence of local leaders to maintain church vitality. The apostolic strategy in this regard was the recognition and installation of a cadre of leaders from among the more mature believers in a given locality. Therefore, this article examines the nature of local leadership in the early house churches.

DESCRIPTION

Local leaders were natives of an area who had been appointed or confirmed by traveling apostolic workers to take on responsibilities for church health and growth in their immediate vicinity. They were 'home grown' leaders.

---

[1] Acts 2:46, 5:42, 8:3, 10:1-48, 12:12, 16:14-15,29-34, 18:8, 20:6-8,20; Rom 16:3-5; 1 Cor 16:15,19; Col 4:15-16; Philem 1:2; 2 John 1:10

[2] Roger Gehring (2004), *House Church and Mission: The Importance of Household Structures in Early Christianity*, Hendrickson Publishers; Robert Banks (1994), *Paul's Idea of Community*, Hendrickson Publishers; Del Birkey (1988), *The House Church: A Model for Renewing the Church*, Herald Press; F.V. Filson (1939), "The Significance of the Early House Churches", *J. Biblical Literature*, 58:105-112.

The New Testament record utilizes several different terms for local leaders, namely 'presbyter' (Greek = *presbuteros,* meaning 'elder'), 'bishop' (Greek = *episkopos,* meaning 'overseer'), and 'pastor' (Greek = *poimen,* meaning 'shepherd'). Significantly, from a cross-comparison of the key scriptures on local leadership[3] it is evident, in effect, that presbyter = elder = bishop = overseer = pastor = shepherd. These terms refer to one and the same person, though each highlights a specific role or duty. This is demonstrated ably by New Testament professor Gerald Cowen.[4]

There are two passages in particular, though, that are important in this regard which interchangeably utilize all these terms in addressing the same group of people. In some cases the noun form of the original Greek words above are used and in other cases it is the verb form. Nonetheless, these passages demonstrate indeed that each of these names referred to the same person(s).

In the first of these scenarios, on his way to Jerusalem the apostle Paul organized a meeting with all the local leaders of the church from the city of Ephesus not only in order to instruct them further but also perhaps as a last farewell, knowing that he was soon to be arrested by Roman authorities for his preaching activities. The Scripture describes the circumstance this way:

> And from Miletus he sent to Ephesus and called to him the **elders** of the church. And when they had come to him, he said to them,… "Be on guard for yourselves and for all the flock, among which the Holy Spirit has made you **overseers** to **shepherd** the church of God which He purchased with His own blood."[5]

In the second case, the apostle and elder Peter was writing to believers that were scattered over several regions of the Roman world, encouraging them to stand firm in the face of the challenges posed by the world, the flesh, and the devil in living a holy life pleasing to God. Near the end of his letter, he turned his attention to the local leaders of the various churches. He instructed them to fulfill their responsibilities faithfully before God in caring for the believers in their charge, saying:

> Therefore, I exhort the **elders** among you as your fellow elder and witness of the sufferings of Christ, and a partaker also of the glory that is to be revealed, **shepherd** the flock of God among you, exercising **oversight** not under compulsion, but voluntarily, according to the will of God.[6]

---

[3] Acts 14:23, 20:17,28; Eph 4:11; Philip 1:1; 1 Tim 3:1-7; Titus 1:5-9; James 5:14; 1 Pet 5:1-3

[4] Gerald Cowen (2003), *Who Rules the Church?* Broadman and Holman Publishers, pp.5-16.

[5] Acts 20:17-18,28 (NASB, emphasis added).

[6] 1 Pet 5:1-2 (NASB, emphasis added)

Therefore, any distinction between elder, presbyter, bishop, overseer, pastor, and shepherd by the creation of a formal, local, leader-over-leader hierarchy would have gone against the apostolic pattern. Thus, 'elders', by far the most common term used for local church leaders, were the primary facilitators of household churches in the first century.

ROLE

Elders were the primary, but not the only, nurturers, teachers, influencers, and patrons of a community of Christian believers. Since the role of elders was local and ongoing, they were to be readily available to address all manner of needs among believers.

Firstly, elders were to function as nurturers and encouragers in matters of the heart. When someone was sick, they were called upon to visit the ill person, anoint them with oil, and pray because of the spiritual experience that they could bring to bear upon such a difficult situation.[7] They were to be "gentle, uncontentious" as well as "hospitable, loving what is good, sensible, just, devout, self-controlled" in their dealings with people.[8]

Secondly, elders were to function as instructors and teachers in matters of the mind. When someone needed clarification on a scriptural matter, they were to become directly involved, even going so far as dealing decisively with any false teachers that might seek an audience with the church.[9] This was such an important role for local leaders that the apostle Paul encouraged believers to respect and honor those elders in the church who especially extended themselves in the study of the Scriptures and in teaching.[10]

Thirdly, elders were to have a good deal of influence generally within their spiritual community. The writer of Hebrews, for example, encouraged Christians to 'obey' (Greek = *peitho*, meaning to 'be persuaded or convinced by') and 'submit' (Greek = *hupeiko*, meaning to 'yield or give in') to their leaders.[11] Similarly, when major decisions affecting the strategic direction of the church were made, elders were key people in the process.[12] However, this did not mean a blind and unthinking submission to leadership, but rather a willingness to go along with elders when there was an impasse. The authority of local leaders, though, was held in check by the involvement of the entire body at various decision-making moments.[13]

Fourthly, elders also often acted as patrons and patronesses for the early Christian communities by making available their own homes for church meetings. In ancient society it was common for an entire household and

---

[7] James 5:14
[8] 1 Tim 3:3, Titus 1:8 (NASB)
[9] 1 Tim 3:2; Titus 1:9-11
[10] 1 Thess 5:12-13; 1 Tim 5:17-18
[11] Heb 13:17
[12] Acts 15:2-6,22
[13] Matt 18:15-17; Acts 15:22

associated persons in that circle to be converted to a particular faith upon the conversion of the head of the family, i.e. *pater familias* and/or *mater familias*. In the case of Christian conversions, it became very natural for household leaders to open their homes to the apostles to establish a church there. We see a number of such examples in the New Testament record such as that of Cornelius the Roman officer, Lydia the merchant, the Philippian jailer, Crispus the leader of a synagogue, and Stephanas' household in the city of Corinth.[14] Moreover, where appropriate, the head(s) of the household became the leader(s) of that house church.[15] New Testament scholar Roger Gehring describes this phenomenon in his examination of the early house churches of the New Testament era:

> The private homes of wealthy members served Paul, his coworkers, and the other Pauline Christians as gathering points, as meeting rooms for fellowship, prayer, instruction, and the Lord's Supper. The homeowners made such worship services possible through their patronal hospitality, that is, by providing a place for assembly and, if needed, materials—for example, for the agape meal and the Lord's Supper. These patrons and patronesses offered the congregation and the itinerant missionaries protection in the face of the urban authorities and assumed leadership responsibility for the political affairs of the church. Often the hosts of a house church grew into a church leadership role because of their natural position, education, gifts, and talents. Thus house churches were a kind of training ground for future leaders for church and mission.[16]

Fifthly, elders were also responsible in their role as patrons and patronesses to personally alleviate any financial hardships that other believers in their care may have been facing. Rather than receiving financial support from the church, they were expected to provide financial assistance to others from their own resources. On one occasion, the apostle Paul assembled the elders of the Ephesian church together and encouraged them to follow his example in this regard, saying:

> I have coveted no one's silver or gold or clothes. You yourselves know that these hands ministered to my own needs and to the men who were with me. In everything I showed you that by working hard in this manner you must help the weak and remember the words of the Lord Jesus, that He Himself said, 'It is more blessed to give than to receive.'[17]

---

[14] Acts 10:1-48, 16:14-15, 16:31-34, 18:8; 1 Cor 1:16, 16:15

[15] Roger Gehring, *House Church and Mission*, Ibid, pp.103,155,194.

[16] Roger Gehring, *House Church and Mission*, Ibid, p.226.

[17] Acts 20:33-35 (NASB)

Finally, there was also the emergence at times of other local leaders called 'deacons' (Greek = *diakonos*, meaning 'servant' or 'minister'). Deacons assisted elders in managing the organizational affairs of the church, particularly when it came to finances and material needs.[18] These were perhaps supplemental roles that were filled only depending on the need. This can be inferred from Paul and Timothy's discussions regarding both elders and deacons in Ephesus and Philippi, while only elders are mentioned to the apostle Titus as he nurtured the churches of Crete.[19] Both elders and deacons (if present) led the church as parents would lead a family, not in a dictatorial manner but through their humble and loving attitude and hard work.[20]

ORGANIZATION

Paul wanted elders appointed in each church and town.[21] There initially may seem to be some uncertainty about the exact distribution of elders because of the multi-purpose use of the term 'church' (Greek = *ekklesia*)[22] which could refer to an individual home-based church, a citywide church, or a regional church. Several observations, though, can be made from the available data.

The first-century Jewish synagogue system provided the cultural and religious background for the early Christian house churches. It is significant that a team of elders was responsible for each local synagogue.[23] This is confirmed by the New Testament Scriptures which describe synagogue "officials" or "elders" in the context of a local Jewish community.[24]

Moreover, the biblical record lends itself to a plurality of local leaders managing a given Christian community, rather than any one individual. The Scriptures speak most often of "elders" and "overseers" in the plural.[25]

In addition, steps made by some local elders to pursue power and position even during the apostolic period were denounced by the apostles Paul, Peter, and John.[26] Only in the post-apostolic period did the early church father Ignatius of Antioch (c.100) formally promote the false unbiblical distinction between a one-man ruling bishop/pastor and his assisting group of elders/presbyters.[27]

---

[18] Acts 6:1-6; 1 Tim 3:8-10

[19] Philip 1:1; 1 Tim 3:1,8; Titus 1:5

[20] Matt 20:25-28; 1 Thess 5:12-13; 1 Pet 5:3; Heb 13:7

[21] Acts 14:23; Titus 1:5

[22] Acts 8:1, 9:31, 11:26; Rom 16:1-5; 1 Cor 1:2, 16:19; 2 Cor 1:1; 1 Thess 1:1; 2 Thess 1:1

[23] Richard Ascough (1998), *What are they saying about the Formation of Pauline Churches?* Paulist Press, p.13.

[24] Mark 5:22; Luke 7:1-5; Acts 13:15 (NASB)

[25] Acts 11:30, 14:23, 15:2-6,22, 16:4, 20:17, 21:18; Philip 1:1; 1 Tim 4:14, 5:17; James 5:14; 1 Pet 5:1 (NASB)

[26] Acts 20:29-30; 1 Pet 5:3; 3 John

[27] See the seven *Letters of Ignatius* to the churches.

Thus, each house church would most likely have had a small group of co-equal elders working as a team as the ideal. Elders, in turn, were part of a larger citywide or regional team that worked as a network of house churches.

QUALIFICATIONS

The apostles provide guidelines regarding the qualifications of elders.[28] The particulars listed were necessary prerequisites in order that elders would fulfill their duties successfully. They recognized that if local workers were weak in any one of these areas, it could hinder the spiritual growth of Christians and potentially be an obstacle to others coming to faith for the first time. Both character and competence had to be evident in local church leaders. The apostles specified three broad categories, namely character, basic management skills, and an ability to teach.

Regarding character, the apostles insisted on elders being above reproach in general, but specifically they were to be free from addiction to alcohol, devout, generous, gentle, hardworking, hospitable, just, prayerful, prudent, respectable, reputable among those outside the church, self-disciplined, sensible, slow to anger, temperate, uncontentious, not greedy for money, not stubborn, and not a recent convert lest they fall prey to pride.

Concerning basic management skills, the apostles counseled that elders be able to supervise their own households well, particularly their children, as indicators of being able to manage the church. Moreover, they were to competently address the very real needs of the poor among them, the needs of other Christians in far off lands, and the funding needs for apostolic mission work.[29]

With regard to teaching, the apostles wanted to ensure that sound doctrine found a place among the early house churches. However, an even stronger emphasis was placed on the ability of elders to deal with false teachers who found a hearing in certain circles, upsetting whole families, in some cases being motivated by financial greed. Why? This was so because of several false schools of doctrine that attempted to infiltrate the churches.[30] The Judaizers wrongly insisted on the need for observing the Jewish ritual of circumcision for non-Jewish Christians before they could be acceptable to God and the church. The Gnostics taught a dualistic stream of thought that viewed the material world as fully evil and the spiritual world as fully good, thereby wrongly denying the physical incarnation of Christ and wrongly decrying marriage and food. The Religionists wrongly insisted on the observance of special days, months, seasons, and years as a sign of true spirituality. Such were some of the challenges facing local elders and all believers in maintaining sound theology in the life of the early church.

---

[28] Acts 20:28-35; 1 Thess 5:12-13; 1 Tim 3:1-13, 5:17-18; Titus 1:5-16; James 5:14-18; 1 Pet 5:1-3

[29] Acts 11:27-30, 20:33-35; Rom 15:25-28; 1 Cor 9:1-14, 16:1-4; 2 Cor 9:1-15

[30] Gal 4:8-11, 5:1-12; Col 2:16-17,20-23; 1 Tim 4:1-8; 2 John 1:7-11

TRAINING

Although there is no detailed account concerning the development of local leaders, several hints appear in the scriptural record.

Firstly, *apostolic coaching* was directly involved in the training and selection of local leaders. This was especially the case when a new church was started as the first generation of leaders emerged. On five separate occasions, Paul stayed locally for 1½ to 3 years to ensure that local churches were healthy and strong, including the proper training of elders.[31] Paul would sometimes gather local elders together for a private meeting apart from the rest of the church to discuss leadership issues.[32] In other situations Paul, as the more experienced apostle, gave the responsibility of appointing elders and deacons to younger apostles like Timothy and Titus.[33]

Secondly, a *discipleship chain* mentality was evident. Paul saw his job not simply as gaining many followers and doing the work himself, but in making capable leaders of younger apostles (i.e. Timothy), the local leaders they trained (i.e. faithful men), and the next generation that followed in local leadership (i.e. others also).[34] It is significant to notice that Paul's practice was to have direct apostolic involvement in a church only temporarily until it was well established; subsequent generations of leaders were to be trained and appointed locally.

Thirdly, an *apprenticeship model* would have also been employed. This would have been in imitation of how Jesus himself trained his followers, who were sent on practical assignments to preach and heal from village to village.[35] As such, preparation of local leaders would have consisted of practical on-the-job experiences as they labored side-by-side with and learned from the example of apostolic workers. Interestingly, this was also a culturally accepted manner in which to equip trainees in various trades.

ACCOUNTABILITY

If an elder had seriously erred in any regard, it was the responsibility of an apostolic worker in relationship with that church or another local elder to address the problem. But this step was only to be taken after the evidence of two or three witnesses was brought to bear.[36] In a well-known case, a local elder named Diotrephes attempted to gain personal prominence and power, refused to work with traveling Christian workers, rejected letters to the church from the apostle John, and even expelled believers who would not abide by his directives. The Scripture reports on the situation:

---

[31] Acts 18:11, 19:10, 20:31, 24:27, 28:30
[32] Acts 20:17
[33] 1 Tim 3:1-13; 2 Tim 2:2; Titus 1:5-9
[34] 2 Tim 2:2
[35] Mark 3:13-15; Luke 9:1-6, 10:1-11
[36] 1 Tim 5:19

> I wrote something to the church; but Diotrephes, who loves to be first among them, does not accept what we say. For this reason, if I come, I will call attention to his deeds which he does, unjustly accusing us with wicked words; and not satisfied with this, neither does he himself receive the brethren, and he forbids those who desire to do so, and puts them out of the church.[37]

The apostle John, also a local elder himself, made plans for a personal visit to deal with the situation. Diotrephes, in effect, created a pyramid leadership scheme that placed himself above others in authority as the 'senior', 'lead', or 'ruling' elder within his house church and/or the citywide network of house churches. Such naked pursuit of power was severely criticized by Jesus, the apostle Paul, and the apostle Peter.[38]

FINANCIAL SUPPORT

What about the monetary support of local leaders? Unlike traveling leaders who clearly did receive material assistance,[39] local house church leaders carried out their ministries on an unpaid, volunteer basis. There is one passage in the New Testament, however, which is often put forward as an argument for financial support of local elders. In writing to his co-apostle Timothy about elders in the city of Ephesus, Paul states that they should receive "double honor" since, by analogy, an ox should not be muzzled while it is treading grain and workers deserve their wages.[40] However, there are four reasons why this does not refer to financial or material support.

First, the actual word for 'honor' (Greek = *time*) is also used over 40 times in other places in the New Testament, having the force of respect or value, but not finances. Another perfectly good Greek word for pay, wages, or salary (Greek = *misthos*) is used 38 times in the New Testament which, significantly, is not present in the phrase 'double honor'. In some scriptural instances, *time* might be stretched to possibly include financial gifts (among other things) given to departing apostolic teams and to widows, though this is not certain even from the context.[41] Additionally, there is one occasion in ancient literature when the Greek word *time* refers specifically to a physician's monetary honorarium, though this is from third century BC Greek writings, is a rare usage of the term, and is far removed in context and time from the writings of Paul.[42] However, *time* does not specifically refer to finances or money in the New Testament writings.

---

[37] 3 John 1:9-10
[38] Matt 20:25-28, 23:6-12; Acts 20:29-30; 1 Pet 5:3
[39] Matt 27:55; John 12:4-6, 13:29; Luke 10:1-9; 1 Cor 9:1-18; Philip 4:14-19
[40] 1 Tim 5:17-18 (NASB)
[41] Acts 28:10; 1 Tim 5:3
[42] Steve Atkerson, "Should Pastors And Missionaries Be Salaried?" (www.ntrf.org)

Second, while meeting with these same elders of Ephesus on another occasion, Paul encouraged them to follow his example by working hard with their own hands to meet their material needs and the needs of others.[43] Elders were to give to the church financially, not take from it. It would certainly be a major contradiction if Paul were to suggest financial support for elders on one occasion and then on another to completely discourage it.

Third, in first century Jewish synagogues—as a precursor to the early Christian house churches—the team of elders that managed the affairs of the Jewish community did so on a voluntary unpaid basis.[44] This influence certainly would not have been lost on Paul in organizing house churches.

Fourth, there would not necessarily have been any practical reason for the early house churches to ever pay local elders. A small team of four or five unpaid elders could have easily facilitated a New Testament style house church—which often had no more than 20 to 40 members—without requiring financial support.

Consequently, the weight of the evidence is that the phrase 'double honor' refers not to financial support at all, but rather to the rightful rewards of elders being the increased respect, appreciation, and admiration they rightfully gain from the people they serve and lead.[45] Certainly, if an elder suddenly faced a personal financial crisis or if the house church wanted to give them an occasional gift, they certainly would have been free to do so.[46]

Thus, local house church elders were unpaid volunteers who had other employment like everyone else in the house churches.

CONCLUSIONS

This article has examined briefly the nature of local leadership in the early household churches. These 'elders' were the primary nurturers, instructors, influencers, and patrons of local Christian communities. Their qualifications, training, and accountability ensured that they facilitated the local church with both competence and character. They accomplished their ministries in co-equal teams on a voluntary unpaid basis. They worked both with other local believers and traveling apostolic teams to accomplish God's purposes.

STUDY QUESTIONS

1. What five other names are 'elders' known by in the New Testament?
2. What primary roles did elders have in leading their church community?
3. What is the evidence that local leaders were unpaid volunteers?

---

[43] Acts 20:33-35
[44] R.C.H. Lenski (1946), *The Interpretation of St. Paul's Epistles to the Thessalonians, to Titus, and to Philemon*, Wartburg Press, p.683.
[45] A good parallel passage is 1 Thess 5:12-13
[46] Gal 6:6

Chapter 8

THE MISSION AND THE CHURCHES

ROBERT BANKS

Robert Banks received his Ph.D. from Cambridge University (United Kingdom). He is a biblical scholar and practical theologian who has held academic positions in his home country of Australia and in the United States. Through books such as Paul's Idea of Community, Going to Church in the First Century, and The Church Comes Home (and their translation into several other languages), as well as through his ministry of planting, nurturing, and networking house churches, he has helped shape the house church scene not only in Australia but in several places overseas. [The following was adapted from Robert Banks (1994), Paul's Idea of Community, Hendrickson Publishers, Ch.16. Used by permission of the publisher].

INTRODUCTION

Paul's work existed as a separate entity with a life of its own alongside the local churches founded and supported by it. But just as Paul's apostolic career has a history that is independent of the communities fathered by him, the reverse is also true. His communities tended to move away from close dependence on Paul. In fact, clear differences existed between Paul's mission and the churches at the level of the principles upon which they operated. The precise points where these differences occur can now be plotted. At first sight the structure of Paul's mission has certain similarities with that of the churches founded by him. So, for example: (a) there is an extensive use of family terminology between those involved in the work, viz., father[1], son[2], brother[3], sister[4]; (b) there are gifts and ministries in evidence among the group, viz., apostles[5], prophets[6], evangelism[7], serving[8], healing[9]; and (c) there is a strong note of equality present among its

---

[1] Philip 2:22
[2] Philem 1:10
[3] 1 Cor 1:1, 16:12,20; 2 Cor :1, 2:13, 8:18,22,23; Eph 6:21; Philip 2:25, 4:21; Col 1:1, 4:7-9; 1 Thess 3:2; Philem 1:1,20
[4] Rom 16:1; Philem 1:2
[5] Gal 1:1 et al.
[6] Acts 15:32; Rom 16:7; 2 Cor 8:23
[7] 2 Cor 8:18,20
[8] 2 Cor 8:20
[9] Acts 28:8-9

members, indicated by Paul's way of referring to them as fellow-workers[10], fellow-soldiers[11], fellow-servants[12], and by the types of people represented, viz., Jews and Gentiles, men and women, slaves and free. Alongside these similarities, however, exist some real differences between the work and the churches.

DIFFERENCES BETWEEN PAUL'S MISSION AND HIS CHURCHES

Character

In the first place, Paul's whole operation has a specialized character. It exists for a specific and limited purpose. Unlike the churches, its basis lies not just in Jesus' death and resurrection and the Spirit's fruit and gifts. Nor is its goal primarily the welding together of its members into a common life. Like the members of the churches, members of Paul's mission must possess gifts and the maturity that goes with them. Experience of Christ and the Spirit, however, are not in themselves sufficient to qualify someone for inclusion in the mission. Paul's mission is unique. It is itinerant, not local, and does not constitute itself chiefly by gathering. It is constantly on the move and is more marked by the dispersion of its members than by their assembling. This does not mean that those involved in it never 'churched' together. In some measure that must have happened among those who were traveling together, especially when no local churches were in the vicinity. But this was not the main purpose of the group.

Function

In the second place, nowhere do we find any hint of the 'body' metaphor, so frequently used of the church, being applied to this group. Those involved in Paul's mission were not primarily participating in a common life—though that certainly did occur—but rather sharing in a common task. Hence the description *ergon*, work, which lies at the root of so much of Paul's thinking about this.[13] The members were more other-directed than inner-directed. Paradoxically, this may have led to their sharing "all things in common" more than the communities founded by them. For example, whatever Paul earned at his trade seems to have gone into funding his missionary enterprise[14]; gifts from his churches were presumably treated in the same way.[15] The 'work' may be viewed as a sort of mobile commune in which all resources are pooled. Unlike the churches, however, it has as its focal point not a group of people but one person: Paul himself. They were drawn into the orbit of Paul's own ministry and became an extension of it. So this work

---

[10] Rom 16:3,9,21; 1 Cor 3:9, 16:16; 2 Cor 8:23; Phil 2:25; Col 4:11; Phm 1:1
[11] Philip 2:25; Philem 1:2
[12] Col 4:7
[13] 1 Cor 3:13-15, 9:1, 16:10; Philip 2:3; Gal 6:4
[14] Acts 20:34
[15] Philip 4:14-16

has as its basis Paul's commission and certain relevant gifts that can help fulfill it and has as its purpose the preaching of the gospel and the establishing of churches. In contrast, the churches have as their foundation the message preached by Paul and the reality of the Spirit and have as their goal the growing harmony and maturity of all who belong to them.

Gifts

In the third place, despite the variety of gifts represented in the mission, not all those listed by Paul as occurring in congregational contexts are present. Most prominent are those gifts that can be aimed towards outsiders rather than the Christian group. What we have here is a concentration of gifts, with the most significant ones disproportionately present. Paul's entourage consists essentially of a group of specialists, whose gifts have to do with the most fundamental areas of religious life.

Evangelism, rather than edification, is the primary task—even though, as churches are founded in various places, edification of church members also takes place. The activities of Paul's co-workers are directed outside the group to a different circle; they frequently exercise their gifts outside the home in places where people gather, e.g., religious buildings, lecture halls, debating forums, market places, etc.

Some in the church had similar gifts for commending the Christian message to outsiders, and these were also chiefly employed outside the local gathering.[16] On a smaller scale their activities would run parallel to Paul's work, related to the church from which they had come but not strictly 'church' activities.

Both the churches and Paul's mission had some members with evangelistic gifts that were exercised in similar ways. The main differences between the two groups is that Paul and those centered around him and his mission, had a much larger focus on evangelistic gifts, to the exclusion of the many other gifts seen in the churches.

Authority

Fourthly, for all that he says about the cooperative nature of his work, Paul himself was not only the main influence in the group but the one around whose personal authority its activities centered. Paul regarded his ministry to the Gentiles as divinely granted and, after his break with Barnabas, assumed a position of authority among his assistants that he did not allow those in the churches subsequently founded by him to have. There were always several leading figures in his communities,[17] so that a system of checks and balances existed between them. But there is only one Paul. And whereas it is ultimately the whole congregation including its apostle, in whom authority resides, in his work Paul appears quite definitely to be 'in charge'. So, for example, he is the one who "sends" or "leaves" his colleagues to engage in

---

[16] Col 1:7
[17] Acts 13:1-2; Philip 1:1; 1 Thess 5:12-13

various activities[18] and who generally seems to decide what the next step will be throughout the journeyings of the group.[19]

There are only two occasions where Paul is not treated as the authority. The first one is when Barnabas refused to comply with Paul's insistence that Mark should not come with them.[20] Because Barnabas had been the senior member of the duo, this disagreement resulted in the establishing of two separate missionary works. The second occasion is when Apollos, having been urged by Paul to visit Corinth "with the other brethren", declined to do so since "it was not at all his will to go now."[21] Since Apollos was engaged independently in evangelistic activity he did not come under Paul's authority. That Paul wanted Barnabas and Apollos to yield to his wishes does not mean that he was authoritarian in manner of that consultation with his fellow-workers was absent. The nature of Paul's relationship with his colleagues and the consideration of both Paul's desires and those of his colleagues is beautifully displayed in his exclamation to the Corinthians: "But thanks be to god who puts the same earnest care for you into the heart of Titus. For he not only accepted our appeal, but being himself very earnest he is going to you of his own accord."[22]

INTERRELATIONSHIP BETWEEN PAUL'S MISSION AND HIS CHURCHES

Mutual Participation

Despite their different orientations, the 'work' and the 'churches' participate in each others' activities in various ways. Paul and those involved in other missions seek to nurture the small communities they have founded and lead them to Christian adulthood. They carry out this responsibility by making personal visits of longer or shorter duration, writing letters to help them with their problems, sending emissaries as their personal representatives, and praying constantly for their welfare and progress.[23] But always Paul is moving on, "making it [his] ambition to preach the gospel, not where Christ has already been named, lest [he] build on someone else's foundation."[24]

For their part, the churches seek to forward the pioneering work in which Paul and other apostles are engaged. They fulfill this in the following ways: by *transmitting* the Spirit's call of one of their members to the work of evangelism and *commissioning* that person to whom the Spirit has given the

---

[18] 1 Cor 4:17; 2 Cor 8:18ff; Eph 6:22; Philip 2:19,23,25,28; Col 4:8-9; 1 Thess 3:2; Philem 1:12

[19] Acts 16:9, 18:1,18-21, 19:21, 20:13,16-17 et al.

[20] Acts 15:36-41

[21] 1 Cor 16:12

[22] 2 Cor 8:16,17 (RSV); see also 2 Cor 8:6, 9:5, 12:18; Philip 4:2

[23] Rom 1:8ff; 1 Cor 1:4ff; 2 Cor 1:3ff, 13:9; Philip 1:3ff; Col 1:3ff; 1 Thess 1:2ff; 2 Thess 1:3ff, 3:1ff

[24] Rom 15:20; cf. 2 Cor 10:13-16

gift for the task[25]; by *participating* in the work that results, whether as members of the sponsoring church or of churches founded by the mission, through forwarding financial aid[26], praying for its success[27], and maintaining personal contact through letters or visits[28]; by *assembling* to hear from those involved in the work everything that had taken place[29] and *sending* representatives to other churches to defend their activities when they come under suspicion.[30] In all these ways they actually 'participate' in the apostolic mission and are members of it. This provides the model for their involvement and evangelistic work. The principles under which Paul's mission operated do not in all respects conform to those he impressed upon the churches that he founded. Some overlap occurs but, as has been shown, there is a quite intentional divergence between them. The two groups are independent and assist one another in their work, but the purpose for which each exists, the skills upon which each depends, and the authority through which each lives are not identical. This once again prompts the question: did the churches founded by Paul really possess as independent a life as his mission had apart from them? How subservient were the churches to him, his associates, and other apostles? To answer this question we must compare the role of leading local members temporarily or intermittently caught up in Paul's missionary work with the role of permanent colleagues chosen by Paul who have only an occasional contact with particular local churches.

Local Co-Workers

The first group, the local members, comprises those instrumental in founding a church and maintaining personal contact with Paul as it developed. Since they engaged in these activities they were also involved in his work. That is why he speaks of them as "fellow-workers" and "laborers". Participating in church is one thing, commencing a church is another; the latter quite possibly depended upon a prior call, either directly from God or mediated through Paul. Stephanas and his household almost certainly fell into this category.[31] So too Philemon, Apphia, and Archippus.[32] This group also includes others who, like Epaphras, independently evangelized their own home cities and founded communities but then maintained contact with Paul.[33] For this reason Paul designates Epaphras a "fellow-slave" and "servant."

---

[25] Acts 13:1-3

[26] Philip 4:14-16

[27] Rom 15:30-32; 2 Cor 1:11; Eph 6:18-20; Phlp 1:19-20; Col 4:18; 1 Thess 5:25

[28] 1 Cor 1:11, 7:1, 16:17-18; Philip 2:25, 4:18; Col 1:17 et al.

[29] Acts 14:26, 18:22-23

[30] Acts 15:1ff

[31] 1 Cor 16:15

[32] Philem 1:1-2

[33] Col 1:7, 4:12

Although the communities did not elect representatives to lead their gatherings, from time to time they did set aside certain people to perform particular extramural tasks on their behalf. When certain functions had to be fulfilled elsewhere it was impracticable for the community as a whole to carry them out. Instead, it deputized one or more members for tasks such as a journey to Paul taking monetary aid or news of the community's progress. Epaphroditus carried out this task on behalf of the community at Philippi. Paul describes him as his "fellow-worker" and "soldier" and as the Philippians "apostle" and "servant."[34] Another example is those people "accredited by letter", who assisted in carrying the collection to Jerusalem—something Paul also refers to as a "work."[35] In this instance, there is only a temporary and limited commission to fulfill.

All such people, insists Paul, are to be given their due honor by the communities who commissioned them or whom they represent, not because of any superior position or rank they possess, but on account of the helpful services they perform. So with Epaphroditus in mind, Paul encourages his readers to "honor such people. For he nearly died for the work of Christ, risking his life to complete your service to me."[36] We find here a further application of the principles of recognition that underlies Paul's whole approach to servanthood within the community. The worth of these people and the acknowledgment they should enjoy are determined by the quality of their labors, not by any inherent status.

Itinerant Colleagues

We turn to the second group, Paul's intermediate colleagues. Paul certainly instructs the churches to graciously receive such people when they are in the vicinity. But when he commends them, he does so based on the nature and quality of their work, not the position they hold in his missionary organization or have by right.

For example, when Timothy is sent by Paul to Corinth to remind the community of his message, his position in the church on arrival is not automatically guaranteed by his connection with Paul's mission. Paul has to urge them to "put him at ease" among them and "not to despise him" since "he is doing the work of the Lord as I am."[37] He should be accepted because he performs the mission god has given him to fulfill. Doubts also existed about the way the same community would accept Titus, but Paul's mind was eventually "set at rest" when he heard that they had received him with the respect due to him on account of his work.[38]

---

[34] Philip 2:25
[35] 2 Cor 8:19
[36] Philip 2:29-30; cf. 1 Cor 16:17-18; 2 Cor 8:9; Col 4:13
[37] 1 Cor 16:10-11a
[38] 2 Cor 7:13-15

The sending of Tychicus to Collossae, Timothy to Philippi and Thessalonica, and Titus to Corinth again illustrates the temporary commission such associates of Paul have. Their worth is endorsed on the grounds of their activities and sense of commitment to the task. He reminds the Corinthians that Titus is his "partner and fellow-worker in your service" who, "being very earnest", journeys to them "of his own accord."[39] Of Timothy Paul says, "I have no one like him, who will be genuinely anxious for your welfare" and goes on to add, "But Timothy's worth you know, how as a son with a father he has served with me in the gospel."[40] He describes Tychicus as "a beloved brother and faithful minister and fellow servant in the Lord" and says that he has "sent him for this very purpose."[41] Paul consistently appeals to their faithful performance of the work entrusted to them, not to any honorific position they have been given. The authority these people exercise when they visit the local communities does not differ in principle from that of residents in the community who have special functions to fulfill.

PAUL'S MISSION COMPARED TO OTHER ITINERANT ACTIVITY

Generally

At this point we can sum up what has been said about the structure and character of Paul's missionary work and compare this with other kinds of itinerant activity in Jewish and Graeco-Roman circles around the same time. Traveling was quite widely undertaken in the first century, if mainly by those in business or by the well-to-do. Philosophic 'missionaries' toured the ancient world disseminating their views. Stoic and Cynic philosophers in particular sometimes operated in this way, their travels and methods being celebrated in historical romances[42] and derided in satirical essays.[43] We know from the book of Acts that Jewish exorcists traveled around the synagogues of the Dispersion[44], while the gospels tell us that (individual?) Pharisees journeyed by land and sea to make Gentile converts.[45] Just how frequently any of this took place is hard to say; there is little evidence to draw upon. However, there are precedents for the sort of traveling and preaching activity in which Paul was involved.

Is there any parallel to the size of his missionary apparatus or to the complex network of relationships built up around it? So far as one can trust the evidence, Cynic philosophers like Diogenes seem to have moved around mainly as individual teachers. Some itinerants, such as the 'prophet'

---

[39] 2 Cor 8:17,23
[40] Philip 2:19-23 (RSV); cf. 1 Thess 3:1-8
[41] Col 4:7-8
[42] E.g. Philostratus, *Appollonius of Tyana.*
[43] E.g. Lucian, *The False Prophet.*
[44] Acts 19:13-15
[45] Matt 23:15

Alexander, traveled with a single partner. Others who journeyed with a group, like Apollonius, did so with "disciples", a "scribe", and "secretary", not with genuine co-workers.[46] The 'Sophists' sought payment for their services, a right Paul consistently declined to press. Paul's 'search and destroy' visit to Damascus may suggest that Pharisees traveled with ancillary help to assist them, but this may be affected by his working under the high priest's direction.[47] Apart from the New Testament, we do not really have any evidence for Pharisaic proselytizing in the Diaspora. On Jewish territory outside Judaea, according to the Gospels, Pharisees generally appear in a group.[48]

In general, Paul's enlistment of full and part-time helpers on his later missionary journeys, at times swelling his company of co-workers substantially, has no parallel in the field of contemporary religious propagation. This could also be said of his mission's continuing close involvement—through messengers, letters, and prayers—in the communities founded by it, and their participation—through visits, letters, gifts, and prayers—in its ongoing work. The new dynamic in the Christian message and the new quality of life created by it apparently could not be contained within conventional itinerant activities, whether religious of philosophic.

A Specific Case

The encouragement, collection, and transport of financial aid from the Gentile churches for the poor among the saints in Jerusalem were an important aspect of Paul's work.[49] This inquires closer inspection because it possesses, externally at least, some parallels with another Jewish institution. The similarities between this and the annual payment of the Temple tax[50] throughout the Dispersion have frequently been noted. Both involved extensive itinerant activity, the creation of groups to oversee the collection and payment, and the acknowledgment of Jerusalem as a distinctive religious center.

But there are significant differences. Paul's collection has a specific basis, for it expresses the gratefulness of the Gentile churches for the foundational preaching in Jerusalem. It is also a cosmopolitan affair in that involves both Jews and non-Jews in giving. Additionally, it possesses a social objective in its aim to alleviate the needs of the poor. All this marks it off from the legal and cultic character of the Temple tax. There are other differences between these two collections. On is voluntary, the other

---

[46] See Dio Chrysostom, *Orations* 8-9; Lucian, *The False Prophet* 6; Philostratus, *Appolonius* 1.18, 4.37-38, 9.19,21,24 (Demetrius in 4.25 and 42.31 was originally independent).

[47] Acts 9:7

[48] Mark 2:24, 3:6, 8:11, 10:2; Luke 5:17, 13:31, 15:2, 16:14, 17:20

[49] Rom 15:24ff; 1 Cor 16:1-4; 2 Cor 8-9; cf. Acts 11:27-30; Gal 2:8-10

[50] Matt 17:24-27

compulsory. One is gathered in individual homes, the other at central collecting points. One is paid to those within the Jerusalem community for charitable disbursement, the other to the Temple authorities. So again, we have only general parallels between these two institutions. Though Paul may have modeled this aspect of his work upon the Temple tax payment, it differs from the Jewish institution at most levels of its operation.

CONCLUSIONS

Not only is Paul's conception of the *ekklesia* distinctive, but his conception of the *ergon* is as well. These two, the church and the work, should never be confused, as they generally have been in subsequent Christian thinking. Paul views his missionary operation not as an *ekklesia* but rather as something existing independently alongside the scattered Christian communities. Only in a secondary way does it provide the organizational link between the local churches, suggesting the basis for a wider conception of *ekklesia* of a 'denominational' kind. Paul's mission is a grouping of specialists identified by their gifts, backed up by a set of sponsoring families and communities, with a specific function and structure. Its purpose is first the preaching of the gospel and the founding of churches, and then provision of assistance so that they may reach maturity. While this clearly involves interrelationship with the local communities, Paul's work is essentially a service organization whose members have personal, not structural, links with the communities and seek to develop rather than dominate or regulate.

STUDY QUESTIONS

1. Can you recall some specific differences between the nature and purpose of local churches and that of Paul's traveling mission? What would be some specific similarities?
2. How did authority and decision-making function within these early traveling 'apostolic bands'?
3. What practical lessons can be applied today in linking local house church networks and traveling ministries?

Chapter 9

THE FIVE-FOLD MINISTRY AND THE FOUNDATIONS
OF THE EARLY CHURCH

WILLIE JOUBERT

Willie Joubert has a Ph.D. degree in theology (University of South Africa) and a Masters degree in Semitic Languages (University of Pretoria). His ministry experience includes teaching at university and ministering in denominational and non-denominational churches. He has written a number of books on house churches. He is currently a house church practitioner living just outside Hamilton, Ontario, Canada.[Adapted and used by permission of the author. Email: breakthrough_prayer@hotmail.com].

INTRODUCTION

Presently, we will consider the so-called five-fold ministry of apostle, prophet, evangelist, pastor, and teacher in the first century church. Though there is the suggestion by some writers that, in fact, there were pairings and overlap in these ministries that resulted in the recognition of only a three-fold or four-fold ministry during the New Testament era, this chapter will examine the early church with the assumption that they utilized a five-fold ministry. As we shall see, these were foundational factors in the proper development of the life and mission of the early Christian communities.

THE IDENTITY AND PURPOSE OF THE FIVE-FOLD MINISTRY

What are the five-fold ministries? The ministries of apostle, prophet, evangelist, pastor, and teacher in the early church were gifts and callings that were distributed among some believers in the Body of Christ. These people functioned primarily in one or two of these roles, but also functioned in the others on occasion. The word 'apostle' (Greek = *apostolos*) means someone sent as an ambassador on a mission with authority to do the work. The word 'prophet' (Greek = *prophetes*) refers to an inspired speaker speaking forth the word of God. The word 'evangelist' (Greek = *euaggelistes*) means someone who communicates the good news of Christ to non-believers. The word 'pastor' (Greek = *poimen*) refers to being a shepherd teaching others how to care for a flock. The word 'teacher' (Greek = *didaskalos*) describes an instructor who is able to effectively communicate ideas and concepts.

Where did these five ministries originate? The early church believed that when Jesus was resurrected and afterward ascended into the heavenly realm, he took the mantle of his own ministry and divided it into five ministries to be distributed as gifts to the church. We are told that,

> To each one of us grace was given according to the measure of Christ's gift. Therefore it says, 'When He ascended on high, he led captive a host of captives, and He gave gifts to men'...And he gave some as apostles, and some as prophets, and some as evangelists, and some as pastors and teachers.[1]

What role did the five-fold have in the early church? Paul employs the metaphor of a physical edifice to explain the matter. The church was like a building being constructed from the ground up to be a dwelling place for the Lord himself. The materials used for this construction project, however, were not bricks and mortar but, rather, people who were being fitted together. This divine blueprint included Jesus as the corner stone, the apostles and prophets, and every believer, in fact:

> So then you are no longer strangers and aliens, but you are fellow citizens with the saints, and are of God's household, having been built upon the foundation of the apostles and prophets, Christ Jesus Himself being the chief corner stone, in whom the whole building, being fitted together is growing into a holy temple in the Lord, in whom you also are being built together into a dwelling of God in the Spirit.[2]

What were the practical implications on the life and mission of the early church of the five-fold ministry? Paul later uses a body metaphor to explain that the apostles and prophets mentioned above—along with those with strong abilities as evangelists, pastors, and teachers—were there to help encourage the maturing of every Christian believer, individually and as a corporate entity. These five ministries were to work in unity in maturing the church by equipping and releasing all believers into their call and ministry. The idea was that the whole church would do the work of ministry as Jesus did.[3] This maturity included not only the ability to discern true from false doctrine, but also the ability of every believer to contribute fully to the unfolding plans of God in the world:

> It was he who gave some to be apostles, some to be prophets, some to be evangelists, and some to be pastors and teachers, to prepare God's people for works of service, so that the body of Christ may be built up until we all reach unity in the faith and in the knowledge of the Son of God and become mature, attaining to the whole measure of the fullness of Christ. Then we will no longer be infants, tossed back and forth by the waves, and blown here and there by

---

[1] Eph 4:7,8,11 (NASB)
[2] Eph 2:19-22 (NASB)
[3] John 14:12

every word of teaching and by the cunning and craftiness of men in their deceitful scheming. Instead, speaking the truth in love, we will in all things grow up in him who is the head, that is, Christ. From him the whole body, joined and held together by every supporting ligament, grows and builds itself up in love as each part does its work.[4]

JESUS WAS THE KEY MODEL OF THE FIVE-FOLD MINISTRY GIFTS

While he was on earth, the Lord Jesus provided the model for how each of the five-fold gifts could ideally function. Certainly, this was the primary example to which the early church would have referred in understanding how it was to carry out its mandate.

Jesus was an Apostle

Jesus was the key apostle, for he was sent by the Father on a mission with the goal to finish the work.[5] Not only was Jesus sent, but he also sent his disciples in a similar way.[6] Moreover, he sent the disciples recognizing that, "All authority in heaven and on earth is given to me. Therefore go and make disciples of all nations, baptizing them in the name of the Father and of the Son and of the Holy Spirit, and teaching them to obey everything I have commanded you. And surely I am with you always, to the very end of the age."[7]

Jesus was a Prophet

When Jesus raised a young man from the dead, the people recognized that a prophet was among them.[8] Jesus also prophetically spoke regarding the destruction of Jerusalem and the signs of the end times.[9] After his resurrection, he appeared to many, including the two men on their way to the town of Emmaus. He joined their conversation and asked what they were talking about. They replied, "We talk about Jesus of Nazareth. He was a prophet, powerful in word and in deed before God and all the people."[10]

Jesus was an Evangelist

He had a heart for the lost and reached out to them. Because of this, he was often criticized, for he tended to reach out to those rejected by society and by the religious establishment.[11] One such occasion was his encounter with a man named Zaccheus, the rich tax collector. Jesus spotted him in a tree where he climbed to get a glimpse of Jesus. When Jesus saw him, he called

---

[4] Eph 4:11-16 (NIV)
[5] John 3:16, 4:34; Heb 3:1
[6] Luke 10:1-11; John 20:21
[7] Matt 28:18-20 (NIV)
[8] Luke 7:16
[9] Matt 24:1-34
[10] Luke 24:19 (NIV)
[11] Matt 9:10-12, 11:19

and visited him at home and enjoyed a meal there. The story ends with Jesus saying: "Today salvation has come to this house, because this man, too, is a son of Abraham. For the Son of Man came to seek and save what was lost."[12]

Jesus was a Pastor

He referred to himself as the Good Shepherd (or pastor) who had real compassion for his sheep to the point of self-sacrifice. He explained: "I am the good shepherd. The good shepherd lays down his life for his sheep...I am the good shepherd. I know my sheep and my sheep know me – just as the Father knows me and I know the Father – and I lay down my life for my sheep."[13] Christians knew that this was exactly what he did on a lonely hill outside Jerusalem, nailed to a cross, where he laid down his life for them. After that, as the Good Shepherd, he appointed others to shepherd the flock, like Peter whom he called again at the Sea of Galilee and three times charged to take care of the flock and feed the lambs.[14] Jesus' example as shepherd was such that this Peter wrote to church elders that they were to shepherd God's flock, since they had been appointed its overseers by God himself and were accountable to Christ, the Chief Shepherd.[15]

Jesus was a Teacher

He taught with authority so that people were amazed. This first happened when he taught what we know as the Sermon on the Mount: "When Jesus had finished saying these things, the crowds were amazed at his teaching, because he taught with authority, and not as their teachers of the law."[16] Nicodemus, the Pharisee who paid him a secret visit, also recognized that Jesus was a teacher who had come from God.[17] He taught with authority and in word and in deed, knowing that he was sent as a teacher. Just before he was arrested and crucified, Jesus washed the feet of the disciples, and when he finished he affirmed to them that he indeed was their teacher and Lord, as they had previously recognized.[18]

THE HOLY SPIRIT AND THE FIVE-FOLD MINISTRY GIFTS

Jesus was not the only model of the five-fold ministry. Let us also consider how the early church experienced the work of the Holy Spirit.

The Holy Spirit was an Apostolic Spirit

He was sent by Jesus and by the Father to guide and teach and strengthen the early church as it stepped forward into God's purposes. During the last few

---

[12] Luke 19:9-10 (NIV)
[13] John 10:11,14-15 (NIV)
[14] John 21:15-19
[15] 1 Peter 5:1-4 (NIV)
[16] Matt 7:28-29 (NIV)
[17] John 3:2
[18] John 13:13-17

hours that Jesus spent with his disciples, he told them ahead of time that a day would come when the Spirit of God would be sent to them after his departure.[19] Yet, the Holy Spirit was also a sending Spirit that launched believers into new endeavors. During a prayer meeting of prophets and teachers, the Spirit nudged those gathered to recognize that Paul and Barnabas had been set apart for the specific purpose of taking the good news of Christ to the Gentile world.[20]

The Holy Spirit was a Prophetic Spirit

Prophecy, simply put, was experienced as a speaking forth of revelation from the Holy Spirit. He was understood by the early church to be, in fact, the author of prophecy. Peter wrote about their witness regarding Jesus and how that confirmed the word of the prophets and then added the following: "Above all, you must understand that no prophesy of Scripture came about by the prophet's own interpretation. For prophecy never had its origin in the will of man, but men spoke from God as they were carried along by the Holy Spirit."[21]

The Holy Spirit was an Evangelistic Spirit

He brought conviction of sin in order to draw people to God.[22] This role of the Spirit was clearly revealed on the day of Pentecost when Peter spoke and explained to the crowd about the resurrection and that the risen and exalted Christ "has received from the Father the promised Holy Spirit and has poured out what you now see and hear. Therefore let all Israel be assured of this: God has made this Jesus, whom you crucified, both Lord and Christ. When the people heard this, they were cut to the heart and said to Peter and the other apostles, 'Brothers, what shall we do?'"[23] The presence of the Holy Spirit caused the witness of Peter to bring conviction leading to the salvation of 3,000 people that day.

The Holy Spirit was a Pastoral Spirit

The very essence of the Spirit was understood to be pastoral, and this is why he came alongside early believers to help them in their weakness and intercede for them, as Paul wrote, "In the same way the Spirit helps us in our weakness. We do not know what we ought to pray for, but the Spirit himself intercedes for us with groans that words cannot express. And he who searches our hearts knows the mind of the Spirit, because the Spirit intercedes for the saints in accordance with the will of God."[24] The Spirit was also intent on ensuring that elders (or pastors) were placed in the church

---

[19] John 14:25-26, 15:26-27 (NIV)

[20] Acts 13:1-4

[21] 2 Peter 1:20-21 (NIV)

[22] John 16:8-11

[23] Acts 2:32-37 (NIV)

[24] Rom 8:26-27 (NIV)

to take care of other believers. For instance, meeting with the elders from Ephesus in Miletus, Paul spoke to them and charged them to care for the people, saying, "Keep watch over yourselves and all the flock of which the Holy Spirit has made you overseers. Be shepherds of the church of God."[25]

The Holy Spirit was a Teaching Spirit

The early church knew that the Spirit was intensely interested in teaching them everything they needed to know and understand. In speaking to the disciples, Jesus once said, "He who does not love me will not obey my teaching. These words you hear are not my own; they belong to the Father who sent me. All this I have spoken while still with you. But the Counselor, the Holy Spirit, whom the Father will send in my name, will teach you all things and will remind you of everything I have said to you."[26] Later that night he also said the following to them: "I have much more to say to you, more than you can now bear. But when he, the Spirit of truth, comes, he will guide you into all truth. He will not speak on his own; he will speak only what he hears, and he will tell you what is yet to come."[27]

THE PRACTICAL ROLE OF THE FIVE-FOLD IN BUILDING THE EARLY CHURCH

How did this work in practical terms? How did God build the church in the first century? Consider the metaphor of a building being built from stones. The five-fold worked together as a construction team. Using Jesus as the cornerstone, they laid foundations and applied the plumb line to build a solid and enduring building. The apostle kept the overall view in mind, overseeing the team, and working with the prophet to start and finish the building. The prophet saw the potential of each living stone and worked with the teacher to shape it into the form it should be. The prophet also directed the evangelist to potential future quarries to cut out more stones. The pastor worked with the evangelist to pick up the newly blasted stones and move them to the building site.

In other words, early churches often started with an initial core group, which determined the size, shape, and strength of the resulting community of believers in the long-term. Core groups were often formed or undergirded in the initial stages by apostles and prophets.[28] Apostles were considered first in time, rank, and order. The anointing of the apostle was a pioneering anointing. They moved with more power and authority than anyone else in the church. They needed this as they were called to move into new geographic territories, break into new cultural contexts, and begin new churches. Prophets were second in rank, and they had the ability to see and

---

[25] Acts 20:28 (NIV)
[26] John 14:24-26 (NIV)
[27] John 16:12-13 (NIV)
[28] Acts 8:14-17, 10:24,44-48, 16:9-15

picture the shape and size of the church. Apostles and prophets worked as a team through revelation to begin a new church or work.[29] Sometimes they were called in to deal with problems and set things in order in existing churches. The evangelist's job was to find non-believers and speak to them about Christ so that they might come to faith and be added to the church.[30] The teacher was the one anointed to instruct new believers in Christian belief and lifestyle, making sure that their doctrine was sound.[31] The pastor (or shepherd) was the one who nursed and cared for believers, making sure that they were spiritually healthy overall.[32] Many of the early churches were linked together by traveling teams that were composed of several people from the five-fold ministry. We also note that at times there was overlap in these roles from person to person and from situation to situation.

There were specific individuals who were recognized as functioning at high levels in one or several of the five-fold gifts. Paul, Barnabas, Timothy, and Silvanus were known as apostles with the specific task of going to the Gentiles.[33] Peter and John were known both as apostles and elders (or pastors).[34] There were also many unnamed elders (or pastors) in Jerusalem and Ephesus.[35] Paul and Barnabas, along with Simeon, Lucius, and Manaen, were identified as being prophets and teachers.[36] Philip was known as an evangelist, while his daughters were called prophetesses.[37] Anna, who was an old woman when Jesus was born, was a prophetess waiting with fasting and prayer for God's redemption of Israel.[38] Apollos the apostle[39] also excelled as a teacher and evangelist, as did many unnamed others.[40] However, it was functioning in these gifts, rather than having the title, which identified a person's real role and calling. Finally, there were also many warnings to the early churches to be on guard against false apostles, prophets, teachers, and pastors,[41] implying the existence of genuine ones.

Every believer, however, was understood to have a deposit of the five-fold. If people were sitting passively and not released to do the works of Christ, it was not the church that Jesus came to establish. This did not mean that every believer was a high level apostle, prophet, evangelist, pastor,

---

[29] Acts 13:1-3, 16:9-15
[30] Acts 8:5-13,26-40
[31] Acts 18:24-25
[32] Acts 20:17,28; 1 Tim 3:1-7; Titus 1:5-9; 1 Pet 5:1-3
[33] 1 Cor 9:1-2,6; Gal 1:1, 2:7-9; 1 Thess 1:1, 2:6
[34] Compare 1 Pet 1:1 and 1 Pet 5:1; Compare Luke 6:13-14 and 2 John 1:1
[35] Acts 15:4, 20:17,28
[36] Acts 13:1
[37] Acts 21:8-9
[38] Luke 2:36
[39] 1 Cor 4:6,9
[40] Acts 18:24-26; 1 Cor 4:15; James 3:1
[41] Acts 20:29-30; 2 Cor 11:13; Rev 2:2, 20

teacher, or had all the other gifts.[42] However, every believer could function in these to a certain degree. Everyone could be sent forth to accomplish some task or mission, no matter how simple or small. Everyone could speak forth a word from the Lord. Everyone was to be willing to share the gospel with someone. Everyone should have had a pastoral heart to care for others. Everyone was to be empowered to instruct someone in the truth. Corporately, every church had the five-fold Spirit operating when they met. The fruit of the five-fold ministry was fully functioning churches where members were equipped and released in their gifts. Paul and Sosthenes, for example, encouraged the Corinthian church to grow in their understanding and use of their many spiritual gifts.[43] Jesus, notably, did not wait to first perfect his disciples. He sent them out and then sat down with them afterwards to debrief and train.[44] Note that he even allowed Judas to do ministry. Peter was not quite perfect. John and James had some problems with envy and were power hungry at the time. Paul, moreover, stated that Christians were to engage the tasks that God had for them, saying, "For we are His workmanship, created in Christ Jesus for good works, which God prepared beforehand, that we should walk in them."[45] It was in the process of doing ministry that members of the early churches were equipped to become effective.

CONCLUSIONS

This article has examined the New Testament evidence for the existence and function of the so-called five-fold ministries of the apostle, prophet, evangelist, pastor, and teacher. We have discovered that Jesus Christ was the key model for the early church in this regard. Additionally, the Holy Spirit functioned as a five-fold Spirit to empower and direct the entire church to become all that it was meant to be.

STUDY QUESTIONS

1. Can you recall some specific examples from the New Testament of each of the five-fold gifts?
2. Can you describe a typical scenario in how a five-fold team might work together to start a new church?
3. Which of the five-fold gifts do you seem to function in most easily? What are some examples?

---

[42] 1 Cor 12:29-30
[43] 1 Cor 12:1-12,27-28, 14:1-40
[44] Luke 9:1-10, 10:1-11
[45] Eph 2:10 (NASB)

Chapter 10

APOSTOLIC STRATEGIES FOR GROWING AND CONNECTING THE EARLY HOUSE CHURCHES

Rad Zdero earned his Ph.D. degree in Mechanical Engineering from Queen's University (Kingston, ON, Canada) and is the manager of a hospital-based orthopaedic research lab. He has participated in, led, and started house churches and cell groups since 1985. He is currently part of HouseChurch.Ca (www.housechurch.ca), which is a church planting team developing a network of house churches in the greater Toronto area and beyond. He is the author of The Global House Church Movement (2004). Email: rzdero@yahoo.ca.

INTRODUCTION

Not long after Jesus Christ gave his disciples the mandate of taking his life-giving message far and wide did the Spirit of God empower the early believers to do so on the day of Pentecost. Along with that mandate came the desire to fulfill their mission in a way that was true to the heartbeat, mindset, and even methodology of the Master. As the early Christians spread the message of Jesus Christ across the Mediterranean world, they planted communities of faith in new linguistic, cultural, and geographic soil. These initial efforts then became the beachheads for further penetrating the new contexts with the gospel message. The use of simple, small, grassroots house churches was their preferred method, as an analysis of Scripture shows[1] and as confirmed by a number of scholars.[2] Yet, the simplicity of their approach was complicated by the very practical challenge of growing and connecting these house churches into a healthy, vibrant, and cohesive movement. The outward thrust of the burgeoning Christian mission needed to be balanced by an inward pull of Christian fellowship and partnership. These efforts can be diagrammatically represented as shown in Figure 1. Let us now turn to an examination of how the first Christians did just this.

---

[1] Acts 2:46, 5:42, 8:3, 10:1-48, 12:12, 16:14-15,29-34, 18:8, 20:6-8,20; Rom 16:3-5; 1 Cor 16:15,19; Col 4:15-16; Philem 1:2; 2 John 1:10

[2] Roger Gehring (2004), *House Church and Mission: The Importance of Household Structures in Early Christianity*, Hendrickson Publishers; Robert Banks (1994), *Paul's Idea of Community*, Hendrickson Publishers; Del Birkey (1988), *The House Church: A Model for Renewing the Church*, Herald Press; F.V. Filson (1939), "The Significance of the Early House Churches", *J. Biblical Literature*, 58:105-112.

- 119 -

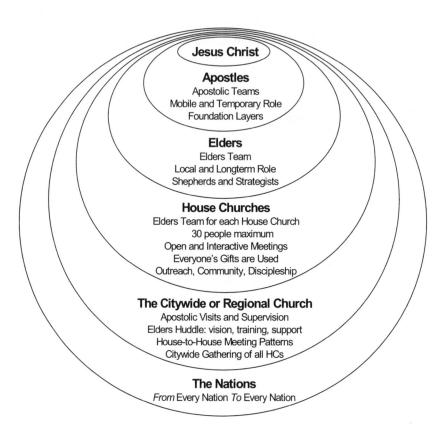

Figure 1. The Early Church as an Organized House Church Movement. The expanding circles of influence flowed from Jesus Christ to the nations of the earth. The outward thrust of the gospel through evangelism and house church planting was balanced by the inward pull of fellowship and partnership between local and translocal elements. This brought cohesion to the early church as a movement during the New Testament era.

HOW DID THE EARLY HOUSE CHURCHES GROW?

The message of Christ spread through a variety of methods capitalized on by the first Christians. The six primary factors were prophetic direction, public proclamation, private conversation, power encounters, persecution, and planting new house churches. The New Testament shows that these were not expensive and highly organized programs dependent on mere human genius, but rather natural, spontaneous, passionate, prayer empowered, and Spirit-led expressions of faith. Thus, the general principle of first-century outreach can best be described as wherever, whenever, whoever, and however.

Prophetic Direction

The early church was open to the supernatural prophetic ways that God revealed which new territories or new people were to be reached. These episodes are particularly telling as human agency in the decision-making process was limited, other than in the practical execution of what the Spirit directed.

Visions and words were given when significant cultural or geographic barriers were to be crossed by the church. Several examples are noteworthy. Culturally, the first significant spiritual launch into the non-Jewish world came as the result of visions given to both the apostle Peter and a non-Jew, the Roman soldier Cornelius.[1] Geographically, Paul and Barnabas were specifically identified and sent out to new territorial frontiers by a word from the Spirit during a prayer meeting of prophets and teachers.

> Now there were at Antioch, in the church that was there, prophets and teachers: Barnabas, and Simeon who was called Niger, and Lucius of Cyrene, and Manaen who had been brought up with Herod the tetrarch, and Saul. And while they were ministering to the Lord and fasting, the Holy Spirit said, "Set apart for Me Barnabas and Saul for the work to which I have called them." Then, when they had fasted and prayed and laid hands on them, they sent them away.[2]

Later, Paul and his team were specifically forbidden by the Spirit to go to Asia and Bithynia, but were given a vision to travel to Macedonia where they would find the first receptive European converts.[3] Moreover Philip, the one-time ordinary table-server in the Jerusalem church, was given explicit directions from the Spirit as to where to go and who to talk to about Christ.[4] His obedience to the Spirit resulted in the conversion of an Ethiopian royal official, probably the first carrier of the faith into continental Africa.

---

[1] Acts 10:1-48
[2] Acts 13:1-3
[3] Acts 16:6-15
[4] Acts 8:26-40

Public Proclamation

A very common apostolic practice was that of verbal proclamation of the message of Christ in a public setting. The strategy used by the apostolic bands was to find an area in a town that acted as a natural gathering place for its citizens, whether it was a riverbank, a synagogue, the Jerusalem Temple courts, a lecture hall, or a marketplace. They would then verbally present the good news of Christ. Typically, they would tailor their message to suit their hearers, thereby making it seem less foreign.

Paul, for example, appealed to his well-educated Greek listeners by weaving into his talk references to Greek religion and poetry as a connection point.[5] Similarly, when talking with a Jewish audience, apostles and evangelists would relate how Christ was the fulfillment of many Old Testament prophecies and was, in fact, the long-awaited Jewish Messiah.[6] In both situations, anyone who responded positively to the message of Christ would either be encouraged to join an existing home church or, if this was a new work in the area, would be encouraged to open up their own home as the first spiritual beach-head in that town. This approach in looking for a person of peace was implemented by both Peter and Paul on numerous occasions.[7] Yet, it was the training exercise that Jesus gave to his first circle of followers which served as the ultimate model for later imitation:

> After this the Lord appointed seventy-two others and sent them two by two ahead of him to every town and place where he was about to go. He told them, "The harvest is plentiful, but the workers are few. Ask the Lord of the harvest, therefore, to send out workers into his harvest field. Go! I am sending you out like lambs among wolves. Do not take a purse or bag or sandals; and do not greet anyone on the road. *When you enter a house, first say, 'Peace to this house.' If a man of peace is there, your peace will rest on him; if not, it will return to you. Stay in that house, eating and drinking whatever they give you, for the worker deserves his wages. Do not move around from house to house.* When you enter a town and are welcomed, eat what is set before you. Heal the sick who are there and tell them, 'The kingdom of God is near you.' But when you enter a town and are not welcomed, go into its streets and say, 'Even the dust of your town that sticks to our feet we wipe off against you. Yet be sure of this: The kingdom of God is near.'"[8]

---

[5] Acts 17:16-28

[6] Acts 2:14-40, 7:1-54, 9:16-42, 17:2-3

[7] Acts 2:1-3:26, 5:12-14, 6:9, 8:5-8, 9:20, 13:14-16, 14:1-7, 16:13-18, 17:1-5,17, 18:4,24-28, 19:8-10

[8] Luke 10:1-11 (NIV, emphasis added); see also Luke 9:1-6

Private Conversation

Jesus often gave attention to specific individuals who showed openness to his message. This would certainly have served as a poignant example of the worth and need of the individual to the early Christians. His one-on-one interactions with Zaccheus the tax collector, the Samaritan woman at the well, Nicodemus the prominent teacher, and a Jewish man born blind that Jesus healed, are just some of the numerous individual encounters that have been preserved in the New Testament record.[9]

Not surprisingly, subsequent Christians followed the example of Jesus in seeing the importance of focused interactions with individuals. These were not programmed or planned endeavors, but rather spontaneous interactions during the daily ebb-and-flow of life. Whether they were walking by the roadside, languishing in jail, visiting someone's home, or when hosting a non-believer at a home meeting, ancient Christians were awake to the opportunities of sharing Christ in a natural unforced conversational way.

Noteworthy in this regard, are the significant missional obstacles that were surmounted because of these seemingly insignificant and quiet efforts.[10] The first Gentile convert was Cornelius the Roman centurion, whose responsiveness to God and the apostle Peter's message resulted in the salvation of many. The first African convert was an Ethiopian eunuch, who believed and was baptized as a result of his discussion with Philip. The first European convert was Lydia the Macedonian merchant, who came to faith during a riverside conversation with Paul. The first apostle to the Gentiles was Saul of Tarsus, whose conversion was confirmed and clarified during his private interaction with Ananias.

Power Encounters

Other common features accompanying both public proclamation and private evangelistic conversation were supernatural healings and exorcisms, sometimes referred to as 'power encounters'. There are several stirring New Testament reports of large groups responding positively to the message brought by Christians because of the miracles that were done by God through their hands.

In Jerusalem, so much healing and demonic deliverance were wrought through the apostles' hands that large crowds were even coming from neighboring cities. Some were laying their sick on the ground in the streets hoping that Peter's shadow would pass over them and heal them. Consequently, a steady stream of people was added to the church.[11]

In Samaria, Philip began to publicly proclaim Christ to the people. The record informs us that the crowds were paying attention to his message specifically because they saw the signs he was performing, namely the

---

[9] Luke 8:49-56, 19:1-10; John 3:1-21, 4:4-42, 9:1-41, 19:33-38

[10] Acts 8:26-39, 9:1-20, 10:1-48, 16:9-15, 16:25-34

[11] Acts 5:12-16

casting out of unclean spirits and the healing of the lame and paralyzed, resulting in the baptism into the faith of many. This then led to a visit by the apostles to the region, resulting in the Samaritans receiving the Holy Spirit through the laying on of hands and hearing the message of the Lord proclaimed verbally.[12]

In Ephesus, Paul and some other believers began to proclaim the word of Christ and confirmed the content of their message with extraordinary miracles, such that even handkerchiefs and aprons were carried away from physical contact with Paul's body and used to actually heal many diseases and cast out evil spirits.[13]

Even a seemingly dire situation like a stormy shipwreck on the island of Malta was used by God to open an effective door for ministry for Paul and his team. To the astonishment of the islanders, Paul went unharmed after he sustained a viper bite while stoking a fire, causing many islanders to mistake him for a god. But, it was the healing of the leading islander's father from fever and dysentery at the hands of Paul that caused many with diseases to seek him for their own healing. The apostolic team then left the island, well respected and well supplied for their next journey.[14]

Persecution

Christians in the first century often enjoyed good rapport with their neighbors, as in the early days of the church in Jerusalem and later in the regions of Judea, Galilee, and Samaria.[15] Any oppression they may have experienced was often at the hands of unruly mobs, limited to one locality, and directed at specific individuals (e.g. Peter, John, Stephen, Paul)[16] rather than at the entire church as such.

However, more significant moments of persecution did happen from time to time, occurring on four notable occasions: Saul of Tarsus was instrumental in a great persecution of Christians in Jerusalem in about AD 35[17]; the Roman emperor Claudius exiled Jews and Christians from Rome in AD 49[18]; the emperor Nero arrested and tortured believers in Rome in AD 64[19]; and the emperor Domitian persecuted Christians in Rome and Asia Minor in the mid-90s.[20]

---

[12] Acts 8:5-17,25

[13] Acts 19:9-12

[14] Acts 28:1-10

[15] Acts 2:46-47, 5:12-16, 9:31

[16] Acts 4:13-23, 5:18, 6:8—7:60, 12:1-18, 19:23-41

[17] Acts 8:1-4, 9:1-2

[18] compare Suetonius, *Life of Claudius* (25.4), with Acts 18:2

[19] see ancient Roman historian Tacitus, *Annals* (15.44).

[20] C.C. Richardson (ed.) (1970), *Early Christian Fathers*, Collier Books, pp.34,37; see also Rev 1:9-11 which reports the apostle John and the churches in Asia Minor experiencing persecution in the mid 90s AD.

Probably the most infamous series of external forces amassed against the Christian community in Jerusalem began with the arrest and beating of Peter and John for their public preaching activities in the Temple courts and escalated in the arrest and beating of many, if not all, of the apostles for the same reason.[21] However, in neither of these situations was the Christian community as a whole destabilized or forced to flee; in fact, this seemed to give the believers a greater sense of boldness to carry on. Tensions with the authorities, though, finally culminated in the execution of the non-apostle Stephen during a theological dispute,[22] which served as a trigger point for a citywide house-to-house rampage against all Christians at the hands of a zealous young Pharisee named Saul of Tarsus. The New Testament record describes it this way:

> And on that day a great persecution arose against the church in Jerusalem; and they were all scattered throughout the regions of Judea and Samaria, except the apostles. And some devout men buried Stephen, and made loud lamentation over him. But Saul began ravaging the church, entering house after house; and dragging off men and women, he would put them in prison. ***Therefore, those who had been scattered went about preaching the word.***[23]

The outcome of this event, rather than impeding the church, was the dispersal of many away from the center of the trouble to the peripheries. There they continued speaking the message of Christ and, based on their prior habits, would have likely established many home-based fellowships in the outlying areas.

Planting New House Churches

The scriptural record informs us that the result of the prophetic direction, public proclamation, private conversation, power encounters, and persecution elucidated above was the establishment of home-based churches spread all across the Roman Empire in cities like Jerusalem, Caesarea, Corinth, Ephesus, Philippi, Colossae, Laodicea, Troas, and even Rome itself.[24] Wherever the apostles and other believers went, they would find someone willing to hear their message about Christ. Upon a positive response by such a 'man of peace', it was quite natural for the Christian heralds to be invited into the person's home to establish a Christian fellowship that functioned as a base of operations to reach out to the surrounding area. This pattern emerges so strongly in the New Testament era under both favorable and unfavorable circumstances that it can be argued to

---

[21] Acts 4:1-21, 5:12-42
[22] Acts 6:8—7:60
[23] Acts 8:1-4 (NASB, emphasis added)
[24] Acts 2:46, 5:42, 8:3, 10:1-48, 12:12, 16:14-15,29-34, 18:8, 20:6-8,20; Rom 16:3-5; 1 Cor 16:15,19; Col 4:15-16; Philem 1:2; 2 John 1:10

have been a deliberate strategy, rather than merely a default strategy due to persecution or poverty. But, what would happen when the groups became especially large and could not be accommodated comfortably by the host home? Although never stated explicitly, whenever a house church grew to exceed the physical limitations of the host home, it is safe to conclude that Christians would simply multiply the group into two or send a few people out to start a new home church. This can be inferred from two facts. First, a given town or city often contained multiple homes that hosted Christian groups, such as in Jerusalem, Corinth, Ephesus, and Rome. Second, the first-century church never constructed special buildings for their meetings. The consequence was an early Christian movement that was growing ever outwardly by planting and multiplying new congregations.

HOW WERE THE EARLY HOUSE CHURCHES CONNECTED?

Was the early church a scattered bunch of house groups peppered across the vastness of the Roman Empire, going it alone? Or, was there a kind of glue that bound them together to guarantee doctrinal accuracy, sustainable growth, and clear vision? Biblically, the theology promoted by the apostles that the church is united and that the Body of Christ is one, was played out in their efforts to connect—relationally if not organizationally—into a cohesive body. Sociologically, the idea and reality of belonging to an expanding global movement certainly added a sense of being part of something bigger than just one's own house church and gave believers a bigger vision for what God was doing in the world at large and what their role in that was. There were several key components working simultaneously toward this end, namely house-to-house meetings, large group meetings, and traveling apostolic workers.

House-to-House Meetings

Although not described in detail, there is some indication from the biblical account that some sort of face-to-face contact between individual house churches existed in a given city or region. A glimpse is given of such a house-to-house pattern actually functioning in Jerusalem. Shortly after Pentecost, the Jerusalem church found itself numbering in the thousands. The believers apparently "broke bread in their homes and ate together" and met from "house to house", which would be a natural thing to do for those seeking to live a shared life together.[25] In addition to the existence of individual Christian house fellowships in Jerusalem, these phrases may suggest some combination of one house group visiting another house group, numerous members of a house church taking turns to open up their homes for gatherings, and/or individuals participating in more than one home gathering. The details of how this would have taken place are unclear and were probably determined based on the situation in the absence of any

---

[25] Acts 2:46, 5:42 (NIV)

apostolic instruction. That this house-to-house pattern was organized or scheduled on a rotating basis is possible, although there is no hard evidence for it from the scriptures.

Large Group Meetings

The record shows that all individual believers and house churches considered themselves part of a single citywide church. As such, for both Jewish and Gentile Christians, citywide gatherings were employed as part of the experience of being a Christian. Yet, large group meetings were often occasional and special events rather than frequent and ongoing features of daily church life. They were no competition to the dominant practice of home-based churches.

Regarding the Jewish Temple, the church in Jerusalem made use of it for large group events as a supplement to home group meetings. First, believers frequented the Temple courts, possibly *en masse*, often for evangelism, healing events, teaching, and/or prayer.[26] Second, large group gatherings also happened when there was a controversial topic that needed to be discussed. For example, believers met over the controversial topic of what to do with non-Jews who were becoming Christians. Should they be required to uphold Jewish religious customs because of the Judaic roots of Christian faith, or were they free of that obligation? This was an issue, we are told, which engaged the apostles, the elders, and, to some degree, the whole church in the process.[27] This may also have taken place, at least in part, in an area of the Temple courts that could accommodate such a gathering.

Regarding Jewish synagogues, they were used by Jewish Christians to spread the message of Christ to their fellow Jews.[28] They often did so until they were ousted or gained converts, who were then invited into a home setting.[29] It is noteworthy that archaeological and literary evidence strongly suggests that even first-century synagogues were private homes (i.e. house synagogues)—with some exceptions like Luke 7:1-5—opened up to the local Jewish public for prayer, Bible reading, and sharing a meal on the Sabbath.[30] In one situation, Paul was barred from his evangelistic preaching in a synagogue and, as a last resort, rented a lecture hall in the school of Tyrannus to continue the same work.[31]

Regarding the legendary upper room, a look at the case of the 120 Jewish believers meeting together shows that this was a significant milestone that

---

[26] Acts 2:46, 3:11, 5:12, 5:42

[27] Acts 15:6,12,22

[28] Acts 13:14-16, 14:1-7, 17:1-5, 18:4,24-28

[29] Acts 18:4-8; compare with Acts 16:13-15

[30] Roger Gehring, *House Church and Mission*, Ibid, pp. 30,82,89; Richard Ascough (1998), *What are they saying about the formation of Pauline churches?* Paulist Press, pp.12-14.

[31] Acts 19:8-12

saw the birth of the church at Pentecost. [32] We note, though, that this was a unique event (occurring only once) of short duration (about 10 days) for a specific purpose (prayerfully waiting for the Spirit to empower believers). As such, this was a catalyst for the house church movement soon to come.

Regarding the Gentile believers outside Judea, they too had a sense of connectedness to one another as underscored by Paul addressing all believers in a city or region as a single church body.[33] Thus, they too may have all gathered together as a larger body occasionally in some open field, on a hillside, or in a rented space, for a specific purpose. For example, when an apostle like Paul visited, he would visit each house church and family home personally and also gather all the house church elders in that city for some public endeavor, either for an evangelistic purpose or for training.[34]

Traveling Apostolic Workers

Itinerant workers in the early church who had the responsibility of coaching the growing house church movement did so primarily in two ways, namely personal visits, letters, and training of local leaders. The purpose of both was the instruction, correction, and encouragement of believers as well as for preaching and healing engagements in public places to reach not-yet-Christians. They were, in effect, circuit riders.

Apostolic Visits

Personal visits to churches were a common feature of apostolic activity. A well-known example is that of Paul and Barnabas, who undertook a journey to personally deliver an important letter from Jerusalem back to their home in Antioch.[35] After they completed their mission, they set out to visit every city where they had preached in order to strengthen the churches there.[36] What they did in each city is uncertain, although some clues are given during Paul's visit to the church of Ephesus. Once there, he called the elders of the citywide church together and reminded them of how he taught them "publicly and from house to house",[37] indicating both a citywide and circulating house church pattern employed by the apostle. Paul was also concerned to see local church leaders appointed during such visits in each church and town.[38] On five separate occasions, for example, Paul stayed locally for one and a half to three years to ensure that local churches were indeed healthy and strong and that local leaders were properly trained.[39]

---

[32] Acts 1:13—2:4; another similar event may have occurred later in Acts 4:31-32, but the details about the group's size or the meeting place are uncertain.

[33] Rom 1:7; 1 Cor 1:2; Gal 1:1; Eph 1:1; Philip 1:1

[34] Acts 20:17-21

[35] Acts 15:23-29

[36] Acts 15:36-41

[37] Acts 20:20

[38] Acts 14:23; Titus 1:5

[39] Acts 18:11, 19:10, 20:31, 24:27, 28:30

Others involved in this kind of work included Peter, John, Apollos, and a number of Paul's traveling companions.[40] For those engaged in this kind of mobile ministry, there was a great deal of personal risk because of the physical dangers of traveling widely in the first century as well as the high financial cost and effort to do so.[41] That they did so at all is a testament to both their courage and conviction that God was calling them to give their lives for the Body of Christ and see the Jesus movement continually expand.

Apostolic Letters

To supplement personal visits, there was also ongoing communication through letters, fully half of the New Testament being written to local Christian groups. In one instance, Paul specifically instructs his readers to circulate his letter to Christians in a neighboring city and make certain to obtain their own copy of the letter he wrote to these neighbors.[42] On other occasions, there is strong encouragement by apostolic workers and local overseers to the churches to value their written communications as authoritatively as their personal visits.[43] In writing to his fellow apostolic workers Timothy and Titus, Paul provides guidelines regarding the qualifications of local elders and deacons.[44] Although less physically risky for the writers, there was a different kind of danger—more insidious and subtle—that accompanied this kind of work, that of deceit. There was even an apparent attempt by some individual or groups to forge a letter using Paul's name to promote their particular teaching to a group of Christians.[45]

CONCLUSIONS

This article has examined the apostolic strategies employed to expand and network the early house churches into a cohesive movement. Practical steps were taken by believers to do so, occurring often enough that a pattern seems to emerge. Human habits were tempered by the Holy Spirit's guidance, which was necessary in particular when linguistic, cultural, and geographic barriers needed surmounting for the gospel of Christ to spread.

STUDY QUESTIONS

1. How did the early church grow? Identify specific mechanisms.
2. How did the apostles connect the early house churches together?
3. Describe the relationship between traveling and local leaders that was necessary for the early Christian movement to grow.

---

[40] Acts 8:14-25, 10:1-48, 18:24-27, 20:4-6; 1 Cor 9:5; 1 Pet 5:1
[41] 2 Cor 11:26-28
[42] Col 4:16
[43] 2 Thess 2:15, 3:14
[44] 1 Tim 3:1-13; Titus 1:5-9
[45] 2 Thess 2:2

Chapter 11

ECCLESIOLOGICAL AND MISSIONAL SIGNIFICANCE OF THE EARLY HOUSE CHURCHES

ROGER W. GEHRING

Roger Gehring, Ph.D. (University of Tubingen, Germany), is Adjunct Professor at George Fox Evangelical Seminary (Portland, OR, USA). He has also served on staff with Campus Crusade for Christ since 1972 at Arizona State University, the Free University in Berlin, and Justus Liebig University in Giessen, Germany. [The following is adapted from Roger Gehring (2004), House Church and Mission: The Importance of Household Structures in Early Christianity, Hendrickson Publishers, Ch.6. Used by permission of the publisher].

FUNCTION AND SIGNIFICANCE FROM JESUS TO PAUL

As in ancient society generally, the *oikos* represented the basic unit for community life for the early Christian movement. Houses were more or less the architectural, social, and economic foundation of urban and inter-regional missions and incubators of local church life. In an embryonic sense, this was true in the earliest days of Jesus' village and regional missional ministry, even more so in the city outreach of the primitive church in Jerusalem, in the city and regional mission of Antioch, and in the worldwide center-oriented missional outreach of Paul. The following section summarize once again the ecclesiological and missional functions and significance of the house from an architectural, socio-economic, and ecclesiological point of view, this time giving special attention to the overall strengths and weaknesses of the house church model.

THE HOUSE AS A BUILDING (ARCHITECTURAL SIGNIFICANCE)

It is known that believers utilized private houses for worship and ministry in a variety of different ways in early Christian missions. Three basic options need to be distinguished. (a) A room, usually the triclinium of a private domestic house, was made available at specific times for religious purposes without architectural changes to the structure of the house (*house church*). (b) A room (or several rooms) in a private domestic house was (were) used exclusively for religious purposes with perhaps an architectural adaptation of the house. (c) An architecturally adapted house (*church house*) or a public building (*hall church*), belonged to a private individual but was used exclusively for religious purposes. Even though all three types existed during the New Testament period the last two were the exception. The existence of the last two types during our time frame cannot be documented with certainty archeologically due to a lack of positive evidence. Of course, the existence of the first type cannot be archeologically documented *per definitionem*, as it was not physically changed or remodeled and thus left no archeological evidence of Christian usage. An exception to the rule is the house of Peter in Capernaum, which was possibly used before 70 C.E. for Christian meetings. We also must keep in mind that particularly wherever synagogue communities converted either partially or as a whole to the messianic faith, entire (public) buildings could have been dedicated for worship and ministry use. Here again we do not have entirely convincing evidence. Possibly one confirmation of this view can be seen in the emergence of early house churches that are often described as filial or contrast groups to the synagogue.[1] Only the first type of house church can be exegetically documented with certainty in the New Testament, but then repeatedly: to begin with, before Easter in the ministry of Jesus (the house of Peter in Capernaum), next in the primitive church in Jerusalem (the house with the upper room; the house of Mary, mother of John Mark), and finally in the Pauline mission (e.g., the house of Aquila, Gaius, Philemon, and Lydia).[2] Much later (starting with the third century) we see a growing tendency toward buildings owned by the congregation and used exclusively for religious purposes. Then with Constantine we see the beginning of a period characterized by large basilical church buildings. In remote, un-christianized regions all three types of house church continued to exist well into the fourth and fifth centuries C.E.

One important result of our examination can be seen in that we were able to demonstrate credibly the historic reliability of the pertinent New Testament references to houses and house churches in the missional outreach of Jesus and in the Jerusalem church. As mentioned, the majority of studies on early Christian house churches up until now have taken for granted that we stand on firm ground historically only with the references to house churches in the undisputed Pauline Epistles.

From an architectural point of view, the house offered certain strengths by providing space used in a variety of ways for missional outreach. To begin with, it needs to be pointed out that houses differ architecturally from one another. For the time period of the early Christian mission, Palestinian, Greek, and Roman types of private houses come into question. They were easily adapted, and they provided Christians with a low cost venue for assembly. With relatively little effort it was possible to establish a Christian presence in the everyday life of ancient cities. At least in the early days, the triclinium (often in conjunction with the courtyard [cf. Capernaum][3] or atrium) provided an ideal room for teaching and preaching ministries,

---

[1] Cf. in Philippi: Acts 16:13ff, 30ff; in Corinth: Acts 18:1–8; cf. also James 2:2f.
[2] Acts 16:14-15; Rom 16:3-5,23; 1 Cor 16:19; Philem 1:2
[3] Mark 2–4.

catechetical instruction for baptism, and other missional activities. The triclinium was also a room well suited for prayer meetings, table fellowship, and the celebration of the Lord's Supper (cf. the primitive church in Jerusalem). Because of the physical limitations of the triclinium, the numerical size of the first house churches was relatively small (on average, twenty to forty persons; in very few exceptional, cases up to a hundred). Hence, by necessity these first Christian communities were small, family-like groups, in which individual pastoral care, intimate personal relationships, and accountability to each other were possible. "One reason for the house church's powerful impact on its environment is found in the fact that it was not possible to grow beyond the parameters of a small group due to a lack of space."[4]

The house also provided other rooms that could be made available for missional outreach, such as guest rooms that served as quarters for travelers or for missionaries who stayed for longer periods of ministry at one location (e.g. Jesus in Capernaum; Paul in Corinth with Prisca and Aquila). The workplace was often also located in the house and was also put to effective missional use. For instance, Paul took advantage of the workplaces (e.g., in the house of Aquila) to generate opportunities for evangelistic conversations with business contacts.

At the same time, however, the private house also had its architectural limitations and weaknesses. The relatively small capacity of the triclinium was not only a positive factor, as by necessity it limited the potential number of participants for the worship service. Once the congregation outgrew the capacity of the living room, another homeowner with a large enough house had to be found who was also willing to make his home available to the church—something that, of course, could not be taken for granted. An additional architectural weakness of a private house can be seen in its lack of features that were important for worship services and other activities in the life of the church. For instance, most houses did not have a built-in facility for baptism. Some Palestine houses containing *miqva'ot* may have been the exception to this rule.[5] Perhaps this is the reason that in the New Testament we hear relatively often of the baptism *of* a house, but never of a baptism *in* a house.

The architectural anonymity of a private house must be viewed with ambivalence. On the one hand, without an intentional Christian alteration, a

---

[4] H.J. Klauck (1981), *Hausgemeinde und Hauskirke im fruhen Christentum*, SBS 103, Stuttgart: Katholisches Bibelwerk, p.100.

[5] For the archaeological evidence for ritual baths in Jerusalem see N. Avigad (1983), *Discovering Jerusalem*, Thomas Nelson, pp. 139–143; For Herodian Jericho see E. Netzer (1982), "Ancient Ritual Baths (Miqvaot) in Jericho", pp.106–119, in *The Jerusalem Cathedra* (vol. 2), L.I. Levine (ed.), Yad Izhak Ben-Zvi Institute.

private house did not outwardly testify to the faith. On the other hand, the anonymity could provide a certain protection in times of persecution, in which the private home became a hiding place for missionaries and church members.[6] This anonymity, however, was neither easy, nor always possible, to preserve (e.g. in Jerusalem).[7] The renovation of a house or building would have caught the attention of the surrounding neighborhood, as such a project would have had to be financed and then tackled by a team of craftsmen and manual laborers.[8] If they had not noticed before, others would now begin to realize that this was a meeting place for Christians.

THE HOUSE AS A COMMUNITY (SOCIOECONOMIC SIGNIFICANCE)

Christians were not the first and only religious group to meet in private homes. For example, members of the cult of Mithras, the mystery associations, and particularly the Jews in their house synagogues followed this pattern as well. Here the total (Mithras) or partial (Judaism) independence from historically established holy sanctuaries in specific locations is evident. The Christians also chose a socially and legally accepted form for their religious assemblies. In particular, the example of the mystery cults illustrates "how natural it would have been in those days for others in society to view and to accept the Christians as another religious association."[9]

From the very beginning and then continuing throughout the first, second, and third phases of the movement, an integration of the Christian community with the social and economic infrastructure of the ancient *oikos* can be observed. The household codes, as found in Colossians and Ephesians, represent the socioethical correspondence to *oikos* structures of earlier congregations against the backdrop of the *oekonomica* (household management literature). Even in the earliest days, with the firm expectation of the imminent return of Christ, potentially lasting social structures emerged in house churches. Because families formed the core of house churches from the onset, they needed special instruction and exhortation, which for us has become historically tangible in the household codes of Colossians and Ephesians. Hence, it is not necessary to understand the household codes either as a reaction to the crisis that arose in the second (and third) generation as a result of the delay in the second coming or as a protest reaction against the eschatological enthusiasts. The household code in Colossians could have emerged early on as 'tradition' with a possible origin from within the missional context of the Pauline house churches.

---

[6] Acts 12:12ff

[7] cf. Acts 8:3

[8] L.M. White (1990), *Building God's House in the Roman World*, Johns Hopkins University, pp.146-7.

[9] P. Stuhlmacher (1989), *Der Brief an Philemon (3rd ed.)*, EKKNT 18, Benziger, p.72.

The integration of *oikos* structures also had a positive consequence in the relationship between church and public. With the decision to adopt *oikos* structures, the house churches corresponded closely with the ancient society around them, as the ancient *oikos* reflected the social order of that time (status, station, rank, position, class, profession), comprised of almost all the different social strata. As a result, the composition of the early Christian movement was not limited to specific groups in the population. Christians were therefore positioned to reach all levels of society with the gospel. This becomes evident in Colossians and Ephesians, but particularly in the Pastoral letters. Christians are encouraged to reflect a household ordered by God in Christ in their own families and house churches, where they were to project an image of order inwardly and outwardly and live an exemplary life with the goal of reaching others with the gospel. The integration of the house church within the *oikos* had a positive effect not only for the spread of the gospel; it also enabled continuity, duration, and tradition. With the integration into *oikos* infrastructures, the Christian church became capable of long-term survival and was given the potential to transition from one generation to the next.

Another socio-economic factor in early Christian missions was *patronage*. Most scholars agree that the role it played in missional outreach and church development cannot be overemphasized. By making their houses available for Christian assembly, householders provided and guaranteed the material and organizational foundation for church development. Early Christians took advantage of the social network in the household, profession, guild, and association of the householder to promote missional outreach and congregational development. The contacts of the *pater familias* with powerful individuals in urban government and society were often quite useful, particularly in times of crisis.[10] The publicly respected householder was able to provide legal protection and a certain social legitimacy for the faith community that met in his home. The extended family, including slaves, clientele, and friends, as well as the contacts of the householder with his professional colleagues and business partners offered an entire network of relationships. Once accepted by the householder, Paul, his co-workers, and many other Christians became trusted insiders within this network of relationships and as a result were able to quickly reach out and touch the lives of large numbers of people for Christ.

The socioeconomic system of ancient patronage served also to support the local and interregional mission. This can be observed even prior to Easter in Jesus' village and regional missional outreach from Capernaum into the entire area of the so-called evangelical triangle.[11] Here a complementary relationship existed between the itinerant missionaries and

---

[10] Acts 17

[11] Capernaum, Bethsaida, and Chorazin.

the sedentary followers of Jesus, in which a kind of patronage played an important role. The significance of the system of patronage becomes all the more obvious in the Pauline mission. Householders, men and women of means, enabled the mission journeys of Paul and his co-workers through their hospitality and other material support (e.g. by covering travel costs). Moreover, the ancient *oikos* served as a source of candidates for the Pauline missional enterprise. Both householders (Stephanas from Corinth) and the members of their households made themselves available to the local and regional mission. The house and household were a training ground for co-laborers and leaders for missional outreach. Household heads, their slaves, and clientele were all able to develop their organizational, administrative, and (particularly the house fathers) their teaching skills even prior to their conversion to Christianity in the context of the ancient *oikos*, so that by the time they came to faith, they were in many ways ready-made house church leaders.

With the catchword "hospitality" we are reminded of yet another benefit of the ancient *oikos* for mission. The early Christian houses and house churches were places where Christian hospitality was practiced by and for Christians and non-Christians alike in a very concrete way. In house churches it was possible both for Christians and non-Christians to experience the safety and security of the family of God. Closely connected with this was early Christian brotherly love, which was able to unite radically different social groups into one community. Our investigation has clearly confirmed the results of recent research indicating that the members of the first Christian churches cannot be categorized exclusively as having originated from one social level, but rather from nearly all existing strata. Both the make-up of the Pauline churches and the household code tradition in Colossians, Ephesians, and the Pastoral letters reflect a high level of social stratification, which demonstrates that house churches embraced individuals from many different social backgrounds: householders and slaves, Jews and Gentiles, men, women, and even believing children. The growth of the Christian movement impacted nearly every social level.

The only way that this could have led to lasting success was to develop a sense of unity, which would be able to prevail even against the unavoidable conflict from the different behavioral patterns of each of these social groups.[12] In all three phases of early Christian missions the house church provides one very important explanation with regard to how it was possible for Christianity to succeed in integrating individuals from such different social backgrounds into one cohesive unit. Gal 3:27, Col 3:11, and the Christian household codes are evidence for the exceptional community-building power and capability for social integration of the early Christian

---

[12] G. Schollgen (1988), "Hausgemeinde, OIKOΣ-Ekklesiologie, und monarchischer Episkopat", *Jahrbuch fur Antike und Christentum*, 31:74-90.

house churches. The concept of church as the family of God became the social model and affected the way Christians related one to another. Christian brotherly love, theologically rooted in the Pauline doctrine of justification by faith, transcended all social barriers including those separating masters from slaves and Jews from Gentiles. Through the penetrating power of the gospel even the *oikos* structures underwent a partial transformation. In the small, family-like setting of the house church, individuals from extremely different social backgrounds were united into one new community. Inwardly, early house churches provided Christians with a training ground for practicing brotherly love and had a powerful integrating effect. Outwardly, house churches were display cases illustrating brotherly love to non-Christians, and as such they had a dynamic missional impact.

There is one further characteristic of ancient patronage that can be seen as a positive factor in early Christian missions. In those days it was generally expected that the subordinate members of the household would accept the religion of the head of the house. Although this was easier to enforce in smaller families than in larger ones and although a relaxation of this practice can be observed during the imperial period, there is some indication in the New Testament that not only individuals but entire houses were baptized (cf. the *oikos* formula in Acts). This obviously accelerated the spread of the gospel. One additional positive aspect of this phenomenon is the solidarity that grew out of this, which was effective even during, but particularly after, conversion. Seekers and new believers were supported from the very beginning in their decision for Christ by the rest of the household. Still, one possible consequence of the baptism of all or most of the subordinates in the household was that some may not have made a personal commitment to Christ or had any faith of their own.

Our study also revealed that the integration of the church and missional outreach into the ancient household had other drawbacks from a socioeconomic point of view. The missional impact of the householder, for instance, was not automatically positive. If the patron of a house church was appreciated and respected in the neighborhood and city, then this usually had a positive effect on the reputation and missional outreach of the church as well. If, however, the opposite was true of the householder, it became a liability for the church, in some cases even limiting its missional fruitfulness in that city. In light of this, the instructions given in the Pastoral Epistles appear all the more understandable.

An uncritical integration of the social order of the *oikos* into the house church often led to social problems as well. Because of the strong social position of the householder, it was possible for unhealthy, over-reliant relationships to develop. Pagan *oikos* structures such as the client system could continue to exist under a Christian cloak. Moreover, there existed the danger that an overly dependent relationship could develop with individual leaders who had powerful, charismatic personalities. Just because someone was wealthy and educated did not guarantee his or her positive theological and spiritual development. Householders who fell into error were often capable dragging their entire house church down with them, which could then lead to tension and conflict within the local church as a whole at that location (cf. the Pastoral Letters).

Simply gathering in a house did not automatically lead to the reconciliation of individuals from diverse backgrounds in the church. Meetings in a house Mithraeum were exclusively for men; the members of *collegia* were most often from the same social level. The membership in house synagogues was a bit more socially diverse, but even here there was the tendency toward community formation according to profession and nationality, which also led to exclusiveness. As a rule, Christian house churches integrated a large diversity of individuals from a variety of backgrounds. This is primarily related to, and grew out of, the inner structure of this new faith.[13] Christ had enabled salvation for everyone; consequently, diversity was supposed to live in loving unity one with the other. This is the reason Paul fought so hard against the separation of house churches according to nationality in Antioch. The Corinthian example also illustrates how social differences can negatively affect the house church. Even though the assembly in a house had increased potential for becoming and sustaining an accepting, loving, and supporting community, it did not always guarantee it.

THE HOUSE AS A CHURCH (ECCLESIOLOGICAL SIGNIFICANCE)

Our study has shown that, in all three phases of early Christian mission the house served as the basic foundation for all church life. Even before Easter it can be observed that the house of Peter in Capernaum, the "cradle of the emerging church"[14], was the operational base for the missional outreach of Jesus, a place where Jesus exercised his teaching and healing ministry, and an assembly place for the family of God consisting of Jesus and his disciples. Houses also served as bases of operation, meeting places for prayer, table fellowship, and teaching in the missional outreach of Jesus' disciples. Later, in the primitive church in Jerusalem, houses were used for assembly, community formation and fellowship, prayer, teaching, and for the celebration of the Lord's Supper. It is legitimate here to speak of house churches as churches in the full sense, as all of the ecclesiological elements that constitute the church are observable. The house churches enabled the celebration of a specifically Christian worship service. Christians met in the

---

[13] Gal 3:27f

[14] S. Loffreda (1993), "La tradizionale casa di Simon Pietro a Cafarnao a 25 anni dalla sua scoperta", pp.37-67, in *Early Christianity in Context: Monuments and Documents*, F. Manns and E. Alliata (eds.), SBF.CMa 83, Franciscan Printing Press.

temple for prayer, the teaching of the Word, and the proclamation of the gospel, but it was only in houses that the celebration of the Lord's Supper was possible. This use of houses is continued then in Antioch and in all phases of the Pauline mission.

One important question addressed during our study was the relationship between the house church and the local church, with all its ecclesiological implications. In the New Testament the relationship between house church and local church varied from city to city and area to area. On the one hand, we find references in Acts to several houses that served as meeting places in Jerusalem; on the other hand, two centers are particularly singled out,[15] the first place of assembly of the Jerusalem church in the upper room, the other in the house of Mary, mother of John Mark. It is possible that these two house churches were the meeting place for the Hebrew- and the Greek-speaking congregations respectively. As a result of the rapid growth of the primitive church in Jerusalem, the number of house churches multiplied even in the earliest days.[16] Opposite these house churches we find the whole Jerusalem church, which met regularly in the temple. A plurality of house churches within the whole local church can already be observed in the primitive church in Jerusalem.

It is almost certain that a plurality of house churches existed in Rome, each with a different orientation.[17] Due to the size of the city and the large number of groups there, it is highly unlikely that all Roman Christians met regularly at one place as the whole local church. Christians met in different private homes in Corinth as well. Paul, however, places a high value on a regular assembly of the whole local church there; accordingly we can assume that it happened. It can be asked whether the regular gathering of the whole church was to celebrate the Lord's Supper. It appears to us that the transition between house church and local church with regard to the content of the worship service was fluid. In any case, we can be certain that a plurality of house churches existed alongside the whole local church in Corinth. There are indications of a plurality of house churches as well in Antioch, Thessalonica, Ephesus, Philippi, and Laodicea.

The existence of a plurality of house churches led us to the question how Paul theologically defined the relationship between the individual congregation and the local church and between the whole church at any one location and the whole worldwide church. How are the two series of ecclesiological assertions to be resolved in Paul's understanding of the church: the unity of the whole worldwide church, on the one hand, and, on the other, the position of the individual congregation? Does the unity of the whole church have priority over the individual congregation or vice versa?

---

[15] Acts 1:12ff and 12:10b–17

[16] Acts 2:42–47; 5:42

[17] Rom 16

The decisive ecclesiological passages in the undisputed Pauline letters speak for the priority of the individual congregation over the whole worldwide church.[18] In particular, the plurality of house churches within the whole local church as it can be demonstrated for the Pauline mission is an empirical expression of this priority. The emphasis that Paul himself placed on the dignity of the individual congregation documents it theologically as well.[19]

An additional question emerged from our study, whether the structure of the ancient *oikos* had any influence on the organization of the house church and on the development of leadership structures. There are a number of indications in the Jerusalem church that wealthy homeowners enjoyed special authority as the householders and hosts of the church that met in their house due to their social position in the group. After all, the community assembled in the social context of *their* houses with their own built-in authority patterns. We can assume that at least some of these hosts became leaders of these house churches. It is possible that in time some of those who formed the circle of seven around Stephen and later those who were designated elders were elected from this group of house church leaders and thus formed a kind of house church board or council. We do not, however, have certain evidence of this. The book of Acts gives the impression that in the beginning the term "elder" was merely a designation of age or possibly an honorific title, but in time it indeed became a title of office.[20]

In the Pauline mission, then, it becomes very clear how household structures influenced the organization and leadership structures of house churches. It was most likely the Hellenists that brought the house church organizational forms (from Jerusalem) to Antioch, as we were able to determine an organizational transition from the primitive church in Jerusalem to the mission church in Antioch.[21] In both locations early Christians met in small house churches. This organizational structure is then transferred from Antioch to the worldwide Pauline center-oriented mission enterprise. As we saw, it was an integral part of Paul's missional approach to attempt to win one or more houses over to the Christian faith early on in his mission at that location, and so the conversion of the head of the household was top priority.[22] This was due in part to the significant role these householders played in Pauline missional outreach; among other things, they made worship services possible by providing the congregation with a place to assemble.

---

[18] This is however not to be understood absolutely.

[19] Eph 4 and John 17 provide a balance.

[20] Acts 15:4, 6, 22, 41; 16:4, 21:18

[21] R.W. Gehring (2000), *Hausgemeinde und Mission*, BWM 9, Giessen, Germany: Brunnen, pp.196-8and 212-4.

[22] This approach (householder evangelism) is something realized at least in a preliminary form even before Easter in the ministry of Jesus and his disciples.

We discovered considerable evidence for concrete leadership structures in the Pauline house churches. Paul used a number of terms in his undisputed letters that indicate leading, teaching, administrative, and supportive functions of men and women. Particularly in the absence of Paul and his full-time co-workers, the group that was most likely to assume responsibilities—such as providing a meeting place, leading the assembly and (communion) meals, church organization, representation of the church toward city officials and possibly other churches—was that of the householders. Because of their position in ancient society, it would have been natural for them to emerge into leading and possibly teaching roles in the church that met in their home. This is not to say, however, that the homeowners were the only ones who took on leadership responsibilities in house churches. Surely there were other gifted members of the congregation who also assumed leading, teaching roles.

In the undisputed Pauline Letters, nothing is said about the official installation of church leaders through Paul or anyone else. This could be related to the fact that it did not appear necessary because leadership structures were already built in to the ancient household. Consequently, leaders emerged from below, out of the house church setting. The acceptance and the recognition of these leaders both by the congregation itself and by Paul, however, was the precondition for this type of house church leadership structure.

As we saw, *episkopoi* are plainly documented as a designation of office for the Pauline mission churches (Phil 1:1 in plural!). Given the plurality of house churches at any one location with householders as their hosts and leaders, it can be assumed that the overseers mentioned in Phil 1:1 were the leaders of house churches in the city of Philippi. This view is later confirmed in the Pastoral Letters. The house church setting provides a plausible explanation for the presence of a plural number of *episkopoi* at one location, a title that had become a formal designation for office by the time the Pastoral Letters were written.

In some respects the architectural and particularly the social image of the ancient *oikos* becomes the determining image for ecclesiology, church development, leadership structures, and the social relationships of Christians in community. The well-organized household became the model for a well-organized church. This is related in particular to the fact that many house churches were small, close-knit groups with a nuclear family as their core. Consequently, it was quite natural that household patterns impressed themselves upon the social reality of the congregation. The house churches of the Pastoral Letters understood themselves essentially as the "household or family of God" and it is therefore fully legitimate to speak here of an *oikos* ecclesiology. It seemed logical and natural that one single overseer should lead the house church just as the household was led by one house father and this is indeed the conclusion to which the Pastoral letters came.

In the Pastoral Letters we see the extension of the office of overseer from the basis of existing episcopal-patriarchal structures to the level of the house churches, on the one hand, and from the basis of the existing presbyterial organization to the city level, on the other hand. At the very latest with the writing of the Pastoral Letters, the title "elder" is to be understood as the designation of a formal office. One important result of our study is the finding that the presbyterial structure with an office of elder, as it was in effect in the Pastoral Letters and possibly already in the primitive church in Jerusalem, could not have been a mere copy of Jewish tradition. If some scholars have correctly understood the ancient and in particular the Jewish use of the title "elder" as an honorific, then no such office existed either in a communal or in a synagogal form.[23] This would mean that with regard to the development of the office of elder the Christian contribution was much greater than is generally assumed.

These organizational structures are also indication that the church of the Pastoral Letters already shows signs of institutionalization. This is not necessarily negative (see below). Institutionalization is unavoidable for an organization that wants to continue existing and growing beyond its first generation. It was precisely the formation of church leadership and organizational structures the led to the stabilization of the church. As these leadership structures emerged from the household setting, it can be said that the integration of the church into the *oikos* insured long-term stability and enabled the continued transmission of the gospel into the future. Thus house churches became 'tradition bearers' of the Christian faith for generations to come. Hence, they enabled the tradition, continuity, and duration of the church.

We also uncovered in the house church model, however, structural weaknesses which can lead to divisiveness, disunity, and the formation of splinter groups within the local church as a whole. As in the early days in the life of the Corinthian church, the existence of several house churches in one city became a problem indeed for the churches in the Pastoral Letters. Not only could an unhealthy dependence on a house church leader with a strong, charismatic personality develop. In addition to this danger from within, house churches encountered one from without. An isolated house church, in particular one with weak leadership, was quite vulnerable to those who attempted to lead members of the church astray spiritually and theologically.[24] All of these dangers, which were inherent to the house

---

[23] A.E. Harvey (1974), "Elders", *Journal of Theological Studies*, 25:318-31; R.A. Campbell (1993), "The Elders of the Jerusalem Church," *Journal of Theological Studies*, 44:511-28; R.A. Campbell (1994), *The Elders: Seniority within Earliest Christianity*, Studies of the New Testament and Its World, T&T Clark.

[24] Titus 1:11

church setting, demanded a consolidation of organizational and leadership structures at the level of the local church as a whole. Ideally, these dangers can be countered with a local and supralocal organizational infrastructure, including the formalization of offices for specific leadership functions. The Pastoral Letters testify most unambiguously of such a development.

The early Christian house churches also exhibited a number of weaknesses from an ecclesiological perspective. The main problem lies in the one-sidedness of an *oikos* ecclesiology, which could lead to a narrow understanding and practice in the life, organization, and theology of the church. It can become particularly critical, if ecclesiology and church order are developed exclusively from the Pastoral Letters without sufficient consideration given to other ecclesiological assertions in the New Testament, especially those found in the other Pauline letters. The New Testament as a whole did not elect the *oikos* as its primary ecclesiological image, and thus it exercises a healthy caution over against these potentially negative tendencies. The *oikos* as a theological concept must be integrated into New Testament ecclesiology and at the same time confined by it.

STUDY QUESTIONS

1. What was the role of the household leader in the early house churches?
2. What was the relationship between a house church and the entire church in a city or area?
3. What were the strengths of the first century household approach to mission?
4. What were the challenges that house churches faced in the New Testament era?

Chapter 12

WERE PERSECUTION, POVERTY, AND PROGRESSION THE REAL REASONS FOR FIRST CENTURY HOUSE CHURCHES?

STEVE ATKERSON

Steve Atkerson holds an M.Div. from Mid-America Baptist Theological Seminary, served seven years as one of the pastors of a Southern Baptist church, began working with house churches in the late 1980s, and is now elder of a house church in Atlanta, GA, USA. He travels widely teaching and training leaders on the basics of New Testament church life. Books he has edited and contributed to include Toward A House Church Theology, Ekklesia: To the Roots of Biblical House Church Life, The Practice of the Early Church: A Theological Workbook (Leader's Guide), and The Equipping Manual. He is part of the team at The New Testament Restoration Foundation (www.ntrf.org). [Used by permission of the author. Email: nt_restoration_foundation@juno.com].

INTRODUCTION

That the first century church held its meetings primarily in private homes is common knowledge and has been documented extensively by biblical scholars.[1] A brief survey of the New Testament record attests to this fact as well.[2] Any public places that were utilized—such as the Temple, synagogues, lectures halls, or the outdoors—were used occasionally or transitionally, either for teaching by an apostolic team visiting town, an evangelistic outreach event, special prayer meetings, or important decision-making moments, rather than for the regular church meetings of believers.[3] Less well known is the fact that the early church continued this practice of home meetings for hundreds of years, long after the New Testament writings

---

[1] Roger Gehring (2004), *House Church and Mission: The Importance of Household Structures in Early Christianity*, Hendrickson Publishers; Robert Banks (1994), *Paul's Idea of Community*, Hendrickson Publishers; Del Birkey (1988), *The House Church: A Model for Renewing the Church*, Herald Press; F.V. Filson (1939), "The Significance of the Early House Churches", *J. Biblical Literature*, 58:105-112.

[2] Acts 2:46, 5:42, 8:3, 10:1-48, 12:12, 16:14-15,29-34, 18:8, 20:6-8,20; Rom 16:3-5; 1 Cor 16:15,19; Col 4:15-16; Philem 1:2; 2 John 1:10

[3] Acts 1:13—2:4, 2:46, 3:11, 5:12, 5:42, 13:14-16, 14:1-7, 15:6,12,22, 17:1-5, 18:4,24-28, 19:8-12, 20:17-21

were completed. Graydon Snyder observed that the New Testament church started as a house church movement and remained so up until about the year AD 300.[4] Furthermore, there is no evidence that any home during that period was ever converted into a special building devoted solely to religious services for Christians.[5] Why were house churches the norm for so long?

PERSECUTION?

The most common suggestion given for the existence of early house churches was the continual pressure of persecution by governmental or religious authorities. However, this does not fit the evidence that is available.

Firstly, persecution was not always a factor. It is often overlooked, for example, that the followers of Jesus sometimes met in homes while simultaneously "enjoying the *favor* of all the people"[6] as they did in Jerusalem. Also, in the first few years after Pentecost as the church spread, the Scripture reports that "the church throughout all Judea and Galilee and Samaria *enjoyed peace*, being built up; and going on in the fear of the Lord and in the comfort of the Holy Spirit, it continued to increase."[7] Moreover, the situation in Samaria when Philip the evangelist preached the gospel was such that "the multitudes with one accord were giving attention to what was said by Philip, as they heard and saw the signs which he was performing...and there was *much rejoicing in that city*."[8]

Secondly, Paul the apostle gives instructions regarding non-Christians visiting the house churches, saying that, "if the whole church comes together and...some unbelievers come in"[9], then they were to make some adjustments to the flow and content of the meeting. It is possible, therefore, that unbelievers also attended church meetings from time to time, suggesting that where they met was not always a secret to outsiders. This would have been an unlikely practice if believers were continually in the throes of persecution.

Thirdly, it is simply not true that all the early believers were always persecuted everywhere and all the time. Persecution prior to around AD 250 was localized (e.g. in a given city),[10] often the result of mob hostility (e.g.

---

[4] Graydon Snyder (1991), *Church Life Before Constantine,* Mercer University Press, p.166.

[5] Graydon Snyder, Ibid., p.67.

[6] Acts 2:46-47 (NIV, emphasis added)

[7] Acts 9:31 (NASB, emphasis added)

[8] Acts 8:6,8 (NASB, emphasis added)

[9] 1 Cor 14:23 (NIV)

[10] see Acts 18:2 and Suetonius (*Life of Claudius, 25.4*) for persecution under Claudius in 49 AD; see Tacitus (*Annals, 15.44*) for persecution under Nero in 64 AD; see Rev 1:9 and Will Durant (1944), *Caesar and Christ—The Story of*

the stoning of Stephen or the attacks on Paul),[11] and/or directed at specific Christians that would venture to preach and heal publicly (e.g. Peter, John, Stephen, Paul),[12] rather than because of the empire-wide decree of a Roman ruler. Interestingly, Roman officials are often presented in a somewhat favorable light by the New Testament writers, since they intervened to protect Christians from unlawful local harassment by unbelieving Judaism.[13] Prior to AD 250, Christianity was illegal, but generally tolerated. The simple fact is that widespread and systematic persecution did not occur until emperor Decius in AD 250, followed by Gallus (AD 251–253), then Valerian (AD 257–259), and finally Diocletian (AD 303–311).[14] Someone, somewhere, could have constructed a special church building in the 200 years prior to Decius, but significantly, no one ever did.

Fourthly, when persecution did erupt, meeting in homes did not keep Saul, for example, from knowing exactly where to go to arrest Christians. We are told that "Saul began ravaging the church, *entering house after house*; and dragging off men and women, he would put them in prison."[15] Nonetheless, the presence of persecution would not necessarily rule out a deeper, more purposeful preference for smaller, house-sized congregations.

POVERTY?

Another common idea is that poverty was a deciding factor in explaining the total absence of church buildings during New Testament times. Again, the evidence speaks to the contrary.

The construction of special buildings for meetings or worship was a common feature of first century Mediterranean religion. The Jews had the Temple in the city of Jerusalem, as well as synagogues in many towns and cities. In Capernaum, for example, in Jesus' day, the Jews pleaded with Jesus to heal a Roman centurion's servant, saying, "He is worthy for You to grant this to him; for he loves our nation, and it was he who built us our synagogue."[16] The Gentiles, similarly, had various temples dedicated to the worship of gods and goddesses that acted as patrons for a specific group or for an entire city, as they did for the goddess Artemis in the city of Ephesus.[17] Thus, as Christian converts from Judaism and paganism, many would certainly have been able to afford the construction of places for the

---

Civilization: Part III, Simon and Schuster, pp.292,592-593,647, for persecution under Domitian in the 90s AD.

[11] Acts 7:54-60, 19:23-41

[12] Acts 4:13-23, 5:18, 6:8—7:60, 12:1-18, 19:23-41

[13] Acts 16:35, 17:6-9, 18:12-16, 19:37-38, 23:29, 25:18-20, 25:24-27, 26:31-32

[14] Williston Walker (1970), *A History of the Christian Church,* Charles Scribner's Sons, p.43.

[15] Acts 8:3 (NASB, emphasis added)

[16] Luke 7:4-5 (NASB)

[17] Acts 19:27-28

church to gather if they had desired. However, all this was a feature curiously absent among the first Christians.

Furthermore, there were some anonymous rich people among God's elect, as made clear from the scriptural record. For example, the advice that Timothy received was to "instruct those who are rich in this present world not to be conceited or to fix their hope on the uncertainty of riches, but on God, who richly supplies us with all things to enjoy. Instruct them to do good, to be rich in good works, to be generous and ready to share, storing up for themselves the treasure of a good foundation for the future, so that they may take hold of that which is life indeed."[18] Moreover, Paul rebukes the rich in Corinth for slighting the poor by refusing to eat the Lord's Supper along with them: "Or do you despise the church of God, and shame those who have nothing? What shall I say to you? Shall I praise you? In this I will not praise you."[19] Also, James warned against showing favoritism toward those who came to the church gathering wearing a gold ring and fine clothes,[20] indicating such persons were indeed involved with the church. There were also other anonymous believers of some influence and position mentioned elsewhere.[21]

Additionally, there were, in fact, Christians of some societal position and/or wealth that are specifically named in the New Testament, like the Ethiopian royal official, Cornelius the Roman officer, Lydia the merchant, Erastus the city treasurer, Zenas the lawyer, possibly some relatives or associates of Rome's emperor himself, and Philemon the slave owner.[22]

Certainly, there were many churches and individuals who suffered from material need in the first century, due to famine, widowhood, or other circumstances.[23] However, as we have seen, there were also a number of believers that were of some means. Therefore, poverty alone, clearly, was not a deciding factor in the lack of church buildings and the predominant use of house-based congregations during the first century.

PROGRESSION?

Some think that God intended for the practice of meeting in homes to be a legitimate phase of the church's early development, an initial but transitory step toward later maturity. Thus, house churches were characteristic of the church in its infancy, but not in its maturity. It was right and natural, they argue, for the church to grow beyond these early practices and develop ways that are far different than, but in the spirit of, the practices of the apostles as

---

[18] 1 Tim 6:17-18 (NASB)
[19] 1 Cor 11:22 (NASB)
[20] James 2:1-4, 5:1-6
[21] Acts 17:4, 1 Tim 6:17
[22] Acts 8:26-39, 10:1-2, 16:14; Rom 16:23; Philip 4:22; Philem 1:16; Titus 3:13
[23] Acts 2:43-45, 4:32-35, Acts 11:27-30 (cf. Rom 15:25-28, 1 Cor 16:1-4; 2 Cor 9:1-15; Gal 2:1,9-10); 1 Tim 5:3,9,16

recorded in Scripture. Thus, centuries later, the erection of special church buildings is seen as a good and positive development in the history of Christianity.[24]

Yet, the apostles intended for churches to adhere to the specific patterns that they originally established, either through their direct command or their repeated practice. For instance, the Corinthians were praised for holding to the apostles' traditions for church practice.[25] Sweeping appeals for holding to various church practices were made based on the universal practices of all the other churches.[26] The Thessalonians were directly commanded to hold to the traditions of the apostles.[27] The early church understood that the apostles were handpicked and personally trained by the Lord. If anyone ever understood the purpose of the church, it was these men. The practices that they established for the church's corporate activities were certainly in keeping with their understanding about the purpose of the church. Respect for the Spirit by whom they were led, persuaded the first century believers to prefer apostolic modes of organization to any alternative that any of their own creative thinking might otherwise suggest.

Also telling is the total absence of any instruction in the New Testament regarding the construction of special buildings for worship. This is in contrast to Old Testament legislation, which contained very specific blueprints regarding the tabernacle and, later, the temple in Jerusalem. When the New Testament writers did touch upon this subject, they pointed out that believers themselves were the temple of the Holy Spirit, living stones that come together to make up a spiritual house with Jesus Christ as the chief corner stone.[28] Even the Lord Jesus, in conversation with a Samaritan woman, said, "Woman, believe Me, an hour is coming when neither in this mountain, nor in Jerusalem, shall you worship the Father…God is spirit, and those who worship Him must worship in spirit and truth."[29] Therefore, the early church understood that an attachment to special places and sacred spaces was no longer the norm for Christian believers.

A PURPOSEFUL PATTERN?

Might the apostles have laid down a purposeful pattern of home-based churches? What practical effects would meeting in a home have had on the early followers of Jesus? The apostles' belief concerning the function of the

---

[24] Along with special church buildings, the rise of one bishop presiding over all churches in a city, the development of a hierarchical leadership system, and even the eventual merger of church and state after Constantine (4th century) are often also seen as either positive or at least natural occurrences.

[25] 1 Cor 11:2

[26] 1 Cor 11:6, 14:33b-34

[27] 2 Thess 2:15

[28] 1 Cor 3:16, 6:19; Eph 2:19-22, 1 Pet 2:4-5

[29] John 4:21,24

church was naturally expressed in the form that the church took. Some of the distinct practices of the early house churches are worth considering.

A Theology of Community

The overarching significance of the house churches was in their theology of community. The church was depicted by apostolic writers in terms which describe a family. Believers were children of God[30] who were born into God's family.[31] God's people were, thus, seen as part of God's household.[32] They were called brothers and sisters.[33] Consequently, Christians were to relate to each other as members of a family.[34] Out of this theological point arose many church practice issues. The question became, what setting best facilitated their functioning as God's family?

The Lord's Supper as a Full Meal

Many scholars are persuaded that the Lord's Supper was originally celebrated weekly as a full, fellowship meal, i.e. the Agape Feast.[35] Each local house church was to be like a family,[36] and one of the most common things families did was to eat together. Early church meetings centered around the Lord's Table, with tremendous times of fellowship, community, and encouragement.[37] Rather than a funeral-like atmosphere, the Lord's Supper was in anticipation of the Wedding Banquet of the Lamb.[38] The larger an individual congregation, the less family-like it would have become, and the more impersonal and impractical the Lord's Supper as a true meal would have been.

Interactive Church Meetings

Early church meetings were clearly interactive.[39] Any person could participate verbally. The prerequisite for anything said was that it be edifying and designed to strengthen the church. Such participatory meetings were best suited to living room sized gatherings, composed of people who all knew each other and were true friends. These participatory meetings would have been impractical for large numbers.

---

[30] 1 John 3:1

[31] John 1:12-13

[32] Eph 2:19; Gal 6:10

[33] Rom 16:2; Philem 1:2

[34] Rom 16:13; 1 Tim 5:1-2

[35] Roger Gehring (2004), *House Church and Mission*, Hendrickson Publishers, pp.171-177; Robert Banks (1994), *Paul's Idea of Community*, Hendrickson Publishers, pp.80-85; Del Birkey (1988), *The House Church*, Herald Press, pp.122-124,131-133.

[36] Titus 5:1-2

[37] Luke 22:16-19, 29-30; Acts 2:42, 20:7; 1 Cor 11:17-34

[38] Rev 19:6-9

[39] 1 Cor 14; Eph 19-20; Col 3:16; Heb 10:24-25

The 'One Another' Commands

The Scriptures are full of the 'one another' commands. Church was to be about accountability, community, and maintaining church discipline.[40] These ideals were best accomplished in smaller congregations where people knew and loved each other. Church was to be about relationships. A large auditorium of people, most of whom would have been relative strangers to each other, would not have easily achieved these goals. The early churches, therefore, met in homes to foster the simplicity, vitality, intimacy, and purity that God desired for his church.

Leadership and Decision-Making Patterns

The New Testament church had clearly identified local leaders called elders/presbyters, pastors/shepherds, or bishops/overseers. These terms were simply different names used for the same person(s) that functioned as leaders.[41] Yet, these leaders led more by example and persuasion than by command. The elder-led consensus of the whole congregation was paramount in decision making.[42] Achieving consensus was possible in a house church where everyone knew each other, loved each other, was patient with one another, and was committed to one other. Larger fellowships would have damaged relationships and lines of communication.

A Strategic Approach to Evangelism

The first century church turned its world upside down,[43] and it did so using the New Testament house church model. House churches were low cost, led by ordinary people, could reproduce quickly, and had great potential for growth through evangelism. God did not equate church size with church ability. Paul reminded believers that "God chose the foolish things of the world to shame the wise; God chose the weak things of the world to shame the strong. He chose the lowly things of this world and the despised things — and the things that are not — to nullify the things that are, so that no one may boast before him."[44]

---

[40] Matt 18:15-20; Rom 12:10, 12:16, 15:7, 15:14, 16:16; 1 Cor 1:10, 12:25, 16:20; 2 Cor 13:12; Gal 5:13,26; Eph 4:2, 4:32, 5:21; Philip 4:2; Col 3:9,13, 3:16; 1 Thess 3:12, 4:9,18, 5:11,13,15,25; 2 Thess 1:3; Heb 3:13, 10:24, 13:1; James 4:11, 5:9,16; 1 Pet 1:22, 3:8, 4:7-11, 5:5,14; 1 John 1:7, 3:11,23, 4:7,12; 2 John 1:5

[41] The interchangeability of these terms can be determined from a cross comparison of key scriptures: Acts 14:23, 20:17,28; Eph 4:11; Philip 1:1; 1 Tim 3:1-7; Titus 1:5-9; James 5:14; 1 Pet 5:1-3. For a detailed scholarly discussion on New Testament local leadership, see Gerald Cowen (2003), *Who Rules the Church?* Broadman and Holman Publishers.

[42] Matt 18:15-20; Luke 22:24-27; John 17:11, 20-23; Acts 15:22; 1 Cor 1:10, 10:17; Eph 2:19-20, 4:13-17; Philip 2:1-2; 1 Pet 5:1-3

[43] Acts 17:6

[44] 1 Cor 1:27-29 (NIV)

Financial Support of Traveling Leaders and the Poor

The New Testament writers urged the generous support of traveling leaders like apostles and evangelists, as well as the poor.[45] First century believers were better able to fund church planters and assist the poor because they met as house churches, without the financial burden that would have come had they constructed special buildings like their Jewish and pagan contemporaries.

House Churches were Small in Size

Since they met almost exclusively in private homes, the typical congregation of the apostolic era was small. No specific number is ever given in Scripture, but there were generally no more people than could fit comfortably into the average living-room. The pattern was for smaller, rather than larger, churches. Biblical scholar Robert Banks notes that during the first century, "The entertaining room in a moderately well-to-do household could hold around thirty people comfortably—perhaps half as many again in an emergency...A meeting of the "whole church" may have reached forty to forty-five people...but many meetings may well have been smaller. The average membership was around thirty to thirty-five people...Even the meetings of the "whole church" were small enough for a relatively close relationship to develop between the members. So long as they preserved their household setting, this was bound to be the case."[46]

CONCLUSIONS

Persecution, poverty, and progression are not adequate reasons to explain the phenomenon of first century house churches. Rather, the apostolic church did not erect church buildings in large part because they simply did not need them. God intended the typical church to be smaller and intimate, rather than larger and impersonal. The letters which were written to the various New Testament churches were, in fact, written to individual house churches and/or citywide house church networks. Thus, the instructions contained in them were geared to work best in smaller congregations.

STUDY QUESTIONS

1. What are the three most common reasons given for the existence of home-based churches in the apostolic era? Discuss each briefly.
2. Can you describe the theological and strategic reasons why the early believers may have chosen to deliberately meet as smaller house-sized congregations?

---

[45] Luke 10:1-11; 1 Cor 9; 3 John 5-8
[46] Robert Banks (1994), *Paul's Idea of Community*, Hendrickson, pp.35-36.

Chapter 13

THE AUTHORITY OF 'APOSTOLIC TRADITION' IN THE NEW TESTAMENT ERA

STEVE ATKERSON

Steve Atkerson holds an M.Div. from Mid-America Baptist Theological Seminary, served seven years as one of the pastors of a Southern Baptist Church, began working with house churches in the late 1980s, and is now elder of a house church in Atlanta, GA, USA. He travels widely teaching and training leaders on the basics of New Testament church life. Books he has edited and contributed to include Toward A House Church Theology, Ekklesia: To the Roots of Biblical House Church Life, The Practice of the Early Church: A Theological Workbook (Leader's Guide), and The Equipping Manual. He is part of the team at The New Testament Restoration Foundation (www.ntrf.org). [Used by permission of the author. Email: nt_restoration_foundation@juno.com].

INTRODUCTION

Let us suppose a brand new, first century congregation in Alexandria, Egypt, wrote a letter to the 12 apostles in Jerusalem. Imagine that this church consisted of Jewish believers who had heard the gospel on a visit to Jerusalem.

Now, back home in Egypt, they did not know how to function as a new body of believers. They may have sent a letter to the apostles in which they asked a series of questions about church life such as the interactive nature of church meetings, how often believers should meet, the best location for such gatherings, whether they should build a special church building once they grew numerically, the proper qualification and role of church leaders, whether church leaders should be paid money for their ministry, whether decisions should be made by consensus of all the believers or only by those in leadership, how often they should celebrate the Lord's Supper, who they should baptize, and so forth.

How would the apostles have answered? Would they have written that each church was free to do whatever it wanted? Would they have perhaps encouraged each fellowship to independently pray and follow the Holy Spirit's leading? Would they have suggested that each congregation should be unique and different, free from apostolic influence? Or conversely, might they have replied with very specific instructions for church life, with a particular way of doing things, a definite agenda, and unmistakable congregational guidelines?

An analysis of the New Testament writings suggests that the apostles indeed had a definite and particular way in which they organized churches and encouraged them to function. The evidence further asserts that they intended all congregations to follow these same apostolic traditions and that these traditions were in fact meant to be seen as authoritative.

APOSTOLIC AUTHORITY WAS ROOTED IN CHRIST'S AUTHORITY

Early believers recognized that if anyone understood the purpose of the church it would have been the apostles and, consequently, in the absence of Christ's personal physical presence, it was safest to recognize the authority of the apostles and to adhere to their guidance.

Firstly, believers would have known that the apostles were hand-picked and personally trained by Jesus for three years. The gospel record reveals that "[Jesus] went up to the mountain and summoned those whom He Himself wanted, and they came to Him. And He appointed twelve, that they might be with Him, and that He might send them out to preach, and to have authority to cast out demons."[1]

Secondly, Jesus sent the Holy Spirit to teach the apostles things he had not taught them before. Thus, whatever Jesus taught his apostles about the church was naturally reflected in the way they subsequently set up and organized churches. Jesus confirmed that this kind of guidance would be with the apostles when he said, "the Helper, the Holy Spirit, whom the Father will send in My name, He will teach you all things, and bring to your remembrance all that I said to you."[2] Later, Jesus said to the apostles that "when He, the Spirit of truth, comes, He will guide you into all the truth; for He will not speak on His own initiative, but whatever He hears, He will speak; and He will disclose to you what is to come."[3]

Thirdly, during his earthly ministry, Jesus made a statement to his inner circle of followers that showed how he viewed the authority that he himself had vested in them. Speaking to his original group of 12, the Lord said, "The one who listens to you listens to Me, and the one who rejects you rejects Me; and he who rejects Me rejects the One who sent Me."[4]

Fourthly, there was an understanding that the Lord Jesus appeared to the apostles over a 40 day period after his resurrection in order to give them additional instruction: "To these He also presented himself alive, after His suffering, by many convincing proofs, appearing to them over a period of forty days, and speaking of the things concerning the kingdom of God."[5]

Thus, the implication of the above understanding would certainly have been far-reaching in the minds of first century believers. Listening to

---

[1] Mark 3:13-15 (NASB)
[2] John 14:26 (NASB)
[3] John 16:13 (NASB)
[4] Luke 10:16 (NASB)
[5] Acts 1:3 (NASB)

apostolic instruction meant that believers applied their teachings and practices as fully as possible. Any other ideas or practices that early churches may have had, even in light of perhaps changing local circumstances, were to be always evaluated carefully under the influence of apostolic directives.

HOLDING TO APOSTOLIC TRADITION WAS PRAISEWORTHY

Paul again urged the Corinthians, "Follow my example, as I follow the example of Christ."[6] The immediate context concerns seeking the good of others so as to glorify God and bring them to salvation. The word "follow" is from *mimatai,* the basis for "mimic." Paul wanted the Corinthian believers to imitate him in that regard. Apparently they were doing well in imitating him in other matters as well, since Paul stated in the very next verse, "I praise you because you remember me in everything, and hold firmly to the traditions, just as I delivered them to you."[7] Let us examine this verse.

What is a "tradition"? The regular Greek word for "teaching" is *didaskalia* (the basis for "didactic"), but significantly that is not the word used here. Instead, *paradosis* (tradition) is used. Although the Greek word for tradition, *paradosis,* was a technical term in Judaism for oral transmission of religious instruction, in this context it almost certainly does not refer to teaching, but rather to religious traditions regarding worship.[8] A tradition is usually thought of as a custom or a certain way of doing things. It is an inherited pattern of thought or action. A popular definition might be, "things people *do* on a regular basis." This same Greek word (in verb form) is used in regard to the practice of the Lord's Supper (i.e. that it was passed on).[9] The point of these traditions was that they were something that was passed on for others with the expectation that they would be followed. Here we see an apostle praising a church for holding to his traditions.

Consider the word "everything" as Paul used it. It means "all that exists," or at least, "all that pertains to the subject." When Paul wrote "everything", what did the early believers understand him to mean? His use of the word "everything" certainly suggests that Paul's intended application was larger than just the exhortation regarding evangelism.[10] Might "everything" have also included church order? Indeed it did.

What do the words "just as" indicate about the extent of compliance with Paul's traditions? Christians adhered to every iota, or at least were expected to. They were not to be haphazard about it. Paul praised them for holding to his traditions exactly as he had passed them on. The apostles evidently

---

[6] 1 Cor 10:31—11:1 (NIV)

[7] 1 Cor 11:2 (NASB)

[8] Gordon Fee (1987), *New International Commentary on the New Testament,* William B. Eerdmans Publishing, p.499.

[9] 1 Cor 11:23

[10] 1 Cor 10:31-11:1

desired for churches to precisely mimic the patterns they established. Yet the word "traditions" is in the plural. Paul apparently had in mind more than just one tradition, but all the traditions he passed on to the churches.

This habit of using specific examples as general guidelines to be applied diligently to unforeseen or unspoken situations is part of the fabric of the Old Testament. This fact would not have been lost on the apostles. Mosaic legislation, for example, was paradigmatic in nature. It was case law. Only a few, sample, legal examples were recorded by Moses. The believer was expected to apply those case studies to other areas of life not specifically mentioned. For instance, the corners of fields were to be left unharvested for the poor to gather and eat.[11] Nothing was said about olive groves. Did this mean that a wheat farmer alone was burdened with feeding the poor, but that the man with an olive grove could harvest every last olive? Certainly not. Every farmer, regardless of the crop, was to leave a similar portion of his harvest to meet the needs of the poor. Similarly, adherence to apostolic tradition was paradigmatic in nature. If the early believers observed that the apostles were pleased when churches followed specific traditions, then they were expected to apply that example to other patterns they saw modeled by the apostles in their establishment of churches.

An interesting paradox can be observed about "tradition." The same word (*paradosis*) used by Paul was also used by Jesus to the Pharisees, "Why do you break the command of God for the sake of your tradition?"[12] Jesus confronted the tradition of the Pharisees, but Paul blessed the Corinthians for following the tradition of an apostle. Pharisaic tradition broke the command of God. Apostolic tradition, however, was seen as consistent with the commands of Jesus. Holding to the tradition of the apostles was thus praiseworthy, as proven by Paul's praise for the Corinthians. Therefore, house churches did not develop their own church practices apart from that handed down to them by the apostles themselves.

HOLDING TO APOSTOLIC TRADITION WAS TO BE UNIVERSAL

We also read that Paul planned to send Timothy to Corinth. Timothy was to remind the Corinthians of Paul's lifestyle so that they could imitate him. The immediate context concerns Paul's faithfulness in service and his humility as an apostle. Thus Paul wrote,

> I urge you to imitate me. For this reason I am sending to you Timothy, my son whom I love, who is faithful in the Lord. He will remind you of my way of life in Christ Jesus, which agrees with **what I teach everywhere in every church**.[13]

---

[11] Lev 19:9-10, 23:22
[12] Matt 15:1-3
[13] 1 Cor 4:16-17 (NIV, emphasis added)

Notice the uniformity of practice reflected in Paul's words. His way of life in Christ was consistent with what he taught everywhere in every church. There was a lifestyle tradition that grew out of Paul's teachings. His belief determined his behavior. His doctrine naturally determined his duty. In similar fashion, the apostles' beliefs about the function of the church would surely have affected the way they organized churches, which would be in line with the axiom that form always follows function. Though the direct import is far afield from church practice, to also imitate the apostles' ways regarding church life would have been the obvious choice for any fellowship in the first century.

Paul quieted those inclined to be contentious about head coverings by appealing to the universal practice of all the other churches: "If anyone wants to be contentious about this, we have no other practice—nor do the churches of God."[14] This final statement was designed to win over the contentious people and settle any argument. Regardless of the proper application of head coverings, the point is that Paul expected all the churches to be doing the same thing. Just to realize that one was different was argument enough to silence opposition. Obviously, prior emphasis had been given to certain practices that were supposed to be done the same way, everywhere. This indicates a uniformity of practice in all New Testament churches.

In a passage about church meetings, Paul mentioned something else that was to be true universally: "As in all the congregations of the saints, women should remain silent in the churches."[15] Regardless of the correct application of this verse, notice how Paul again appealed to a universal pattern that existed in all the churches as a basis for obedience.

Finally, note how Paul chided his readers, "Did the word of God originate with you? Or are you the only people it has reached?"[16] The obvious answer to both questions was 'no'. This further indicates a uniformity of practice among New Testament churches. In some respect, the Corinthians were doing something differently from what all the other churches were doing. Evidently all the churches were expected to follow the same patterns in their church meetings. These two questions were designed to pull the Corinthians back into line. Holding to apostolic traditions was to be universal in the first century.

HOLDING TO APOSTOLIC TRADITION BROUGHT GOD'S PEACEFUL PRESENCE

"Rejoice in the Lord always, I will say it again: Rejoice! Let your gentleness be evident to all. The Lord is near. Do not be anxious about anything, but in everything, by prayer and petition, with thanksgiving, present your requests

---

[14] 1 Cor 11:16 (NIV)
[15] 1 Cor 14:33b-34 (NIV)
[16] 1 Cor 14:36 (NIV)

to God. And the peace of God, which transcends all understanding, will guard your hearts and your minds in Christ Jesus."[17] The main point here is that by rejoicing in the Lord we can gain God's peace, regardless of circumstances.

In the next paragraph, the church at Philippi was given the recipe for how to obtain God's peace. Paul wrote, "Finally, brothers, whatever is true, whatever is noble, whatever is right, whatever is pure, whatever is lovely, whatever is admirable – if anything is excellent or praiseworthy – think about such things. Whatever you have learned or received or heard from me, or seen in me – put into practice. And the God of peace will be with you."[18]

The Philippians were instructed to put into practice 'whatever' they learned, received, heard from Paul, or saw in Paul. The primary application in context concerned imitating Christ's humility, putting others first, and rejoicing in the Lord. By extension, however, this 'whatever' most likely also included the way that Paul organized churches. The apostles held to a definite pattern for setting up the early churches. To bypass apostolic tradition in this area was to also bypass God's blessing. The apostles believed that fellowships which followed their pattern for church life would enjoy much more of God's peaceful presence.

HOLDING TO APOSTOLIC TRADITION BROUGHT ORDER

In a passage that deals directly with church practice, Paul wrote, "The reason I left you in Crete was that you might straighten out what was left unfinished."[19] This specifically concerns the appointment of qualified elders in every city. Similarly, in a passage about the practice of the Lord's Supper, Paul wrote, "The rest I will *set in order* when I come."[20] It is evident from these scriptural passages that the apostles did indeed have a definite way they wanted certain things done regarding the church. It was not left up to each individual assembly to find its own way of doing things. There was obviously some kind of order, pattern, or tradition that was followed in organizing the churches which would minimize chaos and bring appropriate order to the early house churches.

HOLDING TO APOSTOLIC TRADITION WAS COMMANDED

The Thessalonians were instructed to "stand firm and hold to the traditions which you were taught, whether by word of mouth or by letter from us."[21] Here, they were specifically commanded to hold to the traditions of the apostles, whether received orally or in writing. The 12 apostles were not able to be present everywhere to tell early believers in person what to do.

---

[17] Philip 4:4-7 (NIV)
[18] Philip 4:8-9 (NIV)
[19] Titus 1:5 (NIV)
[20] 1 Cor 11:34 (KJV, emphasis added)
[21] 2 Thess 2:15 (NASB)

However, they did send letters that discussed the practices they expected the early churches to follow. The overall context refers to eschatological events, and not specifically to church practice. However, the word "traditions" is in the plural, since the author had more in view that merely the tradition about Christ's Second Coming.

Interestingly, rather than "traditions," the NIV renders this "teachings." This may be because a tradition (*paradosis*) can include a teaching (*didaskalia*), and the immediate context concerned the apostles' oral traditions about 'end times' eschatology. However, the KJV, ASV, RSV, and NASB Bible versions translate it as "traditions," which is also a valid translation of *paradosis*. The importance of the various "traditions" passages such as this must have been grappled with by the early churches, especially those that were independently minded. Yet, in the end, this verse indicates that adherence to apostolic traditions was actually commanded and not merely suggested.

A similar attitude toward tradition is expressed elsewhere: "keep aloof from every brother who leads an unruly life and not according to the traditions which you received from us. For you yourselves know how you ought to follow our example."[22] The specific context here refers to gainful employment versus being idle and lazy. In context, this tradition refers to a practice more so than a doctrine.

CONCLUSIONS

In this article, the nature of apostolic tradition and authority and the way in which the early churches complied with apostolic guidance have been briefly examined. It is evident that there was a normative church practice in all the churches. Individual churches were not left to their own devices or wisdom in organizing their communities. It was not just apostolic teaching and doctrine to which the first believers adhered, but also to apostolic tradition and practice as revealed by the letters the apostles sent to the churches, by their verbal instructions, and by their example. These traditions would have included the way the early churches were organized and the way they functioned. It may be that these patterns of church practice are part of what gave the early church its missional dynamic.

STUDY QUESTIONS

1. What is the difference between a 'teaching' and a 'tradition'?
2. Name specific 'traditions' or 'patterns' that the apostles passed on to the early churches by their example, by word of mouth, or by letter.
3. Why were the early churches expected to follow these 'traditions'?

---

[22] 2 Thess 3:6-7a (NASB)

PART 3

HOUSE CHURCH AND
SMALL GROUP MOVEMENTS
THROUGH THE AGES

Chapter 14

WHY DO HOUSE CHURCHES AND SMALL GROUPS PERSIST THROUGHOUT CHURCH HISTORY?

MIKE BARNETT

Mike Barnett, Ph.D. (Southwestern Seminary, Fort Worth, Texas, USA), earned his doctorate in church history and is currently the Elmer V. Thompson Professor of Missionary Church Planting at the seminary and school of missions, Columbia International University (Columbia, South Carolina, USA). He and wife Cindy served 12 years with the International Mission Board, working in the 10/40 Window. He has a business background and continues to work in international business development. Mike recently co-authored Called to Reach: Equipping Cross-Cultural Disciplers (2007). Email: mcbar@pobox.com.

INTRODUCTION

Through the ages, the pendulum has swung from one ecclesiological paradigm to another. The Jewish sect called 'The Way' became a movement of 'Christians' in Antioch. About 250 years later, this illegal, empire-wide, oppressed church was first tolerated (AD 313) and then lauded as the only acceptable, legal, imperial religion.

From generation to generation, schools of thought and their parallel methodologies rose to prominence only to be followed by opposing, reforming, frequently grassroots, lay-led movements. For example, Aquinian scholasticism, the official method of teaching in the late Middle Ages, produced a biblical and spiritual vacuum that was filled by the new way (*via moderna*) of learning, taught by young monk professors like Martin Luther at the University of Wittenberg.[1] This paved the way for the reformation of the church and the beginnings of the enlightenment and the modern age. Institutional systems of faith and practice were redirected and reformed, sometimes with a more biblical and spiritual basis. Still, new challengers to the status quo arise and the pattern continues to this day. Action and reaction, ebb and flow, back and forth, the moods and movements of the church shifting according to the times, cultures, and contexts.

Yet, throughout the many pendulum swings, house churches and small groups are evident. An often overlooked and maligned form of church, house-based churches simply never went away. From the first century homes of the likes of Lydia to communities of Benedictine monks, followers of

---

[1] Timothy George (1988), *Theology of the Reformers*, Broadman Press, p.43.

Christ met in homes for worship, ministry, and service. As expanding bands of disciplers reached beyond the infrastructure of the established church, they congregated in houses. Often persecuted and pushed underground, dissenters against man-made and self-serving institutions of Christendom encouraged one another around the hearth of the home.

Monastic beginnings often took root in small, intimate, and informal gatherings on the edges of conventional church venues. Martin Luther's dining room 'table talks' among family and students fueled the theological fervor of the Reformation in the 16th century. Indeed, he proposed that German believers should "assemble by themselves in some house to pray, to read, to baptize and to receive the sacrament and practise other Christian works."[2] Ulrich Zwingli's 'prophecy meetings' with his students in the Grossmünster library served as the seedbed for what became an Anabaptist movement of house churches.[3] John Wesley's small 'classes' and 'bands' often met in church classrooms or homes. Today, around the world, small groups of believers meet in homes to worship Jesus Christ and encourage each other in their life and work.

Why has God always seen fit to use the house-sized church? What patterns can we glean from this legacy of home-based groups?

WHOSE HISTORY?

Before we ponder lessons from the past, perhaps we should state the obvious—the rationale for searching history for patterns and lessons for today. Simply put, it is God's history!

When we study the history of the church, its nature and character, we examine the record of God's work. By recognizing consistent patterns—those pendulum swings—we gain insights into God's plan and method. We learn what works for God's glory and what does not. We recommit ourselves to proven practices. We recognize wayward direction and correct our course before the damage has been done. We take courage to reform the church in the image intended by God, not ourselves. We stay on track with God's plan for proclaiming the gospel among all peoples on earth. As the proverb says, "there is nothing new under the sun."[4]

Let us, therefore, learn from what has gone before. Let us glean from the past those effective principles and practices for the sake of the future. After all, it is God's story.

THE PERSISTENCE OF HOUSE CHURCHES AND SMALL GROUPS

In the first century AD, we see that the first pattern for church, for a community of believers in Jesus Christ, was that of meeting in small groups

---

[2] Martin Luther (1526), *Preface to the German Mass and Order of Divine Service.*
[3] William R. Estep (1986), *Renaissance and Reformation*, Eerdmans, p.173.
[4] Ecc 1:9 (NASB)

in homes. Roger Gehring's landmark scholarly book *House Church and Mission*[5] masterfully takes us back to the roots of this persistent presence of house churches in the history of God's work. He focuses on the ministries of Jesus and the apostles. Even the most zealous house church advocate can learn from this thorough study of the ministry of Jesus and his first followers. Truly, the house and home served as the center of gravity for Jesus' ministry. No wonder the early Jesus movement swept through the Roman empire house-to-house. It was modeled by the Master.

In the early fourth century AD, when the newly crowned emperor Constantine endorsed Christianity as a legal, and later favored, faith it seemed for a time that the house church had served its purpose. This 'Christianization' of the Roman empire[6] initiated the institutionalization of government sponsored and financed church life. The emperor financed the construction of church buildings throughout the Mediterranean world. To this day, ruins of ancient basilicas dot the shoreline of North Africa. As Christianity eventually became the *only* legal religion, there was no longer a need to meet in homes. The basilica became the place to be seen. The Sunday gathering for worship was a highly visible and public affair.

Some of the faithful, however, soon sensed the essence of the faith was being sacrificed on the altar of institutionalized Christianity.[7] At first, it was the hermit monks and, thereafter, communities of monks who began to recapture the essentials of the faith. The small meeting house of worship was no longer the mainstay of Christianity, but it persisted nonetheless among these monastic communities.

Then, throughout the Middle Ages, small groups of dissenters, reformers, and faithful followers of Jesus Christ met in houses often in the shadows of cathedrals.[8] Waldensians, Hussites, Lollards, Hutterites, Mennonites, Moravian Brethren, Methodists, and others reveal the persistence of home groups in God's story. A marvelously preserved example of the medieval house church survives in Tewksbury, England. During times of severe persecution of English Baptists in the late 17th century, a small congregation gathered regularly in a house on a side street literally yards from the local cathedral. Tourists today can remove the wooden planks in the floor of the original house and discover a hidden baptistery where the faithful conducted believer's baptism.[9]

---

[5] Roger Gehring (2004), *House Church and Mission: The Importance of Household Structures in Early Christianity*, Hendrickson.

[6] M. Cunningham (2002), *Faith in the Byzantine World*, InterVarsity Press, p.19.

[7] Henry Chadwick (1993), *The Early Church [Revised Edition]*, ch.12.

[8] John Driver (1991), *Radical Faith: An Alternative History of the Christian Church*, Pandora Press; Peter Bunton (2001), *Cell Groups and House Churches: What History Teaches Us*, House to House Publications.

[9] Ferrell Foster, "Baptists Reconnect with Their Heritage of Liberty," www.bgct.org/texasbaptists/Page.aspx?&pid=1182&srcid=733

Even in the modern era, house churches and small groups persist.[10] Wave after wave continues. In the 20th century, lay renewal movements meet in houses. In the 1960s, the Jesus Movement often abandoned the traditional church venue for a less formal house environment. In more traditional churches, as Sunday morning 'Sunday Schools' or Bible studies gave way to multiple worship services, weekday house groups took up the slack for the sake of more intimate interaction within the body of believers. The recently documented 'New Monasticism' movements in North America regularly meet in homes.[11] Many mega-churches also promote their 'cell groups' as integral to the health of their larger congregation.

The pendulum has swung, from the temple to the homes of followers of 'The Way'. House churches and small groups remain. They simply will not go away. A study of history reveals a simple but profound association. When and where the kingdom of God expands beyond former geographical and spiritual borders, there is the house church and small group. It is so subtle that we miss it. When God moves to expand his kingdom on earth beyond its borders, he uses the home-based fellowship. It is undeniable. There must be a reason. What can we learn from this providential persistence?

EXPANSION OF THE KINGDOM

One of the positive outcomes of house churches and small groups throughout church history has been the expansion of God's kingdom. What was the primary venue for the expanding gospel throughout the Roman empire? The house church. How did the invading Germanic tribes of Northern Europe receive the gospel? From traveling families of Celtic missionaries. Where did the faith thrive among these Celtic immigrant families? Around the modest hearths of their simple medieval villages. How did God carry the gospel from Persia to China from the 7th to the 14th centuries? Through Nestorian merchant missionaries. Though material evidence is limited, we can assume that initially these marketplace missionaries practiced their faith in their caravans—ancient mobile homes. When the gospel spread from the original colonies of America into the frontier lands, it flowed through the log cabins of pioneers. Throughout the oppression of communist China and the former Soviet Union, the church first survived, then thrived, in homes. In recent decades, when the Cuban government suppressed Christianity, believers found refuge in house churches. The largest house church movement in history is no longer a secret as tens of millions of Chinese Christians worship today in homes.

REFORMATION

Another outcome of house churches and small groups throughout the ages serves as a reminder to the church universal not to get caught in the very

---

[10] David Garrison (2004), *Church Planting Movements*, Wigtake Resources.
[11] Rob Moll, "The New Monasticism," *Christianity Today*, Sept. 2005, p.39.

human trappings of institutionalization. As we review the history of the church, we see that the church needs reforming from time to time. When the church needs to return to its most basic and biblical roots, God uses house churches and small groups. The chapters of church history are full of accounts of a few bold disciples, gathering together to worship and serve God, to act in faith for the purpose of returning the church to its biblical and foundational roots. When God desires reformation of the church, he often inspires young reformers to carry the day.

No better example of this radical faith and action for the sake of reform exists than that of the early 16th-century Swiss Anabaptists. On January 21, 1525, a dozen mostly young men, students of Master Ulrich Zwingli, pastor of the Great Church of Zurich, gathered in the home of their colleague and friend, Felix Manz. After months of disputation and reasoning with the religious and political leaders of the city, they were prepared to stand against what they viewed as the corruption and extra-biblical practices of the church. They were even ready to oppose their beloved teacher, Zwingli. With great anxiety and awareness of the severe consequences of their pending actions, they prayed to God for direction and mercy. George Blaurock then stood up and asked to be baptized—as an adult and without the presence of any ordained minister officially sanctioned by the government. Congrad Grebel then took a dipper of water and poured it over the head of the kneeling Blaurock, a former monk. The deed was done. And the others soon followed suit. Thus began a movement of house churches that swept through Europe and laid foundations for all 'Free Church' traditions today. Indeed, the consequences of this move were severe. By the end of the decade, almost all twelve were dead, mostly at the hands of the executioners of the traditional church. But the seeds of reform had been planted in hundreds of house churches from Switzerland, to Moravia, and eventually throughout Europe.

LESSONS LEARNED

As we read the history of God's house churches and small groups, we should keep in mind these basic lessons or observations.

First, the persistence of house-sized and home-based groups throughout church history speaks to the importance that God himself places on this ecclesiological form. The Christian church began as a home-based phenomenon led by the Savior himself. In spite of the institutionalization of Christendom, it seems evident that God still intends for believers to gather in their homes for worship, study, friendship, and mutual service to the body of Christ and surrounding community. The mere fact that this has been, and still is, a viable and powerful expression of Christian community should grab and hold our attention.

Second, history reveals that when and where God is actively expanding his kingdom on earth, there is the house church and small group. It is undeniable. For the past 2000 years, God expanded his church by using simple saints who speak and live the good news of Jesus Christ as they go about their daily lives. The gospel flows from the house through the marketplace and back. Never has this been so obvious as today, serving as living testimony to the strategic nature of the house-based church. Those seeking to serve God in his mission among the nations must pay attention.

Finally, when the church needs reforming, do not be surprised if the house church or small group serves as the foundation. In our 21st-century world, what better place is there to reestablish the basics of Christianity than the home?

CONCLUSIONS

What do these few lessons from the history of house churches and small groups teach us? Members of these grassroots faith communities can celebrate who they are as modern (or postmodern) representatives of God's historic home-based church. They should be diligent as they model a true community of faith in Christ. They should be bold as they reach beyond existing borders of church with the gospel. They should be humble as they seek to reform and recreate biblical Christianity. Skeptics of the house church and small group should take care not to dismiss them as less than legitimate forms of church. Let us all learn our lessons from history. Let us all listen to the encouragements and warnings coming from the homes of believers. Let us encourage those who are called to lead and serve God in this way. May we all learn lessons from God's unfolding drama.

STUDY QUESTIONS

1. What were some of the factors motivating the revitalization efforts of various movements in church history?

2. What are your own motivations for being involved in the house church movement?

3. What practical lessons can you apply to your house church network today?

Chapter 15

THE FALL AND RISE OF THE CHURCH: THE PRINCIPLE OF RESTORATION

NATE KRUPP WITH JANICE WOODRUM

Nate Krupp has been calling the church to be all that God would have it be for over 40 years. He was led to Christ in 1957 by two converted Jews while an engineering student at Purdue University. He and his wife, Joanne, pioneered Lay Evangelism, Inc., have served with Youth With A Mission (YWAM), are professors with Christian Leadership University, and oversee the work of Preparing the Way Publishers. They have had a house-church understanding since 1966. Nate has written over 20 books on evangelism, prayer, Bible study, and the church, including The Church Triumphant at the End of the Age (1988). Janice Woodrum is preparing a second edition of The Church Triumphant at the End of the Age. With her husband, Dave, she will be assuming the oversight of Preparing the Way Publishers in 2007. [Adapted and used by permission of the author. Email: kruppnj@open.org].

INTRODUCTION

One of the features of church history has been 'The Fall and Rise of the Church'. By 'fall' is meant the process of drifting away from the pattern, power, and purposes of the church as revealed in the New Testament. By 'rise' is meant the process of recovery of these same patterns, power, and purposes through individuals and movements that God saw fit to use. Both of these have occurred simultaneously through the ages. This is not to say that any particular movement or individual was completely free from their own biases or that they were always in full obedience to what God was asking of them. Rather, God in his wisdom has chosen to use flawed individuals to restore things to a flawed church structure in order to prepare a spotless bride—the church—for Christ. Therefore, this chapter looks briefly at the principle of 'restoration' in the Scriptures and church history.[1]

WHAT IS 'RESTORATION'?

The word *restore* means "to bring back into existence or use, to bring back to a former or normal state, to bring back to health or strength, to put back to a former place or rank."[2]

---

[1] For a more detailed examination see Nate Krupp (1988), *The Church Triumphant at the End of the Age*, Preparing the Way Publishers

[2] *Webster's Dictionary of the English Language* (1983), Based on *The Random House Dictionary (Classic Edition)*, Random House, Inc.

The Hebrew word most often translated *restore* in the Old Testament is the word *shub*. It has the basic meaning "to turn back, return." It is most frequently translated return (263 times), returned (151 times), restore (59 times), again (54 times), turn (53 times), bring back (45 times), and brought back (31 times).[3]

The Greek word most often translated *restore* in the New Testament is the word *apokathistemi*, which means "to restore, give back."[4] The noun form is used only once: "...until the period of restoration of all things about which God spoke by the mouth of His holy prophets from ancient time."[5] The verb form is most often used in connection with Jesus healing people[6], meaning that their bodies were being restored.

Thus, we can define *restoration* as a returning or bringing back to a former, original, normal, unimpaired state of health, soundness, or vigor.

RESTORATION IN THE BIBLE

As we study the pages of the Bible, we see that God is a God of restoration. When Abimelech mistakenly took Abraham's wife Sarah to be his wife, God spoke to him in a dream and told him to restore her to Abraham.[7] Reuben wanted to restore Joseph unharmed to his father.[8] Joseph predicted that the cupbearer would be restored to his place of responsibility.[9] Moses restored Pharaoh's hand.[10] The Israelites prayed to God for restoration from their calamities.[11] David cried out for God to restore to him the joy of salvation.[12] God was committed to restoring the nation Israel to their land, inheritance, and blessings when they backslid, if they would but return to him.[13] David says that God "restores my soul."[14] God restored Job's fortunes.[15] Nebuchadnezzar is restored to sanity and his throne after he acknowledged God.[16] God promises to restore to Israel that which has been taken away.[17]

---

[3] *New American Standard Bible Concordance* (1975), The Lockman Foundation, Holman Publishers, pp.1011,1602.
[4] *New American Standard Bible Concordance,* Ibid., pp.1011,1634.
[5] Acts 3:21 (NASB)
[6] Matt 12:13; Mark 3:5, 8:25; Luke 6:10
[7] Gen 20:7
[8] Gen 37:22
[9] Gen 40:9-13
[10] Exod 4:7
[11] Psalm 60:1, 80:3,7,19
[12] Psalm 51:12
[13] Deut 30:2; Psalms 85:1, 4, 126:4; Isa 1:26, 49:8; Jer 15:19, 16:15, 27:22, 29:14, 30:3, 30:18, 31:23, 33:7; Ezek 16:53; Joel 3:1, Amos 9:14
[14] Psalm 23:3
[15] Job 42:10
[16] Dan 4:34-37
[17] Joel 2:25-27

People are restored to health by God.[18] Those who fall into sin, God desires to see restored.[19] The disciples were expecting Elijah (John the Baptist) to restore all things.[20] Just before Jesus' ascension, the disciples were asking Jesus if now was the time that he was going to restore the kingdom to Israel.[21] God's plan of restoration of his people, Israel, also included the calling of the Gentiles.[22] And someday Jesus will return to earth to restore all things to their condition before Adam's fall.[23] And so forth, through the rest of the Bible.[24] This principle of restoring things to their rightful place, based on the biblical principle, is a part of the Judeo-Christian heritage. We find it in our conscience, our laws, and in our understanding of proper social behavior. What a God he is—committed to a full restoration of all things!

THE FALL OF THE CHURCH

In this section we want to look at the principle of restoration as it relates to church history. This writer believes that all of church history is a cycle, or circle. The early church that we read about in the first century AD could be called the early, apostolic, New Testament church. It was characterized by purity, authority, power, purpose, principle, and pattern, as well as by a certain degree of fruitfulness. Though flawed individuals comprised the New Testament church, it was God's standard for the entire subsequent church age. Arthur Wallis puts it this way:

> In the New Testament we have a clear picture of the early Church. It wasn't a perfect Church because it was composed of human beings, and they are never perfect. However, the early Church was perfect in constitution, perfect in the revelation on God's mind, received through His holy apostles and prophets. They had complete light and thus had no need to progress into fuller revelation in the ensuing centuries. Through the apostles, the early Church received in the First Century a complete revelation of the mind of God. This revelation is, of course, contained in our New Testament. But also, as they walked in the light of this revelation, not only the revelation but they themselves became a model of God's intention.[25]

---

[18] Isa 38:16; Jer 30:17; Matt 12:13, 15:31; Mark 3:5, 8:25; James 5:15
[19] Gal 6:1
[20] Matt 17:11
[21] Acts 1:6
[22] Acts 15:12-21
[23] Acts 3:18-21; Rom 8:18-23
[24] Num 35:25; Deut 22:2; 1 Sam 12:3; 2 Sam 9:7, 16:3; 1 Kings 12:21, 20:34; 2 Kings 8:6; 2 Chron 24:4; Ezra 2:68
[25] Arthur Wallis, "Revival and Recovery," in Frank Bartleman (1982), *Another Wave of Revival*, Whitaker House, pp.155-156.

It was not long until this early church began to fall away from this state. In fact, it began to fall away even during New Testament times. The apostle Paul warned the leaders of the church in Ephesus that men would arise from among their own ranks who would lead believers astray:

> I know that after my departure savage wolves will come in among you, not sparing the flock; and from among your own selves men will arise, speaking perverse things, to draw away the disciples after them. Therefore be on the alert, remembering that night and day for a period of three years I did not cease to admonish each one with tears.[26]

Paul also wrote to Timothy that the Spirit of God foresaw that some true believers would even be swept up by the allure of strange teachings and practices that would lead them to abandon the faith:

> But the Spirit explicitly says that in later times some will fall away from the faith, paying attention to deceitful spirits and doctrines of demons, by means of the hypocrisy of liars seared in their own conscience as with a branding iron, men who forbid marriage and advocate abstaining from foods, which God has created to be gratefully shared in by those who believe and know the truth.[27]

The apostle John records that even in his day there were false teachers that were not acknowledging that Jesus Christ had actually come in the flesh, perhaps being precursors of the Gnostic groups that were to come to prominence in the second and third centuries:

> For many deceivers have gone out into the world, those who do not acknowledge Jesus Christ as coming in the flesh. This is the deceiver and the antichrist.[28]

Jesus Christ himself, appearing in a vision to John on the island of Patmos, called on five of the seven first century churches of Asia to repent.[29] A number of things were displeasing to the Lord, including the emergence of the Nicolaitans, who began a trend of creating a rigid distinction between Christian leaders and ordinary Christians, and false prophetesses like Jezebel, who was bringing immorality into the church:

> Yet this you do have, that you hate the deeds of the Nicolaitans, which I also hate...Thus you also have some who in the same way hold the teaching of the Nicolaitans. Repent therefore.[30]

---

[26] Acts 20:29-31 (NASB)
[27] 1 Tim 4:1-3 (NASB)
[28] 2 John 1:7 (NASB)
[29] Rev 2 and 3
[30] Rev 2:6,15,16 (NASB)

> But I have this against you, that you tolerate the woman Jezebel, who calls herself a prophetess, and she teaches and leads My bondservants astray, so that they commit acts of immorality and eat things sacrificed to idols.[31]

The church continued to decline, losing its evangelical faith, the power and gifts of the Holy Spirit, and the simple pattern of church life, in part, through some of the sincere but unfortunate decisions made by the Early Church Fathers.

Eventually, the Roman emperor Constantine legalized Christianity in the fourth century AD and offered the church power, prestige, and position, which led to state-church partnership, special church buildings, a rigid clergy system, and an influx of formalism and laxity into the churches. This reached a low point during the Dark Ages, which saw the established Roman Catholic church introduce special clergy clothing (500), image and relic worship (786), holy water (850), canonization of dead saints (995), celibacy of the priesthood (1079), religious crusades and persecution of heretics (1000-1600), the teaching of purgatory (1439), and the eventual placement of church tradition on an equal footing with the Bible (1545).

THE RISE OF THE CHURCH

Starting in the 150s and accelerating about the year 1200, the Holy Spirit has been restoring the church to New Testament Christianity, step by step, movement by movement.

The Montanists (c.150) reminded the church about the need for the full operation of the spiritual gifts and disciplined living. The Monastics (c.300) brought back the idea of true community and focused devotion to God through prayer and meditation. The Priscillianists (c.350) brought back the importance of small groups for discipleship. The Celtic Missionary Movement (400s–700s) through believers like Patrick and Colomba restored the practice of traveling apostolic teams that would plant churches in unreached areas. The Waldenses (1100s and 1200s) utilized traveling preachers, home meetings, and the priesthood of all believers. Through John Wyclife (c.1350) came wide distribution of the Bible among the people.

The Reformation brought about the rediscovery of justification by faith in Christ alone through Martin Luther (c.1520). God used the Anabaptists (c.1500s) to restore water baptism for believers only. The Quakers (c.1600s) put into practice open church meetings where everyone could participate as the Lord prompted them. The Methodists (1700s) incorporated small discipleship groups, traveling preachers and teachers, and outdoor evangelism and helped usher in the Great Awakening. A vision to evangelize the world returned to the church through the Moravians (1700s), William Carey (1800s), and others. An emphasis on the person and work of

---

[31] Rev 2:20 (NASB)

the Holy Spirit returned to the church through the Pentecostals and Charismatics (1900s). In the 20th century, we have seen a restoration of personal evangelism and discipleship through the Navigators, Campus Crusade for Christ, the cell group movement, and many others. Others, too, have observed a similar phenomenon:

> God is not just dealing with the Church in this manner because of a lack of something better to do. God has a glorious plan which He is in the process of working out in His dealings with man. Each new visitation brings us just that much closer to the end product. Each new step or portion of truth brings us ever closer to the fully restored Church that will be a fit, or suitable, Bride for His Son. The Church will indeed be a help meet for the Son of God. It will be a glorious Church without spot or wrinkle or any such thing (Ephesians 5:27).[32]

> Ever since the early Church fell from New Testament purity and life, she has been like a backslider, fallen from the summit of apostolic days—though destined to return and yet enter into the full blessing of the Father's house....But steadily, relentlessly, the might Spirit of God has been moving on, restoring that which was lost and heading things up toward the great prophetic revelation of the Body of Christ in unity and fullness: even one Body, full matured 'unto the measure of the stature of the fullness of Christ!'[33]

> Events in the history of the churches in the time of the Apostles have been selected and recorded in the book of Acts in such a way as to provide a permanent pattern for the churches. Departure from this pattern has had disastrous consequences, and all revival and restoration have been due to some return to the pattern and principles contained in the Scriptures.[34]

CONCLUSIONS

The idea of the cyclic fall and rise of God's people is evident in Scripture. We have also provided an overview of how this concept of restoration applies to church history, with the hope that Christian believers today will be open to God's plans to bring the church to a renewed state of vigor.

STUDY QUESTIONS

1. What is meant by the term 'restoration' as it relates to the church?
2. Describe some of the steps in the 'fall' and 'rise' of the church.
3. What implications are there for the house church movement today?

---

[32] Dick Iverson (1975), *Present Day Truths*, Bible Press, p.52.

[33] Frank Bartleman (1982), *Another Wave of Revival*, Whitaker House, p.135.

[34] E.H. Broadbent (1999), *The Pilgrim Church*, Gospel Folio Press, p.26.

Chapter 16

THE EARLY CHURCH FATHERS AND HOUSE CHURCHES: THE SUBTLE SHIFT TOWARDS FORMALISM (AD 100 – 300)

BERESFORD JOB

Beresford Job is an itinerant Bible teacher traveling throughout England and America. He is an elder in the Chigwell Christian Fellowship (www.house-church.org), a biblically-based house church he helped establish in the mid-1980s. He is part of the team at the New Testament Restoration Foundation (www.ntrf.org). [Used by permission of the author. Email: talk2ccf@hotmail.com].

INTRODUCTION

It is a simple fact that, when we approach the New Testament, we see the apostles starting churches which were both uniform and universal when it comes to structure and practice. Paul's constant testimony is that he taught the same things in every church.[1] He even uses this fact of established uniformity as an unanswerable argument against those who would try to do things differently.[2] Peter's corroboration that Paul's writings (at least, those in the New Testament) were inspired Scripture further strengthens this idea[3] and demonstrates the complete unity of the apostles in regards to what they taught by way of both doctrine and practice. However, a subtle but significant shift can be detected in the post-apostolic period leading up to the First Council of Nicea in AD 325. This shift involved a move away from apostolic church patterns as found in the New Testament towards a more centralized and formalized system. This was primarily done at the hands of those known collectively as the Early Church Fathers. The purpose of this chapter is to provide an overview of this shift, arguing that its legacy has been a generally unhelpful one for the church universal. It is also worth noting that this shift elicited many later church revitalization movements throughout church history.

NEW TESTAMENT CHURCH PATTERNS

The existence and nature of New Testament patterns for the early house churches as instituted by the apostles have been previously described in

---

[1] 1 Cor 4:17, 7:17, 11:16, 14:33
[2] 1 Cor 14:36-38
[3] 2 Pet 3:15-16

great detail elsewhere by biblical scholars.[4] That the apostles implemented these patterns deliberately as the blueprint to be followed by all churches everywhere can be seen from an examination of their writings.[5] Presently, however, we will only briefly summarize several aspects that constituted the general biblical structure of church life and mission which were universal in the New Testament era churches.

Firstly, New Testament churches were governed through the consensual involvement of all the believers. Leadership at the local level was by a plurality of leaders who had been recognized and raised up for such leadership from within whatever church they were to lead. But, they were not considered to be executive or hierarchical. That is, they were not seen as being in authority over the church, but simply part of the consensual process, as were non-elders, since "when decisions were made, they were made by the whole company of believers, not simply the officials."[6] Moreover, these leaders were variously designated in Scripture as elders/presbyters, shepherds/pastors, and overseers/bishops. Each of these terms referred to one and the same person, though describing their differing roles. Professor of church history, A.M. Renwick, summarizes this nicely:

> When we come to consider the permanent officers of the Church we find that in the days of the Apostles elders and deacons were appointed and their duties defined. The office of elder is variously described in the New Testament as bishop, pastor, teacher, preacher, minister and steward. The various terms mentioned referred to the same officer, but each presented a different aspect of their work. Thus 'pastor' indicated their duty to 'shepherd the flock' of Christ. Bishop, a word used to translate the Greek *'episkopos'*, indicated that as 'overseers' they had to 'feed the Church of God' (Acts 20). That the *'presbuteros'* and *'episkopos'* (elder and bishop) were the same is shown by many facts...Furthermore, the qualifications for bishop and elder were the same. Scarcely any scholar today would dispute the words of the late Dr. J.B. Lightfoot, Bishop of Durham, and an undoubted authority: 'It is a fact now generally recognised by theologians of all shades of

---

[4] Roger Gehring (2004), *House Church and Mission: The Importance of Household Structures in Early Christianity*, Hendrickson Publishers; Robert Banks (1994), *Paul's Idea of Community: The Early House Churches in their Cultural Setting*, Hendrickson Publishers; Del Birkey (1988), *The House Church: A Model for Renewing the Church*, Herald Press.

[5] 1 Cor 4:17; 1 Cor 11:2; 1 Cor 11:16; 1 Cor 14:33,36-38; Philip 4:9; 2 Thess 2:15; See also Steve Atkerson, "Apostolic Tradition: Obsolete?" (www.ntrf.org).

[6] Donald Guthrie (1981), *New Testament Theology*, InterVarsity Press, p.741.

opinion, that in the language of the New Testament the same Officer in the Church is called indifferently bishop, and elder or presbyter.'[7]

Secondly, New Testament churches met in the homes of those who constituted them. This kept the numerical size of each church small. It is a simple fact that, every time the New Testament locates a particular and specific church, it is always in someone's house.[8] Meeting in homes perfectly complemented both the nature of a church as an extended family of God's people and the interactive format of the gatherings they would have. There were occasional meetings in a larger public context for evangelism, healing, or teaching, being sometimes held outdoors.[9] However, these rallies in no way competed with the clearly dominant practice of house-to-house gatherings. The late scholar, Dr. Colin Hemer, explains that "the earliest Christians had no special buildings, but met in private houses, as mentioned in several places in the New Testament."[10]

Thirdly, when New Testament churches met on the first day of the week they primarily engaged in the Lord's Supper and participatory worship meetings. Like two sides of the same coin, both parts of the gathering were integral to the whole and utterly consistent with the nature of what was going on. The heart of the gathering was the Lord's Supper which was observed as an actual meal which all those gathered shared and ate together.[11] The loaf and cup were partaken of in the context of those present eating together what was their main meal of the day. New Testament scholar Donald Guthrie remarks that "in the early days the Lord's Supper took place in the course of a communal meal. All brought what food they could and it was shared together."[12] Moreover, they would have a time of corporate worship whereby the format was that all were free to participate as the Spirit led.[13] No one person convened the gathering from the front. Indeed, in a house, with all gathered in a circle around the perimeter looking at each other, there was no front from which to lead. Prayer, sung worship, the gifts of the Spirit, testimony, and teachings would emerge from all gathered. Professor of Religious Studies, John Drane, describes the participatory nature of meetings in the early house churches in this way:

---

[7] A.M. Renwick (1958), *The Story of the Church*, InterVarsity Press, pp.20-21.
[8] Acts 20:6-8; Rom 16:3-5,23; 1 Cor 16:19; Col 4:15; Philem 1:1-2
[9] Acts 1:13-17, 2:46, 3:11, 5:12,42, 19:8-10, 20:20
[10] Tim Dowley (ed.) (1988), *A Lion Handbook - the History of Christianity*, Lion Publishers, p.58.
[11] 1 Cor 11:20-34
[12] David and Pat Alexander (eds.) (1978), *The Lion Handbook of the Bible*, Lion Publishers, p.594.
[13] 1 Cor 12:7-10; 1 Cor 14:26; Col 3:16; Heb 10:25

> In the earliest days...their worship was spontaneous. This seems to have been regarded as the ideal, for when Paul describes how a church meeting should proceed he depicts a Spirit-led participation by many, if not all...There was the fact that anyone had the freedom to participate in such worship. In the ideal situation, when everyone was inspired by the Holy Spirit, this was the perfect expression of Christian freedom.[14]

THE SUBTLE SHIFT OF THE EARLY CHURCH FATHERS

The men collectively known as the Early Church Fathers were the most influential leaders of the Christian churches in the immediate centuries following the death of the apostles and the closure of the canon of Scripture. They should, of course, have kept everyone on the path laid down by the apostles as recorded in the ever-increasing amount of New Testament writings becoming available to them through the years. What they did, rather, was to lead the churches down a completely different path towards centralization and formalism in the church's life, mission, and organization. Though these men were undoubtedly sincere in their faith in Christ and in their concern for the churches, the fact remains that the changes they implemented were a departure from both the mindset and methodology of the apostles. Let us now turn to some of the specific shifts that the Early Church Fathers brought into the churches.[15]

Clement of Rome

Clement was one of the early leaders of the church in Rome. He wrote a letter to the Corinthian Church in about AD 95, as Paul had once done. He died several years later in AD 100. He writes:

> The high priest has been given his own special services, the priests have been assigned their own place, and the Levites have their special ministrations enjoined on them. The layman is bound by the ordinances of the laity.[16]

Around the very same time that John the apostle is likely putting the finishing touches to the book of Revelation on the Isle of Patmos, we here have Clement of Rome suggesting the idea of applying the Old Testament Levitical priesthood to the Christian churches. Here, as early as AD 95, we have the introduction of the concept that church leadership ought to be that of priesthood, with the inevitable resultant distinction being made between

---

[14] John Drane (1999), *Introducing the New Testament*, Lion Publishing. p.402.

[15] All quotes from the Early Church Fathers are taken from Henry Bettenson (1969), *The Early Christian Fathers: A Selection from the Writings of the Fathers from St. Clement of Rome to St. Athanasius*, Oxford University Press. Used with permission.

[16] *First Epistle of Clement to the Corinthians.*

"priest" and "people". The clergy/laity divide, which negatively influenced Christianity for the next two millennia, did not originate with either Jesus or his apostles, and has therefore nothing whatsoever to do with the teaching of the New Testament. It rather originated with Clement, who took church leadership as set up by the apostles in the form of a non-hierarchical, plural, co-equal, indigenous group of elders, and put in its place a special "priesthood" quite separate from the ordinary "laity".

Ignatius of Antioch

Ignatius wrote seven letters to different churches while traveling to Rome where he was eventually martyred around AD 110. He wrote the following:

> Your reverend presbytery is tuned to the Bishop as strings to a lyre...Let us be careful not to resist the Bishop, that through our submission to the Bishop we may belong to God...We should regard the Bishop as the Lord Himself...[17]

> I advise you to always act in godly concord with the Bishop, presiding as the counterpart of God, and the presbyters as the counterpart of the council of the Apostles...As the Lord did nothing without the Father, either by Himself or by means of the Apostles, so you must do nothing without the Bishop and the presbyters.[18]

> ...respect the Bishop as the counterpart of the Father, and the presbyters as the council of God and the college of the Apostles: without those no church is recognised.[19]

> Let no-one do anything that pertains to the church apart from the Bishop...it is not permitted to baptise or hold a love-feast independently of the Bishop. But whatever he approves, that is also well pleasing to God.[20]

Notice what Ignatius suggests. The "presbytery" (from which comes the English word "priest") is now referred to as a "reverend" presbytery. It is growing both in importance and spiritual authority. Moreover, non-hierarchical co-equality is gone too, and this "ordained ministry" is now headed up by a Bishop. Note also the astounding authority ascribed to the

---

[17] *Letter of Ignatius to the Ephesians.*
[18] *Letter of Ignatius to the Magnesians.*
[19] *Letter of Ignatius to the Trallians.*
[20] *Letter of Ignatius to the Smyrneans.*

Bishop. He is to be looked upon "...as the Lord Himself." Such was the Bishop's control and authority that churches, in fact, now needed to obtain his permission even to baptize new believers or have a love-feast.

The Didache

This manual for church order is a second century document probably originating from the Christian community of Alexandria, Egypt. The Greek word *didache* literally means 'teaching', which is exactly what this manuscript does. It deals with all manner of practical advice, from the daily affairs of the church to living a moral lifestyle to how churches are to discern whether the traveling apostles and prophets they welcome are true or false teachers. Here is a sample that illustrates, once again, a shift away from apostolic practices:

> Before the baptism, moreover, the one who baptizes and the one being baptized must fast, and any others who can. And you must tell the one being baptized to fast for one or two days beforehand. Your fasts must not be identical with those of the hypocrites. They fast on Mondays and Thursdays; but you should fast on Wednesdays and Fridays.[21]

Though the advice, on the surface, appears sound and perhaps even helpful, it betrays a level of formality with regard to both baptism and fasting that was not evident in the early Christian house churches of the first century. Regarding baptism, there are numerous examples in the New Testament of new believers being baptized as soon as they professed faith in Christ,[22] rather than needing to go through a preparatory or probationary period as advised above. Regarding fasting on special days, the apostle Paul strongly encourages believers not to become enslaved to the superstitious idea of holding one day in spiritually higher esteem than another,[23] contrary to the advice given above which proposes a degree of routine formalism.

Tertullian

A widely respected but controversial apologist and philosopher in his time, Tertullian was converted in AD 193. His many writings date from AD 196 to 212. He lived in Carthage in Africa. He writes:

> The supreme priest (that is the Bishop) has the right of conferring baptism: after him the presbyters and deacons, but only with the Bishop's authority. Otherwise the laity also have the right...how much more is the discipline of reverence and humility incumbent upon laymen (since it also befits their superiors)...It would be idle for us to

---

[21] *The Didache* (Public Domain Text)
[22] Acts 2:36-41, 8:35-38, 10:43-48, 16:13-15
[23] Rom 14:1-12; Gal 4:8-11; Col 2:16-17

suppose that what is forbidden to priests is allowed to the laity. The distinction between the order of clergy and the people has been established by the authority of the Church.

Another 90 years have passed from the time of Ignatius, and there is now a full-blown priesthood, under the authority of a Bishop, with said priests considered the superiors of the mere laity, and with the Bishop regarded as supreme. In his statement that the clergy/laity divide, "...has been established by the authority of the Church", we can see how Tertullian and the other church leaders of the day are claiming divine authority to sanction their own system. Church leaders are now, in effect, beyond question or challenge.

Cyprian of Carthage

Cyprian lived in the same place as Tertullian, but some years later. He became a Christian in Carthage in AD 246 and was made bishop there within two years. Fifty years later, one might be amazed to discover that the 'priesthood' has developed even further and is now considered to be an actual sacrificing one. It was now understood to be actually mediating between God and those who are not priests. Writing of the Lord's Supper, Cyprian declares:

> If Christ Jesus our Lord and God is Himself the High Priest of God the Father, and first offered Himself as a sacrifice to the Father, and commanded this to be done in remembrance of Himself, then assuredly the priest acts truly in Christ's place when he reproduces what Christ did, and he then offers a true and complete sacrifice to God the Father, if he begins to offer as he sees Christ Himself has offered.

What eventually became the full-blown Roman Catholic mass is here in germinal form as early as AD 250. And, of course, the supremacy of the bishop over the priesthood soon led to even more layers of priestly hierarchy culminating, of course, in the very bishop of bishops, namely the Pope.

THE LEGACY OF THE EARLY CHURCH FATHERS

We see how, little by little, the Early Church Fathers took Christian churches from being a proliferation of small, grassroots, localized extended families, and made them instead into a worldwide hierarchical religious corporation. It is evident too how this first error, which was their foundational one, made it inevitable that more errors would soon follow. Their incorrect teaching about the very nature of the leadership and government of the church gave Christian leaders, in the form of Priests and Bishops, such authority that whatever else they taught was accepted, virtually automatically, as being from the Lord. It was indeed a seedbed and from it sprang more false teachings and practices. Suffice it to say, that once a hierarchical 'expert' leadership was in place, every other aspect of church life was removed and replaced with a centralized and formalized system. Once ecclesiastical experts were at the helm, it was thought best if non-leaders were not involved. Not only did the participatory nature of church meetings cease to exist, virtually every other aspect of biblical practice disappeared or was significantly altered. All of this quite naturally paved the way for even more changes that were brought about when Christianity was legalized in the early fourth century by the Roman emperor Constantine.

CONSTANTINE'S REVOLUTION

It is often suggested that Constantine's revolution in the early 300s was the sole reason for many of the departures from apostolic practices that have characterized churches throughout history. However, nothing could be further from the truth, as we have seen. What happened with Constantine was merely the consequence and final result of the changes that had already begun to occur. If such changes had not already occurred, then Constantine's claimed embracing of the Christian faith would have had an entirely different outcome. It is plain, therefore, that the marriage of Christianity with the Roman Empire would never have happened had it not been for what the Early Church Fathers had previously done by shifting church life and practice away from the apostolic patterns of the New Testament.

Constantine's revolution merely made the resultant religious multinational institution official and utilized it for the political purpose of unifying the Roman Empire.[24] He offered believers something which they readily accepted, namely the political backing and power of the Roman Empire. Because church gatherings had already been turned into the opposite of what they started out as and had become formalized religious services instead, any actual need to limit numbers and meet in believers' homes was gone. The offer of pagan temples in which to meet, and the promise of religious officialdom, was, understandably, irresistible to those whose mindset regarding church life was now so different and who had also just emerged from a period of persecution under the rein of the Roman emperor Diocletian. Notably, it is unimaginable that Jesus, the apostles, or the churches of New Testament times would have ever accepted such an offer from the civic or religious authorities of their day.

CONCLUSIONS

This article has briefly examined the shifts brought about by the Early Church Fathers away from the practices of the New Testament apostles towards formalism in church life, mission, and organization. This prepared the way in the early 300s for partnership with the Roman Empire, which

---

[24] Henry Chadwick (1993), *The Early Church*, Penguin Books, chapters 8 and 9; Will Durant (1944), *The Story of Civilization: Part III - Caesar and Christ*, Simon and Schuster, pp.653-664; E.H. Broadbent (1931), *The Pilgrim Church*, Gospel Folio Press, chapter 2.

officially sanctioned further erroneous teachings and practices in the Christian churches.

STUDY QUESTIONS

1. Can you recall the apostolic patterns of the New Testament for church life and mission?
2. Can you recall what specific shifts in leadership were brought about by the Early Church Fathers?
3. What was the Roman emperor Constantine's role in changing the nature of the church?
4. Specifically, how can you guard against the development of formalism in your house church network?

Chapter 17

Constantine's Revolution: The Shift from House Churches to the Cathedral Church (AD 300 and Beyond)

Rad Zdero

Rad Zdero earned his Ph.D. degree in Mechanical Engineering from Queen's University (Kingston, ON, Canada). He has participated in, led, and started house churches and cell groups since 1985. He is currently part of HouseChurch.Ca (www.housechurch.ca), which is a church planting team developing a network of house churches in the greater Toronto area and beyond. He is the author of The Global House Church Movement (2004). [Used by permission of the author. Email: rzdero@yahoo.ca].

INTRODUCTION

The aim presently is to provide an overview of the process of institutionalization that the early Christian churches underwent. This occurred initially only gradually and almost imperceptibly through the sincere but, at times, ill-advised work of the Early Church Fathers. This was then given official sanction and vigorously propelled forward in the early fourth century AD by the Roman emperor Constantine (b.272-d.337). H.A. Drake, professor of history and renowned scholar on Constantine, observes the following:

> The impact of Constantine on Christianity can be summarized fairly quickly: during the thirty years of his reign, more change took place in the status, structure, and beliefs of the Christian Church than during any previous period of its history.[1]

To be sure, many of Constantine's modifications to the church brought a healthy sense of stability and security to the Christian faithful. However, these changes overall were also a significant shift away from the patterns of the New Testament as established by the first generation of apostles. This mixed legacy of Constantine's revolution, in turn, would require a type of counter-revolutionary activity by the many revitalization movements that emerged time and again throughout church history.

---

[1] H.A. Drake, "The Impact of Constantine on Christianity," in *The Cambridge Companion to the Age of Constantine*, Noel Lenski (ed.) (2006), Cambridge University Press, p.111.

THE FIRST THREE CENTURIES BEFORE CONSTANTINE

The Church of the New Testament Era

In the first century AD, a mere 40 days after his resurrection from the dead, Jesus Christ entered the heavenly realm to sit at the right hand of Power. After three long years of public ministry, punctuated by victories and challenges, he left a noble commission of making disciples of all nations to his small motley crew of followers.[2] Yet, not many years later, first century believers had become known as those that had turned the world upside down.[3] They were able to make good strides in their journey of spreading the message of Christ to the then-known world through the empowerment that they received from the Spirit of God.[4] In the process, they birthed new communities of faith in new linguistic, cultural, and geographic soil. Their preferred strategy—initially forged by the apostles themselves—was that of an expanding network of simple, small, reproducible, grassroots house churches, as borne out by even the briefest survey of Scripture[5] and described in detail by scholars.[6] These home-based and house-sized groups were characterized by Spirit-led participatory meetings, consensus decision-making, the Lord's Supper as a full meal, baptism of adults immediately upon profession of faith, co-equal teams of unpaid leaders, and recognition of apostolic teachings and practices as authoritative in all respects. House churches were networked together through occasional citywide meetings and by traveling apostolic teams that circulated from group-to-group and city-to-city.

The Early Church Fathers[7]

In the second and third centuries, the Jesus movement continued to expand its influence through the faithful witness of its adherents. Bright minds, brave hearts, and able hands were put to the task of preaching the gospel, healing the sick, casting out demons, clothing the naked, fighting false

---

[2] Matt 28:18-20

[3] Acts 17:6

[4] Acts 1:8

[5] Acts 2:46, 5:42, 8:3, 10:1-48, 12:12, 16:14-15,29-34, 18:8, 20:6-8,20; Rom 16:3-5; 1 Cor 16:15,19; Col 4:15-16; Philem 1:2; 2 John 1:10

[6] Roger Gehring (2004), *House Church and Mission: The Importance of Household Structures in Early Christianity*, Hendrickson Publishers; Robert Banks (1994), *Paul's Idea of Community*, Hendrickson Publishers; Del Birkey (1988), *The House Church: A Model for Renewing the Church*, Herald Press; F.V. Filson (1939), "The Significance of the Early House Churches," *J. Biblical Literature*, 58:105-112.

[7] Henry Chadwick (1993), *The Early Church (Revised Edition)*, Penguin Books, Copyright © Henry Chadwick, 1967, 1993, chapters 2 to 7; Henry Bettenson (1969), *The Early Christian Fathers: A Selection from the Writings of the Fathers from St. Clement of Rome to St. Athanasius*, Oxford University Press.

teachings, and facing both sword and flame, believers preferring to die for Christ rather than live for Caesar.

Many spiritual giants emerged during this era, especially those collectively known as the Early Church Fathers. Ignatius of Antioch (c.35-c.107) wrote seven powerful letters to the churches while being taken by soldiers to Rome where he was literally thrown to the lions in the Coliseum.

Justin Martyr (c.100-165), a one time pagan philosopher, turned to Christ and thereafter used his verbal and written skills in rationally defending the Christian faith against skeptical philosophers, antagonistic governors, argumentative rabbis, and so-called Gnostic Christians, eventually being scourged and beheaded for his beliefs.

Cyprian of Carthage (d.258), a pagan rhetorician who converted to Christianity only 12 years before his martyrdom, became an important Christian leader whose writings influenced thinking on the nature of the church, Christian leadership, and the sacraments. These are but a few of the characters in a long line of Christian martyrs, thinkers, and influencers.

Yet, subtle shifts began to creep in amongst the churches. The Early Church Fathers, whose sincerity should not be doubted, nevertheless, advocated for moves away from apostolic approaches, toward a more institutionalized understanding of the church. These shifts included the development of clergy who were distinct from the ordinary so-called lay Christian, a hierarchical approach to one-man leadership, formality in worship meetings, a pre-baptism probationary period for adults, the beginning of infant baptism, the observance of special holy days, a gradual rejection of miracles and spiritual gifts, and a rigidity in doctrine.

Doubtless, some of the centralization and control were well-meaning responses by the Early Church Fathers to the external challenges posed by heretical fringe groups that were gaining momentum (e.g. the Gnostics) and Roman imperial policies that vacillated between grudging tolerance (e.g. emperor Trajan) and outright persecution (e.g. emperors Decius, Gallus, Valerian, and Diocletian) of the Christian faithful.

To be sure, there were similar challenges that even the first century churches faced, which the letters of the apostles often addressed and which Jesus himself denounced in the book of Revelation.[8] However, the apostles eventually died and were not able to check these tendencies personally in later generations.

This was all merely a preparation phase for the coming full-fledged institutionalization of Christianity under the emperor Constantine in the early fourth century AD, which finally displaced the early grassroots house churches with 'The Cathedral Church'. This institutionalization, as we shall see, affected the church's freedom, faith, form, and function.

---

[8] Rev 2:1—3:22

ENTER CONSTANTINE[9]

Early Life and Training

Constantine (born Flavius Valerius Constantinus) was born in the town of Nish (in modern-day Serbia) in about AD 272 to Constantius Chlorus and his legal concubine Helena. Constantius eventually left Helena, who was not of noble stock, to marry Theodora, the stepdaughter of the emperor Maximian. Constantius was a 'Caesar', a lesser title than that of 'Emperor' (or 'Augustus'), being responsible for the western Roman empire. Constantine received a reasonable education, being raised in camps and barracks and taking up soldiering eagerly to fight in the wars against Egypt and Persia. He was also well-versed in Latin literature, exceptional in speaking Greek, and adept at philosophy.

Although he was kept away from his father by the eastern Roman emperor Galerius, in late AD 305 Constantine escaped and rode across Europe to join his father's army in Gaul (modern-day France) to fight the invading Franks in a British campaign. After Constantius died at York in AD 306, his army immediately proclaimed his son Constantine not just as a mere Caesar, but as the new emperor of the west. However, Constantine, having a politically savvy mind, accepted only the lesser title. He went on to fight the Franks successfully, feeding the kings of his defeated foes to the beasts in the amphitheaters.

Vision and Victory at the Bridge

By AD 308, political intrigue resulted in rivalries that culminated in the emergence of six self-proclaimed 'Emperors'—none wanting the mere title of 'Caesar'—Constantine being one of them. By AD 310, Constantine had eliminated one of his rivals, Maximian, by attacking him in Marseilles, capturing him, and allowing him to commit suicide. By AD 311, Constantine crossed the Alps, defeated an army at Turin, and then moved towards Rome itself. By AD 312, he faced another rival, Maxentius, a mere nine miles north of Rome. Though having only 20,000 soldiers under his command compared to Maxentius's 100,000, Constantine forced his opponent to fight with only the Milvian Bridge as an escape route. As a military leader, Constantine was known for his ability and willingness to act quickly and boldly in battle. Constantine won the day handily. Maxentius, however, died in the river. This victory won Constantine unrivalled rule in the western part of the empire, the east being ruled by his ally Licinius.

---

[9] H.A. Drake, Ibid., pp.111-136; Noel Lenski, "The Reign of Constantine," in *The Cambridge Companion to the Age of Constantine*, Noel Lenski (ed.) (2006), Cambridge University Press, ch.3; "Constantine the Great," in *Catholic Encyclopedia* (www.newadvent.org/cathen/12429b.htm); Will Durant (1944), *The Story of Civilization: Part III—Caesar and Christ*, Simon and Schuster, pp.653-664.

What is of greater relevance to the present examination is the source of Constantine's victory, which is said to have been due to both a heavenly vision and a dream that he received while preparing to face his rival Maxentius. Constantine was adjured to paint the symbol ☧ onto the shields of his soldiers, by which he was assured success in battle. In separate accounts written by contemporaries of Constantine, the pictogram possibly represented the Christian cross and/or the first two letters 'Chi-Rho' of the Greek form of the name 'Christ':

> Constantine was directed in a dream to cause the heavenly sign to be delineated on the shields of his soldiers, and so to proceed to battle. He did as he had been commanded, and he marked on their shields the letter X, with a perpendicular line drawn through it and turned round thus at the top, being the cipher of Christ. Having this sign (XP), his troops stood to arms.[10]

> [Constantine] said that about noon, when the day was already beginning to decline, he saw with his own eyes the trophy of a cross of light in the heavens, above the sun, and bearing the inscription, 'Conquer By This.'[11]

Constantine's Conversion

Whether the combination of the vision and dream marked the occasion of Constantine's genuine conversion to Christianity or whether his subsequent patronage of the church was motivated more by political ambition have been the subject of many discussions among a previous generation of scholars. Today's historians, though, remind us that in the context of the late ancient mindset, there was no such contradiction in the fusing of religion and politics. In fact, some of Constantine's predecessors had infused their reigns with themes borrowed from Greco-Roman mythology. The importance of the vision/dream, however, lies in the fact that Constantine and his allies in the Christian church would later consciously interpret this event as a divine call to Constantine to govern the empire. It was seen as heavenly sanction for Constantine's earthly reign. In his case, the call came from the god of the Christians. This was the decisive moment for everything else that followed with regard to the changes that the Christian church was to experience.

---

[10] Schaff, Philip (trans.), *Fathers of the Third and Fourth Centuries: Lactantius, Venantius, Asterius, Victorinus, Dionysius, Apostolic Teaching and Constitutions, Homily*, see section entitled "Lactantius: Of The Manner In Which The Persecutors Died," chapter 44 (public domain text.)

[11] Schaff, Philip (trans.) (1890), *Eusebius Pamphilius: Church History, Life of Constantine the Great, and Oration in Praise of Constantine*, Christian Literature Publishing Co., see section entitled "Life of Constantine," book 10, chapter 28 (public domain text.)

Constantine's Impact on Freedom: The Edict of Milan[12]

In AD 313, within several months of the Milvian triumph, Constantine and Licinius met in Milan to solidify their alliance. There they decided to craft a common policy regarding empire-wide religious toleration, which became known as the Edict of Milan. Later, in writing to a governor about these matters, the co-rulers summarize the edict and their original reasons for it:

> Perceiving long ago that religious liberty ought not to be denied, but that it ought to be granted to the judgment and desire of each individual to perform his religious duties according to his own choice, we had given orders that every man, Christians as well as others, should preserve the faith of his own sect and religion....When I, Constantine Augustus, and I, Licinius Augustus, came under favorable auspices to Milan and took under consideration everything which pertained to the common weal and prosperity, we resolved among other things, or rather first of all, to make such decrees as seemed in many respects for the benefit of every one; namely, such as should preserve reverence and piety toward the deity. We resolved, that is, to grant both to the Christians and to all men freedom to follow the religion which they choose, that whatever heavenly divinity exists may be propitious to us and to all that live under our government.[13]

What this meant, in effect, was that a general amnesty was given to groups that were persecuted by previous regimes. What lay behind this decision? The co-emperors reveal that they see a link between divine favor and the prosperity of the state. Not willing to risk the anger of any of the gods and, hence, any harm to the welfare of the empire, they wish to appease any and all deities by allowing their adherents to perform their ritual obligations. Officially at least, because of the non-specific identity of the "deity" mentioned, the empire would no longer force any one particular set of beliefs on its citizenship. Though displaying at times a syncretistic attitude by his embrace of pagan rituals and support of pagan temples publicly, Constantine would increasingly favor Christianity, as his patronage of the church and involvement in its internal affairs would soon testify. Licinius, to the contrary, became once again known as a persecutor of the Christians,

---

[12] H.A. Drake, Ibid., pp.121-123; Will Durant, Ibid., pp.654, 657-658.;
"Constantine the Great," in *Catholic Encyclopedia*
(www.newadvent.org/cathen/12429b.htm)
[13] Schaff, Philip (trans.) (1890), *Eusebius Pamphilius: Church History, Life of Constantine the Great, and Oration in Praise of Constantine*, Christian Literature Publishing Co., see section entitled "Church History," book 1, chapter 5.2-4 (public domain text.)

deposing and executing some bishops and barring Christian assemblies near the Armenian frontier. This gave Constantine a public pretext for seizing the eastern half of the empire in AD 324 and executing Licinius the following year. This left Constantine as sole ruler of the empire.

CONSTANTINE'S IMPACT ON FAITH: THE NICENE CREED[14]

In the eastern part of the empire, in about AD 318, a theological scuffle began to brew which centered primarily around the ideas of Arius, a priest from the city of Alexandria. Put simply, Arius proposed that just as earthly fathers exist before their earthly sons, so too must the heavenly Father precede the Son. This implied that there was a time when the Son did not exist. Though Arius stressed that this 'birthing' of the Son occurred before the existence of time and space, his doctrinal rivals seized on the opportunity to suggest that this was tantamount to saying that the Son was a mere creature who, consequently, had no real power to eternally save those that believed in him. A central tenet of Christian faith was at stake. After failing to reconcile Arius with the Alexandrian bishop by appealing to reason and suggesting the matter was trivial, Constantine began to make plans for convening the first ever empire-wide church council to deal with the issue.

In AD 325, no fewer than 318 bishops, along with an array of accompanying priests, met in the town of Nicea, just southeast of modern-day Istanbul. Most of the participants were from the eastern provinces, the controversy being largely ignored in the western empire. They all met in the hall of an imperial palace. Constantine showed himself to be an able and congenial facilitator, appealing to both sides in the conflict to be reconciled to one another peaceably, both in his opening speech and during the general proceedings of the meetings. His primary aim, it became clear, was a resolution of the dispute, rather than in the correctness of the council's final verdict on the Arian controversy. To this end, Constantine oversaw the creation of the tangible outcome of the council—the Nicene Creed—which affirmed that the Son was indeed co-eternal with the Father. This not only allowed the church to formulate an important doctrinal statement that would wield a massive influence on its future up to the present day, but also committed Constantine to an increasingly clear allegiance to Christianity in his own day.

All but two of the bishops signed the Nicene declaration. Arius, along with the two refusenik bishops, was excommunicated from the church and exiled by the emperor. Arius's books were ordered to be burned, their concealment punishable by death. However, only a few years later, Constantine reversed his own opinion about the council's conclusions, sending Athanasius—a champion of the Nicene council's conclusions who

---

[14] H.A. Drake, Ibid., pp.123-130; Henry Chadwick, Ibid., pp.125-132; Will Durant, Ibid., pp.658-661.

had become the new bishop of Alexandria in 328—into exile for refusing to accept Arius fully into the church, thereby fueling the controversy again. These actions were not to be atypical in Constantine's long career as emperor. Forgetting about the toleration that he espoused in the Edict of Milan, Constantine was not averse to occasionally prohibiting the meetings of perceived heretics and pagans and ordering the destruction of their meeting places.[15] He leveled the temple of Aphrodite in several cities, as well as destroying other shrines. However, there is no hard evidence that he pursued an empire-wide policy of temple destruction.

CONSTANTINE'S IMPACT ON FORM: THE CHURCH BUILDING[16]

Like his predecessors, Constantine as an emperor would have had various responsibilities, motivations, and challenges in engaging in both public and private construction campaigns. He would have seen it as his duty to found new cities, reestablish old cities that had undergone decay, refurbish older public buildings, and erect new buildings. His motivations would likely have included some mixture of personal political statement, practical public need, and the display of his generosity to the citizenship. Such campaigns no doubt required an emperor to both find and commit large sums of money, land, energy, and other resources.

Unlike his predecessors, though, Constantine publicly identified himself as protector and patron of the Christian religion. This reality would find tangible expression in an unprecedented way—the first ever construction of public buildings for exclusive use by Christians. It is a well established fact that Christian congregations of the first several centuries were primarily home-based and house-sized groups. Constantine's beneficence would ultimately alter the complexion and status of the formerly maligned and fringe Christian communities and propel them to respectability and, inevitably, popularity.

In the early 320s, Constantine began his campaign by erecting the basilica of St. John Lateran in Rome, which was built on a grand scale seemingly appropriate for use by the important bishop of Rome. By design, it was meant to be seen as more than a mere meeting place for the local Christian community—it was a symbolic gesture. The edifice was a large structure over 300 feet long, equipped with rows of columns, an open beam roof, clerestory windows, and lands that provided the necessary income for its daily maintenance. It also faced east towards the rising sun, mimicking the manner in which pagan temples were oriented. A large circular

---

[15] A.D. Lee, "Traditional Religions," in *The Cambridge Companion to the Age of Constantine*, Noel Lenski (ed.) (2006), Cambridge University Press, pp.172-176.
[16] Mark J. Johnson, "Architecture of Empire," in *The Cambridge Companion to the Age of Constantine*, Noel Lenski (ed.) (2006), Cambridge University Press, pp.278-297.

baptistery was constructed on the east side, its roof propped up by a ring of eight pillars and the baptismal font encircled by silver statues of stags apparently drinking from the water. The building's appearance would not have struck Roman citizenry of the time as unusual, since it was somewhat similar to civic public basilicas and halls to which they were accustomed.

Though most of Constantine's many ensuing church building projects were focused on Rome, there were Christian communities in other parts of the empire which were to soon have their own meeting place, some even more luxurious than the basilica of St. John Lateran. Towns and cities in modern day Italy, France, Turkey, North Africa, and Israel were the sites for these edifices. Professor Mark Johnson summarizes the emperor's vast construction campaign:

> Constantine followed his predecessors in this regard; indeed, he would surpass most of them...Beyond the usual motivations, an important aspect of Constantine's building program was the fact that, for the first time in Roman history, an emperor was actively involved in the promotion of the Christian religion. Previously the growing Christian communities in the cities of the empire had never enjoyed the privilege of meeting in public buildings and had instead been relegated to house-churches, the residences of wealthy congregants that were often left as legacies to the local Christian community. The growth of Christianity and the emperor's involvement with it demanded a massive new building campaign that would both accommodate the day-to-day needs of the various Christian congregations throughout the empire and also honor the sites most significant to the faith. A need and an opportunity had arisen, and Constantine responded with the resources of an emperor to take advantage of that opportunity and meet that need.[17]

CONSTANTINE'S IMPACT ON FUNCTION: THE RISE OF THE CLERGY[18]
During Constantine's reign, both bishops and priests saw their function and status rise in the eyes of the empire and the Christian community. No longer were they to be harried as leaders of a fringe sect but, rather, they were to be hailed as trusted servants of God and the emperor.

The ascension of the clergy was endorsed by Constantine in his appointment of Christian leaders to civil servanthood and in granting them authority to act as virtual judges in the churches. Church courts, which were

---

[17] Mark J. Johnson, Ibid., pp.278-279.
[18] Henry Chadwick, Ibid., pp.131-132; Will Durant, Ibid., pp.656-657; "Constantine the Great," in *Catholic Encyclopedia* (www.newadvent.org/cathen/12429b.htm)

already in existence, were now recognized by the empire. By AD 325, the churches in the eastern provinces had become accustomed to being organized in the same hierarchical manner as was the empire, along provincial lines. More and more, therefore, the bishops were effectively treated as the emperor's political aides.

The emperor Constantine also provided the churches and their leaders with financial gifts and tax exemptions, as well as allowing them to receive bequests. The church in Rome, for instance, from AD 314 to 336 annually received 963 kilograms of gold, 5300 kilograms of silver, and revenues from landed properties totaling 148 kilograms of gold.[19] The money was administered by the bishops themselves, becoming at times an occasion for temptation and abuse. Such wealth and influence, though, were also often used generously by the clergy in assisting and advocating on behalf of criminals, prisoners, widows, orphans, and other unfortunates.

In return for such promotions, the actions of bishops now became monitored more stringently than they had been previously. The law now forbade any overly ambitious bishops from moving from smaller to larger sees and required the consecration of a new bishop by a minimum of three other bishops from within the same province. Moreover, veto power was given to a metropolitan—a regional bishop of bishops—within his jurisdiction over lesser bishops, thus concentrating church authority within the hands of fewer and fewer individuals.

The upshot of this rapid process, according to Constantinian scholar H.A. Drake, was that "When [Constantine] died in 337, Christian leaders had assumed the rank, dress, and increasingly the duties of the old civic elite."[20] Within a few decades, any uncertainty that may have lingered regarding the proper role of the Christian clergy in public life and its link to the empire, had vanished. Oxford and Cambridge professor Sir Henry Chadwick explains that,

> By the end of the fourth century the Church had virtually captured society. In worldly terms of status and social influence, the episcopate of even moderately important cities had become an established career to which a man might aspire for reasons not exclusively religious. Many local churches had become substantial landowners, supporting numerous poor folk. A bishop was expected by his people to be the advocate of their secular interests as well as their spiritual pastor.[21]

---

[19] Georges Depeyrot, "Economy and Society," in *The Cambridge Companion to the Age of Constantine*, Noel Lenski (ed.) (2006), Cambridge University Press, p.248.

[20] H.A. Drake, Ibid., p.111.

[21] Henry Chadwick, Ibid., p.174. Used by permission of Penguin Books Ltd.

ASSESSING CONSTANTINE'S LEGACY TO CHRISTIANITY

When it comes to fairly assessing the overall legacy of Constantine to the Christian church, we must readily admit that it is a difficult task. One's final conclusion will inevitably be influenced by one's initial assumptions about the appropriateness of the merger of empire and church. At best, Constantine's legacy is a mixed one. In the long-term, in this author's view, the negative consequences of his reign far outweigh any positive value brought to the church, as summarized below.

Freedom

The Edict of Milan provided Christians, and others, liberty in choosing to associate or not associate with the various religious options available at the time. This increased the acceptability of the Christian religion in the eyes of the broader citizenship of the empire, effectively ended the era of persecution—though Constantine himself deviated from this on occasion—and exposed more people to the Christian message. Soon enough, though, becoming a Christian became a popular fad, resulting in an influx of nominal, insincere, and opportunistic people into the churches. The consequence was a dilution of spiritual passion and a heightened laxity among so-called believers. This, in part at least, caused an exodus of the more ardent into the deserts to form some of the early monastic communities where prayer, study, meditation, and flight from worldly corruption could find a haven.[22]

Faith

The Nicene Creed introduced specific formulations for expressing the basic tenets of the Christian faith. This helped solidify a theological center of gravity which would become useful in distinguishing orthodox from heterodox or heretical teaching. Soon enough, though, these same recipes were used in justifying the persecution of so-called heretics and the suppression of views contrary to that officially sanctioned by the state supported church. By the end of the fourth century under the emperor Theodosius I, official legislation against heretical sects and pagans was passed. This opened the door for pressurization and persecution by the so-called Christian empire of any and all that disagreed with its theology.[23]

Form

The construction campaign of Constantine introduced, for the first time in history, the idea of a Christian church building, thereby forever altering the outward form of the church. This provided Christians with a sense of physical safety, security, and stability that was unknown to them before. Soon enough, though, the fact that a large number of attendees could now physically fit inside a church building actually altered the nature of the

---

[22] Henry Chadwick, Ibid., ch.12.
[23] Henry Chadwick, Ibid., pp.167-171.

church meeting itself permanently. No longer were Christian meetings small, intimate, and interactive, but rather large, impersonal, and spectator-type experiences. Not many years later, both Basil the Great (c. AD 330-379) and John Chrysostom (c. AD 347-407) introduced complex and choreographed ceremonies for Christian worship services which, though beautiful in their own right, finally eliminated any active, spontaneous, or creative participation by ordinary believers.[24]

Function

The rise in status of Christian leaders inside and outside the church changed the way they functioned within their congregations. Constantine's support gave Christian leaders a great deal of official influence within the empire which no doubt quickened its Christianization and brought about more humane laws. Soon enough, though, power corrupted the wielders of power and led to a hierarchical system that made clergy more prone to authoritarianism in their exercise of church leadership, shifted political power increasingly into the hands of the clergy, and greatly widened the gap between clergy and laity.[25]

CONCLUSIONS

The great changes in the Christian church's mindset and methodology that were propelled forward under the emperor Constantine have been examined. We have seen how grassroots Christianity, as expressed in the early house churches, finally gave way to 'The Cathedral Church'. The legacy of this for the church universal in the short- and long-term has been a mixed one, requiring church revitalization efforts by numerous individuals and movements throughout history.

STUDY QUESTIONS

1. What are the pros and cons of Constantine's legacy to the church?
2. Explain what is meant by 'The Cathedral Church'?
3. Was there a need for eventual church revitalization?
4. What practical steps can today's house church movements take to avoid eventually becoming like 'The Cathedral Church'?

---

[24] *The Divine Liturgy of St. Basil* and *The Divine Liturgy of St. John Chrysostom*
[25] See also H.A. Drake (2002), *Constantine and the Bishops: The Politics of Intolerance,* The Johns Hopkins University Press; Bill Leadbetter (2002), "Constantine and the Bishop: The Roman Church in the Early Fourth Century," *Journal of Religious History*, vol.26, no.1, pp.1-14; Richard Hanson (2000), *Christian Priesthood Examined*, Lutterworth Press; G. Bowersock (1986), "From Emperor to Bishop: The Self-Conscious Transformation of Political Power in the Fourth Century AD," *Classical Philology*, vol.81, no.4, pp.298-307; Henry Chadwick (1979), *The Role of the Christian Bishop in Ancient Society*, Center for Hermeneutical Studies in Hellenistic and Modern Culture.

Chapter 18

CHURCH REVITALIZATION MOVEMENTS USING HOUSE CHURCHES AND SMALL GROUPS (AD 150 - 1500)

NATE KRUPP WITH JANICE WOODRUM

Nate Krupp has been calling the church to be all that God would have it be for over 40 years. He was led to Christ in 1957 by two converted Jews while an engineering student at Purdue University. He and his wife, Joanne, pioneered Lay Evangelism, Inc., have served with Youth With A Mission (YWAM), are professors with Christian Leadership University, and oversee the work of Preparing the Way Publishers. They have had a house-church understanding since 1966. Nate has written over 20 books on evangelism, prayer, Bible study, and the church, including The Church Triumphant at the End of the Age (1988). Janice Woodrum is preparing a second edition of The Church Triumphant at the End of the Age. With her husband, Dave, she will be assuming the oversight of Preparing the Way Publishers in 2007. [Adapted and used by permission of the author. Email: kruppnj@open.org].

INTRODUCTION

After the death of the first generation of apostles who authored the New Testament, the church eventually began to drift away from the purity, power, purposes, principles, patterns, and fruitfulness that God had intended. But God is a merciful God. He is a God of restoration who desires that all things be brought back to their original state, including the church. He has purposed to have "a radiant church, without stain or wrinkle or any other blemish, but holy and blameless."[1] God desires a people who are "mature, attaining to the whole measure of the fullness of Christ."[2] God has shown his commitment to restoring his church to the Christianity of the New Testament. The Holy Spirit, early in church history, began this process of restoration, often making use of household meetings and/or small groups. This chapter provides a brief overview of some of the key movements and individuals that God utilized to bring about some measure of revitalization to the church at large in the period AD 150 to 1500. Their influence is felt even today, whether we realize it or not, in the daily life of individual believers and churches. These movements engaged their task often in the face of opposition from both civic and religious authorities.

---

[1] Eph 5:27 (NIV)
[2] Eph 4:13 (NIV)

MONTANUS (AD 156 - 400)[3]

One of the early movements of restoration began about AD 156 with the appearance on the scene of Montanus of Phrygia (Asia Minor). He appeared at a time when much of the church had become cold and formal, the gifts of the Spirit had largely ceased to operate, and there was lax discipline. Montanus called for holy living, greater church discipline, and preached the return of Christ. He was assisted by two prophetesses. The spiritual gifts of speaking in tongues and prophecy were in operation. There were itinerant preachers supported by the believers. The movement spread widely to Greece, Italy, Gaul (France), and North Africa. The most noted convert from the more organized church to Montanism was the scholar Tertullian, in North Africa, in the early 200s. Tertullian wrote that, "Where but three are, and they of the laity also, yet there is a church", showing that the Montanists had a somewhat fluid and decentralized understanding of the nature of the church. In the east, tensions with the established church caused a separation, though in the west the Montanists remained as societies within the church for many years. The movement continued into the 400s.

CHRISTIAN COMMUNITIES (AD 280 - 550)[4]

The decline of spirituality in the churches provoked some to efforts of reform, just as it had the Montanists. For others, the solution was to withdraw from the organized church and society and find a deeper walk with God in another setting. At first, there were those who withdrew completely and became Christian hermits. Notable among these was Anthony in Egypt, who was born about AD 250. One day, he heard Jesus' words, "If thou wilt be perfect, go and sell what thou hast and give to the poor." He immediately sold and gave away inherited land to the village, sold his possessions, and gave the proceeds to the poor. He moved outside the village and later to a fort on a mountain, where he gave himself to prayer and fasting for 20 years. The emperor Constantine wrote him for counsel. Anthony died in AD 356 at the age of 105. His example was contagious, and soon hundreds were imitating him. These hermits, living in a cave or a hut, were sometimes close enough to one another to make fellowship possible.

This led to the next step, the development of a Christian community, or monastery. One of the early pioneers of monasteries was Pachomius, who also lived in southern Egypt, from AD 286 to 346. In the monastery, a number of Christians could live together and seek God in a spiritual setting. They lived lives of chastity, poverty, and discipline. They gave themselves to a strict schedule of work, fasting, prayer, Bible study, memory, and

---

[3] John Driver (1999), *Radical Faith: An Alternative History of the Christian Church*, Pandora Press, ch.4; E.H. Broadbent (1999), *The Pilgrim Church*, Gospel Folio Press, pp.35-36.
[4] John Driver, Ibid., ch.5.

meditation. Each of these early monasteries was led by a 'father' and made up of a cluster of several 'tribes'. Each tribe was in turn comprised of three or four 'houses'. Each house was managed by a household 'chairman' or 'chief', who was charged with the spiritual and material well being of the small group of believers that lived there.[5]

Monasteries for women also developed. In time, the separated life of the monastery became the way of life for thousands throughout much of Europe, North Africa, and as far east as Mesopotamia. It was in a monastery in Bethlehem that Jerome translated the Latin version of the Bible around 400. In the fifth and sixth centuries, practically every church leader had received his early Christian formation at one of the monasteries. One of the most famous was founded by Benedict in AD 529, about 85 miles southeast of Rome.

For centuries, monasteries provided a deepening effect upon the Christian church, although they sometimes tended to overemphasize pious living through strenuous personal effort.

PRISCILLIAN (AD 340 - 385)[6]

Priscillian was a Spanish nobleman of wealth, position, education, and personal charisma. In his early years, he was more fascinated by Greek philosophy than by Christianity. He was eventually converted to Christianity and was baptized. Priscillian was a diligent student of the Bible and began to preach and teach, although only a layman. Through his oratorical abilities and reputation for a rigid ascetic lifestyle, he drew a significant following. He started a movement of 'brotherhoods' throughout Spain, Portugal, and France in which only baptized believers could participate. These small groups met in homes for Bible study and prayer. Both men and women participated and were free to use their skills and abilities during these gatherings. A significant number of bishops and priests joined him in asserting the independence of each local congregation, which caused tension with the official state church. Some falsely accused Priscillian of teaching Gnostic-Manichaean dualism, which suggests that physical matter is evil. This charge may have arisen, in part, because of the practice of celibacy by members of Priscillian's groups. Criticism from other church leaders led to Priscillian's excommunication by a church synod held at Saragossa in 380. In defiance, he was ordained to the priesthood and became the bishop of Avila. Along with several compatriots, Priscillian went to Rome to seek that help of Pope Damasus in having his excommunication revoked. The Pope denied him an audience. The Roman emperor Maximus wanted to eliminate the tensions that existed between the state church and this movement. Eventually, Priscillian and six of his friends were arrested and beheaded in

---

[5] *The Rule of Pachomius*
[6] E.H. Broadbent, Ibid., pp.58-62; *Catholic Encyclopedia* (www.newadvent.org/cathen/12429b.htm)

Trier, France, despite the great protest of Priscillian's former opponents, the eminent bishops Martin of Tours and Ambrose of Milan. Their bodies were returned to Spain, where they were celebrated as martyrs. After Priscillian's demise, the movement grew for the next 200 years despite continued persecution.

THE CELTIC MISSIONARY MOVEMENT (AD 432 - 800)[7]

While the western church in southern Europe was departing from New Testament Christianity, there was a movement in northern Europe, unattached to Rome, that was more true to the New Testament. During the Dark Ages, Ireland stood out as a beacon. From the sixth to the eighth centuries, it was the most advanced nation in western Europe. Free from the disastrous invasions of the barbarians, the church kept the lamp of learning burning when the lights were going out all over Europe. During the sixth and seventh centuries, the Irish church became one of the greatest missionary churches of all times. Patrick came from Scotland to Ireland in the 400s. God used him to restore the practice of small groups of traveling missionaries that planted churches all over the country, baptizing thousands into their new found faith in Christ. In 563, the Irish church sent Colomba (521-596) to Scotland. He was a man of zeal, piety and prayer, and he performed many miracles. On the island of Iona, he built a monastery which became a strategic center for the training of missionaries. For over 200 years, missionaries went out from the monasteries of Ireland and Scotland to all parts of the British Isles and Europe. They had no official connection with the Roman church until AD 664.

THE WALDENSES (AD 1100 - 1300)[8]

There emerged in the late 1100s and early 1200s in central and western Europe large grassroots movements of Christianity. Some groups held to teachings that were solidly biblical, though others gathered around ideas that could be considered heterodox. Their appeal to the average person allowed them to sweep through towns and villages with their simple message about Christ and Christian living. Common features among them included the absence of a formal priesthood, the recognition of all believers as priests, governance of churches by elders chosen by lot, house meetings, and the use of finances to assist the sick, the poor, and traveling missionaries who preached the gospel among the unreached.

One of the largest of these groups became known as the Waldenses, gaining their name from Peter Waldo (1140-1218), a wealthy merchant and banker in Lyons. Upon being impressed with the brevity and insecurity of life, he inquired of a priest what he must do to secure heaven. The priest, quoting from Matthew 19:21, said, "If you would be perfect, go, sell what

---

[7] K. Latourette (1975), *A History of Christianity*, Harper & Row, pp.342-349.

[8] John Driver, Ibid., ch.7; E.H. Broadbent, Ibid., ch.5.

you possess and give to the poor, and you will have treasure in heaven; and come, follow Me." In 1176, Waldo paid his creditors, provided for his wife and children, and gave the rest to the poor. He then enlisted two priests to translate portions of the Bible into French. Waldo then made a diligent study of the New Testament, memorizing long passages. He undertook to imitate Christ, traveling about without purse and preaching in cities and countryside. Soon others joined him.

The Waldenses sought to adhere strictly to the Scriptures and to revive the simple practices of the apostolic age. They first appeared in southern France. They soon spread to Spain, Italy, Germany, Austria, and Bohemia. Called the Poor Men of Lyons, they went out preaching two by two. Their meetings often happened outdoors after nightfall under the facilitation of one of their traveling preachers. After an opening prayer and a sermon, they proceeded back into their homes for dinner, prayer, discussion, and eating the Lord's Supper.

The Waldenses were humble and simple folks who dressed simply, labored with their hands, remained chaste, refused to go to taverns and dances, shunned anger, and believed that great wealth was evil. They memorized large portions of Scripture in the local language. Some, in fact, memorized the entire New Testament and portions of the Old Testament. They increasingly came to believe that no teaching except Christ's was binding on them.

They were excommunicated by the Archbishop of Lyons and also by Pope Lucius III in 1184 for their unauthorized preaching. After Waldo's death, the Roman Catholic church condemned the Waldenses outright at the Fourth Lateran Council (1215) and promptly excommunicated and punished those who continued their involvement in the Waldensian movement.

THE MYSTICS (AD 1100 - 1500)[9]

There have always been those individuals known as mystics, who have sought God with all of their hearts and have spent many hours a day in prayer, drawing near to and receiving from him. But in the 1100s and succeeding centuries their numbers were increasing.

One of these mystics was Bernard of Clairvaux. His life was spent largely in a monastery, which he founded in 1115 at the age of 25. It was the Cistercian order and was located at Clairvaux in France. He was deeply moved by the love of Christ and was deeply committed to him. His life was one of deep contemplation as he attempted to live a life of silence and prayer. He wrote of "longing for the Bridegroom's presence." But Bernard had a practical side to him and was not able to give himself wholly to prayer because of his love for the church and the needs of men. He, in fact, became

---

[9] Nate Krupp (1988), *The Church Triumphant at the End of the Age*, Preparing the Way Publishers, pp.81-82.

a leading figure in the Western church and exerted great influence through his writings and preaching, even helping to heal a schism which had developed by the almost simultaneous election of two popes. But he was first and foremost a mystic who raised the spiritual level of the entire Roman Catholic church and attracted thousands to the way of mysticism.

There were also some wonderful women among the mystics. One of the most well known was Hildegarde (1098-1179). She entered a Benedictine monastery at age eight and spent her life in monasteries. She often had visions, exercised the gift of prophecy, and spoke of the end of the world. She also carried on an active correspondence with popes, emperors, and princes. There was also Bridget of Sweden (1303-1373), the wife of a prominent noble and the mother of eight. She had many revelations, exercised the gift of prophecy, founded an order for women, and once rebuked the King of Sweden for oppressive taxation and injustice to the poor. Catherine of Siena (1347-1380), starting at the age of 12, spent six years in private in a room set apart by her parents. She later exercised the gifts of healings, and counseled hundreds, including the Pope, and died at the age of 33.

There were many other mystics and monastic orders with similar tendencies. The orders included the Carthusians, which were started in AD 1084 by Bruno, and included the founding of many centers of hermits. They were men of great austerity, giving themselves to reading, praying, fasting, laboring, and the copying of Scriptures. In the 1300s to 1500s, other mystics arose throughout much of Europe, in countries like France, England, Italy, Germany, Spain, and the Low Countries (today's Holland and Belgium). This included the Brethren of the Free Spirit, the Friends of God, the Brothers and Sisters of the Common Life, Thomas a Kempis, and Teresa of Avila.

Truly, God was getting the attention of a growing number of people and drawing them into deeper communion with himself.

FRANCIS OF ASSISI (AD 1181 - 1226)[10]

Francisco Bernardone was born in Assisi, Italy, the son of a rich cloth merchant. In 1209, at the age of 27, he heard the call, "Preach, the Kingdom of heaven is at hand, heal the sick, cleanse the lepers, cast out demons, provide neither silver nor gold in your purses." He immediately made this Scripture the rule of his life. A year later, Francis and 11 companions journeyed to Rome to seek papal permission to pursue their ministry, which was reluctantly granted. They utilized small groups of traveling apostolic teams to spread their message, selling all they had and going out barefoot, two by two, preaching the Kingdom of God, singing, calling men to repentance, praying for the sick, and helping the poor. They sought to

---

[10] John Driver, Ibid., ch.8.

imitate Jesus and obey him in every way. They slept in hay lofts and ate whatever was offered to them. This order was called the Brothers Minor. A second order for women, the Poor Ladies, came into being. A third order, the Order of Penitants, was founded in 1221. Members of this order were allowed to stay in the world, work, and hold property, but they were to live simply, give alms, and be loyal members of the Catholic Church. Francis of Assisi was a man of purity of purpose and humility of spirit. Some historians believe that he more than any other person saved the medieval church from complete collapse. The Franciscans were intensely missional and were soon found throughout Europe, and in Africa and Asia, and later in North and South America. They sought to bring nominal Christians to a deeper faith and to win non-Christians.

JOHN WYCLIFE AND THE LOLLARDS (AD 1324 - 1384)[11]

John Wyclife spent most of his adult life as a leading professor at Oxford University in England. In the last 10 years of his life, he became very outspoken in his radical views concerning the papacy and other church matters. He insisted that Christ alone was the head of the church and that the pope was antichrist. He held that every person held an equal place in the eyes of God and that the mediating priesthood and the sacrificial masses were not essential. Wyclife challenged the whole range of medieval beliefs and practices including pardons, indulgences, absolutions, pilgrimages, the worship of images, the adoration of the saints, and the distinction between venial and mortal sins. He concluded that where the Bible and the church do not agree, we must obey the Bible, and where conscience and human authority are in conflict, we must obey conscience. To further his views, Wyclife led a group of scholars at Oxford to translate the Bible from Latin into the English vernacular of his day. And like Francis of Assisi, over 150 years earlier, he sent men out in small teams, two by two, to preach and to distribute the Bibles and reformation tracts. They were called 'poor priests' or Lollards. Wyclife was the first of the Protestant reformers. In 1406, the English parliament took a stand against the Lollards, and in 1428 Wyclife's remains were dug up and burned.

JOHN HUS (AD 1369 - 1415)[12]

In 1382, Bohemia (western Czech today) and England were more closely linked together by the marriage of Anne of Luxemburg, sister of the King of Bohemia, to King Richard II of England. Students began to travel back and forth between Oxford and Prague, and so did the writings of Wyclife.

One of those most greatly influenced was John Hus, a professor at the University of Prague. He was soon translating Wyclife's writings into

---

[11] John Driver, Ibid., ch.9.
[12] Donald Durnbaugh (1968), *The Believers' Church*, The MacMillan Company, pp.51-53; E.H. Broadbent, Ibid., pp.143-144.

Bohemian. Hus became a powerful preacher in the most influential churches in Prague and in 1409 also became leader of the national Bohemian party at the University. He was soon an outspoken national leader for church reform and for the political and religious rights of the people. His teachings were similar to Wyclife's. He was soon branded a heretic by the clergy and was excommunicated by the Pope.

In 1412, Hus left Prague to preach from place to place. All of Bohemia was astir. Hus was arrested and on July 6, 1415, was burned at the stake. His last words were, "Lord, into Thy hands I commend my spirit." Hus became a national hero. His followers became known as the Bohemian Brethren, and were the spiritual ancestors to the Moravians. For some time they continued meeting secretly in small groups. By 1467, they had become a more clearly defined body known as Unitas Fratrum, or the Unity of Brethren.

SAVONAROLA (AD 1452 - 1498)[13]

As in England and Bohemia, God had his prophet for Florence, Italy. Savonarola spent his early years in a Dominican monastery. In 1481, he transferred to a monastery of reformed Dominicans in Florence. About 1491, he began to preach against the sins of the day, especially those of the clergy, and called for repentance before God's judgment fell upon the city. His preaching caused a great transformation of the city—women began to dress plainly, merchants became honest, there was much reading of the Bible, and more was given to the poor. In 1497, Pope Alexander VI excommunicated Savonarola, and on May 23, 1498, he and two of his associates were hanged and their bodies burned. In time, the people of Florence returned to their old ways, but God's prophet had spoken.

CONCLUSIONS

The tide of those committed to a return to the Christianity of the Bible was rising over the centuries. As we have seen, one of the strategies God often used was the concept of the 'small group'. Some of these small groups traveled abroad to spread the good news through public and private preaching as well as to start new churches, much as the early apostolic bands did in the New Testament era. Other small groups were stationary and functioned like house churches, being integral to the day-to-day spiritual life of a local community of Christian believers. Both expressions of the small group—the local and mobile—served to expand and solidify the church at large and the movements with which they were associated.

STUDY QUESTIONS

1. What were some of the factors motivating various revitalization efforts?
2. What role did household churches and small groups have?
3. What practical lessons can your house church network apply today?

---

[13] Latourette, Ibid., pp.671-675.

Chapter 19

CHURCH REVITALIZATION MOVEMENTS USING HOUSE CHURCHES AND SMALL GROUPS (AD 1500 - 1800)

PETER BUNTON

Peter Bunton ministers with Dove Christian Fellowship International (www.dcfi.org), giving oversight to churches in Europe, as well as serving as director of Dove's missions office. He holds a Master's degree in missiology (All Nations Christian College, England) and has also led a house church in England. He has researched and written on small groups in the years following the Reformation. [Adapted from Peter Bunton (2001), Cell Groups and House Churches: What History Teaches Us, House to House Publications. Used by permission of the publisher].

INTRODUCTION

The Reformation of the 1500s was a seismic event in the history of the church. Theology changed radically, birthing the Protestant churches. The Reformation opened the way also for new forms of small group and house church meetings to take place in the centuries which followed. This chapter will provide an overview of some of those groups. Whatever terminology was employed as names for these groups, they all, to some extent or another, can be seen as forerunners of contemporary forms of church, such as cell groups and house churches.

MARTIN LUTHER (1483-1546)

While not actually beginning small house church meetings himself, it is important to take note that Luther's theology provided a belief system in which home fellowship could be legitimized. In this regard, Luther's teaching on the priesthood of all believers is particularly noteworthy as it allowed for all Christians, even lay people, to meet together and minister to one another. Luther wrote:

> Scripture expressly tells us to "encourage the fainthearted" (1 Thessalonians 5:14) and "a dimly burning wick should not be quenched" (Isaiah 42:3), but rather nurtured... Therefore the Spirit reminds and admonishes us everywhere that Christians have authorization from God himself to teach and console one another....You should listen to me when I comfort you...I on the other hand, should listen to and believe you...There is tremendous

weight in the word of the brother.[1]

Rather radically for the time, this mutual ministry even applied to the hearing of confession and granting of absolution:

> [For all are able] most freely to hear the confession of secret sins, so that the sinner may make his sins known to whomever he will and seek pardon and comfort, that is, the word of Christ, by the mouth of his neighbour.[2]

Luther, however, not merely provided a theology which would legitimate home fellowship meetings, but he wrote, in his *Preface to the German Mass* of 1526, of his vision to add to congregational worship the meeting of true believers in home fellowships:

> Those, however, who are desirous of being Christians in earnest, and are ready to profess the Gospel with hand and mouth, should register their names and assemble by themselves in some house to pray, to read, to baptize and to receive the sacrament and practise other Christian works. In this Order, those whose conduct was not such as befits Christians could be recognized, reproved, reformed, rejected, or excommunicated, according to the rule of Christ in Matt. xviii. Here, too, a general giving of alms could be imposed on Christians, to be willingly given and divided among the poor, after the example of St. Paul in 2 Cor. ix. Here there would not be need of much fine singing. Here we could have baptism and the sacrament in short and simple fashion: and direct everything towards the Word and prayer and love. Here we should have a good short Catechism about the Creed, the Ten Commandments, and the Lord's Prayer.[3]

In this *Preface* Luther is, in effect, advocating some form of 'believers' meeting', a meeting of the true church from within the visible church (an *ecclesiola in ecclesia*, "little church within the church"). He continues by recommending some form of covenant between believers (the writing of names as a commitment) and that the meetings be held in homes. He states that one of the chief purposes for the groups was accountability and church discipline. The very reference to Matthew 18 indicates a belief that two or three gathering actually was a meeting of the church.

---

[1] David Zersen (1981), "Lutheran roots for small group ministry", *Currents in Theology and Mission,* Vol.8, p.235.

[2] P. Avis (1983), "Luther's Theology of the Church", *The Churchman*, Vol.97, No.2, p.109.

[3] Martin Luther (1526), *Preface to the German Mass and Order of Divine Service.*

Luther himself, however, did not actually implement such a plan. In fact, in the above mentioned preface he continues by stating that he did not see an urgent need to bring about such a transformation, and that he did not have enough people to help him do so. He was, in fact, not at all trusting of what the German people would do with his proposal. The preface continues: "For we Germans are a wild, rude, tempestuous people; with whom one must not lightly make experiment in anything new, unless there be most urgent need"!

Notwithstanding the above, it is entirely possible to see how later movements could appeal to Luther and this text of the *Preface to the German Mass* for legitimization of their small groups meeting within the context of a larger congregation (the *ecclesiolae in ecclesia* concept), or even the notion of the independent believers' churches, as many have done.

THE RADICAL REFORMATION (16TH CENTURY)

The Radical Reformation, largely developing into Anabaptism, emphasized the concept of the Believers' Church—as opposed to the concept of the 'state church' or *corpus Christianum*, where all within a given territory are deemed to be Christians and church members. The Radical Reformation stressed discipline, that all were ministers and priests (the universal priesthood) and primitivism, which is the desire to return to the New Testament church in its belief, practice, and structures. In the Radical Reformation, this strong motivation to be the true church is shown by one of its leaders, Georg Witzel (1501-1573), who said:

> Which is the true [church]? The ancient apostolic. My wish, my yearning is that the world may go back to a true apostolic church. The Acts and the writings of the Great fathers and ancient bishops show the way on which we must go back to it. The apostolic church flourished to the time of Constantine. From then on it was perverted, because the Bishops went over to the world...[4]

In many ways this growing movement, as it began in Switzerland, was a network of small groups often meeting secretly in homes. Such a network was encouraged by Zwingli (1484-1531), one of the main Reformers, and began in 1520. In the next three years, there was a wave of small group meetings in the Allied District of Zurich. These groups were often spontaneous rather than initiated by leadership. Many of these groups began to consider the role of civil authority and the practice of baptism in the Scriptures. Because of their threat to the theology of the newly reformed church, as well as to the civil authorities, the city council of Zurich banned small group meetings on January 18, 1525. On January 21, a group of about 12 men met once again in defiance of the ban and (re)baptized each other. This is usually considered the starting date of Anabaptism.

---

[4] F.H. Littell (1964), *The Origins of Sectarian Protestantism,* Macmillan, p.77.

Subsequent to the birth of Anabaptism, small groups continued, particularly as a means of spreading the Anabaptist message. The Nikolsburger Articles of 1527 states that, "The gospel is not to be preached openly in churches, but only in secret byways and privately in houses."[5]

Small groups were part of early Anabaptism missionary strategy. They had also produced the leaders of Anabaptism, many of whom had been trained in biblical interpretation and self-expression in the house meetings before the ban of 1525. These small groups were not *ecclesiolae* within the church of the masses; they were the beginnings of a movement of churches built on the ecclesiology of the believers' church.

MARTIN BUCER (1491-1551)

A key figure in the Reformation of the church in the 16th century was Martin Bucer, who spent most of his life in Strasbourg, in Alsace. Bucer believed the church to be where the word of God was purely preached, willingly heard, and where people were subject to Christ; this would be evidenced by the fruits of the Holy Spirit. He believed, moreover, that it was not possible ever to see the true church; the latter was certainly not the visible church consisting of all those baptized in a given area. He recognized that this outer church (the actual church) collected both the good and the bad within it. The true church, however, was a community of those led by the Spirit.

By the mid-1540s, after some 20 years of his attempts to reform the church by teaching, writing, establishing various church ordinances as well as disciplinary procedures, Bucer was very disappointed with the church and the morals of many within it. He lamented the deficiencies of the Strasbourg church because he saw her defective apostolicity, that is, that the church was not being faithful to the New Testament pattern. It was not a question merely of returning to the doctrine of the New Testament but also to its patterns and forms of community—it is the latter which would show the contemporary church to have apostolic faithfulness.

In 1547, Bucer decided to be even more zealous and radical in church reformation. The following actions of Bucer have been described as an attempt at a "second reformation."[6] This "second reformation", which was to begin small groups, called "christliche Gemeinschaften" (Christian communities), began early in 1547. Bucer saw these groups as the means of bringing "the church to rest and unity." They were for aiding growth into holiness, both personal and in the whole parish. Within the communities there was open, honest fellowship, confession of sin (Bucer believed that corporate confession in public worship was not sufficient), accountability,

---

[5] Littell, Ibid, p.130.
[6] Werner Bellardi (1934), *Geschichte der "Christlichen Gemeinschaften" in Strassburg (1546-1550),* M.Heinsius Nachfolger.

including granting others permission to address issues seen in the member's life. There was also, to some degree, a sharing of goods and mutual practical provision for one another. Discipline was also exercised, ultimately in excommunication.

Such groups were Bucer's attempt to restore primitive Christianity. Indeed, he taught that partaking in such little communities modeled on the New Testament was the only way to keep the Ten Commandments. Each group remained connected to others. The leaders were to meet each week, and every one to two months there should be a meeting of all groups in the parish for teaching. This has some semblance of the structure that Wesley was to establish some 200 years later!

Bucer was much criticized for practicing excommunications and for what others believed was the implication that there were two classes of Christians, those in the parish and those in the communities. Perhaps the critical issue, however, was that the civil authorities believed that the *Gemeinschaften* gave power of discipline and punishment to the church, not the state. If the latter were to exercise its magisterial discipline properly, then the *Gemeinschaften* were unnecessary. In November 1547, Bucer yielded somewhat and gave the civil authorities greater power over the *Gemeinschaften*. This, however, did not satisfy his opponents, and in January 1548, the *christliche Gemeinschaften* were banned. Officially they ceased to exist, although in effect they continued in the form of one large group for each parish.

THE PURITANS (16TH AND 17TH CENTURIES)

Puritanism was a form of spirituality which developed in England and then the English colonies. The initial Puritans were those dissatisfied with the form and life being developed within the Anglican church. They wished to stress greater 'purity' (hence 'Puritanism') in doctrine, ecclesiology, and life. Emphasis was laid on depth of spiritual and devotional life and its outworking into the ethical and moral sphere. These goals of a deeper life and rectitude in behavior were to be accomplished through a number of instruments. Personal devotional life was to be developed through reading of the Scriptures and other devotional works (of which the Puritans wrote many). In addition, great emphasis was placed on the continual preaching of the Word of God.

With the regular Sunday service not lending itself to some of the chief aims of the Puritans, such as practical application of the preaching heard, and with the necessity to be about one's devotional more often than Sundays, it should not be too surprising to see the development of various small group meetings within Puritanism (usually called 'conventicles'). In 1596, John Udall in his *Certaine Sermons* wrote:

> After that the sermon is done, we ought at our coming
> home to meet together, and say one to another: "come, we

have all been where we have heard God's word taught; let us confer about it, that we may not only call to rememberance [sic] those things that every one of us have carried away, but also that one may have the benefit of the labours of others."[7]

Puritan conventicles met, however, not just on Sundays but in homes at other times, some weekly, others bi-weekly or monthly. John Eliot wrote that in them "we pray, and sing, and repeat sermons, and confer together about the things of God."[8]

Under the leadership of one minister at least, Cotton Mather (1663-1728), in New England, a veritable network of conventicles within his congregation was developed. Mather formed about 13 or 14 conventicles, each with around 12 members. They met in homes for prayer, Bible study, reading of sermons and devotional diaries. People were divided into groups according to gender and stage of life, as well as according to standing (e.g. tradesmen) and race.

That such conventicles were successful in their aims of transforming lives can be seen in the comments of Richard Baxter (1615-91) in his classic *Gildas Salvianus: The Reformed Pastor* (1656). He spoke of house meetings as bringing "more outward signs of success with most that do come than from all my public preaching to them."[9] Some 100 years later, John Wesley was to make a similar observation. Among the Puritans, therefore, conventicles did much in fostering personal piety and the moral and ethical outworking of faith.

THE QUAKERS (17TH CENTURY)[10]

George Fox (1624-1691) was the key figure of the early Quaker movement, also sometimes referred to as the Society of Friends. He was born in northern England in the town of Drayton-in-the-Clay in Leicestershire and grew up in a devout home. His father Christopher, a poor but honest weaver, was nicknamed 'Righteous Christopher' by the townsfolk. His mother Mary was the descendent of a family who had experienced martyrdom for their beliefs. Fox's education was minimal and informal, having grown up far

---

[7] John Tiller (1982), *Puritan, Pietist, and Pentecostalist: Three types of Evangelical Spirituality*, Grove Books, p.10.

[8] Charles E. Hambrick-Stowe (1994), "Ordering their Private World—What Puritans Did to Grow Spiritually", in *Christian History,* Vol. XIII, No. 1, p.18.

[9] Baxter 1656:10, in Michael Green (1970), *Evangelism in the Early Church*, Hodder & Stoughton, p.219.

[10] Donald Durnbaugh (1968), *The Believers' Church: The History and Character of Radical Protestantism*, The MacMillan Company, pp.106-117; John Driver (1999), *Radical Faith: An Alternative History of the Christian Church*, Pandora Press, ch.15; E.H. Broadbent (1999), *The Pilgrim Church*, Gospel Folio Press, pp.261-265.

from any major centers of religious, economic, or political influence and opportunity.

Most of his late teenage years and early twenties were spent traveling England and sharing his concerns about the beliefs and practices of the established Christian churches of his day. He did not have any real success in either a personal spiritual awakening or in attracting fellow pilgrims in his journey of questioning the contemporary religious climate of England. He spent much time in prayer and fasting, hoping that his own sense of spiritual distress would be relieved. Then, one day during his travels, after he had all but given up on trying to find answers to his own inner spiritual conflict, he had a significant experience that gave his soul peace:

> When all my hopes in them and in all men were gone, so that I had nothing outwardly to help me, nor could I tell what to do, then, oh, then, I heard a voice which said, "There is one, even Christ Jesus, that can speak to thy condition"; and when I heard it, my heart did leap for joy...My desire after the Lord grew stronger, and zeal in the pure knowledge of God, and of Christ alone, without the help of any man, book, or writing. For though I read the Scriptures that spoke of Christ and of God, yet I knew Him not, but by revelation, as He who hath the key did open, and as the Father of Life drew me to His Son by His Spirit.[11]

Fox was later to have a profound experience standing atop Pendle Hill, from which he saw a great mass of people that would receive his message. This signaled the beginning, in many ways, of the Quaker movement. Soon after, Fox began to gain a hearing for his message of salvation in Christ. The Quakers drew 20,000 converts in the first five years of their mission. Many of the early Quakers also went forth two by two throughout the British Isles, continental Europe, America, and the West Indies, among other places, determined to take the gospel to the whole world.

But with this kind of growth, they inevitably attracted severe persecution both from religious and civil authorities. They were jailed, beaten, and ill-treated. As the movement grew, there was seldom a time when there were less than 1,000 Quakers in prison at a given moment.

The Quakers emphasized several aspects of genuine Christian faith and practice. The work of the Spirit was to be active in a believer's life. Every person had an inner light and seed that merely needed to be awakened by their acceptance of Christ. They advocated for complete non-violence, solidarity with the poor and ordinary laborers, and equality between the genders.

---

[11] George Fox, *Journal*, Chapter I.

Their 'church' meetings were informal and Spirit-led as believers waited for a prompting from the Spirit before speaking. To eliminate false divisions between sacred and secular places of worship, they preached the message of Christ in the open air and met in people's homes for small group gatherings. They also organized a system of monthly, quarterly, and yearly meetings to deal with practical matters, such as assisting the families of those in prison for their faith. There was also a group of traveling 'public friends' that circulated among other Quaker meetings, thereby bringing cohesion to the movement as a whole.

Quakers were also critical of both Catholic and Protestant churches with their 'steeple-houses' and paid clergy. This attitude towards the established churches, which the Quakers saw as deeply flawed, is summarized by George Fox:

> I declared unto them that the Lord God had sent me to preach the everlasting gospel and Word of life amongst them, and to bring them off from all these temples, tithes, priests, and rudiments of the world, which had been instituted since the apostles' days, and had been set up by such as had erred from the Spirit and power the apostles were in. Very largely was I opened at this meeting, and the Lord's convincing power accompanied my ministry, and reached the hearts of the people, whereby many were convinced; and all the teachers of that congregation (who were many) were convinced of God's everlasting truth.[12]

THE PIETISTS (17TH CENTURY)

'Pietism' is a term used to describe those within the Protestant church (and occasionally affecting some within the Roman Catholic Church), that stressed the need for a living relationship with God and for this to overflow in the fruit of good works. Subsequent to Luther, the Reformation churches had stressed the need for doctrinal orthodoxy as the priority. The Pietists, while wishing to stand on the doctrinal truths of the Reformation, believed that following Christ was more than mere intellectual assent to orthodoxy— it involved personal renewal.

Johann Arndt (1555-1621)

Perhaps the defining works of Pietist spirituality came from Johann Arndt, who wrote works such as *True Christianity* (1606) and *A Paradise Garden Full of Christian Virtue* (1616). In the latter we read:

> Ah, give me grace that I may help relieve and not make greater my neighbor's affliction and misfortune, that I may comfort him in his sorrow and all who are of a grieved spirit, may have mercy on strangers, on widows and

---

[12] George Fox, *Journal*, Chapter VI.

orphans, that I readily help and love, not with tongue, but in deed and truth. The sinner says the wise man ignores his neighbor, but blessed is he who has mercy on the unfortunate.

Pietism stressed conversion and a personal relationship with God as a gracious gift from him, a transformed life shown by the fruit of good works, a belief in the Bible as the Word of God, which was not only for doctrine but to effect everyday life.

To the Pietist, the study of Scripture became important in the pursuit of godliness. They, in fact, saw themselves as completing the Reformation, which to them had largely been a *reformatio doctrinae* but not a *reformatio vitae* (a reformation of doctrine rather than a reformation of life). Such a reformed life would necessitate the direct application of biblical insights to everyday life involving the laity's using the Scriptures for themselves.

A common phenomenon among the Pietists was the establishment of small groups, usually called *collegia* or *collegia pietatis* (groups of piety), to study the Scriptures and promote holiness and good works. Such groups existed in the Reformed churches in Holland and the German states, as well as in Lutheran churches and in various radical or independent groups.

Philip Jakob Spener (1635-1705)

Perhaps the largest body of Pietists and its most influential thinkers like Spener, were within the Lutheran church. Lutheran Pietists wished to complete Luther's reformation and believed that the establishment of *collegia* would complete the Reformation in the area of ecclesiastical structures. Philip Jakob Spener is perhaps the most influential of all Pietists, largely due to his writings and his clear enunciation not just of doctrines, but of a seminal program for church renewal. Spener stressed that the church was not the building but the people, including those in house group meetings:

> [By church] one doesn't mean the building that is dedicated to the worship of God and is used for that purpose. Such churches of which we speak are "meeting houses." One understands by the word "church," however, the gatherings of Christians, in general as well as in certain special groups. The former is the universal; the latter are the singular churches.[13]

Spener clearly saw that public preaching was not enough to help people grow in their walk with God, and that all were ministers before God. His program for new meetings was set out in 1669:

---

[13] From "Of the Christian Church" (preached 1687), in Howard Snyder (1989), *A Signs of the Spirit — How God Reshapes the Church,* Academie Books/Zondervan, p.90.

It is certain, in any case, that we preachers cannot instruct the people from our pulpits as much as is needful unless other persons in the congregation, who by God's grace have a superior knowledge of Christianity, take the pains, by virtue of their universal Christian priesthood, to work with and under us to correct and reform, as much in their neighbors as they are able according to the measure of their gifts and their simplicity.[14]

Spener wrote that Jesus had taught in homes, that the early church had met in homes, and that in starting these small group meetings, he was reintroducing the "apostolic kind of meetings".

Jean de Labadie (1610-1674)

Labadie, a Frenchman and former Jesuit living in Holland, established small groups or *collegia* to help people separate themselves from the world as much as possible and to seek mystical union with God. These *collegia*, held twice daily, both morning and evening, were to be the instrument for reformation within the Reformed communion. Labadie attempted to popularize these small groups in his writings. He even wrote in his book, *La réformation de L'Eglise par le pastorate (The Reformation of the Church by the Pastorate*, 1667), that establishing small groups should be one of the main occupations of the pastor. His groups were for both men and women together, although only the men were permitted to speak.

Other *collegia* in Holland during this period tended to be held on Sunday afternoon or a weekday evening. They were presided over by the pastor. The content included singing, reading and discussion of Scripture, discussion of the sermon, and prayer. They also existed for the fostering of *koinonia* (fellowship) as they believed the early church had experienced it. This provides some hint of primitivism, the desire to return to the early church, which was to play a large part in the forming of cell groups in many of the 17th and 18th century movements.

Theodor Untereyck (1635-1693)

One of the most influential figures within German Reformed circles in the 17th century was Theodor Untereyck. In 1665, he began small groups in Mühlheim. On Sundays, he met with interested men, while his wife led a women's group every weekday from 11 am to 12 noon. She also led groups on Wednesdays and Saturdays for servant girls, while Untereyck held a group for children.

What was the response of the church authorities to this explosion of small groups? Interestingly, in the case of the German Reformed Church, it

---

[14] Jacob Spener, *Erbauliche Evangelische — und Epistolische Sonntags — Andachten*, Frankfurt, 1716:638, in Theodore G. Tappert (trans.) (1964), *Pia Desideria (by Philip Jacob Spener)*, Fortress Press, p.13.

was favorable in many cases. The Synod of Cleve in 1674 instructed ministers to permit conventicles, allowing individuals to invite their immediate neighbors into their houses for the purpose of reading the Bible, singing, praying and repeating the morning sermon.

The influence of Pietism's small groups upon the German states was such that, by 1687, even some civil authorities were advocating cell meetings. In that year the town council of Wesel decreed that "Almighty God is to be served not only public in the congregations of the church, but also privatum," that is, in small house groups!

THE MORAVIANS (18TH CENTURY)

Count Nicolaus Ludwig von Zinzendorf (1700-1760), an aristocrat raised in a Pietist Lutheran family and in Pietist educational institutions, allowed the settlement in 1722 of religious refugees from Moravia and Bohemia (a remnant of the *Unitas Fratrum* or *Unity of the Brethren* church) on his lands in Saxony, later to be called Herrnhut. A religious community developed in the succeeding years, with strong small group structures. In time, the Moravians became the largest Protestant missionary movement in the world to that date.

For the Moravian, faith was highly experiential, emphasizing the joy of knowing Christ, (*Glückseligkeit* in German). There was a strong emphasis on the priesthood of all believers, with people serving according to gifts. This allowed for the release of women to ministry and leadership responsibilities within their community. Zinzendorf stressed the communal nature of the Christian faith, where unity, holiness, and intimate fellowship went hand in hand. Zinzendorf stated: "I am not willing to see Christianity without community."[15] Within their larger community, they believed that there needed to be small fellowships to aid believers to live a holy life of service to God.

Bands

One key for living a godly life was the participation in small fellowships called bands, (*Banden* in German), which were later called *Kleine Gesellschaften* (little societies). These were originally just two to three people, later comprising between five and nine. Members were of the same sex and marital status.

People chose to associate with those whom they trusted. Initially they met weekly, but as time progressed, they tended to meet more frequently, at times even daily. Meetings were usually for one hour but could last three hours if the members so desired. Band meetings were held outdoors or in homes, but not in church buildings. It is possible for us to know so much of

---

[15] Quoted in "The Moravian Church in the World 1457-1957" in *International Review of Mission,* XLVI: No. 184 (Oct 1957), p.422.

the detail of what actually took place in band meetings as minutes were kept and placed in the community's official diaries.

The bands flourished, spreading to nearby towns and even to the universities of Jena and Tübingen. By 1732, Hernnhut had 500 residents and 77 bands. In 1733 there were 85 bands, and by 1734 there were 100 bands.

John Wesley, on his visit in 1738, wrote in his journal that he found "about ninety bands, each of which meets twice at least, but most of them three times a week, to 'confess their faults one to another, and pray for one another, that they may be healed.'"

The Herrnhut official diary describes that the inception of the bands arose due to the lack of deep fellowship and lack of discussion concerning one's personal walk with God. For Zinzendorf, an honest and open speaking of one's spiritual state was necessary. These groups were to foster that need:

> Tell one another sometimes how it stands with their heart.
> For that is the only Way to get an upright and honest Flock,
> viz. to habituate them to express the true and proper Sense
> of their Mind; or at least, certainly not to pretend such a
> Thing, if it be not indeed so.[16]

Zinzendorf described the bands as those "who converse on the whole state of their hearts and conceal nothing from each other, but who have wholly committed themselves to each other's care in the Lord...cordiality, secrecy and daily intercourse is of great service to such individuals and ought never to be neglected."

The bands also provided the Herrnhut community with a useful and efficient way of providing pastoral care, playing a vital role in maintaining the stability and health of the wider community. In addition to self-disclosure, the contemporary reports of band meetings show that members were free to bring their observations of one another and confront in love.

Biblical Justification for Bands

The Moravians had biblical and theological justifications for bands. Firstly, the biblical pericope of Mary's visit to Elizabeth (Luke 1:39), the text used for preaching on July 2, 1727. Spangenberg (1704-1792), Zinzendorf's co-leader and eventual successor, comments that:

> Mary's visit to Elizabeth, which is remembered this day in
> Christendom, and the divine movement which these two
> sisters felt on that occasion in their, as yet hidden, children,
> have been brought by them [the Moravians] into gatherings
> of God's children, at which the Saviour is always the third

---

[16] Zinzendorf, *Twenty-one Discourses or Dissertations upon the Augsburg Confession, Which is also the Brethren's Confession of Faith: Deliver'd by the Ordinary of the Brethren's Churches before the Seminary*, F. Okeley (trans.), Bowyer, 1753:243-44, in Howard Snyder, Ibid, p.149.

man, and into the *Banden* and *Gesellschaften*...[17]

Whenever two believers were to gather, Christ would be there as the "third man," and bands were recovering the spiritual dynamic as experienced in this passage of the Bible. Secondly, we find Zinzendorf providing biblical justification for mutual confession, from Galatians 6:1-2 and James 5:16. Zinzendorf, therefore, saw the formation of bands as a return to the New Testament practice. Thirdly, Zinzendorf believed that Jesus often chose to work in small groups:

> But we must always remain with a small number. He called the twelve, he withdrew with his disciples, that is twelve people without sisters, and even reduced this to a group of four on Tabor and on the Mount of Olives, and finally to three when he was on the cross.[18]

Diaspora Societies

The different type of small group advocated by the Moravians was the Diaspora Society. These societies were established as missionaries traveled through different lands, seeking to bring together groups of believers for fellowship and unity.

Each group consisted of people from one denomination, but they were linked together in a broad ecumenical network. At such meetings, usually in homes, there was prayer, singing, reading and discussion of sermons (often Zinzendorf's), but not the Lord's Supper, nor the study of Scripture, so as not to encourage individualistic interpretations which might encourage separatist tendencies.

They were very similar to the Spenerian *collegia pietatis,* that is, for mutual edification rather than theological disputes. However, they were ecumenical in scope and intent. In 1745, 159 such societies had been formed in the Baltic alone, of which 88 were Lutheran, 38 Reformed, 30 Moravian, and three others.

Zinzendorf sent Friedrich Wilhelm Biefer to Basel in Switzerland in 1738. Biefer experienced a small revival with between 500 and 600 Swiss being converted. These were established into 32 cell groups. Biefer was in fact forced to leave, whereupon he spent three months in Geneva and founded a further six cells.

At the Synod of Zeist in 1746, it was reported that the *Unitas Fratrum* stood in connection with 540 societies, not including the 159 in the Baltic.

---

[17] Spangenberg, *Leben des Herrn Nicolas Ludwig Grafen und Herrn von Zinzendorf und Pottendorf,* 1772-75:432, in Peter Frör, "Gruppenseelsorge in der kirchlichen Tradition: das Beispiel der Banden Herrnhuts", in *Perspektiven der Pastoralpsychologie,* R. Riess (ed.) (1974), Göttingen: Vandenhoeck & Ruprecht, p.84 (my translation).

[18] Zinzendorf, *Rede vom Grund-Pläne unserer Heidenmissionen,* in Bintz (ed.) (1979), *Texte zur Mission,* Wittig Verlag, p.99 (my translation).

Moravian bands and classes fostered a spiritual passion which included a commitment to missions. This, in turn, led to the formation of many other groups in the lands to which their missionaries went.

THE METHODISTS (18TH CENTURY)

John Wesley (1703-1791) was the founder of the Methodist movement, which began in Great Britain in the 18th century. As many came to faith in Christ, Wesley and his co-leaders established a vast and interlocking network of groups to turn these raw converts into mature disciples and many into leaders. From the first meeting of the first group of students at the University of Oxford in 1729, until his death in 1791, Wesley tirelessly preached Christ and founded multiplying small groups. By 1791, there were 72,000 Methodists in Great Britain and 57,000 in America. By 1798, a few years after Wesley's death, there were over 100,000 members of Methodists societies in Great Britain. Around one in 30 adult men in England was a Methodist. The role of cell groups was crucial in the building of this movement of Christian disciples. The movement was linked, in particular, through a cadre of 'circuit riders' who traveled from group to group, teaching believers and preaching evangelistically in the open air. In 1748, Wesley wrote *A Plain Account of the People called Methodists* (available in *Works* VIII: 248-268) which provides us with much of our understanding of his thinking behind his formation of the various groups. A number of sections from this work are quoted below. Of the various structures Wesley put in place, particular attention should be given to the classes and bands, which were key to Wesley's strategy.

Classes

Class meetings became the cornerstone of Wesley's method. The term derives from the Latin *classis* meaning *division*. Wesley had grown dissatisfied with his existing system of pastoral supervision He witnessed the regression of many who had responded to his field preaching and was at pains to provide a solution. The class meeting was that solution. Having been developed in Bristol, where the 1,100 society members were placed in classes of 12, Wesley implemented in April 1742 the same design in London. From this point, it was no longer possible to be a member of a society unless also a member of a class. The 426 members in London (plus 201 on trial) were divided into 65 classes. By December 1743, all 2,200 members were in classes.

Class meetings were formed according to geographic location. They consisted of both men and women, and people of different social backgrounds, ages, and maturity in the Christian faith. Initially, they met in homes, shops, and attics. At a later stage, as the Methodists owned or constructed their own buildings, in small rooms on the premises. The format was usually the singing of a hymn, the leader's opening with a statement as to his spiritual condition, followed by others so doing, including testimony or admission of sin. Visitors could attend, but every other meeting was only for the members. After two visits, one had either to join or cease to attend.

Wesley noted that where he merely preached, the seed fell by the wayside, but where classes were established there was lasting fruit. The primary purposes of classes were discipleship and discipline, but they were also evangelistic as more professed conversion in class meetings than in the preaching services. *A Plain Account* states:

> By the blessing of God upon their endeavors to help one another, many found the pearl of great price. Being justified by faith, they had "peace with God, through our Lord Jesus Christ." These felt a more tender affection than before, so those who were partakers of like precious faith; and hence arose such a confidence in each other, that they poured out their souls into each other's bosom.... Indeed they had a great need to do so; for the war was not over, as they had supposed; but they had still to wrestle both with flesh and blood, and with principalities and powers: so that temptations were on every side; and often temptations of such a kind, as they knew not how to speak in class; in which persons of every sort young and old, men and women, met together.

Bands

A second type of fellowship group was the band. These were small groups of the same sex, same marital status, and of similar age. Wesley's goal for Methodism was "to spread scriptural holiness throughout the land"; this was to entail both ethical morality and inward purity. The classes were to deal with the former; the bands the latter. Wesley's approach was largely to change the behavior first and the motives second. Although strongly encouraged, attendance at the bands was not compulsory (perhaps explaining why they did not multiply in the same way that the classes did). They were for the purposes of achieving "closer union" and for honest divulging of sins and temptations faced. Wesley explained their purposes in *A Plain Account:*

> These, therefore wanted some means of closer union; they wanted to pour out their hearts without reserve, particularly with regard to the sin which did still easily beset them and the temptations which were most apt to prevail over them. And they were the more desirous of this when they observed it was the express advice of an inspired writer: "Confess your faults one to another, and pray for one another, that ye may be healed."

Bands were for those "who seem to have remission of sins." Each member was to speak in turn. Because they were strictly for believers, unlike class meetings, it was hoped that the bands would consist of more mature members than the classes, hence, there was no leader who interrogated others but individual initiative in self-disclosure. Wesley, however, left little to chance, and in 1738 (*Works* VIII: 272-3), drew up a list of questions to be used:

1. What known sins have you committed since our last meeting?
2. What temptations have you met with?
3. How were you delivered?
4. What have you thought, said, or done, of which you doubt whether it be sin or not?
5. Have you nothing you desire to keep secret?

OBSERVATIONS FROM HISTORY

Having briefly surveyed some of the small group and home fellowship meetings which flourished in the centuries subsequent to the Reformation, it might be beneficial to make a few observations. The above examples show that believers meeting in small groups for edification, discipleship, accountability, and outreach occurred in many varying settings–in different countries and cultures, in differing denominations, and among distinctive social classes. There is a universality to these basic believers' gatherings. Despite the above diversity of location, ecclesiastical tradition and social constituency, it is possible to discern a number of common characteristics, perhaps not present in all those investigated, but nonetheless common to most. Certain theologies and beliefs tend to lead to the establishment and on-going support of small groups. These provide the value system in which small groups will flourish, for groups and small fellowships are not a structural exercise but the outworking in life of a deep value system. Among such characteristics, the following may be found.

The Corporate Nature of Christianity

There was a strong belief in the corporate nature of Christianity rather than the individual. Zinzendorf was "not willing to see Christianity without community." Wesley knew of neither solitary religion nor solitary holiness—both were social. Bucer stressed the passages of Scripture which taught on communal life, such as the book of Acts, chapters 2 and 4.

The Organic Church

Church was seen in essence not as an organization, nor something to which all belong, nor as the building but as something living, perhaps invisible. It is body or family rather than organization. It is the coming together of believers in itself which is church, as Spener wrote: "One understands by the word "church," however, the gatherings of Christians, in general as well as in certain special groups. The former is the universal; the latter are the singular churches." Not everyone in this study would have stated it this way, but, in essence, for many there was such an organic, family understanding of church. Zinzendorf used familial vocabulary (fellow believers were "God's children") or terms of endearment (gatherings of Christians were the "little flock").

Experiential Faith

Zinzendorf stressed *Glückseligkeit*, the joy of knowing Christ. Wesley described his conversion as his "heart strangely warmed."[19] God was to be experienced and lives changed. Faith was not simply a matter of correct belief. Reformation was not merely that of doctrine, but of life.

The Priesthood of All Believers

All Christians were to minister. This was stressed less among some. In other movements, however, this was vital to the health and life of the group. Spener, in *The Spiritual Priesthood*, wrote that all believers were to edify one another, teach, and admonish. Within Herrnhut, virtually all the leadership was lay, as was the majority of missionaries sent to other lands. Wesley built his movement on lay leaders and lay preachers. Methodist group multiplication would not have been achievable without lay ministry and lay leadership.

Volunteerism

Volunteerism, that is, a personal decision to join the group was unlike the membership of the territorial churches. There is, therefore, an aspect of the believers' church ecclesiology evident to some extent in all the movements in question. This is controversial, as some (Luther and Bucer, for example) would have strenuously denied their adherence to such a position; nonetheless, it is valid. In the *Preface to the German Mass,* Luther called for the gathering of those "who are desirous of being Christians in earnest, and are ready to profess the Gospel with hand and mouth." Bucer called for the formation of "true" Christian communities who were serious in their walk with God.

Furthermore, in Pietism, Moravianism, and Methodism there was a clear distinction between the true believer and the non-believer. Pietism stressed either the process (*Busskampf*—the struggle resulting from conviction) or the standing (*Wiedergeburt*—rebirth) which separated the two. Moravianism stressed the resultant state after *Wiedergeburt*, namely *Glückseligkeit*, joyous blessedness. Methodism spoke of "awakened persons" or those "who seem to have remission of sins." The believer could demonstrate his theological and juridical position by choosing to join a *collegia*, that is, a band or small group of some name. The commitment level was high, particularly in Moravianism and Methodism, with strict group boundary maintenance and expulsion for lack of participation or attendance. Whether seeking to express oneself as the true, invisible church within the visible (*ecclesiola in ecclesia*) or as some kind of sectarian movement (Methodism), some expression of the believers' church theology is evident.

---

[19] *Journal*, 24 May, 1738.

Spiritual Growth

A developmental understanding of life, growth, and sanctification seems to underpin many of these movements and how they were structured. This was true of Bucer and of many of the Pietists. Arndt, one of the most influential of the Pietists, wrote in *True Christianity*:

> As there are different stages and degrees of age and maturity in the natural life; so there are also in the spiritual. It has its first foundation in sincere repentance, by which a man sets himself heartily to amend his life. This is succeeded by a greater illumination, which is a kind of middle stage. Here, by contemplation, prayer, and bearing the cross, a man is daily improving in grace, and growing up to perfection. The last and most perfect state is that which consists in a most firm union, which is founded and cemented by, pure love. This is that state which St. Paul calls "the perfect man" and "the measure of the stature of the fullness of Christ." (Ephesians 13)

This work was to influence Wesley, who discovered the text in 1736 and published extracts from it. From this understanding of human development, Wesley divided people accordingly so they could be taught and helped in line with the needs appropriate to their stage in the Christian life. As Zinzendorf was to say: "God is adapting Himself to the varied ways of each man, woman and child, going his specific ways with them in each place...."[20]

Mutual Confession

Mutual lay confession, rather than confession solely between the believer and God, was also present. While not wishing to place an intermediary between the individual and God and holding to the Reformation doctrines, we have seen the belief that confession to one another was important for overcoming sin and growth in holiness. This was evidenced in the writings of Luther and in the meetings of the Moravian and Wesleyan bands.

Church Discipline

There was a belief in church discipline and that small groups were to be the place to restore an effective biblical discipline. In the *Preface to the German Mass,* Luther wrote that "those whose conduct was not such as befits Christians could be recognized, reproved, reformed, rejected, or excommunicated, according to the rule of Christ in Matthew xviii." Bucer, the Moravians, and the Methodists would expel people from bands for such things as non-attendance, stealing, wife-beating, and the like. Ethical standards were to be maintained through discipline.

---

[20] *Manorial Injunctions and Prohibitions*, 1727.

Primitivism

Many of the groups were motivated by primitivism, that is, the desire to return to the New Testament church, holding that this period in church history showed both an efficacy and vitality which the church in their day needed. It was in the formation of various small fellowships which provided a way to produce such holiness and vitality once again.

Multiplication and Movement

In addition to the above observations concerning beliefs and values, we can of course draw many valuable lessons from studying such groups in the history of the church. At this stage we will draw just two crucial lessons: multiplication and movement.

Many of the groups flourished and were successful because they did not grow too large as an individual group. When numerical growth occurred, movements such as the Moravians and Methodists multiplied their groups. Each group was not allowed to grow too large, because the benefits of the sharing, prayer, and accountability occurred in the more intimate nature of the meeting—which required that the membership be small in number. Spener, in fact, found that when his group grew to about 50 people, it was not as effective and lost its vitality.

The second key lesson is that groups succeed when they are part of a broader and larger network. Some of the groups, such as the Pietist *collegia*, occurred in many places, but they were not really part of a defined movement or network. The Quaker, Moravian, and Methodist groups, however, sat clearly within something larger, where there was apostolic leadership of the movement that could articulate vision, theology, and methodology, as well as give oversight through band leaders' meetings or, in the case of the Quakers and Methodists, itinerant circuit riders that traveled and strengthened the faith of the various groups. History shows that a small group or house church being part of a wider movement is crucial for its life, health, growth, and long-term effectiveness.

STUDY QUESTIONS

1. What were some of the factors motivating the revitalization efforts of the movements examined?

2. What were some of ways that the house churches and small groups were linked together?

3. What practical lessons can you apply to your house church network today?

Chapter 20

A BODY KNIT TOGETHER

TERTULLIAN (AD 155-223)

Tertullian was born Quintus Septimius Florens Tertullianus in the city of Carthage (North Africa) to a Roman centurion officer. By profession he was an advocate in the law courts. He was a pagan until midlife, sharing all the typical anti-Christian prejudices. In the late 190s, he was firmly converted to the Christian faith, embracing it with the ardor that was to later characterize his Christian writings and becoming the pastor of the church at Carthage. In about AD 206, he joined the growing Montanist movement which sought to restore passionate spirituality, holy living, discipline, an informal leadership style, and prophetic gifts to the church. As a Montanist Christian, he wrote strongly against the increasing laxity and formalism he perceived in the more established church and felt that "Where but three are, and they of the laity also, yet there is a church." He opposed the idea of Christians serving in the military, questioned the value of patriotism, and felt that a martyr's death was the noblest one for a follower of Christ. Tertullian is considered to be one of the early church's greatest and most controversial theologians, writing both for Christian and Roman audiences. He is especially known to many by his phrase, "The blood of the martyrs is seed" [The text below is an excerpt from Tertullian's work entitled Apology (chapter XXXIX) and is in the public domain.]

I shall at once go on, then, to exhibit the peculiarities of the Christian society, that, as I have refuted the evil charged against it, I may point out its positive good. We are a body knit together as such by a common religious profession, by unity of discipline, and by the bond of a common hope.

We meet together as an assembly and congregation, that, offering up prayer to God as with united force, we may wrestle with Him in our supplications. This violence God delights in. We pray, too, for the emperors, for their ministers and for all in authority, for the welfare of the world, for the prevalence of peace, for the delay of the final consummation. We assemble to read our sacred writings, if any peculiarity of the times makes either forewarning or reminiscence needful. However it be in that respect, with the sacred words we nourish our faith, we animate our hope, we make our confidence more steadfast; and no less by inculcations of God's precepts we confirm good habits.

In the same place also exhortations are made, rebukes and sacred censures are administered. For with a great gravity is the work of judging carried on among us, as befits those who feel assured that they are in the sight of God; and you have the most notable example of judgment to come when any one has sinned so grievously as to require his severance from us in prayer, in the congregation and in all sacred intercourse. The tried men of our elders preside over us, obtaining that honour not by purchase, but by established character.

There is no buying and selling of any sort in the things of God. Though we have our treasure chest, it is not made up of purchase-money, as of a religion that has its price. On the monthly day, if he likes, each puts in a small donation; but only if it be his pleasure, and only if he be able: for there is no compulsion; all is voluntary. These gifts are, as it were, piety's deposit fund. For they are not taken thence and spent on feasts, and drinking-bouts, and eating-houses, but to support and bury poor people, to supply the wants of boys and girls destitute of means and parents, and of old persons confined now to the house; such, too, as have suffered shipwreck; and if there happen to be any in the mines, or banished to the islands, or shut up in the prisons, for nothing but their fidelity to the cause of God's Church, they become the nurslings of their confession.

But it is mainly the deeds of a love so noble that lead many to put a brand upon us. *See*, they say, *how they love one another*, for themselves are animated by mutual hatred; how they are ready even to die for one another, for they themselves will sooner put to death. And they are wroth with us, too, because we call each other brethren; for no other reason, as I think, than because among themselves names of consanguinity are assumed in mere pretence of affection. But we are your brethren as well, by the law of our common mother nature, though you are hardly men, because brothers so unkind. At the same time, how much more fittingly they are called and counted brothers who have been led to the knowledge of God as their common Father, who have drunk in one spirit of holiness, who from the same womb of a common ignorance have agonized into the same light of truth!

But on this very account, perhaps, we are regarded as having less claim to be held true brothers, that no tragedy makes a noise about our brotherhood, or that the family possessions, which generally destroy brotherhood among you, create fraternal bonds among us. One in mind and soul, we do not hesitate to share our earthly goods with one another. All things are common among us but our wives. We give up our community where it is practiced alone by others, who not only take possession of the wives of their friends, but most tolerantly also accommodate their friends with theirs, following the example, I believe, of those wise men of ancient times, the Greek Socrates and the Roman Cato, who shared with their friends the wives whom they had married, it seems for the sake of progeny both to themselves and to others; whether in this acting against their partners' wishes, I am not able to say. Why should they have any care over their chastity, when their husbands so readily bestowed it away? O noble example of Attic wisdom, of Roman gravity—the philosopher and the censor playing pimps!

What wonder if that great love of Christians towards one another is desecrated by you! For you abuse also our humble feasts, on the ground that they are extravagant as well as infamously wicked. To us, it seems, applies the saying of Diogenes: "The people of Megara feast as though they were going to die on the morrow; they build as though they were never to die!" But one sees more readily the mote in another's eye than the beam in his own. Why, the very air is soured with the eructations of so many tribes, and curioe, and decurioe. The Salii cannot have their feast without going into debt; you must get the accountants to tell you what the tenths of Hercules and the sacrificial banquets cost; the choicest cook is appointed for the Apaturia, the Dionysia, the Attic mysteries; the smoke from the banquet of Serapis will call out the firemen.

Yet about the modest supper-room of the Christians alone a great ado is made. Our feast explains itself by its name. The Greeks call it *agape*, i.e., affection. Whatever it costs, our outlay in the name of piety is gain, since with the good things of the feast we benefit the needy; not as it is with you, do parasites aspire to the glory of satisfying their licentious propensities, selling themselves for a belly-feast to all disgraceful treatment, but as it is with God himself, a peculiar respect is shown to the lowly. If the object of our feast be good, in the light of that consider its further regulations. As it is an act of religious service, it permits no vileness or immodesty. The participants, before reclining, taste first of prayer to God. As much is eaten as satisfies the cravings of hunger; as much is drunk as befits the chaste. They say it is enough, as those who remember that even during the night they have to worship God; they talk as those who know that the Lord is one of their auditors. After manual ablution, and the bringing in of lights, each is asked to stand forth and sing, as he can, a hymn to God, either one from the holy Scriptures or one of his own composing—a proof of the measure of our drinking.

As the feast commenced with prayer, so with prayer it is closed. We go from it, not like troops of mischief-doers, nor bands of vagabonds, nor to break out into licentious acts, but to have as much care of our modesty and chastity as if we had been at a school of virtue rather than a banquet. Give the congregation of the Christians its due, and hold it unlawful, if it is like assemblies of the illicit sort: by all means let it be condemned, if any complaint can be validly laid against it, such as lies against secret factions. But who has ever suffered harm from our assemblies? We are in our congregations just what we are when separated from each other; we are as a community what we are individuals; we injure nobody, we trouble nobody. When the upright, when the virtuous meet together, when the pious, when the pure assemble in congregation, you ought not to call that a faction, but a *curia*-[i.e., the court of God.] ■

STUDY QUESTIONS

1. What was the interplay between spontaneity and structure in the early church meetings described by Tertullian?

2. In your view, which factors helped develop cohesiveness in the Christian communities presented?

3. How was money viewed and utilized by the early Christians?

4. What lessons can be applied to your network of house churches?

Chapter 21

CONFESSION

PATRICK OF IRELAND (AD 390-460)

Patrick was born in Britain to socially well-placed parents, his father being a deacon in the village church. Christianity, however, held no interest for Patrick, who preferred to go off with friends. At the age of 16, he was captured by Irish raiders, brought over to Ireland by ship, and sold into slavery, where he shepherded a large flock of sheep that belonged to a pagan chieftain-king. During this trying time, he began to fervently pray to the God that his Christian grandfather had told him about. One night he heard a voice that told him, "Soon you will go to your own country". That night, he began his escape after six long years of servitude. He made a 200-mile trek to a port, managed to secure passage aboard a ship, and landed on the coast of Gaul (France) three days later. In Gaul, he sought out the famous bishop Germanus of Auxerre, who saw to it that the young Patrick would become trained in a knowledge of the Scriptures. He eventually returned to his native land of Britain. But his stay was not to be permanent. In a late night vision, he received a commission to return to Ireland. In AD 430, Patrick, the former slave, now returned as a missionary to show a people gripped in superstition and paganism how to be free in Christ from the slavery of sin. For the next 30 years, Patrick spread the message of Christ all over Ireland. Using the strategies of traveling apostolic teams and open air preaching, he established hundreds of churches, monasteries, and schools which sent forth missionaries for the next several centuries to Scotland, England, France, Germany, and Belgium. So many people were baptized as Christian converts that Ireland was nicknamed "The Isle of Saints". It was not until AD 664 that this Celtic missionary movement came under the authority of the Roman Church. [The following text is entitled Confession and was written by Patrick as an old man. It is in the public domain.]

1. I, Patrick, a sinner, a most simple countryman, the least of all the faithful and most contemptible to many, had for father the deacon Calpurnius, son of the late Potitus, a priest, of the settlement of Bannavem Taburniae; he had a small villa nearby where I was taken captive. I was at that time about sixteen years of age. I did not, indeed, know the true God; and I was taken into captivity in Ireland with many thousands of people, according to our deserts, for quite drawn away from God, we did not keep his precepts, nor were we obedient to our priests who used to remind us of our salvation. And the Lord brought down on us the fury of his being and

scattered us among many nations, even to the ends of the earth, where I, in my smallness, am now to be found among foreigners.

2. And there the Lord opened my mind to an awareness of my unbelief, in order that, even so late, I might remember my transgressions and turn with all my heart to the Lord my God, who had regard for my insignificance and pitied my youth and ignorance. And he watched over me before I knew him, and before I learned sense or even distinguished between good and evil, and he protected me, and consoled me as a father would his son.

3. Therefore, indeed, I cannot keep silent, nor would it be proper, so many favours and graces has the Lord deigned to bestow on me in the land of my captivity. For after chastisement from God, and recognizing him, our way to repay him is to exalt him and confess his wonders before every nation under heaven.

4. For there is no other God, nor ever was before, nor shall be hereafter, but God the Father, unbegotten and without beginning, in whom all things began, whose are all things, as we have been taught; and his son Jesus Christ, who manifestly always existed with the Father, before the beginning of time in the spirit with the Father, indescribably begotten before all things, and all things visible and invisible were made by him. He was made man, conquered death and was received into Heaven, to the Father who gave him all power over every name in Heaven and on Earth and in Hell, so that every tongue should confess that Jesus Christ is Lord and God, in whom we believe. And we look to his imminent coming again, the judge of the living and the dead, who will render to each according to his deeds. And he poured out his Holy Spirit on us in abundance, the gift and pledge of immortality, which makes the believers and the obedient into sons of God and co-heirs of Christ who is revealed, and we worship one God in the Trinity of holy name.

5. He himself said through the prophet: 'Call upon me in the day of trouble; I will deliver you, and you shall glorify me.' And again: 'It is right to reveal and publish abroad the works of God.'

6. I am imperfect in many things, nevertheless I want my brethren and kinsfolk to know my nature so that they may be able to perceive my soul's desire.

7. I am not ignorant of what is said of my Lord in the Psalm: 'You destroy those who speak a lie.' And again: 'A lying mouth deals death to the soul.' And likewise the Lord says in the Gospel: 'On the day of judgment men shall render account for every idle word they utter.'

8. So it is that I should mightily fear, with terror and trembling, this judgment on the day when no one shall be able to steal away or hide, but each and all shall render account for even our smallest sins before the judgment seat of Christ the Lord.

9. And therefore for some time I have thought of writing, but I have hesitated until now, for truly, I feared to expose myself to the criticism of men, because I have not studied like others, who have assimilated both Law

and the Holy Scriptures equally and have never changed their idiom since their infancy, but instead were always learning it increasingly, to perfection, while my idiom and language have been translated into a foreign tongue. So it is easy to prove from a sample of my writing, my ability in rhetoric and the extent of my preparation and knowledge, for as it is said, 'wisdom shall be recognized in speech, and in understanding, and in knowledge and in the learning of truth.'

10. But why make excuses close to the truth, especially when now I am presuming to try to grasp in my old age what I did not gain in my youth because my sins prevented me from making what I had read my own? But who will believe me, even though I should say it again? A young man, almost a beardless boy, I was taken captive before I knew what I should desire and what I should shun. So, consequently, today I feel ashamed and I am mightily afraid to expose my ignorance, because, [not] eloquent, with a small vocabulary, I am unable to explain as the spirit is eager to do and as the soul and the mind indicate.

11. But had it been given to me as to others, in gratitude I should not have kept silent, and if it should appear that I put myself before others, with my ignorance and my slower speech, in truth, it is written: 'The tongue of the stammerers shall speak rapidly and distinctly.' How much harder must we try to attain it, we of whom it is said: 'You are an epistle of Christ in greeting to the ends of the earth ... written on your hearts, not with ink but with the Spirit of the living God.' And again, the Spirit witnessed that the rustic life was created by the Most High.

12. I am, then, first of all, countryfied, an exile, evidently unlearned, one who is not able to see into the future, but I know for certain, that before I was humbled I was like a stone lying in deep mire, and he that is mighty came and in his mercy raised me up and, indeed, lifted me high up and placed me on top of the wall. And from there I ought to shout out in gratitude to the Lord for his great favours in this world and for ever, that the mind of man cannot measure.

13. Therefore be amazed, you great and small who fear God, and you men of God, eloquent speakers, listen and contemplate. Who was it summoned me, a fool, from the midst of those who appear wise and learned in the law and powerful in rhetoric and in all things? Me, truly wretched in this world, he inspired before others that I could be—if I would—such a one who, with fear and reverence, and faithfully, without complaint, would come to the people to whom the love of Christ brought me and gave me in my lifetime, if I should be worthy, to serve them truly and with humility.

14. According, therefore, to the measure of one's faith in the Trinity, one should proceed without holding back from danger to make known the gift of God and everlasting consolation, to spread God's name everywhere with confidence and without fear, in order to leave behind, after my death,

foundations for my brethren and sons whom I baptized in the Lord in so many thousands.

15. And I was not worthy, nor was I such that the Lord should grant his humble servant this, that after hardships and such great trials, after captivity, after many years, he should give me so much favour in these people, a thing which in the time of my youth I neither hoped for nor imagined.

16. But after I reached Ireland I used to pasture the flock each day and I used to pray many times a day. More and more did the love of God, and my fear of him and faith increase, and my spirit was moved so that in a day [I said] from one up to a hundred prayers, and in the night a like number; besides I used to stay out in the forests and on the mountain and I would wake up before daylight to pray in the snow, in icy coldness, in rain, and I used to feel neither ill nor any slothfulness, because, as I now see, the Spirit was burning in me at that time.

17. And it was there of course that one night in my sleep I heard a voice saying to me: 'You do well to fast: soon you will depart for your home country.' And again, a very short time later, there was a voice prophesying: 'Behold, your ship is ready.' And it was not close by, but, as it happened, two hundred miles away, where I had never been nor knew any person. And shortly thereafter I turned about and fled from the man with whom I had been for six years, and I came, by the power of God who directed my route to advantage (and I was afraid of nothing), until I reached that ship.

18. And on the same day that I arrived, the ship was setting out from the place, and I said that I had the wherewithal to sail with them; and the steersman was displeased and replied in anger, sharply: 'By no means attempt to go with us.' Hearing this I left them to go to the hut where I was staying, and on the way I began to pray, and before the prayer was finished I heard one of them shouting loudly after me: 'Come quickly because the men are calling you.' And immediately I went back to them and they started to say to me: 'Come, because we are admitting you out of good faith; make friendship with us in any way you wish.' (And so, on that day, I refused to suck the breasts of these men from fear of God, but nevertheless I had hopes that they would come to faith in Jesus Christ, because they were barbarians.) And for this I continued with them, and forthwith we put to sea.

19. And after three days we reached land, and for twenty-eight days journeyed through uninhabited country, and the food ran out and hunger overtook them; and one day the steersman began saying: 'Why is it, Christian? You say your God is great and all-powerful; then why can you not pray for us? For we may perish of hunger; it is unlikely indeed that we shall ever see another human being.' In fact, I said to them, confidently: 'Be converted by faith with all your heart to my Lord God, because nothing is impossible for him, so that today he will send food for you on your road, until you be sated, because everywhere he abounds.' And with God's help this came to pass; and behold, a herd of swine appeared on the road before

our eyes, and they slew many of them, and remained there for two nights, and the were full of their meat and well restored, for many of them had fainted and would otherwise have been left half dead by the wayside. And after this they gave the utmost thanks to God, and I was esteemed in their eyes, and from that day they had food abundantly. They discovered wild honey, besides, and they offered a share to me, and one of them said: 'It is a sacrifice.' Thanks be to God, I tasted none of it.

20. The very same night while I was sleeping Satan attacked me violently, as I will remember as long as I shall be in this body; and there fell on top of me as it were, a huge rock, and not one of my members had any force. But from whence did it come to me, ignorant in the spirit, to call upon 'Helias'? And meanwhile I saw the sun rising in the sky, and while I was crying out 'Helias, Helias' with all my might, lo, the brilliance of that sun fell upon me and immediately shook me free of all the weight; and I believe that I was aided by Christ my Lord, and that his Spirit then was crying out for me, and I hope that it will be so in the day of my affliction, just as it says in the Gospel: 'In that hour', the Lord declares, 'it is not you who speaks but the Spirit of your Father speaking in you.'

21. And a second time, after many years, I was taken captive. On the first night I accordingly remained with my captors, but I heard a divine prophecy, saying to me: 'You shall be with them for two months.' So it happened. On the sixtieth night the Lord delivered me from their hands.

22. On the journey he provided us with food and fire and dry weather every day, until on the tenth day we came upon people. As I mentioned above, we had journeyed through an unpopulated country for twenty-eight days, and in fact the night that we came upon people we had no food.

23. And after a few years I was again in Britain with my kinsfolk, and they welcomed me as a son, and asked me, in faith, that after the great tribulations I had endured I should not go anywhere else away from them. And, of course, there, in a vision of the night, I saw a man whose name was Victoricus coming as it from Ireland with innumerable letters, and he gave me one of them, and I read the beginning of the letter: 'The Voice of the Irish', and as I was reading the beginning of the letter I seemed at that moment to hear the voice of those who were beside the forest of Foclut which is near the western sea, and they were crying as if with one voice: 'We beg you, holy youth, that you shall come and shall walk again among us.' And I was stung intensely in my heart so that I could read no more, and thus I awoke. Thanks be to God, because after so many years the Lord bestowed on them according to their cry.

24. And another night—God knows, I do not, whether within me or beside me—...most words... which I heard and could not understand, except at the end of the speech it was represented thus: 'He who gave his life for you, he it is who speaks within you.' And thus I awoke, joyful.

25. And on a second occasion I saw Him praying within me, and I was as it were, inside my own body, and I heard Him above me—that is, above my inner self. He was praying powerfully with sighs. And in the course of this I was astonished and wondering, and I pondered who it could be who was praying within me. But at the end of the prayer it was revealed to me that it was the Spirit. And so I awoke and remembered the Apostle's words: 'Likewise the Spirit helps us in our weakness; for we know not how to pray as we ought. But the Spirit Himself intercedes for us with sighs too deep for utterance.' And again: 'The Lord our advocate intercedes for us.'

26. And then I was attacked by a goodly number of my elders, who [brought up] my sins against my arduous episcopate. That day in particular I was mightily upset, and might have fallen here and for ever; but the Lord generously spared me, a convert, and an alien, for his name's sake, and he came powerfully to my assistance in that state of being trampled down. I pray God that it shall not be held against them as a sin that I fell truly into disgrace and scandal.

27. They brought up against me after thirty years an occurrence I had confessed before becoming a deacon. On account of the anxiety in my sorrowful mind, I laid before my close friend what I had perpetrated on a day—nay, rather in one hour—in my boyhood because I was not yet proof against sin. God knows—I do not—whether I was fifteen years old at the time, and I did not then believe in the living God, nor had I believed, since my infancy; but I remained in death and unbelief until I was severely rebuked, and in truth I was humbled every day by hunger and nakedness.

28. On the other hand, I did not proceed to Ireland of my own accord until I was almost giving up, but through this I was corrected by the Lord, and he prepared me so that today I should be what was once far from me, in order that I should have the care of—or rather, I should be concerned for—the salvation of others, when at that time, still, I was only concerned for myself.

29. Therefore, on that day when I was rebuked, as I have just mentioned, I saw in a vision of the night a document before my face, without honour, and meanwhile I heard a divine prophecy, saying to me: 'We have seen with displeasure the face of the chosen one divested of [his good] name.' And he did not say 'You have seen with displeasure', but 'We have seen with displeasure' (as if He included Himself). He said then: 'He who touches you, touches the apple of my eye.'

30. For that reason, I give thanks to him who strengthened me in all things, so that I should not be hindered in my setting out and also in my work which I was taught by Christ my Lord; but more, from that state of affairs I felt, within me, no little courage, and vindicated my faith before God and man.

31. Hence, therefore, I say boldly that my conscience is clear now and hereafter. God is my witness that I have not lied in these words to you.

32. But rather, I am grieved for my very close friend, that because of him we deserved to hear such a prophecy. The one to whom I entrusted my soul! And I found out from a goodly number of brethren, before the case was made in my defence (in which I did not take part, nor was I in Britain, nor was it pleaded by me), that in my absence he would fight in my behalf. Besides, he told me himself: 'See, the rank of bishop goes to you'—of which I was not worthy. But how did it come to him, shortly afterwards, to disgrace me publicly, in the presence of all, good and bad, because previously, gladly and of his own free will, he pardoned me, as did the Lord, who is greater than all?

33. I have said enough. But all the same, I ought not to conceal God's gift which he lavished on us in the land of my captivity, for then I sought him resolutely, and I found him there, and he preserved me from all evils (as I believe) through the indwelling of his Spirit, which works in me to this day. Again, boldly, but God knows, if this had been made known to me by man, I might, perhaps, have kept silent for the love of Christ.

34. Thus I give untiring thanks to God who kept me faithful in the day of my temptation, so that today I may confidently over my soul as a living sacrifice for Christ my Lord; who am I, Lord? or, rather, what is my calling? that you appeared to me in so great a divine quality, so that today among the barbarians I might constantly exalt and magnify your name in whatever place I should be, and not only in good fortune, but even in affliction? So that whatever befalls me, be it good or bad, I should accept it equally, and give thanks always to God who revealed to me that I might trust in him, implicitly and forever, and who will encourage me so that, ignorant, and in the last days, I may dare to undertake so devout and so wonderful a work; so that I might imitate one of those whom, once, long ago, the Lord already pre-ordained to be heralds of his Gospel to witness to all peoples to the ends of the earth. So are we seeing, and so it is fulfilled; behold, we are witnesses because the Gospel has been preached as far as the places beyond which no man lives.

35. But it is tedious to describe in detail all my labours one by one. I will tell briefly how most holy God frequently delivered me, from slavery, and from the twelve trials with which my soul was threatened, from man traps as well, and from things I am not able to put into words. I would not cause offence to readers, but I have God as witness who knew all things even before they happened, that, though I was a poor ignorant waif, still he gave me abundant warnings through divine prophecy.

36. Whence came to me this wisdom which was not my own, I who neither knew the number of days nor had knowledge of God? Whence came the so great and so healthful gift of knowing or rather loving God, though I should lose homeland and family.

37. And many gifts were offered to me with weeping and tears, and I offended them [the donors], and also went against the wishes of a good

number of my elders; but guided by God, I neither agreed with them nor deferred to them, not by my own grace but by God who is victorious in me and withstands them all, so that I might come to the Irish people to preach the Gospel and endure insults from unbelievers; that I might hear scandal of my travels, and endure man's persecutions to the extent of prison; and so that I might give up my free birthright for the advantage of others, and if I should be worthy, I am ready [to give] even my life without hesitation; and most willingly for His name. And I choose to devote it to him even unto death, if God grant it to me.

38. I am greatly God's debtor, because he granted me so much grace, that through me many people would be reborn in God, and soon a after confirmed, and that clergy would be ordained everywhere for them, the masses lately come to belief, whom the Lord drew from the ends of the earth, just as he once promised through his prophets: 'To you shall the nations come from the ends of the earth, and shall say, Our fathers have inherited naught hut lies, worthless things in which there is no profit.' And again: 'I have set you to be a light for the Gentiles that you may bring salvation to the uttermost ends of' the earth.'

39. And I wish to wait then for his promise which is never unfulfilled, just as it is promised in the Gospel: 'Many shall come from east and west and shall sit at table with Abraham and Isaac and Jacob.' Just as we believe that believers will come from all the world.

40. So for that reason one should, in fact, fish well and diligently, just as the Lord foretells and teaches, saying, 'Follow me, and I will make you fishers of men,' and again through the prophets: 'Behold, I am sending forth many fishers and hunters, says the Lord,' et cetera. So it behoved us to spread our nets, that a vast multitude and throng might be caught for God, and so there might be clergy everywhere who baptized and exhorted a needy and desirous people. Just as the Lord says in the Gospel, admonishing and instructing: 'Go therefore and make disciples of all nations, baptizing them in the name of the Father and of the Son and of the Holy Spirit, teaching them to observe all that I have commanded you; and lo, I am with you always to the end of time.' And again he says: 'Go forth into the world and preach the Gospel to all creation. He who believes and is baptized shall be saved; but he who does not believe shall be condemned.' And again: 'This Gospel of the Kingdom shall be preached throughout the whole world as a witness to all nations; and then the end of the world shall come.' And likewise the Lord foretells through the prophet: 'And it shall come to pass in the last days (sayeth the Lord) that I will pour out my spirit upon all flesh, and your sons and daughters shall prophesy, and your young men shall see visions and your old men shall dream dreams; yea, and on my menservants and my maidservants in those days I will pour out my Spirit and they shall prophesy.' And in Hosea he says: 'Those who are not my people I will call my people, and those not beloved I will call my beloved, and in the very

place where it was said to them, You are not my people, they will be called 'Sons of the living God'.

41. So, how is it that in Ireland, where they never had any knowledge of God but, always, until now, cherished idols and unclean things, they are lately become a people of the Lord, and are called children of God; the sons of the Irish [Scotti] and the daughters of the chieftains are to be seen as monks and virgins of Christ.

42. And there was, besides, a most beautiful, blessed, native-born noble Irish [Scotta] woman of adult age whom I baptized; and a few days later she had reason to come to us to intimate that she had received a prophecy from a divine messenger [who] advised her that she should become a virgin of Christ and she would draw nearer to God. Thanks be to God, six days from then, opportunely and most eagerly, she took the course that all virgins of God take, not with their fathers' consent but enduring the persecutions and deceitful hindrances of their parents. Notwithstanding that, their number increases, (we do not know the number of them that are so reborn) besides the widows, and those who practise self-denial. Those who are kept in slavery suffer the most. They endure terrors and constant threats, but the Lord has given grace to many of his handmaidens, for even though they are forbidden to do so, still they resolutely follow his example.

43. So it is that even if I should wish to separate from them in order to go to Britain, and most willingly was I prepared to go to my homeland and kinsfolk—and not only there, but as far as Gaul to visit the brethren there, so that I might see the faces of the holy ones of my Lord, God knows how strongly I desired this—I am bound by the Spirit, who witnessed to me that if I did so he would mark me out as guilty, and I fear to waste the labour that I began, and not I, but Christ the Lord, who commanded me to come to be with them for the rest of my life, if the Lord shall will it and shield me from every evil, so that I may not sin before him.

44. So I hope that I did as I ought, but I do not trust myself as long as I am in this mortal body, for he is strong who strives daily to turn me away from the faith and true holiness to which I aspire until the end of my life for Christ my Lord, but the hostile flesh is always dragging one down to death, that is, to unlawful attractions. And I know in part why I did not lead a perfect life like other believers, but I confess to my Lord and do not blush in his sight, because I am not lying; from the time when I came to know him in my youth, the love of God and fear of him increased in me, and right up until now, by God's favour, I have kept the faith.

45. What is more, let anyone laugh and taunt if he so wishes. I am not keeping silent, nor am I hiding the signs and wonders that were shown to me by the Lord many years before they happened, [he] who knew everything, even before the beginning of time.

46. Thus, I should give thanks unceasingly to God, who frequently forgave my folly and my negligence, in more than one instance so as not to

be violently angry with me, who am placed as his helper, and I did not easily assent to what had been revealed to me, as the Spirit was urging; and the Lord took pity on me thousands upon thousands of times, because he saw within me that I was prepared, but that I was ignorant of what to do in view of my situation; because many were trying to prevent this mission. They were talking among themselves behind my back, and saying: 'Why is this fellow throwing himself into danger among enemies who know not God?' Not from malice, but having no liking for it; likewise, as I myself can testify, they perceived my rusticity. And I was not quick to recognize the grace that was then in me; I now know that I should have done so earlier.

47. Now I have put it frankly to my brethren and co-workers, who have believed me because of what I have foretold and still foretell to strengthen and reinforce your faith. I wish only that you, too, would make greater and better efforts. This will be my pride, for 'a wise son makes a proud father'.

48. You know, as God does, how I went about among you from my youth in the faith of truth and in sincerity of heart. As well as to the heathen among whom I live, I have shown them trust and always show them trust. God knows I did not cheat any one of them, nor consider it, for the sake of God and his Church, lest I arouse them and [bring about] persecution for them and for all of us, and lest the Lord's name be blasphemed because of me, for it is written: 'Woe to the men through whom the name of the Lord is blasphemed.'

49. For even though I am ignorant in all things, nevertheless I attempted to safeguard some and myself also. And I gave back again to my Christian brethren and the virgins of Christ and the holy women the small unasked for gifts that they used to give me or some of their ornaments which they used to throw on the altar. And they would be offended with me because I did this. But in the hope of eternity, I safeguarded myself carefully in all things, so that they might not cheat me of my office of service on any pretext of dishonesty, and so that I should not in the smallest way provide any occasion for defamation or disparagement on the part of unbelievers.

50. What is more, when I baptized so many thousands of people, did I hope for even half a jot from any of them? [If so] Tell me, and I will give it back to you. And when the Lord ordained clergy everywhere by my humble means, and I freely conferred office on them, if I asked any of them anywhere even for the price of one shoe, say so to my face and I will give it back.

51. More, I spent for you so that they would receive me. And I went about among you, and everywhere for your sake, in danger, and as far as the outermost regions beyond which no one lived, and where no one had ever penetrated before, to baptize or to ordain clergy or to confirm people. Conscientiously and gladly I did all this work by God's gift for your salvation.

52. From time to time I gave rewards to the kings, as well as making payments to their sons who travel with me; notwithstanding which, they seized me with my companions, and that day most avidly desired to kill me. But my time had not yet come. They plundered everything they found on us anyway, and fettered me in irons; and on the fourteenth day the Lord freed me from their power, and whatever they had of ours was given back to us for the sake of God on account of the indispensable friends whom we had made before.

53. Also you know from experience how much I was paying to those who were administering justice in all the regions, which I visited often. I estimate truly that I distributed to them not less than the price of fifteen men, in order that you should enjoy my company and I enjoy yours, always, in God. I do not regret this nor do I regard it as enough. I am paying out still and I shall pay out more. The Lord has the power to grant me that I may soon spend my own self, for your souls.

54. Behold, I call on God as my witness upon my soul that I am not lying; nor would I write to you for it to be an occasion for flattery or selfishness, nor hoping for honour from any one of you. Sufficient is the honour which is not yet seen, but in which the heart has confidence. He who made the promise is faithful; he never lies.

55. But I see that even here and now, I have been exalted beyond measure by the Lord, and I was not worthy that he should grant me this, while I know most certainly that poverty and failure suit me better than wealth and delight (but Christ the Lord was poor for our sakes; I certainly am wretched and unfortunate; even if I wanted wealth I have no resources, nor is it my own estimation of myself, for daily I expect to be murdered or betrayed or reduced to slavery if the occasion arises. But I fear nothing, because of the promises of Heaven; for I have cast myself into the hands of Almighty God, who reigns everywhere. As the prophet says: 'Cast your burden on the Lord and he will sustain you.'

56. Behold now I commend my soul to God who is most faithful and for whom I perform my mission in obscurity, but he is no respecter of persons and he chose me for this service that I might be one of the least of his ministers.

57. For which reason I should make return for all that he returns me. But what should I say, or what should I promise to my Lord, for I, alone, can do nothing unless he himself vouchsafe it to me. But let him search my heart and [my] nature, for I crave enough for it, even too much, and I am ready for him to grant me that I drink of his chalice, as he has granted to others who love him.

58. Therefore may it never befall me to be separated by my God from his people whom he has won in this most remote land. I pray God that he gives me perseverance, and that he will deign that I should be a faithful witness for his sake right up to the time of my passing.

59. And if at any time I managed anything of good for the sake of my God whom I love, I beg of him that he grant it to me to shed my blood for his name with proselytes and captives, even should I be left unburied, or even were my wretched body to be torn limb from limb by dogs or savage beasts, or were it to be devoured by the birds of the air, I think, most surely, were this to have happened to me, I had saved both my soul and my body. For beyond any doubt on that day we shall rise again in the brightness of the sun, that is, in the glory of Christ Jesus our Redeemer, as children of the living God and co-heirs of Christ, made in his image; for we shall reign through him and for him and in him.

60. For the sun we see rises each day for us at [his] command, but it will never reign, neither will its splendour last, but all who worship it will come wretchedly to punishment. We, on the other hand, shall not die, who believe in and worship the true sun, Christ, who will never die, no more shall he die who has done Christ's will, but will abide for ever just as Christ abides for ever, who reigns with God the Father Almighty and with the Holy Spirit before the beginning of time and now and for ever and ever. Amen.

61. Behold over and over again I would briefly set out the words of my confession. I testify in truthfulness and gladness of heart before God and his holy angels that I never had any reason, except the Gospel and his promises, ever to have returned to that nation from which I had previously escaped with difficulty.

62. But I entreat those who believe in and fear God, whoever deigns to examine or receive this document composed by the obviously unlearned sinner Patrick in Ireland, that nobody shall ever ascribe to my ignorance any trivial thing that I achieved or may have expounded that was pleasing to God, but accept and truly believe that it would have been the gift of God. And this is my confession before I die. ∎

STUDY QUESTIONS

1. How did Patrick's slavery, servitude, and obscurity train him for his eventual mission?

2. A milestone in Patrick's life was the late night vision of a man named Victoricus, who beckoned him to return to Ireland. What milestone in your life has caused you to be 'sent forth'?

3. Patrick felt a very clear calling to the Irish people. For which neighborhood, city, people group, or other context might you feel called to plant house churches?

4. How can the concept of 'apostolic teams' help with effectively planting networks of house churches?

Chapter 22

THE TESTAMENT

FRANCIS OF ASSISI (AD 1181-1226)

Francis was born in the town of Assisi, Italy, about 60 miles northeast of Rome. In his early years, he worked for his father, a rich cloth merchant. At the age of 20, along with others that were conscripted, he went to battle defending his home town against neighboring Perrugia. Upon returning home, he was in poor health physically and emotionally. At 27, he reached a spiritual crisis, responding to a call to preach the kingdom of God and serve the world's poor and outcast. The following year, Francis, along with 11 companions, went to Rome to secure papal recognition from Innocent III of their newly formed order. Upon receiving recognition and ordination as priests, any ambivalence Francis may have felt toward the established church authorities vanished. While in Rome, he was deeply moved at the sight of beggars on the steps of St. Peter's Cathedral, so much so that he exchanged his clothes with one of them and spent the rest of the day begging. After selling some of his father's merchandise to finance his mission to the poor, he was quickly disinherited. Over the next few years, he and his associates, went abroad barefooted, two by two, speaking the message of Christ, calling people everywhere to repent, singing, helping the poor, assisting farmers with their labors, praying for the sick, and gaining a considerable following. They begged for their food and slept in hay lofts. And so was restored the concept of the traveling apostolic bands. The revitalization work of the Little Brothers, as they were called, has often been credited as having prevented the utter collapse of the corrupt medieval church. The text below was written shortly before Francis' death to combat what he perceived to be compromise within the movement. [The text was taken from Paschal Robinson (trans. and ed.)(1906), The Writings of Saint Francis of Assisi, The Dolphin Press. It is in the public domain].

The Lord gave to me, Brother Francis, thus to begin to do penance; for when I was in sin it seemed to me very bitter to see lepers, and the Lord Himself led me amongst them and I showed mercy to them. And when I left them, that which had seemed to me bitter was changed for me into sweetness of body and soul. And afterwards I remained a little and I left the world. And the Lord gave me so much faith in churches that I would simply pray and say thus: "We adore Thee Lord Jesus Christ here and in all Thy churches which are in the whole world, and we bless Thee because by Thy holy cross Thou hast redeemed the world."

After that the Lord gave me, and gives me, so much faith in priests who live according to the form of the holy Roman Church, on account of their order, that if they should persecute me, I would have recourse to them. And if I had as much wisdom as Solomon had, and if I should find poor priests of this world, I would not preach against their will in the parishes in which they live. And I desire to fear, love, and honor them and all others as my masters; and I do not wish to consider sin in them, for in them I see the Son of God and they are my masters.

And I do this because in this world, I see nothing corporally of the most high Son of God Himself except His most holy Body and Blood, which they receive and they alone administer to others. And I will that these most holy mysteries be honored and revered above all things and that they be placed in precious places. Wheresoever I find His most holy Names and written words in unseemly places, I wish to collect them, and I ask that they may be collected and put in a becoming place. And we ought to honor and venerate all theologians and those who minister to us the most holy Divine Words as those who minister to us spirit and life.

And when the Lord gave me some brothers, no one showed me what I ought to do, but the Most High Himself revealed to me that I should live according to the form of the holy Gospel. And I caused it to be written in few words and simply, and the Lord Pope confirmed it for me. And those who came to take this life upon themselves gave to the poor all that they might have and they were content with one tunic, patched within and without, by those who wished, with a cord and breeches, and we wished for no more.

We clerics said the Office like other clerics; the laics said the Paternoster, and we remained in the churches willingly enough. And we were simple and subject to all. And I worked with my hands and I wish to work and I wish firmly that all the other brothers should work at some labor which is compatible with honesty. Let those who know not [how to work] learn, not through desire to receive the price of labor but for the sake of example and to repel idleness. And when the price of labor is not given to us, let us have recourse to the table of the Lord, begging alms from door to door.

The Lord revealed to me this salutation, that we should say: "The Lord give thee peace." Let the brothers take care not to receive on any account churches, poor dwelling-places, and all other things that are constructed for them, unless they are as is becoming the holy poverty which we have promised in the Rule, always dwelling there as strangers and pilgrims.

I strictly enjoin by obedience on all the brothers that, wherever they may be, they should not dare, either themselves or by means of some interposed person, to ask any letter in the Roman curia either for a church or for any other place, nor under pretext of preaching, nor on account of their bodily persecution; but, wherever they are not received let them flee to another land to do penance, with the blessing of God.

And I wish to obey the minister general of this brotherhood strictly and the guardian whom it may please him to give me. And I wish to be so captive in his hands that I cannot go or act beyond his obedience and his will because he is my master. And although I am simple and infirm, I desire withal always to have a cleric who will perform the office with me as it is contained in the Rule.

And let all the other brothers be bound to obey their guardian and to perform the office according to the Rule. And those who may be found not performing the office according to the Rule and wishing to change it in some way, or who are not Catholics, let all the brothers wherever they may be, if they find one of these, be bound by obedience to present him to the custos who is nearest to the place where they have found him.

And the custos shall be strictly bound, by obedience, to guard him strongly day and night as a prisoner so that he cannot be snatched from his hands until he shall personally place him in the hands of his minister. And the minister shall be firmly bound by obedience to send him by such brothers as shall watch him day and night like a prisoner until they shall present him to the Lord of Ostia, who is master protector, and corrector of this brotherhood.

And let not the brothers say: This is another Rule; for this is a remembrance, a warning, and an exhortation and my Testament which I, little Brother Francis, make for you, my blessed brothers, in order that we may observe in a more Catholic way the Rule which we have promised to the Lord. And let the minister general and all the other ministers and custodes be bound by obedience not to add to these words or to take from them.

And let them always have this writing with them beside the Rule. And in all the Chapters they hold, when they read the Rule let them read these words also. And I strictly enjoin on all my brothers, clerics and laics, by obedience, not to put glosses on the Rule or on these words saying: Thus they ought to be understood; but as the Lord has given me to speak and to write the Rule and these words simply and purely, so shall you understand them simply and purely and with holy operation observe them until the end.

And whoever shall observe these things may he be filled in heaven with the blessing of the Most High Father and may he be filled on earth with blessing of His Beloved Son together with the Holy Ghost, the Paraclete, and all the Powers of heaven and all the saints. And I, Brother Francis, your little one and servant, in so far as I am able, I confirm to you within and without this most holy blessing. Amen. ■

STUDY QUESTIONS

1. How does Francis view poverty, labor, and humility?
2. How does Francis view clergy, hierarchy, and church buildings?
3. Though Francis embraced the established church of his day, he sought its renewal from within. Would this work in your context?

Chapter 23

YET THE LORD'S POWER WENT OVER ALL

GEORGE FOX (1624-1691)

George Fox, the founder of the Quakers (also called the Society of Friends), grew up in a religious home. He spent his late teenage years and his early twenties traveling England and sharing his concerns about the practices of the established Christian churches, but without any real success. After a profound experience standing atop Pendle Hill, in which he saw a great crowd of people that would receive his message, he began to gain a hearing rapidly through his preaching efforts. Many of the early Quakers went forth two by two throughout England and eventually all across the world. They drew 20,000 converts in the first five years of their mission and attracted severe persecution both from religious and civic authorities. The Quakers emphasized the work of the Holy Spirit in a believer's life, the inner light and seed in each person, personal holiness, open Spirit-led believers' meetings, complete non-violence, solidarity with the poor and ordinary laborers, equality among the genders, and criticism of both Catholic and Protestant churches with their 'steeple-houses' and paid clergy. To eliminate false divisions between sacred and secular places of worship, they preached the gospel of Christ in the open air and met in people's homes for small group gatherings. [The public domain text below is a series of excerpts from George Fox - An Autobiography, edited with an Introduction and Notes by Rufus M. Jones (1908)].

ON RECEIVING GOD'S MANDATE ON PENDLE HILL

As we travelled we came near a very great hill, called Pendle Hill, and I was moved of the Lord to go up to the top of it; which I did with difficulty, it was so very steep and high. When I was come to the top, I saw the sea bordering upon Lancashire. From the top of this hill the Lord let me see in what places he had a great people to be gathered.

ON PREACHING THE GOSPEL

I directed them to the Divine Light of Christ, and His Spirit in their hearts, which would let them see all the evil thoughts, words, and actions that they had thought, spoken, and acted; by which Light they might see their sin, and also their Saviour Christ Jesus to save them from their sins. This I told them was their first step to peace, even to stand still in the Light that showed them their sins and transgressions; by which they might come to see they were in the fall of old Adam, in darkness and death, strangers to the covenant of promise, and without God in the world; and by the same Light they might see Christ that died for them to be their Redeemer and Saviour, and their way to God.

ON THE VICTORIOUS ADVANCE OF GOD'S WORD

Since these meetings have been settled, and all the faithful in the power of God, who are heirs of the gospel, have met together in the power of God, which is their authority, to perform service to the Lord, many mouths have been opened in thanksgiving and praise, and many have blessed the Lord God, that ever He sent me forth in this service. For now all coming to have a concern and care for God's honour and glory, and His name, which they profess, be not blasphemed; and to see that all who profess the Truth walk in the Truth, in righteousness and in holiness, as becomes the house of God, and that all order their conversation aright, that they may see the salvation of God; they may all see and know, possess and partake of, the government of Christ, of the increase of which there is to be no end. Thus the Lord's everlasting renown and praise are set up in the heart of every one that is faithful; so that we can say the gospel order established amongst us is not of man, nor by man, but of and by Jesus Christ, in and through the Holy Ghost. This order of the gospel, which is not of man nor by man, but from Christ, the heavenly man, is above all the orders of men in the fall, whether Jews, Gentiles, or apostate Christians, and will remain when they are gone. For the power of God, which is the everlasting gospel, was before the devil was, and will be and remain forever. And as the everlasting gospel was preached in the apostles' days to all nations, that all nations might, through the divine power which brings life and immortality to light, come into the order of it, so now the everlasting gospel is to be, and is, preached again, as John the divine foresaw it should be, to all nations, kindreds, tongues, and people.

ON ORGANIZING MEETINGS ACROSS THE NATION

Then I was moved of the Lord to recommend the setting up of five monthly meetings of men and women in the city of London (besides the women's meetings and the quarterly meetings), to take care of God's glory, and to admonish and exhort such as walked disorderly or carelessly, and not according to Truth. For whereas Friends had had only quarterly meetings, now Truth was spread, and Friends were grown more numerous, I was moved to recommend the setting up of monthly meetings throughout the nation. And the Lord opened to me what I must do, and how the men's and women's monthly and quarterly meetings should be ordered and established in this and in other nations; and that I should write to those where I did not come, to do the same.

* * *

For meetings were very large, Friends coming to them from far and near; and other people flocking in. The powerful presence of the Lord was preciously felt amongst us. Many of the world were reached, convinced, and gathered to the Truth; the Lord's flock was increased; and Friends were greatly refreshed and comforted in feeling the love of God. Oh the brokenness that was amongst them in the flowings of life! so that, in the power and Spirit of the Lord, many together broke out into singing, even with audible voices, making melody in their hearts.

* * *

I answered to this purpose: "Christ's promise was not to discourage many from meeting together in His name, but to encourage the few, that the fewest might not forbear to meet because of their fewness. But if Christ hath promised to manifest His presence in the midst of so small an assembly, where but two or three are gathered in His name, how much more would His presence abound where two or three hundred are gathered in His name?"

ON CHALLENGING THE RELIGIOUS STATUS QUO

Now there were many old people who went into the chapel and looked out at the windows, thinking it a strange thing to see a man preach on a hill, and not in their church, as they called it; whereupon I was moved to open to the people that the steeple-house, and the ground whereon it stood were no more holy than that mountain; and that those temples, which they called the dreadful houses of God were not set up by the command of God and of Christ; nor their priests called, as Aaron's priesthood was; nor their tithes appointed by God, as those amongst the Jews were; but that Christ was come, who ended both the temple and its worship, and the priests and their tithes; and that all should now hearken unto Him; for He said, "Learn of me"; and God said of Him, "This is my beloved Son, in whom I am well pleased; hear ye Him." I declared unto them that the Lord God had sent me to preach the everlasting gospel and Word of life amongst them, and to bring them off from all these temples, tithes, priests, and rudiments of the world, which had been instituted since the apostles' days, and had been set up by such as had erred from the Spirit and power the apostles were in. Very largely was I opened at this meeting, and the Lord's convincing power accompanied my ministry, and reached the hearts of the people, whereby many were convinced; and all the teachers of that congregation (who were many) were convinced of God's everlasting truth.

ON SOCIAL JUSTICE

When I was at Mansfield, there was a sitting of the justices, about hiring of servants; and it was upon me from the Lord, to go and speak to the justices, that they should not oppress the servants in their wages...I exhorted the servants, to do their duties, and serve honestly. And they all received my exhortation kindly; for I was moved of the Lord therein. Moreover I was moved to go to several courts and steeple-houses at Mansfield, and other places, to warn them to leave off oppression and oaths, and to turn from deceit to the Lord, and do justly.

* * *

In the morning, after I had spoken to them again concerning the meeting, as I walked upon a bank by the house, there came several poor travellers, asking relief, who I saw were in necessity; and they gave them nothing, but said they were cheats. It grieved me to see such hard-heartedness amongst professors; whereupon, when they were gone in to their breakfast, I ran after the poor people about a quarter of a mile, and gave them some money.

* * *

We stayed there the weekly meeting, which was a large one, and the power and life of God appeared greatly in it. Afterwards we passed to a province meeting, which lasted two days, there being one about the poor, and another meeting more general; in which a mighty power of the Lord appeared. Truth was livingly declared, and Friends were much refreshed therein.

ON PHYSICAL AND EMOTIONAL TRIALS

I was so exceeding weak, I was hardly able to get on or off my horse's back; but my spirit being earnestly engaged in the work the Lord had concerned me in and sent me forth about, I travelled on therein, notwithstanding the weakness of my body, having confidence in the Lord, that He would carry me through, as He did by His power.

* * *

As I was walking down a hill, a great weight and oppression fell upon my spirit. I got on my horse again, but the weight remained so that I was hardly able to ride. At length we came to Rochester, but I was much spent, being so extremely laden and burthened with the world's spirits, that my life was oppressed under them. I got with difficulty to Gravesend, and lay at an inn there; but could hardly either eat or sleep.

* * *

Here I lay, exceedingly weak, and at last lost both hearing and sight. Several Friends came to me from London: and I told them that I should be a sign to such as would not see, and such as would not hear the Truth. In this condition I continued some time. Several came about me; and though I could not see their persons, I felt and discerned their spirits, who were honest-hearted, and who were not. Diverse Friends who practiced physic came to see me, and would have given me medicines, but I was not to meddle with any; for I was sensible I had a travail to go through; and therefore desired none but solid, weighty Friends might be about me.

Under great sufferings and travails, sorrows and oppressions, I lay for several weeks, whereby I was brought so low and weak in body that few thought I could live. Some that were with me went away, saying they would not see me die; and it was reported both in London and in the country that I was deceased; but I felt the Lord's power inwardly supporting me. When they that were about me had given me up to die, I spoke to them to get a coach to carry me to Gerrard Roberts's, about twelve miles off, for I found it was my place to go thither. I had now recovered a little glimmering of sight, so that I could discern the people and fields as I went, and that was all. When I came to Gerrard's, he was very weak, and I was moved to speak to him, and encourage him.

After I had stayed about three weeks there, it was with me to go to Enfield. Friends were afraid of my removing; but I told them I might safely go. When I had taken my leave of Gerrard, and was come to Enfield, I went first to visit Amor Stoddart, who lay very weak and almost speechless. I was moved to tell him that he had been faithful as a man, and faithful to God, and that the immortal Seed of life was his crown. Many more words I was moved to speak to him, though I was then so weak I was hardly able to stand; and within a few days after, Amor died.

I went to the widow Dry's, at Enfield, where I lay all that winter, warring in spirit with the evil spirits of the world, that warred against Truth and Friends. For there were great persecutions at this time; some meeting-houses were pulled down, and many were broken up by soldiers. Sometimes a troop of horse, or a company of foot came; and some broke their swords, carbines, muskets, and pikes, with beating Friends; and many they wounded, so that their blood lay in the streets.

Amongst others that were active in this cruel persecution at London, my old adversary, Colonel Kirby, was one. With a company of foot, he went to break up several meetings; and he would often inquire for me at the meetings he broke up. One time as he went over the water to Horsleydown, there happening some scuffle between some of his soldiers and some of the watermen, he bade his men fire at them. They did so, and killed some.

I was under great sufferings at this time, beyond what I have words to declare. For I was brought into the deep, and saw all the religions of the world, and people that lived in them. And I saw the priests that held them up; who were as a company of men-eaters, eating up the people like bread, and gnawing the flesh from off their bones. But as for true religion, and worship, and ministers of God, alack! I saw there was none amongst those of the world that pretended to it. Though it was a cruel, bloody, persecuting time, yet the Lord's power went over all, His everlasting Seed prevailed; and Friends were made to stand firm and faithful in the Lord's power.

ON PERSECUTION

On a lecture-day I was moved to go to the steeple-house at Ulverstone, where were abundance of professors, priests, and people. I went near to priest Lampitt, who was blustering on in his preaching. After the Lord had opened my mouth to speak, John Sawrey, the justice, came to me and said that if I would speak according to the Scriptures, I should speak. I admired him for speaking so to me, and told him I would speak according to the Scriptures, and bring the Scriptures to prove what I had to say; for I had something to speak to Lampitt and to them. Then he said I should not speak, contradicting himself, for he had said just before that I should speak if I would speak according to the Scriptures.

The people were quiet, and heard me gladly, till this Justice Sawrey (who was the first stirrer-up of cruel persecution in the north) incensed them against me, and set them on to hale, beat, and bruise me. But now on a sudden the people were in a rage, and fell upon me in the steeple-house before his face, knocked me down, kicked me, and trampled upon me. So great was the uproar, that some tumbled over their seats for fear. At last he came and took me from the people, led me out of the steeple-house, and put me into the hands of the constables and other officers, bidding them whip me, and put me out of the town.

They led me about a quarter of a mile, some taking hold by my collar, some by my arms and shoulders; and they shook and dragged me along. Many friendly people being come to the market, and some to the steeple-house to hear me, diverse of these they knocked down also, and broke their heads so that the blood ran down from several; and Judge Fell's son running after to see what they would do with me, they threw him into a ditch of water, some of them crying, "Knock the teeth out of his head." When they had haled me to the common moss-side, a multitude following, the constables and other officers gave me some blows over my back with their willow rods, and thrust me among the rude multitude, who, having furnished themselves with staves, hedge-stakes, holm or holly bushes, fell upon me, and beat me on my head, arms, and shoulders, till they had deprived me of sense; so that I fell down upon the wet common.

When I recovered again, and saw myself lying in a watery common, and the people standing about me, I lay still a little while, and the power of the Lord sprang through me, and the eternal refreshings revived me; so that I stood up again in the strengthening power of the eternal God, and stretching out my arms toward them, I said, with a loud voice, "Strike again; here are my arms, my head, and my cheeks." There was in the company a mason, a professor, but a rude fellow, who with his walking rule-staff gave me a blow with all his might just over the back of my hand, as it was stretched out; with which blow my hand was so bruised, and my arm so benumbed, that I could not draw it to me again. Some of the people cried, "He hath spoiled his hand for ever having the use of it any more." But I looked at it in the love of God (for I was in the love of God to all that persecuted me), and after awhile the Lord's power sprang through me again, and through my hand and arm, so that in a moment I recovered strength in my hand and arm in the sight of them all. Then they began to fall out among themselves. ∎

STUDY QUESTIONS

1. What do you make of Fox's challenge to the religious status quo?
2. The Quakers separated from the established churches of the day. What are the pros and cons of working inside, outside, or alongside the established churches today for the house church movement?

Chapter 24

A PLAIN ACCOUNT OF THE PEOPLE CALLED METHODISTS

JOHN WESLEY (1703-1791)

John Wesley was an Anglican priest and began his religious career in various parishes. He eventually returned to Oxford and, along with his brother Charles and friend George Whitefield, began a small group for accountability, prayer, Bible study, communion, and works of charity. After an unfruitful period as a missionary in America, Wesley returned to England in a deep spiritual crisis. Following a series of inner experiences of spiritual empowerment, Wesley followed Whitefield's example of preaching outdoors to crowds. Thus began the Methodist movement, which became a key element in the First Great Awakening. Over the next five decades, Wesley gathered thousands of converts from the outdoor preaching efforts of the Methodist circuit riders into home 'cell groups' of 6 to 12 people for accountability, discipleship, care for the sick, and collection of money for the poor. At John Wesley's death, the Methodist movement in Britain and the United States was composed of approximately 10,000 home cell groups and over 100,000 people. Though not a pure house church network, the Methodist movement shared many similar characteristics. [The following full text of A Plain Account of the People Called Methodists is in the public domain. Numbered subtitles in bold print below do not appear in the original text and have been inserted here for study purposes by the Editor].

1. SMALL BEGINNINGS

Reverend and Dear Sir,

Some time since, you desired an account of the whole economy of the people commonly called Methodists. And you received a true, (as far as it went), but not a full, account. To supply what I think was wanting in that, I send you this account, that you may know, not only their practice on every head, but likewise the reasons whereon it is grounded, the occasion of every step they have taken, and the advantages reaped thereby.

But I must premise, that as they had not the least expectation, at first, of any thing like what has since followed, so they had no previous design or plan at all; but every thing arose just as the occasion offered. They saw or felt some impending or pressing evil, or some good end necessary to be pursued. And many times they fell unawares on the very thing which secured the good, or removed the evil. At other times, they consulted on the most probable means, following only common sense and Scripture: Though they generally found, in looking back, something in Christian antiquity likewise, very nearly parallel thereto.

About ten years ago, my brother and I were desired to preach in many parts of London. We had no view therein, but, so far as we were able, (and we knew God could work by whomsoever it pleased him,) to convince those who would hear what true Christianity was, and to persuade them to embrace it. The points we chiefly insisted upon were four:

First, that orthodoxy, or right opinions, is, at best, but a very slender part of religion, if it can be allowed to be any part of it at all; that neither does religion consist in negatives, in bare harmlessness of any kind; nor merely in externals, in doing good, or using the means of grace, in works of piety (so called) or of charity; that it is nothing short of, or different from, "the mind that was in Christ;" the image of God stamped upon the heart; inward righteousness, attended with the peace of God; and "joy in the Holy Ghost." Secondly , that the only way under heaven to this religion is to "repent and believe the gospel;" or, (as the Apostle words it), "repentance towards God, and faith in our Lord Jesus Christ." Thirdly, that by this faith, "he that worketh not, but believeth on him that justifieth the ungodly, is justified freely by his grace, through the redemption which is in Jesus Christ." And, lastly, that "being justified by faith," we taste of the heaven to which we are going; we are holy and happy; we tread down sin and fear, and "sit in heavenly places with Christ Jesus."

2. THE NEED FOR CHRISTIAN FELLOWSHIP

Many of those who heard this began to cry out that we brought "strange things to their ears;" that this was doctrine which they never heard before, or at least never regarded. They "searched the Scriptures, whether these things were so," and acknowledged "the truth as it is in Jesus." Their hearts also were influenced as well as their understandings, and they determined to follow "Jesus Christ, and him crucified." Immediately they were surrounded with difficulties; — all the world rose up against them; neighbors, strangers, acquaintance, relations, friends, began to cry out again, "Be not righteous overmuch; why shouldest thou destroy thyself?" Let not "much religion make thee mad."

One, and another, and another came to us, asking, what they should do, being distressed on every side; as every one strove to weaken, and none to strengthen, their hands in God. We advised them, "Strengthen you one another. Talk together as often as you can. And pray earnestly with and for one another, that you may 'endure to the end, and be saved.'" Against this advice we presumed there could be no objection; as being grounded on the plainest reason, and on so many scriptures both of the Old Testament and New, that it would be tedious to recite them. They said, "But we want you likewise to talk with us often, to direct and quicken us in our way, to give us the advices which you well know we need, and to pray with us, as well as for us." I asked, Which of you desire this? Let me know your names and places of abode. They did so. But I soon found they were too many for me to talk with severally so often as they wanted it. So I told them, "If you will all of you come together every Thursday, in the evening, I will gladly spend some time with you in prayer and give you the best advice I can."

Thus arose, without any previous design on either side what was afterwards called a 'Society'; a very innocent name, and very common in London, for any number of people associating themselves together. The thing proposed in their associating themselves together was obvious to every one. They wanted to "flee from the wrath to come," and to assist each other in so doing. They therefore united themselves "in order to pray together, to receive the word of exhortation, and to watch over one another in love, that they might help each other to work out their salvation." There is one only condition previously required in those who desire admission into this society, — "a desire to flee from the wrath to come, to be saved from their sins." They now likewise agreed, that as many of them as had an opportunity would meet together every Friday, and spend the dinner hour in crying to God, both for each other, and for all mankind.

It quickly appeared, that their thus uniting together answered the end proposed therein. In a few months, the far greater part of those who had begun to "fear God, and work righteousness," but were not united together, grew faint in their minds, and fell back into what they were before. Meanwhile the far greater part of those who were thus united together continued "striving to enter in at the strait gate," and to "lay hold on eternal life." Upon reflection, I could not but observe, this is the very thing which was from the beginning of Christianity. In the earliest times, those whom God had sent forth "preached the gospel to every creature." And the *oi akroatai*, "the body of hearers," were mostly either Jews or Heathens.

But as soon as any of these were so convinced of the truth, as to forsake sin and seek the gospel salvation, they immediately joined them together, took an account of their names, advised them to watch over each other, and met these *kathcoumenoi*, "catechumens," (as they were then called,) apart from the great congregation, that they might instruct, rebuke, exhort, and pray with them, and for them, according to their several necessities. But it was not long before an objection was made to this, which had not once entered into my thought: — "Is not this making a schism? Is not the joining these people together, gathering Churches out of Churches?"

It was easily answered, if you mean only gathering people out of buildings called churches, it is. But if you mean, dividing Christians from Christians, and so destroying Christian fellowship, it is not. For (1.) These were not Christians before they were thus joined. Most of them were barefaced Heathens. (2.) Neither are they Christians, from whom you suppose them to be divided. You will not look me in the face and say they are. What! drunken Christians! cursing and swearing Christians! lying Christians! cheating Christians! If these are Christians at all, they are devil

Christians, as the poor Malabarians term them. (3.) Neither are they divided any more than they were before, even from these wretched devil Christians. They are as ready as ever to assist them, and to perform every office of real kindness towards them. (4.) If it be said, "But there are some true Christians in the parish, and you destroy the Christian fellowship between these and them"; I answer, That which never existed, cannot be destroyed. But the fellowship you speak of never existed. Therefore it cannot be destroyed. Which of those true Christians had any such fellowship with these? Who watched over them in love? Who marked their growth in grace? Who advised and exhorted them from time to time? Who prayed with them and for them, as they had need?

This, and this alone, is Christian fellowship: But, alas! where is it to be found? Look east or west, north or south; name what parish you please: Is this Christian fellowship there? Rather, are not the bulk of the parishioners a mere rope of sand? What Christian connection is there between them? What intercourse in spiritual things? What watching over each other's souls? What bearing of one another's burdens? What a mere jest is it then, to talk so gravely of destroying what never was! The real truth is just the reverse of this: We introduce Christian fellowship where it was utterly destroyed. And the fruits of it have been peace, joy, love, and zeal for every good word and work.

3. THE DEVELOPMENT OF 'CLASSES'

But as much as we endeavored to watch over each other, we soon found some who did not live the gospel. I do not know that any hypocrites were crept in; for indeed there was no temptation: But several grew cold, and gave way to the sins which had long easily beset them. We quickly perceived there were many ill consequences of suffering these to remain among us. It was dangerous to others; inasmuch as all sin is of an infectious nature. It brought such a scandal on their brethren as exposed them to what was not properly the reproach of Christ. It laid a stumbling-block in the way of others, and caused the truth to be evil spoken of. We groaned under these inconveniences long, before a remedy could be found. The people were scattered so wide in all parts of the town, from Wapping to Westminster, that I could not easily see what the behavior of each person in his own neighborhood was: So that several disorderly walkers did much hurt before I was apprised of it.

At length, while we were thinking of quite another thing, we struck upon a method for which we have cause to bless God ever since. I was talking with several of the society in Bristol concerning the means of paying the debts there, when one stood up and said, "Let every member of the society give a penny a week till all are paid." Another answered, "But many of them are poor, and cannot afford to do it." "Then," said he, "put eleven of the poorest with me; and if they can give anything, well: I will call on them weekly; and if they can give nothing, I will give for them as well as for myself. And each of you call on eleven of your neighbors weekly; receive what they give, and make up what is wanting." It was done.

In a while, some of these informed me, they found such and such an one did not live as he ought. It struck me immediately, "This is the thing; the very thing we have wanted so long." I called together all the Leaders of the classes, (so we used to term them and their companies,) and desired, that each would make a particular inquiry into the behavior of those whom he saw weekly. They did so. Many disorderly walkers were detected. Some turned from the evil of their ways. Some were put away from us. Many saw it with fear, and rejoiced unto God with reverence. As soon as possible, the same method was used in London and all other places. Evil men were detected, and reproved. They were born with for a season. If they forsook their sins, we received them gladly; if they obstinately persisted therein, it was openly declared that they were not of us. The rest mourned and prayed for them, and yet rejoiced, that, as far as in us lay, the scandal was rolled away from the society.

It is the business of a Leader, (1.) To see each person in his class, once a week at the least, in order to inquire how their souls prosper; to advise, reprove, comfort, or exhort, as occasion may require; to receive what they are willing to give, toward the relief of the poor. (2.) To meet the Minister and the Stewards of the society, in order to inform the Minister of any that are sick, or of any that are disorderly and will not be reproved; to pay to the Stewards what they have received of their several classes in the week preceding. At first they visited each person at his own house; but this was soon found not so expedient. And that on many accounts: (1.) It took up more time than most of the Leaders had to spare. (2.) Many persons lived with masters, mistresses, or relations, who would not suffer them to be thus visited. (3.) At the houses of those who were not so averse, they often had no opportunity of speaking to them but in company. And this did not at all answer the end proposed, — of exhorting, comforting, or reproving. (4.) It frequently happened that one affirmed what another denied. And this could not be cleared up without seeing them together. (5.) Little misunderstandings and quarrels of various kinds frequently arose among relations or neighbors; effectually to remove which, it was needful to see them all face to face. Upon all these considerations it was agreed, that those of each class should meet al together.

And by this means, a more full inquiry was made into the behavior of every person. Those who could not be visited at home, or no otherwise than in company, had the same advantage with others. Advice or reproof was given as need required, quarrels made up, misunderstandings removed: And after an hour or two spent in this labor of love, they concluded with prayer and thanksgiving. It can scarce be conceived what advantages have been reaped from this little prudential regulation. Many now happily experienced that Christian fellowship of which they had not so much as an idea before.

They began to "bear one another's burdens," and naturally to "care for each other." As they had daily a more intimate acquaintance with, so they had a more endeared affection for, each other. And "speaking the truth in love, they grew up into Him in all things, who is the Head, even Christ; from whom the whole body, fitly joined together, and compacted by that which every joint supplied, according to the effectual working in the measure of every part, increased unto the edifying itself in love."

But notwithstanding all these advantages, many were at first extremely averse to meeting thus. Some, viewing it in a wrong point of light, not as a privilege, (indeed an invaluable one), but rather a restraint, disliked it on that account, because they did not love to be restrained in anything. Some were ashamed to speak before company. Others honestly said, "I do not know why; but I do not like it." Some objected, "There were no such meetings when I came into the society first: And why should there now? I do not understand these things, and this changing one thing after another continually." It was easily answered: It is pity but they had been at first. But we knew not then either the need or the benefit of them. Why we use them, you will readily understand, if you read over the rules of the society. That with regard to these little prudential helps we are continually changing one thing after another, is not a weakness or fault, as you imagine, but a peculiar advantage which we enjoy. By this means we declare them all to be merely prudential, not essential, not of divine institution.

We prevent, so far as in us lies, their growing formal or dead. We are always open to instruction; willing to be wiser everyday than we were before, and to change whatever we can change for the better. Another objection was, "There is no scripture for this, for classes and I know not what." I answer, (1.) There is no scripture against it. You cannot show one text that forbids them. (2.) There is much scripture for it, even all those texts which enjoin the substance of those various duties whereof this is only an indifferent circumstance, to be determined by reason and experience. (3.) You seem not to have observed, that the Scripture, in most points, gives only general rules; and leaves the particular circumstances to be adjusted by the common sense of mankind. The Scripture, for instance, gives that general rule, "Let all things be done decently and in order." But common sense is to determine, on particular occasions, what order and decency require.

So, in another instance, the Scripture lays it down as a general, standing direction: "Whether ye eat or drink, or whatever ye do, do all to the glory of God." But it is common prudence which is to make the application of this, in a thousand particular cases. "But these," said another, "are all man's inventions." This is but the same objection in another form. And the same answer will suffice for any reasonable person. These are man's inventions. And what then? That is, they are methods which men have found, by reason and common sense, for the more effectually applying several Scripture rules, couched in general terms, to particular occasions. They spoke far more plausibly than these, who said, "The thing is well enough in itself. But the Leaders are insufficient for the work: They have neither gifts nor graces for such an employment." I answer, (1.) Yet such Leaders as they are, it is plain God has blessed their labor. (2.) If any of these is remarkably wanting in gifts or grace, he is soon taken notice of and removed. (3.) If you know any such, tell it to me, not to others, and I will endeavor to exchange him for a better. (4.) It may be hoped they will all be better than they are, both by experience and observation, and by the advices given them by the Minister every Tuesday night, and the prayers (then in particular) offered up for them.

4. HUNGERING FOR MORE

About this time, I was informed that several persons in Kingswood frequently met together at the school; and, when they could spare the time, spent the greater part of the night in prayer, and praise, and thanksgiving. Some advised me to put an end to this; but, upon weighing the thing thoroughly, and comparing it with the practice of the ancient Christians, I could see no cause to forbid it. Rather, I believed it might be made of more general use. So I sent them word, I designed to watch with them on the Friday nearest the full moon, that we might have light thither and back again. I gave public notice of this the Sunday before, and, withal, that I intended to preach; desiring they, and they only, would meet me there, who could do it without prejudice to their business or families. On Friday abundance of people came. I began preaching between eight and nine; and we continued till a little beyond the noon of night, singing, praying, and praising God.

This we have continued to do once a month ever since, in Bristol, London, and Newcastle, as well as Kingswood; and exceeding great are the blessings we have found therein: It has generally been an extremely solemn season; when the word of God sunk deep into the heart, even of those who till then knew him not. If it be said, "This was only owing to the novelty of the thing, (the circumstance which still draws such multitudes together at those seasons,) or perhaps to the awful silence of the night:" I am not careful to answer in this matter. Be it so: However, the impression then made on many souls has never since been effaced. Now, allowing that God did make use either of the novelty or any other indifferent circumstance, in order to bring sinners to repentance, yet they are brought. And herein let us rejoice together. Nay, may I not put the case farther yet? If I can probably conjecture, that, either by the novelty of this ancient custom, or by any other indifferent circumstance, it is in my power to "save a soul from death, and hide a multitude of sins," am I clear before God if I do it not, if I do not snatch that brand out of the burning?

As the society increased, I found it required still greater care to separate the precious from the vile. In order to this, I determined, at least once in three months, to talk with every member myself, and to inquire at their own mouths, as well as of their Leaders and neighbors, whether they grew in grace and in the knowledge of our Lord Jesus Christ. At these seasons I likewise particularly inquire whether there be any misunderstanding or difference among them; that every hindrance of peace and brotherly love may be taken out of the way. To each of those of whose seriousness and good conversation I found no reason to doubt, I gave a testimony under my own hand, by writing their name on a ticket prepared for that purpose; every ticket implying as strong a recommendation of the person as whom it was given as if I had wrote at length, "I believe the bearer hereof to be one that fears God and works righteousness." Those who bore these tickets, (these *sumbola* or *tesserae*, as the ancients termed them, being of just the same force with the *epistolai sustatikai*, commendatory letters mentioned by the Apostle), wherever they came, were acknowledged by their brethren, and received with all cheerfulness. These were likewise of use in other respects. By these it was easily distinguished, when the society were to meet apart, who were members of it, and who not. These also supplied us with a quiet and inoffensive method of removing any disorderly member. He has no new ticket at the quarterly visitation; (for so often the tickets are changed); and hereby it is immediately known that he is no longer of the community.

The thing which I was greatly afraid of all this time, and which I resolved to use every possible method of preventing, was, a narrowness of spirit, a party zeal, a being straitened in our own bowels; that miserable bigotry which makes many so unready to believe that there is any work of God but among themselves. I thought it might be a help against this, frequently to read, to all who were willing to hear, the accounts I received from time to time of the work which God is carrying on in the earth, both in our own and other countries not among us alone, but among those of various opinions and denominations. For this I allotted one evening in every month; and I find no cause to repent my labor. It is generally a time of strong consolation to those who love God, and all mankind for his sake; as well as of breaking down the partition-walls which either the craft of the devil or the folly of men has built up; and of encouraging every child of God to say, (O when shall it once be!) "Whosoever doeth the will of my Father which is in heaven, the same is my brother, and sister, and mother."

5. THE DEVELOPMENT OF 'BANDS'

By the blessing of God upon their endeavors to help one another, many found the pearl of great price. Being justified by faith, they had "peace with God, through our Lord Jesus Christ." These felt a more tender affection than before, to those who were partakers of like precious faith; and hence arose such a confidence in each other, that they poured out their souls into each other's bosom. Indeed they had great need so to do; for the war was not over, as they had supposed; but they had still to wrestle both with flesh and blood, and with principalities and powers: So that temptations were on every side; and often temptations of such a kind, as they knew not how to speak in a class; in which persons of every sort, young and old, men and women, met together. These, therefore, wanted some means of closer union; they wanted to pour out their hearts without reserve, particularly with regard to the sin which did still easily beset them, and the temptations which were most apt to prevail over them. And they were the more desirous of this, when they observed it was the express advice of an inspired writer: "Confess your faults one to another, and pray one for another, that ye may be healed." In compliance with their desire, I divided them into smaller companies; putting the married or single men, and married or single women, together.

The chief rules of these bands (that is, little companies; so that old English word signifies) run thus: — "In order to 'confess our faults one to another,' and pray one for another that we may be healed, we intend, (1.) To meet once a week, at the least. (2.) To come punctually at the hour appointed. (3.) To begin with singing or prayer. (4.) To speak each of us in order, freely and plainly, the true state of our soul, with the faults we have committed in thought, word, or deed, and the temptations we have felt since our last meeting. (5.) To desire some person among us (thence called a Leader) to speak his own state first, and then to ask the rest, in order, as many and as searching questions as may be, concerning their state, sins, and temptations." That their design in meeting might be the more effectually answered, I desired all the men-bands to meet me together every Wednesday evening, and the women on Sunday, that they might receive such particular instructions and exhortations as, from time to time, might appear to be most needful for them; that such prayers might be offered up to God, as their necessities should require; and praise returned to the Giver of every good gift, for whatever mercies they had received.

In order to increase in them a grateful sense of all his mercies, I desired that, one evening in a quarter, all the men in band, on a second, all the women, would meet; and on a third, both men and women together; that we might together "eat bread," as the ancient Christians did, "with gladness and singleness of heart." At these love-feasts (so we termed them, retaining the name, as well as the thing, which was in use from the beginning) our food is only a little plain cake and water. But we seldom return from them without being fed, not only with the "meat which perisheth," but with "that which endureth to everlasting life." Great and many are the advantages which have ever since flowed from this closer union of the believers with each other. They prayed for one another, that they might be healed of the faults they had confessed; and it was so. The chains were broken, the hands were burst in sunder, and sin had no more dominion over them. Many were delivered from the temptations out of which, till then, they found no way to escape. They were built up in our most holy faith. They rejoiced in the Lord more abundantly. They were strengthened in love, and more effectually provoked to abound in every good work.

But it was soon objected to the bands, (as to the classes before), "These were not at first. There is no Scripture for them. These are man's works, man's building, man's invention." I reply, as before, these are also prudential helps, grounded on reason and experience, in order to apply the general rules given in Scripture according to particular circumstances. An objection much more boldly and frequently urged, is, that "all these bands are mere Popery." I hope I need not pass a harder censure on those (most of them at least) who affirm this, than that they talk of they know not what; they betray in themselves the most gross and shameful ignorance. Do not they yet know, that the only Popish confession is, the confession made by a single person to a Priest? — and this itself is in nowise condemned by our Church; nay, she recommends it in some cases. Whereas, that we practice is, the confession of several persons conjointly, not to a Priest, but to each other. Consequently, it has no analogy at all to Popish confession. But the truth is, this is a stale objection, which many people make against anything they do not like. It is all Popery out of hand.

And yet while most of these who were thus intimately joined together, went on daily from faith to faith; some fell from the faith, either all at once, by falling into known, wilful sin; or gradually, and almost insensibly, by giving way in what they called little things; by sins of omission, by yielding to heart-sins, or by not watching unto prayer. The exhortations and prayers used among the believers did no longer profit these. They wanted advice and instructions suited to their case; which as soon as I observed, I separated them from the rest, and desired them to meet me apart on Saturday evenings. At this hour, all the hymns, exhortations, and prayers are adapted to their circumstances; being wholly suited to those who did see God, but have now lost sight of the light of his countenance; and who mourn after him, and refuse to be comforted till they know he has healed their backsliding. By applying both the threats and promises of God to these real, not nominal, penitents, and by crying to God in their behalf, we endeavored to bring them back to the great "Shepherd and Bishop of their souls;" not by any of the fopperies of the Roman Church, although, in some measure, countenanced by antiquity. In prescribing hair-shirts, and bodily austerities, we durst not follow even the ancient Church; although we had unawares, both in dividing *oi pistoi*, the believers, from the rest of the society, and in separating the penitents from them, and appointing a peculiar service for them.

Many of these soon recovered the ground they had lost. Yea, they rose higher than before; being more watchful than ever, and more meek and lowly, as well as stronger in the faith that worketh by love. They now outran the greater part of their brethren, continually walking in the light of God, and having fellowship with the Father, and with his Son Jesus Christ. I saw it might be useful to give some advices to all those who continued in the light of God's countenance, which the rest of their brethren did not want, and probably could not receive. So I desired a small number of such as appeared to be in this state, to spend an hour with me every Monday morning. My design was, not only to direct them how to press after perfection; to exercise their every grace, and improve every talent they had received; and to incite them to love one another more, and to watch more carefully over each other; but also to have a select company, to whom I might unbosom myself on all occasions, without reserve; and whom I could propose to all their brethren as a pattern of love, of holiness, and of good works.

They had no need of being incumbered with many rules; having the best rule of all in their hearts. No peculiar directions were therefore given to them, excepting only these three: — First . Let nothing spoken in this society be spoken again. Hereby we had the more full confidence in each other. Secondly . Every member agrees to submit to his Minister in all indifferent things. Thirdly . Every member will bring, once a week, all he can spare toward a common stock. Every one here has an equal liberty of speaking, there being none greater or less than another. I could say freely to these, when they were met together, "Ye may all prophesy one by one," (taking that word in its lowest sense,) "that all may learn, and all may be comforted." And I often found the advantage of such a free conversation, and that "in the multitude of counselors there is safety." Any who is inclined so to do is likewise encouraged to pour out his soul to God. And here especially we have found, that "the effectual fervent prayer of a righteous man availeth much."

6. LEADERSHIP AMONG THE METHODISTS

This is the plainest and clearest account I can give of the people commonly called Methodists. It remains only to give you a short account of those who serve their brethren in love. These are Leaders of classes and bands, (spoken of before), Assistants, Stewards, Visitors of the sick, and Schoolmasters. In the third part of the "Appeal," I have mentioned how we were led to accept of Lay-Assistants. Their office is, in the absence of the Minister, (1.) To expound every morning and evening. (2.) To meet the united society, the bands, the select society, and the penitents, once a week. (3.) To visit the classes once a quarter. (4.) To hear and decide all differences. (5.) To put the disorderly back on trial, and to receive on trial for the bands or society. (6.) To see that the Stewards, the Leaders, and the Schoolmasters faithfully discharge their several offices. (7.) To meet the Leaders of the bands and classes weekly, and the Stewards, and to overlook their accounts.

But, long before this, I felt the weight of a far different care, namely, care of temporal things. The quarterly subscriptions amounted, at a mean computation, to above three hundred pounds a year. This was to be laid out, partly in repairs, partly in other necessary expenses, and partly in paying debts. The weekly contributions fell little short of eight pounds a week; which was to be distributed as every one had need. And I was expected to take thought for all these things: But it was a burden I was not able to bear; so I chose out first one, then four, and after a time, seven, as prudent men as I knew, and desired them to take charge of these things upon themselves, that I might have no incumbrance of this kind. The business of these Stewards is: To manage the temporal things of the society. To receive the subscriptions and contributions. To expend what is needful from time to time. To send relief to the poor. To keep an exact account of all receipts and expenses. To inform the Minister if any of the rules of the society are not punctually observed. To tell the Preachers in love, if they think anything amiss, either in their doctrine or life.

The rules of the Stewards are, (1.) Be frugal. Save everything that can be saved honestly. (2.) Spend no more than you receive. Contract no debts. (3.) Have no long accounts. Pay everything within the week. (4.) Give none that asks relief, either an ill word or an ill look. Do not hurt them, if you cannot help. (5.) Expect no thanks from man. They met together at six every Thursday morning; consulted on the business which came before them; sent relief to the sick, as every one had need; and gave the remainder of what had been contributed each week to those who appeared to be in the most pressing want. So that all was concluded within the week; what was brought on Tuesday being constantly expended on Thursday.

I soon had the pleasure to find, that all these temporal things were done with the utmost faithfulness and exactness; so that my cares of this kind were at an end. I had only to revise the accounts, to tell them if I thought anything might be amended, and to consult how deficiencies might be supplied from time to time; for these were frequent and large, (so far were we from abundance), the income by no means answering the expenses. But that we might not faint, sometimes we had unforeseen helps in times of the greatest perplexity. At other times we borrowed larger or smaller sums: Of which the greatest part has since been repaid. But I owe some hundred pounds to this day. So much have I gained by preaching, the gospel!

But it was not long before the Stewards found a great difficulty with regard to the sick. Some were ready to perish before they knew of their illness; and when they did know, it was not in their power (being persons generally employed in trade) to visit them so often as they desired. When I was apprised of this, I laid the case at large before the whole society; showed how impossible it was for the Stewards to attend all that were sick in all parts of the town; desired the Leaders of classes would more carefully inquire, and more constantly inform them, who were sick; and asked, "Who among you is willing, as well as able, to supply this lack of service?" The next morning many willingly offered themselves. I chose six-and-forty of them, whom I judged to be of the most tender, loving spirit; divided the town into twenty-three parts, and desired two of them to visit the sick in each division.

It is the business of a Visitor of the sick: To see every sick person within his district thrice a week. To inquire into the state of their souls, and to advise them as occasion may require. To inquire into their disorders, and procure advice for them. To relieve them, if they are in want. To do any thing for them, which he (or she) can do. To bring in his accounts weekly to the Stewards. Upon reflection, I saw how exactly, in this also, we had copied after the primitive Church. What were the ancient Deacons? What was Phebe the Deaconess, but such a Visitor of the sick? I did not think it needful to give them any particular rules beside these that follow: — (1.) Be plain and open in dealing with souls. (2.) Be mild, tender, patient. (3.) Be cleanly in all you do for the sick. (4.) Be not nice. We have ever since had great reason to praise God for his continued blessing on this undertaking. Many lives have been saved, many sicknesses healed, much pain and want prevented or removed. Many heavy hearts have been made glad, many mourners comforted: And the Visitors have found, from Him whom they serve, a present reward for all their labor.

7. CARING FOR THE POOR AND SICK

But I was still in pain for many of the poor that were sick; there was so great expense, and so little profit. And first, I resolved to try, whether they might not receive more benefit in the hospitals. Upon the trial, we found there was indeed less expense, but no more good done, than before. I then asked the advice of several Physicians for them; but still it profited not. I saw the poor people pining away, and several families ruined, and that without remedy. At length I thought of a kind of desperate expedient. "I will prepare, and give them physic myself." For six or seven and twenty years, I had made anatomy and physic the diversion of my leisure hours; though I never properly studied them, unless; for a few months when I was going to America, where I imagined I might be of some service to those who had no regular Physician among them. I applied to it again. I took into my assistance an Apothecary, and an experienced Surgeon; resolving, at the same time, not to go out of my depth, but to leave all difficult and complicated cases to such Physicians as the patients should choose. I gave notice of this to the society; telling them, that all who were ill of chronical distempers (for I did not care to venture upon acute) might, if they pleased, come to me at such a time, and I would give them the best advice I could, and the best medicines I had.

Many came: (And so every Friday since:) Among the rest was one William Kirkman, a weaver, near Old Nichol-street. I asked him, "What complaint have you?" "O Sir," said he, "a cough, a very sore cough. I can get no rest day nor night." I asked, "How long have you had it?" He replied, "About threescore years: It began when I was eleven years old." I was nothing glad that this man should come first, fearing our not curing him might discourage others. However, I looked up to God, and said, "Take this three or four times a day. If it does you no good, it will do you no harm." He took it two or three days. His cough was cured, and has not returned to this day. Now, let candid men judge, does humility require me to deny a notorious fact? If not, which is vanity? to say, I by my own skill restored this man to health; or to say, God did it by his own almighty power? By what figure of speech this is called boasting, I know not. But I will yet no name to such a fact as this. I leave that to the Revelation Dr. Middleton. In five months, medicines were occasionally given to above five hundred persons. Several of these I never saw before; for I did not regard whether they were of the society or not. In that time seventy-one of these, regularly taking their medicines, and following the regimen prescribed, (which three in four would not do), were entirely cured of distempers long thought to be incurable. The whole expense of medicines during this time, was nearly forty pounds. We continued this ever since, and, by the blessing of God, with more and more success.

But I had for some years observed many who, although not sick, were not able to provide for themselves, and had no one who took care to provide for them: These were chiefly feeble, aged widows. I consulted with the Stewards, how they might be relieved. They all agreed, if we could keep them in one house, it would not only be far less expensive to us, but also far more comfortable for them. Indeed we had no money to begin; but we believed He would provide "who defendeth the cause of the widow:" So we took a lease of two little houses near; we fitted them up, so as to be warm and clean. We took in as many widows as we had room for, and provided them with things needful for the body; toward the expense of which I set aside, first, the weekly contributions of the bands, and then all that was collected at the Lord's Supper. It is true, this does not suffice: So that we are considerably in debt, on this account also. But we are persuaded, it will not always be so; seeing "the earth is the Lord's, and the fulness thereof."

In this (commonly called The Poor-house) we have now nine widows, one blind woman, two poor children, two upper-servants, a maid and a man. I might add, four or five Preachers; for I myself, as well as the other Preachers who are in town, diet with the poor, on the same food, and at the same table; and we rejoice herein, as a comfortable earnest of our eating bread together in our Father's kingdom. I have blessed God for this house ever since it began; but lately much more than ever. I honor these widows; for they "are widows indeed." So that it is not in vain, that, without any design of so doing, we have copied after another of the institutions of the Apostolic age. I can now say to all the world, "Come and see how these Christians love one another!"

8. CARING FOR CHILDREN

Another thing which had given me frequent concern was, the case of abundance of children. Some their parents could not afford to put to school: So they remained like "a wild ass's colt." Others were sent to school, and learned, at least, to read and write; but they learned all kind of vice at the same time: So that it had been better for them to have been without their knowledge, than to have bought it at so dear a price. At length I determined to have them taught in my own house, that they might have an opportunity of learning to read, write, and cast accounts, (if no more,) without being under almost a necessity of learning Heathenism at the same time: And after several unsuccessful trials, I found two such Schoolmasters as I wanted; men of honesty and of sufficient knowledge, who had talents for, and their hearts in, the work. They have now under their care near sixty children: The parents of some pay for their schooling; but the greater part, being very poor, do not; so that the expense is chiefly defrayed by voluntary contributions. We have of late clothed them too, as many as wanted. The rules of the school are these that follow:

First. No child is admitted under six years of age. Secondly. All the children are to be present at the morning sermon. Thirdly. They are at school from six to twelve, and from one to five. Fourthly. They have no play-days. Fifthly. No child is to speak in school, but to the masters. Sixthly. The child who misses two days in one week, without leave, is excluded the school. We appointed two Stewards for the school also. The business of these is, to receive the school subscriptions, and expend what is needful; to talk with each of the masters weekly; to pray with and exhort the children twice a week; to inquire diligently, whether they grow in grace and in learning, and whether the rules are punctually observed; every Tuesday morning, in conjunction with the masters, to exclude those children that do not observe the rules; every Wednesday morning, to meet with and exhort their parents, to train them up at horne in the ways of God. A happy change was soon observed in the children, both with regard to their tempers and behavior. They learned reading, writing; and arithmetic swiftly; and at the same time they were diligently instructed in the sound principles of religion, and earnestly exhorted to fear God, and work out their own salvation.

9. BENEVOLENT FUNDS FOR THE NEEDY

A year or two ago, I observed among many a distress of another kind. They frequently wanted, perhaps in order to carry on their business, a present supply of money. They scrupled to make use of a pawnbroker; but where to borrow it they knew not. I resolved to try if we could not find a remedy for this also. I went, in a few days, from one end of the town to the other, and exhorted those who had this world's goods, to assist their needy brethren. Fifty pounds were contributed. This was immediately lodged in the hands of two Stewards; who attended every Tuesday morning, in order to lend to those who wanted any small sum, not exceeding twenty shillings, to be repaid within three months. It is almost incredible, but it manifestly appears from their accounts, that, with this inconsiderable sum, two hundred and fifty have been assisted, within the space of one year. Will not God put it into the heart of some lover of mankind to increase this little stock? If this is not "lending unto the Lord," what is? O confer not with flesh and blood, but immediately join hands with God, to make a poor man live!

I think, Sir, now you know all that I know of this people. You see the nature, occasion, and design of whatever is practiced among them. And, I trust, you may be pretty well able to answer any questions which may be asked concerning them; particularly by those who inquire concerning my revenue, and what I do with it all. Some have supposed this was no greater than that of the Bishop of London. But others computed that I received eight hundred a year from Yorkshire only. Now, if so, it cannot be so little as ten thousand pounds a-year which I receive out of all England! Accordingly, a gentleman in Cornwall (the Rector of Redruth) extends the calculation pretty considerably. "Let me see," said he: "Two millions of Methodists; and each of these paying two-pence a week." If so, I must have eight hundred and sixty thousand pounds, with some odd shillings and pence, a-year. A tolerable competence! But be it more or less, it is nothing at all to me. All that is contributed or collected in every place is both received and expended by others; nor have I so much as the "beholding thereof with my eyes." And so it will be, till I turn Turk or Pagan. For I look upon all this revenue, be it what it may, as sacred to God and the poor; out of which, if I want anything, I am relieved, even as another poor man. So were originally all ecclesiastical revenues, as every man of learning knows: And the Bishops and Priests used them only as such. If any use them otherwise now, God help them! I doubt not, but if I err in this, or any other point, you will pray God to show me his truth.

To have "a conscience void of offense toward God and toward man" is the desire of, Reverend and dear Sir, Your affectionate brother and servant,

John Wesley

STUDY QUESTIONS

1. Describe Wesley's understanding of what it means to follow Christ.
2. How did the Methodists use 'small groups' and 'circuit riders'?
3. How did the Methodists practically help the poor and the sick?
4. Which factors in your immediate context help or hinder the kind of revitalization that the Methodists saw in their own day?

Chapter 25

WHY SO FEW REVIVALS?

CHARLES FINNEY (1792-1875)

Charles Finney was born in Connecticut (USA) into a Puritan family and grew up in western New York state, at that time a frontier area with few religious or educational opportunities. He was educated in New England and New Jersey, where he took up the study of law. Though curious, his personal pride and skepticism prevented him from fully embracing Christian faith until the age of 29 while practicing as a lawyer. Soon after, he experienced a powerful baptism in the Holy Spirit and almost immediately began to preach. During the next 50 years, he conducted meetings in many leading American and British cities, with almost 500,000 people turning to Christ due to his traveling evangelistic ministry. It has been estimated that 85% of those confessing Christ in his meetings remained committed to their Christian faith in the long-term. One of the most significant ventures for which God used Finney was a campaign planned for the small town of Rochester (New York, USA) in 1830. Most churches partnered together and prayed for this revival day and night. Then, Finney preached. The result was the conversion of 10% of the town, including many leading business and professional people. Finney was also a key Christian leader who publicly spoke out against the evil of slavery in the USA. In 1833, he became president of Oberlin College (Ohio, USA), where he continued to train students for Christian ministry until just a few weeks before his death at the age of 83. His writings on the topic of revival have had worldwide circulation and have made a major impact on many subsequent ministries. He is considered to be one of the greatest evangelists of all time. [The following is from Charles Finney's book Revival Fire (Chapter 9 – Why So Few Revivals?). The text below is in the public domain.]

I am rejoiced to perceive that the inquiry is beginning to agitate the Church, "Why are there not more revivals, as well as why is their character so changed?" The inquiry is also made, "What can be done to promote them, and to promote them under a desirable and permanent type?"

Now, my dear brethren, I hope and trust that you will not be offended with me if I speak my mind on this subject with great plainness. The circumstances of the Church, the decline of revivals, and the whole aspect of the Christian world, demand it. I have seen in the public papers various reasons assigned for this declension of revivals, this absence of revival influence, this powerless preaching of the gospel.

Now it does appear to me that we who are ministers, instead of looking abroad and searching for the fundamental difficulty beyond and out of ourselves, should see that whatever else may be an occasion of the great falling off and decline in revivals, our own spiritual state is certainly one, if not the primary and fundamental, reason of this decline. Want of personal holiness, unction, power in prayer, and in preaching the Word, the want of holy living and consecration to the work of self-denial, and energetic effort in the ministry, - these, no doubt, are the principal reasons why revivals are so few and far between, and of so superficial character at the present day.

The fact is, ministers have turned aside, in a great degree, to vain janglings; have given up their attention to Church politics, Church government, and ecclesiastical proceedings of various kinds. The ministers have been diverted, to an alarming and most injurious extent, from promoting revivals of religion out of the Church and holiness in the Church.

I appeal to you, my brethren, of all denominations, if it is not a fact in your own experience and observation, that ministers have to a great and alarming extent suffered themselves to be diverted from the direct work of promoting the conversion of sinners and sanctification of the Church. This is too notorious to need any proof. The journals of the day, the movements of ecclesiastical bodies, the doctrinal collisions, and - shall I say? - ambitious projects, that have come up and figured before the public within the last few years, bear no dubious testimony to the fact that the great mass of ministers are turned aside from promoting revivals and the holiness and entire consecration of the Church.

Now, my beloved brethren, while this is so, does it not become us to take this home, confess it, bewail it, and first of all understand that whatever else needs to be corrected and set right, we must ourselves repent and receive a new unction for the work?

Beloved brethren, it is of no use for us to go abroad and search for reasons, while the principal of all the reasons lies at our own door. While our hearts are cold, our zeal in revivals abated; while we are turned aside, and running here and there to attend Conventions, Councils, ecclesiastical bodies; while we are engaged in reading the vituperative publications of the day, and entering into Church politics and jangling about Church government and all these things—it is no wonder that both the Church and the world are asleep on the subject of revivals.

Until the leaders enter into the work, until the ministry are baptized with the Holy Spirit, until we are awake and in the field with our armor on, and our souls anointed with the Holy Spirit, it certainly ill becomes us to be looking around at a distance for the cause of the decline of revivals.

I have no doubt that there are many causes which, the Lord willing, we will search out. But this is the first, the greatest, the most God-dishonoring of all—that the ministry are not in the work, that the shepherds have in a measure forsaken their flock; that is, they are not leading them into the green pastures and beside the still waters, are not themselves so anointed and full of faith and power as to be instrumental in leading the Church into the field for the promotion of revivals.

To a considerable extent the Churches seem not to be well aware of the state of the ministry, and for the reason that they themselves are in a state of decline. The decline of vital godliness in the ministry has been, of course, the occasion of so much decline in the Churches that they are hardly aware either of their own state or of the spiritual state of the ministry.

Now, my dear brethren, I hope it will not be said that, by writing in this way, I am letting down the influence of the ministry and encouraging a fault finding spirit in the Church. I would by no means do this.

But I think that we may rest assured that, unless we are frank enough, and humble enough, and honest enough, to look the true state of things in the face, confess, forsake our sins, and return to the work and engage in the promotion of revivals,

God will undoubtedly rebuke us, will raise up other instruments to do His work, and set us aside; will alienate the heart of the Churches from us, destroy our influence with them, and raise up, we know not whom, to go forth and possess the land.

Among all the Conventions of the present day, I have thought that one of a different character from any that have been might be greatly useful. If we could have a Ministerial Convention, for prayer, confessing our faults one to another, and getting into a revival spirit, and devising the best ways and means for the universal promotion of revivals throughout the length and breadth of the land, I should rejoice in it. It has appeared to me that of all the Conventions of the day, one of this kind might be the most useful.

What shall we say, brethren? Are we not greatly in fault? Have not the ministry, to a great extent, lost the spirit of revivals? Is there not a great lack of unction and power amongst us? And have we not suffered ourselves to be greatly and criminally diverted from this great work?

If so, my dear brethren, shall we not return? Shall we not see our fault, confess it to the Churches, to the world, and return, and, in the name of the Lord lift up our banner?

I hope my brethren will bear with me, while I further insist on the general delinquency of ministers, especially of late, in regard to revivals.

There has been so manifest and so lamentable a falling off from a revival spirit among the ministers of Christ as to become a matter of general, if not universal, observation. Nothing is more common than the remark that ministers, as a general fact, have lost the spirit of revivals, have become very zealous in ecclesiastical matters, censorious, afraid of revivals, of revival men and measures, and that they do little or nothing directly for the promotion of revivals of religion.

Now I do not think that this is a universal fact, but as a general remark it is too obvious to need proof, and I think must be conceded by all.

Now, dearly beloved brethren, unless there is a spirit of a revival in the ministry, it is in vain to expect it in the Church. The proper place for the shepherd is before or in advance of the sheep. The sheep will follow him whithersoever he goes; but if he attempt to drive them before him, he will scatter them in every direction. If the shepherd fall away from a revival spirit, the sheep will naturally decline also. If he advance in the work of the Lord, they will almost as a thing of course follow him wherever he leads.

The greatest of all difficulties in the way of the promotion of revivals has been a superficial work of grace in the hearts of ministers themselves. If this is not true, I am greatly mistaken.

My brethren, believe me, I speak not this censoriously or in the spirit of fault-finding; it is the full and deliberate conviction of my own mind - an opinion formed, not hastily, but from protracted observation, and from an intimate acquaintance with great numbers of the ministers of Christ of different denominations.

While the ministers of Christ are filled with the Spirit of God, the Church, as a general thing, will not backslide. I say as a general thing. There may, in some instances be influences brought to bear on the churches that will divert them from the promotion of holiness in their own hearts and the conversion of the impenitent, in spite of all that the most wakeful and vigilant ministry can do. Great political excitements, great commercial embarrassments, great depressions or elevations in the business and pecuniary state of the Church or the world, may, in a great measure, divert the mass of professors of religion for a time from deep spirituality, although the ministers maybe awake.

And yet it is my deliberate opinion that a thoroughly wakeful, prayerful, energetic ministry, by their influence, would generally, if not universally, prevent all the calamities and disturbances, by so deeply engaging the Church and the community in general on religious subjects, that war, great political excitements, great commercial excitements, speculations, or embarrassments, would not be likely to occur. However this may be, I can not believe it to be otherwise than a general truth, that if the ministry are baptized with the Holy Spirit, and deeply anointed with the revival influence, so the Church will be—"Like priest like people."

And now brethren, it does seem to me that when we ourselves are thoroughly in a revival spirit, our call to the Churches to arise and engage in the general promotion of revivals will be immediately responded to on the part of the Church. Let the ministry only come out in the true spirit of revivals, and I doubt whether any minister in the land can preach for three Sabbaths to his Church, in the Spirit, without finding the spirit of revival waking up in the Church. Let this experiment once be tried; let us wake up to the importance of this subject, confess and forsake our own sins, and cry aloud to the Church, and spare not: let us lift up our voice like a trumpet, and rally the host of God's elect; and if they are deaf to the call, then let us inquire most earnestly what is next to be done. But until we are anointed to the work, do not let us tempt the Lord or abuse the Church, by looking out of ourselves and away from ourselves for the cause of decline in revivals.

Do not misunderstand me. I know that the Church is in a state of decline, and needs greatly to be quickened and aroused; but I am confident that the prime cause of this decline in the Church is to be found in the fact that the ministers have been diverted from their appropriate work. And I am also confident that the only remedy for this state of things is, first and foremost of all, for ministers to come into a deeply spiritual and revived state of mind. And as soon as this comes to pass, there will be a general revival. And I am not looking for it to come unless ministers do thoroughly wake up to their own state and the state of the Church. ∎

STUDY QUESTIONS

1. How do you respond to the idea of 'personal revival' in the life of the Christian? Can you claim such an experience as your own?

2. Why does Finney place such an emphasis on the need for Christian leaders to take initiative in stirring up passion within the church? Does this apply to leaders in house church networks?

3. How can partnership between mass evangelism ministries like that of Charles Finney's and house church networks help retain the fruits of evangelistic harvest? Is this a practical reality in your context? Is such a thing even desirable?

PART 4

HOUSE CHURCH MOVEMENTS
ON THE
WORLD SCENE TODAY

Chapter 26

The 10 Universal Factors in Church Planting Movements Today

David Garrison

David Garrison, Ph.D. (University of Chicago, USA), is the author of four books on missions, including his most recent work entitled Church Planting Movements: How God is Redeeming a Lost World (2004), available at www.FreshWindDistributing.com. He has been a missionary in Hong Kong, Egypt, Tunisia, Europe, and India. He has served as the Associate Vice President for Global Strategy at the Southern Baptist Convention's International Mission Board (IMB) before assuming the position of IMB's Regional Leader for South Asia. Garrison is internationally acknowledged as a pioneer in the understanding of Church Planting Movements. [Used by permission of the author. Email: dgarrison@wigtake.org].

Introduction

In recent years, there has been an explosion in the growth of biblical Christianity around the world. In northern India, 4,000 churches were planted in a mere decade. In Latin America, two Baptist unions overcame government persecution to grow from 235 to 3,200 churches in eight years. In China, 160,000 Chinese were baptized in a single year. In Ethiopia, a decade of Marxist persecution failed to halt the growth of a Pentecostal denomination from 5,000 to 50,000 members through underground house groups. In Cuba, a petrol crisis sparked the growth of between 6,000 and 10,000 multiplying house churches from 1992 to 2000. In the USA, Dove Christian Fellowship's three cell groups numbering 25 people grew to 80 cell church networks on five continents encompassing over 20,000 people in a 20 year period. What is happening in all the places? The answer: God is bringing people to himself through Church Planting Movements. *A Church Planting Movement is a rapid and multiplicative increase of indigenous churches planting churches within a given people group or population segment.* After surveying these phenomena around the world, we found at least 10 elements present in every one of them. While it may be possible to have a Church Planting Movement without them, we have yet to see this occur. Any missionary intent on seeing a Church Planting Movement should consider these 10 elements.

1. Prayer

Prayer has been fundamental to every Church Planting Movement we have observed. Prayer typically provides the first pillar in a strategy coordinator's master plan for reaching his or her people group. However, it is the vitality of prayer in the missionary's personal life that leads to its imitation in the life of the new church and its leaders. By revealing from the beginning the source of his power in prayer, the missionary effectively gives away the greatest resource he brings to the assignment. This sharing of the power source is critical to the transfer of vision and momentum from the missionary to the new local Christian leadership.

2. ABUNDANT GOSPEL SOWING

We have yet to see a Church Planting Movement emerge where evangelism is rare or absent. Every Church Planting Movement is accompanied by abundant sowing of the gospel. The law of the harvest applies well: "If you sow abundantly you will also reap abundantly." In Church Planting Movements, hundreds and even thousands of individuals are hearing the claims that Jesus Christ has on their lives. This sowing often relies heavily upon mass media evangelism, but it always includes personal evangelism with vivid testimonies to the life-changing power of the gospel. The converse to the law of the harvest is also true. Wherever governments or societal forces have managed to intimidate and stifle Christian witness, Church Planting Movements have been effectively eliminated.

3. INTENTIONAL CHURCH PLANTING

In every Church Planting Movement, someone implemented a strategy of deliberate church planting before the movement got under way. There are several instances in which all the contextual elements were in place, but the missionaries lacked either the skill or the vision to lead a Church Planting Movement. However, once this ingredient was added to the mix, the results were remarkable. Churches don't just happen. There is evidence around the world of many thousands coming to Christ through a variety of means without the resulting development of multiple churches. In these situations, an intentional church-planting strategy might transform these evangelistic awakenings into full-blown Church Planting Movements.

4. SCRIPTURAL AUTHORITY

Even among non-literate people groups, the Bible has been the guiding source for doctrine, church polity and life itself. While Church Planting Movements have occurred among peoples without the Bible translated into their own language, the majority had the Bible either orally or in written form in their heart language. In every instance, Scripture provided the rudder for the church's life, and its authority was unquestioned.

5. LOCAL LEADERSHIP

Missionaries involved in Church Planting Movements often speak of the self-discipline required to mentor church planters rather than do the job of church planting themselves. Once a missionary has established his identity as the primary church planter or pastor, it's difficult for him ever to assume a back-seat profile again. This is not to say that missionaries have no role in church planting. On the contrary, local church planters receive their best training by watching how the missionary models participative Bible studies with non-Christian seekers. Walking alongside local church planters is the first step in cultivating and establishing local leadership.

6. LAY LEADERSHIP

Church Planting Movements are driven by lay leaders. These lay leaders are typically bivocational and come from the general profile of the people group being reached. In other words, if the people group is primarily non-literate, then the leadership shares this characteristic. If the people are primarily fishermen, so too are their lay leaders. As the movement unfolds, paid clergy often emerge. However, the majority—and growth edge of the movement—continue to be led by lay or bi-vocational leaders. This reliance upon lay leadership ensures the largest possible pool of potential church planters and cell church leaders. Dependence upon seminary-trained—or in non-literate societies, even educated—pastoral leaders means that the work will always face a leadership deficit.

7. CELL OR HOUSE CHURCHES

Church buildings do appear in Church Planting Movements. However, the vast majority of the churches continue to be small, reproducible cell churches of 10-30 members meeting in homes or storefronts. There is a distinction between cell churches and house churches. Cell churches are linked to one another in some type of structured network. Often this network is linked to a larger, single church identity. The Full Gospel Central Church in Seoul, South Korea, is perhaps the most famous example of the cell-church model with more than 50,000 individual cells. House churches may look the same as cell churches, but they generally are not organized under a single authority or hierarchy of authorities. As autonomous units, house churches may lack the unifying structure of cell churches, but they are typically more dynamic. Each has its advantages. Cell groups are easier to shape and guide toward doctrinal conformity, while house churches are less vulnerable to suppression by a hostile government. Both types of churches are common in CPMs, often appearing in the same movement.

8. CHURCHES PLANTING CHURCHES

In most Church Planting Movements, the first churches were planted by missionaries or by missionary-trained church planters. At some point, however, as the movements entered a multiplicative phase of reproduction, the churches themselves began planting new churches. In order for this to occur, church members have to believe that reproduction is natural and that no external aids are needed to start a new church. In Church Planting Movements, nothing deters the local believers from winning the lost and planting new cell churches themselves.

9. RAPID REPRODUCTION

Some have challenged the necessity of rapid reproduction for the life of the Church Planting Movement, but no one has questioned its evidence in every CPM. Most church planters involved in these movements contend that rapid reproduction is vital to the movement itself. They report that when reproduction rates slow down, the Church Planting Movement falters. Rapid reproduction communicates the urgency and importance of coming to faith in Christ. When rapid reproduction is taking place, you can be assured that the churches are unencumbered by nonessential elements and the laity are fully empowered to participate in this work of God.

10. HEALTHY CHURCHES

Church growth experts have written extensively in recent years about the marks of a church. Most agree that healthy churches should carry out the following five purposes: 1) worship, 2) evangelistic and missionary outreach, 3) education and discipleship, 4) ministry and 5) fellowship. In each of the Church Planting Movements we studied, these five core functions were evident. A number of church planters have pointed out that when these five health indicators are strong, the church can't help but grow. More could be said about each of these healthy church indicators, but the most significant one, from a missionary vantage point, is the church's missionary outreach. This impulse within these CPM oriented churches is extending the gospel into remote people groups and overcoming barriers that have long resisted Western missionary efforts.

STUDY QUESTIONS

1. Would the application of the above 10 principles in your context be desirable or practical?

2. Which factors above seem suited for use particularly in starting house church networks? Which factors would be more challenging?

3. Can you identify one or two scriptural examples of each of the above factors?

Chapter 27

40 TRENDS THAT ARE RESHAPING THE CHURCH TODAY

ROBERT FITTS, SR.

Robert Fitts, Sr., with his wife Joni, has spent over 50 years serving the Lord as pastor, teacher, missionary, evangelist, children's worker, and author. His writings and travels have touched many nations. Robert travels internationally encouraging the formation of a 4H strategy that includes house churches, home bible colleges, houses of prayer, and healing rooms (www.robertfitts.com). [The following excerpts from Robert Fitts' book, Breaking Through The Stained Glass Barrier, are used by permission from the author. Email: robertjoni@aol.com].

INTRODUCTION

No one who has his eyes open and his ears attuned to present trends can deny that a new reformation is taking place in the church today. In a symbolic sense, it is like we are at a momentous time of breaking through a stained glass barrier. It is a time of breakthrough! We are breaking through religious barriers that have hindered the growth of the church for centuries! Multitudes are beginning to see and understand what it is to be free from religiosity and traditionalism. More and more honest seekers are taking the risk and walking out into the fresh air and sunshine of a new day of freedom in Christ!

The following 40 trends are only part of what God is doing in the earth today to bring the church, the Body of Christ, out of traditionalism, institutionalism, and commercialism back to the dynamic simplicity of the early church. Not every trend cited is a trend within the house church movement alone. Some of these trends are beginning to go forward in all kinds of churches worldwide. Not every trend has to do with the nature and function of church. Some of them deal with coming out of darkness into light concerning the teachings of the church. Some of what I have called a 'trend' is actually more of a beginning than a trend. However, I have felt it to be the beginning of something that will go on and become a trend that will bring the present day church back to the simplicity and power of the first century church. As we think of the trends of the church today, we must not forget to factor in the divine plan of God. We need to see this picture as God sees it.

1. FROM THE SANCTUARIES TO THE STREETS

As we read through the life of Jesus in the New Testament, with very few exceptions it is difficult to find him organizing a religious gathering or an evangelistic meeting, or in fact, any kind of meeting. It seems that all of his large meetings, such as the feeding of the 5000 or the multitudes that gathered on the shores of the Sea of Galilee, took place more or less spontaneously as crowds would gather to hear what he was saying and to be healed of their diseases. People knew he had power to help them and they did not wait for a special meeting to get that help. Most of his earthly ministry happened as he walked among the people, taught them, and responded to needs as they confronted him. Jesus' strategy was to go where the people were, see the needs and minister to those needs. We find him healing a man at the Pool of Siloam as he walked by; feeding the hungry, ministering, teaching in the Temple, on the streets, at the beach, in the synagogues or on a mountainside. Jesus' primary ministry was spontaneous responses to the needs of people as he walked through each day. In every place where he found people in need, he met that need in the power of the Holy Spirit. He said we would do the same.

2. FROM CHRISTIANITY TO CHRIST

The word 'Christianity' is not found in the Bible. It is a word we use to designate a religious system. The early church did not build a system or priesthood, or denomination, or mission, or organization. They were "the followers of the Way." (Acts 22:4, NLT). It was a way of life. But deeper than that, it was a new relationship with God. It was Christ in you! It was God living inside every follower of the Way. Jesus said, "he who abides in Me and I in him, he bears much fruit." (John 15:5, NASB). That is exactly how we are to operate. God is in me doing the same kind of works Jesus did. Paul had grasped this truth when he said, "I have been crucified with Christ; and it is no longer I who live, but Christ lives in me." (Gal 2:20, NASB). In another place he says, "For to me, to live is Christ." (Philip 1:21, NIV). Again he said that the "mystery" that had been hidden from ages and from generations was, "Christ in you, the hope of glory." (Col 1:27, NIV). Christ in me is the *only* hope of glory, which means the outshining radiance of God coming through me at all times. May the eyes of our understanding may be enlightened, that we may know and enjoy the riches freely given us in Christ.

3. FROM CHURCH HOUSES TO HOUSE CHURCHES

For the first 250 to 300 years of the Christian movement there were no church buildings. We are told that during that period of time the church grew faster and with more power to leaven all of society than at any other time in history. Of course it takes more than changing the size of the gatherings to return to the dynamic power and simplicity of the early church, but it's a good place to start. A close friend of mine, Dr. John Amstutz, a leader in the Four Square movement, wrote me a very balanced letter about the desirability of house churches while also making room for other ways to gather together and worship Jesus. In the letter he said: "If the fulfillment of the Great Commission is our goal, then let's use any legitimate means available to get the job done. I believe there is no more effective way than planting new churches to fulfill this goal, and house churches is one of the most efficient ways of planting churches."

4. FROM UPWARD TO OUTWARD GROWTH

God is teaching us to pray for the rapid multiplication of house church networks, and it is stretching our faith. It stretches my faith to pray for the birth of one house church. It is harder to pray and believe for two or more. It is more of a challenge to pray for the multiplication of house church networks, but in India they pray for "The rapid multiplication of house church networks!" However difficult that may seem, I am sensing that we are to pray and believe the day will come when we will witness in North America what is now happening in China, India, and Africa, and is beginning to happen in Latin America—*the rapid multiplication of house church networks!* We will continue to pray till we see it happening all over the world!

5. FROM 'PROFESSIONAL PASTORS' TO 'HOME GROWN PASTORS'

Many of those who desire to serve God as leaders in the church go away to Bible colleges and seminaries with their hearts full of faith, fervor and zeal, then come away with most of that faith, fervor, and zeal all washed away in the sea of intellectualism. In the average Bible college or seminary the students are trained to serve the churches as a special priesthood. They are no longer classified as a layman. But, let's not forget that the veil of the temple was rent from top to bottom when Christ died on the cross, signifying that the old was gone and the new had come. There is no room in the Kingdom of God anymore for a system of clergy on one level with God and the layman on another level. There should be nothing that we wear, or say, or do as pastors, evangelists, prophets, teachers, and apostles that is calculated to set us apart as a different breed of 'holy men' or a special priesthood. Jesus is our High Priest and every born-again believer is a priest unto God and unto men. There is no longer a priesthood separate from the common people. We are all a 'kingdom of priests'. And that includes every believer. As the priest in the Old Covenant would go before God in behalf of men, so are we to stand before God in intercession and prayer for the lost and needy and share the good news of God's love and forgiveness to all men everywhere.

6. FROM SPECIAL DAY CHRISTIANS, TO EVERY DAY CHRISTIANS

One of the things my parents taught us was that you are not supposed to work on Sunday. Back in those days people would preserve garden vegetables and fruits in jars. Mother said if we canned on Sunday, it would likely spoil, for you had violated the Sabbath. It was almost like a curse would be on that food. Religion opens the door to a lot of superstition. Jesus came to fulfill the symbolism of every holy place, every holy thing, and every holy day. Jesus is our Sabbath rest for we have entered into his finished work (Heb 4). Paul, an apostle in the early church, was given the revelation of the gospel of the grace of God beyond all his contemporaries. In his letter to the Colossian believers he makes it clear that Jesus is our Sabbath when he says, "Therefore do not let anyone judge you by what you eat or drink, or with regard to a religious festival, a New Moon celebration or a Sabbath day. These are a shadow of the things that were to come; the reality, however, is found in Christ." (Col 2:16-17, NIV). If we walk in the light that Paul walked in, we will not put any special significance on one day above another, nor will we put our brothers and sisters down who still do not see this truth. The more truth and light we walk in, the more freedom, liberty, joy and peace we have. God is bringing us out of religiosity into reality.

7. FROM HIERARCHY TO SERVANT LEADERS

The dictionary definition of hierarchy is, "a ruling body of clergy organized into orders or ranks, each subordinate to the one above it." The keyword in that definition is the word "above." Wherever there is a ladder-oriented organizational structure, there will always be those whose ambition and desire is to climb up one more rung of that ladder till they reach the top. The urge to be "above" is almost irresistible to the flesh. Hierarchy is a system of this world, not of the kingdom of God. Jesus said the kingdom of God is a brotherhood. "You are not to be called 'Rabbi' for you have only one Master and you are all brothers. And do not call anyone on earth, 'father', for you have one Father and he is in heaven. Nor are you to be called 'teacher' for you have one Teacher, the Christ. The greatest among you will be your servant. For whoever exalts himself will be humbled and whoever humbles himself will be exalted." (Matt 23:8-12, NIV). How refreshing it is to find a servant leader whose aim is to pour out his life for the saints and for the life of the world!

8. FROM WEEKLY WORSHIP TO CONSTANT WORSHIP

We often call the Sunday morning service at church a 'Worship Service'. The word 'Worship' is a contraction of two words; *worth* and *ship*. When we 'worth-ship' God, we are declaring his worth; how much we value our God! He is worthy of our praise. Paul says "Therefore I urge you, brothers, in view of God's mercy, to offer your bodies as living sacrifices, holy and pleasing to God, which is your spiritual worship." (Rom 12:1, NIV) Paul brings us down to the "bottom line" where true worship really starts. Spiritual worship starts with a total surrender of myself to God. That act of submission carries over into all the activities of every moment of every day. We are worshipping God all day long if we are in his will. Doing the will of God from the heart is an act of worship, no matter where we are or what we are doing. I may be sweeping or mopping the kitchen floor, taking out the trash, washing dishes, driving to the store to get groceries, taking a bath, or writing a letter, but everything I do, if I am doing God's will, becomes an act of worship. Singing his praises certainly has its place, but we put too much emphasis on how we sound or whether or not it is producing goose bumps on our goose bumps. We tend to worship our worship and praise our praise. The singing that really matters comes after that act of spiritual resignation to God. The singing of songs and hymns that does not begin with that full and complete consecration of our lives to God is not worship at all.

9. FROM BRINGING 'COME TO' TO 'GO TO' CHRISTIANITY

Pray the following prayer sincerely everyday and eventually you will become a minister and an evangelist wherever you go, all day, every day!

"Father, give me a divine appointment today with someone who is hungry for God or sick, or in need. Give me sensitivity to know when that happens, and give me grace to minister the love of Jesus in the power of the Holy Spirit."

God will always answer that prayer. You may miss a day or two now and then, but if you faithfully make that your prayer every morning, some time during the day the Holy Spirit will nudge you and say, "This is the one. Tell him about Jesus!" or "This is the needy person that you can help, or the sick person you can minister to in the name of Jesus." When God sets up the appointment, you can be certain you are dealing with the right person and that the seed or the deed will fall on prepared and fertile ground. They are either hungry to know God or they have a need that you can help fill, whereby you show them the love of God. They may be sick, which gives an opportunity to minister healing in the name of Jesus. These divine appointments often lead to a prayer to receive Jesus.

10. FROM SYMBOLISM TO REALITY IN THE LORD'S SUPPER

Jesus said, "Unless you eat the flesh of the Son of Man and drink his blood, you have no life in you." (John 6:53, NIV). Those words were easy to misunderstand because, when he said that, all except the 12 disciples went away and walked with him no more. It sounded too ridiculous to them! Who but an egomaniac would ever be so brazen as to utter such words? And how could anyone ever fulfill such an outlandish command? But Jesus went on to say, "The words I have spoken to you are spirit and they are life." (John 6:63, NIV). They had to be understood in the spirit and not with the natural mind. That which is spirit is real, not symbolic. It is real to believers. They that eat the bread and drink the cup in the communion service are indeed (spiritually, not literally) eating his flesh and drinking his blood. They are eating of the bread that came down from heaven. Jesus said, "I am the living bread that came down from heaven. If anyone eats of this bread, he will live forever." (John 6:51, NIV). Watchman Nee said that when the house churches in China, called "little flocks," started taking the Lord's Supper every time they met, it brought a dramatic new flow of life into the whole movement just before the blood bath took place when the Communists took over China in 1949.

11. FROM DENOMINATIONS TO SPIRIT-LED NETWORKS

Denominations and Christian organizations can become a problem when they cause division in the Body of Christ. It opens the door to a subtle snare, a spirit of divisiveness. The Hebrews were one people with one God, one nation, one religion, and one army, but there were 12 tribes, each having its own identity, its own space in the camp, and its own flag. So there can exist different groups with specific designations or names without a spirit of division and sectarianism. These 'Spirit-led networks' come together by divine direction and not by the organizational skill of men. There is a free flow of liberty and freedom in each house church without any legalistic pressures from a denominational headquarters, and there is no "I am of Paul. I am of Apollos, I am of Cephas" spirit entrenched in the fellowship. Sectarianism is a spirit. It is a spirit of exclusivity. You can be non-denominational and be very exclusive in your spirit toward anyone and everyone who does not understand and teach the Bible just like you do. You can be the most dedicated house church adherent and still be divisive. That is the crux of the problem…and that is what the word heresy means…divisiveness. There are people in denominational churches with open hearts and there are people in the house church movement with open hearts. We need to receive our brothers and sisters everywhere, regardless of their denominational label or organizational affiliation. And that includes house churches too!

12. FROM SOCIAL RESPECTABILITY TO SALT AND LIGHT

When Paul and his team arrived in Thessalonica and began sharing the good news about Jesus, they caused quite a stir. Several Jews and a great multitude of Greeks received the message of salvation, but the unbelieving Jews gathered together a crowd and set the whole city in an uproar. They shouted, "These men who have turned the world upside down have come here also" (Acts 17:6, ESV). A strong, vital, Spirit-filled, anointed church will be sending out teams to turn the world upside down, which, in reality, is turning it right-side up! This is done by the bold proclamation of the simple message of God's love and forgiveness as well as seeing the Lord confirm our words with signs following. This is the ministry of Jesus being multiplied in the lives of his followers. When Jesus sent out his disciples, he commanded them to do the same things he was doing. "He gave them authority to cast out demons and to heal all kinds of disease and illness." (Matt 10:1, NLT). He still does it that way today!

13. FROM PERFORMANCE TO PARTICIPATION

"When you meet, one will sing, another will teach, another will tell some special revelation God has given, one will speak in an unknown language while another will interpret what is said. But everything that is done must be useful to all and build them up in the Lord." (1 Cor 14:26, NLT). There was no such thing as a clergy-laity distinction in the early days of the church. All believers were taught to do the works of Jesus and proclaim the good news. The ground is level in the kingdom of God. Servant leaders are not ladder climbers. The special priesthood and the distinction between the 'clergy' and the 'laity' emerged over a long period of time. This certainly does not mean that God has done away with leaders in the Body of Christ. There will always be leaders. God gave these ministries to the church. Apostles, prophets, evangelists, pastors and teachers are gifts from God to his people. These all have their place and function. We will only be blessed when receive them in the name of Jesus and hear what they have to say. But, *all* of us are commanded to go into all the world to preach the gospel to everyone in the power of the Holy Spirit. *All* of us can bring our spiritual gifts, talents, and words from God to the meetings for the strengthening of the church. *All* of us have that privilege and responsibility for we are a kingdom of priests.

14. FROM TEMPLE-BASED CHURCH TO HOME-BASED CHURCH

It may surprise many people that house churches have been around longer historically than the 'liturgical' churches (like the Catholic, Orthodox, Lutheran, or Episcopal) or the 'Evangelical' churches (like the Baptist, Methodist, Presbyterian, or Pentecostal). And today, worldwide, there are more informal house church meetings and more people that meet in house churches every week than in either liturgical or Evangelical churches. Of course this includes China, India, Africa and many other countries around the world which are beginning to explode with house church movements. According to church history there were no church buildings for the first 250 years of the spread of the gospel into all nations. But, the house church is mentioned often in the New Testament. (Acts 2:26, 20:20, 28:30-31; Rom 16:5; 1 Cor 16:19; Col 4:15; Philem 1:2). This is how the first century church spread throughout the known world within a very short time. They were not slowed down by the need to buy land, build buildings or hire a staff. They just did church in homes and found that it worked just as well for them as it did for Jesus.

15. FROM THE SEMINARY SYSTEM TO THE APPRENTICE SYSTEM

Paul says, "The things you have heard me say in the presence of many witnesses, entrust to reliable men who will also be qualified to teach others." (2 Tim 2:2, NIV). We can see four generations in that verse. The first generation is Paul; second, Timothy; third, reliable men; and fourth, others. That sets the stage for amazing multiplication as it develops. Just before the start of the Second World War, Dawson Trotman was a sailor on a battleship in the Pacific Fleet. He was a dedicated Christian who believed in Paul's method explained in 2 Timothy 2:2. He led another sailor to the Lord and began to 'entrust' the things of God to this young man. By the end of World

War II Dawson Trotman's ministry had multiplied to such an extent that there were disciples on every ship in the Pacific fleet. Out of that 'one on one' experience, he formed a ministry called *The Navigators* who now have disciples in nearly every country in the world and are still growing. Classroom teaching like that found in seminaries and Bible schools has its strong points, but it is significant that Jesus chose to call his students alongside him while he lived life and ministered the word of God on a daily basis. He went from town to town, from place to place, doing the works of God in the presence of his students (disciples) and teaching them to do the same things he was doing. He not only told them how (classroom) he showed them how (workshop). Even with all our modern methods and tools of education designed for the classroom, the apprentice system is still unbeatable. More than that, it is essential!

16. FROM TENTH TO TOTAL GIVING

Most of us were taught that when we give our tithes and offerings to God, we are to expect nothing in return. In one sense this is true. We *are* to give without expecting anything in return from the one to whom we give. But all through the Bible when God admonishes us to give, there follows a promise of blessing to the giver. There are passages that encourage us to give, followed with the promise of material blessing (Prov 3:9-10; Prov 11:25; Luke 6:38; 2 Cor 9:7-8). These verses and many others make it clear that we are not only to give generously to the Lord but we are to look to the Lord to fulfill his promises to bless those who give. We cannot ignore any of God's promises without offending his goodness and mercy toward us. The reason these promises have not been fulfilled in many lives is because we have been taught to give without any expectation of return; that it is wrong to give expecting something in return. It is not wrong to give and then expect God to do what he has clearly promised in his word that he would do. For many years I gave, expecting nothing in return and that is just what I received. Then one day I saw my error and began to give with expectation of material blessing. I have found that Jesus keeps his promises to the one who is trusting in his promises.

17. FROM SELECTIVE SUBMISSION TO TOTAL SUBMISSION

In the late 1970s and early 1980s I got excited about what was then called "The Discipleship Movement" or the "Shepherding Movement". I fed on the teachings of the main leaders by cassette tapes and ultimately joined the movement, submitting myself to the oversight of one of the leaders of that movement. One of the main problems, however, was what I call, 'Selective Submission'. After four years, my family and I walked away from it and felt a huge release! To me, those four years were like going to a university and coming away with a degree in 'How to Recognize Legalism in the Body of Christ'. Since that time, if anyone asks me the question, "Who is your covering?" or "Who are you accountable to?" or "Who are you submitted to?" I look straight into their eyes and say, "I am accountable to *you* and if you have a word from the Lord to me or a word of wisdom, or caution, or admonition, or encouragement, I am listening." That person has the responsibility to deliver that word and I have the responsibility to weigh it to see if it is truly a word from the Lord or not. If I am submitted to the King of the kingdom, I am automatically submitted to his delegated authority wherever it crosses my path.

18. FROM TITLES TO FUNCTION

There is a fine line between title and function. So, what's the difference? I was standing in the hallway of a church, talking to Bill, the pastor of the church when one of his church members passed by and said, "Hi, Bill!" The pastor immediately called him back and said, "My name is Bill, but you are to address me as 'Pastor Bill,' okay?" It was an embarrassing moment for me and especially for the poor church member. There are many ways to show respect for our spiritual leaders without violating the command of Christ to avoid the use of titles. But why would our Lord make a point of forbidding us to use titles? Is it not an obvious fact that titles are intended to impress, to intimidate and to establish a sense of superiority or importance upon those who use them? Why should it be necessary for God's people to boast about any of their accomplishments? The most obnoxious of all religious titles is 'Reverend'. The word 'reverend' is only used one time in the Bible. Here it is: "He sent redemption unto his people: he hath commanded his covenant forever: holy and reverend is his name." (Psalm 111:9, KJV). Isn't it God's name, not ours, that is "holy and reverend?" May God help us to take the words of Jesus at face value in this matter (Matt 23:1-12) and refuse to be entangled in this subtle snare of using impressive titles!

19. FROM INDEPENDENCE TO INTER-DEPENDENCE

Everything that belongs to Jesus belongs to me, and I belong to everything that belongs to him. That's what it means to be an heir of God and a joint heir with Jesus. I am a member of every church in town and every other ministry that belongs to Jesus. A 'joint heir' does not own half of the inheritance, he owns it all and so does every other joint heir! Every joint heir owns it all...jointly...at the same time. I do not have the same measure of responsibility for every other church or ministry, but it still belongs to me and I belong to it. On the other hand, every ministry that God has given me belongs to every other believer, too. We are members one of another, bone of his bone and flesh of his flesh. We do not have the same level of involvement or responsibility in God's kingdom, but we all own it jointly. How does this play out in practical ways? It should cause us to pray for and bless one another; to give us a sense of oneness or unity; to melt away a feeling of competition, and to dissolve the walls that separate us. It should also cause us to fellowship with one another and even admonish one another when necessary, even though we may not attend the same fellowship. All the 'one another' verses in the New Testament were directed to the citywide church, not to a local fellowship.

20. FROM PAPER MEMBERSHIP TO BODY MEMBERSHIP

One of the most subtle and grievous problems in the Body of Christ today is that of paper membership. This is a practice that goes directly against the warning Paul gave to the elders not to "draw away disciples after themselves." Consider his words to these elders, "I know that after I leave, savage wolves will come in among you and will not spare the flock. Even from your own number men will arise and distort the truth in order to draw away disciples after them." (Acts 20:29-30, NIV). "But isn't that the way it should be?" some will say. "How can anyone be a member of more than one congregation and how can they have more than one pastor?" The book of Acts presents one church, one Body of Christ to which all believers felt joined. This comes across loud and clear! It was the Lord who added new converts into the membership. It is the Holy Spirit who baptizes us all into the Body of Christ, which includes all believers everywhere! (Acts 2:47; 1 Cor 12:13). And do not believe the deception that we are to 'make covenant' with those with whom the Lord has given you relationship in your local church. We are already in covenant with every other believer in the world! When we take communion we are celebrating the one covenant of blood that joins every member to every other member of the Body of Christ. We are all born into the same family through faith in the Lord Jesus Christ. There is only one Body, and we are all members one of another.

21. FROM THE WHEEL TO THE VINE

Many traditional churches are recognizing the need for small groups that meet weekly in homes for the purpose of encouraging and strengthening one another in their walk with Jesus. This is like a wheel which has spokes going out in all directions and coming together at the hub, the center of the wheel. A church which starts midweek cell meetings led by its members will certainly strengthen and multiply its evangelistic outreach. This is the picture of Pastor Cho's church in South Korea, which is the largest church in the world and has been instrumental in spinning off many other large congregations and thousands of cell groups! And many churches today adopt this approach. We praise God for it!

But, the early church grew even faster by taking a different path that was like a vine. The 'vine' church could be compared to a strawberry plant. It grows out in all directions, multiplying itself over and over as it puts new roots down, giving birth to multitudes of baby strawberry plants which, in turn, put out vines that put down roots that give birth to more and more strawberry plants (2 Tim 2:2). The most dramatic growth in the history of the church since the first century is taking place now in China, India, and Africa. And they are all house church movements. This should stand as proof that the advance of the kingdom of God through the rapid multiplication of house church networks is thoroughly embedded in the history of the church, both in ancient times and in modern times, right up to the present. The Chinese house church movement has the following motto: "It is good to lead someone to Christ. It is better to start a house church. It is best to start a house church network." In India they say: "Everyone can start a church. Every home can become a church. Every church can become a Bible School."

22. FROM ORGANIZATIONAL UNITY TO SPIRITUAL UNITY

"As for the one who is weak in faith, welcome him, but not to quarrel over opinions." (Rom 14:1, ESV). "Accept one another, then, just as Christ accepted you, in order to bring praise to God." (Rom 15:7, NIV). Unity is an attitude. It is an attitude of the heart. It is lovingly receiving each other as members of the same body even though we may not agree on all points of doctrine or methodology. If you have come out of darkness into his marvelous light by being born of the Spirit through faith in Jesus Christ, then God is your Father and I am your brother. We will probably never see everything alike until we get to heaven, but we are still one through the blood of the everlasting covenant. Denominational walls are getting thinner and thinner throughout the world, and the day will come when we will not be looking over any walls. Oh, Father, hasten the day when we will see and experience this kind of unity in the church worldwide!

23. FROM SEEKING PATTERNS TO SEEKING GUIDANCE

The early church did not look for a 'pattern' in the Old Testament for fulfilling Jesus command to go into all the world and preach the good news, and they did not have the New Testament to read, for it had not yet been written. They had Jesus' example, and they depended on the Holy Spirit through prayer. That was their strategy, and that still works today. If I am looking for a pattern to follow, that strategy is the predominant pattern we find in the New Testament. Several years ago I worked with four different churches that tried to copy the methods of pastor Yonggi Cho of Korea. After all, he had built the largest congregation in the world and the largest in the history of the church. He had the ear of every church leader in the world. We were listening, too, but all four churches failed to grow by meticulously trying to copy Cho's methods. A few years later I was listening to an interview of Dr. Cho on the radio. When asked, "What is your formula for success in building such an enormous congregation?" He gave his formula for success: He said "I just pray and obey". That formula will work in any country, among any people, of any culture, at any time, by any church!

24. FROM 'US AND THEM' TO JUST 'US'

One of the problems among some house church people is that of a critical attitude toward the traditional church. It is true that God is dealing with some very basic problems that exist in the traditional church. But he will also deal with a sour, sick, ugly attitude toward any part of the Body of Christ. We cannot afford to nurture an attitude of antagonism toward the people of God, no matter what their problems might be. They belong to us, and we belong to them. God is purging, burning, scourging, transforming, teaching, and bringing his people out of the old and into the new, out of the problems and into the provision of his grace. This is the ministry of the true intercessor. *The problems of the church, the whole church, are our problems for we are the church! It is not us and them...it is just US!* There are not two bodies of Christ...just one. And when one part of the Body suffers, the whole Body feels the pain.

25. FROM PLANNED CHURCH TO SPONTANEOUS CHURCH

Certainly we will plan and we will attend our regular church meetings, but we will also be open to spontaneous church! Jesus did not say that he would be in the midst of two or three who come together in his name to study the Bible, or pray, or sing praise. He said, "Where two or three come together in my name." The phrase, "in my name" refers to those who are called by his name because they have been born again and they belong to him, flesh of his flesh and bone of his bone, named by his name. The Body of Christ, the church, is made up of people and is to function as church in every area of life, not just in so called 'religious' gatherings inside the walls of a 'sanctuary'. Let us determine to recognize and honor the presence of Jesus every time we get together with another believer, no matter what the occasion. We may be amazed at what will happen!

26. FROM BONDAGE TO FREEDOM FOR WOMEN

More and more books are being written today to point out the need for women to be released to function in the Body of Christ. A number of Scriptures indicate this need (Gen 1-3; Acts 2:17-18; 1 Cor 11:3-16, 14:34-40; Gal 3:28, Eph 5:21-33; 1 Tim 2:8-15). "In the last days, God says, I will pour out my spirit on all people. Your sons and daughters will prophesy, your young men will see visions, your old men will dream dreams. Even on my servants, both men and women, I will pour out my spirit in those days, and they will prophesy." (Acts 2:17-18, NIV). "You are all sons of God through faith in Christ Jesus, for all of you who were baptized into Christ have clothed yourselves with Christ. There is neither Jew nor Greek, slave nor free, male nor female, for you are all one in Christ Jesus." (Gal 3:26-28, NIV). It is not insignificant that the largest church in the world, located in Seoul, Korea, began its explosive growth when it defied the traditions of the church and of Korean culture and allowed women to do the work of the ministry. Read the life and ministry of Dr. Paul Yonggi Cho, the pastor of that church. You will be amazed! The amazing multiplication of house churches taking place at this time in China and India is being initiated mainly by young people and the majority of them are girls. Will we, also, be brave enough to release the other half of God's army so that the world can be reached for Christ?

27. FROM OLD COVENANT TO NEW COVENANT

Many of the most entrenched problem areas in churches today come from either ignorantly or stubbornly hanging on to the shadows and types of the Old Covenant. The vestments, the altar, the emblems, the priestly garments, the incense, the special priesthood, the stilted language, the tithes to the priestly tribe, the teachings, special holy days, the temple, and the temple furniture all tend to hold the people under a certain bondage to the old covenant. There is no special priesthood anymore. The church of God is a kingdom of priests who offer up the sacrifice of praise to God continually and point men to Christ as the lamb of God who takes away the sin of the world. We need to read the book of Hebrews (chs. 8-10) again and again till we see clearly that we are living under a new covenant. Some of the things we are still doing are no longer to be done, the special priesthood being the most prominent and most destructive to the covenant of grace. Let us embrace fully the freedom of the new covenant in Christ!

28. FROM ARBITRARY GUIDELINES TO BIBLICAL GUIDELINES FOR APPOINTING ELDERS

God has ordained civil authority (Rom 13:1-2) and spiritual authority (1 Tim 3:1-7; Titus 1:5-9). Men have abused civil authority and spiritual authority, but that does not negate the fact that these authorities exist and they are for our good, for God is good and he only designs good for us. Some would like to totally obliterate the whole idea of spiritual leaders who have some measure of spiritual authority in the kingdom of God, but that will never happen. Just remember that those in authority will answer to God for how they exercise that authority. It is not primarily a matter of how much intellectual training leaders have, but it is first the character of the individual that matters, such as purity, truth, devotion, anointing, and faithfulness. He is not to be a novice, but neither is he required to have a degree in theology. We do not have to appoint elders as soon as we plant a house church. A study of Paul's first missionary journey shows that you can plant churches first and appoint leaders later. In most cases that is probably the best way. It gives leaders that God has gifted and anointed and called time to begin doing the work of leading and becoming recognized as leaders before they are commissioned as elders. Let them function in their office for a time, and then let them be recognized for what they are. They are elders.

29. FROM MY PASTOR TO MY APOSTLES, PROPHETS, EVANGELISTS, AND PASTOR/TEACHERS

When Paul called the leaders of the Ephesian church together he refers to all the saints who lived in Ephesus as 'the flock' and not 'the flocks' as if there were more than one flock of God's sheep in that city (Acts 20:17-38). There was only one flock and the elders were all commissioned by Paul to shepherd that one flock. They all collectively went about to watch over, feed, and nurture the flock. They were not to divide up the flock till all the sheep had their own favorite shepherd and every shepherd had his own following. How would it sound if I said, "My Apostle", or "My Prophet" or "My Evangelist?" Sounds very strange to me and completely unscriptural! It should sound just as strange to say, "My Pastor" when it implies that you only have one pastor and could not possibly have pastoral input from more than one spiritual leader. Pastors are to function for the whole Body of Christ like the other offices on the equipping team. They all have a mandate from the Lord to "Feed my sheep" anywhere, anytime, to any of God's people as the Lord may direct them. Likewise I must remain open to apostolic, prophetic, evangelistic and pastoral input wherever it crosses my path. There is already a lot of cross-pollinating going on within the Body of Christ, which has not been happening for centuries. The trend is definitely toward more networking among denominations, churches and ministries. Pastors are getting together in many cities across America to pray together. We praise God for this new day!

30. FROM RAISING UP LEADERS TO APPOINTING SERVANTS

The phrase 'raising up' gives the impression that in order to be a leader you have to be 'raised up' or elevated above the common, ordinary people. In some of the older church buildings, especially in Europe and New England, the pulpits were raised high above the people, so high that the speaker had to climb a winding stairway to reach it. This gives the wrong impression, to say the least! In reality the process God usually employs to prepare true leaders rather than 'raising up' would more accurately be described as, 'battering down' leaders! You may be going through the 'battering' process and know what I mean. The process of spiritual preparation that God puts us through to become servant leaders inclines us to be servants rather than "lords." (Matt 23:6-12). The 'clergy-laity' system has fostered the idea that the common people should be pouring out their lives to minister to the spiritual leader, as if that leader were a sort of 'queen bee' of the hive; that they are more important and need lots of attention. Another way the clergy put themselves above the common people is to quote the Scripture from the Old Testament, "Touch not God's anointed." As if the pastor is anointed and the people are not. The New Testament makes it clear that all believers are anointed; not just certain leaders (1 John 2:26-27). It will not take long to discern if you are following a servant leader or not. The servant-leader pours out his life for others. He lives to give. Let us believe for more servant leaders!

31. FROM LOCAL VISION TO WORLD VISION

A very encouraging word concerning the progress of the Christian movement into all the world came to me recently by email about a book that describes a tidal wave of Christianity. From this and other reports that come to me from week to week, it is clear that the church is returning to the simplicity of the book of Acts and the gospel is going forth with greater speed and power. Read and rejoice!

> Dr. Philip Jenkins, distinguished professor of History and Religious Studies at Penn State University....shocked and probably panicked some of America's political and media elite with his acclaimed book, *The Next Christendom: The Coming of Global Christianity*. Jenkins argues the greatest movement of the past century was not communism or capitalism. Do the math and the winner is Spirit-filled Christianity, or what he terms in his study as "Pentecostalism". 'The modern Pentecostal movement begins at the start of the 20th century,' Jenkins said. 'So, say this begins with a few hundred, a few thousand people...today you're dealing with several hundred million people, and the best projections are by 2040s or 2050s, you could be dealing with a billion Pentecostals worldwide. By that stage there will be more Pentecostals than Hindus. There are already more Pentecostals than Buddhists.' Jenkins says in just 20 years, two-thirds of all Christians will live in Africa, Latin America or Asia. (Source: CBN, www.cbn.com/CBNNews/News/030819a.asp)

> The mission agency, *Christian Aid*, was founded in 1953 by Bob Finley, who worked closely with Billy Graham. It was one of the first American mission agencies to support local missionaries instead of (expensive) Americans, particularly in nations where Evangelical Christians are an oppressed minority. Today, they support 90,000 missionaries, and are training 40,000 mission workers in hundreds of Bible schools. They plant over 52,000 new churches every year! That's 1,000 each week. (Sources: www.christianaid.org; Friday Fax 2004, Issue 46, 26 November, 2004)

32. FROM BUILDING MY EMPIRE TO BUILDING HIS KINGDOM

Church, in many countries, has become big business, especially in the USA! Whether it is taught or not in the seminaries and Bible colleges, the philosophy of success that is embraced by many pastors and leaders is that success is measured in 'nickels and noses'. A big offering and a big attendance on Sunday morning brings with it the sweet smell of success! In addition to a large following and a good income, it helps to have an astonishingly beautiful building, usually called, 'the sanctuary'. However, it is the primary task of church leaders to "equip the saints for the work of the ministry" according to Ephesians 4:11-13. The following is a word from Rick Joyner concerning this need to equip the saints:

> I have asked in many conferences and large churches how many people know their ministry, or the gifts of the Spirit that have been given to them. Usually the result is that less than 5 percent know the answer to this question. How would you be doing if only 5 percent of your body was working? Yet, this is the present state of the body of Christ. Obviously this is because there are very few true New Testament ministries now in the church or they would be "equipping the saints to do the work of the ministry" as we are told in Ephesians 4:12. For this reason the modern church probably has more in common with a spectator sport than the biblical model we have of the church - you basically have a few people playing the game and everyone else watches and cheers them on. However, this will begin to change, and change quickly. We have come to the time of the restoration of all things, and it will begin with the church being restored to her purpose, and maturing in it as a light to all people of what they were created to be.

The local churches are the primary equipping and sending agencies. We live in a time when Bible colleges and seminaries have tried to take over this responsibility, and it is just not working! The best way to equip men and women to do the work of the ministry is to have them begin doing it right there in the local assemblies. Let's equip and release any army of men and women to open their homes to plant churches that reach the neighborhoods and cities!

33. FROM INTELLECTUALISM TO SUPERNATURAL ANOINTING

Jesus said to his disciples after his resurrection, "This is what is written: The Christ will suffer and rise from the dead on the third day, and repentance and forgiveness of sins will be preached in his name to all nations, beginning at Jerusalem. You are witnesses of these things. I am going to send you what my Father has promised; but stay in the city until you have been *clothed* with power from on high." (Luke 24:45-49, NIV, emphasis added). The primary equipment of the early apostles and evangelists was not intellectual furniture, but a divine touch from God that enabled them to do the works of Jesus in the power of the Holy Spirit. It was not just the words of Jesus that attracted the crowds. It was mainly the miraculous works of God that he was doing. These included healing the sick, raising the dead, casting out demons, walking on water, feeding a multitude with a handful of food, turning water into wine, calming the storm with a command of authority, withering a fig tree with a word, exposing the inward thoughts of people, disarming his detractors with irresistible logic, telling people details about themselves that only they would know, and predicting things to come!

Here is a list of things we count as essential in our day for taking the gospel into all the world: television, computers, radio, telephones, airplanes, automobiles, newspapers, magazines, books, organizations, temples, sanctuaries, buildings, and lots of money! We may say, "But there is nothing wrong with using every available means to take the good news to all the world." And we would be right, but it still stands that the baptism in the Holy Spirit was the only equipment Jesus mentioned both in Luke 24 and in Acts 1 as essential preparation to becoming effective in getting the gospel into all the world. This is not to minimize the training that his disciples had in walking with Jesus for three years, but still Jesus said in effect, "Go, but don't go until you receive the power of the Holy Spirit." May we too as the church pray for God's anointing power to accomplish God's purposes!

34. FROM REJECTING TO ACCEPTING ONE ANOTHER

We can only work closely with a very small group, but we can receive, accept, and bless every other believer God brings across our path. Not everyone will be excited and blessed that you are seeking to multiply house churches throughout the city. Some may ask, "But won't all these little house churches scattered throughout a city cause division and disunity in the Body of Christ within the city?" As a matter of fact, little churches cause no more division than big ones. Very large churches and very small churches have the same challenge when it comes to unity. We may not be able to have 'organizational unity' with our brothers and sisters who do not yet see the validity of the house church vision, but we can have spiritual unity. Let us be open to spiritual unity, the citywide church, and the diversity of believers!

Some years ago when I began to understand how free I was to fellowship with all believers within my town, I started saying, "I'm a member of every church in town." That sounded really good to me, but it sounded like heresy to some of my friends. But I have held my ground and I still say, "I'm a member of every church in my town, your town and every other town, because there is only one Body of Christ in all the world." We are one! We are born into spiritual unity "for there is one Lord, one faith, one baptism, one God and Father of us all." We are members one of another whether we know it or not and whether we like it or not! That's just the way it is! To acknowledge that truth and live as if it is true is "to preserve the unity of the Spirit in the bond of peace." (Eph 4:3, NASB).

35. FROM LAW KEEPING TO LIVING BY GRACE

It is a sad fact that a great segment of the Body of Christ is either bordering on law keeping as the means of salvation or they are blatantly teaching salvation by works rather than salvation by grace through faith. This is not something new. It was the most serious disagreement within the early church. The question was then as it still is today, "Are we saved by grace as a gift of God or by keeping the commandments of God, or by a mixture of the two?" Many are beginning to see what Paul saw so clearly and to embrace their freedom and to stand fast in that freedom. There will always be religious leaders who are ready to bring you right back under the bondage of law keeping. The Bible says it like this, "It is for freedom that Christ has set you free. Stand firm, then, and do not let yourselves be burdened again with a yoke of slavery...you who are trying to be justified by law have been alienated from Christ; you have fallen away from grace." (Gal 5:1, 4, NIV). It is a matter of much rejoicing that this is a day in which the message of grace is beginning to be caught by the Body of Christ worldwide. There is no greater bondage than religious bondage, but Jesus said, "Then you will know the truth, and the truth will set you free." (John 8:32, NIV). Let us daily thank God that we are saved by grace through faith, not by works, lest any man should boast!

36. FROM OVERWHELMING OVERSIGHT TO RESTFUL OVERSIGHT

A few years ago while making the transition from serving as pastor of a traditional church to getting involved in the house church movement, I began to pray that God would show me what changes this would involve. Over a period of a few weeks the Lord showed me that there was a lot more rest to be enjoyed as pastor of a church than I had ever thought. God began to show me some things through several parables, one of which was that of the fire on the beach. I was down on the beach early in the morning as was my custom when we lived in Laguna Beach, California a few years ago. I used to go down to the beach almost every morning with a beach chair, some matches and old newspapers, some books and my Bible. There was always plenty of driftwood that I could gather off the beach to build my fire. On this particular morning I built my fire as usual and after an hour or so, I took a walk on the beach. When I returned the fire had died down. I found some more wood and stoked the hot coals, then put the wood on the coals. In less than a minute I had a good fire going again. I sat down to enjoy the fire a little longer before going back to the house for breakfast. As I sat there, looking into the fire, the Lord spoke to me, "That's how the church is. It is like watching over this fire. The church is a spiritual fire and when it dies down, you can help rekindle the flames as you see the need. You cannot bring the fire of my Spirit, but you can help set the stage for his coming. I want you to enjoy overseeing the church. All you have to do is just be ready to stir the coals and put on more fuel. The fire burns of its own accord. This is the nature of the church and this is the work of an elder." Let us rejoice in the freedom that comes with releasing the entire Body of Christ to minister!

37. FROM "WE WILL BUILD" TO "I WILL BUILD"

At times we are guilty of changing the words of Jesus to mean what we think they ought to mean. When Jesus said, "I will build my church", we think it ought to mean, "*We* will build *his* church" with his help, of course! So we set out to do the work that only Jesus can do. It is true that we are laborers together with God, and we sincerely want him to help us build his church, but we seem to have forgotten that it is Jesus who is doing the work and we are coming along side to help *him*. He must take the initiative and when we see what he is doing, it is our part to co-labor with him. Jesus said, "Lift up your eyes and look on the fields that are ready for harvest." The only field that most churches can see is the immediate field that will build their own congregation.

There must be a lifting up of our vision to include the nations of the world! Jesus said, "Go into all the world." If we intend to be like Jesus and obey the commands of Jesus, we must embrace a world vision; a vision to evangelize the nations of the world. And it is beginning to happen in more and more churches. But, let us remember that it is his work and his church, not ours!

38. FROM PROGRAMS TO PRAYER

Some time ago, I was studying how central prayer was to the church in the book of Acts. As I was going through this study I noticed a pattern begin to emerge. I saw three things come together that I had never noticed before. First, prayer. The church took time to pray in concentrated, corporate prayer. Second, miracles. God worked with them, confirming their word with signs following. Third, explosive growth. There was a notable extension of the kingdom of God as people saw the miracles, heard the word of God and came to the Lord. When reading the book of Acts one cannot help but notice this pattern repeating over and over again. There's something to it!

The church of Jesus Christ worldwide has been involved in a powerful prayer movement for the past 25 or more years and we are beginning to get wonderful reports of revivals, releases, breakthroughs, and multitudes coming out of darkness into the light. In a recent report from George Otis Jr. producer of the *Transformations* videos, we are told that 157 cities and nations on five continents are experiencing transforming revival. Restoring community life and hope, reducing crime and addiction, with thousands coming to faith.

God is leading us in this ministry of church planting and church multiplication to emphasize prayer. All the rest will come to birth as we pray and seek God with all our hearts. In all of the various ministries we teach the people to pray daily the following prayer. This is a prayer that will make every believer a missionary wherever they are 24 hours a day, seven days a week. Pray this prayer sincerely at the beginning of each day and teach it to your church, and you will see miracles begin to happen on a daily basis:

> *Father, give me a divine appointment with someone today who is hungry for God or sick or in need. Give me sensitivity to know when that happens and grace to minister the love of Jesus in the power of the Holy Spirit.*

39. FROM SINNERS TO SAINTS

It is when I see that I am holy that I become holy. Wow! That is a powerful statement! As a new believer I was taught to say, "I am just a sinner, saved by grace." We all felt that was the only humble and truthful position to take. As time went on I began to see that there is not one instance in the New Testament where believers are called sinners. In every case they are called 'saints' meaning 'holy ones'. There are many statements about those who are in Christ that make it clear that we are to confess our righteousness and our holiness in Christ. Never in ourselves, but always considering our position in Christ (1 Cor 1:30-31; 2 Cor 5:17).

To be righteous is to be declared 'not guilty' even though we are guilty. The innocent one has suffered for the guilty one, and the broken law has been satisfied. To be holy, is to have clean hands and a pure heart. This is what we have as our heritage in Christ. Jesus said, "Now you are clean", and that means NOW we are clean, by the blood of the Lamb. It is for me to begin to confess that NOW I am clean. I am committed to never again declare that I am a sinner, for by Jesus blood I have been declared justified and sanctified through the redemption that is in Christ Jesus. There is not one place in the entire New Testament where a born-again believer is called a sinner. They are always called saints, and that is what we are after we are justified and sanctified by the blood of Jesus!

40. FROM RELIGION TO RELATIONSHIP

Dick Eastman, in his book *Beyond Imagination - A Simple Plan to Save the World*, says, "Early in my ministry, a wise colleague and mentor told me, 'Dick, God's plans are always incredibly simple and unusually inexpensive. So if things start getting terribly complex and amazingly expensive, you might rethink whether it's God's plan after all.'" When we look today at the institution we call 'Christianity', the amazing pomp and ceremony, the huge sanctuaries and expensive cathedrals, the stilted language, priestly garb, intricate liturgy, mysterious rituals, and complicated theologies, it is hard to find Jesus in the midst of it all. But his life, his teachings, and his ministry to people still stand as our model. We cannot do better than to follow his example in how to evangelize the world.

The fastest growing segment of the Body of Christ worldwide is the Pentecostal movement that started on the day of Pentecost. It was strong for about 300 years, then went into an eclipse during the dark ages. Then there was a sudden resurgence back in 1900 at the Azusa Street meetings under the leadership of James Seymore. If there was one thing that was outstanding in that movement, it is the stark similarity to the ministry of Jesus and the apostles. Pentecostals spend much time in prayer crying out to God for miracles, signs and wonders just like the early church did in Acts 4:29-30 and they receive the same anointing. "Now, Lord, consider their threats and enable your servants to speak your word with great boldness. Stretch out your hand to heal and perform miraculous signs and wonders through the name of your holy servant Jesus. After they had prayed the place where they were meeting was shaken. And they were all filled with the Holy Spirit and spoke the word of God boldly." (Acts 4:29-30, NIV).

Jesus himself did no miracles until after he received that anointing. Afterwards he came forth in the power of the Holy Spirit to boldly preach the kingdom of God, heal the sick, cast out demons, and raise the dead. He is our example. He is our model, not only for living, but also for how to extend the kingdom of God in the earth. And it is a simple relationship with him and the receiving of his power that will propel us forward!

CONCLUSIONS

In all of the above, we have sought to awaken the Body of Christ to the tremendous trends and opportunities that await us in this day of visitation. Will we stand up and step out to do the will of the Father to fulfill our part of reaping this end time harvest? May God help us to take that first step and trust him to use us in bringing in this harvest!

STUDY QUESTIONS

1. Reflect on the practical implications for the worldwide church and for you personally based on the statement, "from complexity to simplicity".

2. Reflect on the statement, "Get empowered by the Spirit before you get busy with ministry"?

3. Which of the trends or opportunities above seem to you the most difficult to implement? Why?

Chapter 28

Case Study (China): China's House Church Movement

Paul Hattaway

Paul Hattaway is the director of Asia Harvest (www.asiaharvest.org), an inter-denominational ministry dedicated to evangelism and church planting in the restricted countries of Asia. The ministry works alongside Asian church leaders, helping and equipping them to reach the lost. [The following is taken from Paul Hattaway (2003), Back to Jerusalem: Three Chinese House Church Leaders Share Their Vision To Complete The Great Commission, Piquant Editions/Gabriel Resources, pp.1-16. Adapted and reprinted with permission from the publisher, www.piquant.net].

Introduction

Over the past five decades something remarkable has started to take place throughout the length and breadth of China: the emergence of a viable New Testament Christianity. Few secular sources report the unfolding of this dramatic event, which has the potential to change the entire social and moral structure of the nation if it continues unabated. Estimates of the total number of Christians in China today vary, but I believe a figure of between 80 million and 100 million Protestants to be realistic, in addition to at least 12 million Catholic believers meeting in both registered churches and illegal house church gatherings. Although these numbers still represent only a small minority of the 1,300 million souls inhabiting China today, the growth of the church is spectacular and unparalleled in Christian history when it is considered that there were only about 700,000 Protestants and three to four million Catholics in China at the time the communists took power in 1949. This chapter explores the history and nature of the Chinese house church movement.

Getting Acquainted

At the dawn of the new millennium, I had the privilege of meeting with a number of Chinese house church leaders. These men and women were unremarkable in themselves. Most came from simple farming backgrounds, yet to be in their presence was an exhilarating experience. I was aware—as many Christians around the world are—that China has been experiencing a revival of Christianity in recent decades that has had an impact on many parts of their vast nation. I had read reports of mass conversions, secret baptisms, and brutal persecution.

During that special meeting the leaders of each house church network, or 'family', testified about what God was doing in their midst and reported on the growth their churches were experiencing. They had been asked some time before to research the number of church fellowships and believers in their networks as accurately as possible. The top leaders asked their provincial and regional leaders to submit reports. These people then gathered the statistics from grassroots house church leaders, who operate at the city and county level.

The information was then collated by the top leaders, who were gathered at the special meeting. The combined total membership of the house church networks present at the meeting came to 58 million people, while the net growth rate of each church group was reported to be between 12.5% and 17.5% per year. Some experts estimate that 30,000 Chinese are coming to Christ each day, which works out to more than 10 million new believers annually.

Even though the number of conversions in China today does not yet match the birth rate (approximately 55,000 babies are born each day), at the present rate of growth the church in China may soon be expanding at a faster numerical rate than the country as a whole.

As I chatted with these leaders, I learned more of their zeal, love and sacrificial commitment to the cause of Christ. These were not merely believers, they were disciples of Jesus. They did not preach a 'ticket to heaven' gospel, they preached and demonstrated the reality of the kingdom of God. They had paid a great price for their witness. Every single Christian leader in the meeting had spent time in prison, and many had been subjected to severe torture, humiliation, and deprivation. You would never know it, however, as they were the most joyful and sincere people you could ever hope to meet. Their joy was not a superficial emotion but a reality that came from deep within their souls—a supernatural kind of joy that only those who have truly enthroned Jesus Christ as the master and lover of their souls can ever experience.

One lunchtime I asked several church leaders how many Christians they thought there would be in China in 20 or 30 years time if the gospel continued to blaze its way through the nation as it had been doing for the previous decade. "200 million believers?" I asked with a smile on my face. "300 million?"

The Chinese brothers didn't answer. They understood my question, but didn't understand my lack of faith! After repeating the question, one leader, with a puzzled look on his face, said, "Of course in 20 or 30 years all of China will know the Lord!"

I have learned not to impose my limited Western thinking on the Chinese church. They believe that part of their mandate from God is to completely evangelize their whole nation and to make China "the first truly born-again Christian country in Asia." Don't be surprised if they succeed!

HUDSON TAYLOR AND THE MISSIONARY ERA

Undoubtedly, the most famous Protestant missionary to China was James Hudson Taylor, the founder of the non-denominational China Inland Mission. He is fondly remembered by house church leaders in China today. One key figure in the house church movement talks about the deep respect he has for Taylor:

> The vision of the house churches in China today is not only to saturate our own country with the life and presence of the Lord Jesus Christ, but also to impact all the remaining Muslim, Buddhist and Hindu nations with the gospel. This is why we are so thankful for the impact Hudson Taylor made on our country. His example was one of single-minded passion to see God's kingdom come. Like a mighty soldier he marched into pioneer areas where the Name of Jesus Christ had never been uttered before. Today the house churches in China have caught that same vision. It is as though Hudson Taylor handed a flaming torch to the Chinese church and asked us to continue the race towards the finish line.

Although most books about Hudson Taylor's Ministry tend to focus on Western missionary methods, a careful examination of the work of the China Inland Mission reveals that these missionaries increasingly saw their role as being trainers and facilitators of local Chinese Christian leaders. Simply speaking, it was their Chinese co-workers who did most of the front-line work, while the Western missionaries increasingly supported and encouraged their efforts from the background. Early in his career, Taylor wrote:

> The harvest here is indeed great, and the laborers are few and imperfectly fitted for such a work. And yet grace can make a few feeble instruments the means of accomplishing great things - things greater than even we can conceive.[1]

Decades later there was a clear shift in Taylor's strategy as he realized that the Chinese church would never fully grow and mature as long as missionaries remained in leadership and decision-making positions within the Body of Christ. Note the change of emphasis in the following passage:

> I look upon foreign missionaries as the scaffolding around a rising building. The sooner it can be dispensed with, the better; or rather, the sooner it can be transferred to other places, to serve the same temporary use, the better.[2]

---

[1] Theodore Mueller (1947), *Great Missionaries to China*, Zondervan, p.111.
[2] George Sweeting (1985), *More than 2000 Great Quotes and Illustrations*, Word Publishing, p.184.

In an ethnocentric and proud nation like China, an effective indigenous strategy was essential. The Chinese masses would never embrace a 'foreigner's religion'. The appearance and structure of Christianity had to change before the Chinese would accept it.

Alas, many missionary organizations did not share Hudson Taylor's insights, and continued to act like parents to the fledgling Chinese church. Not surprisingly, China continued to view Christianity as a Western religion and its Chinese adherents as traders and slaves of their Western masters. A common Chinese saying at the time was "One more Chinese Christian equals one less Chinese."

The 1920s were "a high-watermark for the missionary enterprise in China."[3] More than 10,000 foreign missionaries were scattered throughout the land. Many were fully committed, sacrificial Christians and God used them in different ways, but once the church had taken root their role clearly should have been to step aside and let the Chinese lead and direct their own congregations.

One of the most telling indictments of the missionary enterprise in the early 20th century is not found in any words or sermons but in a picture taken at a key conference held in 1907 at the Martyr's Memorial Hall in Shanghai. The meeting was called to plan for the future of Christianity in China, yet close inspection of the attendees reveals a room full of black-suited Western missionaries. Shockingly, a mere handful of Chinese pastors felt comfortable enough to attend this key meeting to determine the future of the Chinese church. They were largely lost among the 800 foreign delegates to the meeting. The 1907 meeting was just one of a series of conferences in Shanghai dating back to 1877, all of which were dominated by the foreign missionary force.

The church in China continued to grow slowly during the missionary era, but not at the pace or in the form necessary for the world's largest nation to experience Christ's salvation in the way God wanted them to. Christians remained marginalized within Chinese society. The church with all its Western trappings had erected physical, spiritual, and cultural walls between the Chinese Christians and the unsaved millions surrounding them.

Towards the close of the 19th century, missionary zeal in Britain started to wane and many church leaders wanted to forget about evangelizing the world and to confine their Christian work to their home parishes. One Christian statistician announced that the work of foreign missionaries in China had been an abject failure. His research indicated that at the rate the gospel was advancing, it would take another 27,000 years for the conversion rate in China to draw level with the birth rate! It was estimated that even if

---

[3] Archie R. Crouch, Steven Agoratus, Arthur Emerson, and Debra E. Soled (eds.) (1989), *Christianity in China: A Scholar's Guide to Resources in the Libraries and Archives of the United States*, M.E. Sharpe, p.xxxi.

the population of China remained static, it would take another 1,680,000 years to convert them![4]

God, however, had other ideas. He would not allow the Chinese masses to languish in their sin and spiritual darkness while the glorious news of the victory of his beloved Son on the cross remained unheralded in the world's largest nation.

THE START OF PERSECUTION AND REVIVAL

On October 1, 1949, Mao Zedong climbed a podium in Beijing's Tiananmen Square and announced the birth of the People's Republic of China.

For the first few years the Communists stood back and watched the church. To the surprise of many Christians, things continued largely unchanged. Like a tiger stocking its prey, the government was waiting for the most opportune time to strike. And strike it did in the early 1950s, when persecution commenced in full fury. Hundreds of church leaders were arrested, taken away during the night. Many died and were never heard of again. Others were sent to prison labor camps where they suffered silently for decades before being released into a changed China that looked little like the one they had known.

G. Campbell Morgan once stated, "Satan's first choice is to cooperate with us. Persecution is only his second-best method." Sensing that the faithful believers in China would never compromise their inward trust in God, the devil and his evil forces tried to destroy the earthen vessels that contained this eternal treasure.

When persecution broke out against Christians throughout China in the 1950s there was no limit to the savagery displayed. Brother Yun recalls what took place when the persecution began:

> In just one city in China, Wenzhou in Zhejiang Province, 49 pastors were sent to prison labor camps near the Russian border in 1950. Many were given sentences of up to 20 years for their "crimes" of preaching the gospel. Of those 49 pastors, just one returned home. Forty-eight died in prison. In my home area of Nanyang believers were crucified on the walls of their churches for not denying Christ. Others were chained to vehicles and horses and dragged to their death. One pastor was bound and attached to a long rope. The authorities, enraged that the man of God would not deny his faith, used a makeshift crane to lift him high into the air. Before hundreds of witnesses, who had come to falsely accuse him of being a "counter-revolutionary", the pastor was asked one last time by his persecutors if he would recant. He shouted back, "No! I will never deny the Lord who saved

---

[4] *North China Herald*, June 1, 1888, p.513.

me!" The rope was released and the pastor crashed to the ground below. Upon inspection, the tormentors discovered the pastor was not fully dead, so they raised him up into the air for a second time, dropping the rope to finish him off for good. In this life the pastor was dead, but he lives on in heaven with the reward of one who was faithful to the end.[5]

By 1953 almost all foreign missionaries had been expelled from China. Some refused to go willingly and were imprisoned for years. Many faithful missionaries who had served China with their lives now stood on the outside. Their work had suddenly been taken away from them. Reading the missionary newsletters and magazines from the early 1950s, it is clear that few of the expelled missionaries could see the hand of God anywhere in their bitter experience. Most believed their expulsion was a victory for the devil, and many lamented the death of the Chinese church. The general consensus was that there was no way the fledgling believers left behind the Bamboo Curtain could survive the brutality of a totalitarian regime hell-bent on destroying Christianity once and for all. Several articles suggested that if and when China's doors ever reopen, the missionary enterprise would have to begin all over again. They were wrong!

History and hindsight show that God's control of events is absolute. Although the persecution that occurred (and continues to occur) in China is unquestionably diabolical in nature, the evidence strongly suggests that God allowed it to happen so that his bride would be purified and equipped to bring more glory to her bridegroom.

One of the missionaries who had been expelled from China in the early 1950s was David Adeney of the Overseas Missionary Fellowship (formerly called the China Inland Mission). He later wrote:

> When all missionaries left China, the West was sometimes guilty of unbelieving pessimism. Seeing a weak and divided church, we felt we had failed. We knew many dedicated men and women and outstanding spiritual leaders. But could they, a tiny minority, stand against the mighty tide of a triumphant communist ideology that proclaimed the "Kingdom of man"—with no place for a crucified Savior? With no news of those we loved, our prayers became general and sporadic; most of us failed to enter into a continuous preserving prayer of faith. Now, as we hear of faithful witness in the midst of trial and great poverty, we feel rebuked for our lethargy, easy-going ways, affluence and lack of concern for the poor.[6]

---

[5] Brother Yun, *The Heavenly Man*, pp.20-21.
[6] David H. Adeney (1985), *China: The Church's Long March*, Regal Books: Ventura, CA, USA, p.206.

The brutal persecution resulted in the church being stripped of all the external things associated with Christianity. Church buildings were confiscated and either demolished or used as warehouses, gymnasiums or storage facilities. Bibles and hymn books were burned, while almost the entire church leadership was removed. Unable to continue as they were used to, many Chinese Christians fell away. Some denied Christ and betrayed fellow believers. Those who decided to remain true to Jesus Christ found all of their religious props removed, leaving only one foundation that could not be moved—the Lord Jesus Christ himself.

HOW THE CHINESE COMMUNISTS PAVED THE WAY FOR REVIVAL

Indeed, Chinese believers today joyfully explain that the Communist authorities, despite their efforts to demolish Christianity, actually paved the way for the rapid spread of the gospel. Before 1949 there was very little infrastructure in China, and linguistic, cultural, and geographic barriers greatly hindered the advance of the gospel. The Communists changed all this. Here are just some of the ways the policies of the government prepared the ground for the revival of Christianity:

- Much of China's idolatry was removed during the Cultural Revolution. Thousands of temples and idols were smashed, creating a spiritual void in the hearts of hundreds of millions of people.

- The government's attempts to remove God and deny the existence of the supernatural resulted in mass conversions to Christ when people personally experienced the reality of God and miracles.

- Train lines, roads and airports were constructed, enabling evangelists to easily travel to areas that were formerly inaccessible.

- Mandarin was adopted as the official language of China and is now used in all education and media. Formerly there were thousands of dialects that made communication of the gospel problematic.

- Large-scale literacy projects were undertaken, resulting in multitudes of people being able to read God's word for the first time.

- Control of the media resulted in a hunger and respect for the printed word. Christian organizations have taken advantage of this, printing tens of millions of Bibles and Christian books, while radio ministries were quick to broadcast the gospel by short wave radio into China. Millions of Christians in China trace their salvation to radio ministry.

- During the excesses of the Cultural Revolution people were forced to denounce their wrongdoings and reform their lives. The 'culture of confession' this created makes it much easier for people to repent and confess their sins to God when they hear the gospel.

It's little wonder that Christians in China today have a very deep realization of the sovereignty of God and his absolute control over human affairs! Despite living in the midst of a system dedicated to destroying them, Christians have learned to have no fear—not because they enjoy persecution and torture, but because they have met God and have been deeply transformed.

Surely the authorities in China have long been confused and amazed at how the church continues to grow and flourish despite their most brutal attempts to crush, seduce, and deceive believers. In their spiritual blindness they can't see they are fighting against a power far greater than their own, the power of Almighty God!

David Adeney was one former missionary astounded by what he found when China's iron doors slowly creaked open again in the late 1970s, after almost three decades of silence. While most expected to find the church had been completely obliterated, reports began filtering out that a great miracle had taken place! Somehow, in a way only God could do, the church in China had not merely survived the brutality of the past 30 years, but had actually grown and flourished! Amazing testimonies were received of how pastors were released after 20 years or more of imprisonment, and went home wondering whether they could find anyone who remembered their name. When they reached home, they found that not only had people been praying for them all those years, but their church fellowships had grown three, five, or ten times as large as before their imprisonment!

THE STRENGTHS OF CHINA'S HOUSE CHURCH MOVEMENT

In his book *China: The Church's Long March*,[7] Adeney joyfully documented the strengths the Chinese house churches had developed during their years of hardship. The following are some of the most important:

1. *The house churches are indigenous.* They have cast off the trappings of the West and have developed their own forms of ministry. The dynamics flow from their freedom from institutional and traditional bondage.

2. *The house churches are rooted in family units.* They have become part of the Chinese social structure. The believing community is built up of little clusters of Christian families.

3. *The house churches are stripped of nonessentials.* Much that we associate with Christianity is not found in Chinese house churches today. Thus they are extremely flexible. One believer remarked, "In the past we blew trumpets and had large evangelistic campaigns. Some believed, but not great numbers. Now we have very little in equipment ... and many are coming to the Lord."

---

[7] David H. Adeney, Ibid., pp.146-165.

4. *The house churches emphasize the lordship of Christ.* Because Jesus is the head of his body, the church must place obedience to him above every other loyalty; it cannot accept control by any outside organization. The word of God is obeyed and every attempt to force unscriptural practices on the church is resisted.

5. *The house churches have confidence in the sovereignty of God.* When there was no hope from a human point of view, Christians in China saw God revealing his power and overruling in the history of their day.

6. *The house churches love the word of God.* They appreciate the value of the Scriptures and have sacrificed in order to obtain copies of the Bible. Their knowledge of the Lord has deepened as they have memorized and copied the word of God.

7. *The house churches are praying churches.* With no human support and surrounded by those seeking to destroy them, Christians were cast on God, and in simple faith expected God to hear their cry. Prayer was not only communion with God but also a way to share in the spiritual conflict.

8. *The house churches are caring and sharing churches.* A house church is a caring community in which Christians show love for one another and for their fellow countrymen. Such love creates a tremendous force for spontaneous evangelism.

9. *The house churches depend on lay leadership.* Because so many Chinese pastors were put into prison or labor camps, the house churches have had to depend on lay leaders. The leadership consists of people from various walks of life who spend much time going from church to church teaching and building up the faith of others.

10. *The house churches have been purified by suffering.* The church in China has learned firsthand that suffering is part of God's purpose in building his church. Suffering in the church has worked to purify it. Nominal Christianity could not have survived the tests of the Cultural Revolution. Because those who joined the church were aware that it was likely to mean suffering, their motivation was a genuine desire to know Jesus Christ.

11. *The house churches are zealous in evangelism.* No public preaching was allowed. People came to know Christ through the humble service of believers and through intimate contact between friends and family members. The main method of witness in China today is the personal lifestyle and behavior of Christians, accompanied by their proclamation of the Gospel, often at great personal risk.

STUDY QUESTIONS

1. Recall the strengths of the Chinese house churches. Which of these is most lacking in your own house church network? What are you going to do about this?

2. Recall the ways that government policy actually helped the house churches flourish in China. Which similar factor in your region or nation can you capitalize on in the same way?

3. Hudson Taylor encouraged foreign missionaries to help the Chinese church get started, but emphasized their temporary and supportive role. How might this parallel the role of 'apostles' and 'apostolic teams' in raising up house church networks today?

4. The Chinese church believes that part of its mandate from God is to completely evangelize the whole nation. Take a few moments right now to pray that God would build in you the willingness to have this kind of faith for your city, region, or nation.

Chapter 29

CASE STUDY (INDIA):
HOW 100,000 HOUSE CHURCHES
WERE STARTED IN FIVE YEARS

VICTOR CHOUDHRIE

Victor Choudhrie is a well-respected and accomplished former cancer surgeon. He received his training in India and is a fellow of the Royal College of Surgeons in the U.K., the American College of Surgeons, and the International College of Surgeons. In 1992, he and his wife Bindu began a full-time church planting ministry that has resulted in thousands of house churches planted in India and around the world. He is the author of Greet the Ekklesia in Your House (2005) [Adapted and reprinted by permission from the author. Email: vchoudhrie@gmail.com].

INTRODUCTION

The house church movement in India or for that matter, anywhere else in the world, is not new. It is at least 2000 years old and has continually been a factor in the revitalization of the church at large through the various movements that God brought forth into the story of the church. In fact, the family (i.e. the household) has been the focus of the Almighty from the very beginning of human history. He told Moses to tell the fathers to teach the laws and the statutes to their children and grandchildren in a household situation.[1] Our Father in heaven has been orchestrating history, from the time of Queen Esther when her cousin Mordecai, the Prime Minister of Persia, sent thousands of administrators to India, which was one of the 127 provinces under his jurisdiction. Much later the British would do the same. There is evidence of synagogues and Jewish influence in many parts of India even today. The Scriptures clearly tell us that on the day of the birth of the church, on the day of Pentecost, devout Jews from every nation under heaven were present in Jerusalem.[2] It is possible that there were devotees from India also, who brought back the gospel to India, which spread through families and homes, as there is no evidence of any church buildings for many centuries. The intent of this chapter is to provide an overview of the more recent explosion of Christianity in modern-day India. The spiritual 'forest fire' in India has seen the emergence of 100,000 house churches in a few short years, from 2001 to 2006.

---

[1] Deut 6:3-6
[2] Acts 2:5

THE MIXED SUCCESS OF WESTERN MISSIONARY EFFORTS

With the onslaught of Buddhism, Islam, and the upsurge of Hinduism, the house church movement would die, only to be revived again in the 19th century after the arrival of the British. This would be followed by an army of missionaries from the West which initiated a vigorous church planting movement. Unfortunately, this time they came with the Western baggage of denominationalism, church buildings, reverends, mission compounds, theological seminaries, Christmas, Easter, and other traditions. The system would fail to penetrate even 1% of the population. What little the Western missionaries had accomplished is now suffering alarming attrition, especially by losing the younger generation. But the system continues regardless, since that is the power of 'traditions'. However, I believe our Father has had enough of this approach. He is particularly sore at being thrown out of the household and put in a lifeless building in the hands of holy men, silent women, and a disenchanted younger generation. He is now making a belated attempt to get back into the family and promote the simple, organic, relational household church. The family now has to model their homes as the household of the heavenly Father and be accountable to each other as much as to him.

After over a century of work, the Western missionary Visa was suddenly stopped by the government of India in the 1950s, which resulted in the exodus of foreign missionaries. This was followed by a mass migration of evangelists and pastors from South India to North India, who penetrated many unreached areas. However, they brought their own 'traditions' with them and were often busy producing their own kind, rather than espousing gospel essentials that would result in strong New Testament Christians. This was followed by large healing and deliverance crusades, but unfortunately very little attempt was made to disciple and flock the seekers that came.[3] Where such an attempt was made, it was to assimilate them into Western-style churches, which were not culturally acceptable to such seekers. Consequently, very little real fruit remained. However, this did succeed in waking up the sleeping devil in the form of fundamentalist high caste Hindus who saw the danger of Dalits—the low caste oppressed untouchables—abandoning Hinduism fully and, thus, changing their rulership equation. The situation has now worsened, and persecution of the visible Christian church is rampant.

A NEW KIND OF LEADERSHIP

The 1990s saw a mass prayer and intercessory movement in which millions prayed for the breaking down of spiritual strongholds and for the redemption of this country. This was followed by a humble church planting effort, which is now steadily growing and has the potential to become a mighty stream in

---

[3] Matt 12:30

one generation. Fueling this movement under the guidance of the Holy Spirit is a small number of highly committed national level house church advocates. The majority of them are not trained in theological seminaries, but they come from a secular professional background and bring their entrepreneurial skills to the table.

A New Kind of Resource People

Men and women of God came from all over the world and brought a new message and methodology. Millions prayed for India in 1993 through the effort of AD 2000, led by Luis Bush who coined the term '10/40 Window'. The prayer effort saw a great sense of freedom from demonic oppression in this country, including a sudden improvement in the economic situation, from grinding poverty to a net exporter of food grains as well as software technology. Barbara Femrite from the USA and Zach Fomum from Cameroon would come and teach us how to pray and wage spiritual warfare and completely change the prayer scenario of this country. Believers are now prayer walking all over, demolishing the strongholds, and claiming and possessing territories. John Robb of World Vision would come and create awareness about people groups all over India. Wolfgang Simson from Germany came and spoke about the house church to anyone who cared to listen. Roy Wingerd came and spread the DAWN strategy all over the country and changed freelance preaching to purpose-oriented research and an information-based strategy. Gene Davis came and adopted the country in general, but the gypsy Banjaras in particular, and modeled how focused networking with resources abroad and the church planters in the harvest fields could create synergy for explosive church growth. Bruce Carlton from the International Mission Board (Southern Baptist Convention) came and started training strategy coordinators. The international grant makers would rise up to the occasion and selectively fund church planting movements. Many of God's other people would come with different gifts and skills and add to the momentum. Passionate believers would arise in India from east to west and from north to south who would adopt regions to bring about church planting movements. All this created an unprecedented partnership, which has resulted in at least 100,000 house churches in about five years, from the year 2001 to 2006.

A New Kind of Training

The main approach has been training of large numbers of master trainers from the grassroots harvest field. Almost all the major agencies and individuals involved in advancing the kingdom are involved in training church planters. Thousands of young people have undergone short- or long-term formal and informal training programs. The best product comes not from the seminaries or Bible schools, but from those who have been practically trained in the harvest field. Long training in Bible schools resulted in them being long on theology but short on discipling and church planting skills and vice versa. Some of the original master trainers come from the traditional church, but the vast majority and certainly leaders with a wider scope of 'apostolic' responsibility are coming from the harvest field. This is the same pattern that Paul followed in which he extracted the Messianic Jews from the local synagogues to plant his first house churches, wherever he went. Then came Timothy, Titus, and Lydia. Then the Gentiles completely took over the leadership. Paul never imposed outside leadership on the emerging house churches, but appointed local elders. Wherever this system is not followed in India, then weak house churches emerge, deficient in reproductive genes that fail to multiply spontaneously. Instead of obedience to the heavenly Father, sycophancy and chasing the 'funding fathers' with mighty dollars becomes rampant in these leaders.

A NEW KIND OF CHRISTIANITY

There is a fundamental difference between house churches compared to what has been happening in the traditional churches of India. In the house churches, 'one-man' ministry and 'one-day' meetings do not happen. Rather, church life is based on participatory meetings[4] and practical ministry.[5] Here the new comer or the seeker is treated like an honored guest like in any family situation. Every one makes a serious attempt to disciple them after they confess "truly God is among you" and is added to the household church. From that moment, they are a full member, which means they can participate in all the activities of the house church including discipling, baptizing, and equipping others. The activities include apostolic teaching, fellowship (koinonia), table fellowship, prayer, signs and wonders, and sharing of material resources. Shared meals and breaking bread from house to house are an integral part of the gatherings.[6] The New Testament church was known for extravagant giving, signs and wonders, and great boldness in speaking the word of God as a mark of transformation. The bench mark of unity 'of being one heart and one soul', is not just praying together but sharing all your resources, so much so that no one lacks anything.[7] Worship is not accompanied by loud music, as the persecuted church functions mostly under the radar to avoid detection. Any vibrantly growing church, anywhere in the world, will suffer persecution if it is growing exponentially among the people of other faiths. Non-invasive churches that do not intentionally demolish the devil's domain will have no such problem. In the New Testament church, the best form of tithing was not giving to fruitless church programs, but helping the poor and the itinerant missionaries. And where two or three congregate in Jesus' name, then he is present, thus,

---

[4] 1 Cor 14:23-31
[5] Acts 2:42-47
[6] Acts 20:7
[7] Acts 4:31-35

constituting an authentic church with all the power of heaven and earth.[8] These little house churches in India are like the starfish, the more you divide them the more they replicate. Jesus said, "Do not be afraid, little flock, for your Father has chosen gladly to give you the kingdom."[9]

STRENGTHS

The great strength of the house church movement—and the Indian church in general—is that it is led by very committed Indian leaders. Even more important is the fact that there are thousands of bivocational leaders who, like Paul, earn their own living and contribute their time, talent, and might in advancing the kingdom. This army is steadily growing. They follow the Luke 10 technique of finding a 'person of peace' among their friends or extended families and plant house churches. They are the people who will finally finish the task of discipling this nation. All they need is continuous mentoring, encouragement, and upgrading of their skills. Literally hundreds of thousands of Indians live outside the country, and some of them are Christians. Now the house church planters have started going, not just to the West, but to neighboring countries like Nepal, Bhutan, Tibet, Uzbekistan, Kazakhstan, Myanmar, and even to the Gulf and African countries. This is a healthy development. Birthing of new missions, partnerships, alliances and networks, with the completion of the task of the Great Commission in mind is a very good and healthy sign for India's church.

WEAKNESSES

Firstly, the great weakness of the house church movement—and the Indian church in general—is that there is a great mismatch between the 'people group' oriented harvest force (skilled in a local cultural context) and the harvest field (which is multi-cultural, multi-religious, and multi-linguistic). Often, the church expects the lost to come to it, whereas Jesus expects the church to go wherever the lost are and make them his disciples.[10]

Secondly, an oligarchy of Western church leadership, that controls, manages, manipulates, and hordes the international forums with their superior communication and multi-tasking skills, refuses to hand over the baton to the sons of the Indian soil.

Thirdly, even though our National Constitution gives equality to women, the church refuses to do so. Many leaders come embedded in 'traditional' baggage and refuse to empower women, who form 70 to 80% of the congregation. What a loss that is to the harvest force!

Fourthly, it is also very difficult for church leaders to accept plurality in five-fold ministry leadership and the priesthood of all believers.[11] Vertical

---

[8] Matt 18:18-20
[9] Luke 12:32 (NASB)
[10] Matt 28:19; John 20:21
[11] Eph 4:11; 1 Pet 2:9

hierarchical leadership is still rampant in the churches, instead of the scriptural model of flat horizontal servant leadership. The churches need to understand that they have to pastor the whole city and not just one congregation.[12] We need pastors who will launch believers out into the harvest field.

Fifthly, another weakness is that the vast majority of the villagers are non-literates and, therefore, communication of the gospel has to change from the traditional intellectual discourses to story telling. Christ was a great story teller, and he did not teach anything without the parables.[13] There is an urgent need to convert non-literates into 'Oral Bibles' through systematic story telling, if we are to reach the bulk of India.

Sixthly, library research on the harvest force, the harvest field, and spiritual mapping has resulted in information overload. Not enough field research and mapping has been done on the task accomplished and the task that remains. No research has been done about different successful methodologies, so that others do not have to repeat the same mistakes. This is of prime importance to those in the harvest field.

Finally, the role of the electronic media (e.g. television and radio) has been very disappointing. In spite of astronomical claims, so far they have been used only as evangelistic tools with celebrity evangelists catering mostly to Christians. They need to be transformed into vehicles for discipling the nation through planting radio churches. It is of paramount importance to understand that behind every response card from a seeker is a 'person of peace', who has the potential to plant a multiplying house church.

CONCLUSIONS

This is a 'kairos' moment for India. God is putting all the necessary pieces of the jigsaw puzzle in the appropriate places. Even though the picture is far from complete, God knows what he is doing, and we just have to be obedient. There is much land to be possessed, and all hands on board must be gainfully harnessed.

STUDY QUESTIONS

1. What 'traditional' baggage did Western missionaries bring with them in the 19th century? Why did this strategy fail to penetrate Indian culture?
2. Describe the recent Indian strategy for planting multiplying house churches?
3. What are some of the strengths and weaknesses of the current house church movement in India?
4. What lessons apply specifically to your context?

---

[12] Jer 29:7
[13] Matt 13:34

Chapter 30

CASE STUDY (PHILIPPINES): FROM TRADITIONAL PASTOR TO HOUSE CHURCH PLANTER

EMAN ABREA

Eman Abrea has a B.Th. degree from the Philippine Missionary Institute (Silang, Cavite, Philippines). He has been a Christian leader in various contexts, including pastoring traditional churches, planting traditional churches, and training missionaries and pastors. Since 2002, he has been pioneering the development of house churches in his home country of the Philippines. Email: eman1227@yahoo.com.

INTRODUCTION

Among the fastest growing Christian groups in the Philippines are Couples for Christ (4 million people since 1994), El Shaddai (3 million people since 1983), Assemblies of God (2,853 churches in 2001), Jesus is Lord (1 million members since 1983), and Center for Community Transformation (almost 2,000 house-fellowships since 1992).[1] The last statistic is particularly telling—because Philippine society is family-based, an additional strategy of house church networks is viable if the country is to be reached with the message of Jesus Christ. The aim of this article is to provide an overview of the development of a new house church network in the Philippines.

PASTORING A TRADITIONAL CHURCH

I started to gradually grasp the concept of 'house churches' during the time that I pastored a traditional church which was dying, the growth being merely biological. In 1984, during my first year of pastoring, we experienced growth from more or less 30 attendees to more than 100. All the leaders and members of the church were happy about this growth, in spite of the fact that I had no real experience pastoring any church previously. After a year, the growth became stagnant due to many factors, including my study in a Bible School to finish my Bachelor's degree in theology. I was in school from Monday to Friday and then went back to the church during weekends. I had no time to oversee the life of the church. After my graduation, I continued my ministerial work on a full-time basis from 1986 to 1992. Because my minor was in Biblical Studies, I started to compare existing

---

[1] David Lim, "How Then Shall We Worship? A Biblical Theology of Public Worship", unpublished article, December 2005.

traditional churches to the pattern of the New Testament. During my research, and through much prayer and reflection, I discovered that both Evangelical and non-Evangelical churches were very far from the practice of the New Testament church—non-hierarchical team leadership that encouraged the priesthood of all believers. Although I understood these things, I still continued with my traditional manner of pastoring because I had no idea how to do it otherwise based on my experience.

PLANTING A TRADITIONAL CHURCH

After eight years of pastoral work in the church, I sensed the leading of the Lord to start a church planting work in a nearby neighborhood. Through the help of new friends and other saints from the church, we started to plant another church in the area in 1992. By God's grace, the people were very receptive to the gospel. We began conducting a dozen home Bible studies weekly on a regular basis within a span of six months. We were excited about this result. Because our effort was concentrated mainly on this ministry, it was easy to open new home Bible studies. Many families were saved, converted to Christ, and grew in the fruit and gifts of the Holy Spirit. But because of our traditional thinking, naturally the next step was to congregate these believers into one church building, where we could worship, study the Scripture, fellowship, pray, tithe, etc.

Our focus on winning souls for Christ *outside* the church building shifted to feeding the sheep, caring for them, and encouraging them to regularly participate in the various programs we offered *inside* the church building. People were encouraged to come to Sunday school, worship services, prayer meetings, fellowship, training, etc. Due to these major changes, the growth of the church ceased. Previously, our battle cry was "Win souls for Christ by going to their homes"! But, now the important thing became encouraging the homes and families to come to the 'church'. So, counting the number of attendees was now the major focus. Previously, fellowship and relationship with every home Bible study group was real, intimate, and growing because of their size—about 5 to 14 people per group. But, now intimacy was lost when we came together as a big group inside the church building.

STARTING A CROSS-CULTURAL TRAINING CENTER

The year 1997 was a major change in my life when my friend—then a Chief Operating Officer of Asian Center for Missions (ACM), a missions arm of the Christian Broadcasting Network—chose me as the coordinator for the South Luzon area of the Philippines. During those years (1997-2000), I was deeply involved in promoting, recruiting, interviewing, training, overseeing, and sending missionaries to the '10/40 Window' countries. Because of my new ministry, the Lord gave me the opportunity to minister in Thailand, Vietnam, Hong Kong, mainland China, and the United Arab Emirates. I knew how to work in a free country as well as in a restricted nation. Because of this exposure, I internalized all my experiences and began studying the best way to propagate the gospel of Christ in different countries.

At about this time, I met Dr. David Lim, who is a proponent of the house church movement in the Philippines. I invited him to discuss the topic of leadership in the context of Asian culture. While attending his classes for a week, he also discussed the concept of house churches. When I heard it, my mind was opened—"this is it!" I thought to myself. Praise God, the Lord answered my years of prayer, research, reflection, and study of the biblical concept of the church! The fire started burning within my heart to apply what I had learned. At the end of 1999, I felt the leading of the Lord to resign from ACM and from the church that we planted and organized, which was our source of financial support. I embarked on a new journey of house church planting.

STARTING HOUSE CHURCHES

While meditating on the Gospels and the book of Acts for many months, I heard a message from the Lord—"Go back to Jesus Christ, study his life and ministry, follow his pattern to start a house church." This period was intense because I needed to obey the Lord. The implication of this decision was to start living by faith on a daily basis. My family and I had no options, but to surrender our will, fears, and future to the mighty and loving hands of our Father in heaven. In the end, we resigned from ACM and the church we had planted. But our relationship with them remained as friends and partners in God's kingdom.

From 2000 to 2002, we kept praying for God's direction because we did not know how to start house churches. One day, I saw a copy of *Acts Magazine* where Roberts Fitts' article was published, with the title, "The Church in the House."[2] I started reading it and reflected on its content. After contacting him, he told me to first plant a house church with my family. So, I encouraged my wife and children to have a worship service in our home every Sunday morning. We stopped attending 'church' and started *being* the church. Initially, some of our friends thought we were falling away from the faith because they did not see us attending any activities in church buildings.

Despite this, God worked mightily during our gatherings in the home. During one meeting, I meditated on the words of Christ: "What do you want me to do for you?"[3] We asked our children what their response would be if Jesus was standing in front of them and asked them this question. Our daughter closed her eyes and answered, "Lord Jesus, please touch my stomach because it's painful." Suddenly she shouted, "Wow, the pain is gone! Thank you Jesus!" Our son was also encouraged to do the same and asked the Lord, "Jesus, please heal my headache." He too shouted and said,

---

[2] See also Robert Fitts (2001), *The Church in the House: A Return to Simplicity*, Prepare the Way Publishers.
[3] Mark 10:51 (NIV)

"My head is now okay! Thank you Lord!" These were some examples of God's confirmation to continue obeying his will to start a house church movement.

From our home, some of our friends joined with us to start another house church. As a result, we developed a core group with whom we had regular prayer, fasting, fellowship, and accountability. Through this core group, we started planting house churches in the provinces of Laguna, Cavite, and Batangas. God also opened a way for us to connect with others in the country doing the same thing. Even our former traditional congregation where I had pastored in the early 1980s was also encouraged enough to plant 20 house churches within a year aside from their church planting work in Hong Kong and China! In the span of just over a year, through our own efforts and our partners in different provinces, by God's grace we could safely say that we had planted almost 50 house churches. Even though we had little experience, the Lord was faithful to fulfill all his promises to us. We did different things on a trial and error basis, but we kept going on in spite of many hardships, discouragement, and lack in many things. We had one goal—to please our Master!

EXPANDING THE VISION

We have also helped pastoral movements in different provinces in the Philippines to share and to cast the vision of simple and reproducible house churches. We wish to help them unite as one Body of Christ. We also helped prepare, organize, and coordinate the 1st Asian House Church Leaders Conference in 2006, which was held in the Philippines. There were 46 participants altogether, with representatives from China, Hong Kong, India, Indonesia, Korea, Japan, Philippines, and the USA. This was an historic meeting that gathered key leaders from Asian countries to meet face to face, to have fellowship with one another, to share experiences, to learn from each other, and to propagate the kingdom of God in Asia and the whole world.

LESSONS LEARNED

Though we have had many successes so far, these have not come without challenges and failures. In our first year of planting house churches, for example, we were like mushrooms sprouting and scattering in different places and provinces. But, the house churches that we planted were slowly dying, and some of them were absorbed by the traditional churches. We would encourage anyone at the initial stages of starting a house church network to consider the following lessons we learned:

- *Ministry Focus*—while planting and overseeing house churches, we also had ministries in Hong Kong and mainland China. By doing these simultaneously, the tendency was to neglect the house churches. Therefore, as the Lord leads, seek to make planting house churches the main focus.

- *Leadership Training*—if we had developed strong, trusted, servant leaders, the growth and the expansion of the house churches would have been a steady one during our first year. The leaders we had, however, did not demonstrate the proper level of commitment to the work. So, the house church flocks were attacked by the enemy in different ways. Therefore, be sure about the commitment of leaders to the vision.

- *Experienced Coaches*—because we were novices in this new ministry at the time, we did not know what to do in many instances. Our tendency was to try new things, which most of the time were wrong and impractical. We ourselves were not well-equipped. Before planting these house churches, it would have been best to have an experienced house church planter go with us, train us, coach us, and encourage us the way the Lord Jesus did with his 12 disciples. The role of a discipler—or team of disciplers—is very important in this regard.

- *Financial Support*—we had no financial support in starting the work, as well as no job or business to sustain the needs of our families. We were not able to follow-up with the house churches we had started on a regular basis. It is hard to start any ministry without the assurance of its sustainability. Thus, funding sources should be secured, as the Lord leads, for traveling house church planters.

CONCLUSIONS

I have attempted to explain how God has led us on our journey in starting a house church network in the Philippines. Though we have had successes, there have been many challenges and lessons learned along the way, which we expect will give us greater strength in working with the Holy Spirit in developing the house church movement in our nation in the upcoming years.

STUDY QUESTIONS

1. Can you recall some of the significant milestones in the author's journey leading up to starting his first house church? What are yours?
2. Can you recall some of the hard lessons learned during the first year of house church planting? How can you apply these lessons?
3. Read Mark 10:51. What would you have Jesus do for you right now?

Chapter 31

CASE STUDY (PHILIPPINES):
THE WANDERER—UNPLANNED HOUSE CHURCH PLANTING

ROMULOS 'MOLONG' NACUA

Molong Nacua is a house church planter in the Philippines. He also travels extensively training Christians in saturation house church planting as a strategy to reach his nation for Christ. He has ministered in the context of both traditional churches and the house church movement for many years. Email: chm_intl@yahoo.com.

INTRODUCTION

Over 90% of people in the Philippines are affiliated at least in name with some form of Christianity. Great strides by evangelicals have also been made in the 1980s and 1990s in terms of numerical growth and unity. However, the challenges the country faces include shallow discipleship at the grassroots, second-generation nominalism, and poverty. A strategy of house church planting can be a viable alternative to meet these challenges. In this article, I hope to give a brief but adequate account of my own story as a 'wandering' house church planter and how our regional apostolic team has helped give rise to 400 house churches in the Visayas region of the Philippines.

A SOLID BUT TRADITIONAL CHRISTIAN BACKGROUND

I have been in the traditional church ever since I became a Christian. For over 10 years, I served the church with my whole heart. I had been literally joining Bible studies every night with my pastor, being a part of a worship team, and doing evangelism myself or with a group. I have also been a church stage decorator, a church painter, a church electrician, a church caretaker, a church round-the-clock security guard, and a church janitor. It was the best place I ever found on earth to offer my ability, talents, gifts, time, and energy. I did this all as a volunteer. And for all those years, I never missed a single Sunday church service. Yet, I remained deeply unsatisfied.

I got saved at a camp, and that very day I knew the Lord was calling me to pastor a church. At the same time, I was aware that it would be a process. It was not until nine years later that I finally started a traditional church in our house. For the first couple of months, I was involved with 21 Bible studies each week, 12 of which I led. I was also engaged in prayer meetings, youth night, Sunday night services, a twice weekly crusade that stretched out for six months, weekly discipleship training, overnight prayer meetings, and other special events.

However, it was all draining my strength. I began to feel bored and confused and finally asked God "Why?" I believed that when God called someone to pastor, he would tell them what kind of church it should be. And I began questioning myself too. I told God in my prayers, "Be it a traditional church or a cell church, as long as it comes from you, I will do it." The house church concept, though, at that time never came to my mind. This was simply because, in my view, it was merely an immature way of doing church. The phrase 'house church' here in the Philippines is often seen as a 'not yet' full-grown church, a 'baby church', a 'phase one' church that someday may become a 'real' church once it has enough members to warrant a larger meeting place, like a hall or building.

'Homes' and 'Houses' Everywhere!

To deal with my confusion, I began seeking the Lord and searching the Bible for a way of doing church for me. I did find books on church planting, but they did not fit what I was called to do. As I continued reading, especially the Gospels, Acts, and the letters of Paul, my mind always stuck on the word 'homes' and 'house.' Jesus ministered in the house, preached and taught in the house, healed in the house, ate in the house, and trained his disciples to find a house of peace. There were also households of faith, the household of Stephanas and others, the church in the house, and just "houses" everywhere! And then I also began reading phrases like, "they have turned the world upside-down," and "they have filled Jerusalem with their teaching." I concluded, then, that if I wanted to see their results in evangelizing my world, then I had to follow their principles!

Trial and Error Can Start House Churches

In the year 2000, a few of us began the adventure of starting house churches, with only the word of God as our training resource. It was simply quite exciting. We decided not to rent or build any church buildings and started thinking of our gatherings in homes, not as Bible study ministries, but as church in a revolutionary way. We started 13 house churches in our first year! We gathered our groups together to meet in one place, and we numbered around 180 people in three cities. This was quite a large gathering, especially since traditional church membership here in the Philippines is from 50 to 120 people.

"If you mix the rabbits with the elephants," as someone said in the house church movement, "the rabbits will die eventually." We indeed mixed the traditional church concept with the house churches we had started. We did get rid of the building, but traditional mentality prevailed. We had a program with a master of ceremonies, a Sunday school teacher, a worship team, a testimony time, a preaching time, a tithe, an altar call, and a benediction. In other words, we became a traditional church that was meeting in houses!

We did all of that for three long years from year 2000 to 2003. While doing this 'trial and error' church planting, I continually visited Christian bookstores in search of books on house churches, but failed to find even one book. I really thought I was alone in this journey, but I held on to what I felt to be the right thing. Then, one day, a friend handed me a copy of *Acts Magazine*. It was an old 1995 issue. The article was entitled "The Church in the House", by Robert Fitts, Sr. Then and there, I found myself floating in the air reading his article from cover to cover! Then I reached the end of the article where Robert said, "I predict that in the year 2000, house churches will spring up all over the earth..." And, indeed, we were part of this in the year 2000 without realizing it. Later, I found Wolfgang Simson's book *Houses that Change the World* in one of the bookstores and also Rad Zdero's book *The Global House Church Movement*. Since then, we have been in constant communication with these people.

THE VISAYAS HOUSE CHURCH NETWORK

Since that time, I have become part of an apostolic team that meets monthly for the purpose of discussing our vision of starting house churches in the Visayas region of the Philippines. There are now 400 house churches associated with the work of this team. We are looking forward to doubling this number yearly as we continue training house church planters. We have developed the H.O.U.S.E.C.H.U.R.C.H. strategy for our network of house churches.

H—House of Peace. We encourage our house church planters to find people in the community that 'offer a meal' as an initial sign from Luke 10 that they are open to the gospel. Eating is still a mark of hospitality to most Filipinos and, thus, speaks a message of acceptance.

O—Ongoing Follow-up. Leaders should visit those families twice-a-week to really listen to their needs.

U—Unsaved People. Experience has taught us that is it much easier to start a house church with non-believing people, rather than those who already have a background of religious affiliation. The exceptions are those Christians who are truly hungry for ministry.

S—Someone Needs to Go with You. Jesus sent the disciples two by two. We want to make sure that people have the chance to learn from each other and support each other while house church planting.

E—Establish Your Relationship with the Family. Most of those we train are young people, so we implore them to respect their elders by addressing them in culturally appropriate ways, such as 'Nanay' and 'Tatay', 'Mam' and 'Sir.'

C—Congregate. After a month or two of visits with an interested family—which involves eating, sharing, praying, and listening—we encourage them to invite their neighbors to these get-togethers or other more special events like birthdays.

H—Huddle. Some sort of singing or games are used to make the host family and any newcomers feel at ease. We try to create a celebratory environment when we start house churches.

U—Unify. After the host family has become friends with their neighbors and a critical mass has been reached, we would encourage a regular get-together in that house. We might say something like this: "Since we know each other already and we live in the same community, why don't we gather together in this house once or twice each week?"

R—Represent the House Church Concept. This is the time when we introduce the idea of having a simple church in the host home. We share basic concepts of what the church is and how they can meet in someone's home as a Christian church. Sharing some verses from the Bible helps them understand more.

C—Create Your Own Time Management. Flexibility is the key to cater to all kinds of people, especially those who have different schedules and lifestyles that may not be mainstream, like street people, taxi drivers, inmates, the hospitalized, the elderly, etc.

H—House Church Established! And finally, after getting to know each other's needs and availability, a house church can be established.

ON THE ROAD AGAIN

My calling is to start house churches, train others to do so, and link with other house church planters wherever the Lord leads me in the Philippines. One traditional church, for instance, where I have been invited to speak many times, eventually asked me about house churches. We held seminars on house churches and, at the same time, modeled house church meetings during dinner. This traditional church has had a heart for reaching the mountain people, but has failed to bring people to their church building and has faced financial challenges in funding another building in the area. But now, they plan to start planting house churches among the mountain people.

Similarly, in another city, a church struggles because their building will be reclaimed by the owner. After my speaking engagement there, they called the leadership and had a short meeting regarding what their next move was. The pastor called me and asked me to share about house churches. The night before, he and I had a little discussion about house churches, but I did not know that they were facing a building problem. What happened as a result was a rapid planting of five house churches in five different neighborhoods with five of the church's leaders leading them. Later, the pastor asked me about what he should do now. I suggested that he start a house church in his own house, gather all the house churches in a big place once a month, and have weekly church planter training and progress reports. From time to time, I have also had the privilege of teaching house church principles to 15 to 25 students in one of the Bible schools. They have decided that, during their year long studies, they will start planting house churches in their community until they graduate. This has become a sort of practical ministry workshop for the students. The dean of the school and the small band of student church planters has allowed me to coach them as they continue in these endeavors.

Though I work closely with my team and travel often, I also work with other house church leaders in the Philippines for greater impact. Some networks have focused on college students. Some leaders are in particular cities or towns. Another dear partner works in the mountain area. We have different assignments, yet work together for a greater purpose—saturation house church planting. Our next move will be to have a corporate gathering of house church leaders and have the Lord's Supper together to speak for unity in the Body of Christ. This will hopefully lead to citywide gatherings of Christians in each city, so that we can speak as one voice to the world that we love one another.

STUDY QUESTIONS

1. Can you recall what each of the letters of the H.O.U.S.E.C.H.U.R.C.H. strategy represent?

2. Can planting house churches by 'wandering' work effectively in your context?

3. What does this story tell you about God's ability to spontaneously open doors of opportunity?

4. What specific lessons from this story can you apply in your effort to plant house churches?

Chapter 32

CASE STUDY (CAMBODIA): A HOUSE CHURCH EXPLOSION IN THE WAKE OF THE KHMER ROUGE

DAVID GARRISON

David Garrison, Ph.D. (University of Chicago, USA), is the author of four books on missions, including his most recent work entitled Church Planting Movements: How God is Redeeming a Lost World (2004), available at www.FreshWindDistributing.com. He has been a missionary in Hong Kong, Egypt, Tunisia, Europe, and India. He has served as the Associate Vice President for Global Strategy at the Southern Baptist Convention's International Mission Board (IMB) before assuming the position of IMB's Regional Leader for South Asia. Garrison is internationally acknowledged as a pioneer in the understanding of Church Planting Movements. Adapted from David Garrison (2004), Church Planting Movements, Wigtake Resources. [Adapted and used by permission from the author. Email: dgarrison@wigtake.org].

INTRODUCTION

Cambodia was one of the greatest victims of the decades-long Vietnam War. As the South Vietnamese government fell in 1975, Cambodia saw Pol Pot and his murderous Khmer Rouge rise to power. Before the Khmer Rouge were forced from power in 1979, 3.3 million of Cambodia's less than 8 million citizens had been murdered, starved, or driven from the country. The Khmer Rouge aimed its wrath at anyone with leadership potential: adults, urbanites, and the educated. Their paranoia also led them to attack anything perceived to be foreign, a judgment that fell heavily upon Christianity. By the 1980s, the fledgling Evangelical population in Cambodia, which had never exceeded 5000, was reduced to less than 600. However, the 1990s saw the emergence of a church planting movement in the nation, reaching tens of thousands of people, mostly by saturation house church planting.

SMALL BEGINNINGS, BIG ENDINGS

One of the chief agents God used to spark the Cambodian movement was a young Southern Baptist missionary couple named Bruce and Gloria Carlton.[1] The Carltons entered Cambodia as Strategy Coordinators in 1990.

---

[1] Bruce Carlton (2000), *Amazing Grace: Lessons on Church Planting Movements from Cambodia*, Mission Educational Books.

Although Bruce was already an experienced church planter, he determined that he would not plant any churches in Cambodia. Instead, he vowed to train Cambodians to launch a movement.

Bruce began by recruiting a promising Cambodian layman to assist him in translating a book he was writing on church planting. As the project unfolded, Bruce transferred his own vision and skills into his Cambodian brother. Within a year, the Cambodian apprentice had recruited eight other Cambodian men and a woman, all of them anxious to learn how to plant churches. The Carltons taught personal evangelism, how to study the Bible, church planting, and church leadership. The training was intensely practical, always aimed more at application than information.

By 1992, these house church planters had multiplied the original house church into six house churches. In 1993, the number climbed to 10 and then 20 the following year. Over the next three years, the number of Baptist house churches climbed to 43, then 78, and then 123. By 2001, Southern Baptists indeed reported 220 house churches with more than 10,000 members. The typical house church was comprised of 30 to 50 people. Other Christian groups planting churches also experienced great growth, such that the total Christian population in the country exceeded 60,000.

PRINCIPLES OF THE MOVEMENT

In his account of why this particular Church Planting Movement unfolded, Carlton cited the importance of prayer. "Over the past six years," he said, "there has been more mobilized prayer for the people of Cambodia than at any time in their history." Prayers were aimed at protecting church planters and opening the hearts of lost Khmer people. God answered on both accounts. Prayer was integrated into the lives of the new believers in Cambodia. They evidenced a strong sense of God's direct involvement in their lives. Signs and wonders, exorcisms, healing, and other manifestations of God's power were common-place.

Training was another key to the success of Cambodia's Church Planting Movement. Carlton established the first Rural Leadership Training Program (known as RLTPs) in the country. The RLTPs became vital to the Church Planting Movement in Cambodia. Later, missionaries observed that, "where there were RLTPs in place, church planting always followed." The RLTPs consisted of eight modules of training, each one lasting two weeks, so that the entire program could be completed in about two years. Since most of the church leaders were bivocational, the pastors could not afford to be away from their homes for more than two weeks at a time. Furthermore, the meals for the trainees were provided by newly started churches in the area, and if the training went more than two weeks, the poor church members would be hard-pressed to continue making this sacrifice. In a remote province near the Vietnam border, one could see where an RLTP center has been instrumental in spawning more than 40 new church starts. Dusty roads winding through acres of banana groves leads to village after village, each with scores of

Cambodian believers meeting in thatched-roof homes. Each village church tells a similar story. They have been believers for less than six years. They meet regularly with 30 to 50 members. Each house church has reproduced itself several times over the previous year.

Carlton also implemented a lifelong mentoring approach to leadership training. "I call it the 222 Principle," he said. "It's based on 2 Timothy 2:2 where Paul told Timothy: '...the things you have heard me say in the presence of many witnesses entrust to reliable men who will also be qualified to teach others.'"[2] Carlton applied the 222 Principle as a means of multiplying the personal mentoring approach to leadership development. "Never do anything alone," he told the church planters, evangelists, and church leaders. "Always take someone with you so that you can model for them the vision, skills, and values that shape your life."

At their departure in 1996, the Carltons left behind a small missionary band with a passionate commitment to serve the growing churches of Cambodia. It was this band that carried on the spiritual legacy of the Carltons, helping to plant 220 house churches that reached 10,000 new believers by 2001.

THE MOVEMENT WANES

By the year 2000, though, the Cambodia Church Planting Movement had mostly passed. Before the movement began to wane, other denominations and mission agencies such as the Christian and Missionary Alliance, Overseas Missionary Fellowship, Four-Square Gospel, Presbyterians, and Campus Crusade for Christ all reaped a harvest in Cambodia. In the end it suffered, not from lack of missionary attention, but from too many well-intentioned intrusions from the outside. Foreign funds went to subsidize pastors and church planters who had previously done the work without remuneration. Salaries led to a sort of professional minister class that created a gap between church leaders and common laypersons. Funds also accelerated the rate of institutionalization of training, ministry, and leadership. With funds and institutions came internal conflict within denominational hierarchies over who would control these resources.

CONCLUSIONS

The account above is but one of many similar stories across Southeast Asia that relate how God is bring the masses to himself through the simple strategy of saturation house church planting.

STUDY QUESTIONS

1. Which specific factors helped in the house church planting movement?
2. Which specific factors caused the movement to eventually falter?
3. Would training centers help plant house churches in your context?

---

[2] 2 Tim 2:2 (NIV)

Chapter 33

CASE STUDY (MYANMAR): PLANTING HOUSE CHURCHES IN A BUDDHIST COUNTRY

RAM KHAW LIAN

Ram Khaw Lian holds a doctor of ministries degree (D.Min.) from Union Theological Seminary (Manila, Philippines). He is the founder and director of Myanmar Christian Institute and is a house church strategist ministering in his homeland of Myanmar. Email: lianram@gmail.com.

INTRODUCTION

Today, the Union of Myanmar—formerly known as Burma—is composed of eight major tribes (Burmans, Karens, Kachins, Chins, Shans, Mons, Kayas, and Rakhines) that form a single nation. There are 135 races and languages. Myanmar peoples are very religious and have devoted themselves to Buddhism since the 11th century. Buddhism was already deeply rooted when the first missionary, Adoniram Judson, came to the city of Yangon—formerly known as Rangoon—in 1813. Therefore, Judson said, "it is easier to extract a tooth from a live tiger's mouth than to convert a Burmese Buddhist to Christian faith."[1] But Judson did not give up his vision, although he knew it would be very difficult. Instead, he gave up his life to Christ for Myanmar. God blessed him, and he became one of the most famous missionaries in the world. However, the nation still remains gripped in the teachings of the Buddha. It is in this context that a new house church planting strategy is being currently developed to reach the nation for Christ.

THE STATUS OF HOUSE CHURCHES IN MYANMAR

In 1978, my father received Christ as his personal Savior and Lord, so he was very active in witnessing for Christ to his friends. Before that, he was just a nominal Christian and worked hard to support his family. But, his life and vision were totally changed after he accepted Christ. He and his friends shared the good news wherever they went. Eventually, they were expelled by the traditional church, and they began to have a worship service in our home. That was my first experience as a child of worshipping together as a household. They were just newly converted born-again Christians, but they were able to lead the house church. My father acted as the pastor, although he was just a farmer and an uneducated man. God blessed our house church and increased the number of church members. Eventually, they built a

---

[1] Gerald H. Anderson (ed.) (1968), *Christ and Crisis in Southeast Asia*, Friendship Press, p.27.

church building and affiliated themselves with the Assemblies of God Churches of Myanmar in 1982. I believe, at the time, that there were many house churches started by such lay pastors, but they would soon join traditional churches because there was no access yet to teaching materials regarding New Testament house church patterns, structures, and philosophy. This trend has continued in recent years. According to one magazine, in 2004 there were more than 150 churches led by Chin pastors, almost 95% of whom were having 'traditional' worship services in houses or apartments.[2] There are likely to be many other similar groups in the city of Yangon among the other tribes. Every year, God raises up many house-sized churches in Yangon, though the pastors are unaware of the patterns and philosophy of New Testament house churches, which involves participatory meetings, lay leadership, and multiplication growth.

THE BIRTH OF THE 'HOUSEHOLD CHURCH MISSION' TEAM

God gave me a desire to establish Myanmar Christian Institute (MCI) in order to train church planters while I was studying in the Philippines. I graduated in 2004 and returned back home. I almost gave up on this vision because most of my friends convinced me that ministry could not happen without money or sponsors.

Then God gave me a vision to start MCI from my small rented house and to hold classes for busy ministers and laymen and women who wanted to study the Scriptures regarding missions and church planting. We were able to start classes in September of 2004 with 20 students and three lecturers. By March 2006, we happily saw our first graduating class of 23 students. They are currently involved in missions and church planting across the country. By September 2006, there were 50 students enrolled and seven volunteer lecturers. All this has happened by God's grace!

During this time, I still desired to plant new churches in Myanmar, but did not know how to do so because of a lack of resources, or so I thought. In April 2005, a missionary friend gave me a book entitled *The Global House Church Movement*.[3] I really thanked God for this book because I now had a low-cost strategy to reach Myanmar for Christ—saturation house church planting! We received a shipment of free copies of the book from the author's house church network in Canada for our entire class at MCI. All the students were very interested in house church planting.

We then formed Household Church Mission (HCM) in November 2005. Several months later, I planted a prototype house church in my home. Presently, more than 10 students are actively involved in house church planting and have already established a prototype network of 18 house

---

[2] Yangon Chin Christian Interdenominational Fellowship Magazine, 2004, pp.229-246.
[3] Rad Zdero (2004), *The Global House Church Movement*, William Carey Library.

churches. To push the mission forward, we have developed an exciting vision and mission statement:

The HCM Vision
"To see 1,000 house churches planted
by the year 2030"

The HCM Mission
"Train leaders to
start a church from their homes and
multiply as God leads them to
serve the world for Christ"

In our country, many Christians fail to start a church or ministry because they continue waiting for sufficient materials or funds or sponsors, but God gave me a vision and practical strategy to start both a Bible school and a church planting team.

CHALLENGES FACING THE HOUSE CHURCH

The entire New Testament was written within the context of Roman and Jewish persecution. Asians today are living in the midst of suffering, whether they look for it or not. To be Asian is to suffer. The majority of Christian believers today are undergoing some form of religious, political, or cultural oppression.[4] Struggling is part of life for church planters in our country. To confirm this idea, I distributed 100 questionnaires to pastors in our capital city of Yangon, and 75 were completed and returned back to me. According to the results, 95% of pastors agreed that wolves—from the church and the community—and a lack of resources are the two greatest hindrances to any kind of pioneer church planting. This will also be faced by our house church team as we proceed.

The Wolves

The wolves are coming from within the church and from outside the church to destroy the ministry of church planting. Jesus said, "I am sending you out like sheep among wolves. Therefore, be as shrewd as snakes and as innocent as doves. Be on your guard against men; they will hand you over to the local councils and flog you in their synagogues. On my account you will be brought before governors and kings as witnesses to them and to the Gentiles."[5] This statement of Jesus is still relevant to church planters in our country. Jesus knows our struggles. The seven churches in Asia Minor also dealt with sustained political and religious persecution, as well as

---

[4] Vinay Samuel (1989), *Let Asia Hear His Voice*, Asia Lausanne Committee for World Evangelization, Quezon City, Philippines, p.190.
[5] Matt 10:16-18 (NIV)

experiencing the infiltration of secularism into the lives of believers.[6] In the same way, Christians in general are facing a three-fold crisis of faith, which will also affect our team as they seek to launch a house church movement.

Lack of Resources

We need resources for reaching the lost for Christ and planting new house churches in Myanmar.

First, most of the house church planters need strategy coordinators or coaches who are able to help them spiritually, emotionally, and physically. Most of the strategy coordinators with organizations like the Southern Baptist Convention and Gospel for Asia are successful in seeing church planting movements among unreached people groups because they are committed to coach and assist their church planters.

Second, most of our house church planters need financial resources. We do not need financial assistance to construct church buildings because we are committed to a house church planting ministry. But, we still need help to support the ministry and family of house church planters, since many are quite poor. Though God can and has in the past sent ravens to feed prophets and manna to feed a whole nation, he often sends you and me to meet a need. I often meet and talk with pioneer church planters in Yangon city, and I ask them, "What is the thing you most need for your ministry?" Almost all of them say, "We need financial assistance to support our families and ministry." My heart is always deeply touched. I want to help them, but am unable to. I sometimes feel just like the man who says, "Go, I wish you well; keep warm and well fed, but does nothing about his physical needs."[7]

Today, many Christian leaders are good at talking and writing, but few are good at doing. Therefore, this is a time to live as the apostles lived. They shared each other's spiritual and physical needs and preached the good news to unbelievers.

OVERCOMING THE CHALLENGES

First of all, we can overcome our struggle of temptation through 'prayer'. Jesus said, "Watch and pray so that you will not fall into temptation."[8] The temptation is to be unfaithful in the face of threatening circumstances confronting our house church team. It is easy to be unfaithful to God's calling when our condition is bad for us and our family. That is why many pastors leave the traditional church and go to rich countries in order to have a better life for their families. During this time, prayer is a vital weapon in overcoming these problems: "Prayer has become the first priority of every church planting movement strategist."[9] Without prayer, it is impossible to

---

[6] Vinay Samuel, Ibid., p.191.

[7] James 2:16 (NIV)

[8] Matt 14:38

[9] D. Garrison (2004), *Church Planting Movements,* Wigtake Resources, p.173.

have success in missions and church planting. Therefore, I organized the "House of Prayer Movement" (HOPM). The purpose of HOPM is to equip believers to pray together with their families every night, to equip every believer to participate in the ministry of house church planting, and to equip every house church and family to adopt a child of unbelievers in order win lost souls. In addition, the students of MCI have worked hard to produce the first edition of a new "House of Prayer" journal for September 2006. The goal of HOPM is to see a great house church planting movement that will reach Myanmar for Christ.

Secondly, we can overcome our struggle of facing the wolves through 'love and careful living'. The desire of the wolves is to destroy the ministry of pioneer house church planters and expel him or her from their community. Sharing the gospel is very good and is the main task of the house church planter, but if we share the good news with unbelievers carelessly, sooner or later, the house church planter will be arrested or expelled from the community. Therefore, living as shrewd as snakes and as innocent as doves is very important. This will enable the planter to remain in the community and reach it for Christ. The best and most relevant tool in this regard is the strategy of "incarnational missions", which involves a combination of friendship evangelism, church multiplication, and a simple lifestyle.[10] The basic requirement to accomplish this is "Loving God and others as yourselves". Love for God is why Adoniram Judson gave his life for Myanmar. If one really loves God, offering one's life for others is possible.

Finally, we can overcome our struggle concerning financial needs through 'living by faith'. In November 1997, I prayed to God like this: "Lord, give me 20,000 Kyats for the application cost of my passport, if you really want me to study in the Philippines". As I prayed, God granted me a passport, as well as my airfare for the trip to Manila, but he did not give me a sponsor. I prayed as much as I could for a sponsor, but no answer came. Then God gave me boldness to step out by faith. I did not have any sponsors. I did not have any money. I did not even know who would pick me up at the airport in Manila. But, the Holy Spirit spoke to me with a soft voice in my heart and said, "If you believe, you will see the glory of God". I gained new strength to step out by faith. So, I flew to Manila by faith, and God granted everything I needed, one step at a time. I stayed and studied for six years with a full scholarship in the seminary. God trained me to trust him for all my financial needs while I was in the Philippines, so I have been confident in starting Myanmar Christian Institute (MCI) and Household Church

---

[10] David Lim and Steve Spaulding (2003), *Sharing Jesus in the Buddhist World,* William Carey Library, p.73; Ram Khaw Lian (2004), *The Incarnation as a Mission Strategy for Reaching Out to Buddhists in Myanmar,* A Dissertation of Doctor of Ministry at Union Theological Seminary, Philippines.

Myanmar (HCM) without any sponsors. Ironically, many of my friends have thought that I must have had outside support, because almost all who establish Bible schools in Myanmar have sponsors from abroad.

Living by faith is very hard, especially in 'third world countries'. But the joy of our spirits is incomparable to anything else in the world when God gives us victory in ministry. In my life, God has given me the vision and methods to start a new ministry, but he provided the resources one at a time depending on the need. I seldom received help from expected sources, but God met my needs in surprising ways.

CONCLUSIONS

In the country of Myanmar, having a traditional worship service in a house or apartment is common, but there is a lack of thought given to a New Testament ethos for these groups. About 95% of pastors in Yangon city do not know much about the house church movement. Their vision is to eventually build mega-churches, rather than house church networks or church multiplication teams. Thus, to see a healthy and vibrant house church explosion in the nation in the years ahead, Myanmar needs strategists who have passion for the nation, practical love for house church planters, and experience as part of the house church movement.

STUDY QUESTIONS

1. What are the vision and mission of the Household Church Myanmar team?
2. What are the practical challenges facing the establishment of multiplying house churches in Myanmar?
3. Does your house church network have a vision or mission statement? If not, spend some time prayerfully crafting one.

Chapter 34

CASE STUDY (ETHIOPIA): HOW AN UNDERGROUND CHURCH SURVIVED PERSECUTION

VISION VIDEO / EASTERN MENNONITE MISSIONS

The following transcript is taken from the film "Against Great Odds" (1992), a production of Eastern Mennonite Missions (www.emm.org) and distributed by Vision Video (www.visionvideo.com). Adapted and used by permission.

INTRODUCTION

In Ethiopia, the story is told that many years ago, God created the world, forming humans out of baked clay. Those who came out too dark, God sent to the south. Those who came out pasty white, he threw to the north. But those who came out just right, he put in his chosen land—Ethiopia. Ethiopians are a proud people. Except for a brief Italian occupation, Ethiopia, unlike other African countries, has never been colonized by a foreign power. During the decade between 1982 and 1992, the world witnessed a dramatic new chapter of church history in Ethiopia. The Meserete Kristos Church along with other Evangelical groups were outlawed by the Marxist regime. They became a people hidden from view. Yet, this period saw an explosion of Christianity through underground 'home cell groups' across the nation. This resulted in a tenfold increase of the Meserete Kristos Church from 5,000 to 50,000 believers.

THE EARLY DAYS OF THE MESERETE KRISTOS CHURCH

Christianity is not a modern implant in Ethiopia—the Orthodox church was born more than 1600 years ago. Today, about half of the population is Orthodox. Ethiopia developed severe economic problems during the 20th century reign of Haile Selassie. Suffering from the costs of civil war and from a feudal system of land ownership, Ethiopia had become one of the world's poorest countries.

Individuals such as Bati welcomed the North American missionaries who brought new ideas embedded in a holistic understanding of Christianity. Bati was among the first to join the new church in the early 1950s. He recalls those early days with the missionaries. "We had good times together. We used to sit in the shade of the big trees at the hospital compound. I taught them Amharic, and they taught me English."

The early missionaries opened hospitals and started schools. Most of the time people came to get an education and get jobs and to learn the English language from American expatriates who were working in hospitals and schools. But through close contact with these Christian missionaries, the Ethiopians became interested in learning the Bible. Gebreselassie remembers that, "We really loved each other. We felt like brothers and sisters in the Lord. There was no discrimination. No segregation. We felt very close to each other."

Many indigenous believers might have been content to model a church in the mold of their missionary mentors. Not so for these fiercely independent people. In 1959, when the Ethiopian believers organized their church, they rejected Western labels, calling themselves the Meserete Kristos Church, which in Amharic means, "A Church Founded on Christ." Alemu recalls that "In the establishment of the Meserete Kristos Church, there is one very important point that the early missionaries did—they gave leadership to the nationals."

In the 1960s, a group of young Christians in Nazareth, influenced by the Pentecostals, or "Pentes" as they were known, formed a prayer group. They called themselves "Heavenly Sunshine." "The mission people rented a house," Mekonnen says, "where we could meet together, and there we had times of prayer and times of healing."

Solomon, one of the original members, remembers the grandiose ambitions of those early days at the Heavenly Sunshine Chapel. "At that time", he says, "we were thinking of evangelizing the whole nation. That was our vision, our dream." Alemu adds that "with that, the revival movement began, and that also slowly began to affect the Meserete Kristos Church."

A MARXIST REGIME COMES TO POWER

Then came political upheaval. In 1974, emperor Haile Selassie was overthrown and replaced with a Marxist-Leninist dictatorship under the ruthless control of Lt. Col. Mengistu.

"In the beginning," reports Amha, "Mengistu and his compatriots never thought of destroying the church or working against the church but after being indoctrinated with Marxist thought, they became anti-church, especially the evangelical church."

Shemsu remembers that "the situation of those early revolutionary days couldn't be predicted, but we were aware that the revolutionists were against the work of God."

"When the revolution came," adds Kedir, "we knew very well that it was going to be very, very bad and very harsh because we had been hearing about what was happening to Christians in the communist countries and in Eastern Europe."

On January 24, 1982, the government, fearful of the young church's evangelistic zeal and its popularity with young people, outlawed the

Meserete Kristos Church. Their schools, hospitals, and church buildings were confiscated and in some cases used for political indoctrination.

"I was angry with the government, of course," admits Kedir. "They took our church buildings and used them for other purposes. In fact, at one point I wished the Lord would curse the earth and make the earth open up and swallow the church building. There was much fear. There was a dread among the church leaders, because six of our church leaders were thrown in jail in Addis Ababa."

Many were imprisoned, for political and religious reasons.

Shemsu was one of the first of the six church leaders to be arrested and imprisoned. "We were put in a place in a room [with] dimensions of less than four by four meters, and I was the last one to come in that cell, and already there [were] 31 individuals in the room. The sleeping situation was tight—head to foot. During the night, if you want to change, you can't turn from right to left, there is no space so you have to ask the cooperation of others. And it was an interesting room where they had no window. Only one door. On top of the door they have a little opening where they have barred space for breathing ventilation. When you have somebody sick with diseases, it was very, very tough. We pick the sick one to that opening space where he could put his nose to breathe. Otherwise, the air was not sufficient for him."

THE CHURCH CHANGES ITS STRATEGY AND STRUCTURE

With leaders in prison, assembly forbidden, and no place to gather, the future of the Ethiopian church looked bleak. For a time, Christians worshiped any way they could. Often this meant singing and talking while traveling in the privacy of a car or truck. But more was needed if the church was to survive.

"At the beginning," Alemu remembers, "there was fear and uncertainty, but later on believers began to feel that this can't go on."

Kedir says that "the Lord laid it on my heart, in consultation with the Nazareth elders, that I should take responsibility for bringing together the leaders from other churches for planning."

Alemu reports that "people really believed from their heart that they had to meet together to grow together. If they were alone, they couldn't discuss spiritual matters. They couldn't really share from the word of God and also share their problems in prayer."

"We came together secretly," Kedir admits, "in a brother's home in Addis [Ababa] after one year of hard work, to organize the church again. We met at night to avoid being followed. We knew the officials were watching us."

"So the elders met there," Alemu recalls, "and they began to think how to organize ourselves as an underground church."

The group discussed dividing the believers into small groups for worship and nurture.

Alemu describes the process. "The evangelists began to divide the believers into small groups to meet in different homes, and the numbers were kept to between five and seven in the beginning."

The leaders assigned the believers to cell groups, based on geographical areas. In the capital city of Addis Ababa, this task became easier when a newly completed map of the city fell into the hands of Shemsu, one of the members. "As soon as I got hold of that city map, I took it to my home church in Addis Ababa."

Next began the difficult task of convincing members to go along with the cell group plan, as Kedir explains. "Before the church buildings in Nazareth were closed we tried to form cell groups. But they weren't successful."

Bedru brings to mind that "the tradition in the church was to go out into the place where there is a church service or a church to worship and there you worship, you sing, and then go back home. The home was mainly for the family, not for others to be included in worship, singing, and other Christian services."

"Before the underground days," Zinna recollects, "we gathered for Sunday worship, we had fellowship and then forgot everything when we left. After we went underground, then we began to reach every individual member in the cell groups, teaching and nurturing them."

The idea caught on. Members overcame their initial fears, and the cell group movement took off.

"So others said, 'Why not we open up our homes?'" Bedru remembers. "So slowly the number of cell groups increased as we get more houses. In fact, we are saying that God closed one church but now we are having more than 2,000 churches."

Almaz left her homeland of Eritrea and came to Addis Ababa in search of the Meserete Kristos Church. But soon after she arrived, she heard the bad news. "I remember praying," she recounts, "'Oh Lord, I gave up the world to follow you. I gave up my family and my friends. I came here to worship, and now the church is closed. I have no place to go'. I sat in my apartment and wept, and then I prayed again and the Lord told me, 'The house built with hands is closed, but the real church is not. The holy temple is the body of Christ—it's the body of believers.'"

The cell groups helped members shift from the idea of church being a building to church being a people.

A NETWORK OF UNDERGROUND 'HOME CELL GROUPS'

The cell group movement grew and so did the risk of discovery. To avoid the danger of government informants, only members were allowed to participate in cell groups. "The believers were afraid of having newcomers or strangers in their meetings," says Alemu.

Precautions needed to be taken when using the phone to set up meetings. If, for instance, a communion service was planned, members would use code language, saying, "We should take glasses and bread to that house."

Alemu also recalls that "we were also told how to come in two by two or even just one by one over a long period of time. Maybe taking a half an hour or so when the first person and the last one would come in. Also we tried to take different routes. If the house had three or four directions from which we come into the house, we came in different directions."

"Sometimes," explains Aster, "the cell groups would have tea cups ready and some food, so if the soldiers came to catch us, then we would say we are having a fellowship meal, or we are having a party with friends."

Ironically, not all religious groups suffered the same kind of persecution. The Orthodox and Muslims enjoyed relative freedom during this time of oppression. Zinna, from the village of Wonji, tells of one group that was discovered by the authorities. "A cell group was caught while they were praying and studying the Bible, and the soldiers took them to the Town Dwellers Association office. They asked, 'Why do you meet? You know this is forbidden.' The group leader said, 'No, the Muslim and the Orthodox believers are worshiping openly, so why should we be deprived of our right to worship God?' He told the soldiers they would continue to openly worship the Lord."

With a new church structure emerging, the leaders realized they needed new teaching materials. "Many of the instructional materials [were] developed and written after the church went underground," says Alemu. A primitive press was established in this building on the mission compound. "We had a committee that was responsible for instruction for educating believers," explains Alemu, "and that committee would meet and choose the material. We would edit it, and then we would mimeograph it and staple it. Then we would just pray and hope that God would protect people taking these things from place to place from being caught."

Prayer was a constant and powerful part of each cell group's routine. "A great change came upon us," asserts Gebreselassie, "after we began to fast and pray together. One day as we prayed, the Holy Spirit came upon each one of us like in the book of Acts."

Any occasion became an opportunity to utilize the power of prayer, even sitting down to a snack. Some of the cell group's services lasted all night, with members sleeping only an hour or two before going to work the next morning. One of the key prayer concerns, of course, was for church leaders such as Shemsu, who remained in prison.

Shemsu recounts how "inside, we were kept in the spirit of the church members outside. You could really feel the prayers of our own congregations and the prayers as well as those in America and in the world. All the Christians were supporting [us through their] prayers. All that [helped us] really [feel] alive in that prison."

Singing helped believers cope with the pain and uncertainties of imprisonment and oppression. Members of the Meserete Kristos Church developed their own style of music during the years of persecution.

Pharaoh's sword pursued the people
But the people were spared on the shore of the sea
By a great victory we have received our inheritance
By Your shepherding we have come this far

The words sung often had double meaning. They told biblical stories, but expressed current experiences.

"God used music in a special way," says Tamarat. "Several of us were called to this ministry. Believers did not know each other outside their cell groups. Music helped bring us together. We used to go from cell group to cell group and lead with music."

"Sometimes we had to keep quiet," adds Alemu, "even in singing we couldn't sing out loud. If we wanted to sing, we had to sing very softly and very low."

Cell groups often ate together. In Ethiopia, eating is an occasion that binds people into closer fellowship and friendship. Traditional meals of injera (a pancake-like bread) and wat (a stew), were common occurrences at these non-traditional gatherings. Eating together, along with the coffee ceremony, strengthened the bonds of Christian community.

SIGNS, WONDERS, AND EVANGELISM

The government drove the church underground, but the church did not become invisible. Menoro, a member of the Meserete Kristos Church and a worker at the mission hospital in Nazareth, recalls when the new government ordered the cross in the hospital chapel removed. "When the Marxist regime took over, the officials told me they wanted the cross destroyed. Of course, the cross was built into the wall, so it was quite difficult for them to destroy it completely. But they wanted to paint over it, and they asked me as the maintenance person to do this. We painted it, and the cross came out even more distinctly. Then we tried another paint, and it still came out distinctly. We tried five times, but it remained visible." As did the Meserete Kristos Church.

Members looked for opportunity to share their faith with neighbors and friends. The underground church discovered a new role for funerals—they were a time for open evangelism. Church leaders had learned this practice from an earlier visit to the Soviet Union.

"What we learned from the registered church," reports Bedru, "was that the only time and place they can witness to others is in their workplace, or when they have weddings, or when they have at least a funeral. But that point had really helped us, and we started to use that."

Some of the church's new members, like Paul of the early church, had been its former persecutors. Ahma was one of those people. "After the revolution started, I began to read Mao's works and Lenin's works. I accepted the Marxist teaching and started to fight against the Christian religion."

Ahma had a change of heart when an interrogator accidentally shot herself with her own pistol. "I began to think," conceded Ahma, "there must be a God who is paying retribution to those that are doing the wrong thing. I accepted Jesus Christ. I closed the door and prayed. I decided to follow Jesus."

Ahma's associates quickly noticed the change and forced him out of their circle of friends. "After I became a Christian, I could not do the things I did before. I quit drinking and participating in their evil acts of arresting people. And I quit informing them of what Christians were doing."

A few brave Christians risked being arrested by witnessing openly on the streets. Haragewein would prepare herself with a bottle of water for passers-by to drink, and handfuls of tracts. Then she would venture out into the streets of Addis Ababa. "I go out in the morning and come back at night," she explains. "I do not choose where I go. I preach to everybody. I don't care what tribe, whether they are priests or prostitutes, on the bus, on the street, anybody I find."

In one instance, the soldiers even assisted her in her work.

"I was distributing tracts at Market Square one day," Haragewein recalls, "when a man refused the tract I offered him. He was about to strike me, when a soldier pointed his gun at the man and said, 'Take it.' I said, 'Please don't do anything to him.' Finally, the man was so afraid he took the tract."

The cell structure also provided a system for spreading the church from its urban locale into other parts of Ethiopia, particularly the rural areas.

Mulugetta describes how "our members who go to different parts of the country because of the job assignment. And they testify to others and they gather together in the group. And this group grows a little by little and then [starts] another group."

The rapid growth in membership forced the church to rethink leadership patterns.

Bedru explains that "in the previous situation, we have only the pastor or the elders who would be preaching or the evangelists. But now when you have cell groups in many houses, you need many people to serve there."

Many of these leaders were women. In fact, eventually two-thirds of the church's lay workers were women. "Before the Marxist takeover," Aster says, "we used to contribute to the church by making hand crafts and sewing different types of clothing for the poor. After the authorities took our sewing machines, cloth, and scissors we were left with little to work with. Because of that, we women became engaged in teaching and other ministries."

THE UNDERGROUND DAYS END

The Marxist government fell in early 1991. After a decade underground, the Meserete Kristos Church reemerged into the light of day. Members of the church gathered at meeting halls throughout Ethiopia for their first public worship service in a decade in over 500 Sundays—their faces spoke of immense joy. They greeted each other like long-separated friends.

Aster exclaims, "Just praise the Lord for this opportunity. The Lord has really helped us to grow together in these ten years as an underground church."

Mekonnen recognizes that "today God gave us a second chance, and this victory, and we are worshipping there, and we are singing there. I feel it is a victory for us which God has given us, and I should just rejoice."

One of the most moving differences the Meserete Kristos members notice with their newly found freedom is their singing. Mekonnen suggests that "when we are really in that group, being seven or five, like that, we are not able to sing loudly. But now there are 500 to 600 to 1,000 people together, and you see different faces—the youngsters and older women and older men. It is really enjoyable now."

Worshiping in buildings that still bear the reminders of their recent oppressors, the believers know that they have much to be thankful for.

"One thing that we really are grateful to the Lord for," asserts Tamarat, "is that the times of persecution and times of tribulation were very short compared to what they had in Eastern Europe and Soviet Russia."

The church members are also grateful for the new freedom in teaching children about spiritual matters. "The Lord loves these children," Mulunesh says. "Tomorrow they'll be the leaders, and I want to bring them on the right path so that they will be capable leaders."

Believers are also grateful for the strengths they gained in their decade underground. Gebreselassie believes that "prayer revolutionized the life of the church, just as it did in the days of the apostles." Prayer continues to be so important, in fact, that even during these mass worship sessions, a group of believers meets separately and engages in special prayer for the church worshipers participating in the service.

The church experienced another change—a dramatic increase in numbers. In 1982, the Meserete Kristos Church was composed of 5,000 members. "Before we go to underground we had 14 congregations," recalls Kassa, "and then after the underground [in] this time of freedom, we have 53 congregations."

With a total membership of 50,000 and growing so fast that current church buildings cannot begin to contain all who gather, the church's remarkable success has also created huge challenges. "How to nurture those that come in hundreds and in thousands?" asks Alemu. "That I see as a big challenge in the future."

Even though the church is free to meet in the open, the members are determined to see the cell groups remain a key part of church life. "It is important for the life of the church to meet in small groups," insists Kedir. "I hope this lesson will remain alive in our hearts as it was in the underground days."

"The church grows through challenges," suggests Kassa, "and without challenges there wouldn't be any growth."

Erupting conflicts among the country's many tribal groups are a major source of concern for the church. "We as Christians rejoiced when the war was over," says Mekonnen. "But then we learned of new fighting, so once again we need to pray for peace."

The church is determined not to bring tribal conflicts within its own walls. Shemsu says that "at church, we are from all different tribes in Ethiopia. We have different bodies, we have different responsibilities also. As church, we are committed to the gospel. We are committed to peace."

One mark of maturity for the Meserete Kristos Church is their concern for witness beyond the boundaries of Ethiopia.

"In the early days," Bedru recalls, "missionaries were coming from the north to the south to evangelize. But now I think it should be the time for missionaries to go from the south to the north, and the riches of the north has to come down to the south, so that it can feed and fill them. There must be a mutual exchange I think. And God is going to do this. This is my vision."

AN UNCHARTED FUTURE

Although the church is free to worship for the time being, the risk of religious or political persecution remains. But it is a risk that these believers are prepared for.

"A true church," claims Mekonnen, "a church that is following the ways of God, that is Christ-like, will always face persecution, and we as a true evangelical church will openly preach and witness to people."

"Even today," says Shemsu, "we know that it is possible to go back to prison or to have another kind of hardship, if it is necessary, but God is with us. We are strengthened day by day."

As their worship service ends, and the members of Ethiopia's Meserete Kristos Church return to their homes for another week of work and witness, they marvel at the amazing way in which God has worked in their lives, even during a decade of oppression.

"Some 25 years ago," asserts Shemsu, "we were praying for God to give us people to fill the bench in the churches we had. Today, we are praying to God to give us benches for the people that come or shelter for them to stand under. God is not finished with us. He is still working on us. He makes us perfect for Christ. He will continue creating us."

STUDY QUESTIONS

1. Why were members of the Meserete Kristos Church initially resistant to the idea of church meetings in homes?
2. What advantages did meeting in this format afford believers?
3. How did the role of women change during the underground days?
4. When government persecution ended, the underground church regained its former church buildings. In your opinion, how great is the danger of returning to 'the old way of doing things' because of this?

Chapter 35

CASE STUDY (RUSSIA): THE HOUSE CHURCH MOVEMENT OF MOTHER RUSSIA

HAROLD ZIMMERMAN

Harold Zimmerman is the founding director of Home Fellowship Leaders International (www.homefellowshipleaders.com), a mission agency that empowers the house church movement around the globe [Used by permission of the author. Email: mail@homefellowshipleaders.com].

INTRODUCTION

Russia is a vast land with a complex history. Christian faith was firmly established at the baptism of Vladimir, ruler of Kiev, in AD 988. For close to 1000 years, the Russian Orthodox Church was a mainstay of the people's sense of identity, being tightly interwoven with the fabric of society, all the way from the peasantry to the aristocracy. After the October Revolution of 1917, the Communist rule of Russia saw the establishment of collective farming villages. These villages generally had about 400 residents that worked the farm. Most villagers made less than 20 U.S. dollars per month. Because these villages were built under Communism, they do not have church buildings in them. There are around 38,000 such villages in Russia today. After the fall of the Soviet system in 1991, a spiritual void in the land left many Russians prone to the allure of religious cults, though the number of Christian churches of all types also doubled in the 1990s. For more than 10 years, Home Fellowship Leaders International has been supplying literature to a growing number of Russian house churches, numbering almost 800 groups currently. God is calling us to equip and enable the established groups to send out missionaries to these villages and start at least one house church in each village. This is but one tool among many that God is using today to reach the people of the vast land of Russia.

THE VISION

There is a tremendous ministry possibility in Russia, and God is calling us to meet that need. The people in many villages are hungry to hear the gospel. The people are very poor, and home fellowships allow them to meet without the need to construct a building. In small groups, they can learn about the Bible and what God has promised to his children. They can make the decision to follow Jesus, be baptized by both water and the Holy Spirit and become true disciples of Christ. The first house church in each village can then establish more groups within their own village. In this way, soon everyone can be involved with a local home church. And the good news of

Christ can be spread throughout Russia. This is already happening. Many believers go out to villages in their area and start home groups. They have no formal training, using only our *Home Fellowship Guide* and lessons provided by the Home Fellowship Leaders International team. They have a burning desire to spread the message of Christ. The vision is that God will establish thousands of new house churches as the vehicle with the anointing of the Holy Spirit to bring redemption to the people and land of Russia.

THE STRATEGY

Home Fellowship Leaders International sees the house church approach as a way of nurturing new believers toward spiritual maturity. We are dedicated to providing materials at no cost to challenge house churches to grow and multiply, to reach out to those around them with the message of Christ. The concept involves practical training, just as Jesus trained his disciples using an apprenticeship model. Our materials empower Russians who have the desire to share the good news of Christ to start a home fellowship as a host or hostess and, in time, to become spiritual grandparents in the church of Jesus Christ. Our materials are available to all house church leaders, leaders discipling new believers, those affiliated with traditional churches, those not affiliated with traditional churches, and those house church leaders that minister to what we call 'wounded eagles.' These are people who have, at some time or another, been hurt in relationships with Christians or have come to believe that God is not there for them. We know that God wants everyone to be a disciple of Jesus Christ. A universal fellowship of disciples is what we believe in, regardless of church affiliation. Jesus said, "For where two or three have gathered together in My name, there I am in their midst."[1] We believe this is the church, when Christ is in our midst.

GROWING STRONGER THROUGH HOUSE CHURCHES

The purpose of a recent trip to Russia—one of almost 30 visits—was to see how house churches are working in Russian culture. It was once again exciting to see the fruit of our work in the lives of Russian believers. On the trip, my companions and I had a chance to see very poor villages and also great historical riches of the Kremlin in Moscow.

During our visit to Russia we went to Moscow, then took a train ride to Izhevsk. In the 10 days of our trip, we visited several groups. Two groups were in the city of Izhevsk and two in the surrounding villages five to six miles outside of Izhevsk. We also visited an orphanage and local television show. On the television show, we talked about the gospel and house fellowships—what we are doing and what is happening.

We found that most of the new traditional churches (Charismatic and Pentecostal) are facing serious difficulties because they cannot register. If they cannot register, then they cannot operate as a church. The law, which

---

[1] Matt 18:20 (NASB)

the Russian government passed several years ago, is now coming into effect. Leaders of churches are very concerned about what is happening. Pressure is mounting because the churches that are younger than 15 years could not register and, even if they could register, the government was not accepting what was happening in registration

This is where Home Fellowship Leaders International really comes into play. Almost 800 house churches are using our literature. Since we are not a registered organization in Russia—Russian law does not require home fellowships to register—the government has not done anything against the home fellowship movement so far.

We visited villages that are wide open to the gospel. There are hardly any churches of any kind there, so the villagers, mostly senior citizens, are very excited to hear the message of Jesus Christ.

We attended house church meetings and were delighted to see that they use our materials which are designed to help for the ordinary unschooled believer to lead meetings and teach Bible lessons. We also see that in this time of persecution coming against the young churches, believers are using the house churches as an option for meeting together and still functioning as a church. This is an option of spreading the gospel.

In one house church that we attended, things were moving really well—people were very involved in sharing the gospel with others. There were about 30 people in attendance. Three persons accepted the Lord that night and two others were baptized in the Holy Spirit. Christians were learning to share the gospel and were being filled with the Holy Spirit and love. Praise the Lord for this move of the God within the house churches!

We also found in some of the new churches and fellowships, that Jewish people are deeply involved. Many Jewish people are intermarried with Russians and are involved in sharing the gospel and organizing house churches as well. We personally met several Jewish people in the fellowships laboring for the gospel along with Russian believers.

It was very encouraging for us to see the strong faith of Russian believers that is growing in spite of persecution, accusation, and rejection. The house church leaders sacrifice much while serving very poor villagers. Sometimes they have to walk to be able to reach the villages, where there is no transportation or even roads. Some of them walk through the thick woods in the Russian winter just to be able to lead their meetings and share Christ with the villagers. We were elated to find believers depending on the Lord for everything and growing stronger in faith and in the grace of God through the house church movement.

STUDY QUESTIONS

1. What are the pros and cons of using a common 'study guide' for a house church network?
2. In your opinion, what are the strengths and weaknesses of the Russian house church movement.

Chapter 36

Case Study (Britain): A Retrospective on the British House Church Movement of the 1970s

John Noble

John Noble has been involved in the British house church movement and charismatic renewal since coming back to the Lord in the late 1950s. He led a network of churches called Team Spirit until it linked in with the Pioneer network in 1993. He has been Chairman of the National Charismatic Leaders Conference since 1984 and is an international speaker and author. He and his wife Christine also give leadership to Spiritconnect (www.spiritconnect.org), which is a group of churches within Pioneer (www.pioneer.co.uk). They have five children and 15 grandchildren and have always lived in community or extended family situations. Email: john@spiritconnect.org.

Introduction

During the late 1960s and early 1970s, a home-grown and decentralized British house church movement emerged.[1] By 1979, a total membership of 50,000 people and hundreds of churches could be counted, at a time when many traditional denominational churches were in decline. In addition to activating the faith of participants, it brought revitalization to British Christianity in general. The early practice of meeting in homes eventually waned, though, giving way to gatherings in more public places like school halls and buildings. Thus, the movement later became popularly known as 'New Churches' rather than as 'house churches', though some continue in this form presently. A number of lessons can be gleaned that may benefit others called by God to move in this direction, but who wish to see the longer term survival of a purer house church model.

Why House Churches in Britain?

In China, in the 1950s, it was initially persecution which drove people to meet in their homes. Now, however, many Chinese believers are doing so as

---

[1] W.J. Hollenweger, "The House Church Movement in Great Britain," *Expository Times*, 1980, Vol.92, No.2, pp.45-47; N.G. Wright, "Restorationism and the 'House Church' Movement," *Themelios*, 1991, Vol.16, No.2, pp.4-8; Andrew Walker (1986), *Restoring the Kingdom: The Radical Christianity of the House Church Movement*, Hodder and Stoughton.

a deliberate strategy to reach their nation. In other parts of Asia, house churches have become an obvious way to reach and retain poorer, scattered people in rural areas. More recently, in North America, many are starting house churches as a missional and biblical strategy to reach people for Christ, while some are, in part, also responding to the impersonal mega-church scene.

House churches in Britain, however, emerged for quite different reasons to those in other parts of the world in the last century. British house churches have followed a long tradition of people who challenged the establishment and the spread of formal religion which seemed to deny the power of the gospel and the Holy Spirit. Of course, many of today's denominations started in house or cottage meetings, not least Methodism with Wesley's class meetings in the 1700s. Indeed, his thinking, which went far beyond the discipleship group, is revealed in the early Methodist hymns, which often envisaged loving communities living in peace with 'a little church in every house.' Among many other movements in Britain, the Quakers in the 1600s also started by meeting in their homes and preaching the gospel in the open air, eliciting a harsh reaction from both the civil and religious authorities of the day.

MY PERSONAL JOURNEY

My own journey into a house church began just after I was married in 1958. Having dabbled in the occult and come face-to-face with a personal devil, my wife Christine and I turned to the Bible, which was very much a part of my upbringing in the Salvation Army. There we discovered a personal Jesus who had power over evil spirits and who also brought a dynamic church into being, which was both fluid and mobile—a church which would flow into every corner of society and into the furthest flung parts of the globe. I was so excited that I began to testify about our deliverance and preach about this simple, but powerful kind of New Testament church. I was welcomed in all sorts of denominational churches, mission halls, and Brethren groups where hungry Christians sensed it was time for a change.

After some years preaching and also connecting into the charismatic renewal, which began to sweep through many traditional churches, I realized that few understood or, if they did understand, were unwilling to face the radical changes necessary to turn their churches around to become strong, flexible, Spirit-filled communities. At this point, Christine and I heard the Lord calling us to build a working model. We opened our home to a few friends and some young people who had been touched through our ministry. We were almost totally rejected by all those we had come to know and love through our ministry in the churches. We felt alone and thought we were the only ones who had seen this fresh revelation of church, but were soon to discover that others dotted around the country were feeling the same. Small home churches began to spring up everywhere, many having been put out of, or asked to leave, their denominations.

It must be remembered that, at this time, only 0.5% of the church in Britain could be described as Evangelical, let alone Pentecostal or Charismatic. Liberalism was rife even among those, like the Baptists, where you would lease expect it. Generally, ordinary people were leaving the church in large numbers. Had the churches responded to the message which was coming forth, who knows whether the house church movement would have come into existence at all? Certainly, the home would have featured strongly in any reshaping or restructuring, as there was a major emphasis on relationships, community, and 'church' invading all of life, not just meetings.

MUCH MORE THAN CHURCH IN THE HOUSE

In Luke 10, when Jesus sent out his disciples in pairs to heal the sick and share the good news, he encouraged them to find the 'person of peace' in whose home they could stay. Then he commanded them to 'eat and drink whatever they give you'. Having made a relational connection they could then be about their kingdom business. In a similar way, homes and food and drink were at the center and also the means of building trust in the communities that the British house churches were seeking to reach.

While church in the home featured strongly in all that emerged, developing spiritual communities which could influence the locality was also extremely important. In the church we planted in 1967 in North East London, around 200 people lived within 400 meters of one another, sharing their lives and possessions. This greatly impacted the streets where we lived as well as the banks, schools, and businesses in the small urban area in which we were located. But what was it that drew people together in such strong commitment? At the heart of our vision was a Jesus-centered kingdom message which brought the natural and spiritual realms together and dealt a fatal blow to the evil sacred/secular divide. We saw that the kingdom of heaven was coming to earth, and the church was Christ's body through which it would be ushered right into the real world in which we lived. The grace of God, relationships, freedom in Christ, the baptism in the Holy Spirit, and a fresh understanding of the unity of all God's people encouraged an earthy, non-religious Christianity where diversity and creativity were welcome.

New worship songs abounded and quickly travelled around the world, spreading the message even where ministry was unwelcome. Apart from what was happening in homes, large auditoriums like London's Royal Albert Hall were filled with joyfully worshipping saints. The communities grew as leaders around the British Isles connected with one another. Soon 'apostolic' teams were formed to care for the increasing number of house churches which were emerging and looking for advice, ministry, and prophetic input. These teams became the basis for the numerous networks which exist today with their Bible weeks, leadership events, training programs, social projects, international links, and varying degrees of support structure. It is significant that the tag 'house churches' soon gave way to 'New Churches', as we moved into rented rooms in pubs, schools, and any other suitable buildings. Indeed, today more and more 'New Churches' are buying or building premises of their own, mostly with a strong involvement in the surrounding community.

FAILURES AND VICTORIES

It is important to recognize that the different groupings have been tested in a variety of ways, often around their strengths. In 1976, a wider leadership group which represented the majority of house churches in existence, suffered a painful split which is still difficult to put down to a single primary issue. Personality, theology, differing styles of leadership, and understanding of church authority all played their part. Strong friendships of years were shattered and individuals, ministries, and churches found themselves having to choose sides. My friend, Gerald Coates, labeled it 'the great split forward' as he believes it freed us up to pursue our different callings. Later, our own church and its church plants in North East London were devastated after 15 wonderful years of friendships, ministry, and life together. It may be that perhaps we began to preach the 'gospel of our relationships' or the 'gospel of our church' as opposed to the 'gospel of Jesus'—the Lord will not share his glory with another. Most of the British networks have been tested in one way or another, some even in recent years. These challenges have come over such issues as authority and discipleship, differing ecclesiologies, failure to release one another, revival fatigue, and so on.

God has continued to work, however, and many wonderful things have happened. First, there was a great turnaround in the rejection we experienced from our denominational brothers and sisters. Seeing God's blessing being outpoured upon us and experiencing their own, we began to find one another again and hold joint meetings. Second, we experienced a growing co-operation among charismatic Evangelicals from different denominations through events such as 'Spring Harvest' which drew tens of thousands together each year. Soon, churches and Christians from all backgrounds began to come together in social and missional projects. This persists to this day and is growing as the multiplying numbers of black churches join in 24/7 prayer, Soul in the City, Merseyfest, great prayer gatherings, and the like. In 2008, three major youth works are combining to facilitate HOPE 2008 in which "the whole nation is to be reached, with the whole gospel, by the whole church, for a whole year." There is great anticipation, as this is being widely owned by many churches and organizations.

WHAT OF THE FUTURE?

Recently, we had the privilege of meeting with the present Archbishop of Canterbury, Dr. Rowan Williams, with 30 other charismatic 'New Church' and denominational leaders. We had asked him to come and share his perspectives on 'Fresh Expressions', the Anglican initiative to explore new ways to be church in today's changing world. He spoke with enthusiasm and excitement about some of the things he sees emerging in the Church of England. While he does not wish to dispense with the traditions and liturgy which many Anglicans love, practice, and enjoy, he realizes that many un-churched people cannot immediately relate to these things and some may never do so. He and others are encouraging a new generation of Anglicans to experiment and move outside the recognized channels of the parish system to discover how to connect with the many groups and sub-cultures which make up our British society today.

In some parts of what was the house church movement, the networks have become quite focused on their own particular vision from the Lord. However, others are beginning to sense God's calling to work across the streams. There is a growing realization that, if we believe there is only one church, then we must also behave as one church. This does not mean a mega organization, but rather recognition of those Christians in our locality with whom we can co-operate. This can bring our diversity and our distinctives together for the blessing and benefit of the area where God has placed us. In other words, we know we cannot fulfill God's purposes for our villages, towns, and cities alone.

CONCLUSIONS

The turnaround in the spiritual life of the church in Britain was matched by a new openness in society in the 1970s. This came about, I believe, for two primary reasons. First, the outpouring of the Holy Spirit in charismatic renewal crossed denominational lines. Second, the house church movement was open to the radical changes needed to see the whole church restored to her former simplicity and glory. Though the British house church movement eventually waned and gave way to a more traditional way of organizing and understanding itself, there are signs of yet another resurgence of house churches in recent years. This will hopefully, once again, bring fresh vigor to the Body of Christ at large.

STUDY QUESTIONS

1. What factors brought about the house church movement in Britain in the 1970s?
2. What were the movement's strengths and weaknesses?
3. The house churches eventually moved into their own buildings and other more public meeting places. What are the pros and cons of this decision?
4. What steps can you take to ensure that your house church network will not eventually depart into more traditional ways of organizing and meeting?

Chapter 37

Case Study (USA):
The Story of Church Multiplication Associates—
From California to Chiang Mai in Seven Years

Neil Cole

Neil Cole is the founder of Church Multiplication Associates (www.cmaresources.org), a worldwide network of 1000 'organic' churches that meet in homes, offices, and just about anywhere. His several books include Organic Church: Growing Faith Where Life Happens (2005) and Cultivating a Life for God (1999). Email: neilcole@aol.com.

Introduction

The following tells the story of Church Multiplication Associates, a worldwide family of 'organic churches', sometimes also called 'simple churches' or 'house churches'. We meet in homes, offices, coffee shops, and just about anywhere. At the time of this writing, our estimation is that there have been well over 1000 churches started in 36 states in the USA and in 31 nations around the world in only seven years.

Abandoning All

In 1998, my family and I were commissioned to start something new in the city of Long Beach (California, USA). We came to start new churches among urban post-moderns. Starting a single church was not an option for us; we would settle for nothing less than a church multiplication movement, and we would abandon all things, even successful ones that would hold us back from the goal. I have found there are many effective ministry methods that also hold back multiplication. Success, as defined by most of Christendom, is often counter to healthy reproduction. We were willing to abandon anything that would not multiply healthy disciples, leaders, churches, and movements. For this reason, we also started a new organization, called Church Multiplication Associates (CMA), to develop the resources to accomplish the mission. We selected Long Beach because we were looking for three things: an urban center, an area with a large university system and many young people, and a location by the beach (for baptisms, of course).

Starting Small

We came with a few methods that had proven effective in reproducing disciples. A far greater asset was our desire to learn and hearts willing to listen to what the Spirit had to say. The churches that God started did not look like our plans, but as we followed the leading of the Lord of the harvest, we discovered ways to start churches that were healthy and could reproduce. These new churches were small and met mostly in homes.

I never set out to start 'house churches' and am always a little surprised when I am considered an authority on such. We usually do not call them house churches. Instead, we call them 'organic churches', to emphasize the healthy life and the natural means of reproducing that we longed to see.

We do not mandate that churches remain small and meet in homes; that would miss the point. We seek that churches be healthy and reproduce. The reason our churches actually do tend to stay small is the dynamic life-changing property of a 'band of brothers and sisters' that are actively on mission together. There is an innate quality to our expression of church that causes them to want to remain small, intimate, and involved on mission.

The new churches we saw starting were different from others of which we had been a part. They were the result of planting the seed of the gospel in good soil and watching the church emerge more naturally, *organically.* These organic churches sprang up wherever the seed was planted: in coffeehouses, campuses, businesses, and homes. We believe that church should happen wherever life happens. You should not have to leave life to go to church. Because we were approaching church as a living entity, organic in essence, we followed certain natural phases of development. The result was reproduction at all levels of church life: disciples, leaders, churches, and ultimately movements. In all of life, reproduction begins at the cellular level and eventually multiplies and morphs into more complex living entities. Life reproduces, and usually it develops from micro to macro. Our movement has developed in just such a manner.[1]

As we discovered new things, we shared our learning with others in a training context we called Organic Church Planters' Greenhouse, which consisted of a weekend training retreat followed by regional monthly gatherings of church planters.[2] Soon, organic churches were starting all over the United States and the world. It may seem as though we know something of what we are doing, but we did not start with an ingenious plan. Rather, we learned from our mistakes as well as our accidental successes and passed them on to others. We also have constantly kept our ears open for what others are learning around us. One characteristic of our training resources that is both a blessing and a curse is that they are constantly being changed and improved based on experience out in the field.

IT'S TIME FOR A COFFEE...AND GOD'S VISION FOR A CITY

Our first plan was to start a coffeehouse. We had the whole scenario worked out: who would bake muffins and pastries, who would brew coffee, who

---

[1] Neil Cole (2005), *Organic Church: Growing Faith Where Life Happens*, Jossey-Bass.

[2] To find out more about training opportunities visit: www.cmaresources.org.

would play guitar and sing cool 'Jesus songs' in the corner. We even had a space rented to turn into the business. Then the Lord stepped in and whispered in my ear: "Why start coffeehouses to attract lost people? Why not just go to the coffeehouses where they already are?"

That was a turning point for us. Our original strategy required us to 'convert' people from the coffeehouses they already loved to our coffeehouse, so that we could then convert some to Jesus. The Lord of the harvest, once again, had a better idea. This simple transitional lesson meant the difference between becoming just another attraction-oriented 'come to' form of church to actually becoming a missional and incarnational 'go to' church that goes to the lost.[3] We found that if you want to win this world to Christ, you are going to have to sit in the smoking section.

We found that desperate people were more receptive to the good news of Jesus than people who were content with themselves. Bad people make good soil for the gospel; there is a lot of fertilizer in their lives.

Most Christians today are trying to figure out how to bring lost people to Jesus. The key to starting churches that reproduce spontaneously is to bring Jesus to lost people. We are not interested in starting a regional church, but rather in making Jesus available to a whole region.

For the first seven weeks that my family was in Long Beach, we were homeless. A couple we knew had a house they wanted to rent to us, so we packed up and prepared to move, only to find that the previous tenants had changed their mind about leaving, and so we found ourselves without a home. We stored all our earthly possessions at my office and slept on borrowed beds and couches or in motels. We were a traveling band of nomads, wandering in the wilderness with a dog, a cat, a bird, and children.

For two weeks we stayed in a motel, but we could not keep the pets there. They stayed in my office. So several times a day I would take my dog for a walk. I remember one night I took the dog to the top of Signal Hill, surrounded by the city of Long Beach. While the dog was sniffing every bush, I had a heated discussion with God. Why had we been dislodged from our home? I asked God what he was trying to say to me, and he answered.

In that night I heard the city, and God's voice spoke to my heart. I heard wives and husbands screaming at each other. I heard dogs barking, cars screeching, sirens blaring, and guns shooting. I heard the things that Jesus hears when he listens to the city, and I began to weep. In that moment, the Lord broke my heart for the city and the people of the city enslaved to darkness. I begged God to set the captives free and establish his kingdom in the city of Long Beach as it is in heaven.

After that, the Lord opened up the original house we meant to come to, and we moved in. The new house was a back unit on an alley, but without a

---

[3] M. Frost and A. Hirsch (2003), *The Shaping of Things to Come*, Hendrickson Publishers, pp.18-30.

yard. We still had a dog, so each night I went on prayer walks with the dog (well, at least I was praying, I can't speak for the dog). I found a coffeehouse in my neighborhood that was full of young people who were there every night. I would pray for this place and the people I saw there each night as I walked the dog. I spent hours begging God for the souls of these young people. I began to hang out at this coffeehouse with several of the teammates who joined our work.

We played chess, checkers, or dominoes with the regulars who came to the coffeehouse, and we became part of the crowd. We would listen intently to people's stories and offer compassionate prayer for those who were hurting. We did not really preach at people, but they would often ask us about our spiritual lives. There must have been something attractive about our lives because many were drawn to discover more about Christ.

Before long, my living room was filled with new life. Rather than move to a larger space, we sent small teams of two or three to other coffeehouses to start other churches.

A MOVEMENT IS BORN

In our first year, we began 10 new churches. In our second year, Church Multiplication Associates (CMA) started 18 churches. The next year, we added 52 new starts. The momentum was beyond our expectations. In 2002, we averaged two churches every week being started and had 106 starts. The following year, we saw around 200 starts in a single year. We estimate that close to 400 churches were started in 2004, but counting the churches has become a daunting task. At the time of this writing, our estimation is that there have been well over 1000 churches started in 36 states and 31 nations around the world, in only seven years.

These churches we were starting were small (averaging 16 people) and simple. The term *simple church* began to gain popularity, because we valued a simple life of following our Lord and avoided many of the complexities of the traditional church. Complex things break down and do not get passed on, but simple things are strong and easily reproduced. Ordinary Christians were able to do the extraordinary work of starting and leading churches because the work was simple, the results powerful.

We started articulating this profound goal for CMA: "We want to lower the bar of how church is done and raise the bar of what it means to be a disciple." If church is simple enough that everyone can do it and is made up of people who take up their cross and follow Jesus at any cost, the result will be churches that empower the common Christian to do the uncommon works of God. Churches will become healthy, fertile, and reproductive.

The traditional church has become so complicated and difficult to manage that only a rare person who is a professional can do it every week. Many people feel that to lower the bar of how church is done is close to blasphemous because the church is Jesus' expression of the kingdom on earth. Because church is not a once-a-week service but the people of God's family, what they have actually done is the opposite of their intention. When church is so complicated, its function is taken out of the hands of the common Christian and placed in the hands of a few talented professionals. This results in a passive church whose members come and act more like spectators than empowered agents of God's kingdom.

The organic or simple church, more than any other, is best prepared to saturate a region because it is informal, relational, and mobile. Because it is not financially encumbered with overhead costs and is easily planted in a variety of settings, it also reproduces faster and spreads further. Organic church can be a decentralized approach to a region, nation, or people group and is not heavily dependent upon trained clergy.

CMA's mandate is clear and simple: to reproduce healthy disciples, leaders, churches, and movements to fill the earth with God's kingdom. We have developed some very simple ways to release the power of multiplication at each of these levels of kingdom life and growth. Saturating the globe with healthy and vital disciples is our mandate. It appears that God is fulfilling our deepest desires.

The smallest building block of our movement is not the "organic churches" but the Life Transformation Groups (LTGs).[4] This is a group of two or three people who meet weekly to challenge one another to live an authentic spiritual life. Members of these same-gender groups have a high degree of accountability to one another in how they have walked with the Lord each week, which involves mutual confession of sins as well as reading a large volume of Scripture repetitively. LTGs are also missional, in that they actively pray for the souls of lost friends, family, associates, and neighbors. This is the context in which we multiply disciples, which must come before we multiply churches.

Multiplication growth starts small and with time builds momentum, until it is beyond control. We look forward to times when we are surprised by the kingdom expansion.

PLANTING CHURCHES WITHOUT EVEN KNOWING IT

One evening at one of my own churches, Michael (who paints houses for a living) asked me about the church we had on Gaviota Street in Long Beach. Gaviota is only a few blocks from where I lived at the time. I told him we didn't have any churches on Gaviota...yet (being an optimist I always add, "...yet"). He smiled and said, "Yes, you do." He told me he had been painting a house and noticed that cars started coming to the house across the street. People would pull out guitars, bongos, and Bibles (a sure sign of a church), and go into the house. He went over to introduce himself and mention that he had a church meeting in his home as well. When they saw him, they recognized him and said they were also a part of our network of

---

[4] Neil Cole (1999), *Cultivating a Life for God*, www.cmaresources.org.

churches. A church had started only a few blocks from my home, and I didn't even know about it. When I heard this story, I felt as though we had finally reached a goal of spontaneous reproduction; we were beginning to see things get out of control. We still have much to learn, but God seems to be showing us the way to release spontaneous multiplication.

A couple of us from one of our networks started a new church in an apartment complex in the barrio of East Los Angeles. On a Saturday, we went to the apartments to have a barbecue and baptize new believers. When we arrived, I was surprised to see Carlos, one of our other church planters there. He was also surprised to see me. He led a church that he had already started there in Spanish. Suddenly there were two churches on the block, one in Spanish and one in English. Could it be that we are now bumping into each other?

I went recently on a trip to Asia with Phil Helfer, one of the key leaders and co-founders of CMA. On our return flight, we met a flight attendant who was expecting her first child. As we talked, we found out that she had lived in Long Beach and was a Christian. What we did not find out until a few weeks later is that she was a part of one of our churches. It astounds me that in such a short time we are discovering people in our movement all over the place, even 36,000 feet above the Pacific Ocean.

One church I am a part of has sent missionaries to various parts of the USA in cities like San Francisco, Portland, Salt Lake City, and Denver, and internationally to France, North Africa, Afghanistan, The Canary Islands, Kosovo, Cypress, and Romania. A daughter church from this one has sent missionaries to American cities like Seattle and Phoenix, as well as internationally to places like Bangladesh and Chiang Mai.

This is not the experience of every organic church network. We have also had many leaders disappoint us, churches that failed to live for a long time, and entire networks that have dissolved. Paul also experienced much of the same. Jesus had Judas, Paul had Demas, and we will all have leaders who disappoint us, in fact, this will be the greatest pain any of us feel in ministry. This is the messiness of organic church, but it is worth the pain to see those who do take root, grow, and bear much fruit—30-fold, 60-fold, and 100-fold.

STUDY QUESTIONS

1. What are some of the key ways Church Multiplication Associates are being missional?
2. What is the purpose of the Life Transformation Groups?
3. What are some practical lessons that you can apply to your context?

Chapter 38

CASE STUDY (USA):
A CITY OF HOUSE CHURCH NETWORKS

TONY AND FELICITY DALE

Tony and Felicity Dale are both family doctors, trained at Barts Hospital (London, England). Between them, they have authored many books on healing and medicine, and more recently on house church life and practice. Felicity's two most recent books, An Army of Ordinary People (2005) and the Getting Started Manual (2003) have helped literally thousands of people around the world start churches. Tony and Felicity helped to start House 2 House magazine (www.house2house.com), which they also edit.

INTRODUCTION

God is moving across the USA in extraordinary ways. According to the latest statistics produced by the researcher George Barna, 5 million people in the USA are currently involved in some form of house or simple church. The city of Austin (Texas, USA), where we are based, is probably fairly representative of what God is doing in a university city. This report will cover the story of the network of house churches we are involved in—just a very small part of what God is doing in this city. We will then discuss what is going on at a citywide level.

WANDERING IN THE SPIRITUAL WILDERNESS

It was in 1987 that the Lord led us to move to the USA. We assumed, naively, it was because God wanted to expand the ministry to doctors and nurses that we had been leading in Britain and facilitating in various other countries around the world. However, when God landed us in Texas, knowing no one, God appeared to return to England, and did not show up again in our lives for nine long and difficult years!

During that spiritual sojourn on the backside of the desert, we had much opportunity for reflection. For many years, we had been part of what was known as the 'British House Church Movement'. In the 1970s, all over Britain, churches spontaneously emerged. It was a grass roots movement. Because these churches mostly began in houses, they were known as house churches, but they rapidly outgrew the homes and rented other buildings. Many of these churches were characterized by a non-religious Christianity— life lived from the Spirit within rather than obeying a set of rules, a shared lifestyle, team leadership, and the participation of the whole body.

On our arrival in the USA, we attempted to get involved in the church scene. But the values of the churches we had known in Britain were so different from those of the churches in which we now found ourselves. We made many mistakes, and began moving from church to church, longing for the depth of fellowship we had known in the past.

Finally, we arrived at the point of even taking the quite risky step of delivering an ultimatum to the Lord—either he changed things for us, or we were going to return to Britain where at least we could earn a living.

IT ALL STARTS AT HOME

It was at this point things began to change. We had been involved in a business that brought us into contact with many unbelievers. We invited about a dozen of them to come to our home for pizza and a discussion of business principles. We let them know that we would be using a book reputedly written by the wisest man who ever lived. So, 12 unsuspecting businesspeople came to our house for an interactive discussion based on the book of Proverbs. We used a pattern that we have used many times since then when starting churches with unbelievers. We use three symbols to aid us in our study: a question mark for something not understood, a candle for something that sheds light or brings fresh understanding, and an arrow for something that pierces the heart—i.e. this is God speaking and you know you have to take action. Our discussions were very broad ranging, and over the course of a year, everyone in the group became a follower of Jesus.

At the time, we were taking these new disciples to a church that met about half an hour from our home, but when this church physically moved yet further away, we spoke to the senior pastor. He recommended that we start a church, and used for us a convincing argument, namely that according to Dr. Peter Wagner, statistically the best means of evangelism within the Western context is starting a church.[1]

At the time we had teenagers at home. We started a 'Breakfast Bible Club' for them and their friends. We ran it on a Sunday morning because the Christian kids would be in church, and we wanted to touch unbelievers. So we cooked a huge breakfast, and the kids started coming. They came for the food, but they stayed for the activities afterwards which were all Bible-based. Soon, around 20 of them had given their lives to the Lord. The marked changes in their lives influenced some parents to get involved too.

When we merged the business people's group with the teenagers and their families, there were over 50 of us in our small suburban home. At this point we faced a choice. Would we do what is traditionally done when a church gets too big for a home and rent a building somewhere, or was God leading us to do something different?

We had had nine years to think this one through. As we thought back over our time of involvement in a previous move of God back in Britain— actually a church planting movement—the times we most valued were in the

---

[1] P. Wagner (1990), *Church Planting for a Greater Harvest*, Regal Books, p.11.

early days when the churches were still small and met in homes. Here we could easily obey the 'one anothers' of the New Testament—to love one another, bear one another's burdens, teach and admonish one another, etc. In fact, the more we searched the New Testament, the more obvious it became that it was written from the perspective of small communities of disciples, intimately involved in each other's lives and laying down their lives to spread the gospel in a meaningful way to the world around them. Added to that, we were hearing stories from countries like China where God's kingdom was extending rapidly through multiplication of smaller churches, because it was too dangerous to congregate in larger numbers. The decision was easy! We would not use a traditional model of church, but we would multiply smaller churches that met in homes.

LEARNING THE PRINCIPLES OF GROWTH AND LOSS

Following some mission trips to areas of Africa and India where church planting movements were actually occurring, we realized that churches did not have to grow by slow addition, but multiplication was also possible. The key to this was following the principles in Luke 10, a key passage that God is using all over the world. Luke 10 is the passage where Jesus sends out 70 disciples into various towns and villages. These principles include:

- Hearing from the Lord where he wants us to go
- Prayer that the Lord of the harvest will thrust out laborers into the harvest
- Prayer walking and spiritual warfare
- Finding the person of peace
- Creating a relationship with the person of peace
- Staying in their home and eating with them
- Bringing the God of the supernatural into any areas of need
- Preaching the gospel of the kingdom

As we understood these principles, we grew more rapidly. At this stage, we had several churches that had grown from new believers and some others that were primarily people who had been involved in traditional churches before they had become involved with us. All of us were seeking to reach out. We met together once a month on a Sunday morning for a celebration.

As the house churches grew in number, we ran into some problems. We had quite a number of youth and young adults in their early 20s who had recently become believers. We discovered that mornings did not suit them and, therefore, they did not take part in the celebrations. Another problem surfaced with the house churches we had started in low income housing projects. The kids from these groups had not cleaned up their language! This caused challenges to the families with kids who were being home-schooled. They were not accustomed to foul language being used in church! So the leadership team met together and decided that celebrations did not model what we were trying to live in being house churches. As we prayed and sought the Lord, we sensed that we might do better to only occasionally call all the house churches together if a speaker was coming through town or if there was something we wanted everyone to hear.

This had some other interesting effects we had not anticipated. Many who had become involved from a traditional church background went back to their old churches. To them, they had been coming once a month to the 'real' church, i.e. the celebrations. However, the people who had been birthed into the house church had always wondered why we bothered with celebrations anyway! They preferred the small group meetings. It was a good illustration of Jesus' parable of the wineskins.[2] If you put old wine into new wineskins, some people will say, "The old is better."

OVERLAPPING HOUSE CHURCH NETWORKS

In 2000, we were approached by two leaders from other house church networks in our region, asking if we would join them in starting a magazine that speaks to the house church movement around the country. We agreed, knowing that in many moves of God there had been a magazine that somehow spoke into the movement. They had the idea, but somehow we became primarily responsible for the magazine, which is called 'House2House'. Since that time, God has used this magazine to spark many kingdom expanding ventures around the globe—it has been a real privilege for us to partner with God in this way. This turned our focus away from the city to the rest of the nation and into other nations. But Jesus did not need us for our city. There were many other far more significant works emerging in the city that had little, if anything, to do with us. Because house churches tend to be under the radar—they are not listed in the telephone book—there can be a lot of activity going on without others being aware of it.

For instance, a few years ago, Campus Renewal Ministries, an organization that seeks to unite all the different Christian ministries on campuses across the country for prayer, commissioned a survey of the University of Texas in Austin to see what different groups or subcultures were represented within the University. The survey revealed over 500 distinct groups—for example, Indian students in the Department of Engineering, or students studying art who lived in a particular hall of residence. The different organizations within CRM began to pray and strategize towards a visible expression of the Body of Christ—what they called an 'authentic faith community' (AFC)—being formed in each one of these groups. They trained the students to socialize in areas where the subcultures congregated, and through acts of service and more overt evangelism, reach out to their fellow students. As they became followers of Jesus, they would form them into an AFC. Last school year, they had AFCs in 82 of these subcultures. This has now grown to over 100 AFCs across the

---

[2] Luke 5:36-39

campus. The potential for reaching many for Christ is great, seeing that the city of Austin has a large student population of around 100,000.

Similarly, in 2003, we suddenly became aware of a network of more than 30 AFCs in the same area of town where we live. A gentleman who had been on the staff of a mega-church had come to our city with the intention of starting simple expressions of the Body of Christ by reaching out into pockets of lostness. His groups meet all across town, and he and his wife have become good friends of ours.

On another occasion, the part-time student who handled the administration of 'House2House' magazine, asked us if we knew who it was in the north end of our city who had just ordered a second case of one of our books. We had no idea, but we contacted him to find out. A senior executive at one of the major computer companies in the city had recently left the mega-church where he had been on the elder board. While asking the Lord what he should be doing next, he came across one of our books, *Simply Church*.[3] Liking the ideas expressed in it, he bought a case and handed them out to all his friends saying, "If you are interested in church like this, let me know." Now well into his second case of books, he had started a network of six churches in just six months. These churches are heavily involved in social works tied to evangelism and have seen many people find the Lord.

The Lord is also leading some other more traditional churches to move in this direction. An Anglican church in the city has recently broken down into a network of four house churches. And in a neighboring town, a Church of Christ church is actively expanding via house churches. Increasingly, it seems that the Lord is blurring the distinctions.

CONCLUSIONS

The story of our house church network is but one thing that God is doing in our city. Because of the grassroots nature of what is happening, there is an increased desire for connection between the various house churches and similar kingdom ventures. As such, we now meet on a regular basis with leaders of house church networks from every type of background within the greater Austin area. What matters most is the kingdom of God. House churches of all persuasions are working together to expand it.

STUDY QUESTIONS

1. Being 'trained in the wilderness' before being 'launched into ministry' is a theme in the Scripture. What is your personal story in this regard?
2. Luke 10 was an important strategy in this story. Read Luke 10:1-11. How can you apply this to your context in starting house churches?
3. There is a cross-pollination of several independent house church networks in this case study. What are the ways in which God can use this decentralized phenomenon to his advantage?

---

[3] Tony and Felicity Dale (2002), *Simply Church*, Karis Publishing.

Chapter 39

CASE STUDY (CANADA):
HOUSE CHURCHES AND UNIVERSITY STUDENTS

RAD ZDERO

Rad Zdero earned his Ph.D. degree in Mechanical Engineering from Queen's University (Kingston, ON, Canada) and is the manager of a hospital-based orthopaedic research lab. He has participated in, led, and started house churches and cell groups since 1985. He is currently part of HouseChurch.Ca (www.housechurch.ca), which is a church planting team developing a network of house churches in the greater Toronto area and beyond. He is the author of The Global House Church Movement (2004). [Used by permission of the author. Email: rzdero@yahoo.ca].

INTRODUCTION

The New Testament record and church history demonstrate that the spread of the good news of Christ can be accelerated that much more when it happens within the context of a homogenous people group that shares common characteristics among its members, such as language, customs, socio-economics, etc. In a quite real sense, a university campus is the context in which one can find the people group known as 'university students'. In addition to those listed above, this group has the added unifying factors of being within a very narrow age range (i.e. usually between 18-21 years of age for undergraduates) and being encircled by a relatively small geographic boundary (i.e. the campus). It is with this in mind that the following case study is offered, which describes how a house church can function effectively to reach and disciple the university student for Christ. Names of people have been changed to preserve privacy. It is worth noting that in Canada, many mission groups with active campus ministries such as Campus Crusade for Christ, Intervarsity Christian Fellowship, and the Navigators operate in a similar fashion as that described below, with a strong emphasis on Bible study groups and prayer groups that meet in homes, dormitories, cafeterias, and classrooms.

SOWING SEEDS

Bill and Darlene, a missionary couple affiliated with The Navigators of Canada, found themselves stationed at Queen's University in Kingston, Canada. They were to carry on the work pioneered there years before by early Navigator staff. They focused on helping the dozen students in there midst to memorize and study the Bible and apply its principles to their lives. They did this primarily one-on-one, a typical Navigator habit first employed by its founder, Dawson Trotman, during the late 1930s among US Navy men who responded to the gospel. This approach was based on the passage in 2 Timothy 2:2 (NASB), which states: "And the things which you have heard from me in the presence of many witnesses, these entrust to faithful men, who will be able to teach others also." In addition, they would gather these students together in a small group setting for more Bible study, prayer, discussion, and learning in a student house just a few minutes walk from campus. Bill and Darlene were soon joined by a single woman Navigator missionary named Trudy, who was known for her quiet demeanor, but solid and steady walk with the Lord. This trio carried on with their task. Try as they might, the ministry remained modest for some time.

SUDDEN HARVEST

Enter Jenny, a bubbly and bright freshman from Toronto, Canada, who had a solid Christian testimony. She joined the Navigator student group and began to get excited about inviting her fellow university friends, many of whom she had known from her previous church connections. Word spread about the group, and soon the numbers swelled from a modest dozen to four times the size. Three seasoned missionaries. Over 50 energetic university students. What was to be done? Could they handle this kind of growth? Would the student house they were meeting in be able to accommodate these numbers? But more important questions were pressing. How many of these students were really followers of Christ? How many were there merely for social reasons? How could three Navigators effectively take 50 students to the next level of their Christian walk and calling? There was only one thing to do. Multiply student leaders!

TRAINING REAPERS FOR THE HARVEST

Bill, Darlene, and Trudy identified the more mature Christians in the bunch and invited them into a leadership huddle for training that would meet at another Christian student house on campus. This core group of a dozen met every other weekend for teaching, prayer, planning, and relationship building. This was somewhat reminiscent of Jesus' inner circle of 12 'disciples' (i.e. learners) that he trained to one day become 'apostles' (i.e. sent ones). It was with these students that 'third generation ministry' took root. The idea was that the Navigator missionaries were to train the core group, the core group was to train the other students, and the others would then certainly have at least some spiritual influence on their own peers in the daily ebb and flow of student life. This core group was hungry and eager to grow and practically use what they were learning.

HOUSE CHURCH STRATEGY

For the next several seasons, every week would see a large group of 50 students meeting in the original student house. This was a sight to see. There were students sitting on the floor of the living room. Some were sprawled across the top of sofas. Others were standing and leaning up against the walls. A few were sitting in the stairwell. Still others were pushed into the adjoining kitchen for lack of room. It might remind one of the house church at Caesarea, which the apostle Peter had helped form upon the invitation of the Roman officer Cornelius: "And on the following day [Peter] entered Caesarea. Now Cornelius was waiting for them, and had called together his relatives and close friends....[Peter] entered and found many people assembled" (Acts 20:24,27, NASB). As a large group they would spend 45 minutes worshipping the Lord in song, mixed in with testimonies, short teachings, and organizational announcements from various students, the trio of missionaries, and visiting speakers. Then for the next 90 minutes they would break out into six or seven smaller groups into the various rooms of the house for more intensive and interactive prayer, sharing, and Bible discovery. Some groups focused on a particular book of the Bible. Others studied the writings of some Christian author. Still others focused on accountability or were evangelistically tailored towards non-Christian students that would attend. These small groups were composed of the same people each week, so that relationships that were built and content that was studied would carry on uninterrupted. Each of the groups was led by two students from the core student leadership group, or by one of the Navigator missionaries and a student assistant. At the end of the evening, people would stay around for a long time, eat food, chat, and generally enjoy each other's company. These were exciting times!

TIMES OF CHANGE

In 1993, I arrived at Queen's University in Kingston, Canada, to pursue my doctorate in Engineering. Because of my previous heavy involvement with Navigator student ministries at another university for several years prior to that, it was natural for me to join what was happening with this Navigator student 'house church'. At about that time, I had been asked by the National Campus Director of Navigators to consider coming on officially as an 'Associate Navigator', an unpaid volunteer position, to help Bill, Darlene, Trudy, and the student group. I was humbled. I prayed. I reflected. I agreed. About a year later, Bill and Darlene felt called by the Lord to leave the ministry that they had helped undergird and shift to another capacity as Navigators. Soon after, Trudy married another Navigator, named Stan, working at another campus, who then proceeded to move to our campus. Soon, the trio of Navigators at Queen's University had become Stan, Trudy, and me. And for the next couple of years, we worked closely as a team to lead the student house church using the same strategy that had been used up to that point.

A VISION FOR EVANGELISM

Though there was some good discipleship, growth, and fellowship within the house church, Stan, Trudy, and I had a burning desire to mobilize the students to reach out to their non-believing housemates, classmates, and friends with the message of Christ. We used a multi-pronged approach.

In partnership with some of the other Christian student groups, during the university's orientation week we approached students going through the registration line to fill out a simple spiritual interest survey. It was composed of some basic questions designed to gauge their opinions about Jesus Christ. Several weeks later, we used the contact information on the surveys during a follow-up campaign to telephone any non-Christian students interested in finding out more about God and the Bible.

We then invited the new contacts from the surveys to a campus lecture we organized entitled, 'Christianity: So What?!' for which we had scheduled a very dynamic and engaging Christian speaker. This not only engaged a number of volunteer Christian students from our house church to make the necessary phone calls, but also gave them an opportunity to invite other non-Christian friends to the lecture. We videotaped the lecture, which we then showed once or twice in the student house church as training for how to address various philosophical and historical questions that might arise while sharing their faith with their classmates.

We also organized what we called a 'discussion dinner', which involved our bolder Christian students bringing a non-Christian friend to an evening of free pizza, soda pop, a music video, and group discussion. The event took place in my apartment living room. There were 15 of us gathered there, eight Christians and seven non-Christian friends. Just as we began, there was a knock on the door. One of my neighbors from the building had noticed the sign I had posted in the hallway and wanted to participate. So, we invited him in. Though he was clearly drunk, he stayed and participated in the evening's discussion without any disruptions. Later, this neighbor and I developed a good rapport, and I had a chance to clearly explain the good news of Christ to him. In addition, this opened the door for many further spiritual conversations between the Christian students and the friends they had brought to the dinner. The 'discussion dinner' became an ongoing outreach strategy on that campus for several subsequent years.

Moreover, as Navigator staff, we also encouraged the students that we were mentoring one-on-one to begin sharing their faith with their friends in a natural but intentional way. A student that I was discipling weekly desired to learn how to do this better. So, over the course of several months, we began to pray, search the Scriptures, and read articles together on the topic. In addition, we kept each other accountable to share our faith with those around us. Eventually, this student had connected very well with a friend, sharing their faith with them and mentoring them one-on-one. The student was excited! I was excited! This student had caught the vision of 'passing the baton' to the next generation!

Finally, during my time at the university, I also at one point lived in a student house off-campus. I shared my faith openly with my housemates after developing a trusting relationship with them. Two of these students (one of them was a non-Christian) and I eventually began studying the Gospel of Matthew together as a group. We as Navigators not only encouraged but also modeled this type of evangelistic 'Investigative Bible Study' to our Christian students. They could also do this with their friends!

LESSONS LEARNED

There are several things that I learned from this house church experience in a campus context, convincing me that house churches planted among college or university students can be effective.

1. *Students are Open to the Gospel.* This is one of the most developmental times in a person's life. Students are curious, keen, open, and genuinely desire to learn about new ideas and are warm to the idea of making new friends. This goes for Christian and non-Christian students alike.

2. *Students are Open to New Ways of Doing Church.* From my own conversations with the students, some did not consider the house church as truly a 'church' and referred to it rather as a 'fellowship group'. Others, however, recognized that it could legitimately be called 'church' and was probably more practical in meeting their spiritual needs than simply passively attending a traditional Sunday morning church service once a week. In any case, all the students were tremendously open to meeting in homes and using them as a base of operations for worship, prayer, Bible discovery, training, and evangelism.

3. *Students Can Become Effective Leaders.* With the proper coaching, students can become effective leaders. Regarding discipleship, adequately trained Christian students can do a good job of leading a Bible study or prayer group. Evangelistically, in my experience, it could be argued that the students themselves were the 'insiders' among their circle of friends and were more effective in reaching their friends with the gospel than we were as Navigator missionaries.

4. *House Churches with Satellite 'Small Groups' can Work.* House churches can function well when they have both a large group and small group dynamic. In our case, we had a house church of 50 students, which provided the energy beneficial to large group worship and teaching. However, we also had a number of smaller breakout groups meeting in the various rooms of the home, which were especially conducive to intimacy, relationship building, and participatory meetings.

STUDY QUESTIONS

1. In your specific context, can house churches be planted effectively among university students?

2. Reflect on the patience needed to plant a solid house church.

3. How could new house churches have been planted in this case?

Chapter 40

CASE STUDY (CUBA):
HOW FIDEL CASTRO LAUNCHED
10,000 HOUSE CHURCHES

MINDY BELZ

Original publication of this article by Mindy Belz, "Su casa es mi casa", World Magazine, Feb. 6, 1998, Vol. 13, No. 5. Used by permission © WORLD magazine, all rights reserved (www.worldmag.com).

As the Pope visited Cuba, Castro used the occasion to close thriving, numerous Protestant casas culto, house churches.

"What kind of a communist dictatorship is this, anyway?" was the wonder of more than one foreign reporter as Cubans jammed the Plaza of the Revolution, where Pope John Paul II gave his final and most well-attended mass Jan. 25. Towering above a swelling crowd of more than 200,000, a giant depiction of Christ faced one of Che Guevara, Cuba's Marxist revolutionary hero. The Pope used the opportunity to declare, "Cuba has a Christian soul"—a message carried on state-run television, which broadcast the address nationwide. When he spoke on religious freedom, the right of Cubans "to live their faith freely, to express that faith in the context of public life"—on the front row sat dictator Fidel Castro.

Yet for all the anomalies that attended the Roman Catholic leader's landmark visit, several Christian groups found business as usual in the communist nation.

An unidentified number of house churches in Havana were ordered to close by agents of Cuba's National Registry of Associations just hours before the Pope's arrival Jan. 21. In addition, the Baptist Convention of Western Cuba, which reported the closings, was not asked to participate in an ecumenical meeting with the Pope on the last day of his visit, Sunday morning, Jan. 25. The snub came just before the convention began its own national meeting in Havana Feb. 3. The Baptist Convention of Western Cuba is affiliated with the Southern Baptist Convention in the United States and is the largest Protestant denomination, with over 12,000 members, behind Pentecostals. The Eastern Convention is affiliated with American Baptist Convention and is, overall, more charismatic and less conservative.

Neither Compass Direct, which reported the closures, nor WORLD were able to confirm their extent. The number of house churches pressured to close was described as "numerous," and leaders of the Baptist Convention speculated that house churches of other evangelical denominations may have been affected also.

"When agents approached the house churches, they asked to talk to the tenants, who in general are faithful members of local churches," said a Cuban pastor who spoke to Compass Direct. "They were asked to sign a form that committed them to close the house church." The pastor asked not to be identified because of the ongoing risk of harassment.

Government officials gave no reason for the forced closures. The campaign received little public notice in a week dominated by the Pope's daily services. Although the house church sponsors were pressured to sign the form and to hold no future meetings, for most of the leaders this was familiar territory.

"When house churches close, they may open in other parts of the city," said Tomas Diaz, an exiled Baptist pastor, now an American citizen, in Miami. He told WORLD that the house churches are often referred to as "preaching points" to distinguish them from established churches, under whose authority they are often formed.

The number of casas culto, or house churches, in Cuba began a steady increase in the early 1990s when the Cuban economy fell into steep decline. Fuel shortages hindered transportation to such an extent that church members began meeting in smaller groups, in homes easily reached by bicycle or on foot. Authorities would issue no building permits for the construction of new churches, forcing many to meet for worship in their homes. House churches flourished and are now estimated to number 10,000 nationwide.

These gatherings take place at odd times-often a weekday afternoon or evening-to avoid detection. They include Bible study, prayer, and singing. Some are led by an ordained pastor. Most, however, are led by part-time preachers or teachers who function as tentmaking missionaries. They receive support from a larger church or from exiled Cuban Christians abroad. Their fluidity is feeding a revival in Cuba, according to David Lema of the Miami Baptist Association. Their growth led Cuban authorities to force pastors to close house churches sponsored by members of their denominations, or risk imprisonment.

Arrests of prominent house church leaders began several years ago. Orson Vila, a Pentecostal evangelist who oversaw more than 80 Assemblies of God house churches, was arrested in May 1995 and sentenced to nearly two years in prison for holding services in his own backyard. Eliezer Veguilla, a Baptist pastor and medical doctor, was arrested in February 1994. He was ordered to confess to espionage or "sleep with a bear." The bear proved real (and very much alive), waiting for Mr. Veguilla when he was pushed into a basement cell at police headquarters in Havana. This was but one of many forms of psychological torture Mr. Veguilla was to endure during 47 days in prison-the bear was chained to the wall.

Exiled to Miami since September 1995, Mr. Veguilla fears the freedoms in evidence during the Pope's visit may be another kind of psychological torture for evangelicals.

"The visit of the Pope is very important for our country," he told Compass Direct. "In spite of this opening, we continue to hear proof that suffering and repression against the church in Cuba will continue."

Gerardo van Dalen, executive director of the Miami-based Pro-Martyrs Foundation, told the Miami Herald that the Evangelical League of Cuba was warned by the Cuban Secret Police to refrain from all evangelistic activity during the Pope's five-day visit. Nonetheless, evangelical churches in Cuba were able to carry out the planned distribution of nearly one million tracts during that time.

The Western Convention in Cuba is also planning to carry out its convention this month, which will feature a number of Cuban pastors who have been exiled to the United States. Juan Perez, a Baptist pastor who was jailed for six years in Cuba but came to the United States two years ago, said even he was granted a visa by the Castro government to attend the convention.

Nevertheless, Mr. Castro's shutting Baptists out of the meeting with the Pope and shutting down their house groups is an attempt to divide and distract the evangelical churches, Mr. Perez said. The meeting, which involved other Protestant and Jewish groups the morning before the Pope's final mass, included members of the Cuban Council of Churches. The Baptist Convention is not part of the Council.

Mr. Perez agrees with Cuba's Baptist Convention president, Leoncio Veguilla (Eliezer Veguilla's father), who said the government is "playing games" with his denomination. But in this high-stakes game, real lives hang in the balance.

STUDY QUESTIONS

1. What factors initially led to the emergence of thousands of house churches in Cuba?
2. How are the house churches networked together?
3. How is government repression helping fuel the growth of the movement?

Chapter 41

CASE STUDY (BRAZIL):
A HOUSE CHURCH MOVEMENT BECOMES VISIBLE

DANIEL ALLEN

Daniel Allen, M.Div. (Southwestern Baptist Theological Seminary), last served as Assistant Pastor of Green Acres Baptist Church (Tyler, Texas) before beginning service with the International Mission Board (Southern Baptist Convention) in 2000. Currently, he serves as the Strategy Coordinator for the Germanic Team in Brazil. His focus is on training nationals to plant house churches. In 2004, together with Wycliffe Bible Translators and the Brazilian Bible Society, he began facilitating the Hunsriker Bible Translation Project. Hunsriker is a Germanic language spoken in Argentina, Brazil, and Paraguay by more than 2 million people. Email: allen@onmissionwithgod.org.

INTRODUCTION

This article describes the fledging but growing house church movement in Brazil. Briefly, we will look at the present state of Christianity in the country as of 2006, what is taking place in the house church movement, and draw some conclusions regarding its strengths and weaknesses.

THE PRESENT STATE OF CHRISTIANITY IN BRAZIL

Like most Latin American countries, Brazil has a mixed population of peoples that are of European, Indigenous, and African descent. In the late 1980s, after decades of military rule, democracy was reinstituted, providing a burst of optimism. The people saw this as an opportunity for increased political, social, and economic freedom. After 20 years, enthusiasm has been dampened due to a lack of job opportunities, increase in violent crime, and extensive corruption in government and business. These barriers to upward social mobility and mistrust of organizations have led to a deep sense of frustration among many people.

Evangelicals, who had experienced repression under the military regime, welcomed democratization believing that greater religious freedom would bring greater church growth. However, this has not proven to be the case. There is an increasing frustration among church leaders who are dismayed about their stagnant church growth. This is especially true in southern Brazil. In Rio Grande do Sul, the hard numbers of Evangelicals are declining, according to SEPAL (Serviço de Evangelização para America Latina), a non-denominational organization dedicated to evangelism and church planting. Traditionally, the population has been Roman Catholic (80%), but according to government statistics the fastest growing religion in the nation is now spiritism.

THE EMERGENCE OF HOUSE CHURCHES IN BRAZIL

Becoming Visible

Many have questioned whether or not a house church movement exists in Brazil. All indications are that there is a grassroots house church movement. It has become increasingly more visible in recent years. While house churches have existed for some time, they are only now beginning to surface seeking like-minded people to discuss specific issues that relate to house church. Because of their growing visibility, they are learning to speak out in favor of their choice to meet in homes. Even though the movement is young, there are stories coming to us via the web from all over Brazil, from individuals who are finding the movement attractive.

The size of Brazil's house church movement is not easily discovered. Research is showing that the movement cuts across all social and ethnic lines. However, it is the middle-class in Brazil that is most visible at this time. Most of them have come out of mainline Evangelicalism. After drifting between several churches and/or denominations, they are finding the option of meeting in homes intriguing. This is leading them to search for resources. These resources include books, web sites, and believers who are already participating in the house church movement. Part of their interest comes from their desire to be a part of a highly participative and inclusive church that is organic in nature. In recent years there have been several highly esteemed books translated into Portuguese on the topic.[1] These, and other books, are aiding the discussion. It should be understood that the books, sites, and forums are not inspiring the movement, but are instead a direct result of the marketplace.

Loose-knit networks are also beginning to form. The first goal of one network is to promote house church awareness and training on a national level. They have already contacted some international leaders in the house church movement such as Wolfgang Simson. The people involved in these plans are coming from successful business backgrounds and made up of all ages. Almost without exception, those who are participating are calling themselves Evangelicals, but avoid any denominational affiliations. This places the movement in a position that is parallel to traditional Evangelical churches.

Outside and Inside the Established Churches

House churches differ in their view of the established churches. Many choose not to become involved in the more traditional churches (whether

---

[1] David Garrison (1999), *Church Planting Movements* (www.onmissionwithgod.org/português.htm); Wolfgang Simson (1998), *Houses that Change the World*, Paternoster Publishing.

Protestant or Roman Catholic), so that they can freely focus on accomplishing their mission. Some, desiring to renew existing Christian entities, are affiliating themselves formally with denominations.

The oldest known Evangelical house church network grew out of the Roman Catholic Church. In this case, we found a group that has been meeting in homes for the past 20 years and involves hundreds of believers. The founders of the movement were initially Catholic, but after studying the Bible and coming to know Christ, they came to reject Catholic teachings and left. They initially searched for a church home among Evangelicals, but did not find one that fit their expectations. Some sited striking resemblances between Catholic and Evangelical organizations and traditions as their main objection. Like those who come from an Evangelical background, they too are middle-class and identify themselves as Evangelical with no denominational affiliations.

Many Roman Catholics themselves, however, have also formed a kind of house church movement over the past 40 years. They are known as 'Basic Ecclesial Communities' or 'Basic Christian Communities'[2] and are focused on Bible study, prayer, mutual support, and practical service to the community. The groups are often made up of about 40 people and are led either by trained laypersons or clergy. Many people on the fringes have been touched, including the unemployed, the elderly, peasants, laborers, and frustrated youth. Though the movement is formally recognized by the Vatican, some Catholic clergy have had mixed feelings, wanting the communities to have closer ties to local parishes and priests. In 1985, there were approximately 100,000 groups in existence.

Motivations for Involvement

What is motivating Brazilian believers to consider house church as a viable option? There is a profound distrust of political, business, and religious institutions and organizations that few would deny. This distrust has fueled a growing perception that institutions and organizations are too bureaucratic, i.e. not relational in nature. All too common, moral failures among leadership are lending to this perception. Churches and denominations are not above suspicion and are seen as being a part of this problem. They are perceived as inwardly focused and, therefore, more interested in the life of the organization, rather than that of the people. However, it should not be considered as the primary factor. It is not merely a case of disgruntled Christians forming themselves into house churches. It does beg the question whether or not this movement is seeking reform or revolution.

---

[2] Jeanne Hinton (1995), *Walking in the Same Direction: A New Way of Being Church*, WCC Publications, pp.1-4; John Driver (1999), *Radical Faith: An Alternative History of the Christian Church*, Pandora Press, ch.21 *(Editor's note—though this editor does not necessarily endorse every aspect of this movement, it is provided for illustrative purposes.)*

Understanding this issue is the key to understanding what is taking place at this time and why.

Interest is also growing because of a desire among believers to become full participants in the gospel. This is evidenced in web articles and forums. The discussion deals with the issues that surround questions like: What is a house church? What defines it? Where can it meet? How is it organized? Who leads it? How do we handle tithes and offerings? etc. There is also much discussion about the church being organic in nature, like that of family, rather than like an organization. They are not stating that all organization is unnecessary, but rather that they want to participate in church where relationships are family-like.

There are signs that they are approaching this change with a holistic purpose and not simply as another model to place in the church planting portfolio. There is a sincere desire to change the content, rather than merely revolt against the old structure. They are keen on finding what they believe to be the true essence of the church: a spiritual family. Within the movement, the family and its importance is always stressed. This is not a quest for independence through division in order to form a new church or one more denomination. It is a reform, and according to Jamê Nobre, focused upon changing the "the vision, the practice, and the experience of the people of God."[3]

LESSONS LEARNED

There are several lessons that can be learned from the house church movement in Brazil.

First, what works are the informal family-style meetings involving dialogue-based Bible study with a simple meal. The burgeoning discussion in forums and in books is producing an educated first generation of house church participants. The emphasis on the father and empowering him with authority to lead his wife and children spiritually is motivating whole families.

Second, the greatest criticism is that the house churches do not appear durable. Why is this? They are only now beginning to draw a distinction between themselves and home Bible study groups. The observing of the Lord's Supper and carrying out of baptisms by laymen is helping to create this distinction. Covenants for each house church could also be useful in this regard. Moreover, the lack of durability is due more to a lack of vision than a lack of heart. Many have not caught a Matthew 28:18-20 vision to go out and make disciples of all peoples. There is an idea circulating among house church participants that things will happen spontaneously without any plan or strategy. The thought is that, if they live with integrity and passion, then disciples will be made, house churches will be born, the gospel will spread,

---

[3] Jamê Nobre, *A Igreja nas Casas: Revolução ou Reforma?*
(www.odiscipulo.com/php/pagina.php?doc=estudos/ic_revolucao_reforma)

and in the end the church will be reformed. However, Jesus taught and modeled reproduction, and it is lacking at this time. At this point, the movement has been in an experimental phase and needs to make the next crucial step by becoming intentional in their disciple-making and their house church planting. The greatest opportunity for the Evangelical house church movement lies with the masses of lost people and, as of yet, they are not looking in this direction.

STUDY QUESTIONS

1. How are house churches beginning to network with each other?
2. What is motivating people to become involved?
3. Why are some house churches affiliating with established churches, whereas others are not?

Chapter 42

Case Study (Ecuador):
The Story and Strategy of
'The Church in Your House'

Guy Muse

Guy and Linda Muse are missionaries in Guayaquil, Ecuador. They have served in this capacity since 1987 with the International Mission Board (Southern Baptist Convention). Guy received a Master of Music degree in 1986 from Southwestern Baptist Theological Seminary (Ft. Worth, Texas, USA). For more information, please log on to www.guymuse.blogspot.com.

Introduction

Central and Latin America have seen significant growth of biblical Christianity in the last several decades. This article describes the efforts of one missionary band whose focus has been establishing multiplying house churches in Guayaquil, the largest city in Ecuador. The history, values, training program, and methodology of the missionary team are discussed.

A Brief History

We call our church planting network 'La Iglesia en Tu Casa' ('The Church in Your House'). It began in July 2000. Our team at that time was composed of seven missionaries (International Mission Board—Southern Baptist Convention), all assigned to church planting. The team currently consists of two missionaries from the USA and three Ecuadorian church planters, who fully participate in all planning, teaching, decision making, etc.

None of the missionaries actually plant house churches, rather, we are *catalysts* for house church planting. The reason for this is that, if we set out to plant a church, we individually might plant only several new houses churches each year. But as catalysts, the only limitation of church starts is the number of people who respond to the Lord's leading to go out and plant New Testament churches.

Lay leaders, whom we call *servant-leaders,* lead all the house churches. At nearly any given moment, we are training between 20 to 30 men and women who are likewise in various stages of training and starting new house churches. Most of them tend to come out of established traditional Evangelical churches and, thus, carry a certain mindset with them in beginning new works. There have been well above 250 new house churches started since July 2000, though only about half continue to function currently.

OUR GUIDING VALUES

The mission of 'The Church in Your House' has a number of guiding values which we seek to establish firmly as part of our ethos:

- *A Foundation of Prayer.* This is the most important work in which we are engaged (Luke 10:2).
- *Mobilizing the Laity.* The laity is empowered to go and do tasks traditionally assigned only to trained professional clergy (Eph 4:11-12, 1 Pet 2:9-10).
- *Taking the Church to the People.* We desire to be a 'go to' church movement, rather than a 'come to' movement that brings people to the church (Matt 28:18-20, Luke 10:3).
- *Crossing Denominational Lines.* We wish to work with all Great Commission Christians to plant New Testament churches (Eph 4:4-6).
- *Depending on God to Provide Workers.* No recruitment or manipulation is required (Luke 10:2).
- *Women Can Lead.* We wish to empower all believers, including gifted women, to plant house churches (Matt 28:18-20).
- *Christ is Responsible to Build His Church.* It is not our responsibility (Matt 16:18). Our job is the Great Commission.
- *The Missionary Task is to Equip Others.* The job of missionaries is primarily one of praying, modeling, teaching, training, and mentoring (Eph 4:11-12).
- *Strategic Use of Resources.* Locally available and reproducible communication media are utilized, such as radio, brochures, videos, letters, tracts, cassettes, Bibles, etc. We do not use anything from the outside that cannot be done or reproduced locally by the people.
- *Church is a Family Gathering.* This is best held in a home setting and is not a 'traditional church service' (1 Cor 12-14, 14:26).
- *Prayer and Evangelism.* These twin pillars drive the work of planting house churches.
- *Group Multiplication.* Growth happens by reproducing of more and more house churches, not just addition to existing works (e.g. the parables of the kingdom).
- *The Work Belongs to God.* The Lord can do with it and us as he pleases. Change in the way things are done is an on-going process, as God continues to open our eyes to his ways of building the kingdom.

THE LUKE 10 STRATEGY FOR STARTING HOUSE CHURCHES

Gathering the Trainees

Several times a year, we will schedule training sessions for new house church planters. In the past, we relied heavily on Christian radio stations to announce the event. Today, it is more word of mouth as people seek us and ask to be trained. We usually have a group of 20-30 people from a cross-section of all Evangelical denominations in the city. We are using a training manual called C.O.S.E.C.H.A. (HARVEST), with each letter representing a module of preparation. It can be used to plant house churches, cells, and even missions for traditionally oriented churches.

The entire manual can be covered in a single five-hour workshop, or spread out over 10-15 weeks. We are still trying to determine which method is most effective, but both seem to be equally successful in getting people out into the harvest fields. The first meeting is about sharing our vision for reaching 500,000 new souls in the coming five years. Our objective is to get people to understand that it can be done, and how we are going to go about doing it with the Lord's help. The secret is, of course, multiplication of new believers, new leaders, and new house churches. We impart all the basics necessary to plant a house church in a step-by-step fashion.

Applying the Strategy of Luke 10

Over the past five or so years, we have learned much and are continuously evaluating and adjusting our method to ministry and house church planting. Overall, though, our basic approach has been to follow the way Jesus prepared his own disciples in Luke 10:1-9. When Jesus' followers were given the Great Commission in Matthew 28, they knew what to do and how to go about it because they had previously been trained by Jesus himself in the way he wanted them to do the work.

We do not see a need to change our Lord's instructions. Therefore, from the beginning, our way of working has consisted in following the pattern outlined in Luke 10:1-9. We believe our role is to go make disciples. His role is to build his church (Matt 16:18). The pattern from Luke 10 is found in the commands of Christ as, step by step, he outlined how he intended they accomplish the task—*Beseech* the Lord of the harvest for laborers; *Go* out into the harvest fields; *Find* the man of peace; *Stay* in that house; *Minister and Heal* in that home; and *Proclaim* the kingdom of God. We also encourage these new groups to *Meet Like a Family*, rather than organizing a formal 'worship service'. While many things have been tried, the following would be a general summary of how we have sought to carry out these commands.

Beseech

Prayer to the Lord of the harvest to call and send out laborers is always foremost. Luke 10:2b is a daily prayer, is part of our gatherings, is prayed by our house churches, and is taught as a command of Christ. We encourage all believers to pray this prayer. We do not try to talk anyone into planting a house church. This is Christ's responsibility. He must be the one to lay this on someone's heart. Ours is to pray that he would touch hearts and that they would respond. It is up to him to call out the called.

Go

In the first several weeks of training, we make clear that they are to start immediately. They are to pray over their list of lost family/friends/neighbors, witness to those on the list for whom they are praying, personally follow up those who make professions of faith within 48-hours, immediately disciple new believers with our 52-lesson program, and be the church that they are in Christ Jesus as soon as the first baptisms occur.

Find and Stay

Once they find their 'man of peace'—usually their first convert—they are to stay focused on that home and family and begin by gathering in that home. They are to build a spiritual beachhead in that home, from which they are to then reach out to any and all connected with that household. They are not to go to another location until something first becomes established in that household.

Minister, Heal, and Proclaim

It is then important to minister to that family and lead them to becoming followers of Christ through the proclamation of the gospel. We encourage the servant leaders to start as soon as they encounter the 'man of peace', even if it is only one person. The longer they delay in starting, the less likely they will ever do so. Note that training of the servant leaders takes place simultaneously as they begin to minister in the houses. We do not train them, and then send them out. We send them out, and train them as they are actually doing the house church plant. We stress heavily the need to minister to the real needs of the people, not just to invite them to house church meetings. We feel that genuine love for the seekers is what wins them over to Christ. We share with them that the love they show towards these lost friends, family, and neighbors will make more of an impact for the kingdom than any words they might share. Therefore, in our training we stress practical ministry to people, loving them where they are. This is in keeping with Luke 10:9, where Christ says to first heal and then speak. Soon after, these people are loved into the kingdom and begin to grow as they continue to fellowship with one another. Jesus himself weaves them into a local body of believers, an *ekklesia*.

Meet Like a Family

From the very beginning the family, friends, neighbors, and work associates *(oikos)* of the 'man of peace' are invited to join in the house meetings. The meetings themselves are more of an informal 'family gathering' than a formal 'worship service'. This is important. The New Testament church gatherings (1 Cor 14) were quite informal and participative. We try to emulate these ideals and encourage a more relaxed, open time of gathering rather than a structured 'culto' (worship service) in a home. These meetings are modeled in our training, since most have never participated in such gatherings. It is difficult to lead something in a home if they have never experienced it themselves. Each gathering of believers has several parts:

- An informal time of talking, sharing, reading Scripture, discussion of what was read and understood by the group, and a time of singing.
- A more structured time where one of the discipleship lessons is shared in 20 to 30 minutes. Meetings are interactive with everyone participating, including any non-believers who are present.
- A time of praying for individual needs and generally ministering one to another. This usually is also a time of sharing food and refreshments, fellowship, and celebrating together some event, etc.

THE CHALLENGE OF MOBILIZING THE SECOND GENERATION

Though we have planted over 250 house churches in half a dozen years, about half are currently meeting and functioning. We attribute most of this to a combination of several factors. There has sometimes not been a thorough paradigm shift from traditional church values and practices to what we believe are true New Testament principles, traditions, and practices. Spiritual immaturity is also evident in those who began with enthusiasm, but lost focus or became discouraged along the way. Moreover, other Evangelicals have at times aggressively discouraged and questioned the validity of the new work.

While this is a source of concern, we are nevertheless encouraged that those won through the ministry of the new house churches tend to have had genuine salvation experiences. Even though the house church itself may dissolve, the people won in those initial weeks of the new work for the most part tend to remain true to the kingdom, with a high percentage shifting over to existing traditional churches.

In January 2006, we began seeking to implement changes to strengthen current and new works in the future. Every believer within our house church network is now expected to seek to win, baptize, disciple, and teach at least eight others during the year. These eight form their own church planting team and network with one another. Consequently, we now feel there are several requirements for anyone who wants to start a house church. They must be willing to win-disciple-train at least eight others each year. They must be willing to be trained in the basics of evangelism, discipleship, teaching, etc. They must be willing and committed to visit, evangelize, and minister to the local community where the house church is being planted. They must be willing to lead in the house church meetings, especially in the beginning as they are being started with non-believers.

Our greatest struggle continues to be mobilizing the second generation of new Christians to actually go out themselves and repeat the process. The heart of the matter seems to be ingrained in the servant leaders that new believers are 'too tender' and not ready to be released out into the harvest. The same problem we have with the traditional churches comes back to haunt us—the patterns of delaying baptism for new believers and falling back into a traditional worship service meeting where the leader does most of the talking, sharing, and teaching. This, sadly, leads to churches that model a type of church life that is a 'come, sit, and learn', rather than 'let's go out and make disciples of the nations'! As a team, we constantly remind people of these principles, yet once out working in the field, most tend to fall back into the default mode of the ways brought with them from their traditional church backgrounds. Some house church servant leaders, too, soon forget to keep the main thing the main thing—Go, Make Disciples, Baptize, and Teach. All too often, they try to do it all themselves and build the church by adding numbers, rather than training those already won to go out and do the same thing they are doing. Therefore, what we sometimes see are traditional churches meeting in houses winning and baptizing a few per year, versus the multiplication growth that Christ spoke of in the parable of the sower.

CONCLUSIONS

This article has examined some of the successes and challenges faced by our house church planting team in Ecuador. Through a recalibration of our training program, we hope to see a decrease in the attrition rate of the house churches planted, so that a second generation of new believers will catch the vision to reach their nation for Christ.

STUDY QUESTIONS

1. Can you describe the Luke 10 house church planting strategy?
2. What are some of the factors that have led to house churches eventually folding?
3. What specific lessons can one take from this story to ensure that new believers catch the vision to plant house church networks successfully?

Chapter 43

CASE STUDY (LATIN AMERICA): HOUSE CHURCHES IN A ROMAN CATHOLIC CONTEXT

JOHN DRIVER

John Driver was educated at Goshen Biblical Seminary (B.D.) and Perkins School of Theology (S.T.M.). Along with his wife Bonita, John has dedicated himself to over 40 years of missionary work in Spanish-speaking countries in partnership with the Mennonite Board of Missions. He has served in Puerto Rico, Uruguay, Argentina, and Spain. He is the author of over a dozen books. [The following excerpted and revised text is taken from John Driver, "Twentieth-Century Movements: Basic Ecclesial Communities" (ch.21), In: Radical Faith: An Alternative History of the Christian Church (Pandora Press: Kitchener, ON, Canada, 1999). Adapted and used by permission of the publisher. Website: www.pandorapress.com] (Editor's note—though the editor does not necessarily endorse every aspect of this movement, it is provided for illustrative purposes.)

INTRODUCTION

Although analogous communities currently exist on other continents, the variant of 'house churches' known as 'Basic Ecclesial Communities' (BECs) originated in Latin America. In the 1950s, 'experiments' were going on in Brazil, Chile, and Panama. In the 1960s, the communities became popularly known as Basic Ecclesial Communities, or in Spanish as Comunidades Ecclesiales de Base, or CEBs. The name was drawn from the Basic Education Movement, a Brazilian organization which used radio in its teaching program. A desire for locally-based evangelization, and experiments in a lay apostolate, under the auspices of the pastoral program of the national church in Brazil, also contributed to the rise of the communities.

ORIGINS OF BASIC ECCLESIAL COMMUNITIES (BECs)

A Program for Evangelization

In 1956, the bishop of Barra do Pirai, in the district of Rio de Janeiro, initiated a program for evangelization in his diocese. The program was begun after an old woman complained that no priest would serve their neighborhood. This challenge led to serious reflection within the Brazilian church. Did the life of a Christian community depend solely on the presence of a formally trained, ordained priest? The church began preparing lay catechists who would serve, in the name of the bishop, as community coordinators. They would nurture fraternal communion at the local church level. On Sundays and other holidays, people from the neighborhood would meet together for a 'Sunday without mass' or the 'mass without a priest'. In this way, they could accompany, in spirit, the mass being celebrated in the distal mother parish.

Many of the lay catechists were public primary school teachers. The catechists, or community coordinators, assumed responsibilities for the group. They led daily prayer sessions and weekly worship services. They served according to the community's needs, administering baptisms in urgent cases and ministering to the sick and dying. Instead of building chapels dedicated exclusively to worship, they built modest facilities that were used for primary education, sewing classes, religious instruction, and as community centers where neighbors could meet to share their concerns.

In the northeastern region of Brazil, the church made a special attempt to serve people in their struggle for survival. The church looked for viable solutions to the region's pressing social problems of malnutrition, endemic illness, illiteracy, and socio-economic exploitation.

The church raised the people's social consciousness and encouraged the establishment of schools and centers of social welfare. In the process, the Basic Education Movement was born. 'Radio schools' were vehicles for consciousness raising and seedbeds for the church. By 1963, there were 1,410 radio schools in the archdiocese of Natal. The resource helped people learn to read, as well as offering religious instruction. In communities without a priest, people would meet in their homes around their radio to listen to a sermon and recite prayers of the mass, which was being celebrated in the distant parish church.

The Basic Education Movement spread throughout the northeastern and western parts of the country, contributing to the formation of small ecclesial communities, which were more basic than traditional parishes. In this way, a network for education and evangelization was formed. In the process of being evangelized, these communities would also serve as agents for evangelization.

The National Pastoral Program

With the approval of the Brazilian episcopate, a team of 15 priests, nuns, and lay persons dedicated five years to a campaign called "A Better World". They visited parishes throughout the country and offered 1,800 courses in spiritual formation and renewal. The initiative led to an atmosphere of spiritual awakening. People began questioning the social and religious status quo.

The National Bishop's Conference approved an 'emergency plan' which would transform traditional parishes into a network of small communities of faith, worship, and charity. The plan was to develop basic communities within the parishes in which the members would actively participate in the celebration of the Eucharist and other sacraments.

The church in Latin America was concerned about the numerous people who had been baptized, but had virtually no relationship with the church. For geographical and social reasons, many parishioners had little or no exposure to the sacramental expressions of salvation, or to the Bible, or to their spiritual brothers and sisters. These people could hardly be expected to evangelize others or share the message of salvation.

The church's concern about evangelization was combined with a growing sense of responsibility for their poorest parishioners. For this reason, BECs would flourish in those regions most affected by endemic social problems.

BECs have spread throughout Latin America. By 1975, there were 40,000 communities in Brazil, 4,000 in Honduras, and numerous others in Chile, Panama, Ecuador, Bolivia, Columbia, Nicaragua, El Salvador, the Dominican Republic, and Paraguay. BECs are now present in all Latin American countries. Bishops met at the Second General Conference of the Latin American Episcopate in Medellin in 1968 and at the Third in Puebla in 1979 and discussed the development of BECs. Both assemblies wholeheartedly approved of the movement.

THE NATURE AND MISSION OF
BASIC ECCLESIAL COMMUNITIES (BECs)

The Philosophy of BECs

BECs are churches which challenge dominant ecclesiastical and secular structures. Committed to the welfare of humanity, the communities are part of the kingdom of God and denounce the idolatry of sexism, power, and money that characterizes the kingdoms of this world. Their revolutionary stance is viewed with suspicion, but the movement is dedicated to building a new world based on New Testament values. According to the principles that guide BECs, the church is not a powerful society, but a community of communities, committed to Christ and to one another. The fundamental philosophy of BECs has been summarized in the following points by Jose Marins.[1]

1. Church vitality is maximized while its outer structures are minimized.

2. The evangelizing mission of the church and communal witness are focused upon.

3. They are open to other Christian groups through prayer, study, and fellowship.

4. The personal atmosphere calls members to participate in the life of the church.

---

[1] Jose Marins, "Basic Ecclesial Communities in Latin America", *International Mission Review*, 68.271 (1979):235.

5. There is a charismatic understanding of ministry which is not hierarchical.
6. The spiritual focus is on Jesus, not the saints.
7. Catholics who have been baptized, but not evangelized, are participants.
8. Adults, as well as children, receive catechistic instruction.
9. The sacraments are celebrated communally.
10. The clergy are teachers, and lay people participate in the church's ministry.
11. The political dimensions of faith are recovered through service.

Leonardo and Clodovis Boff, Brazilian Franciscan brothers, are among the foremost advocates of BECs. They have defended the movement against the ecclesiastical conservatism of traditional Catholicism. The brothers summarized the principle ecclesiological characteristics of BECs in their book, *Church: Charism and Power*[2], from which the following discussion largely draws.

Concrete Expressions of Communion

BECs are concrete expressions of communion. In contrast to traditional Catholicism, the communities of faith do not depend on the ministry of ordained clergy. Lay people assume responsibility for evangelization and expression of faith. Interpersonal relationships are direct and fraternal. Communities are usually made up of 15 or 20 low-income families. They meet once or twice a week to share their problems and search for communal solutions based on their understanding of the gospel. Under the leadership of a coordinator, who is a member of the group, meetings are spent in Bible study, reflection, and prayer. God's people are part of a community in mission that invited the participation of the poor and outcast. This active community is the real church of Jesus Christ. Admittedly, however, tensions do exist between those who believe that active service best expresses faith and those who believe that faith is strictly sacramental and devotional.

The Gospel and the Communities

BECs are born out of the Bible. People in these communities are guided by the gospel message. Scripture offers good news and is the primary source of hope, promise, and joy. Communities are guided by the Bible through an extensive hermeneutical process. Listening to Scripture leads people to take interest in the problems affecting others in their group. This awareness leads people to reflect on the problems affecting their neighborhood. Eventually, communal reflection urges them to question larger social and economic issues. By these means, the community's social commitment becomes strongly rooted in faith. The community becomes the primary place in which

---

[2] Leonardo Boff (1986), *Church: Charism and Power*, Crossroad.

the Bible is read, heard, and interpreted. The entire community participates in this process.

Successors of the Apostolic Community

BECs represent both new and ancient ways of being a church. Lay people take on important roles in the mission of the church. The witness of these communities is expected to lead to the formation of new communities. In this way, they become true successors of the early apostolic church. The church is continually being renewed and reshaped through the activity of these communities. Further, the communities are family: all are brothers and sisters, and all are participants. Although they are all equals, not everyone participates in the same way. Each serves according to his or her best abilities. Paul the apostle called these abilities 'charisms', or gifts of the Spirit, and they include a wide variety of functions. Coordinators, often women, look out for the well-being of the community and preside over worship services. Other people care for the sick, or counsel the troubled, or teach the young and the old how to read and write.

Signs of the Kingdom

BECs are signs of the kingdom of God and instruments of liberation. They are not sectarian, but are open to secular society. They are rooted in the message of the gospel and reflect on the human problems of injustice and oppression from this perspective. They recognize all forms of violence as sin. Members of BECs have sometimes been repressed and persecuted. Some have become witnesses and martyrs for their cause. But repression has not diminished the strength of the communities. As in the early church, suffering for conscience sake has served to consolidate these communities and increases their courage. This has provided an opportunity for serious reflection on the meaning of innocent and vicarious suffering freely assumed on behalf of others, including the oppressor.

Popular Expressions of Faith

BECs are, in the final analysis, made up of people who are experiencing and celebrating their own liberation. For this reason, the salvation of Jesus Christ occupies the center of each community's life. Overflowing joy is often one of their most visible characteristics and is not diminished by the gravity of their struggles. Popular expressions of faith, often frowned upon by official Catholicism and orthodox Protestantism, abound in these communities. These are authentic expressions of faith made by people who value the symbolic logic of the spirit rather than the rational logic of reason. In BECs, faith and life are seen to be one and the same. Members do not merely celebrate the sacraments, but the sacramental dimension of all life. The lines between the sacred and the profane are muted, allowing worship to take on greater significance in the community. Their worship is marked by liturgical creativity. Long prayers relate problems being faced by members, and celebrate victories and milestones. In their worship, they create new rituals, dramatize Scripture, organize liturgical celebrations, and turn common meals into love feasts.

The Response of the Roman Catholic Church's Hierarchy

BECs have become concerned about reactionary tendencies in the church. At the Fourth General Conference of the Latin Episcopate, held in Santa Domingo in 1992, some members of the established church expressed their desire to place BECs under firmer control. In his inaugural speech at the Conference, the Pope stated that BECs should be officially presided over by a priest. BECs worry that their vital role among the common people will be severely restricted if the communities are controlled by church hierarchy. For a number of years, Rome has put pressure on those Catholic theologians who encourage and defend BECs. Leonardo Boff, for example, chose to withdraw from the Franciscan Order in 1992, so that he could continue to teach and write without facing official censorship.

CONCLUSIONS

The future of BECs is uncertain, but also filled with hope. These communities are at once humanly precarious and authentic signs of God's kingdom in our presence.

STUDY QUESTIONS

1. Reflect on each of the three terms that make up the name 'Basic Ecclesial Community'. What do each of these terms mean for you as you step ahead to start a house church or network of house churches?

2. What can other house church movements learn from the way social and economic concerns are addressed by BECs?

3. Official Roman Catholic authorities have had mixed feelings about the formation of BECs. What might this say about the pros and cons of your house church network working inside the established church?

PART 5

PRACTICAL LESSONS IN STARTING A HOUSE CHURCH NETWORK

Chapter 44

HOW TO START A HOUSE CHURCH

FRANK VIOLA

Frank Viola is an internationally known speaker, a house church planter, and the author of six highly acclaimed books on radical church restoration, including Rethinking the Wineskin, Who is Your Covering?, Pagan Christianity, *and* The Untold Story of the New Testament Church. *Frank lives in Gainesville, Florida, USA. You can visit him at www.frankviola.com.*

INTRODUCTION

In this chapter, we will discuss how to create a 'womb' for a house church— a living organism—to be 'born'. In other words, what are the basic ingredients for experiencing the life of the Body of Christ? How can a people learn to gather under the headship of Jesus Christ instead of the headship of a man? How does one begin a house church? What I will share in this chapter has come out of 18 years of pioneering in the house church phenomenon. I do not claim that they are the only ways to start a house church. Nor do I claim that they cannot be improved upon. They are simply the best ways that I am aware of presently. Eventually, as the original house church prototype is developed and the Lord opens the doors of opportunity, the time for multiplying into a network of house churches may also come.

IDENTIFY A NEW TESTAMENT-BASED CHURCH PLANTING STRATEGY

A careful reading of the New Testament will demonstrate that there were four ways in which churches were planted in the first century. These four means are extremely effective and are discussed at great length elsewhere.[1] Each of these can be considered viable options to start a prototype house church today that can result in a thriving network of house churches. Prayerfully identifying which of the following approaches is most practical and feasible in our situation may be the first step to take:

- *The Jerusalem Strategy* – One church is transplanted into many different cities, thus creating new churches. This occurred during the persecution in Jerusalem, causing many believers to leave the city. As they scattered, they spread the message of Christ. Philip preached, healed, and saw many come to faith in Samaria. Peter and John later strengthened the work.[2]

---

[1] Frank Viola (2003), *So You Want to Start a House Church? First-Century Styled Church Planting Today*, Present Testimony Ministry.
[2] Acts 8:1-40

- *The Antioch Strategy* – Church planters are sent out from a local church to plant churches in new cities. After laying foundations in those new churches, the church planters leave those churches on their own in their infancy. Paul and Barnabas, for instance, were sent out by the Holy Spirit during a prayer meeting of prophets and teachers in Antioch to take the good news of Christ to the Gentile world.[3] This was the initial thrust that propelled them into a traveling church planting ministry for years to come.

- *The Ephesian Strategy* – An older church planter resides in a particular city to plant a church and train younger church planters. He then sends them out to plant new churches in nearby regions. This happened to Paul the apostle, who stayed in Ephesus for three years, preaching, healing, and also sending forth church planters like Timothy into the surrounding region.[4]

- *The Roman Strategy* – Believers from many different churches transplant themselves into a specified city to found one new church. For example, Prisca and Aquila found themselves as part of Rome's variegated Christian body—even hosting a church in their home—after having been previously located in Corinth.[5]

CREATE A CRITICAL MASS OF PEOPLE

The next step for the traveling church planter, the traveling church planting team, or the local believer would be to seek to gather together a group of at least eight adults. In my experience, this number constitutes critical mass for the ground floor of a healthy house church. Anything less is typically unworkable given the small numbers. Depending on what part of the world in which we live, it may be difficult locating eight brave souls who live nearby to step into the adventurous world of meeting in a home without a professional pastor. Sometimes, Christians relocate to another city to be part of an existing house church if they cannot find those of like-minded hearts to gather with in their own town or if their soul-winning attempts do not prove fruitful. This was a practice that was widely used in the first century, and it has great advantages. Nonetheless, here are some feasible ways that have been successfully employed to create a nucleus for a new house church:

- *Prayer* – Undergird everything with travailing prayer. People interested in seeing a house church born in their town should begin to seek the Lord earnestly and regularly, asking him to bring those of like mind and heart across their path. This is no small ingredient or trivial matter. We must remember that unless the Lord builds the house, we will labor in vain.[6]

---

[3] Acts 13:1-3
[4] Acts 19:6-12,22
[5] Compare Rom 16:3-5 with 1 Cor 16:19.
[6] Psalm 127:1

- *Evangelism* – Seek to win souls to Christ in town to create the nucleus of the church. This can happen through many means. Some have used private friendship evangelism, servant evangelism like practical works of love, public street-preaching, passing out literature, investigative Bible study groups, etc.
- *Evangelistic Follow Up* – You and a few others might wish to follow up with new Christians that have recently come to faith at the mass meetings of a mobile evangelistic ministry. Such ministries often partner with local churches and believers with the hopes of integrating new converts into fellowship groups for discipleship. This could be the start of a new house church.
- *Book Group* – Create a book-reading group in town to generate interest in a house church among existing Christians. Many Christians are unaware of the fact that believers actually gather outside the traditional church. Not a few will throw in their lot if they are introduced to such a concept.
- *Literature Distribution* – Pass out ground breaking books and other literature to your Christian friends in town. By ground breaking, I mean those books that have caused you personally to have a paradigm shift regarding the church and have fostered a hunger and thirst within you for Body life.
- *House Church Seminars and Conferences* – Invite a house church planter to the city to host a conference or simply to meet privately with a core group that may form a potential house church. If he is well known, he will no doubt be able to draw seekers and those who are ready to begin gathering.

PRACTICE THE FOUR UNMOVABLE PRINCIPLES

Once the Lord has brought a nucleus of people together who wish to begin gathering, discussing 'The Four Unmovable Principles' with one another right at the start of the house church may be the next step. If the house church can embrace each of these and manage to practice them, it will inoculate it from a bundle of problems and disappointments that surely await.

Principle #1: Become Like Little Children

One sure thing that will kill Body life is the belief that we—as individuals—are more mature, more gifted, and more spiritual than the rest of the group.

Perhaps in our last church we were regarded as spiritual giants. Perhaps we were even a minister in some capacity. Perhaps we have been outside the institutional church for years and have experienced all manner of supernatural activity. Perhaps we were in a house church in the past. So we might be tempted to feel we are more experienced than the rest of the group.

If so, let us please keep this in mind. There is one experience we may have never had. It may be an experience that is totally new to us. It is the experience of being built together with all of the brothers and sisters who are in our present group. It is the experience of being in a face-to-face community with Jesus Christ as the group's only head. This changes the playing field dramatically! And it makes everyone a beginner.

If we will discover Jesus Christ corporately in a fresh way, then we must become like little children. Let us drop our agendas, our ambitions, our view of ourselves, and even our 'ministries', in order to become modest brothers or sisters in Christ.

One of the greatest and most common tragedies of a new house church is for its members to transfer institutional baggage from their religious background straight into the new group. When this happens, the house church becomes nothing more than a scaled-down, small-is-beautiful version of a particular stripe of the institutional church.[7] Further, if the people in the group come from different religious backgrounds, the only chance the house church has for staying together is if everyone agrees to come in with a clean slate.

That being said, if the Lord will lead the group, it will need to unlearn many things. It will need to discard a great deal of baggage. This baggage touches the way people pray, the way they sing, the kinds of songs that are sung, the vocabulary that is used, the way people see themselves, the way the Lord is seen, the way the Bible is approached, the way sharing happens, etc. In short, it touches just about everything!

The most important ingredient for a new house church is to strip down to Christ alone. Doing so will give the Lord the opportunity at teaching the group himself in a new way. He will be free to express himself in a way that is natural, organic, and free of traditional baggage.

So, let us come up to ground zero! Let us put our gifts, our 'ministry', and our ambitions at the foot of his cross. And let God, in his time, raise up whatever he wishes to raise up. We can be assured of this one thing. If we take this step, whatever comes up out of the ground will look quite different from what we may have known in the past. This is the principle of resurrection. It is only by death that new life is produced. And what dies comes back in a different form in resurrection life.

If we are not prepared to do this, we will severely hamstring the church. Therefore, let us come to discover the Lord all over again with the brothers and sisters with whom we will be the church. For it is to such, those who have become like little children, that the kingdom of God is given.

---

[7] By 'institutional baggage', I am referring to those *unhealthy* and *unscriptural* practices and concepts that we have unwittingly absorbed in our previous institutional church experience. Not everything that the institutional church does is unhealthy or unscriptural. I owe my salvation and my baptism to the institutional church!

To put it another way, we are walking into a forest not clearly blazed. We are stepping into a world where most of us have never been. We will be taking responsibility for our meetings and for the affairs of the church. Not as an individual, but as a *people!*

For this reason, it is important that no one become the 'traditional pastor' of the group, performing actively for a passive audience. Participation will come from *everyone* as they learn to function as members of Christ's Body. Leadership will come from the Holy Spirit through the Body. Sometimes it will come from the weakest. Other times it will come from the strongest. Decisions will be hammered out by consensus. Specialized gifts and functions will emerge naturally in time.

Let us burn this into the circuitry of our brains. If someone is functioning as the traditional pastor (whether titled or untitled), his presence will hamper Body life. Consequently, everyone in the group should be on equal footing. Forfeit this and what follows will be of little value to us. The exception to this principle is if the group has a church planter who is there only temporarily to equip the group at the beginning stages. If that is the case, he should be working himself out of a job! He should not meet with the group all the time, and he should have real plans of leaving the group on its own after he lays the foundation. If he does not, he is merely functioning as a traditional pastor, regardless of whether or not he calls himself one.

Principle #2: Our Feelings Will Get Hurt

The institutional church has a way of hiding our flaws. It also has a way of safeguarding and insulating each of us from one another. In a house church, we get to know one another very well. That means that what we are in the natural gets exposed. When pressures come, we see who we really are in the flesh. To wit, authentic church life is a house of mirrors!

One of the most profound things that people learn in a face-to-face community is the utter depths that the fall has marked on their souls. Consequently, it is inevitable that people will hurt one another. This is one of the cardinal laws. Everybody seems normal until we get to know them. This sums up Body life in a house church!

Add to the above the following sentence: We will not get our own way in the church. So, let us learn to surrender. Let us discover the spiritual secret of relinquishing control and forfeiting our way. There is something called a cross. And it is found at full force in Body life. The cross means death to self. It means loss. We will meet the cross in one another. It is inevitable.

Church life is a holy wedding of glory and gore—of agony and ecstasy. This journey can be the most difficult adventure in our lives. But it may very well be the most glorious.

The principle of the cross is designed to transform us. It is designed to bring life to our brothers and sisters in Christ. If we get our own way all or most of the time, then the Lord is not getting his way! If we are forfeiting our way, then we are allowing the Lord Jesus to build his own house, and our labor will not be in vain. If we can understand that the cross is embedded in the DNA of church life, it will spare us from having unrealistic expectations. When someone hurts our feelings, at that moment, our spiritual mettle is being fiercely tested. Our reaction will reveal volumes about us. But this is God's wonderful design of transforming us into his glorious image.

To frame it another way, we will never learn the virtues of forbearance, patience, endurance, longsuffering, extending mercy and forgiveness until we are thrown together with a group of very imperfect people who are putting absolute strains on our Christian character! In addition, someone in the group just may become our own personal tailor-fitted cross!

Consider this image. The members of a house church are living stones that are being welded together to form a dwelling place for the Lord. In order for those stones to be built together, they require a great deal of cutting, chiseling, sanding, and refining. If we can remember that these deeper virtues are being worked out when we face difficulties in the group, it will carry us a long way during the painful periods. The secret: Allow the Lord to thicken our skin so that we will survive Body life.

Principle #3: Be Patient with the Progress of the Group

Meeting in a home does not constitute the birth of church life. A church, in its purest form, takes time to be born. It takes approximately nine months for a person to be born! In that time, the mother experiences growth pains, sickness, uncomfortable positions, as well as major adjustments to her wardrobe and her eating and sleeping patterns.

It is similar with the birth of an *ekklesia*. The church is a living organism. Therefore, it takes time to be born. Starting something is human, but birth is divine. Birthing a church is territory staked out exclusively by divinity. It is not a human proposition.

Therefore, let us be patient. We will be learning to use instincts we have never before used. More importantly, we are beginning a journey to discover our Lord like never before. Not as individuals, but as *a people*.

Before the foundation of a new house can be laid, the lot must be thoroughly cleared. Trees, brush, and debris all must be removed. Our first six months or so are the 'clearing phase' of our life as a new church.

During this clearing phase, a great deal of unlearning will occur. A great deal of de-programming. A great deal of tearing down the old mindset, the old mentality, and the old practices. A discarding of the methods of operation that were picked-up by being part of institutional Christianity. In place of that, there will grow up among the group a new mindset, a new mentality, a new way of operating, and a new way to know the Lord and express him together. This all takes time.

Therefore, Body life demands infinite patience. We may think at times that it cannot possibly work. That it is hopeless. That the die has been miscast, and we were handed the wrong bundle of people. We may feel at times that the group simply refuses to do what we want them to do. The house church will not grow fast enough for us.

Impatience with the birth of church life is a monumental hurdle that many will have to face squarely. Task-oriented, program-driven people will have to face the slow pace of Body life. But no one can hurry the birthing process. This is God's business.

We are moving away from a religious service on Sunday morning where people mostly sit and listen to an organic gathering of new creations who are discovering anew how to express Jesus Christ corporately.

That is no small shift! It is as large as the universe.

So let us persevere, irregardless of how slow the pace. If we can manage to endure, we will discover a Lord who is all-sufficient. But remember, God moves according to his own clock! And his clock virtually always ticks much slower than ours.

Principle #4: People Will Leave the Group

This should be chiseled in marble. Let's face it. In the minds of most Christians, it is strange to go against the conventional current of having a paid pastor, a Sunday school program, a church building, and a church service that is centered on a worship team and a 45-minute sermon.

In the Western world, there are countless options. Westerners are accustomed to choosing from a raft of different automobiles, ice-cream flavors, and brands of cologne. In the city, there are most likely hundreds of churches, Bible studies, and para-church organizations from which to choose.

The situation was drastically different in the first century. There was only one option for a Christian. If someone came to Christ, they became part of the one and only church in their city. And that church met in homes without a traditional-type pastor. In the New Testament era, coming to Christ was the equivalent of being a member of his Body.

What does this mean for house churches? It simply means that the only way they will manage to stay together for the long haul and eventually grow numerically and in quality, is if they have come to the place where they have run out of options!

To put it another way, this way of gathering, though biblical, is not easy for everyone. Meeting in a home without a traditional pastor has significant cost attached to it. The meetings are now in our hands. What to do with the children is now a problem that we as a group must resolve. Difficulties with the other members is a challenge that we must tackle. Add to that, authentic church life will not work if we come to the meetings only to receive and not to give. And giving requires preparation. It requires time. It requires energy.

So let us get clear at the outset that there is an excellent chance that some of the people who are in the house church will not be around a few weeks from now, let alone a few months! Further, there are endless reasons why they will leave.

But here is the most important thing to remember. When someone leaves, we should not pressure or persuade them to stay. And more importantly, let us not speak ill of them when they go!

Further, it is of utmost importance that we refrain from imputing evil motives to their hearts. I have watched the profound destruction that judging motives does to relationships. The damage is devastating, and it has a ripple effect which injures many others.

The Lord Jesus condemned this practice, saying, "Do not judge lest you be judged. For in the same way you judge, you will be judged."[8] These were his thundering words. The Lord then followed this by giving peculiar insight into what happens when a person judges the motives of another. The one who finds fault with his brother and detects a speck of wood in his eye is exposing the fact that he is guilty of having a cedar tree in his own! The speck is actually a small chip off the cedar tree.

Consequently, when someone judges the heart motives of another, they in effect are projecting what is in their own heart onto that person. Simply put, to impute ill motives onto another is to expose what is in our own hearts! Only Jesus Christ has the right and the ability to see into the motives of someone's heart. We have no such right or ability.

Let us take the high road when people leave the group. Accept what they say at face value instead of second-guessing their intentions. In fact, if we really wish to hit a high watermark, bless and speak well of them when they leave and especially after they leave.

To do so incarnates a monumental breakthrough in the kingdom of God. It also speaks volumes about the group, namely, that the house church is not built on fear, elitism, sectarianism, or religious obligation, but on freedom. And an atmosphere of liberty and freedom is an evidence of the presence of God's Spirit. Note that freedom includes the freedom to leave without negative consequences!

So when someone joins the group, recognize that God has brought them. And if they leave, accept that God is removing them. If we can remember that it is God who adds and removes, then we will be better able to leave everyone who crosses our path in the Lord's hands.

By the same token, if we happen to be the one leaving, let us not criticize the group afterwards. The high road for us is to leave quietly, in peace, and to take no one else with us. To do this is to keep our integrity and honor. Neglect this and we have done great damage to the kingdom of God.

CONCLUSIONS

This chapter has briefly examined several ways in which a house church or house church network can begin. In addition, four key principles have been

---

[8] Matt 7:1-2 (NASB)

proposed that should be discussed at the start of a house church that will help ensure a group's long term health and vitality. If a house church can manage to keep them in mind, it will increase its chances for surviving and thriving dramatically.

STUDY QUESTIONS

1. Which New Testament strategy for church planting seems most workable in your situation to see a house church network planted in your area?
2. What can you do right now to begin creating a critical mass for the start of a prototype house church?
3. Which of the 'The Four Unmovable Principles' seems most difficult? Most exciting?

Chapter 45

How to Have Participatory House Church Meetings

Frank Viola

Frank Viola is an internationally known speaker, a house church planter, and the author of six highly acclaimed books on radical church restoration, including Rethinking the Wineskin, Who is Your Covering?, Pagan Christianity, and The Untold Story of the New Testament Church. Frank lives in Gainesville, Florida, USA. You can visit him at www.frankviola.com.

Introduction

In this chapter, we will explore how to have a life-giving participatory house church meeting. The theology, biblical merit, and spiritual benefits of the first century-styled open meeting are discussed elsewhere.[1] The evolution of when and why the open church meeting became extinct in church history and how the performance-spectator, Sunday morning, fixed 'order of worship' replaced it are also examined in detail elsewhere.[2] Presently, rather, we will look at the subject very practically. What follows is what I have discovered over the last 18 years of participating in house church meetings. This chapter is intended to help a new house church learn how to function as a community of believers without a traditional-type pastor or preplanned order of service.[3] The aim is to equip everyone to participate, share, and use their spiritual gifts in the meetings.

Traditional Church 'Services' vs. House Church 'Meetings'

Let us start by saying a few words about the language we have been conditioned to use. It will take some time for a house church to remove these concepts from its thinking and adjust its vocabulary. There are two phrases that we will want to forever strip out of our vocabulary. They are 'church service' (or 'the service') and 'going to church'. First, 'services' belong to institutions. They are ritualistic, performance-based ceremonies. The early Christians never had 'services' in which an active few performed for a passive audience. Instead, they had 'meetings' that were spontaneous, interactive, participatory, and Spirit-led. 'Meeting' is the word that is

---

[1] Frank Viola (2001), *Rethinking the Wineskin: The Practice of the New Testament Church,* Present Testimony Ministry.
[2] Frank Viola (2003), *Pagan Christianity: The Origins of Our Modern Church Practices,* Present Testimony Ministry.
[3] Frank Viola (2006), *Gathering in Homes: Volume 1—Beginning,* Present Testimony Ministry.

employed throughout the New Testament when the early Christians came together to display Christ.[4] Second, we are no longer 'going to church'. The church, or *ekklesia*, is the Body of Christ which assembles together. It is not a place to go. It is not an edifice. We are going to a 'meeting', and we are part of the church.

PRACTICAL ASPECTS OF HOSTING A HOUSE CHURCH MEETING

Let us now move on to practical arrangements for hosting a house church. Some of these issues will be obvious, though some may not be. These suggestions are meant to create an atmosphere conducive to having a participatory meeting with minimal distraction.

Find a Host Home

Hopefully, the person who has the largest living room will be willing to host the meetings. If the person lives 50 miles away from everyone, however, that will not work. It is important to find a home that is central to where most of the group lives. Note also that the person or couple who hosts the meetings understands that they do not own the church, nor are they necessarily automatically the leaders of the group. However, those who are hosting the meetings have the prerogative to lay down some basic house rules about shoes, parking, rooms that are not to be used, etc. And it is important that the group respects these rules. If you have several people who are willing to host the meetings, you may want to rotate homes.

Decide on Time and Frequency of Meetings

First, it is suggested that the house church meet at least once weekly. Everyone should participate in the decision of when and how often to meet, so that everyone is most often available for at least several hours. The group may wish to revisit and negotiate the time and day of the meetings as the group gets larger or based on other issues like child care.

Second, be respectful of the agreed upon times of when a meeting will start or end. Otherwise, people will stop coming to your meetings. Institutional churches can get away with persistent late-comers. But not so with house churches. Open participatory meetings require everyone to be on time. If the meetings always start on time, even among a few, it will provoke most of the others who may have the habit of being late to change their ways. But if the group waits until everyone shows up, people will get the idea that it is acceptable to be late.

Third, announce the time and place of the next meeting. For house churches that rotate time and place, if such an announcement is not made, some people will not show up. The best time to make this announcement is at the end of the meeting with everyone present. House churches that have a regular time and place will, obviously, not need to worry about this factor.

---

[4] Also called "assembling" or "coming together" (Acts 4:31; 1 Cor 14:23, 26; Heb 10:25).

Temperature, Lighting, and Noise

Be aware that once the group shows up, the room will heat up due to body heat and adjustments may need to be made. Also be aware of adequate lighting required if the group will be reading Scripture or watching something on video. Additionally, the hosts may wish to ensure that no noisy distractions occur during the meeting. It is also a good idea for everyone to turn their cell phones off or to set them to 'vibrate'.

Arrange Chairs to Promote Open Sharing

Rather than setting up chairs in rows, chairs can be arranged in a circle or square, which will invite face-to-face communication and bring everyone as close as possible. Those who enjoy sitting on the floor can conveniently sit in the middle of the chairs on top of pillows and/or blankets.

Dress Informally

Dress modestly, but informally, for the house church meetings. Ritualistic services where one watches, listens, and is very minimally involved are not to characterize the meetings. We are through with spectator church. We are learning how to participate in an interactive and informal gathering of God's people. Dressing like we do in our own homes can add to the authentic atmosphere of the group.

Everyone Should Clean Up

If a person is hosting the meetings in their home, the burden of clean-up after the meeting should not fall upon their shoulders exclusively. Instead, the rest of the group should carry the clean-up burden. Everyone can participate in clean-up, or a rotating schedule can be agreed on ahead of time. This would include taking down the chairs, vacuuming the rug, sweeping the floor, cleaning up the kitchen, etc.

Welcome Visitors

If the house church has visitors, someone in the group should ask them to share who they are, where they are from, and what brought them to the gathering. It is also encouraged that house churches follow-up with your visitors. Have someone greet them at the end of the meeting. Get their contact information. Give them a call during the week. Ask them how they liked the meeting, and invite them back. It is essential that you make visitors not only feel welcome, but wanted. If not, you are headed toward devolving into an 'us-four-and-no-more' clique! House churches who suffer from that disease end up losing more members than they gain.

WHAT TO DO IN A PARTICIPATORY MEETING

It is suggested that the content of house church participatory meetings contain seven key elements, namely singing, sharing, eating, playing, praying, handling Scripture, and releasing everyone's spiritual gifts. Every element does not have to be present in every meeting. Rather, the goal is that each element will find its way into the meetings in a spontaneous, natural, interactive, and participatory way as the house church learns to allow the Holy Spirit to lead the gatherings.

Sing Together

Learn to sing as a corporate group of believers. It may be helpful in the first few months of a house church that people learn to sing as the Body of Christ without a song leader, music director, a preplanned order of songs, or any musical instruments. Instead, learn to sing together *acapella*. Why? Because for centuries we Christians have been conditioned to let instruments control our singing. We sit and we wait for an instrument to tell us when to begin singing and when to stop. A song leader can actually distract from corporate singing. By removing instruments and singing *acapella*, we are winning back singing into the hands of all of God's people! Once the house church owns its own singing where there is no song leader present, then musical instruments may be reintroduced without inhibiting Body functioning. Those playing instruments should learn to follow the singing rather than lead it. Musicians should consider the possibility that the Lord would desire for them to lay down their talent at his cross for a season so that his people could rise to their calling of singing corporately. The goal is that you will learn to sing as the Body of Christ without reliance on any props or song leaders, though they might act as a beneficial supplement later on.

Share Together

An important aspect of meeting together is to learn how to share our thoughts, feelings, ideas, concerns, and victories readily with one another. What follows are several exercises that a house church might try. The exercises below may be temporarily used for, say, the initial six months of a house church and are never meant to become a rigid liturgy for the meetings on a long-term basis. The goal is to use them until the house church becomes accustomed to sharing quite naturally and easily with one another, after which such planned exercises will not be necessary and should be dispensed with altogether.

Exercise 1—Share a Teaching. According to the New Testament, churches were planted by the preaching of Jesus Christ. They were typically founded by the speaking of the word of God by a church planter. The word of Christ has incredible community-forming properties that cannot be explained rationally. In the beginning, it is best to invite a church planter to share the riches of Christ with the new house church. This was the New Testament pattern.[5] If this is not possible, get a hold of some good, Christ-centered teaching tape, CD, DVD, or book that the group can agree upon. Each time you come together listen, watch, or read the material. Share with one another what you received from the message. Stay away from asking complex theological questions. Instead, share what ministered to you, what

---

[5] Frank Viola (2003) *So You Want to Start a House Church?: First-Century Styled Church Planting For Today,* Present Testimony Ministry.

touched you, what stirred you, or what new insight you discovered or saw about the Lord and his church.

Exercise 2—Share Your Story. Each time you come together, several of you can tell your life-story. This will include the story of your entire life, your testimony of how you came to Christ, the story of your Christian life up until the present day, your personal aspirations, and what brought you to gather with the present group of believers. Be creative if you like. Include songs, poems, photographs, photo slides, video clips, or anything you wish that will help you to communicate your story. At the beginning stage of a house church, it is not wise to tell unnecessary details about extremely personal matters from your past. Use discernment. Do this every week until everyone has told their story.

Exercise 3—Share a Song. Each week, several people will bring to the meeting one song that has special value to them. The song can be either by a Christian or a non-Christian artist. They will share how they saw the Lord through the song. They will either play the song for the group or sing it for them, or both. They will then take as much time as they need to share how the lyrics and/or the music have special value to them. Namely, how does the song minister the Lord to them? The sharing will be open for group participation and interaction. Everyone in the group is encouraged to comment on each person's song and what they saw through it.

Exercise 4—Share a Scripture. Each week, several people can bring to the meeting a few of their favorite passages from the Bible. They will explain what they understand the passages to mean. They will then encourage the group with why it has special meaning for them. The sharing will be open for group participation and interaction. At this point, we should stay away from complex theological discourses. Sharing should be personal and from the heart.

Eat Together

This is a pillar upon which Body life is built. Have a common meal either before or after your sharing time. If you eat first, some people may have difficulty keeping their eyes open during the sharing. On the other hand, eating before the sharing time allows everyone to socially interact as soon as the meeting begins. The host family may decide to prepare the meal, or everyone can bring something. If you have people in your group who are desperately poor and cannot contribute by bringing food, ask them to help cook some of the meal. Encourage them to contribute in some way instead of continually coming empty handed. Eating is a family activity. It helps to build solidarity among family members. People feel much freer and less inhibited to share their lives and thoughts over a meal. There is a mysterious element in a meal that binds people together in an uncommon way. For this reason, the early Christians ate together frequently. They understood themselves to be the household or family of God.

Play Together

Making play a part of our church life is an indispensable ingredient for success. One of the most important things we can learn is how to avoid being overly 'religious' or 'serious'. We are discovering how to be authentic with one another and how to cultivate a feeling of safety with one other. We are also learning to change years of traditional mindsets. Often, whenever Christians meet together in a church setting, it is exceedingly difficult for them to be anything but serious and formal. We hide behind a mask. Our vocabulary, our style of speaking, and our praying all changes when we get together with others for a Christian meeting. The early church was born in an atmosphere of informality. The Body of Christ breathes the air of informality. It is void of ritualism, legalism, professionalism, and religiosity. By learning to get to know one another in an informal, non-religious atmosphere, we are providing a womb for authentic Body life to be born. Religiosity is not spirituality. The former will bring death to a group of Christians. Therefore, learn how to appropriately have fun, tell jokes, share stories, and play with any children in the group.

Pray Together

In the beginning of the house church experience, it is recommended that prayer come slowly and naturally. Many people have learned very poor habits of prayer. Consequently, it is vital that we rediscover prayer from the ground up.[6] We do not want to bring into the new house church experience old modes of traditional praying that are counterproductive, lifeless, and artificial. Let us discover prayer anew and afresh.

Handle Scripture Together

Another aspect of healthy Body life is learning how to discover and apply the message of the Bible together in a living way. The message of the Bible is Jesus Christ.[7] Believers can discover how to know Christ through their handling of Scripture together. Unfortunately, many Christians have only learned to approach Scripture one way, namely from a 'rationalistic' perspective. This has caused much division and harm to the Body of Christ. Using the Scripture can either bring death or life. It can divide or unify. It can reveal Jesus Christ or it can give dead information. The use of Scripture should primarily be done devotionally. Learn to use it as a vehicle for discovering the Lord. In many of today's house churches, much of the time this will happen in a quite natural way as someone spontaneously shares with the group what they have learned from the Scripture recently about the Lord. Occasionally, there may be someone in the group that has a teaching gift who will provide some insights from the Bible in a more directive

---

[6] Rosalind Rinker (1992), *Learning Conversational Prayer*, Liturgical Press.
[7] Luke 24:22; John 5:39. Paul's entire message was Christ. He consistently used the Scriptures to unveil the Lord.

fashion from time to time. In both cases, the house church meeting should be flexible enough so that plenty of response and interactive discussion from all present can happen. Make your focus Jesus Christ and seek to discover him in Scripture. This is the secret to finding life and fostering unity by using the Bible.

Release All Spiritual Gifts

Some final remarks should be made here about the idea of 'spiritual gifts' (i.e. Greek = *charismata*). The early church recognized that every believer had a skill or capacity that they had the privilege and responsibility of bringing to church meetings.[8] In addition to those already discussed above, they included more dramatic things like supernatural utterances, prophecy, words of wisdom, words of knowledge, miracles, distinguishing of spirits, etc. These were incorporated into the meetings in a way that was rather spontaneous as the Spirit of God directed. Today's house churches are encouraged not to fall prey to the extremes of rejecting these genuine manifestations of the Spirit's work (i.e. 'charisphobia'), nor of equating genuine Christian maturity exclusively with dramatic displays of these gifts (i.e. 'charismania'). Rather, let us be open to how God would lead our house church. Keep in mind that the Holy Spirit has come to testify of Jesus Christ. So, authentic spiritual gifts will make Christ, and not the Holy Spirit, the gifts, nor the gifted person, the focus and the center of our meetings.

CONCLUSIONS

We have examined briefly some of the key ingredients necessary for a healthy and thriving participatory church meeting, as well as some practical suggestions for hosting such gatherings. The elements of singing, sharing, eating, playing, praying, handling Scripture, and releasing gifts should find their way into the participatory meetings in a spontaneous, interactive, participatory, and Spirit-led manner.

STUDY QUESTIONS

1. Which traditional church practices or mindsets do you perhaps have that will be difficult to leave behind as you start a house church?
2. Which aspect of participatory meetings is most exciting to you? Most challenging?
3. How can you practically ensure that the group does not drift towards having a fixed 'order of service'?

---

[8] 1 Cor 12:1-12, 14:26

Chapter 46

TRUE COMMUNITY: DOING LIFE TOGETHER AS A HOUSE CHURCH

RAD ZDERO

Rad Zdero earned his Ph.D. degree in Mechanical Engineering from Queen's University (Kingston, ON, Canada) and is the manager of a hospital-based orthopaedic research lab. He has participated in, led, and started house churches and cell groups since 1985. He is currently part of House Church.Ca (www.housechurch.ca), which is a church planting team developing a network of house churches in the greater Toronto area and beyond. He is the author of The Global House Church Movement (2004). [Used by permission of the author. Email: rzdero@yahoo.ca].

INTRODUCTION

Life as part of a house church or house church network can be exhilarating because of the close-knit nature of the relationships that are developed over time. However, the opposite is also true—when tensions and conflict arise, they can be significant. Everything is amplified in a house church that is attempting to experience 'true community'. Along with this, come the more mundane realities of being in relationship to one another and doing things together, as we seek to deepen our relationship with God. These practical realities include spending quality and quantity time together, conflict resolution, decision-making, children, money, baptisms, weddings, and hosting. A brief discussion about such matters is offered here.

WHAT IS 'TRUE COMMUNITY'?[1]

The dictionary defines community as "a social group whose members live in a specific locality, share government, and have a common heritage."[2] This description suggests there is a good deal of overlap between the lives of the members of a community, geographically, governmentally, and historically. These strands connect individuals into a group such that they will have shared experiences and understandings.

For the Christian, more importantly, the idea of community is inherent in the triune nature of God, where there is a mutual and eternal flow of love between the Father, the Son, and the Holy Spirit. This serves as the primary

---

[1] For a more detailed discussion on the concept of community, see Dietrich Bonhoeffer (1954), *Life Together*, Harper and Row.
[2] *Webster's Dictionary of the English Language*, based on *The Random House Dictionary (Classic Edition)*, Random House, Inc., 1983.

model for us in understanding how we are to relate with one another. We have been designed by God with the deep awareness of our need for connection with others. We were never meant to be alone.

As the church, then, we can taste some of this here and now, with God and with each another, since we have the Spirit of God dwelling in each of us. Combining the various images and words found in the New Testament, we could define Christian community in this way: *True Community is God's children, called out of the world, gathered into spiritual families, and sharing life together.*[3]

But some questions naturally arise at this point. How is this to be realized on a day-to-day basis? What happens when there is a rupture in such relationships? What mundane aspects of house church life serve to create true community? Are there pragmatic issues that a house church must deal with in this whole process? Let us turn now to some of these practicalities for house churches.

QUALITY TIME AND QUANTITY TIME

House church is not only about a series of meetings that happen weekly in someone's home. A key ingredient is building spiritually transforming relationships in the context of the ebb and flow of daily life and ministry. For the sake of accountability, encouragement, mentoring, and leadership development, the 'meetings between meetings' on informal and planned levels are vital. A house church is meant to be a family, a 24-hour-a-day, 7-day-a-week community, which is the crucible God uses to change our lives.

This requires both quality and quantity time with each other. This is about mutual life-on-life ministry and about giving each other permission to enter into each other's lives. We should not underestimate the power of spending time together walking, eating, shopping, playing sports, mowing the lawn, watching a movie, going for a coffee, etc. In these informal times, it has been said that 'more is caught than is formally taught'. This may be further supplemented by communally living together as a 'household' church or by having several families move into the same neighborhood or apartment building.

Robert Coleman, in his classic book *The Master Plan of Evangelism*, makes the following astute observation about how Jesus informally trained his 12 disciples and built a sense of group identity among them:

> The time which Jesus invested in these few disciples was so much more by comparison to that given to others that it can only be regarded as a deliberate strategy. He actually spent more time with his disciples than with everybody else in the world put together. He ate with them, slept with them,

---

[3] This concise and helpful definition was provided to me by Jason Johnston (www.housechurch.ca).

and talked with them for the most part of his entire active ministry. They walked together along the lonely roads; they visited together in the crowded cities; they sailed and fished together on the Sea of Galilee; they prayed together in the deserts and in the mountains; and they worshiped together in the synagogues and in the Temple.[4]

CONFLICT RESOLUTION

True community is the place where you will always be in conflict with someone about something. Theology, personality, preferences, learning styles, life choices, etc. These are but a few of the things that often seem to cause conflict even between well-meaning Christians. And in the case of house churches, where the relationships are more intense because of the smaller number of people, the potential for great tension is ever-present. Yet, it may be that these are the very things that God wants to use to challenge us to be more patient, more generous, more forgiving, more understanding, and more committed to one another, as we seek God together.

How can some of these conflicts be avoided altogether early on? Some house churches and house church networks may choose to craft a simple mission or covenant statement together that can then be given to any new people considering joining the group. This can eliminate any misunderstandings about certain values and beliefs held strongly by the group. The statement may be a one page document outlining central theological views (e.g. the Triune nature of God, the authority of the Bible, etc.), practical aspects of house church ministry (e.g. the role of women, the place of the supernatural, etc.), or even views related to certain issues that the group feels convinced about (e.g. human sexuality, pacifism, just war, taxes, the ecology, the poor, evangelism, etc.). It may be wise to have these views clearly communicated early on—even if only verbally—so that unnecessary conflicts and surprises do not arise later, resulting in hurt feelings, broken relationships, and disillusionment.

How can a house church deal with overt sin? Being offended by a brother or sister in Christ is always a hard thing to handle. In a house church, this may be even more destructive because of the intimate relationships that have been forged over time. The offense may be a petty or careless behavior (e.g. a sarcastic remark, a disapproving look, etc.), or perhaps a major breach of trust (e.g. theft, sexual harassment, adultery, etc.). If the offense is rather minor, only a short conversation with the offender may be necessary to clear up any misunderstandings. For more serous matters, the counsel of Jesus is especially meaningful.[5] We are to go to the person privately to deal with the issue and seek resolution and reconciliation with them. If the person is not responsive, then we are to take along someone else (perhaps a witness to the

---

[4] Robert Coleman (1994), *The Master Plan of Evangelism*, Revell, p.45.
[5] Matt 18:15-17

offence) with us to confront the person. If there is still no sign of remorse or repentance, then they are to be challenged on their behavior by the house church the next time the group meets. If there is still no change in attitude, then it may be time to ask them to leave the group for a season or, perhaps, permanently. It may be that this will shake up the person to the point where they will experience godly sorrow and choose to be reconciled to God and to people.[6] In very few extreme cases where someone is in physical danger such as child abuse, spousal abuse, or harassment, the civic authorities and other professionals may need to become involved.

We must remember that regardless of the nature of the sin, the goal of the conflict resolution process is not punishment, but rather reconciliation between all parties, for God is a God of reconciliation.[7] We are to forgive others, as we ourselves have been forgiven.[8] We are to love others because God loved us first.[9] We are to forgive not just seven times, but seventy times seven times.[10] We are to be at peace with everyone, as far as it is possible.[11]

DECISION-MAKING

House churches, just like any other close-knit group, are faced with making both simple and difficult decisions on a whole variety of issues that will shape their present and future. Money, children, church discipline, and organizational matters are just some of the things they face.

Many choices set precedents and create patterns that are hard to change later on, for better or worse. The way a house church engages the decision-making process, therefore, is vitally important.

Our pragmatic thinking may take us down the road toward using either some type of democratic voting system in which the majority carries the day. Or, it may seem best to let the recognized leadership team decide on behalf of the group.

It is suggested here that neither of these is as adequate nor as biblical as possible. Rather, a deliberate process should be facilitated or initiated by the leadership team (or anyone else) that involves everyone in the house church and includes some combination of prayer, mutual consultation, consideration of circumstances, and searching the Scriptures.

As we seek the mind of the Lord together sincerely and openly, consensus decision-making can greatly enhance group ownership, mutual appreciation, and honor to Christ as the real leader of each house church. Though this process can take longer than other methods, it is rewarding once a resolution is reached.

---

[6] 1 Cor 5:1-5; 2 Cor 7:8-12
[7] Rom 5:1
[8] Matt 6:12
[9] 1 John 4:19
[10] Matt 18:21-22
[11] Rom 12:18

CHILDREN

One of the first questions that usually arises for people considering involvement in the house church movement is the role of children. Three approaches commonly used are integration, specialization, and parental apprenticeship.

Integration means that some house churches try to incorporate teens and children fully into the meetings, making sure that their needs are met and that they have the opportunity to contribute to the gatherings. These groups value a truly multi-generational approach where younger generations are also given the chance to teach the older ones something. It may be especially easy to integrate everyone during meals, storytelling, testimonies, worship in song, and clean-up.

Specialization means that some house churches have a separate time for the young kids in another part of the home that is focused on meeting their specific needs, e.g. simple Bible stories, practical lessons on how to follow Jesus, learning songs about Jesus, etc. Also, a group of home churches can band together to have some sort of specialized occasional event for children and teens on a larger scale, e.g. birthday party, campout, sporting events, worship times, etc. In the case of older teens or those about to step into college or university, a house church may be completely comprised of and led by young people, with the support and accountability of the house church network they belong to.

Parental apprenticeship means that the responsibility of spiritual guidance rests mainly with the parents during their daily routine dealings with their children. For better or worse, it is often mom and dad that have the biggest influence on a young person's life. Children and young teens tend to imitate what they see in their parents, making this a challenge to moms and dads to really live out the Christian life in front of their kids. Becoming overly dependent on specialized programming does not acknowledge this fact and detracts from the opportunity and responsibility of Christian parents to raise their children in the things of the Lord as they go about the day-to-day activities of family life.[12] Although specialized programming for young children and teens has merit, it should be a supplement to parental mentoring rather than a substitute for it.

MONEY MATTERS

How do house churches spend any money they collect as a group? They do not utilize their money on expensive programs, rent, church building projects, church building mortgages, or supporting professional clergy. Instead, they funnel their money to the poor, to resources for use within the house church and/or network, to support house church planters, and to overseas mercy ministries.

---

[12] Deut 11:19; Prov 22:6

How do they collect this money? There are different practices among house churches concerning church bank accounts, tax deductible donations, and tithing. There are advantages and disadvantages to each of these. Some house churches do not incorporate any of these elements, but rather use money solely for mutual support within the house church as the need arises and in assisting the poor. Money, thus, flows directly from giver to receiver and bypasses middle agencies like the government and denominational finance departments. Other house churches incorporate all three elements and, thus, function like traditional churches, offering tax receipts to donors.

How does this work for a network of house churches? In some networks, each house church will have its own approach since there is no centralized giving scheme or system, e.g. one house church may have a bank account, another may have a shoe box, another may only collect money spontaneously for crisis needs, etc. Some networks, though, choose to have a central bank account shared by all the house churches in their cluster, for use in common outreach and inreach projects.

How does this compare to more traditional churches? More conventional churches can spend up to 80% of their budget simply in supporting their full time minister, expensive internal programs, and paying off the mortgage for the church building. Individual house churches, on the other hand, do not have these expenses. House church networks, though, sometimes partially or fully support apostolic house church planters and/or those who provide coaching. Nevertheless, strictly speaking, a house church cluster with the same number of people as a single traditional church has significantly more financial leverage in supporting overseas missionaries, relief organizations, and local mercy ministries.

BAPTISMS

Because house churches value outreach to non-believers, as well as seeing fringe Christians rededicate themselves to Christ, baptisms will need to occur from time to time. In full-fledged church planting movements around the world, house church baptisms are a very frequent event. The political and cultural situation may also determine whether baptisms can be done publicly or privately. In any case, there are several creative options that are currently being used by house churches around the globe. During the cold season, it is a valid practice to baptize people indoors, either in an indoor community swimming pool or even a bathtub. During the warm season, outdoor baptisms can occur either in a lake, a river, or a backyard swimming pool. In many situations, baptism can occur immediately or very soon after the person's profession of faith, which is the scriptural precedent. In other circumstances, such a thing will be impractical, requiring first that a suitable water source be found. In any case, a celebratory time can follow that includes food, prayer, worship in song, music, etc., which can recall to mind the joy of God and his angels at the person's salvation, which they have now demonstrated publicly by their act of baptism.

WEDDINGS

In most traditional church settings, an ordained priest or minister has the authority from both their denomination and the state to perform weddings. If house church networks are truly to be seen as genuine Christian communities, they must also be given the opportunity to validate and witness—before God—the joining of a woman and man in marriage. Several creative options are available to house churches that can meet both spiritual and legal obligations. First, the happy couple can arrange to have a Christian wedding facilitated by their home church elder(s), apostolic worker(s), or other person in a hall, backyard, or other setting of their choice. This would be followed by a brief separate civil ceremony at city hall to meet government requirements. Second, if there happens to be someone in a home church network that previously has some ordination status or who has a license to perform weddings, then only one ceremony would be necessary.

HOSTING

Choosing a home to meet in for the house church can work in two ways. Some choose to meet in the same home for consistency's sake, because of the size and comfort of the particular home, or because of the obvious knack for hospitality that the hosts have. Others, on the other hand, choose to have a rotating schedule so that everyone has a chance to host by taking on an increased level of ownership for the house church and to avoid overburdening the same host home. Related to this, it is recommended that a home church meet one to three times per week to maintain a sense of connectedness with one another. Meeting less frequently than this will tend to kill momentum. Meeting more frequently may simply lead to burnout, especially for those expected to facilitate or host regularly. In either case, every member of the house church should be involved in clean-up and respect any house rules of the host home, e.g. shoes off at the door, no food or drinks in grandfather's study, etc.

CONCLUSIONS

We have briefly examined some of the more practical issues involved in developing 'true community' in a house church. Though there are no set rules for carrying out some of these activities or for delegating responsibilities, everyone should be involved as much as possible to create a sense of ownership for the group and what God is calling it to be.

STUDY QUESTIONS

1. Comment on the need for both quality and quantity time in relationships.
2. Reflect on this statement: "True community is the place where you will always be in conflict with someone about something."
3. How could a cohesive network of house churches help deal with some of the practicalities of community life discussed?

Chapter 47

THE LORD'S SUPPER: FEAST OR FAMINE?

STEVE ATKERSON

Steve Atkerson holds an M.Div. from Mid-America Baptist Theological Seminary, served seven years as one of the pastors of a Southern Baptist church, began working with house churches in the late 1980s, and is now elder of a house church in Atlanta, GA, USA. He travels widely teaching and training leaders on the basics of New Testament church life. Books he has edited and contributed to include Toward A House Church Theology, Ekklesia: To the Roots of Biblical House Church Life, The Practice of the Early Church: A Theological Workbook (Leader's Guide), and The Equipping Manual. He is part of the team at The New Testament Restoration Foundation (www.ntrf.org). [Used by permission of the author. Email: nt_restoration_foundation@juno.com].

INTRODUCTION

One of the main reasons for house churches to gather according to the New Testament is the eating of the Lord's Supper. Many modern-day house churches have found it to be a great blessing to their life together as the Body of Christ. Therefore, this chapter explores its New Testament foundations and function, as well as providing practical guidelines in implementing it in today's house churches.

THE NEW TESTAMENT FOUNDATIONS FOR THE LORD'S SUPPER

Jesus and the Last Supper

The very first Lord's Supper is also called the Last Supper, because it was the last meal Jesus shared with his disciples before his crucifixion. The occasion for the meal was the Passover. At this Passover Feast, Jesus and his disciples reclined at a table that would have been heaped with food.[1] Jewish tradition tells us that this meal typically lasted for hours. During the course of the meal, "*while* they were eating"[2] Jesus took a loaf of bread and compared it to his body. He had *already* taken up a cup and had them all drink from it. Later, "*after* the supper"[3] Jesus took the cup again and compared it to his blood, which was soon to be poured out for the sins of the world. Thus, the bread and wine of the Lord's Supper were introduced in the context of a full meal, specifically, the Passover meal.

---

[1] Exod 12; Deut 16
[2] Matt 26:26 (NIV)
[3] Luke 22:20 (NIV)

A Sign of the Messianic Kingdom

The Passover celebrated two major events, namely the deliverance of the children of Israel from Egypt and the long anticipated coming Messianic deliverance.[4] First century Jews thought of heaven as a time of feasting at Messiah's table.[5] Soon after that Last Supper, Jesus became the ultimate sacrificial Passover lamb, suffering on the cross to deliver his people from their sins. Jesus keenly desired to eat that last Passover with his disciples, saying that he would "not eat it again until it finds fulfillment in the kingdom of God."[6] Evidently, the fulfillment of this was later written about by the apostle John, who recorded an angel declaring, "Blessed are those who are invited to the wedding supper of the Lamb!"[7] The Last Supper and the early church's Lord's Supper all looked forward to a fulfillment in the wedding supper of the Lamb.

The Church and the Lord's Supper

The most extensive treatment of the Lord's Supper is found in Paul's letter to the Corinthians.[8] Just as the Last Supper was a full meal, so too did the Corinthians understand the Lord's Supper to be a true meal. The word behind "supper"[9] is *deipnon*, which means "dinner, the main meal toward evening, banquet." It never refers to anything less than a full meal. The deep divisions of the Corinthian believers resulted in their Lord's Supper meetings doing more harm than good. They were partaking of the Supper in an unworthy manner. The wealthier people among them, perhaps not wanting to eat with the lower social classes, evidently came to the gathering so early and remained there so long that some became drunk. Making matters worse, by the time that the working-class believers arrived, delayed by employment constraints, all the food had been consumed and they went home hungry. Some of the Corinthians failed to recognize the Supper as a sacred, covenant meal. The abuses were so serious that what was supposed to be the Lord's Supper had instead become their own personal supper. Their sinful selfishness absolutely betrayed the very essence of what the Lord's Supper was all about. From the nature of their abuse, it is evident that the Corinthian church regularly partook of the Lord's Supper as a full meal. The inspired solution for the problem was not that the church cease eating it as a full meal. Instead, Paul advised that they should wait for one another. Only those so famished or undisciplined or selfish that they could not wait for the others were instructed to eat at home.

---

[4] Fritz Reinecker (1980), *A Linguistic Key to the Greek New Testament*, Zondervan, p.207.
[5] Matt 8:11; Luke 14:15
[6] Luke 22:16 (NIV)
[7] Rev 19:9 (NIV)
[8] 1 Cor 11:17-33
[9] 1 Cor 11:20

THE NEW TESTAMENT FUNCTION OF THE LORD'S SUPPER

Remind Jesus to Return

Partaking of the bread and cup as an integral part of the meal originally served several important functions. One of these was to remind Jesus of his promise to return. Reminding God of his covenant promises is a thoroughly scriptural concept.[10] The Lord's Supper is the sign of the new covenant.[11] As with any sign, it is to serve as a reminder.[12] The Greek word translated 'remembrance' is *anamnesis* and means 'reminder'. Thus, the church was to partake of the bread of the Lord's Supper specifically to remind Jesus of his promise to return and eat the supper again, in person. Understood in this light, it was originally designed to be like a prayer asking Jesus to return.[13] Just as the rainbow reminds God of his covenant with Noah, just like the groaning reminded God of his covenant with Abraham, so too partaking of the bread of the Lord's Supper was designed to remind Jesus of his promise to return. Paul confirms this idea by stating that the early church, in eating the Lord's Supper, did actually proclaim the Lord's death until he returns.[14] To whom did they proclaim his death, and why? Arguably, they proclaimed it to the Lord himself, as a reminder for him to return. It is significant that the Greek behind 'until' is *achri hou*. As it is used here, it grammatically can denote a goal or an objective.[15] Paul was instructing the church to partake of the bread and cup as a means of proclaiming the Lord's death (as a reminder) with the goal of ('until') persuading him to come back! Thus, in proclaiming Christ's death through the loaf and cup, the supper looked forward to and anticipated his return.

Create Unity

Just as the form of the Lord's Supper was important—a full fellowship meal that prefigured the wedding banquet of the Lamb—also important were the form of the bread and cup. Mention is made in Scripture of *the* cup of thanksgiving (singular) and of only *one* loaf.[16] The one loaf not only pictures our unity in Christ, but even helps *create* unity! Even so, some in Corinth were guilty of partaking of the Lord's Supper in an unworthy manner.[17] The rich refused to eat the supper with the poor. The rich arrived at the place of meeting so early that when the poor got there later, some of the rich had become drunk, and all the food had been eaten. The poor went home hungry. These shameful class divisions cut at the heart of the unity that the Lord's

---

[10] Gen 9:16; Exod 2:24-25; Ezek 16:60

[11] Matt 26:28

[12] Luke 22:16-19

[13] Matt 6:11

[14] 1 Cor 11:26

[15] Fritz Reinecker, Ibid., p.34

[16] 1 Cor 10:16-17

[17] 1 Cor 11:27

Supper was designed to achieve. The Corinthian abuses were so bad that it had ceased being the Lord's Supper and had instead become their "own" supper.[18] This failure of the rich to recognize the Body of the Lord in their poorer brethren also resulted in divine judgment, with many of them becoming sick and a number having died.[19] Paul's solution to the harmful meetings was that they were to wait for each other and eat together.[20] Part of the reason the Corinthians were not unified is precisely because they failed to eat the Lord's Supper *together*, centered around one loaf and one cup.

Foster Fellowship

In speaking to the church at Laodicea, our resurrected Lord offered to come in and eat with anyone who heard his voice and opened the door, a picture of fellowship and communion.[21] This 'fellowship in feasting' theme is also found in the book of Acts, where we learn that the early church devoted themselves to "fellowship in the breaking of bread."[22] They had fellowship with one another as they broke bread together. Many commentaries associate the phrase "breaking of bread" throughout the book of Acts with the Lord's Supper. This is because Luke, who wrote Acts, recorded in his gospel that Jesus took bread and "broke it" at the Last Supper.[23] If this conclusion is accurate, then the early church enjoyed the Lord's Supper as a time of fellowship and gladness, just like one would enjoy at a wedding banquet.

Partake Together Weekly

How often did the New Testament church partake of the Supper? Early believers ate the Lord's Supper weekly each Lord's Day. Firstly, the technical term, "Lord's Day" is from a unique phrase in the Greek, *kuriakon hemeran*, which literally reads, "the day belonging to the Lord." The words "belonging to the Lord" are from *kuriakos*, which occurs in the New Testament only twice. Paul uses the term to refer to the "Lord's Supper" or the "Supper belonging to the Lord" (*kuriakon deipnon*).[24] The connection between these two uses must not be missed. If the purpose of the weekly church meeting is to observe the Lord's Supper, it only makes sense that this *supper* belonging to the Lord would be eaten on the *day* belonging to the Lord, namely, the first day of the week. John also uses the term in the book of Revelation, indicating that his visions evidently occurred on the first day of the week, the day in which Jesus rose from the dead and the day on which the early church met to eat the supper belonging to the Lord.[25] The

---

[18] 1 Cor 11:21
[19] 1 Cor 11:27-32
[20] 1 Cor 11:33
[21] Rev 3:20
[22] Acts 2:42 (literal translation)
[23] Luke 22:19
[24] 1 Cor 11:20
[25] Rev 1:10

resurrection, the day, and the supper go together as a package deal. Secondly, Luke informs us that "On the first day of the week we came together to break bread."[26] The words "to eat" reflect what is known as a telic infinitive. It denotes a purpose or objective. Their meeting on the first day of the week was for eating!

PRACTICAL CONSIDERATIONS FOR THE LORD'S SUPPER

Practicing the Lord's Supper in the house churches as a full meal today can be a means of great blessing. The atmosphere is not unlike that of a wedding banquet. It is a great time of fellowship, encouragement, edification, friendship, caring, catching up, praying, exhorting, and maturing. Here are some practical considerations concerning its implementation.

Attitude

Be sure the house church understands that the Lord's Supper is one of the main purposes for the weekly gathering. It is neither optional nor secondary to some other type of 'worship service'. Even if all that a house church does on a given Sunday is celebrate the Lord's Supper, it has fulfilled one of its primary reasons for having a meeting that week.

Food

If at all possible, make the meal one that is shared, and purpose to eat whatever is brought. This makes the administration of the food much easier. Trust God's sovereignty! Over-planning the meal can take a lot of the fun out and make it burdensome. The one thing that should be preplanned is who supplies the one loaf and the fruit of the vine. In some house churches, the family that is hosting the meeting always supplies these things.

Giving

Since celebrating the meal is a New Testament pattern and something important to the life of a properly functioning house church, time and money spent by individual families on food to bring is truly a part of their giving unto the Lord. Rather than merely dropping an offering in a plate each week, go to the food store and buy the best food you can afford.

Clean Up

To facilitate clean up, you may want to consider using paper plates and napkins along with plastic forks and cups. Also, since folks sometimes carelessly throw away their utensils along with the rest of their trash, it is better to accidentally throw away a plastic fork than a metal one! To help avoid spills the host family supplies wicker plate holders, which can be reused and do not usually need to be washed.

Logistics

In warm weather it may be appropriate to eat outside. Spilled food and drink is inevitable, and clean up is much easier. A large folding table can be

---

[26] Acts 20:7 (NIV)

placed where necessary and stored away after the meeting. In cold weather, when eating indoors is necessary, consider covering any nicely upholstered furniture with a layer of plastic and then cloth. Since children make the most mess, reserve any available seating at a table for them and insist they use it.

The Cup and Loaf

Some have found that taking the cup and loaf prior to the meal separates it from the meal too much as a separate act. It is as if the Lord's Supper is the cup and loaf, and everything else is the meal. To overcome this false dichotomy, try placing the cup and loaf on the table with the rest of the food of the Lord's Supper. The cup and loaf can be pointed out in advance of the meeting and mentioned in the prayer prior to the meal, but then placed on the buffet table with everything else. This way, believers can partake of it as they pass through the serving line.

Should the loaf be unleavened and the fruit of the vine alcoholic? The Jews ate unleavened bread in the Passover meal to symbolize the quickness with which God brought them out of Egypt. Jesus used unleavened bread in the original Last Supper. Nothing is said in the New Testament, however, about Gentile churches using unleavened bread in the Lord's Supper. Though sometimes in the New Testament yeast is associated with evil,[27] it is also used to represent God's kingdom.[28] This is a matter of freedom. Regarding wine, it is clear that wine was used in the Lord's Supper,[29] because some had become drunk. No clear theological reason is ever given in Scripture, however, for so doing.[30] It would seem to be a matter of freedom for each house church to decide, especially with respect to believers who have had previous addictions to alcohol and who wish to abstain.

When Unbelievers Visit

Should unbelievers be allowed to partake of the Lord's Supper? The Lord's Supper, as a sacred, covenant meal, has significance only to believers. To non-believers, it is merely food for the belly! It is clear from Scripture[31] that unbelievers will occasionally attend house church meetings. Unbelievers get hungry just like believers do, so invite them to eat too. Love them to Jesus! The danger in taking the Lord's Supper in an unworthy manner applies only to believers.[32] Regarding the one cup and loaf, if an unbelieving child desires to drink the grape juice just because he likes grape juice, that is fine. However, if the parents purposely give it to an unbelieving child as a religious act, then that might be a violation of what the Lord's Supper is all about. It would be closely akin to the concept of infant baptism.

---

[27] 1 Cor 5:6-8
[28] Matt 13:33
[29] 1 Cor 11
[30] However, consider Gen 27:28, Isa 25:6-9, Rom 14:21
[31] 1 Cor 14:23-25
[32] 1 Cor 11:27-32

CONCLUSION

The New Testament form of the Lord's Supper has been duly established. It is one of the primary purposes for which the house church is to gather. Eaten as a full meal, the Supper typifies the 'wedding supper of the lamb' and is, thus, forward looking. It is to be partaken of as a feast, in a joyful, wedding atmosphere. A major benefit of the Supper as a banquet is the fellowship and encouragement each member experiences, which can help build unity within a body of believers. These are also symbolic of Jesus' body and blood and serve to remind Jesus of his promise to return.

STUDY QUESTIONS

1. What are the New Testament precedents for the Lord's Supper?
2. What are the benefits of eating the Lord's Supper as a full meal?
3. What practical challenge does your house church network have in implementing this practice regularly?

Chapter 48

MULTIPLYING AND NETWORKING HOUSE CHURCHES THAT SATURATE NEIGHBORHOODS AND NATIONS

NEIL COLE

Neil Cole is the founder of Church Multiplication Associates (www.cmaresources.org), a worldwide network of 1000 'organic' churches that meet in homes, offices, and just about anywhere. His several books include Organic Church: Growing Faith Where Life Happens (2005) and Cultivating a Life for God (1999). Email: neilcole@aol.com.

INTRODUCTION

In our quest to be part of a powerful move of God's kingdom, we often are tempted to think the solution will come from a complex composite of things that produce the results we so desperately long for. We cry out to the heavens for a solution that will finally change the church forever. Many travel every year to new seminars and conferences, buying the latest books and binders full of new methods in our search for the answer. The primal scream of our hearts is a search for spiritual success that will ultimately change the world. To our query of the universe, Albert Einstein once commented, "When the solution is simple, God is answering." In this article, we will describe the practical ideas our team—Church Multiplication Associates—has used to multiply and network house churches that saturate neighborhoods and nations with the message of Jesus Christ.

WHY ARE SIMPLE THINGS BETTER?

The Power of Simplicity

There is something special about the power of simplicity. Many of the most profound things in life are indeed simple. Simple, however, does not mean simplistic. We tend to overlook simple things thinking that anything of value and substance will be complex, require professional oversight and will be very expensive. A valuable lesson that we have integrated into all we do as a church multiplication movement is that 'less is more'. Simplicity is a step *beyond* complexity. It takes great skill and effort to make something simple. It is easy to create something that is complex. But, to design something that is simple and yet profound, however, is a creative challenge. It takes great skill to know what is absolutely essential and what can be discarded.

Jesus said, "Come to Me, all who are weary and heavy-laden, and I will give you rest. Take My yoke upon you, and learn from Me, for I am gentle and humble in heart; and you shall find rest for your souls. For My yoke is easy, and My load is light."[1] For most, discipleship has become so complicated that it is no longer an easy burden and a light load. But Jesus intends for the Christian life to be easy and light and to bring rest to our souls. Fulfillment of the Great Commission is meant to be restful, not stressful!

Simple Things Last, while Complex Things Breaks Down

When we approach disciple making—wanting to pass the baton on to succeeding generations—we must refine the process so that it is simple and transferable. Simplicity is the key to the fulfillment of the Great Commission in this generation. If the process is complex, it will breakdown early in the transference to the next generation of disciples. The more complex the process, the greater the giftedness needed to keep it going. The simpler the process, the more available it is to the broader Christian populace.

Perhaps the reason that we do not see multiplication of disciples more often is that we are trying to do too much too soon in the process. We fail to grasp the fact that discipleship—following Christ in simple obedience—is a life-long pursuit. We, unfortunately, attempt to teach our disciples so much in the first year that we unintentionally sabotage the rest of the years by intimidating them into thinking it is way too hard for common people to do. We tend to over estimate what we can do in a year and underestimate what we can do in three years.

Simple Things are 'Sticky' and Transferable to Others

In the best selling book *The Tipping Point,* Malcolm Gladwell says any epidemic type of expansion requires a "stickiness factor."[2] In other words, the pattern must stick with people in such a way that it is unforgettable and easily passed on to others. It is not enough that it is easy, but it also must capture the imagination and affection of those who will pass it on.

Paul passed on to Timothy truths that were so profound that he would not forget them. They gripped his life and never left him. At the same time, however, the things Paul passed on were simple enough that Timothy could in turn pass them on to others who could then pass them on to others.[3] The gospel itself is the most profound truth mankind has ever received, yet it is simple enough for a child to understand and pass on to others! It is not enough that people *can* pass it on, it is necessary that they will *want* to pass it on. The gospel is good news, and like a profound secret, it should be something that we all want to tell others.

What we need are systems that are practical and profound. They must be both simple and significant! A system that is significant enough to tap into the Christian's internal motivation, yet simple enough that it can be easily

---

[1] Matt 11:28-30 (NASB)

[2] Malcolm Gladwell (2002), *The Tipping Point: How Little Things can Make a Big Difference,* First Back Bay, pp.24-25.

[3] 2 Tim 2:2

passed on from disciple to disciple, such a system will strengthen the church and produce growth that is qualitative and quantitative.

Our criteria to evaluate the ways we function as a movement in order to see multiplication to the ends of the earth are:

- *Received personally.* It has a profound implication. It must be internalized and must transform the soul of the follower.

- *Repeated easily.* It has a simple application. It must be able to be passed on after only a brief encounter.

- *Reproduced strategically.* It has universal communication. It must pass on globally by being translated into a variety of cultural contexts and languages.

Simple Things Keep the Focus on What is Important

Another reason why simple methods are better is that they do not take away the glory from Christ himself. There are many times, unfortunately, that methods can be so impressive that people cease to notice Christ. Yet, Christ chooses to put his glory in weak vessels so that all the glory is retained by him. If people are so impressed with our wineskins (i.e. systems and strategies) that they stop noticing the wine (i.e. the message and person of Christ), then there is a big problem. Simple strategies keep it focused on Christ, not the plans or the people dreaming up the plans.

Jesus spoke of wine and wineskins.[4] Wineskins are important because they carry the wine, but without the wine, the skins are useless. It is good to give some thought to ministry systems, but the systems should not be the main thing. In fact, if done right, they should hardly be noticed at all because the living water has captivated our attention and affection. Simple systems are more likely to allow for this.

Simple Things Can Reproduce Easily

One final reason why simple methods are important is that multiplication becomes much more feasible. Reproduction comes from a natural desire and ability inherent in all healthy living things. Similarly, reproduction of churches should not be hard. It should be natural and even pleasurable. The fact that reproduction is thought to be so hard and painful for churches is evidence of how far removed we are from being healthy and natural. Reproduction is the product of intimacy, and we are created to enjoy intimacy. Even among churches, reproduction is the product of intimacy— with Christ, his mission, his spiritual family, and the lost world.

All reproduction begins at the molecular level and develops from the micro to the macro, from the simple to the complex. It is the same in the kingdom of God. We each began life as a zygote. A zygote is a cell formed by the union of a male seed and a female egg. Life multiplies from there. The moment that conception occurs, all the DNA necessary for the

---

[4] Luke 5:36-39

formation, growth, and development of a mature person is intact. The DNA never changes—it just leads the multiplication process within every tiny cell into forming the complete body. The same can be said for the Body of Christ.

THE DNA OF CHRIST'S BODY

The Key Elements for Healthy DNA

In the organic world, whether crickets or churches, DNA is the internal code that maintains the integrity of each multiplied cell. In every organism, DNA is what encodes each cell with its proper process and place in the body. In the expansion of the kingdom of God, DNA maintains the strength, vitality, and reproductivity of every cell in Christ's body.

Just as the DNA is exactly the same in almost every cell of a body, the DNA is the same throughout the Body of Christ, for all its members and in every cell. The DNA is the pattern of kingdom life, from the smallest unit (the disciple in relationship to Jesus and others) to the largest unit (a family or movement of churches). The pattern is the same, and its expression remains constant.

The DNA of the church can be simplified to three things, namely, divine truth, nurturing relationships, and apostolic mission.[5] They are needed in every part of the church, from its smallest unit to its largest.

- *Divine Truth.* Truth comes from God. It is the revelation of God to humankind. This comes from the Son, the Spirit, and the Scriptures. The Son (Jesus) is both God and human and came to reveal to us in his person what God is like and what God requires. The Scriptures were authored by God and reveal God's unfolding plan for humanity. The Spirit of God is also divine truth, since he brings revelation and direction to believers.

- *Nurturing Relationships.* Humans were never created to be alone. We are social creatures and have an intrinsic need for relationships. Our relational orientation is a reflection of the image of God in us. God himself is relational and exists in a community—Father, Son, and Holy Spirit. God is love because God is relational. To the Christian, God is love because he has always existed in relationship. Is love possible without someone to love? This should be the defining characteristic of our faith. All men should know that we are Christ's disciples by the love that we have for one another.

- *Apostolic Mission.* Apostolic means that someone is sent as a representative with a message. We are here for a purpose. We have been given a prime directive to fulfill—to make disciples of all the nations. This part of us also comes from the nature of God. Jesus is

---

[5] Neil Cole (2005), *Organic Church: Growing Faith Where Life Happens,* Jossey-Bass, pp.109-121.

an apostle. He is the chief cornerstone of the apostolic foundation. Before he left this planet, he sent his disciples into the world with a mission.

Dangers of Genetic Engineering

We live in a day of radical advancement of science and technology spiraling out of control. We now have the ability to clone life and even genetically engineer it. With these advancements comes great responsibility. Medical ethics has taken on a whole new level of significance. When we identify and map the DNA of Christ's body, we also face dangers. Here are some crucial warnings.

Do Not Unravel the DNA

DNA is only potent when it is together. Once the component parts of the DNA are unraveled, they have little or no significance. It is the same in the church. Most churches will gladly exclaim that they have all three portions of the DNA, but they have unraveled it into separate components and so lost its power. "We have excellent preaching on Sundays, which is where we have the divine truth," one will say. "And we have small groups during the week, which are our nurturing relationships; and a strong missions committee, which is our apostolic mission." The key is not in having a separate ministry committee or program to handle each area. DNA must be whole, intact, and in *every* cell. In other words, every meeting, every ministry, every disciple must have all three components *at the same time.* To break down the DNA into separate components and put them in different places and times is to unravel the DNA. Then life and all that comes with it is lost. Mission without love is dead and can actually undermine the cause of Christ.[6] Relationships without truth are dysfunctional and toxic. Truth without application in relationships and mission is delusional.[7] To separate each part is to destroy the whole thing.

Do Not Subtract from the DNA

Whole DNA is crucial to the health and function of the body. It is complete in its simplicity and complexity. To subtract even a portion from it has devastating results. Many churches are given to specialization, thinking they will find a unique niche that makes them special. But if we concentrate on one part of DNA and eliminate any other part we will lose the whole of it— death and mutation are the result. For example, many traditional churches focus on teaching, and if they add anything else, it is an attempt to build stronger relationships. One reason traditional churches are not multiplying is the absence of the outreach chromosome. Many churches need a good dose of apostolic mission. In the human body, to be missing even a single chromosome results in severe retardation, and even death.

---

[6] 1 Cor 13:1–3
[7] James 1:21–25

Do Not Add to the DNA

One extra chromosome in the human gene can result in Down's syndrome and mental retardation. A person with Down's syndrome is a person who can love and be loved, but this syndrome is not the expression of the body and life that God intended for us. It is a corrupted form that prevents the person from maturing and functioning in full capacity. Many traditional churches are unhealthy precisely in proportion to their mutation of DNA. They have added to what God intended, and it has slowed the church and halted all reproduction. It is quite tempting to add 'good' stuff to the DNA. Unfortunately, whatever we add to the three basic components of divine truth, nurturing relationships, and apostolic mission results in bad side-effects—it dilutes the three components, and it elevates the additives to the same stature. It is better to let the DNA remain in its simplicity. All good things can be found within them, so do not dilute the importance of the three or elevate anything else to their level of importance.

THE NETWORKING OF GROUPS:
NATURAL SOCIAL GROUPINGS FOR MAXIMUM IMPACT

Starting Small

The created world has natural boundaries held in place by gravity. The oceans are held in place by the shores. The atmosphere is contained by the weight of earth's gravity. Gravity keeps the solar system contained in orbit around the sun. In a similar way people have natural boundaries in the way that we function best. We are pulled into social groupings of certain sizes by a spiritual gravity inherent with the function of the group.

Jesus, too, conciously stayed in the boundaries of social gravity. Jesus invested most in an inner circle made up of Peter, James, and John, while he lived with a spiritual family of the 12 disciples. He personally trained and deployed the 70. When he ascended into heaven, he left behind 120 disciples. While these groupings were the main focus of his life and ministry in order of priority, he also healed, taught, and fed the multitudes, while appearing to more than 500 followers at the same time after his resurrection.

Jesus also describes the kingdom of God with the parable of the mustard seed, which starts small and then eventually grows very large. He said: "How shall we picture the kingdom of God, or by what parable shall we present it? It is like a mustard seed, which, when sown upon the soil, though it is smaller than all the seeds that are upon the soil, yet when it is sown, grows up and becomes larger than all the garden plants and forms large branches; so that the birds of the air can nest under its shade."[8] The growth of the kingdom of God must start at the smallest of social groupings. Jesus is instructing us that the kingdom of God must start small and grow via multiplication to have great and expansive influence.

---

[8] Mark 4:30-32 (NASB)

If we cannot multiply house churches, we will never see a movement. If we cannot multiply leaders we will never multiply house churches. If we cannot multiply disciples, we will never multiply leaders. The way to see a true house church multiplication movement is to multiply healthy disciples, then leaders, then churches, and finally movements—in that order.[9] Trying to multiply large, highly complex 'macro' organisms without first multiplying and networking on the 'micro' level is impossible.

Therefore, we would suggest that there are five natural sizes for social groupings that should be multiplied and networked together into today's house church movements.

The Inner Circle: Two or Three People

The beginning of every family starts here at this size. The Bible often elevates a group of two or three to significance. Both the Old and New Testaments mention the phrase "two or three". It is interesting that at least 10 times "two or three" is suggested as an ideal size at which to conduct ministry. The Bible does not say "two or more" or "three or less" but always "two or three". Perhaps it is good to have some flexibility without too many options. There are several reasons why this may be the ideal size for effective fellowship and ministry that will penetrate the rest of the church and ultimately the kingdom of God:

- Community is stronger with two or three (Ecc 4:9–12).
- Accountability is stronger with two or three (1 Tim 5:19).
- Confidentiality is stronger with two or three (Matt 18:15–17).
- Flexibility is stronger with two or three (Matt 18:20).
- Communication is stronger with two or three (1 Cor 14:26–33).
- Direction is stronger with two or three (2 Cor 13:1).
- Leadership is stronger with two or three (1 Cor 14:29).

The Family: 12 to 15 People

This is the natural size in which an extended family opperates. It is small enough that all parts can intimately know one another, yet large enough to have significant diversity and group dynamics. Across the world, this represents the size of house churches everywhere. It is a natural sized grouping to operate naturally as a family.

The Team: 70 to 75 People

When it comes to training and deploying leaders as part of a team, this grouping represents the most efficient size to get across pertinent

---

[9] Neil Cole (2007), *Search and Rescue*, Regal Publications. This soon to be published book expands on principles necessary to multiply disciples and presents Life Transformation Groups, a simple reproducible system that is working all over the world.

information, skills, and relationship, while still maintaining quality. When it comes to training leaders in a region through, say, monthly leadership meetings, this is the size of group that is best.

The Network: 120 to 150 People

Malcolm Gladwell, in his book *The Tipping Point*, writes almost spiritually about the significance of the number 150 in the development of movements throughout history.[10] We, too, have found by experience that a house church network will very rarely grow beyond 15 house churches (or 150 people). This boundary is natural. The kingdom does not stop at this boundary. What is necessary beyond this boundary is to reproduce more *networks*, rather than trying to add more house churches to an existing network. Of course, we should always look for opportunities to start new churches, but we will also find that other churches stop meeting and a network of approximately 15 churches will usually remain constant. The key to multiplying networks is to raise up leaders from within who can start and lead new emerging churches in an entirely new network.

The Masses

Beyond the above numbers are the masses. This is a more relative grouping, but in reality, it is a gathering together of the other smaller groups for the purposes of annual conferences, occasional worship and teaching, saturation of cities with the gospel, broader impact on a culture, etc.

MULTIPLICATION AND DEATH

Reproduction always occurs at the microscopic level in every living organism. The human body is replaced by new cells all the time—that is health. Every few months a new person emerges. Imagine what would happen if the cells in the human body decided to stop multiplying. The moment cells stop multiplying, we would have a serious problem—the body would shrivel up and die because the cells that were dying would not be replaced with new ones. Multiplication stops when death occurs. At the same time, death occurs when multiplication stops. Both statements are true.

There is also a spiritual truth that multiplication starts with death. There is a cost involved with multiplication. Jesus said, "Truly, truly, I say to you, unless a grain of wheat falls into the earth and dies, it remains by itself alone; but if it dies, it bears much fruit. He who loves his life loses it; and he who hates his life in this world shall keep it to life eternal."[11]

As disciples, we must deny ourselves, pick up our cross, and follow Christ. This is all about surrender. This is about confession and repentance. This is about obedience. Where these things exist, there is a dying of self, and growth and generation of life will come. Similarly, a great threat to vital Christianity is self-preservation. The threat to the church and any

---

[10] Gladwell refers the "magic number 150", *The Tipping Point,* pp. 169-192.
[11] John 12:24 (NASB)

spontaneous movement is self-preservation, and the simple solution is dying. We must learn to embrace a theology of death to the flesh—as disciples, churches, leaders, and movements—if we want to have a vital expansion of the kingdom. Without death there is no resurrection.

We must be willing to give up more than our time, talents, and treasure—we must start by giving up our *lives* for God's kingdom. If we are willing to die to self in order to follow Christ, then we can see an abundant harvest of souls for the kingdom of God. The Christians of the first century were willing to give up their lives for the kingdom, and they were able to reach the entire known world with the gospel.

Every vital Christian movement throughout church history whose members were willing to surrender their lives for the sake of Christ witnessed dramatic and spontaneous growth. This is one reason churches thrive under persecution—the people of God are forced to decide what really matters most. They die to themselves, their spiritual lives reproduce, and church growth occurs through multiplication.

I have heard that scientific and statistical probabilities demonstrate that if a single shaft of wheat is left undamaged and allowed to freely reproduce and grow, it multiplies into a crop large enough to feed the entire world population—for an entire year—within only eight years. It takes only one apple seed to grow a tree, yet a single apple tree produces enough seed to plant an entire orchard. Multiplication must start small, but with time and generational reproduction it reaches a global level of influence.

How long will it take to reach the world through multiplication? If just *one* Christian alive today were to lead just one person to Christ every year and disciple that person so that he or she would, in turn, do the same the next year, it would take only about 35 years to reach the entire world for Christ! Suddenly, world transformation seems within our grasp. But, it could be even closer than that. If *every* Christian alive today were to reproduce in the same way, the world would be won to Christ in the next two to four years. What if all of us decided to put everything else aside and focus on truly discipling another for just the next few years in a manner that multiplies? We could finish the Great Commission in just a few years.

CONCLUSIONS

It is important that we infuse the healthy DNA of God's kingdom life into the most basic unit of church life in a simple manner that is easily passed on to others. Unless we do this, multiplication and networking of house churches will not come easily nor will it spread fast and far.

STUDY QUESTIONS

1. Describe the three elements for the DNA of Christ's body, the church.
2. Describe the five social groupings that Jesus used in his ministry.
3. How does multiplication and death work together in a healthy organism?
4. What practical lessons can you apply to your house church network?

Chapter 49

HOUSE CHURCHES AND EVANGELISM

RAD ZDERO

Rad Zdero earned his Ph.D. degree in Mechanical Engineering from Queen's University (Kingston, ON, Canada) and is the manager of a hospital-based orthopaedic research lab. He has participated in, led, and started house churches and cell groups since 1985. He is currently part of HouseChurch.Ca (www.housechurch.ca), which is a church planting team developing a network of house churches in the greater Toronto area and beyond. He is the author of The Global House Church Movement (2004). [Used by permission of the author. Email: rzdero@yahoo.ca].

INTRODUCTION

One of the strengths of the house church movement is as a vehicle for the spiritual growth, accountability, and intimacy of people involved. However, the purpose of this chapter is to open up some of the possibilities of utilizing house church networks as vehicles for intentional, creative, and sensitive evangelism. For house church networks to succeed, they must have a healthy emphasis on outreach, otherwise they will soon become ingrown, flounder, and fail. What is given below is an examination of an alternate way of thinking about evangelism specifically in the context of house church networks based on my own personal experience over the years.

TWO APPROACHES TO EVANGELISM

Let us suppose that our sphere of influence as Christians—our city, our neighborhood, our family, our workplace, our friends, our school—is like a flowing river (Figure 1). The river represents the various contexts that we have in which we relate with the lost in the daily ebb and flow of life. Our non-Christian friends are like fish in the river, some are big, some are small, some are easier to get along with than others. Some are very open to engaging on faith issues, whereas others are either indifferent or hostile. There is a significant opportunity to 'be Jesus' and 'see Jesus' and to engage those around us with the good news. What do we do? There are two common approaches, namely *Bridge Fishing* and *Small Boat Fishing*.

Bridge Fishing

Belonging to a tight-knit group that has a somewhat definable goal is, unfortunately, not only a foreign experience to many followers of Jesus, but also to much of larger society. And so, when it comes to evangelism, the Christian approach is often similar to someone who gets their fishing pole,

Evangelism as Fishing

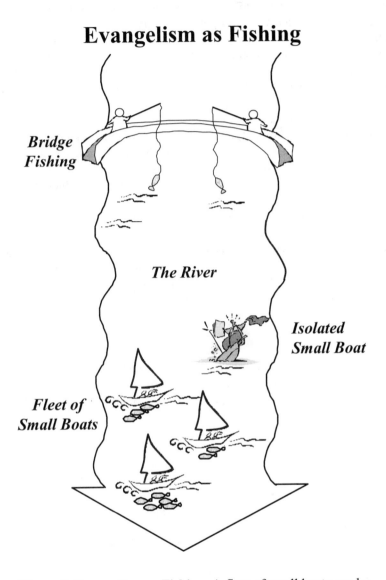

Figure 1. Evangelism as Fishing. A fleet of small boats can be more successful in catching fish than an independent small boat. Similarly, house churches that are part of house church networks will thrive evangelistically better than isolated house churches [Diagram is adaptation of material from Jeremy Horne, former director of The Navigators of Canada (Campus Mission)].

worms it, and positions themselves at the most strategic spot on the bridge. This tactic ensures that we never get wet or dirty or in any kind of real close contact with dirty and smelly fish, until we catch one and pull it up to where we are. In actuality, this might mean that we invite a friend to an 'outreach' event that's coming to town, or we take part in a missions week that our house church is sponsoring by going door-to-door in our neighborhood handing out videos on Jesus, etc.

The advantages of this method are that it is safer, cleaner, and less risky for the person doing the evangelizing. There is not much of a chance that we will have to go to places and be with people that may challenge our moral or theological views. The main disadvantage, though, is that we will never truly be challenged and forced to grow in what we believe by thoughtful non-Christians. And we may never really get to know any non-kingdom friends up close and personal. So, *Bridge Fishing* is more of a 'suck in' rather than a 'go to', periodically going out on evangelism raids rather than becoming an 'insider' in our non-Christian circles. I do not suggest that this strategy has no place at all, because that is in fact how I became a Christian, by someone distributing Bibles. But, there is a complementary approach that may be ideally suited for today's Christians involved in house churches, namely *Small Boat Fishing*.

Small Boat Fishing

Imagine a small boat whose main purpose is to catch fish. The crew of the small boat eats together, socializes, strategizes, encourages every member of the team, and casts out the fishing nets together. They are a unit. They do everything together—move, stop, slow down, speed up, change direction, pull up the nets, put down the nets. They make decisions quickly in a non-bureaucratic manner regarding issues such as when they need to buy new nets, fix the side of the boat, and change directions. But, they are not doing this alone. The small boat is also part of a larger cluster of boats sailing in the same direction as a unified *Fleet of Small Boats*. Why? Because they know that an *Isolated Small Boat* can potentially loose direction and become shipwrecked due to bad weather or perhaps may become easy prey for unsavory pirates.

Similarly, a house church may have decided that it wants to intentionally reach out to friends together as a team. Their main thrust and contribution to evangelism is in their social context. They meet together once a week, pray for each other and their non-Christian friends, learn from each other's attempts at evangelism, brainstorm on overcoming obstacles, invite their seeker friends to social occasions or events, and get into each other's social spheres. They are mobile, flexible, non-bureaucratic, quick to implement decisions and changes, and have support, intimacy, and accountability from each other as part of a team. But, they also realize the benefit of working together with other house churches closely as part of a network which can provide mutual accountability, support, resourcing, and direction.

PRACTICAL EXAMPLES OF SMALL BOAT FISHING

The advantages of small boat fishing far outweigh the potential dangers involved. Let us keep in mind the importance of being an 'insider' and full participant in our non-Christian circles. These strategies are best used outside the actual house church meetings, which should remain focused on the spiritual growth of Christians. Let us now explore six possible scenarios, based on my personal experience in house churches and cell groups.

Discussion Dinners

A discussion dinner is an event hosted periodically (maybe monthly) by the evangelistically oriented house church, in which non-Christian friends come to an evening meal. People gather in the living room for a 10-20 minute presentation about some important questions of life to launch the discussion (e.g. Does God exist?, Why so much suffering?, How do I raise my kids?, Who is Jesus?, etc.). One can use a contemporary and mainstream music video, movie, poem, song, newspaper article, painting, or even Scripture reading. The key here is to make sure that all opinions are valued and allowed to be fully expressed and explored. Non-Christian friends should not feel intimidated or that their opinion is somehow wrong. The purpose for these dinners is to open up the doors for further dialogue. They are not meant to be high pressure situations. Casual, comfortable, and creative are the main ingredients for a good discussion dinner.

Evangelists Anonymous

This is an evangelism support group for those in a house church network that have a particular passion for outreach. They meet together to pray, encourage, brainstorm, and keep each member accountable in their personal one-on-one evangelism efforts in their respective spheres of influence, whether that be at the workplace, in the school, or in the neighborhood. As members help and encourage each other in this endeavor, all will become more motivated and skilled in their own efforts. Suggestions for increasing skills and growing in vision may be for the group to read through some helpful books on 'lifestyle' and 'friendship' evangelism,[1] go through a video learning series,[2] study biblical patterns of mission, go to related seminars, expand their knowledge of the world's religions and pseudo-Christian cults,[3] learn the art of apologetics,[4] and so on.

---

[1] M. Green and A. McGrath (1995), *How Shall We Reach Them?* Thomas Nelson Publishers; M. Green (1995), *One to One*, Random House; R.M. Pippert (1979), *Out of the Salt Shaker and Into the World*, InterVarsity Press.

[2] Jim Petersen (1989), *Living Proof - Sharing the Gospel Naturally*, NavPress.

[3] Huston Smith (1991), *The World's Religions*, Harper SanFrancisco; Walter Martin (1992), *The Kingdom of the Cults*, Bethany House Publishers.

[4] G.A. Boyd and E.K. Boyd (1994), *Letters from a Skeptic*, Chariot Victor Publishing; Paul Little (1988), *Know Why You Believe*, InterVarsity Press.

The Social Butterflies

This house church or small team from the house church network focuses on giving each other opportunities to connect with and engage each other's friends with the good news by merging their social circles together. These people like to socialize with others. They are always eating dinner with people, organizing movie nights, playing sports, playing card games, and going away to the cottage on weekends. They are always including their non-Christian friends so that their friendship networks begin to overlap. In other words, the focus here is on social cross-pollination. The potential here lies in the synergistic and overlapping efforts and talents of each team member with each other's lost friends. The breakthrough that I've been working on with a friend may not come until they connect with another member of the team who perhaps understands them more and is able to connect at a deeper level. What we have here really is the emergence of a community made up of overlapping social circles, with Christians and non-Christians alike, that creates opportunities to dialogue on life, faith, family, work, sports, suffering, and also Jesus.

Service Groups

Imagine if someone in a house church notices that there is something wrong happening in town: there are homeless people in the streets, food banks are running low on donations, soup kitchens are in need of volunteers, etc. This person then rallies a few friends from the house church network, and they decide they need to make a difference, somehow. They start praying, thinking, and doing some research. They come up with the idea of opening up an emergency overnight shelter for homeless people when all other existing shelters and agencies are full. They garner support and advice from existing shelters in town, organize a homeless walk to raise money for their shelter, within a few months are up and running successfully, and are supported greatly by other Christians in town and other agencies with supplies and money. They are able to initially recruit about two dozen volunteers from among the Christian community in town, but also from the community at large, some of whom are non-Christians. Although the main goal of the project is to help the homeless, the project not only strengthens the bonds between the Christians involved, but also creates opportunities to share in word and deed the good news of Jesus to those around them.[5]

Social Issues Discussion Groups

Many in our society are deeply concerned about social issues and are willing to engage and explore societal problems in conversation, for which there are

---

[5] Steve Sjorgen (2001), *101 Ways To Reach Your Community*, NavPress. This resource describes many creative and practical ways for believers to get involved in their community that can provide opportunities to bring the message of Jesus to those with whom they come in contact.

many good resources.[6] Organizing a discussion group that attempts to address and explore various societal problems can be a way of building bridges between Christians and non-Christians. Typical meetings may simply involve discussing a book, magazine article, or newspaper clipping on a certain topic. This provides an opportunity for the believer to learn about issues the church-at-large does not address frequently, to formulate their perspective, and to learn from non-Christians about their views on the environment, AIDS, crime, international relations, abortion, euthanasia, genetic engineering, the media, poverty, homelessness, technology, as well as a host of local concerns. It may be surprising to both believers and non-believers that they share many overlapping perspectives, something that can create friendships and a springboard for dialogue on faith issues.

Investigative Bible Studies

This involves a small team of Christians organizing a weekly Bible study group for their non-Christian friends. It is simply a matter of inviting them. A great approach is certainly one of the Gospels, in which all agree to systematically look through the life of Christ, one chapter at a time on a weekly or monthly basis. Other possibilities may be a topical or thematic introductory look at questions like: Who was Jesus? What about science and faith? Why all the suffering and evil? Is the Bible historically reliable? Does God really care? For instance, introductory courses to the Christian faith such as the ever-popular *Alpha Course*[7] offer a practical and refreshing look at some foundational issues. This Alpha Course is oriented around a meal and lively video presentation, followed by group discussion on the issues addressed. This can quite easily be done in someone's home.

CONCLUSIONS

This chapter has touched on issues related to house church evangelism and offered some practical tips based on my personal experience over the years. May we be creative, intentional, sensitive, and, above all, let us pray and trust God to do something through us to touch the lives of people.

STUDY QUESTIONS

1. Why should a house church have a healthy emphasis on outreach?
2. Why should a house church be part of a cohesive network?
3. Which type of outreach seems most practical for your house church?

---

[6] Ian Bradley (1990), *God is Green: Ecology for Christians*, Doubleday; E.F. Schumacher (1989), *Small Is Beautiful: Economics as if People Mattered*, Harper and Row Publishers; Jacques Ellul (1984), *Money and Power*, InterVarsity Press; Jacques Ellul (1980), *The Technological System*, The Continuum Publishing Corporation.

[7] Nicky Gumbel (1993), *Questions of Life*, Cook Ministry Resources.

Chapter 50

THE FIVE-FOLD MINISTRY: GOD'S RESOURCE FOR MULTIPLYING HOUSE CHURCHES

WOLFGANG SIMSON

Wolfgang Simson travels extensively all over the world, awakening the church to the changes that are taking place through the emergence of the house church movement. He also functions as a strategy consultant, researcher, theologian, and journalist within various networks and regional and global strategy think tanks. He earned his M.Th. degree from the Free Evangelical Theological Academy (Basel, Switzerland) and is the author of the highly acclaimed book, Houses that Change the World. He makes his home in Germany with his family. [The following was taken from Wolfgang Simson (1998), Houses that Change the World, Paternoster Publishing, Ch.4. Adapted and used by permission of the author as the current holder of copyright. Email: wolfsimson@compuserve.com].

INTRODUCTION

Every growth form in life is based on the multiplication of organic cells. This is also true for the church as organic, relational households of God. Once we have discovered that the church is not a series of organized and conducted meetings in religious buildings, but a supernatural communal life form, the species of the people of God, as they follow their Master together, we may have to rethink how this lifeform multiplies in a healthy and organic way. House churches are a multipliable structure. They can literally multiply endlessly. If we have multiplying house churches, which create an exponential growth rate, we need a leadership development structure that grows as fast as the churches multiply. This chapter explores the role of the five-fold ministries of apostles, prophets, evangelists, pastors, and teachers for multiplying house church networks.

MULTIPLY THE FIVE-FOLD MINISTRY ITSELF

The answer to this structural problem for house church movements today is the so-called five-fold ministry, since God "gave some to be apostles, some to be prophets, some to be evangelists, and some to be pastors and teachers, to prepare God's people for works of service, so that the Body of Christ may be built up until we all reach unity in the faith and in the knowledge of the Son of God and become mature, attaining to the whole measure of the fullness of Christ."[1]

---

[1] Eph 4:11-13 (NIV)

The five-fold ministry functions very much as the self-organizing powers of the church. They are part of the built-in 'biotic growth potential', an internal structure, part of the spiritual DNA of the church, which forms itself within the Body of Christ just like a human body forms its own lymphatic system, white anti-body system, a blood circulation system etc., with an amazing and inbuilt ability to grow organically with the general growth of the human body, and maintain or even cure itself. All of those ministries have their own task to fulfill in equipping the saints for the ministry, and constantly circulate through the house churches, like its very own breathing or digestive system.

The most important aspect for house churches is that these ministries can also multiply themselves: apostles spotting and training other apostles, prophets spotting and training other prophets and multiplying themselves through the simple and biblical process of discipleship. This way, the leadership structure can grow exponentially together with a multiplying house church movement. The bottom line is the multiplication and empowerment of more and more people to do the work of God.

The biblical calling of the apostle, prophet, pastor, teacher or evangelist is not at all to assume or usurp 'the ministry' and perform it themselves as others look on, but to train God's people for the ministry, to equip others. In short, an evangelist's true fruit is not a convert, but more evangelists. They are evangelistic, prophetic, teaching, pastoral and apostolic trainers, not demonstrators; teachers, not one-man-shows. The five ministries are given by God to be given away, to be used in equipping others to do the work of the ministry, which ultimately means multiplying the structure through which the ministry is done: the house churches.

THE FIVE FINGERS OF THE HAND

Gerald Coates, leader of the Pioneer movement in England, compared the five-fold ministry with the five fingers of the hand. The Apostle is the thumb. He gives stability, holds the counterbalance, and can literally touch all the other fingers. The Prophet is the indication finger. He points at you and says: "You are the man!" The Evangelist is the Middle Finger, who is the longest of all, and sticking furthest out into the world. The ring finger resembles the Pastor/Shepherd, caring for internal relationships. The small finger is the Teacher: he can worm his teaching deep into any ear.

The Apostle

The apostle is not as far from the herd as the prophet. He is about three miles away, on top of the next hill instead of being on the other side of the hill like the prophet. From this commanding point, he can see the big picture and study his map, looking for the next green pasture. He generally has no time for house visits and small talk; 'the world is his church'. Like Paul, he is never really satisfied: after Rome, he wants to go to Spain! His core word is 'strategy', how to see God's plans come true for nations. Apostles are very much like generals in an army. They carry the main burden and responsibility for the advancement of the cause. The apostolic ministry is a founding ministry, it can create something out of nothing, create a foundation in the desert, and in many ways unites all other gifts in itself. He may function as a supernaturally gifted problem solver and talent spotter. And if the pastor—the word is mentioned only once in the New Testament—is something of the equivalent of a spiritual 'uncle'—very caring and loving, but not ultimately responsible—so the apostles, 22 of them are mentioned by name in the New Testament, are the spiritual fathers who carry the last responsibility, the real agony and joy.

The Prophet

The prophet is way ahead of the herd of sheep, perhaps five miles beyond the next hill. There he hears God's voice and sees visions, enters the throne room of God and glimpses something. It may actually be very good that he is often away from the flock, because few really do understand him. He is interested not so much in people and what they think of him, but he is interested in God's voice for the situation. Added to that, he often has a complicated and disorganized personality exactly because he is so uniquely gifted. Can you imagine spending a relaxed half hour drinking coffee with Jeremiah? Jeremiah would probably tear you and me apart and use the tea for an illustration. A prophet's perspective is radically different to that of the pastor. He hears from God and quite mercilessly questions everything, including the pastor, from God's perspective. That, however, is his healthy and God-given duty. For that reason, there is also a historical tension between the pastor and the prophet: one as a defender of the status quo, who wants to maintain the community; the other who questions everything and is seen (rightly) by many others as a threat, because he disrupts things and wants 'movement now'. The Shepherd, in many pictures, does not only have a stick in his hand to tend the sheep and keep away the wolves, he also may be quick in using that stick to keep away prophets. And yet both views are valid, because both are serving God and the same flock—one with loving attention, the other with a prophetic view. Both are necessary! The prophet's motto, describing his ministry, is 'vision'. Prophets often have the unique ability to see and hear what others do not see nor hear. These supernatural revelations need to go through a process of healthy interpretation in the church and application.[2] The prophet is groomed by a direct calling from God and then usually sent 'pouring water over the hands of a master prophet', as in the case of Elijah and Elisha.[3]

The Evangelist

The evangelist circles the herd, also half a mile away—just enough so that he doesn't smell like the sheep pen and frighten the wild sheep away, but

[2] 1 Cor 14:29
[3] 2 Kings 3:11

close enough to be able to lead them to the herd when he finds a lost sheep. He has three aims and passions: that people find Jesus, find Jesus, and find Jesus. He introduces a healthy outward focus to the churches and is even involved in discipling new believers into maturity by literally 'reading the gospel to them', 'evangelizing' them, filling them with the good news. Biblically, the evangelist does not lead the extension of the churches, but works in partnership with apostolic and prophetic people, who bear the main responsibility for laying the foundations of the churches. The evangelist empowers others to be evangelists, not in order to create evangelistic enterprises in themselves, but for the house churches to become or to remain an evangelistic movement itself.

The Pastor

The pastor, in the charismatic and biblical—not the traditional—sense, is by nature a shepherd; he stands in the midst of the herd of sheep. Everything mills around him; but nowhere in the New Testament do we find a pastor truly leading a congregation. The 'pastor/shepherd' is also known as an 'elder/presbyter' and 'overseer/bishop' in the New Testament[4] and works as part of a co-equal team of other pastors to care for a citywide cluster of house churches. He is by nature a very loving person who can create a family atmosphere; to him, relationships are the most important, simply because he is interested in the herd's long-term spiritual wellbeing. The good shepherd knows the names of the dolls of the children of the adults he is caring for; he is interested in every last detail. There's only one problem: a person's greatest weakness almost always lies in the shadow of their greatest strength. The pastor tends to lose the big picture, because he is 'lost in relationships'. With this ministry usually goes a natural 'professional blindspot'. However, his motto is 'Relationships are everything!' The pastor focuses on redeemed relationship with God, and redeemed relationships with each other, and helps others to function in this relational way also.

The Teacher

The teacher, using the picture of his relationship to the flock of sheep, lives at a critical distance from the herd. He sits on a vantage point half a mile from the herd so that he can send out his dogs in time to deal with a sheep which is misbehaving or separating itself from the herd by eating away unconsciously into the wrong direction. His motto is: 'The truth, and nothing but the truth!' The teacher is interested in quality, in the details even more than he is in the big picture. He is often a 'footnote' person in the truest and best sense of the word, who likes details and needs to know everything exactly. He has a passion for teaching itself, and his gift is to empower others how to teach others, how to teach. He is, like Jesus, his master Rabbi, not so much leaving teaching notes behind, but literally his spirit.

---

[4] Acts 20:17,28; 1 Pet 5:1-4

THE PREDOMINANT ROLE OF APOSTLES AND PROPHETS FOR PLANTING HOUSE CHURCHES

Instead of pastoral, evangelistic, and teaching models of church, apostles and prophets according to the New Testament are to build the churches.[5] As important a role as spiritual hospitals have to play, they cannot replace what apostles and prophets are uniquely gifted for: to build a supernatural base and foundation for a multiplying church movement, to accept nothing as impossible, to respond strategically to visions and supernatural revelations, to be prophetic talent-spotters. They are not so human-centered and felt-need-oriented 'tenders' like good pastors, teachers, and evangelists, but God-centered: they have the God-given ability to see beyond things, beyond human needs and problems, and take hold of the tasks and visions of God. They do not want to just build 'a church', they want the whole city or nation! They live very much in the future, for the future, from the future, getting constantly pregnant with future developments, and can therefore pull and lead the church into the future, and prevent it from becoming a traditional institution only celebrating the past, or a fossilized monument of history long gone.

The church is "built on the foundation of the apostles and prophets, with Christ Jesus himself as the chief cornerstone", writes Paul.[6] Jesus writes to the church in Smyrna "that you have tested those who claim to be apostles but are not, and have found them false"[7] after almost all of 'The Twelve' had died. This suggests the continuation of apostles in the church. In laying the foundation, much of the work of apostles and prophets is not always seen but felt. That is why they are called "first of all"[8] because they are also 'called in' first of all to do the foundational work for 'founding churches', the site spotting, earth moving, excavating, foundation laying, so that others like carpenters and plumbers and electricians can build on that foundation. Would you like to live in a house where the foundations are laid by a carpenter? I admire carpenters, but I would not like to live in a house where the carpenter has laid the foundation. That is simply out of his brief.

Many apostles and prophets today are not in church at all, because they have not much room in traditional churches. They have been pushed to the side, they are often feared because they seem so strong, radical and different, and many have not only been marginalized, but truly rejected, and as a result have given up on church almost completely, maybe with a last flicker and a spark of hope still burning in them. The tragedy of this is that the church is God's mission. Someone needs to find them, go to them, apologize to them profoundly, heal the 'church trauma', speak to that glowing spark and fan it

---

[5] Eph 2:20
[6] Eph 2:20 (NIV)
[7] Rev 2:2 (NIV)
[8] 1 Cor 12:28

into a flame, and then recruit them, helping them to see how God sees them, and release them into their apostolic and prophetic potential for the building up of the church.

AREAS OF RESPONSIBILITY IN THE CHURCH

A house church network is led by a co-equal team of pastors. But, not every individual house church of 15 people will have their own apostles, prophets, evangelists, and teachers sitting all together in one small room. Those ministries are equipping ministries, going beyond the scope of a local house church and functioning translocally, affecting the whole area or, especially in the case of prophets and apostles, even beyond that. Rather than develop layers of hierarchical 'leadership levels', house churches are organically maintained and multiplied through the ministry of specially gifted people. The five-fold ministers are people who have been called by God primarily for one of the ministries of pastor, as well as apostle, prophet, evangelist, or teacher. Those ministers circulate within the house churches 'from house to house' and function as a spiritual blood circulating system nurturing all house churches with the necessary elements to become or remain healthy and therefore multiply. Those ministries are like sinews and joints, linking the various house churches together to be a whole system. Their ministry transcends the individual house church and serves the Body of Christ like a spiritual gene pool, where the house churches of an area or a region can draw upon, and sometimes even goes beyond that.

BUILDING A SPIRITUAL GENE-POOL FOR THE CHURCH OF AN AREA

What is the next step for your area? It depends where you are and what ministries have been founding or dominating your area or even your church in the past. If there was an overabundance of pastoral and evangelistic ministry in your nation or people group, you may need to consider complementing the effects of these good ministries with apostolic and prophetic and teaching ministries, so that the spiritual ground has all the nurture and care it needs to develop strong fruit.

The devil's plan has long been for the pastors to be standing in one corner, the prophets in the other corner looking out of the window, the teachers sitting in the library, the evangelists drinking coffee outside, and the apostles roaming overseas. In order to see the five-fold ministries working together again, they need to be identified afresh. These ministries then need to recognize each other—which might involve some solid repenting to redeem past misunderstandings and correct misconceptions of each other.

Then they need to form teams, usually based on locality—the city, the region, the district, the state, the nation—and start to multiply themselves, prophets multiplying prophets, and evangelists multiplying evangelists 30-, 60-, or 100-fold, and finally forming the equivalent of a spiritual gene-pool, an equipping and resource center for the whole Body of Christ in that locality and beyond. From this leadership pool, the right person with the right gift can be dispatched quickly to add to the spiritual diet if needed somewhere, solve a crisis, or give a specially needed input in any given church or area. Otherwise, the apostolic and prophetic equippers and servants of the Body, similar to civic servants, can form a spiritual senate and council for the city or region or nation, working hard to avoid the formation of another spiritual dominating elite by forgetting titles and fame and being humble and accountable to each other. Their task is to be responsible for the corporate identity, calling and redemptive purpose of the church in a city or region, for truly speaking with one voice to the nation, for citywide celebrations and regular apostolic and prophetic envisioning of the church on a wider basis. Business as usual for them will be to make themselves available to any house church that needs them, constantly circulating 'from house to house', keeping on to pour themselves into God's people as they multiply the house churches.

TALENT SPOTTING AND RECRUITING FOR THE FIVE-FOLD MINISTRY

Research has shown that between 60% and 80% of all Christians do not know their spiritual gifts. How do we help them, and how do we recognize and develop those five ministries?

1. *"A tree is recognized by its fruit."*[9] Others can see in us what we cannot see, the 'specks and planks' in our eyes as well as the supernatural giftings God has given us. So we need to ask them what they see. We can help each other by reflecting on each other's fruit, 'taste it and tell me how we taste', helping each other to identify our gifts and callings. This happens best during the natural and normal life of the house church, or when a group of people ministers together.

2. *Through prophetic ministry.* Prophetic people often simply 'see' how someone else functions; they see a word written all over him, a special sign, they hear a word or see a vision, and so they 'know' by supernatural revelation. I have seen and observed this hundreds of times, and have also seen the joy and liberation in the eyes of countless people who begin to understand who they are in Christ in terms of their ministry and calling.

3. *By spiritual gift analysis.* There are a number of self-evaluating tools available today in many countries called spiritual gift analysis. This is a 'spiritual gift test', where you fill out a form and answer many pointed questions, and may end up knowing more about your spiritual gift and inclination.

4. *By forming a special recruiting ministry.* Most leading companies know that their future depends on the quality of the next generation of their leaders. So they employ so-called human resource companies and placement agencies, or send out their own talent-spotters, who roam the universities and schools to find the kind of gifted people with the right caliber the

---

[9] Matt 12:33 (NIV)

company feels they need to employ. The Body of Christ could learn from that. We need a supernatural talent-spotting ministry or even a plan, systematically identifying and recruiting those gifts in each other and in the churches, and then helping those junior apostles and prophets or pastors-to-be to become an apprentice with their own role model, someone who is miles ahead of them in spiritual maturity and experience in the very ministry area they feel called to serve. Those disciples and apprentices can carry the suitcases of their masters, or 'pour water over the hands' of a senior prophet, and rub off as much as they can, 'catching the spirit' of someone ministering in the spirit; just imitate me, as Paul puts it. As an apprentice without a master does not make much sense economically, a disciple without a master does not make much sense, spiritually.

Avoiding Ministry Projection

One of the greatest errors of our day is that we have allowed and even encouraged 'spiritual gift projection'. Gift projection happens when a Christian who has received a particular spiritual gift assumes—projects!—that his gift is the most natural thing in the world, and that all other Christians would automatically achieve the same results if they acted just as he does. The error is this: God has made each of us unique and given each special gifts. Whoever measures someone else against himself is comparing apples with oranges and is doing himself and others a great disservice. He also complicates the lives of other Christians with unrighteous comparisons and simply sins against the Body of Christ, in which not everyone is a mouth or an ear.

Ministry projection makes the problem worse. At one stage or another, it might be God's plan for a Christian to 'stop having a gift and start becoming one', where someone would stop just prophesying, and starts to become a prophet. In ministry projection, the teacher would look at the evangelist and say: "You and your evangelistic campaigns! Theological training, that's what really counts. You have only one problem: you should be a bit more like me!" The pastor looks with horror at the prophet and says: "You and your visions. Long-term relationships are what counts!" He grasps his shepherd's crook, meant for keeping wolves at bay, and also drives the prophets away.

The Lesson of Liebig

German biologist and chemist Justus von Liebig discovered over 150 years ago that soil only needs basically four fertilizers or minerals for the healthy growth of a plant: nitrogen, lime, phosphates, and potash. As long as all four minerals are present in the soil in sufficient quantity and harmony, growth occurs 'automatically', the soil is truly fertile, and has all it needs to produce a good crop. If one of the fertilizers is lacking, let us say lime, the growth will be limited and halted by this minimizing factor. The soil starves for lime, and you can add as much nitrogen, phosphates and potash as you want, you will not change the situation at all, and even damage it, unless you add lime.

Let us for illustration's sake equate evangelism with phosphate, prophecy with potash, teaching with nitrogen, and pastoring with lime. If you have a soil thoroughly treated with phosphate (evangelism) and nitrogen (teaching), it soon reaches a saturation level where any more of phosphate and nitrogen will actually have a bad effect, it will make the soil acidic and have the opposite results we desire. What the soil needs now is no more phosphate and nitrogen, but potash and lime in sufficient quantity, so that those minerals can catch up and harmony in the soil is restored. This could potentially hurt the producers of phosphate and nitrogen, because they might feel rejected; but in effect they are only complemented by lime and potash, so that their good contribution, together with the other necessary elements, will reduce acidity and make the soil fertile ground again.

Every good agriculturist can test the soil, finding out its quality and what fertilizers it would need in which quantity, in order to produce a good harvest. This would be, in this illustration, the job of the apostle. He would be like the wise farmer who knows which of the four minerals are needed. The apostolic ministry would see which of the four ministries are necessary next in order to create a healthy balance that will truly develop a good soil. In a similar way you may remember the spiritual DNA, made up of the four genetic letters Guanine, Cytosine, Tymine, and Adenin. They are put together in a double helix structure, which defines what letters correspond and complement another genetic letter, and the very way these letters are arranged will define the organism grows. If we equate, for illustration's sake, those four genetic letters with the four ministries evangelism, prophecy, teaching, and pastoring, this creative act of putting them together in the right order would fall into the responsibility of the apostle, God's 'master builder'.

CONCLUSIONS

We have explored one of God's main resources for the maintenance and multiplication of house churches, namely the five-fold ministry of apostles, prophets, evangelists, pastors, and teachers. The house church movement today can benefit greatly by opening itself up to the cohesion and vision that the five-fold ministry can bring. However, trust and teamwork between local and translocal leaders needs to be nurtured to ensure that this is not done in a hierarchical way.

STUDY QUESTIONS

1. Can you describe 'the five fingers of the hand'?
2. What obstacles often prevent the five-fold from functioning freely?
3. What particular role can apostles and prophets play?
4. Pray about whether God is calling you into one of these ministries.

Chapter 51

THE TYPES AND QUALIFICATIONS OF HOUSE CHURCH LEADERS

VICTOR CHOUDHRIE

Victor Choudhrie is a well respected and accomplished former cancer surgeon. He received his training in India and is a fellow of the Royal College of Surgeons in the U.K., the American College of Surgeons, and the International College of Surgeons. In 1992, he and his wife Bindu began a full-time church planting ministry that has resulted in thousands of house churches planted in India and around the world. He is the author of Greet the Ekklesia in Your House (2005) [Adapted and used by permission of the author. Email: vchoudhrie@gmail.com].

INTRODUCTION

The recent explosion of Christianity in modern-day India has resulted in the emergence of 100,000 multiplying house churches in just a few short years, from 2001 to 2006. These households of faith are typically led locally by 'elders' and networked together by the 'five-fold ministries'. With this kind of growth, important issues arise regarding the proper role and appropriate qualifications of such leaders and ministries. Based on Scripture and our practical experience, we offer the following brief insights.

LEADERSHIP TYPES

David Bennett (First Fruits Ministries) has observed five types of leadership, each with differing roles in God's unfolding plan, in the current house church movement of India. They range from the grassroots level to the national level.

The 'Person of Peace'

This is where everything begins. This person may not even be a Christian, like Cornelius, Lydia, or the Samaritan woman. They are local persons who are seekers of truth and are recognized by their hospitality and generosity.[1] This is where signs and wonders are going to take place, people will confess their sins, folks will get baptized, and a house church will be planted. This is where foundational teachings[2] will be given concerning, (a) Repentance from dead works, (b) Faith in God, (c) Doctrine of baptism, (d) Laying on of hands, (e) Resurrection from the dead, and (f) Eternal judgment.

---

[1] Luke 10:5-6
[2] Heb 6:1-2

The Believer

This person is not just a spectator in the church. They are an empowered person who is recognized by their ability to expel demons and pray for the sick, etc.[3] Immediately after their deliverance and salvation, they are given charge of a decapolis (10 cities) to be Jesus' witnesses. Just like in New Testament times, over 80% of the house churches in China, India, and in many other countries, have been planted only after spiritual warfare.

The Disciple

Jesus said, "By this is my Father glorified, that you bear much fruit, and so prove to be my disciples."[4] A true disciple is one who makes disciples. Healing and deliverance crusades do not make you a disciple unless you disciple new believers into the kingdom. Jesus will simply say, "I never knew you",[5] even to those born again people who do signs and wonders, but who do not make disciples. Not "flocking together" lost people is working against Jesus.[6] Discipling includes taking care of both the physical and spiritual needs of the seeker, otherwise there will be the same judgment, since Jesus will also say, "I never knew you", to those who do not feed the hungry.[7] The sign of being filled with the Holy Spirit in the New Testament church was marked not so much by speaking in tongues, but rather by boldness in proclaiming the gospel and for extravagant generosity so that no one lacked anything.[8]

The Elders

Paul, Timothy, and Titus went around appointing 'elders/presbyters' in every church.[9] 'Elders/presbyters' are also known as 'pastors/shepherds' and 'bishops/overseers' in the New Testament.[10] Elder did not mean old in age, but mature in faith. Young people like Titus were authorized to appoint elders. Elders are spiritual father/mother figures, responsible for administration of the church. They mentor the flock and equip them for ministry. Paul never imposed an outsider as a long-term, local elder in any church, but always empowered local persons to be the leaders.

The Five-fold Ministries

The Lord Jesus gave apostles, prophets, evangelists, shepherds, and teachers to his church. Somewhere in history, the role of the apostles and the prophets, who are the foundation layers of the church, was replaced by

---

[3] Mark 16:17
[4] John 15: (NASB)
[5] Matt 7:22,23 (NASB)
[6] Matt 12:28-30 (NASB)
[7] Matt 25:41-46
[8] Acts 4:31-36
[9] Acts 14:23; Titus 1:5
[10] Acts 20:17,28; 1 Pet 5:1-3

shepherds. However, the five-fold ministry is a specialized team that is meant to equip the entire Body of Christ to fulfill its function and should be restored to its proper role among God's people.[11] In particular, apostles, prophets, evangelists, and teachers often have a more short-term but universal scope to their work in evangelizing the lost and starting house churches, while shepherds will lead local house churches over the long-term.

LEADERSHIP QUALIFICATIONS

The qualifications of elders who lead local house churches are well defined in the Scriptures.[12] Normally, they also work together as co-equals as part of a team that manages a citywide cluster of house churches. We look for these same characteristics in the house church leaders of India, both for local house church elders but also for translocal 'five-fold' leaders.

Character Traits

There are 18 character traits which qualify or disqualify a person from holding this position, such as being the husband of one wife, not given to much wine, not greedy for money, not quarrelsome, etc.

Good Manager of their Household

Unless a leader is a good manager of their own household, how can they be a leader in the church? This is especially the case for house church elders, since the church usually meets in their own home. There has to be a natural connection between the way a leader lives their daily life and how they function in their role within the church.

Hospitable

This is a very important qualification because a house church will simply not function otherwise. The entire household, including the spouse and the children, have to acquire this skill to consciously help take care of the needs of the needy and others who come into their home.[13] Discipling cannot be done by Christians isolating themselves, but like their Master, the house churches must find and befriend lost people. Many people will happily gather for a participatory and interactive church in the homes of people who are hospitable to them.

Sound in Doctrine

Leaders are to have head knowledge, which they can obtain from reading widely and from basic Bible training. But they also need experiential and relational knowledge. This means that leaders are equipped with Scripture not only to convict those unbelievers who contradict, but to help make them inheritors of the kingdom. This includes prayer and spiritual warfare.[14]

---

[11] Eph 4:7-16
[12] 1 Tim 3:1-13; Titus 1:5-9
[13] John 13:34,35; Acts 2:42-47, 4:32-37, 20:7; Rev 3:20
[14] Acts 26:17,18

Being sound in doctrine also means finding out the redemptive stories in the history and the mythology of the local people and use them as bridges. For example, Paul used this model of an "unknown god" when visiting Athenian temples and studying their religious books.[15]

Being Fruitful

Local house church elders must see to it that an atmosphere is created in the house church so that when unbelievers and seekers visit, they will be convicted by sound doctrine and loved practically until they realize their need for God. They are then added to the household of God as active members who can fully participate in the meetings and in the life of the house church in general.[16] Precisely because an unbeliever or new believer is encouraged to be active—i.e. the priesthood of all believers—they have a good opportunity to rapidly grow in faith and reach others daily.[17] The Bride of Christ must not be barren but fruitful, multiplying and filling the earth.

CONCLUSIONS

The qualifications for the various types of leaders examined cannot be acquired merely in the theories expounded in the classroom situation, but also in the reality of the harvest field. It means identifying the strengths and weaknesses of the leader. Then they must be practically mentored to rectify the weaknesses and build up the existing strengths until they resonate with the will of God.

STUDY QUESTIONS

1. Prayerfully and carefully read 1 Cor 3:10-15.
2. Based on the leadership types described above, which are you functioning in currently?
3. In your own contribution to the Body of Christ, what strengths and weaknesses do you see?

---

[15] Acts 17:15-34
[16] 1 Cor 14:23-26; 1 Pet 2:9
[17] Acts 16:5

Chapter 52

THE TRAINING OF HOUSE CHURCH LEADERS

VICTOR CHOUDHRIE

Victor Choudhrie is a well respected and accomplished former cancer surgeon. He received his training in India and is a fellow of the Royal College of Surgeons in the U.K., the American College of Surgeons, and the International College of Surgeons. In 1992, he and his wife Bindu began a full-time church planting ministry that has resulted in thousands of house churches planted in India and around the world. The following is adapted from Victor Choudhrie (2005), Greet the Ekklesia in Your House. [Adapted and used by permission of the author. Email: vchoudhrie@gmail.com].

INTRODUCTION

In the Indian house church movement, we train house church leaders practically to plant multiplying house churches through a 15 step approach based approximately on Luke 10:1-17. The goal of those that are trained is to reap the harvest. The problem is that the laborers are few. Yet, for those who do take up the challenge, their job description is to bind the strongman, find the man of peace, plant a multiplying house church, prepare laborers, and reap the harvest.

STEP 1. GO TWO BY TWO

Go, but do not go, unless you are clothed with power (Acts 1:4-8). Do not take excess baggage. You are going as a lamb, and the wolves (evil spirits whose leader is called the 'Strongman') are waiting to welcome you. Go quietly and prayerfully. Focused prayer walking will reveal the legal entry points (the gates of hell). Spy out the land. Remember that you are on a search-and-destroy mission (Luke 10:1,4; Num 13:1-5).

STEP 2. PRAY

There are at least five kinds of prayers you are to pray as you go. First, ask for the nations (people groups or ethnic communities) of that locality because God has asked you to do so (Ps 2:8). Second, pray to the Lord of the harvest for laborers (Luke 10:2; Matt 9:37,38). Third, bind the 'strongman'. Fourth, pray for the 'man of peace' (Luke 10:6). Finally, bless all the families in that location by planting a house church (Gen 12:3).

STEP 3. BIND THE STRONGMAN

Pray against all the strongholds such as centers of occultism, alcoholism, drugs, pornography, smuggling, atheism, idolatry, worship of money, and television/theaters, when used for watching vulgar programming. God wants you to plunder the possessions of the strongman, which includes people, property, and wealth, and make them his possession (Matt 12:29).

STEP 4. FIND THE HOUSE OF PEACE

Finding the 'peaceful home' is central to the strategy of house church planting. It becomes your operational base from where you will launch out. Jesus was a Jewish rabbi who trained Jewish disciples in Jewish homes within the Jewish culture. The 'house of peace' is the most natural place for discipling a people group in its own culture. People are God's tools, and the 'house of peace' is the place where he will transform ordinary people into extraordinary channels of his grace.

STEP 5. EATING, NOT MEETING

Bless every family as you prayer walk (Gen 12:3). Keep prayer walking, binding, loosing, and blessing until the 'person of peace' welcomes you into his home. Eat and sleep there, if appropriate and possible—in any case, develop a strong bond with that family. You are expecting this family to join the household of God; therefore, behave like a member of the household and not just a formal religious visitor (Eph 2:19). Do not go from house to house of non-believers (Matt 10:5). When there are enough believers in the locality, then you can go from house to house (Luke 10:5-8; Acts 20:20). Like Cornelius and Lydia, the 'persons of peace' are God-fearing and influential; otherwise, they would not be able to feed you and take care of you and your companions. They are not necessarily Christians at this point. Once you find them, it is your job to bring them to Christ.

STEP 6. SPIRITUAL WARFARE

The 'person of peace' knows the local people and will gather his friends and relatives into his house, who can be redeemed. First, expel demons and pray for the sick (Matt 10:8; Luke 10:9,17). Wherever Jesus went, he first expelled demons and healed the sick; only then did he teach. Likewise, when Philip the evangelist went to Samaria to preach, the demons came out with a loud voice and the sick were healed. Many New Testament churches were planted after such power encounters. This will produce a healthy awe of the Lord, and people will ask, "What shall we do?" (Acts 8:5,6). One of the first things to teach is spiritual warfare because the expelled demon will return with seven more deadly spirits, and if this person cannot protect himself, his condition will be worse than before. One of the identification marks of a believer is that he can expel demons (Mark 16:17; Luke 10:17).

STEP 7. MAKE DISCIPLES

Jesus modeled lifestyle discipling by living with his disciples, eating the same food, wearing the same clothes, and sharing the same facilities. Jesus taught his disciples by casting out demons, healing the sick, and identifying with the powerless. Discipleship for us will include laying down one's life for the friendly and even for the unfriendly. There are several foundational topics for teaching new disciples (Heb 6:1,2). These include repentance from dead works, faith towards God, the doctrine of baptism, laying on of hands, resurrection from the dead, and eternal judgment. Discipleship is a process, and the end product is a disciple who can faithfully pass on all their teachings and practical skills to others (2 Tim 2:2).

STEP 8. REPENTANCE IS MANDATORY

John the Baptist preached repentance (Matt 3:2). Jesus started his ministry with the same words (Matt 4:17). Jesus' final words to his disciples were that repentance and remission of sins should be preached to all the nations in his mighty name (Luke 24:47). On the day of Pentecost, the apostle Peter also urged his hearers to repent and turn to God (Acts 2:38, 3:19). Repentance is an act, which results in a change of mind, purpose, and action.

STEP 9. REPENTANCE IS A PROCESS

In the Old Testament, the process included confession of sins to two witnesses, restoration of relationship with the wronged person, restitution of losses incurred, taking a bath of purification in a nearby pool, restoration of relationship with God by offering a ram as a sacrifice, and then entering the temple precincts to pray. In the New Testament, repentance would mean taking similar steps except that, instead of a ram, the Lord Jesus himself has now become the sacrifice, once and for all. New disciples must confess all their sins, including generational curses layer by layer, like peeling an onion. Hidden sins will make a person an ineffective Christian (Exod 20:5).

STEP 10. BAPTIZE WITHOUT DELAY

'Mikve' is a Hebrew word for 'bath of purification'. Jews who had committed sin and Gentiles who intended to convert to Judaism came to the temple and took a bath (baptism) of purification in the presence of two or three witnesses, but without the help of a priest. Baptism was a sign of their repentance and personal covenant with God. In New Testament times, they did not go to the temple but took a 'bath of purification' anywhere, like the Ethiopian in a pond, Lydia in a river, and Cornelius in his home. Nowhere is the authority to baptize delegated to any special class of people. Every believer, regardless of gender, is commissioned to baptize (Matt 28:19). All baptisms in New Testament times took place on the same day as their repentance and confession of faith in the Lordship of Jesus. A delay in baptism results in the loss of harvesting of souls (Acts 19:5,6).

STEP 11. TEACH OBEDIENCE

To obey means to come under the authority of Jesus. New believers must discard the devil, their previous master. 'Teaching' takes place through various means. Eating together shows new disciples that being part of the church means being part of the family of God, thereby breaking barriers in societies that are ridden with caste, status, racism, and denominationalism. Praying together demonstrates to new believers their dependence on a generous God that wants to meet their needs and those of others. Serving together illustrates that we are to be concerned with the needs of others in a practical way. Studying the Scriptures together communicates that God's word is the guiding authority for the life and mission of the believer.

STEP 12. SHARE MATERIAL BLESSING

New believers must learn to share their material blessings from day one. Poor widows gave their last dime or their last morsel for the kingdom. Poverty is a curse (Mal 3:8-12; Deut 28:48), which can be broken by giving. Both spiritual conversion and financial conversion are essential (Acts 5:2).

STEP 13. START A HOUSE CHURCH

Use a participatory and interactive format for meetings (1 Cor 14:26-31). Facilitate rather than lead from 'up front'. Encourage everyone to share their dreams, visions, prophecies, revelations, edifications, encouragements, victories, needs, songs, and words of instruction. Emphasize the 'one anothers', which appear many times in the New Testament. Make sure that everyone has the opportunity to participate as the Lord leads the meeting. Do not let the assembly be dominated by only one or two talkative individuals. Encourage the new house church to multiply by sharing their new faith with friends, family, co-workers, etc. House church planting must become a movement of ordinary people (Matt 18:20).

STEP 14. EQUIP THE BODY

The mandate of the church universal is to worship God. One of the best ways of glorifying God is to make disciples (John 15:8). Invite apostles, prophets, evangelists, teachers, and others from the network of house churches in the region. This will soon reveal and strengthen different giftedness in your own house church and create a bond of unity with the visitors. Without apostles and prophets, there will be no adequate and successful church planting activity (Eph 2:20, 4:11,12). Equipping does not mean merely transferring knowledge and information, but transformation. It includes imparting biblically sound house church planting skills, as well as the authority to baptize and serve the Lord's Supper. Avoid or minimize the lecture or sermon method. The early church spread rapidly through interactive meetings and the practical involvement of ordinary believers.

STEP 15. SEND TEAMS

Fast, pray, lay hands on, and send teams to go and repeat the process of planting house churches like in the early church (John 17:18; Acts 13:1-3).

STUDY QUESTIONS

1. Prayerfully and carefully read Luke 10:1-17.
2. How is Jesus' strategy different from what is often done in the church?
3. How can you adapt this strategy to your house church network?

Chapter 53

THE FINANCIAL SUPPORT OF HOUSE CHURCH LEADERS

RAD ZDERO

Rad Zdero earned his Ph.D. degree in Mechanical Engineering from Queen's University (Kingston, ON, Canada) and is the manager of a hospital-based orthopaedic research lab. He has participated in, led, and started house churches and cell groups since 1985. He is currently part of HouseChurch.Ca (www.housechurch.ca), which is a church planting team developing a network of house churches in the greater Toronto area and beyond. He is the author of The Global House Church Movement (2004). [Used by permission of the author. Email: rzdero@yahoo.ca].

INTRODUCTION

A main emphasis of the world house church movement is on a return to the simplicity and strategy of apostolic patterns as found in the New Testament. A significant aspect of this 'restoration' concerns the nature and function of leadership. The apostolic strategy was to implement two types of leadership, namely 'local' and 'traveling' leaders. In order to fully implement this two-pronged approach effectively, issues of role, responsibility, organization, training, accountability, and financial support were addressed by the apostles either expressly in words and/or implicitly in their actions. These topics are dealt with in more detail elsewhere from a New Testament standpoint.[1] Presently, our inquiry will focus on the question of financial support for the two primary types of house churches leaders today, mainly from a practical standpoint.

LOCAL LEADERS

Let us start by describing the scope of responsibility and ministry of the typical local house church leader active in the world today. Today's house church leaders were known in the New Testament by various interchangeable names, namely presbyters = elders = pastors = shepherds = bishops = overseers.[2] They have the character and competence to manage the affairs of the Body of Christ that meets in their home or the host home. Their responsibilities are long-term and local. They function as the primary

---

[1] Rad Zdero (2004), *The Global House Church Movement*, William Carey Library, pp.39-48; Steve Atkerson, "Should pastors and missionaries be salaried?" (www.ntrf.org).

[2] Gerald Cowen (2003), *Who Rules the Church?* Broadman and Holman Publishers, pp.5-16; See also Acts 20:17,28 and 1 Pet 5:1-3

shepherds and strategists for their house church. They have been trained either by traveling church planters, missionaries, and leaders, or by a previous generation of local house church leaders. Their goal is to help other members of the house churches discover, sharpen, and use their spiritual gifts, capacities, and resources to accomplish God's purposes in the church and in the world. They work as part of a small team of leaders as equals to either facilitate a house church or network of house churches in a city or region. They themselves are fathers and mothers, couples and singles, who can relate to the everyday trials and triumphs of others. They are typically carrying out their ministry on a volunteer, unpaid basis. In contrast to their counterparts in traditional churches, they are typically not professionals who have received formal seminary training, nor are they imported from an outside context to be the leaders of a local house church network. They are truly 'home grown' leaders.

Consequently, local house church leaders are encouraged to continue their work for the Lord on a volunteer unpaid basis. Unless the Lord very specifically and clearly asks a local house church leader to receive financial support for a season, they should accomplish their ministries freely, rather than as paid professionals. The following reasons are proposed:

1) *The New Testament Encourages Local Volunteerism.* The New Testament counsels local house church leaders to carry out their ministries as unpaid volunteers. Paul the apostle explicitly encourages this approach to a group of local leaders. He states: "I have coveted no one's silver or gold or clothes. You yourselves know that these hands ministered to my own needs and to the men who were with me. In everything I showed you that by working hard in this manner you must help the weak and remember the words of the Lord Jesus, that He Himself said, 'It is more blessed to give than to receive.'"[3] Note that Paul goes so far as to say that local leaders are to give financial support to those in their spiritual care, rather than receiving from them.[4]

2) *House Churches Are Small and Simple.* There is no practical need for house church leaders today to receive financial support. The usual scope of ministry in a single house church usually involves at most 20 or 30 people. Moreover, the focus of house churches on genuine community, unadorned meetings, and relational evangelism, does not require a high

---

[3] Acts 20:33-35 (NASB)

[4] It is sometimes suggested that 1 Tim 5:17-18 allows for full financial support of local leaders. However, based on linguistic and historical factors, it is more likely that the phrase 'double honor' in this passage refers simply to the respect that a local leader garnered from the members of their Christian community. See Rad Zdero (2004), *The Global House Church Movement*, William Carey Library, pp.42-44, and Steve Atkerson, "Should Pastors and Missionaries be Salaried?" (www.ntrf.org).

degree of organizational maintenance on the part of local leaders. Thus, a small team of three or four leaders can easily facilitate such a group without requiring any kind of funding for themselves.

3) *Everyone Should Minister.* It is desirable to create a real sense of group ownership for the house church or the house church network. It is also advantageous to encourage the practical application of the priesthood of all believers. To do so, all believers should be given the opportunity to minister to both believers and non-believers locally. Conversely, funding local leaders creates a dependence on them to achieve goals, accomplish tasks, and do the work of the ministry. This is a challenge being faced by traditional churches and their paid pastors that we would do well to avoid in the house church movement.

4) *Leaders Should 'Do Life Together' With Others.* House church leaders must be able to effectively carry out their responsibilities before the Lord. They must be able to mobilize their house church to care for itself and reach out to non-believers. To do so, they should be able to empathize with the losses and victories, the drudgery and the excitement, that characterizes the daily lives of those around them. This means experiencing the challenges and responsibilities of maintaining a regular job like everyone else in the church. In this way, local leaders will 'do life together' with others in the house church.

5) *Local Resources May Be Limited.* In many contexts around the world characterized either by poverty or persecution, the financial resources of local house churches will be extremely limited. Members are hard pressed to provide any kind of funding for local leaders even if they desired to do so. Requiring these folks to establish a funding stream that flows in support of local leaders becomes an unnecessary burden and may create more problems than it solves.

6) *Outside Funding Creates Dependence.* Those intent on seeing local house church leaders receive some sort of funding, may appeal to sources outside the vicinity or even the country if local resources are lacking. However, this can hinder the possibility of a genuinely indigenous and reproducible house church movement that feeds only on local resources. Moreover, a stable outside funding source always leads to setting up a system that requires bureaucracy, negotiation, dependence, and waiting.

TRAVELING LEADERS

Let us now move on to describing the typical scope of responsibility and ministry of traveling house church leaders active on the scene today. In the New Testament they are called 'apostles' (Greek = *apostolos*, meaning 'sent one', 'envoy', 'ambassador', or 'messenger'), but they may also have an additional gifting as a prophet, evangelist, teacher, or shepherd. Today, they are commonly called church planters, missionaries, strategy coordinators, regional directors, or circuit riders, but many are increasingly being recognized as having some sort of apostolic function and are being called 'apostles'. Their mandate is temporary and universal. The job of these itinerants is to go to unreached regions to evangelize the populace, baptize new converts, organize new believers into house churches, and train leaders. They circulate from group-to-group and city-to-city to provide ongoing personal teaching, coaching, and problem solving. They are a mixed group in that some have received a seminary education or other formal training, whereas others have not but clearly evidence calling and competence to function as traveling apostles. In contrast to local house church leaders, they are 'outsiders' who have come to start or visit a local house church network. Because they cannot be tied down to local jobs, they often require some sort of ongoing financial support for their ministry. In most cases, they gladly receive such financial assistance, whereas in other cases they are financially independent because of the transportable nature of their trade.

In this light, it is suggested that today's emerging house church movement attempt to provide financial support where possible to traveling leaders. This is to be reserved for those whose ministry involves extensive travel in visiting regional house church networks or those making a geographic move to begin new house church networks in unreached areas or among unreached peoples. The following ideas are offered in support of this practice:

1) *The Lord Jesus Christ Received Material Support While Traveling.* Before the Lord Jesus began his public traveling ministry, he lived a local existence. He would have carried on with the domestic responsibilities of work, family, and friends. Along with his peers, his material sustenance came from farming or a trade. However, when he was in the midst of his traveling ministry, he received financial and material help from a group of faithful women supporters.[5] He also frequently received lodging and food from people who opened their homes to him.[6] Moreover, in training his disciples, he encouraged them to find a 'house of peace' who would offer them hospitality, as they traveled from village to village preaching the kingdom of God.[7]

2) *The Apostle Paul Encouraged Funding for Traveling Leaders.* The apostle Paul counsels traveling house church leaders like apostles to carry out their ministries with the financial support of the churches. He argues for this when writing to the Corinthian church, a community that he was personally involved in raising up. He states: "If to others I am not an apostle, at least I am to you; for you are the seal of my apostleship in the Lord....Who at any time serves as a soldier at his own

---

[5] Matt 27:55-56; John 12:4-6, 13:29
[6] Matt 8:14-15, 9:9-10; Luke 7:36, 10:38-42, 19:2-6
[7] Luke 10:1-11

expense? Who plants a vineyard, and does not eat the fruit of it? Or who tends a flock and does not use the milk of the flock?....If we sowed spiritual things in you, is it too much if we should reap material things from you?"[8]

3) *Traveling Leaders Cannot Maintain Local Jobs.* Because of the temporary and broad nature of apostolic ministry, it becomes nearly impossible for those called to this ministry to maintain a regular job. This would require them to be in a certain place at a certain time for a certain duration, all of which would limit their ability to fulfill their mission. If these folks also have families and younger children that need attention during free time, then it becomes doubly difficult to function as an apostle. There are some exceptions though. Some apostolic people, even while maintaining full-time employment with a regular job, have chosen to maximize their ministries on evenings, weekends, and holidays. Others have gainful employment through freelance work, mobile trades, or as small business owners, which may give them greater flexibility with their time. In these cases, specific ministry funding for them may not be required.

4) *Starting New House Church Networks Takes Time and Energy.* Any start-up venture, whether it is a business, organization, or club, takes time and energy. Starting up a house church network is no different. Traveling apostolic teams that station themselves in a geographic region or among a certain people group to start a new fellowship, may find it beneficial to be financially free in order to be totally committed to that ministry's foundation laying. However, once a church has been established and its leaders identified, the apostolic team should move on to another area to repeat the process. If they decide to settle in that area permanently, they should seek to sever their financial support and seek regular employment, since they are by definition becoming 'home grown' local leaders of the church. As local leaders, they would be encouraged to consider the earlier arguments presented seriously.

5) *Identify Funding Sources.* Financial or material support for traveling apostles or apostolic teams may come in several forms. Regular salaries may be provided by a denomination, mission agency, or network of house churches either periodically or on a long-term basis. Occasional material gifts of money, food, shelter, and travel expenses may be provided by the Christian community that sends or hosts the team.

EXAMPLES OF FUNDING TODAY'S HOUSE CHURCH LEADERS

We will briefly consider several working examples that are similar, but not identical, to the model described above. Do similar funding strategies exist

---

[8] 1 Cor 9:2,7,11 (NASB)

currently somewhere in the world, and are they working well to support house church movements?

The Chinese House Church Movement

The house church movement in China has made a conscious decision to only provide monetary aid to traveling evangelists and church planters.[9] These mobile Christians have the responsibility of starting churches in new unreached areas. Local leaders, however, perpetually remain volunteers. This focuses all of their resources on going into the world and making disciples of all nations for Christ, rather than pouring money into buildings, projects, expensive programs, and local leaders. Given the estimated size, success, and strength of the underground house church movement in China, which encompasses an estimated 80 to 130 million passionate believers,[10] their strategy can serve as a workable example, especially in circumstances that are even more favorable politically and financially than theirs.

The Church Planting Movements of the Baptists

In their work around the world, especially in South East Asia, the Baptists have become involved in full blown church planting movements.[11] These are defined as rapidly growing churches planting churches within a given people group or region. For instance, in Cambodia the Baptists saw the emergence of 220 house churches and 10,000 new believers in less than 10 years. Among the 10 universal elements identified in the majority of these movements is the use of house churches or cell groups, often numbering between 10 and 30 people. Another important factor is the so-called lay led and/or bi-vocational nature of church planters and other leaders. These leaders come from within the people group itself and share in its general demographic characteristics.

The Cuban Petrol Crisis and the House Churches

The 1992 petrol crisis in Cuba caused the island's Protestant Christian leaders to petition Castro's government for permission to reorganize their building-bound congregations into a web of neighborhood house churches. By the year 2000, there were between 6,000 and 10,000 multiplying house churches scattered all over the island, with one house church within walking distance of every 1500 Cubans.[12] Though some of the house churches are led by full-time ordained clergy, this revival is driven mostly by part-time preachers and teachers that travel from group to group.

---

[9] Larry Kreider (2001), *House Church Networks: A Church for a New Generation*, House-to-House Publications, pp.41-42.

[10] Rad Zdero, Ibid, pp.69-71.

[11] David Garrison (2004), *Church Planting Movements*, Wigtake Resources.

[12] Friday Fax, "Cuba: petrol crisis helps church growth – thanks, Castro!", Issue 20, May 25, 2001, fridayfax@bufton.net; Mindy Belz, "Su Casa es Mi Casa", *World Magazine*, Vol. 13, No. 5, February 6, 1998.

CONCLUSIONS

This chapter has described briefly the nature and function of the typical local and traveling house church leaders active in the world house church movement today. Arguments and examples have been presented suggesting that local house church leaders remain as unpaid volunteers, while funding efforts should be made where possible in support of traveling leaders that act in an apostolic fashion.

STUDY QUESTIONS

1. Given your sense of calling and your set of skills, do you feel you can best function as a local leader or as a traveling leader in the house church movement?

2. How does the scope of ministry differ between local and traveling leaders? Is this a good argument for their differing financial support from the house churches? Why, or why not?

3. What is inherent about the nature of apostolic ministry that prevents it from being perceived as a special class of Christians, or which prevents a local church from becoming dependent on it?

PART 6

STRATEGIC DIRECTIONS
FOR LAUNCHING
HOUSE CHURCH MOVEMENTS

Chapter 54

NEW CULTURE, NEW CHURCH: HOW CULTURAL CHANGES IN WESTERN SOCIETY ARE CHALLENGING THE CHURCH TO RETHINK ITS STRATEGY

RICK SHROUT

Rick Shrout's ministry experience includes serving as a home missionary among Native American communities, leadership in cell church ministry, interim pastoral ministry, church planting, and involvement with house church networks. He earned a Master of Religion degree from Warner Pacific College (Portland, OR, USA) with an emphasis in cross-cultural ministry, and is presently enrolled in a Doctor of Ministry program in Leadership in the Emerging Culture through George Fox Evangelical Seminary (Portland, OR, USA). The focus of his doctoral research is on partnerships between traditional churches and house church planters. This will culminate in a book in 2007 that illustrates actual stories of such partnerships across North America with discussion on the essential characteristics of the church. Email: rshrout@mac.com.

INTRODUCTION

At the dawn of the 21st century, the church in the Western nations stands on the edge of a growing cultural divide. A rising current of cultural change is filling the riverbanks of common life with a worldview and lifestyle that many describe as increasingly *postmodern*. Postmodernity has carved its way into the psyche of society in the West. Postmodernity is not necessarily a rejection of *modernity*. Rather, it is simply the cultural climate that has followed the modern era that challenges and brings into question some of the assumptions of modernity that were founded on rationalism, materialism, and reductionism, while giving credence to premodern forms of knowing and interacting with the world. At the same time, postmodernity holds as evidence the dysfunction of modern society—exemplified through the social, moral, and environmental chaos being experienced around the world—arguing that modernity's claim of constructing a better world has fallen far short of what was promised by the glory of science and the sheer determination of human ingenuity. Postmoderns understand that the hunger in the human soul cannot be satisfied by the promises of materialism or through the institutions of modern religion.[1]

---

[1] Jonathan Campbell and Jennifer Campbell (2005), *The Way of Jesus: A Journey of Freedom for Pilgrims and Wanderers [1st ed.]*, Jossey-Bass, p.29.

In light of this unfolding new world, the church is pressed to answer a mounting question: Can the traditional church effectively engage an ever-increasing postmodern world with a transformational gospel? A new kind of church and a new kind of Christian will need to emerge to meet the challenges that a new kind of world will pose.[2]

The church born of modernity—the church in which many of us were nurtured and now serve in as leaders—moves along with little awareness of the massive cultural shifts that demand a meaningful response to the vital questions of our time. In the process, the modern church has become adept at ignoring the cultural changes happening[3] and offers little reality to an emerging generation[4] of postmoderns.[5]

If the church is going to have a credible voice and a missional presence in a postmodern world, then the traditional modern church must consider the planting of new kinds of churches that can effectively demonstrate the kingdom of God within a changing culture in the North American context. It is argued here that one of these new kinds of Christian communities that needs greater consideration is the house church.

MINISTRY IN A POSTMODERN CULTURE

The Challenge of Postmodernity

If postmodernity is a significant cultural current carving its way around the world—especially through Western nations—then we should not ignore its influence as we seek to minister to a world attempting to navigate this culture stream. The need to establish new kinds of churches is imperative. The indicators for this need of new kinds of churches are mounting. Most church growth researchers agree that the church in North America, for example, is in decline.[6] Some are beginning to admit that what was once interpreted as significant church growth in the late 20th century was actually a redistribution of Christians within the consumer environment of modern

---

[2] Brian D. McLaren (2000), *The Church on the Other Side: Doing Ministry in the Postmodern Matrix*, Zondervan, p.14.

[3] G.Barna (1998), *The Second Coming of the Church,* W. Publishing Group, p.2.

[4] The 'emerging generation' is not strictly generational or restricted to 'Gen-Xers.' An increasing number of people with postmodern sensibilities can be found across the generational spectrum.

[5] For many Christians steeped in modernity and Christendom, the church's loss of societal influence calls for sounding an alarm to 'circle the wagons.' Others view this as an opportunity to be a dynamic counter-culture in a post-Christian environment that can profoundly demonstrate the kingdom of God.

[6] During an advance I attended for my doctoral studies with Leonard Sweet in 2003, he stated that 75% of churches in the USA have plateaued or declined in attendance and membership. While 24% of churches are growing, this growth can be attributed to 'migrant worshippers' or church hoppers. Only 1% of churches are growing through reaching non-Christians.

church culture, and that much of this growth was attributed to Boomers returning to their spiritual roots. It is important to understand that not only is there a growing population of postmoderns who are not interested in organized religion or in attending traditional church services,[7] there is a growing population of disillusioned and dissatisfied Christians.

The E.P.I.C. Model of Ministry

I am suggesting that ministry within postmodern culture can be done more effectively in the house church context because postmodern sensibilities parallel the ecclesiological perspectives and affinities of most house churches and other small communities of faith. In support of this thesis, the EPIC[8] model of ministry in the postmodern context, as described by Leonard Sweet, is an excellent and succinct summary of the contextual elements needed for ministry in a postmodern culture— experiential, participatory, image-driven, and connectivity. EPIC pinpoints the heartbeat of postmoderns and their search for meaningful and authentic faith that engages the whole of life. This holistic way of ministry among those in a postmodern culture is one that longs for authentic community, the transcendence of God, and seeing change take place in our very neighborhoods.[9]

The first aspect of EPIC to be considered here is the *experiential* component. Missionaries to postmoderns must seek to rescue experience from the clutches of a rationalistic explanation of reality that has become the hallmark of Christian life within modernity.[10] I am not suggesting that there is no place for propositional truth in the church of the future, but there needs to be a shift in emphasis on the entry point[11] into the community of faith via experience for postmoderns. This is highly significant and should be taken into account when considering philosophies of ministry and learning theories

---

[7] The traditional church born of modernity has been highly invested in the 'attractional' model of evangelism while placing emphasis on ministry as an event on Sunday mornings. I believe the days of the attractional, seeker, facility-dependent church are numbered, but perhaps with a few exceptions.

[8] For a discussion of EPIC, see Leonard I. Sweet (2000), *Post-Modern Pilgrims: First Century Passion for the 21st Century World*, Broadman & Holman.

[9] Robert Webber (2002), *The Younger Evangelicals: Facing the Challenges of the New World*, Baker Books, p.47.

[10] Leonard I. Sweet (1999), *Soultsunami: Sink or Swim in New Millennium Culture*, Zondervan, p.215.

[11] Modernity's emphasis on propositional truth has merit when seeking to communicate what sets Christianity apart from other religions. But, the starting place of conversation with postmoderns is more readily accessible at the place of personal experience and how to live life authentically. Discussion about propositional truth can come later after relationships have developed and the reality of the presence of Jesus demonstrated in common life.

for the church within an emerging culture. Postmoderns seek integrity and intensity, rather than merely clarity.[12]

The second aspect of EPIC that should be considered is the *participatory* component. Participation in genuine experiences is a key ingredient for postmoderns,[13] who believe it is impossible to be totally objective. The observer participates in some fashion with the 'observed'. This has far reaching implications upon our modern understanding of epistemology and theology, and suggests that our understanding of God should have a participatory and subjective component. For example, in matters concerning the traditional church and its top-down leadership model, the participatory component threatens the foundational underpinnings of its hierarchical structure. Postmoderns are not interested so much in sitting under the teaching of a so-called expert authority and then told what to believe, but seek more to be an active participant in the learning process on a personal road of discovery.

The third component of the EPIC model of ministry is *image-driven*. The culture of modernity is word-based. The communication and assimilation of the gospel is profoundly dependent upon text and the explanations and interpretations of words. But in the emerging culture, 'image-based' communication is more significant. Images and *metaphors* are key to the communication of ideas for postmoderns—not the heavy use of words for the presentation of abstract theological propositions. For example, Jesus did not primarily communicate through the exegesis of words, as most modern preachers do today. His exegesis was of images through the use of parables and story.[14] If we are to effectively preach the gospel to postmoderns, it will require greater use of metaphor and narrative. To 'tell the story' of the gospel is a very literal enterprise for postmodern missionaries, and the house church context is well-suited for this task. Yet this goes well beyond homiletic techniques in narrative preaching. This is about sharing personal stories of transformation, and the simple structure and relational lifestyle of house churches allows for and encourages this kind of story telling. In addition, a functioning community of faith is a powerful metaphor that embodies and demonstrates the gospel—a living epistle[15] that a postmodern world can 'read and see' the image of Christ.

The fourth component of EPIC to be considered here is *connectivity*. Avenues of communication have radically changed with the exponential growth of the internet in a cyber world of high-speed bandwidth, connecting and bringing people together through the world-wide-web. Connectivity is

---

[12] Leonard I. Sweet, Brian D. McLaren, and Jerry Haselmayer (2003), *"a" Is for Abductive: The Language of the Emerging Church*, Zondervan, p.120.

[13] Sweet, McLaren, and Haselmayer, Ibid., p.232.

[14] Sweet, *Post-Modern Pilgrims*, Ibid.

[15] 2 Cor 3:2-3

closely related to the idea of community, but with an added nuance that sets it apart. The interdependence of individuals within a group, rather than individualism or communalism, is going to be important in the future.[16] The more interdependent we become, the more important our uniqueness as individuals becomes. This has major implications for our understanding of community. In terms of ministry in the postmodern world, it is more than creating a space that we deem a community of faith. It must go from 'space'—an empty geographical location—to 'place'—a full encounter of authentic connections and relationships. There is a growing desire for personal relationships for postmoderns, who want the opportunity to make a valuable contribution to a community.[17]

Most practitioners of ministry within postmodern culture agree that relationships are key to missional engagement in an emerging culture. This element of human existence has largely been ignored in the modern world and in the church, leading to the belief that individual autonomy is essential for personal fulfillment and wholeness.[18] If this assessment of our modern culture is accurate, and I believe it is, then it is imperative that we consider premodern as well as postmodern perspectives of reality and how these perspectives should inform our ecclesiology and the way we 'do church'.

POSTMODERNITY AND HOUSE CHURCHES

Pre-Constantinian Values

It seems quite apparent that ministry in a postmodern context and the core ecclesiological essentials of the house church run parallel, if not entirely converge, at some points. The postmodern church in many respects is more closely aligned with the church prior to the time of the emperor Constantine, than with that of the modern era.[19] Today's house church advocates agree. And this sentiment for church values prior to Constantine has been the clarion call down through the ages of Christians seeking a more authentic and holistic expression of church life that holds true to the New Testament witness and whole-hearted discipleship. The main concern for Christians living prior to Constantine was how to practically live out the life of a true disciple of Jesus, rather than in clarifying theological matters.[20] It is this kind of holistic and radical faith journey that resonates and connects with postmoderns, and it is this kind of faith expression and commitment that is desired and valued in house church ecclesiology. A Christianity that engages with life at the core of what it means to be human is fundamental to postmodern ministry and life in house churches—experiential, participatory,

---

[16] Sweet, McLaren, and Haselmayer, Ibid., p.72.

[17] Sweet, *Soultsunami: Sink or Swim in New Millennium Culture*, p.221.

[18] John William Drane (2001), *The Mcdonaldization of the Church: Consumer Culture and the Church's Future*, Smyth & Helwys Pub., p.20.

[19] Webber, Ibid., p.217.

[20] Webber, Ibid., p.110.

communal, and connective. It is not necessarily a total rejection of the cognitive emphasis within the church born of modernity, but a longing and commitment to embrace all the components of faith clearly set forth through the testimony of the biblical narrative of God's people and by the example of Christians through the ages.

A Company of Believers

With a voice that sounds as contemporary as the latest scholars in postmodernism, as if speaking to the issue of belonging before believing, Elton Trueblood amazingly wrote over 40 years ago that Jesus' admonition to follow him was an invitation to commitment and involvement in the context of a community, not merely attendance at a church or synagogue service.[21] This resonates with advocates of postmodern ministry and those involved in house churches. Commitment to Christ is not predominantly cognitive assent to propositional truth, but more an invitation to begin a journey with a company of committed people.[22] It is a commitment to one another and to a God who dares lay claim to every area of one's life. It is a call to 24/7 discipleship and the awareness that the Christian life cannot be distilled from real life by a two-hour event on a Sunday morning that is the dominant focus of time and resources within the modern traditional church.

The reality and impact of life lived in the realm of Christian community falls between Sundays in the everyday real world. Postmoderns have a desire for holistic spirituality. The lifestyle associated with a company of committed followers of Jesus can be the touchstone that initiates their exploration of what it means to be part of a Christ-centered community. In light of this, one of the biggest challenges facing the traditional church is to find ways to free the laity and staff from time-consuming assignments and committees that are necessary to keep that attractional church afloat, and release these same people with a missional focus to spend more time with friends, neighbors, and associates in the day to day affairs of life. Businessman and communications expert M. Rex Miller states that "many churches are so fragmented and activity-driven that they have little opportunity to develop strong relational bonds."[23] Because they are free from the demands of program-driven ministry and facility-based obligations, house churches are well suited for the kind of missional focus needed to build relationships with people of a postmodern persuasion.

The commitment to strong community and relationships is undoubtedly one of the greatest similarities between ministry to postmoderns and house churches. Beyond commitment to one another is an appreciation for diversity among postmodern Christians, with an emphasis on being multi-generational, multi-cultural, and postdenominational—convictions that,

---

[21] E. Trueblood (1961), *The Company of the Committed [1st ed.]*, Harper, p.34.
[22] Trueblood, Ibid., p.21.
[23] M. Rex Miller (2004), *The Millennium Matrix*, Jossey-Bass, p.xii.

ironically, contradict certain long-established church-growth principles.[24] This description by Webber of these key features in churches of younger Evangelicals is in sync with key features of many house churches worldwide. The familial setting that crosses the lines of ethnic diversity, gender, age, and denominational background is a powerful current flowing through the house church phenomenon and follows the path of instruction given to New Testament churches—that the *ekklesia* of God is a family comprised of both Gentile and Jew, slave and free, male and female.[25]

The Priesthood of All Believers

The heightened demarcation between clergy and laity within ecclesiastical paradigms of the modern church is an issue clearly in opposition to the nature of leadership in the mind and practice of postmoderns. This is no less true in most house church networks. It is suggested that the postmodern church will eventually endorse and introduce the complete abolishment of the clergy/laity distinction, encouraging all to be fully activated and engaged Christians.[26]

More than one has said that the Reformation was a reformation of 'orthodoxy', but not of 'orthopraxy', and in effect did not restore or reclaim the priesthood of all believers. There is a tremendous desire within house church practitioners to see and experience the functional reality of the priesthood of all believers and not merely give it lip service.[27] This certainly resonates with the cultural proclivity of postmoderns for personal experience and participation. This functional concern lies near the heart of the issues that define an EPIC model of ministry, particularly the elements of experience and participation.

Where post-Constantinian churches—including traditional churches born of modernity—center around the pulpit or liturgy with an elite priesthood dispensing the word of God and sacrament, both postmodern and house church adherents perceive this as a failure to release the church to function as the Body of Jesus, to truly be incarnational, and to embrace Christ as the ultimate leader and shepherd of his people. Along with their early house church counterparts, postmodern Christians try to avoid centralizing leadership into a few hands, turning the meeting place into a sacred location, and over-ritualizing Christian activity.[28]

Eddie Gibbs, professor of church growth at Fuller Theological Seminary, observes that the next generation of churches will work toward

---

[24] Webber, Ibid., p.119.
[25] Acts 2:17; Eph 2:11-22; Gal 3:28
[26] Sweet, *Soultsunami*, Ibid., pp.217-18.
[27] Wayne Jacobsen (1987), *The Naked Church*, Harvest House Publishers, p.75.
[28] Vincent P. Branick (1989), *The House Church in the Writings of Paul*, (Zacchaeus Studies, New Testament), M. Glazier, p.15.

"decentralized networks"[29] that take control out of the hands of a few and enable mutuality, accountability, and shared responsibility within the Body of Christ. This move in the direction of the decentralization of leadership is a critical piece in the ministry to a postmodern culture that house church movements are able to negotiate.

CONCLUSIONS

The shift in ministry in the postmodern world and in the house church movement is, at least in part, a sociological response to modernity. The swelling postmodern cultural currents in the West demand that we ask the question: Is there a need for new kinds of churches? I believe the answer is yes, and that small communities of faith centered on Christ with a missional focus, such as healthy house churches, fit our postmodern culture from a sociological perspective. This is good missiology. And if our ecclesiology is motivated by mission, then this is also good biblical theology. Surrounded by a rapidly changing culture, may we find new ways to be the very hands of Jesus to touch those in a world in desperate need of Christ.

STUDY QUESTIONS

1. Define the term 'postmodern'. Is this good, bad, or neutral?
2. What are the values of the E.P.I.C. model of ministry?
3. What adjustments can or should your house church network make in the light of postmodernity?

---

[29] Eddie Gibbs spoke on the church's changing position in society at the Church Planting Congress in Vancouver (Canada) that I attended (November 19-21, 2003).

Chapter 55

SATURATION HOUSE CHURCH PLANTING

ROBERT FITTS, SR.

Robert Fitts, Sr., with his wife Joni, has spent over 50 years serving the Lord as pastor, teacher, missionary, evangelist, children's worker, and author. His writings and travels have touched many nations. Robert travels internationally encouraging the formation of a 4H strategy that includes house churches, home bible colleges, houses of prayer, and healing rooms (www.robertfitts.com). [The following excerpts are taken from Robert Fitts (2001), The Church in the House. Adapted and used by permission from the author. Email: robertjoni@aol.com].

INTRODUCTION

One of the leading exponents for church planting in this century was the late Donald McGavran. In a *Dawn Report*, Jim Montgomery related the following incident:

> During the last months of Mary McGavran's illness, my wife Lyn would frequently spend time with her. Donald McGavran would be there, too, disregarding his own painful cancer while taking care of his beloved Mary. 'You can be sure Jim and I will continue our commitment to church growth after you're gone,' Lyn said to Donald one day. 'Don't call it church growth anymore,' was his quick response. 'Call it church multiplication!' Two weeks before his death, he said, 'The only way we will get the job of the great commission done is to plant a church in every community in the world.'

There is more interest today in missions, world evangelization and church planting than ever before in history. In AD 100 there were 360 believers for every one believer. In 1500 the ratio was 69 to one. In 1900 it was 27 to one. And in 1990 it was seven to one. Ralph Winter is the founder of the U.S. Center for World Mission. Concerning this shrinking ratio, he says, "In the last 20 centuries the meek have quietly been inheriting the earth!" Just as Jesus predicted, his church is irresistibly penetrating all the earth. We're getting closer to the time when truly the "earth will be filled with the knowledge of the Lord."[1]

---

[1] Hab 2:14 (NIV)

CHURCHES BY THE MILLIONS

When I first read the book by Jim Montgomery, *Dawn 2000*, with a subtitle that I could hardly believe, *Seven Million Churches To Go*, I thought to myself, "How could anyone even dare to think in terms of planting millions of churches?" I hadn't read long before I knew that I could also believe with Jim Montgomery for seven million churches to be planted throughout the world because we are on the leading edge of the strongest missionary movement in history. There is more interest in reaching every tongue, tribe and nation now than there ever has been since Jesus died and rose again and ascended to the Father. Not only in the USA, Canada and England, but from Brazil to South Africa to Russia to Korea to Chile to India to China and throughout the islands of the sea, the cry is:

> *Let's finish the task! Let's fulfill the command of Christ to*
> *preach the gospel to every creature and disciple all the*
> *nations and bring Christ back to reign in righteousness as*
> *the kingdoms of this world become the kingdoms of our*
> *God and of his Christ.*

This movement is gaining momentum daily. The rock that was cut out of the mountain without hands and came crashing down the mountain and smote the feet of the statue in the vision of the prophet Daniel is growing larger each day! It has already crashed into the feet of this world's system and will soon grow into a mountain that will cover the earth with the knowledge of the Lord as the waters cover the sea.

The key to the fulfillment of the Great Commission is to plant churches. The plan that is attracting the attention of many mission strategists these days is to plant a church in every community of from 500 to 1000 people. Saturation church planting! We will have to discard our stained glass concept of church. We can no longer think of church as buildings. We must begin to think of church as people. And that means people coming together in the name of Jesus in homes, shops, offices, factories, stores, schools, mortuaries, parks, jails, prisons, hospitals, deserted buildings, street corners, halls, women's clubs, service clubs, as well as in dedicated church buildings.

CHURCHES IN EVERY NEIGHBORHOOD

Jesus commanded the church to go into all the world and disciple all the nations. According to mission strategists, there are thousands of nations, or ethnic groups. It is also commonly agreed among church leaders that the only way to disciple a nation is to plant churches within that nation. It is further agreed that it will take more than a few churches to disciple a nation. It will require a strategy that envisions *saturation church planting*, which means planting churches in every neighborhood of 500 to 1000 people. This vision for saturation church planting is not only for developing nations. It is for all nations including Europe, Latin America, and the United States. There is no church that is reaching all the unsaved in any city or even a neighborhood. We do not need to fear that saturation house church planting will draw people away from existing churches if we could see it as a multiplying of new congregations. Then every church within a given city could be active in saturating their city with the gospel, rather than trying to build one huge congregation. We need all the help we can get to reach out to those in need. If a house church movement will speed up the evangelization of my city, I want to start as many house churches as I can and see that they multiply. I am also committed to encouraging any traditional pastor in his efforts to multiply congregations within my city or any other city.

CAN WE SIMPLIFY OUR CONCEPT OF 'CHURCH'?

Can we consider simplifying our concept of church so that we can more effectively reach the cities and the nations? How important is it to us to have a large congregation with large offerings and beautiful buildings? We have been led to believe that these are sure signs of success in the ministry, and so we strive to raise up such a congregation. We want to be a success in the eyes of our people, our leaders, and in our own eyes, consequently, we get caught in this web of deception. This produces a spirit of greed, selfishness, pride, and possessiveness. In this climate there is no thought of sending anyone out to the mission field or down the street to start another congregation. The only thought that meets with approval in such churches is something that will add more people to that congregation. The Spirit of God is grieved in such churches. Instead, let us be kingdom minded and focus on developing an army of unpaid leaders to plant simple, inexpensive, welcoming, home-based congregations that could saturate our cities with the good news of God's love and forgiveness through Jesus Christ the Lord!

CAN WE SIMPLIFY OUR CONCEPT OF 'LEADERSHIP'?

Some are concerned that a strategy for multiplying house churches will lead to inept, unqualified leaders. Jesus did not go to the religious institutions of his day to pick the men he would use to lead out in building his church. He chose fishermen and ordinary men whom he empowered with the Holy Spirit. God loves to use little things and weak things:

> For you see your calling, brethren, how that not many wise men after the flesh, not many mighty, not many noble, are called. But God has chosen the foolish things of the world to confound the wise: and God has chosen the weak things of the world to confound the things which are mighty. And base things of the world, and things which are despised, has God chosen, yea, and things which are not, to bring to naught things that are: That no flesh should glory in his presence.[2]

---

[2] 1 Cor 1:26-29 (NIV)

In every movement that has had worldwide significance in the spread of the gospel throughout the history of the church, lay men and women have had a leading role. John Wesley was a man of great learning with years of education and religious training, but as the leader of one of the great revival and church planting movements of history he did not go to the established schools of religious training to find his pastors and leaders. He said:

> Give me 12 men who love Jesus with all their hearts and who do not fear men or devils and I care not one whit whether they be clergy or laity, with these men I will change the world.

And that is just what Mr. Wesley did! To preach the gospel in the open air in Wesley's day was the height of sacrilege and a serious affront to the established church. It was unthinkable in the Church of England to stand outside of the walls of the holy sanctuaries to proclaim the sacred word of God. The Wesley brothers and George Whitefield suffered years of persecution for breaking the long-standing traditions of the established church, but this did not deter them. They knew the Scriptures and were convinced that if Jesus could do it, it was acceptable for them to do the same as well.

Drawing again from the writings of the father of the church growth movement, Dr. McGavran, I quote from his book:

> Develop unpaid lay leaders. Laymen have played a great part in urban expansions of the Church. One secret of growth in the cities of Latin America has been that, from the beginning, unpaid common men led the congregations, which therefore appeared to the masses to be truly Chilean or Brazilian affairs. In any land, when laborers, mechanics, clerks, or truck drivers teach the Bible, lead in prayer, tell what God has done for them, or exhort the brethren, the Christian religion looks and sounds natural to ordinary men. Whatever unpaid laymen, earning their living as others do, subject to the same hazards and bound by the same work schedules, lack in correctness of Bible teaching or beauty of prayers, they more than make up for by their intimate contact with their own people. No paid worker from the outside and certainly no missionary from abroad can know as much about a neighborhood as someone who has dozens of relatives and intimates all about him. True, on new ground the outsider has to start new expansions. No one else can. But the sooner he turns the churches over to local men the better.[3]

---

[3] Donald McGavran (1970), *Understanding Church Growth*, Eerdmans.

David Womack, an Assemblies of God missionary, writes:

> There is only one way the Great Commission can be fulfilled, and that is by establishing gospel-preaching congregations in every community on the face of the earth.[4]

Roger Greenway, a specialist in reaching cities, writes:

> The church's evangelistic task demands that every barrio, apartment building, and neighborhood have a church faithful to God's word established in it.[5]

THE QUALIFICATIONS FOR HOUSE CHURCH PASTORS

Because house church pastors are unpaid and not necessarily seminary trained, does not mean there are no requirements at all for these leaders. The New Testament recognizes the need for qualified individuals to lead these home-based congregations. But, this may be different from what we have traditionally thought and done. The apostles discuss the necessary qualifications for such a pastor.[6] We note, however, that the term pastor (shepherd) is interchangeable with the terms bishop (overseer) and presbyter (elder).[7] Pastors are to be of good character, have basic management skills, and be able to teach. Specifically, the qualifications are: blameless, one wife, believing obedient children, hospitable, lover of the good, self-controlled, holy, disciplined, able to teach, temperate, respectable, not given to much wine, not violent, not quarrelsome, not a lover of money, manages well his own household, mature in the things of the Lord, a good reputation. That's it! These are simply the qualities of a spiritual man; a man fully consecrated to Jesus Christ. The reason we have traditionally put our leaders through such rigorous training in so many different fields of knowledge is that we have moved away from simplicity and into complexity.

THE NEED FOR HOUSE CHURCH PASTORS

Let us believe God for a restoration in these days of godly house church pastors who will open up their homes, reach out to their neighbors, and see their city reached for Christ! We cannot allow the enemy to achieve so great a victory as to deny the church the ministry of those truly called and anointed by God to pastor. We should not reject having unpaid pastors in the house churches because some traditional pastors have been self-centered, self-serving, and abusive in their position of spiritual authority. Where there is the counterfeit, there is always the genuine and the authentic. We have no more right to cancel out the ministry of pastor than we do to cancel out the

---

[4] David Womack (1973), *Breaking the Stained Glass Barrier*, Harper and Row.
[5] Roger Greenway (1979), *Discipling the City*, Baker Book House.
[6] 1 Tim 3:1-7, Titus 1:5-9
[7] Acts 20:17,28-30; 1 Pet 5:1-3; Gerald Cowen (2003), *Who Rules the Church?* Broadman and Holman Publishers, pp.5-16.

ministry of apostle, prophet, evangelist, or teacher. They are all ordained of God to function for the upbuilding of the church. The house church pastor is part of the team to bring the Body up to strength to be able to minister to itself and to reach out to the world. The Scripture says:

> And his gifts were that some should be apostles, some prophets, some evangelists, some pastors and teachers, to equip the saints for the work of ministry...[for]...the building up of the Body of Christ, until we all attain to the unity of the faith and of the knowledge of the Son of God, to mature manhood, to the measure of the stature of the fullness of Christ...from whom the whole body, joined and knit together by every joint by which it is supplied, when each part is working properly, makes bodily growth and upbuilds itself in love.[8]

THE ROLE OF HOUSE CHURCH PASTORS

Some time ago I was praying about how to begin functioning as a pastor. I honestly did not know how far to back off in order to allow the Body to function. "Lord", I prayed, "Give me wisdom in this matter." The Lord heard my prayer and gave me two little parables from my own life that have helped me to understand my role as a pastor. First, he spoke to me using a tomato plant. While eating lunch one day with my wife I remarked how tasty the tomatoes were that we had raised out on our patio. "The tomatoes in the super markets are nothing like these." I said, "These are so much more delicious!" Just as I spoke those words, I heard the Lord say, "How much did you do to bring forth that tomato?" "Not very much," I thought to myself, "I just prepared the soil in a clay pot, bought the tomato plants, put the roots under the soil, and watered them from time to time. A couple of times I put some plant food in the water." "That's how it is with the church." the Lord said. "You didn't have to do very much for those tomato plants to do their thing. You just had to set the conditions for growth and they grew. It is programmed into their genes to work day and night to bring forth those beautiful, red, juicy, delicious tomatoes. So it is with the church. It is organic and if you will just work with me to set the conditions, the church will grow of its own accord. It will produce for I have ordained it to be so."

Not long after that the Lord gave me another analogy that I have remembered and shared with others. I was down on the beach early in the morning as was my custom when we lived in Laguna Beach, California a few years ago. I used to go down almost every morning with a beach chair, some matches and old newspapers, some books and my Bible. There was always plenty of driftwood that I could gather off the beach to build my fire. On this particular morning I built my fire as usual and after an hour or so, I

---

[8] Eph 4:11-13 (NIV)

took a walk on the beach. When I returned the fire had died down. I found some more wood and stoked the hot coals, then put the wood on the coals. In less than a minute I had a good fire going again. I sat down to enjoy the fire a little longer before going up to the house for breakfast. As I sat looking into the fire the Lord spoke to me, "That's how the church is. It is like watching over this fire. You cannot make a fire burn. You can only set the conditions for a fire to burn. Then when it dies down, you can rekindle the flames as you see the need. You cannot bring the fire of my Spirit, but you can help set the stage for his coming. I want you to enjoy overseeing the church. All you have to do is just be ready to stir the coals and put on more fuel. The fire burns of its own accord. This is the work of an elder."

CONCLUSIONS

God is calling us back to simplicity. And he is also calling us to recognize the men and women that he is bringing into leadership as house church pastors. If we will simplify our concept of church, we will automatically simplify our requirements for leadership. And as we simplify our requirement for leadership to reflect New Testament requirements rather than traditional requirements, we will see a releasing of all the saints into ministry and the emergence of church planting movements that can touch every neighborhood!

STUDY QUESTIONS

1. Is the phrase "Seven Million Churches to Go!" more realistic for house churches or traditional churches?

2. As you consider your town or city, name specific things that would have to happen in order to see churches in every neighborhood.

3. How can unpaid house church pastors function in a healthy way as part of the Body of Christ?

Chapter 56

THE SPONTANEOUS EXPANSION OF HOUSE CHURCH MOVEMENTS

JOHN WHITE

John White is a graduate of Fuller Seminary who served as a Presbyterian pastor for 20 years in Denver, CO, USA. He is currently the US Coordinator for Dawn Ministries. The Dawn Vision is for a church (a vibrant family of Jesus) within easy access of every person in North America and beyond Website: www.dawnministries.org/globalministries/north%20america.htm. Email: denverwh@aol.com.

INTRODUCTION

In general, the traditional church could be called the 'The Programmed Church', which uses man's best efforts (e.g. plans, strategies, goals, meetings, etc.) to accomplish God's purposes. This intentional approach is usually characterized by 'the gospel of knowledge and duty'. That is, the assumption that Christians will become more godly and the Great Commission will be fulfilled if only those believers are given more information and are exhorted more forcefully to obey God (i.e., external motivation). While usually well intentioned, my view is that this approach is deeply flawed and is a departure from both the life of Jesus and the life of the early church. The alternative to the program mentality is an intimate, conversational relationship with the Holy Spirit (i.e., internal motivation) resulting organically and spontaneously in the life and mission of the church.

This discussion is also central to the house church movement. The current danger is that this 'program mentality' will be brought along with the many people moving out of the traditional churches and into house church networks. Already, some house churches have become simply traditional churches held in a home. However, house church, properly understood, is much more than a mere change in venue. It is, in fact, an entirely new way of engaging in church life and mission.

With the help of the great English missiologist Roland Allen from the early part of the 20th century and other authors, we will briefly explore three aspects of 'The Spontaneous Church'. The word 'spontaneous' comes from *sponte,* meaning voluntarily, occurring without apparent external cause, unconstrained, and unstudied in behavior.[1] First, we will see that this

---

[1] *Webster's II, New Riverside University Dictionary,* The Riverside Publishing Company, 1994.

concept is rooted in Scripture. It is foundational to the life and ministry of both Jesus and the Holy Spirit and is modeled by the early church. Second, we will explore in greater depth the differences between 'The Programmed Church' and 'The Spontaneous Church'. Third, we will touch briefly on some ways of seeing this New Testament way of life and ministry impact the house church movement.

THE SPONTANEOUS CHURCH IN SCRIPTURE

The life and ministry of the early church grew out of the life and ministry modeled by Jesus before Pentecost and the way it was directed by the Holy Spirit after Pentecost.

The Life & Ministry of Jesus: Nothing on His own Initiative

Even though Jesus was the Son of God, he did not initiate or implement his own plans regarding preaching, healing, raising the dead, choosing the inner circle of 12 disciples, etc. Everything flowed from an intimate relationship with his Father. The Father initiated, and Jesus responded.[2] John 5:19-20 is a foundational passage for understanding the life and ministry of Jesus in this regard. Consider the two following versions of that passage:

> Jesus gave them this answer: "I tell you the truth, the Son can do nothing by himself; he can do only what he sees his Father doing, because whatever the Father does the Son also does. For the Father loves the Son and shows him all he does.[3]

> So Jesus explained himself at length. "I'm telling you this straight. The Son can't independently do a thing, only what he sees the Father doing. What the Father does, the Son does. The Father loves the Son and includes him in everything he is doing.[4]

The Life & Ministry of the Holy Spirit: Nothing on His own Initiative

Perhaps one of Jesus' most surprising statements—at least to those who heard it at the time—was his remark that it was a good thing that he was going away.[5] This began to make sense to his disciples when he explained that he would send the *Paraklete* (Greek = 'counselor') in his place. One of the primary purposes of the *Paraklete* was to enable the disciples to live and minister the same way Jesus did.[6] Jesus described the way communication occurs within the Trinity. The Father told Jesus everything that he was doing.[7] Jesus then told all that he had heard from the Father to the Spirit.[8]

---

[2] John 8:28-29, 12:49-50, 14:10-14, 15:14-15
[3] John 5:19-20 (NIV)
[4] John 5:19-20 (The Message)
[5] John 16:7
[6] John 16:12-15
[7] John 5:19-20, 16:15

The Spirit heard from Jesus and passed that on to believers, as individuals and collectively as the church. Believers were to hear from the Spirit and pass that on to others still. From John 16:12, it is evident that the Spirit functioned the same way Jesus did, that is, he did not initiate on his own. He only made known what he heard from Jesus. Jesus initiated, and the Spirit responded.

The Life & Ministry of the Early Church: Nothing on Its own Initiative

A look at the way the early Christian communities functioned shows that they, too, attempted to do nothing on their own initiative, but waited for the guidance and empowerment of the Spirit.

Jesus as the Builder of the Church. Jesus said he was the head of the church. He made it clear that it was his church, and he was the one who would build it.[9] He called believers to join him in the process. It is also true that he cared more about the fulfillment of the Great Commission than his first followers ever could. Further, he was the expert on incarnational ministry. Christians could learn all of these things from him. Therefore, prayer—especially the aspect of listening—was to be the starting place and the foundation for all future ministry.

Prevenience: He was always Initiating. By saying that it was Jesus who was building his church, believers were reminded that he was always the one who initiated. His initiation was always a response to the prior initiation of the Father. A helpful—though non-biblical—term for this is 'prevenience', which means 'going before' or 'preceding'. In a region or people group, God was always working preveniently, preparing people's hearts to receive the message of Christ before they had even heard it. This can be especially seen in the case of the Samaritan woman, the Roman officer Cornelius, and the cloth merchant Lydia.[10] This understanding changed everything. It meant that it was no longer the believer's job to 'make something happen'. Rather, the early Christians were to see what God was already doing and ask how or if they were to join him. An understanding of and commitment to the prevenience principle was key to the spontaneous nature of the early church.

The structure of the Jewish day illustrates this concept. The day began with sundown. The first thing people did was sleep. This is a picture of 'prevenience'. People then awoke to find a world where God has already been at work. Similarly, the job of the follower of Christ also is to find out what God has already been doing and see how they are to join him in that day. Believers are called to have an awareness that God has already been at work before they ever arrive on the scene, and that their actions as agents of change are always merely responses to God's initiative.

---

[8] John 16:12-15
[9] Matt 16:18
[10] John 4::4-42; Acts 10:1-48, 16:13-15

This prevenient work of God, then, led to the spontaneous life and ministry of the early church. In the biography written by Roland Allen's grandson, Leslie Newbigin writes the following:

> At the center of Allen's message was the conviction that the Holy Spirit is the active agent in the Christian mission. For him Pentecost was the key for the understanding of mission. He could write about "The Spontaneous Expansion of the Church" because he saw it, not as a human enterprise, but as a divine activity. To understand that is to be delivered from the anxieties, the burdens and the sense of guilt which so often form the atmosphere of discussion about mission. Missionary thinking is still pervaded by Pelagianism. Mission is conceived not as a task, rather than as a gift, an over-spill, and an explosion of joy.[11]

The Church's Ministry Inward. How did prevenience impact the way the Body of Christ ministered inwardly to itself, making sure that every individual member was spiritually healthy? Watchman Nee was a Chinese church leader who was used by God in an earlier generation to lay foundations for the modern house church explosion in that country. He describes the kind of participatory, interactive, and yet humanly undirected church meeting that was typical of the early church as described in 1 Corinthians 14:26. The main purpose of first century church meetings was to allow the Spirit to direct and lead the church in how to edify itself, without necessarily having any preplanned human agenda.

The Church's Mission Outward. How did prevenience influence the way the Body of Christ ministered to the world in word and in deed as it sought to fulfill the Great Commission? Rolland Allen goes on further to challenge our thinking about the nature of the early church's worldwide mandate, suggesting that its accomplishment was pursued without any need for external pressure from others. In examining the New Testament, he suggests that,

> ...the same is true of St. Peter and St. John, and of all the apostolic writers. They do not seem to feel any necessity to repeat the great Commission, and to urge that it is the duty of their converts to make disciples of all the nations. What we read in the New Testament is no anxious appeal to Christians to spread the Gospel, but a note here and there which suggests how the Gospel was being spread abroad...for centuries the Christian Church continued to expand by its own inherent grace, and threw up an

---

[11] Hubert Allen (1998), *Roland Allen: Pioneer, Priest and Prophet*, Forward Movement, p.xiii.

unceasing supply of missionaries without any direct exhortation…As I have said spontaneous expansion is spontaneous. It is not created by exhortation. It springs up unbidden. Where men see it they covet it.[12]

Thus, an outflow sprang up unbidden into mission from inside the first century believer who was actively seeking God's presence as an end in and of itself.

IMPLICATIONS FOR THE HOUSE CHURCH MOVEMENT

Understanding some of the differences between many of today's churches and the churches in the New Testament can help us step forward in a more strategic way in the house church movement.

Relationship Rather Than Function

Generally speaking, the church in many parts of the world has focused more on function (task) than on relationship (intimacy). Discipleship especially is seen as a task rather than as a relationship. We have developed programs and tools to accomplish the task, but have often missed a profound connection with the heart of God and others. As a result, the programs have not really worked in many cases. We have to continually exhort people to do the right things. Over time, they give up on the task because their hearts are not engaged. We should take care not to introduce this kind of ethos into the church.

The Toll of the Gospel of Duty and Obligation. Our gospel of duty and obligation ('make it happen') has taken a great toll on believers—especially those in leadership. One of the most difficult places to live as a Christian is in leadership of a church or para-church ministry. There is huge pressure to 'get the job done'. Often this destroys relationships with other leaders and even with God. Often little genuine transformation occurs.[13] There is a high degree of burnout with disastrous consequences for marriages and families.

Mission as a Natural Fruit. The house church model is a new, yet old, wineskin. It is very precious to Jesus and, therefore, it is important to not put the cart (i.e. mission) before the horse (i.e. listening to God). The concern is that house churches not be used simply as tools to get other things done, like evangelism. We must not put the old wine of exhorting people to mission into the new wineskin. Mission is meant to be a natural fruit and not an obligation.

Mission is like Marriage. Consider the analogy of marriage. People get married out of love, not in order to have children. Children are the fruit of relationship. They happen naturally. This is the way God wants to birth things. Again, a movement will only be sustained if mission (children) is the

---

[12] Roland Allen (1962), *The Spontaneous Expansion of the Church*, Eerdmans, pp.7,155. Used by permission of Lutterworth (UK).
[13] George Barna (2005), *Revolution*, BarnaBooks.

fruit of a marriage, not its purpose. What is the primary reason for our existence? Is it relational or functional? In writing about the Trinity, Darrell Johnson says,

> And here is the Gospel: The God who is love draws near to *me*, a sinful, mere mortal, to draw *me* near to Himself, in order to draw *me* within the circle of Lover, Beloved and Love itself. I become a co-lover with God! It is the very reason for my existence.[14]

Internal Rather Than External Motivation

Does motivation for ministry come from the inside or outside? How we answer this question reveals in large part why we make the decisions we make as Christians, both individually and as churches.

Symptom vs. Cause. We all agree that the Great Commission is important. The key issue is how it is to be accomplished. When we consider people not being involved in mission, we need to make sure we are making the right diagnosis. What is the symptom, and what is the cause? Diminished mission may be the symptom and not the cause. By and large, we are all committed to the concept of mission, the expansion of the kingdom. The question is: how does this come about? Is it internally motivated by the Holy Spirit working in the heart of the believer? Or is it externally motivated by teachings, exhortations, and strategies?

Those Who Have 'Life' Don't Need to be Exhorted. The reason that many Christians do not engage in evangelism and missions more is not because they have not been exhorted. It is not because they do not have enough training. Rather, it is that they have so little 'life'. Consider the story of Jesus. People ripped roofs off in order to get to him. Why? Because they saw life in Jesus.[15] When people have that kind of life in them, it will flow naturally into mission. It will flow spontaneously from the inside out. This is a much better model than trying to motivate people from the outside. Roland Allen suggests the following:

> This then is what I mean by spontaneous expansion. I mean the expansion which follows the unexhorted and unorganized activity of individual members of the Church explaining to others the Gospel which they have found for themselves; I mean the expansion which follows the irresistible attraction of the Christian Church for men who see its order life, and are drawn to it by desire to discover the secret of a life which they instinctively desire to share...[16]

---

[14] D. Johnson (2002), *Experiencing the Trinity*, Regent College Publishing, p.63.
[15] John 1:4
[16] R. Allen, *The Spontaneous*, p.7. Used by permission of Lutterworth (UK).

Our Mission: The Manifestation of the Spirit from Within. What is the role of the Christian leader involved in the house church movement? I believe it is one of encouraging people to seek God relationally on an ongoing basis. If people do this thing—the main thing—then mission will naturally flow out of them. Roland Allen remarks that,

> The work of the missionary is education in this sense: it is the use of means to reveal to his coverts a spiritual power which they actually possess and of which they are dimly conscious. As the converts exercise that power, as they yield themselves to the indwelling Spirit, they discover the greatness of the power and the grace of the Spirit, and in so doing they reveal it to their teacher. But we are like a teacher who cannot resist telling their pupils the answer the moment a difficulty arises...The work of the missionary cannot be done by imposing things from without. The one result which he desires is the growth and manifestation of the Spirit from within.[17]

Prevenience Rather Than Programs

Is ministry initiated by us or by God? The answer to this question tells us about who we really think is in charge of the church on a day-to-day basis.

Functional Deism. We have to learn to do nothing on our own initiative. For many of us, we have learned well how to do something, how to engage in activity, how to accomplish tasks. This is the definition of a program—our best efforts to accomplish God's purposes. This is functional deism. God got everything started, gave us instructions, and then left us fully in charge. On a practical level, this denies the role of the Holy Spirit. In principle, we would deny that this is our theology. But the way we have done church exposes our true beliefs. Stated humorously, for many of us as Evangelicals, our trinity in practice has been the Father, the Son, and the 'Holy Strategy'.

Power Evangelism rather than Program Evangelism. When it comes to sharing our faith in Jesus, our preference for program-driven evangelism over power evangelism sometimes also creeps in. In the program-driven approach, Christians are taught that they should witness to everyone they meet regardless of circumstances or timing, with the hope that some will respond positively. However, in power evangelism, not every person that the Christian encounters is to be witnessed to. Rather, it is the Holy Spirit—who knows both the circumstances and timing that will produce fruit—who prods the Christian to witness to a particular person. The Christian's responsibility is simply obedience to the Lord's leading.

Not Both/And. It may be suggested that 'The Programmed Church' and 'The Spontaneous Church' can, and often do, coexist to accomplish God's

---

[17] Roland Allen (1962), *Missionary Methods: Paul's or Ours?* Eerdmans, p.146.

purposes. And that this is acceptable for the house church movement. Though it is true that God has a way of working through our flawed natures and plans to achieve his aims, it is not his preference. Rather, I would argue, God would deeply desire for us to be fully responsive to his plans instead. In a similar vein, Roland Allen believed that fully genuine Christian mission in the world cannot blend the God-initiated with the man-made:

> Nothing could be clearer than that Allen saw "mission" as the "unexhorted and unorganized activity of individual members of the Church" who were impelled by the Spirit. The fact that Allen was not willing to accept a "both/and" perspective was one of the things that got him in so much trouble with the church leaders of his day.[18]

HOW TO BECOME THE SPONTANEOUS CHURCH

Allow me to offer some first steps towards a way of doing and being church that flows spontaneously from conversational intimacy with the Spirit.

Learning to Do Nothing on Our Own Initiative

We have become addicted to taking the initiative, to doing something, to developing programs to accomplish God's purposes. Giving up this addiction is difficult and requires that we go through a period in which unlearn bad habits in order to relearn good habits. The first step in this regard may be that we stop trying to impress God with our ability to achieve things for him. John Piper suggests that,

> [Ps. 50:15] forces on us the startling fact that we must beware of serving God, and must take special care to let Him serve us, lest we rob Him of his glory. This sounds very strange. Most of us think serving God is a totally positive thing; we have not considered that serving God may be an insult to him.[19]

Learning to Listen to the Spirit to Find Out What the Father is Doing

The next step may be that we slow down enough and become quiet enough, so that God then has the opportunity to speak to us things that we otherwise may not be able or willing to hear. We should learn to discern the activity of God already in progress in an individual, a group, and/or a situation.

Learning to Live from Our Heart

Passion comes from calling. Passion comes from one's calling, not from exhortation or from someone else's passion. We should not project our calling or passion onto others. It is better to help them find God's calling for

---

[18] Hubert Allen (1998), *Roland Allen: Pioneer, Priest and Prophet*, Forward Movement, p.xiii.

[19] John Piper (1986), *Desiring God*, (c) 1986, 1996, 2003, Desiring God Foundation, Multnomah Publishers, a division of Random House, Inc., p.138.

them, and let their passion emerge. Let us not promote just one passion, such as evangelism or missions. Rather, let us get people hooked up to God's heart, and let each one find what they are called to do.

Learning to Tell Stories

What, then, is the job of Christian leaders? One aspect of a leader's job description may be to discover and tell stories of spontaneous church and missions—so that others can get excited about it too—rather than pressurizing people to respond dutifully. The answer might not be in revolution or reform, but in the retelling of a new story or of an old story in a fresh and inviting way, the same way the Master did with his parables.

THE KEY TO COMPLETING THE GREAT COMMISSION: FAITHFULNESS

The world has many strategies to reach a large number of people. Jesus has a different plan—he emphasizes the quality of faithful obedience. The Master says, "'Well done, my good servant!' his master replied. 'Because you have been trustworthy in a very small matter, take charge of ten cities.'"[20] The Master also says something quite similar, "His master replied, 'Well done, good and faithful servant! You have been faithful with a few things; I will put you in charge of many things."[21] We may think that the goal of making disciples of all nations is a huge and almost impossible task. We may think that this task will require an immense amount of work by brilliant and highly gifted people. The Master, however, sees this differently. He is prepared to give us not one city but ten! He is not necessarily looking for highly gifted people, but rather highly faithful (i.e. trustworthy and obedient) people. Our job is to be clear about the few, small assignments the Master will give us. If we demonstrate to God that he can trust us with the few and the small, he will indeed give us the many and the large. What is *your* assignment?

STUDY QUESTIONS

1. Describe 'The Programmed Church' vs. 'The Spontaneous Church.'
2. Can both of these approaches coexist within the Body of Christ?
3. In what practical ways would you like to see your house church network become more Spirit-led and spontaneous?

---

[20] Luke 19:17 (NIV)
[21] Matt 25:21 (NIV)

Chapter 57

CAN HOUSE CHURCHES BE PART OF THE REGIONAL CHURCH?

LARRY KREIDER

Larry Kreider serves as the director of DOVE Christian Fellowship International (www.dcfi.org), a global family of cell churches and house church networks. He is the author of numerous books, including House to House: Spiritual Insights for the 21st Century Church (2000) and House Church Networks: A Church for a New Generation (2001).

INTRODUCTION

In the New Testament, each church was identified by its geographical location. The Body of Christ met in house churches within a city, and they were unified by their specific city boundaries: the church of Antioch, the church of Corinth, the church of Jerusalem, the church of Smyrna. Today, however, the church has been divided into many different denominations and ministries within one geographical area. Their doctrinal interpretations and worship styles vary, but each church has its strengths and weaknesses as it empowers people for ministry in their city. Within a city or region, churches of all kinds that intentionally work together can impact their city for God. God is bringing people of various backgrounds and affiliations together in unity and using these connections to accomplish his purposes.

UNITY IN DIVERSITY

In the church, we need to maintain healthy relationships with the spiritual leaders of our own church movement, and we also need to keep healthy relationships with the spiritual leaders of our city or region. When a corporation runs a car through an assembly line, the parts have been gathered from companies all over the world. Similarly, there is a unique mix of denominations and church families in each city. Each church and ministry is to be respected. As we walk together in unity in our region, the Lord will command a blessing.

The Lord is restoring the unity in the church that he prayed for: "That all of them may be one, Father, just as you are in me and I am in you. May they also be in us so that the world may believe that you have sent me."[1] The primary reason Jesus prayed for unity is not simply so that we become one, big family of believers. The ultimate purpose of unity is for the harvest. No one church can reach the harvest themselves. Harvesting is a team effort.

---

[1] John 17:21 (NIV)

Our unity is a witness to a lost and dying world of the reality of Jesus' power to change lives. When the world sees Christians loving each other and working together, despite differences, they cannot deny God's love.

Walls that have divided denominations and churches for centuries are coming down throughout the world at an increasing rate. Pastors in the same town who never knew one another are now finding each other, praying together regularly, and supporting each other. This includes both traditional churches and house churches.

When one studies the revivals found in church history, it is the unity among pastors and church leaders in a region that was often a prerequisite to revival in that region. Apostolic leaders serving towns, cities, and regions carry the mantle of unity that brings revival. There are apostolic leaders who serve in leadership within movements, and some who serve in leadership within regions. Some serve in both areas of leadership. They are not self-appointed, but recognized by the leadership of the church and ministries in the region they represent.

Several new house church leaders I know say that they meet with traditional church pastors in their area on a regular basis. This desire to network comes from a similar desire to receive encouragement from spiritual fathers and mothers. When each house church, although a full church in itself, is committed to network with other churches in their city or region, it keeps them from pride, exclusiveness, and heresy. House churches, and churches of any kind, should never be exclusive entities cut off from the rest of the Body of Christ.

The Lord's plan is for local church leaders in our region to protect us, help us grow, and equip us to be all that we can be in Jesus Christ. Healthy leaders will want to relate closely to the rest of the Body of Christ because they want to be 'one with the Father and each other'.

BELIEVERS CAN CIRCULATE WITHIN THE REGIONAL CHURCH

The heart of the Scriptures teaches us that it is the Lord's desire for us to experience his kingdom being built and expanded in our particular region of the world. Building like this as a regional church is not an attempt to do away with denominations or to compromise the vision to which house church networks are committed. Churches within a collective regional church can maintain their flavor, while working in a unified manner to more effectively share Christ in their geographical area. In short, when unbelievers see the unity of churches in their community, they will be attracted to Christianity. Our God has called us to become one as he and his Son are one, and by this all men shall know that we are his disciples, because we have love for one another. Traditional churches as well as house church networks can work together to represent the church—the Body of Christ—in a region.

Look at what the church in your community could look like in the coming days. Many kinds of churches can work together to form the regional church which will have a significant impact in discipling people and changing lives. Some traditional churches will commission leaders to start house churches and give them the encouragement needed to help them grow. Others will assist house churches in their communities to network together. Still other traditional churches will commission future house church leaders to join with house church networks in their region. On the other hand, even though most house churches will continue to birth new house churches, some house churches might eventually become traditional churches. It is also possible that some people may be in a house church network for a season, and then shift to a traditional church. However, it is the entire church in each of our regions that matters.

LEADERS CAN HELP UNIFY THE REGIONAL CHURCH

Over the next few years, we believe there will be an emergence of spiritual leaders from various backgrounds who will form teams of spiritual leadership to encourage this collective, regional church. These apostolic leaders will serve the church in towns, cities, and regions to resource the Body of Christ. They will not think only in terms of pastoring a church or churches, but will think and pray in terms of sensing a responsibility with other fellow servant-leaders throughout the Body of Christ for their region.

Although these 'leaders of the region' will be concerned about unity, it will not be their focus. Their main focus will be on the Lord and on his mandate to reach the lost as the Lord brings in his harvest. The regional church will include all the types of churches in a geographical location. All church movements operating in a region can have a redemptive purpose to meet the needs of that particular region.

Leaders of all denominations and movements will also be wise to reach out to those within their family of churches that are feeling called to start house church networks to foster this kind of unity.

DOWNSIZING CAN HELP GROW THE REGIONAL CHURCH

Corporations that face an increasingly stiff competition from competitors in the global economy are familiar with the term 'downsizing'. Corporations that downsize rid themselves of unessential costs and liabilities. They may downsize their work force or inventory in order to cut unnecessary costs. This is one way they can continue to exist and expect to be profitable.

Traditional churches and house churches in a region would do well to work together to utilize all their resources more fully. Why not downsize by sharing resources? We believe we will discover myriads of ways that churches can rid themselves of unessential costs and liabilities.

We look forward to the day when we can be so flexible that we will allow church buildings in our communities to be utilized every day of the week. Many traditional churches currently use their buildings for a few chosen meetings (Sunday morning worship service, midweek prayer meeting, etc.), and the church facility remains unused the rest of the week.

A traditional church can offer or rent their facilities to several different house church networks that want to meet in a larger setting each month. The house churches could meet on Sunday nights or on a weeknight when the church does not need its facilities. That would be divine efficiency!

In fact, DOVE Christian Fellowship in our region has launched some new house churches that have come together monthly in the building of a traditional church which is not part of DOVE. When churches share buildings like this, the money that is saved on constructing new buildings and maintaining old buildings can be given to missions and to the poor.

AN EXAMPLE OF THE REGIONAL CHURCH

In most every region or city you will find house churches, as well as more traditional churches. All churches can work together to impact their city.

In 2000, the senior pastor and eldership team of the traditional church where my wife and I served, gave their blessing to our involvement in coaching a new house church network in our area. We are now part of an awesome house church that meets every week in a home in Lancaster County (Pennsylvania, USA). We have a blast each week eating together, praying together, reaching out to non-Christians together, and practically serving one another.

Some of the new believers in our house church have even joined us some Sunday mornings in visiting our previous church. They appreciate the worship experience and the Bible teaching. There have been some house church members who felt called to leave us and join traditional churches.

We also try to find practical ways to serve the more traditional churches in our community. For example, a group of churches in our region was trying to raise enough money to give to a group of missionaries and international church leaders; however, they were not able to raise the money that was needed. Our house church made the decision to give a few thousand dollars to meet the need. Where did we come up with the money? House churches have money! After all, we do not have building mortgages to pay, no pastor salary to pay, and no electric bill to pay. Our leaders are all bi-vocational, and we meet in a home. The mortgage has already been paid. God has blessed the house church financially so we can serve the Body of Christ in our region.

A broader regional unity is also beginning among the churches in our region. During the past few years, a local regional Christian leadership group has emerged and is in place to "empower the church in its many expressions throughout the region."[2] This leadership community is quite diverse. It consists of men and women of tested Christian character and of good reputation within the church and in their spheres of influence in society at large. Pastors, teachers, doctors, legislators, psychiatrists, counselors,

---

[2] www.theregionalchurch.com

ministry leaders, artists, authors, corporate CEOs, and business professionals are joined together in growing relational unity for the sake of the call of Christ to go into all the world with the love of God and the gospel message of salvation through Christ Jesus. Hundreds of Christian leaders in our region are committed to working together as a leadership community regardless of their affiliation. This group is not an organization to join, but a network of leaders devoted to relationships and partnership.

Through prayer and fasting, 20 Christian leaders have emerged to work together on a council to oversee the Christian leadership community. Council members include Christian leaders from many types of churches and key ministry leaders. Some are members of traditional churches, while others are members of new house church networks, but all are members of the Body of Christ in our region.

The vision is to "see the church maturing in Christ, strategically serving together to revitalize the church, give a Christ-centered witness to each resident, and bring transformation to the way of life in this region." This regional team is committed to cooperate in establishing the kingdom of God in the home, neighborhood, community, and marketplace. When the Body of Christ joins in unity like this, we are bound to see results.

One regional member astutely remarks, "The Regional Church represents a very special time in the history of our region. Churches and ministries from a variety of persuasions are coming together, not as an ecumenical movement but as a God-led movement, to see our county impacted by Jesus Christ himself." This effort is an attempt to coordinate, rather than control, the work of God in our region. Cooperative efforts must always have this perspective. We are certainly not yet in revival, but the Lord has brought down walls that had been erected by the enemy between churches and denominations for generations.

CONCLUSIONS

Churches networking effectively in our communities will give the opportunity for thousands of new churches to be planted rapidly all across our nation and in the nations of the world. Is it asking too much for churches to work together like this? Perhaps we have taken the simple gospel and the simple New Testament church and complicated it. Let's get back to the simplicity of the gospel and the simplicity of relational church life.

STUDY QUESTIONS

1. What are some practical ways that traditional churches and house church networks can work together to impact their region?
2. What are the pros and cons of the regional church idea?
3. What practical steps can you take right now to reach out to other Christian believers and churches in your neighborhood, city, or region?

Chapter 58

CAN DENOMINATIONS AND MISSION AGENCIES HELP THE HOUSE CHURCH MOVEMENT?

RAD ZDERO

Rad Zdero earned his Ph.D. degree in Mechanical Engineering from Queen's University (Kingston, ON, Canada) and is the manager of a hospital-based orthopaedic research lab. He has participated in, led, and started house churches and cell groups since 1985. He is currently part of HouseChurch.Ca (www.housechurch.ca), which is a church planting team developing a network of house churches in the greater Toronto area and beyond. He is the author of The Global House Church Movement (2004). [Used by permission of the author. Email: rzdero@yahoo.ca].

INTRODUCTION

A topic of conversation among many is whether denominations and mission agencies (called DMAs from this point forward) can legitimately and feasibly spawn healthy house church movements. Arguments can be made either way as to whether such a thing is possible and/or desirable. The New Testament era church, however, had a theology of unity and utilized a citywide (or regional) church model. The only legitimate biblical reason for division in the Body of Christ—apart from major doctrinal or demographic issues—was geographical distance. Therefore, DMAs are in no way God's best for the Body of Christ. Today's reality, however, is that they do exist. Alongside the many autonomous house church networks in existence around the world, are those who are choosing to work with established Christian organizations to see their house church networks reach their full potential for their own internal health and also for their outward growth through evangelism and church planting. This article provides some preliminary ideas and practical examples of how such partnerships can work effectively.

HOUSE CHURCHES SHOULD COUNT THE COST

House church networks considering joining DMAs should keep several items prayerfully in mind. The issue of such partnerships is a matter of some disagreement among many Christians involved in the house churches. Some are in favor of such efforts because of the accountability, encouragement, and resourcing that can be provided by DMAs. Others are opposed to the idea for theological and practical reasons, being concerned often about undue control from DMAs. Therefore, this author neither encourages nor discourages house churches from participating in DMAs, leaving it up to the conscience and circumstances of individual house church networks.

Advantages

There are a number of advantages to participating in DMAs. Firstly, in some parts of the world such a connection can increase the legitimacy of house churches in the eyes both of Christians and the broader culture. Many people, including non-Christians, are hesitant about joining a house church because of the fear that it may be a cult. A connection to a recognizable DMA can alleviate such concerns. Secondly, DMAs can provide accountability regarding doctrine to prevent house churches from becoming heretical groups focused around an old or new theological error. Thirdly, DMAs can help minimize the possibility of groups being controlled dictatorially by a single leader who abuses group members. Fourthly, DMAs can provide financial and resource support to help launch house church networks that might otherwise have difficulty starting. Fifthly, DMAs can offer house churches a public platform for educating other Christians in the DMA about the option of starting house churches.

Disadvantages

There are, however, also disadvantages in attempting to wed house church networks with DMAs. Firstly, many DMAs have extremely rigid ideas about the role and training of leaders that they will want to impose upon house churches which may not work effectively in the context of home-based congregations. Secondly, DMAs may desire to unduly control or interfere in the local activities of house churches, especially when it comes to administration of the Lord's Supper, baptism, church discipline, and financial decisions. House churches, to the contrary, feel that these issues must be dealt with on a local level. Thirdly, many DMAs may experience turnover in leadership at top levels that becomes unfavorable towards house churches, which could create unnecessary tensions.

DMAs Should Count The Cost

DMAs considering supporting the emergence of house church networks from within their own ranks should be prepared to make the following accommodations for such partnerships to be as healthy as possible.

Realize

DMAs need to understand that New Testament-style house churches have a different ethos than small groups, cell groups, or para-church ministries. They are not appendages of traditional congregations. Rather, they are fully functioning churches in and of themselves that network with others of like mind in their city or region. They do not require nor desire church buildings, expensive programs, professional clergy, or highly choreographed services. Gatherings are open, interactive, and family type meetings around the Lord's Supper as a full meal. They focus on relationships, discipleship, and neighborhood outreach. All of this will require some redefinition on the part of the DMA regarding familiar terms like 'congregation', 'church service', 'pastor/elder', 'discipleship', etc.

Release

DMAs that wish to endorse house church efforts will be faced with the challenge of fully releasing leaders to function according to the ethos built into house church movements. Because house church networks desire to reestablish ancient apostolic patterns and practices for church life, DMAs will need to avoid the temptation of trying to force these leaders into long-established traditional roles and categories. Because they are typically at the grassroots, most house church leaders functioning on local and trans-local levels will be so-called 'lay people'. DMAs will need to give them the same freedom as more traditional leaders to function in their calling from God to lead, train, and oversee the next generation of house church leaders.

Reinforce

DMAs should consider supporting their house church networks the same way they support traditional churches. This includes funneling finances to house church planters, as well as offering these leaders resources in the way of seminary-equivalent courses, church planting workshops, training materials, regional leadership networks, etc. This kind of support may accelerate the emergence of house church networks, which might otherwise lay dormant in isolated and scattered groups.

Recognize

DMAs will need to celebrate and promote the house church networks within their ranks in the same way they do other congregations. In some parts of the world, the only choice most Christians have is that of involvement with a traditional church. However, legitimization by DMAs can offer the additional and valid option of house churches to people that have never been completely at home in more traditional settings. DMAs that support house church movements can also be an example and inspiration to other DMAs not currently involved.

Reform

DMAs should be prepared for the possibility that their house church membership might one day outnumber their traditional church membership. This will, of course, change the complexion of the entire DMA. At such a time, these DMAs might sell all their property, rethink their leadership systems, and reorganize as regional networks of house churches. If a single DMA would do this, this would be a serious call to others toward a significant change in church structure. This would mimic what is already going on in other parts of the world with the house church movement.

EXAMPLES OF DMAs SUPPORTING HOUSE CHURCH MOVEMENTS

In addition to the many autonomous house church movements around the world, a number of DMAs recently are beginning to seriously endorse the emergence of house church networks in both the western and eastern hemispheres. Just a few are listed below for illustrative purposes.

DAWN (Discipling A Whole Nation) is a highly respected mission agency that has been instrumental in many saturation church planting efforts around the globe since its inception, with a strategy for seeing a vital church planted within the reach of every 500 to 1000 people.[1] More recently, the North American DAWN team has envisioned the planting of 4 million house churches with the aim of reaching 40 million Americans and Canadians with the gospel of Jesus Christ. To accomplish this, the team has begun organizing regional roundtables of key house church leaders for the purposes of connection, encouragement, training, and resourcing.

The Evangelical Fellowship of Canada, an umbrella organization that works broadly with the Evangelical movement in the country, has helped launch the Canadian House Church Resource Network.[2] This team is bringing nationwide awareness and connection by building a database of house churches, publishing a newsletter, organizing regional and national consultation groups, and advertising the speaking tours of respected house church consultants.

DOVE Christian Fellowship International is a denomination with churches on five continents.[3] They initially began in the early 1980s in Pennsylvania (USA) with three cell groups encompassing 25 people and have grown to 80 networks of churches involving 20,000 believers by 2004. Their primary approach has been the planting of cell group churches that still retain a church building and weekly Sunday services. More recently, however, they have also embraced the more decentralized concept of house church networks as a genuine move of God in these days. Their international director, in fact, is currently an active member of a house church in the USA.

The Southern Baptist Convention (International Mission Board) has been instrumental in fostering house church planting movements all around the world.[4] The 1990s, for instance, saw International Mission Board missionaries facilitate the planting of 220 house churches in Cambodia that brought in 10,000 new believers. Similarly, International Mission Board missionaries have established over 100 house churches in Guayaquil, Ecuador's largest city. The strategy of house churches and lay leaders has been a deliberate one, with missionaries functioning in the more transient role of launching movements and then moving on. Following this precedent, the Southern Baptist's North American Mission Board has recently commissioned its church planting team to adopt a similar strategy to reach all people groups in the US, the US territories, and Canada.

---

[1] Jim Montgomery (1989), *DAWN 2000: 7 Million Churches To Go*, William Carey Library; www.dawnministries.org/globalministries/north%20america.htm
[2] www.outreach.ca/cpc/housechurches.htm; www.disciplethenations.org
[3] www.dcfi.org; L. Kreider (2001), *House Church Networks*, House to House.
[4] www.imb.org; David Garrison (2004), *Church Planting Movements*, Wigtake Resources.

The Free Methodist Church in Canada has a vision "to see healthy churches within the reach of all people in Canada and beyond" and "aims to develop reproducing churches."[5] Since the mid-1990s, it has come to recognize the cultural shifts happening within the nation and within the church and has also desired to hearken back somewhat to its historical Wesleyan roots, which involved the deliberate use of lay led home cell groups. It has made accommodations in order to embrace forms and models of church that are new to the denomination such as house churches, provided its house church leaders with national platforms to speak about the concept, and officially endorsed these efforts. As such, it is now sponsoring house church planting projects in three Canadian provinces, namely British Columbia, Alberta, and Ontario.

The Evangelical Missionary Church of Canada has recognized the unique challenges and opportunities present within the province of Quebec (Canada) for church planting.[6] The decline in many a Quebecer's formal participation in and connection to their Roman Catholic religious heritage—combined with the growth of secularism, poverty, and the emergence of a number of cultic and New Age groups—offers a unique dilemma for presenting the message of Jesus Christ. As such, the denomination has commissioned a team to launch a network of reproducing house churches that can provide the highly relational Quebecers with a natural context in which to explore the claims of Christ and grow in faith.

AN EXAMPLE OF A PARTNERSHIP AGREEMENT

The following document entitled "We Agree" was crafted jointly by The Free Methodist Church in Canada (www.fmc-canada.org) and one of its house church networks (www.housechurch.ca) to describe the relationship between them, with an eye to maintaining the integrity of both parties. All the members of the house churches were able to read, change, and approve the document before it became part of the denomination's official documentation.

WE AGREE [7]

"We Agree" defines HouseChurch.Ca's relationship to The Free Methodist Church in Canada (FMCiC) and has been approved by the Board of Administration as a working guide as this new form of church is being developed. Communication is key to healthy relationships. This document clarifies how house churches can function effectively within the FMCiC. First we will look at the partnering relationship between the house churches and the FMCiC. Understanding some of the house church distinctives is

---

[5] www.fmc-canada.org; www.housechurch.ca; www.jusnexdoor.ca

[6] www.emcc.ca; email: donald.gingras@videotron.ca

[7] The "We Agree" document is copyrighted by The Free Methodist Church in Canada (www.fmc-canada.org). It is reproduced with their permission.

important in partnering. Next we will focus on the role of approved leaders, and how these leaders fit into the current denominational structure. Finally we explain how the house churches fit into the larger accountability structure of the FMCiC.

1. We Believe in a Clear Partnership Between the House Churches and the FMCiC.

As part of our extended family, we accept The Free Methodist Church in Canada as our spiritual parents. We are not orphans, but are accepted into this wider family, and we are thankful. We accept their guidance and relational responsibility in our lives, as they mutually accept our distinctive qualities as adult children (Romans 15:5-6). We can see at least five unique characteristics of these house churches:

- These small house-sized communities are full functioning churches, not small groups.
- House churches will focus on Christ-centered relationships and might not organize themselves into any form that looks like a "service" or "program."
- Every approved house church leader is released to do every important act of ministry, regardless of ordination status.
- There is no intention of the house churches to ever own real property or buildings specifically used for church gatherings.
- Our intention is to grow by multiplying new house churches, not by simply adding to the existing groups.

We agree that we can better fulfill the great commission together than apart (John 17:23). We view this relationship as a co-operation with God to see His kingdom thrive and expand on this earth until the return of Jesus. Part of this co-operation means understanding the deeper nuances of our house church distinctives.

2. We Believe House Churches will best Multiply through the Intentional Training and Approval of "Non-ordained" Local Leaders.

We believe every person, regardless of race, gender or education, is a potential leader (Galatians 3:28). We also believe that leaders are trained and not necessarily born. This training does not necessitate an official degree, but rather the willingness and openness to be shaped by God's word into a Christ-like person who models and facilitates biblical community. In the place of degree granting institutions, both monthly network training, and continual one-on-one mentorship is essential. It will take exceptional sacrifice by the approved leaders and planters of these new house churches, and so these leaders will need to be exceptional people. Not in the world's standards of power and prestige, but in God's standards of weakness and abandonment to his will.

True leadership can and should administer the most important actions in ministry. This includes baptisms, funerals, marriages and serving communion. We also believe the weight of these actions are heavy enough that only approved leaders with sufficient training should lead these acts. These local leaders would accept the overall responsibility for the people within a local house church.

New house church planters will be released on the basis of their calling, commitment to training, competence to lead and character (1 Timothy 3:2-13; Titus 1:6-9; Galatians 5:22). Even though a new house church might have one or two leaders, we will establish small teams of people whenever possible to start new works. It is through growth by multiplication that we will reach many in Canada and the rest of the world with the good news of Jesus.

Local Leader Qualifications

Local house church activities are led by the full participation of the people within the house church itself, facilitated by a plurality of local leaders. These leaders are Christian men or women who are approved with consensus from the network (HCN) and the local house church, agreeing to the tenants of this document, and who have completed or are currently taking house church leadership training.

Local Leader Job Description

These local leaders are responsible to:

- Model and encourage biblical church values (Loving God, Living Community, Everyone Growing, Everyone Contributing, Depending on God, Responding back to God, Finding Wholeness, Reaching Out, etc.)

- Actively serve people through tasks like: discipleship, organizing gathering times, hosting (cleaning, cooking, welcoming) teaching, being available, following-up, initiating accountability, communicating values, casting vision for multiplying and encouraging & modeling personal evangelism.

- Take overall responsibility that sharing together in the Lord's Supper, Baptisms, Marriages and funerals are administered in a godly and biblical fashion. "Administration" refers to the correct oversight or organization of such event, not necessarily the "hands-on" execution of them. Biblically, the "hands-on" work could be performed by any Christian.

3. We Believe in a Larger Accountability Structure.

We believe that healthy relationships between the local house churches through House Church networks (HCNs) and between the HCNs and the denomination are beneficial. We think this particular kind of connection between the FMCiC and the house churches will provide the best chance for long-term success and multiplication. It allows for both freedom at the grass roots and accountability on a larger level.

House Church Network Level

We are not just planting house churches, but networks of house churches. We call these Local Area Networks "LANs." Some of these networks will eventually develop into networks of networks. In computer terms, these are called "Wide Area Networks" (WANs). In concrete terms, these networks will consist of the leaders of house churches meeting regularly with other house church leaders for training, encouragement, and accountability. They will be tied to one another through relational connections. Most leaders, when first entering a house church network, will work through foundational theological and church practice material. Later these network meetings may become more relational in nature.

Denominational Connection

We propose forming "House Church Networks" (HCNs) as needed. Each of these groups would have a reasonable span of care. They would be led by either an assistant superintendent from within one of the house church networks, or by an approved house church leader who is either ordained within the FMCiC or has been given a lay minister's licence. Like the other networks, the HCNs would be careful to include the eight network values (listen, celebrate, care, strategize, disciple, train, challenge, denominational communication). It is at this HCN level that the house churches could pursue fellowship and society status within the FMCiC.

Accountability of Funds

House Church leaders will be self-supporting and unpaid. We do, however, see the possibility of giving some financial support to network leaders for their time and any costs associated with regional training and networking. For this reason, we view the gathering and dispersing of donations to happen primarily on a house church network level. It would be on this level that the appropriate charity status could be applied. Like any other Free Methodist fellowship or society, it would also be from this network level that any financial support would be given to the FMCiC.

Guiding Principles for the Accountability Structure

- *Accountable vs. Controlled.* The house churches and leaders need biblical accountability—people who will walk beside them spiritually, doctrinally and financially. This functions best through clear lines of relationship developed by the house church networks.

- *Relational vs. Positional.* If the house churches and their leaders know the people to whom they are accountable, they will follow, listen and take guidance. Relationships are key to working well along side denominational and network leaders.

- *Biblical vs. Traditional.* The essence of house church is returning to the biblical roots of that first Christian community. We are thankful that in areas of vision, mission and doctrine, the Free Methodist Church is solidly biblical. House churches and their leaders are given the freedom to act as the Bible, the Holy Spirit, and their communities guide. ■

CONCLUSIONS

We have briefly examined the pros and cons of partnerships between house church networks and DMAs. In many cases, such a connection may not be feasible or desirable for either party. However, we have also seen some examples of how they can work together successfully. If done prayerfully and carefully, the fostering of such partnerships can serve to help coordinate the efforts of established Christian organizations and visionary pioneers in reaching the nations for Christ through saturation house church planting.

STUDY QUESTIONS

1. What are the pros and cons of DMAs and house church networks partnering together?
2. What are some accommodations that DMAs need to implement for such partnerships to work well?
3. Read Luke 5:36-39. How does this apply to the topic at hand?

Chapter 59

CASE STUDY:
CAN A TRADITIONAL CHURCH TRANSITION
TO A HOUSE CHURCH NETWORK?

JERRY STEINGARD

Jerry Steingard, M.Div. (Regent College, Vancouver, Canada), is currently working on his Doctor of Practical Ministry Studies (Wagner Leadership Institute). He has been active in ministry since the 1970s as a cell group leader, an evangelistic coffee house leader, an associate pastor, and as a senior pastor. He is currently team leader of Gateway Harvest Fellowship, a network of house churches in Canada (www.gatewayharvest.com). Email: steingard@sympatico.ca.

INTRODUCTION

I have a few pastoral friends who have resigned their successful congregations once they realized that the majority of the people were not willing to follow them through the transition into a new paradigm and wineskin called house church or simple church. These friends would argue that you cannot transition an existing traditional congregation into this kind of new church. I probably lean in the direction of my pastoral colleagues. However, the bottom line is: "What are you, God, asking me to do? Should I lead my congregation through this transition, or start from scratch with new converts and a small core group of committed believers?" In this article, I hope to share my experience in attempting to lead a traditional church through a transition into a network of house churches.

NEW WINE, NEW WINESKINS

It is true that Jesus said that you cannot put new wine into an old wineskin without breakage and loss. Rather, new wine must be put into new wineskins. Jesus recognized that while some people would be open to change, others would not—to them "The old is good enough."[1] Ralph Neighbour, Jr., the well-known advocate of cell group churches, states:

> For ten years I sought to be a part of bringing renewal to the traditional church. I shared over ten thousand copies of *Touch Basic Training*, and taught over seven hundred pastors of traditional churches. Most of those men found it impossible to add cells to the already cluttered programs of their church.

---

[1] Luke 5:36-39 (NASB)

Twenty-three of them were released by their congregations for trying to insert cell groups into church life. I have come to a conclusion which will guide the rest of the years of ministry the Lord gives me: you cannot put new wine into old skins! I would hope that a reader of this book will understand this, and not attempt to mix this oil with the tepid water of traditional church structures. This guidebook is not written with any thought of, or hope for, the renewal of existing church structures.[2]

PERSONAL PARADIGM SHIFTS

While my wife, family, and I were directing a Christian retreat center and recuperating from pastoral ministry burnout (a common ailment for traditional church pastors), a pastor friend made the mistake of leaving on the kitchen counter a copy of Wolfgang Simson's book, *Houses that Change the World*.[3] Being a book hound, I could not resist reading it. This was a divine appointment for me. It was time for another paradigm shift.

In late 2001, the Lord spoke to my wife and I separately within a few days of each other that we were to move back to our hometown to multiply house churches. Just prior to our move, a good pastor friend in that city, invited us out for lunch and asked us to pray about coming on staff with him as a consultant to lead his congregation through the steps of becoming a network of house churches. Although the church had seen better days and the pastor was burned out, the Lord told him that this church was to be a prototype. He felt that moving in this direction would not only help the church survive, but would be the way towards seeing this word fulfilled. And so we accepted this invitation.

MAKING GRADUAL CHANGES

For six months, we cast vision to the people as well as identified and retooled people in the congregation that were willing to be trained as house church facilitators. This included seminars with Robert Fitts, Sr.,[4] James Rutz,[5] and Tony and Felicity Dale,[6] reading through various books and articles, and question and answer periods. We eventually took small steps to establish half a dozen house churches. We gave people the time to pray about and visit the various house churches, which met weekly, encouraging them to settle into one. Around this time we put our building—an industrial warehouse—up for sale. For our 75 member congregation, maintaining a 250 seat church facility felt like a financial millstone around our necks. In

---

[2] Ralph Neighbour, Jr. (1992), *The Shepherd's Guidebook (3rd edition)*, Touch Publications, p.1.

[3] Wolfgang Simson (1998), *Houses that Change the World*, Paternoster.

[4] Robert Fitts (2001), *The Church in the House*, Preparing the Way Publishers.

[5] James Rutz (2005), *Megashift*, Empowerment Press.

[6] "House2House" magazine, www.house2house.com

keeping with our commitment to make gradual steps, we rented a hall and met two Sundays each month for a celebration service for the first two years until we sensed it was time to change our celebrations to once a month.

Throughout this process, much of my time was spent listening to the complaints and concerns of various individuals and families and seeking to repeatedly recast the vision and reassure them of God's leading. For those who chose to move on to another more traditional church, or drop out of church altogether, we sought to be gracious, understanding, and leave an open door if they ever chose to return. About one third left our group in the first six months, another third were uncertain but willing to suspend judgment to see how it all developed, and a third seemed confident of our new direction and were committed to the process. Eventually, most of the hesitant third also dropped out within two or three years. Of course, it was emotionally painful to lose many quality people and families. We were determined to bless them as they left, but we were committed to staying the course. During this season of change over the past four and a half years, others have come to join our network of house churches, so that our total numbers are roughly the same as when we first started.

UNEXPECTED CHALLENGES AND VICTORIES

Any transitioning process is rarely simple and straightforward. Charles Swindoll has said in the context of remodeling a home, renewal "will take longer than you planned, cost more than you figured, be messier than you anticipated, and require greater determination than you expected."[7] Unexpected variables are inevitably added that can bring either challenges or victories. This keeps us as believers dependent on God, because we live in a world where there really is a spiritual war going on.

Within months of coming on staff in 2002, the congregation found itself going through a grieving process due to the deaths of two women in the church, despite much prayer and fasting. This was quite a blow to all of us. Knowing that change is stressful, we slowed down the transition process and focused primarily on ministering and loving people back to life and faith.

On the heels of seeing two loved ones die, God challenged us not to give up on believing that he could perform signs and wonders in our midst. This is when the Lord beckoned us to establish a downtown outreach ministry, called the Barrie Healing Rooms. Prayer teams consisting of trained volunteers from close to a dozen churches in the area pray and minister God's healing love and grace to the sick in this walk-in clinic. This citywide storefront ministry—as well as other local and global projects—has been financially supported primarily through funds made available by selling our church building. We have seen some wonderful healings, including back problems, cancer, hepatitis C, as well as some 50 salvations in several years.

---

[7] Charles Swindoll, (1980), *Strike the Original Match*, Multnomah Press, p.10.

One of our house churches uses the storefront as a meeting place and is made up of many of the new people we have met and ministered to through this downtown outreach. It has been a stretch for many of us, a sheltered middle class Evangelical group mingling with the poor and marginalized.

With a more streamlined way of being and doing church, I have also had more fun and more quality time with my family and even my neighbors. I have had the privilege of leading more people to Christ one-on-one in the last few short years than in my previous 50 years combined.

LESSONS LEARNED

After four and a half years, have we been successful in completing this transition to a full-fledged house church network? My honest answer would be "No". There are several reasons why this is the case.

First of all, I doubt if any transition is every really complete. We are on a dynamic journey of faith whereby we continually need to change as the Father speaks to us and leads us. Currently, my assessment is that we are a hybrid, somewhere between a cell-group congregation and a house church network. We may have made a number of structural changes congruent with a network of house churches, but I believe the mindset of many of the people has only been partially transitioned or renewed. Like the Israelites, you may get them out of Egypt, but it takes longer to get Egypt out of them! Defaulting one's own spiritual growth and ministry responsibilities to the professional leader is hard to fully deprogram. Although a true priesthood of all believers has not yet fully emerged in our midst, I am seeing some very encouraging progress.

Second, a personal error on my part has been giving too much of my time and energy in seeing apostolic expansion of the downtown Healing Rooms and other exciting inter-church outreach and training ministries established. Rather, I should have spent more time and energy on adequately mentoring and multiplying new house church leaders in our context, who could then in turn mentor and release people in the house churches into their own ministries as believer-priests of God.

CONCLUSIONS

We may find ourselves leading an existing flock into the promised land of new things or having the privilege of birthing our own spiritual sons and daughters into the context of simple and organic house churches. In either case, we will face challenges and experience victories. However, if we seek to wholeheartedly submit to the glorious truth of the word of God, embrace the cross of Christ, and keep in step with the Spirit, we are in for quite a ride.

STUDY QUESTIONS

1. What are some of the paradigm shifts that God has led you through?
2. Is it better to transition an existing group or to start a new work?
3. Read Luke 5:36-39. What does Jesus say about coping with change?

Chapter 60

CASE STUDY:
CAN A TRADITIONAL PASTOR TRANSITION
TO HOUSE CHURCHES?

DAN WILLIAMS

Dan Williams (B.Sc., M.Div., Th.M., M.A.) has been involved with ministry leadership for over 30 years. He has worked as program staff, associate pastor, and senior pastor, as well as having significant para-church experience. A particular focus at every stage has been equipping small group programs. A variety of publications have emerged out of this passion, including 1 Corinthians: The Challenges of Life (2001), Starting (& Ending) a Small Group (1996), and the best-known Seven Myths about Small Groups (2000). Dan's current project involves a house church network (churchwithoutborders), which is supported by Vision Ministries Canada (www.vision-ministries.org). Email: danwilliams@telus.net.

INTRODUCTION

The Christian walk is an important metaphor, but also an ambiguous one. Does it refer to the act of walking or to a path? If a path, are the twists and turns the vital thing, or is it where you are heading? In other words, is it all about the journey or about the destination? For me, the two seem to have been very much woven together. In concert with my wife and friend Sharon, I seem to be heading towards a certain vision of house church, but the specific route has been a big part of the story. What have been the steps from traditional church pastoring to our current adventure in house churches and neighborhood outreach?

THE IMPACT OF AN ORDINARY FOLLOWER OF JESUS

In the mid-1970s, I was deeply impacted by Mike, an ordinary follower of Jesus. Mike is one of my best friends and certainly my first and best discipler. He was eventually the best man at my wedding. Mike was part of a small group of Christians that prayed for me to come to faith, which happened in 1976. Mike conveyed to me from the start that church, real church, has very little to do with real estate or strategic plans. Instead, it has everything to do with being Jesus in the midst of real life.

I first saw Mike sitting on a couch in the university physics building, reading his Bible. I got to know him better as he regularly climbed the stairs to my humble first apartment and helped me learn the basics of the faith. I had no idea that he did not have to do that. He was not an official pastor. He was just a student like me. He was not doing this because of any official structure or formal manual. He was doing it simply because of the call of Jesus on his life.

Then we became roommates. The first thing we did was launch two Bible studies. These groups did not belong to any formal church or organization, but were just groups of people called together to meet with Jesus. Mike has led such groups for years, gatherings that usually maintain, at best, a very loose connection to a traditional church. He has never drawn a salary or aspired to official, public positions of leadership. But, along the way, he has shown himself to be a deep student and teacher of the Scriptures, a man of prayer, a person marked by the fruit of the Spirit, and one who is open to sharing his life and faith and struggles with others. Mike modeled for me from the start what it means to do church in a kingdom way.

THE PARA-CHURCH WORLD

By the time I met my future wife Sharon in 1982, I had been working for InterVarsity Christian Fellowship (IVCF) for several years, specifically in college campus work in the province of British Columbia (Canada).

In para-church work, I was known for pushing the limits, always inventing, trying new things, and going into new fields. This may have as much to do with my personality, as it does my spirituality. Fortunately, most of the innovations came from the Bible. The grounding in the Scriptures that goes along with an IVCF pedigree, reinforced by my early disciplers and solid experience under various Bible teachers, has ensured that my inspiration for ministry came from the Gospels, the Acts, and the various Old Testament foreshadowings of the Christian life. Secondary sources such as books have also been very useful in sharpening my ideas about ministry.

From the very beginning, I have also had a deep commitment to small groups. The best way to get into the Bible, for me, has always been with a group of fellow-travelers, which IVCF has always valued. I grew up in study and prayer groups, spread my wings in outreach groups, went deep in sharing groups, and learned about, led, and launched many small groups.

Being exposed to a para-church ministry model at an early stage instilled in me certain values and standard operating procedures. For me, the key seed principles from these years were:

- *Mission.* Mission is the point. 'Koinonia' fellowship is also essential, but holy huddles by themselves are ultimately doomed. If we are not giving away spiritual life to others, then we do not truly have life ourselves.

- *Wine and Wineskins.* The wine is more important than the wineskins. This means there can be a radical flexibility, regularly and freely reinventing the structures to conserve and convey the good news.

- *The Wine is Essential.* The wineskin is not the end, but only the means. Make sure to drink the wine! The only way forward involves knowing the revelation of Jesus and knowing the Jesus of revelation.

- *Leadership.* Anyone that is committed to the above principles can appropriately be considered for a leadership role. The link between active membership and potential leadership is a strong one.

PASTORING A TRADITIONAL CHURCH

In the context of more traditional churches, I have served as an elder, an assistant pastor, and a senior pastor, having also obtained an M.Div. degree that has been helpful in this regard. In this setting, though, I have always had a deep suspicion about any tendency for church members to hide from the world. For instance, it usually only takes several months for a new follower of Jesus to disconnect from all their non-churched friends and fill every evening with Christian meetings. Resisting this pattern has always been part of my emphasis. The seeds for this approach were planted deep within me early on in my Christian life. My first pastor was very committed to outreach and tried many innovative things. At IVCF, we were always creating platforms to make connections between university students and the gospel. I brought these early lessons into my leadership of traditional churches over the years, applying them in many directions, from young adult events to adult outreach through the Alpha program, from children's programs to evangelism training. A common thread in all this has been looking for ways to encourage Christians to make the shift from a 'come to the church' mentality to a 'go make disciples' attitude. We have always tried to retrofit such a model into existing churches. As a pastor, I have always endeavored to see church planting precisely as taking Jesus—through the Spirit in us—into every corner of the world.

LESSONS LEARNED FROM OUR SHIFT TO HOUSE CHURCHES

Several years ago, my wife Sharon and I finally felt led to 'do church' organically, in the middle of real life, naturally inviting friends and neighbors to join us. We felt that this required me to transition out of my traditional pastoral role. Our dream now is to see the emergence of a network of neighborhood mission outposts, disguised as house churches. The fledgling network we have started is all about the value of doing small things in big ways. In the process, we have learned a number of lessons.

Firstly, there is a cost to leaving behind traditional pastoring. The model we are pursuing now involves bi-vocational ministry. God confirmed our approach by providing a fantastic job and a generous employer. The main challenge here has not been the loss of the pastor's salary, study, parking spot, or library. The main loss has really quite simply been time. There is not enough time currently left over after my regular job for me to make everything happen for the house church ministry. But I am learning in a hard and humble way that doing house church and neighborhood mission is not about me making things happen anyway. Instead, it is all about being with friends committed to one another on the path, committed to hearing the voice of Jesus, and learning how to do church all over again, in the middle of the real world for which he died.

Secondly, I am learning to be more like Jesus by being more open to the needs of others. We are embracing the practice of combining hospitality with being available to help when needed. I have found that after 30 years of following Jesus and having his agenda seep into my pores, I am still a novice when it comes to truly opening up my home and, more importantly, my heart to the stranger. But, we have seen some good things happen. People have shared a few dollars with a family short on cash. A teenage son has sat in the living room and heard his dad pray. Children have invited their friends to an annual backyard club. Our group is trying to sponsor a refugee family to come to Canada. Even so, I am still taking tentative steps when it comes to breaking down the dividing wall and welcoming others to come and taste and see that the Lord is good.

Thirdly, house church is not about the next big project or event. Progress in our network, as measured against the standards of the world and of many denominations, is very slow. But we are learning that faithfulness in small steps of obedience is exactly what we are called to. We are prepared to start small, go slow, grow deep, and allow God to bring the increase in due time.

CONCLUSIONS

My journey has been one of many small steps. From coming to faith through the prayers of a small group of Christian students to growing in my faith in that same context. From coming on staff with a para-church organization that valued small groups to pastoring a more traditional church and emphasizing outreach. God's recent call to me to open up neighborhood mission outposts has been costly, but also immensely rewarding. It is all part of my journey of faith.

STUDY QUESTIONS

1. How can having experience in both small groups and traditional church leadership prepare a traditional pastor to launch a network of house churches?

2. What are some of the challenges that a traditional pastor might face in shifting to house churches?

3. Are you a pastor who is feeling pulled towards making a similar shift? Spend a few minutes right now praying for the Lord's guidance.

Chapter 61

CASE STUDY:
CREATING NETWORKING OPPORTUNITIES FOR
HOUSE CHURCHES IN CANADA

GRACE WIEBE

Grace Wiebe lives just outside Vancouver, Canada. For the past 26 years she has been involved in various aspects of missions and the planting of traditional churches and house churches. For the past 10 years, she has been developing various international, national, and local networks with a vision to see the Body of Christ working together to see God's Kingdom purposes fulfilled among the nations (www.DiscipleTheNations.org). Email: gracew@idmail.com.

INTRODUCTION

Many house churches, especially the first couple years of their existence, tend to be very inward focused due to lack of vision and maturity. Some house churches are very skeptical about connecting with others, even with those in other house churches, for all kinds of reasons, and may not yet have worked through their unresolved questions or issues with regard to traditional churches, denominations, and modern Christendom, etc. Therefore, it is difficult to get an accurate picture of what the house church situation is actually like in Canada. Fortunately, many of these stand-alone groups are beginning to recognize their need to connect with one another in cohesive local, regional, and national networks for long-term health and vitality for the sake of kingdom growth. Thus, the aim of this article is to give an account of how the Canadian House Church Resource Network (CHCRN) has developed and utilized its database, newsletters, website, conferences, etc., in developing regional and national awareness and connectionalism for house churches in Canada. Judging by the constant increase in people contacting the CHCRN, there is likely far more happening than many are aware.

THE HISTORY OF THE CHCRN

A colleague and I had been with the same mission organization for over a decade. This mission agency focuses on planting indigenous house churches internationally, but especially among a particular major world religion. However, over the years, my colleague and I had a growing desire to see house churches planted in Canada, as well, and to see Christianity lived out in radical, Christ-centered, biblical Christian community. Around the beginning of 1999, our Canadian headquarters' office staff was asked to seek the Lord about his directions for how he wanted us to move forward and function in the future. In so doing, God seemed to be giving us some new directions and encouraging us to take some next steps regarding house churches in Canada.

Around April of 1999, I contacted several online missions and church planting resource mailing lists to ask whether anyone knew of others in Canada that were either involved in or interested in house churches. In response I received about 200 emails in a couple of days, requesting the house church resource list I was offering to those that responded, but no one had any information for me about potentially interested Canadians. One significant email I received led to a small, informal meeting with three of us from our city. From that initial visit, the resource network began to take shape as we began to pray, think, gather resources, create a website, develop a database, and network with others that shared a similar vision. During this process, we also forged the following vision statement:

> *By the power and leading of the Holy Spirit, we seek to mobilize, resource, encourage, network, train, and facilitate those that God is raising up in Canada who, while complimenting other forms of Christian gatherings in Canada, share and carry out the vision of establishing Christ-centered, easily reproducible, multiplying house churches in house church networks as a vital part of seeing Canada discipled and taking a more effective role in discipling the nations, in order that Jesus will be glorified as King of Kings among all nations. We desire to see His life lived out through us in every aspect of life.*

Soon there were a growing number of interested parties in my province of British Columbia. We then hosted our first local meeting with about 15-20 people in attendance. It was a very encouraging time as vision was shared and everyone in the room had a heart for the lost. It was affirming for people to realize that they were not alone in this desire and that God was also stirring other hearts in these directions. It was also encouraging for people to know that there was a support network that God was raising up in order to help facilitate what he was putting on the hearts of his people. Since that time, about every three months for a few years or so, we facilitated similar networking meetings. It seemed that those that came and we as the facilitation team were always so encouraged to see how God seemed to keep raising up more and more people in our region.

God also began networking us as a facilitation team with people in other Canadian cities who also shared a similar vision of seeing house church networks developing as a part of God's overall strategy to draw Canada to himself. We sensed that God was leading us to expand nationally and began to pray about bringing additional people to potentially partner with us in order to see God's purposes for house churches in Canada move forward. Thus, a consultation of networkers from across the country was scheduled and was a significant milestone in the development of the broader vision. It was from this consultation that we felt there would need to be both a local and national focus. About a year later, in 2003, we hosted the First National Conference on House Churches in Canada. This was a partnership between various regional networkers/networks and took place one week in several cities in succession across the country. The local networks hosted Wolfgang Simson as the key note speaker for their house church conferences.[1]

THE PURPOSE OF THE CHCRN

Without networking together with other house churches and other house church networks, I believe house churches will become unhealthy and/or die out. We need each other and we need to effectively function together as part of the larger Body and to function in that as the Holy Spirit provides, leads, and enables. Today, the Holy Spirit is gradually leading growing numbers of Canada's house churches to connect with one another, especially regionally. The CHCRN is only one of the vessels God is using to accomplish this in Canada. Notably, inherent in the mandate of the CHCRN is that we remain as a 'network' facilitator, rather than becoming an 'organization'. As such, our desire has only been to act as a 'contact point and resource provider' for house churches in Canada, rather than as a 'control center'. House churches that have contacted us are not asked to become members of an organization or to sign any paper memberships. Rather, we seek to develop deepening, godly relationships to facilitate loose networking among house churches across the country for the following reasons:

- Teamwork can accomplish more than individual efforts
- Resource updates and exchange
- Relationships with others of similar vision can be encouraging
- Prayer to discern God's leading for our neighborhoods, cities, provinces, nation, and world
- Loving accountability between 'peers'
- Awareness about upcoming seminars, conferences, and training events
- Etc.

A TYPICAL REGIONAL NETWORK MEETING

When we began our first regional network gatherings, we focused largely on making connections between people in our region and on giving like-minded people opportunities to share their joys and struggles of where they were

---

[1] Wolfgang Simson (1998), *Houses that Change the World*, Paternoster.

along the journey of considering or transitioning into house churches. We kept everything quite simple and informal in our get-togethers.

The Invitation

Below is some information from one of the initial invitations (without all the details) that was sent out to our region to folks that were potentially interested in starting house churches:

Get-Together for House Church Planters

If you or others you know in the region are interested or involved in the aspect of house churches as a part of seeing this nation reclaimed for the Kingdom of God, we invite you to come meet with us and others who share the vision:

- *Hear about a vision for seeing house churches becoming a growing part of discipling Canada for Christ*
- *Meet others in the region who are also interested in house churches*
- *Share similar vision with each other*
- *Pray for each other about these directions*
- *Discuss some issues regarding house church development*
- *Find out about possible upcoming events and resources on house churches*
- *Consider possible ways to work with the facilitation team to move the vision forward*

Some of you we know or have met before. Others of you may be new to us. We are looking forward to seeing many of you there! If you are not already on our mailing list and would like to receive the invitation once we have the specific location arranged, please let us know.

The Meeting

The format of our times together was very informal. We focused on getting to know one another, hearing each other's hearts, and hearing from God. We sought to be led as the Holy Spirit led. Some of the things we did included:

- Worshipping through singing and prayer
- Introductions. Giving everyone a chance to share a bit about their story of how God led them in this direction, a bit about their vision, as well as their current situation regarding house churches.
- Exchanging resources, networking, talking about upcoming event options, etc.
- Sharing meals together
- Ministering to each other
- Etc.

The Questions

At our first network meetings, common questions that many folks wanted to explore were often very practical in nature. They included the following:

- How do you start a house church?
- What do you do with the children?
- How do you multiply as painlessly as possible once at that stage?
- How do you deal with the responses of others who have negative opinions of house churches?
- What are some helpful resources that we can benefit from?
- Are there some upcoming events to help us move forward in these directions?
- When can we meet again?
- Etc.

The Deeper Issues

As the house churches in our region gained experience over the course of several years and moved past the 'newborn' phase, the local or regional networking get-togethers included discussions on some deeper issues, such as dealing with group finances, church discipline, Body life, developing local teams of apostles, prophets, teachers, evangelists, and pastors to equip the local house churches/networks, effectively reaching out into the marketplace, being part of the city church, etc.

HOUSE CHURCHES ARE IN TRANSITION

Whereas the CHCRN began with a national vision as a catalyst to get things started, followed by developing some local initial foundations which then moved to regional networks, it seems that more recently the focus for the CHCRN and others networkers across the nation has been to focus on what is happening locally and to build up the local house church networks. All of these things—the national, regional, and local networks—are developing simultaneously. As a result, I believe we will see increasing reproduction and kingdom life impacting growing segments of our neighborhoods, cities, and the nation. As the local networks in Canada develop and as trusting relationships between existing house churches becomes established, there is a growing interest in partnering together, as the Holy Spirit leads, in things like occasional corporate worship times together, developing apostolic teams in each region, ministering together in our neighborhoods, cities, and beyond, and partnering together with other believers across the city.

CONCLUSIONS

As I consider all that God has been doing over the years since our initial meeting as a facilitation team, I am truly grateful to the Lord and deeply amazed at how he has indeed done far more than we had asked or imagined, and in quite a short period of time! I believe that in the next few years we will begin to see the 'snowball gathering snow' at a much greater pace than the past several years or so, and that it will not be too long before the house church phenomenon really begins to grow rapidly across Canada.

STUDY QUESTIONS

1. What are some practical steps that the CHCRN took to create national and regional awareness regarding house churches in Canada? What can you do in your context?

2. What are the pros and cons of house churches networking together?

3. How can you prevent a house church 'network' from becoming just another 'organization'?

Chapter 62

CASE STUDY:
CREATING NETWORKING OPPORTUNITIES FOR
HOUSE CHURCHES IN AUSTRALIA

BESSIE PEREIRA

Bessie Pereira, Th.L., was ordained in the Anglican Church in Australia and ministered in five parishes before stepping aside to be involved with the house church movement in 1989. Since commencing a newsletter for house churches, she has seen this work grow to become a significant resource and means of networking for the movement in Australia. Currently, she is director of this team ministry that has become 'OIKOS Australia' (www.oikos.org.au). Email: oikos@optusnet.com.au.

INTRODUCTION

The forerunners of the modern house church movement in Australia were those groups in Canberra that had started in the 1960s with Robert Banks and Geoffrey Moon. These two young Anglican clergymen and Cambridge graduates questioned the hierarchical and paternalistic church structures that led to the disempowerment of ordinary people. They saw simple, small, egalitarian gatherings of church as closer to the biblical norm. In recent years, however, interest has grown significantly. The purpose of 'OIKOS Australia' is to serve the house church movement in our nation. Originally a newsletter, OIKOS has evolved to become more than just that. It has become a resource and a means of networking that grows more personal as relationships have developed. As the house church movement has gained momentum, the ministry has expanded. A major part of the work of OIKOS has been to connect groups and individuals with each other whenever possible. Bringing groups together for celebrations, seminars, and sharing days in various parts of the country is a significant part of our work. Isolated groups have been given opportunities to meet with others in their region. The aim of this article is to give an overview of the practical and tangible ways this has been pursued.

THE ORIGINS OF 'OIKOS'

Years ago in 1989, a typical scene emerged in a backyard in Melbourne, Australia. About 30 adults and what seemed like double the number of children shared a barbeque meal. The men hovered around the focus of this culinary event, while the women chatted in small groups and the children kicked a football around. Eventually, we all wandered inside to sit around the lounge room for the main purpose of the gathering. Very few had met before, but all had come together on that warm summer evening to find out about house churches in our large city.

As we organized the children in another room to view a video, we settled, uncertain as to what we would learn, and less certain as to what we could share. We decided to go around the room and encouraged each person to simply tell their story—what their church background was, why they changed, where God had them then, and how they viewed their situation. The atmosphere in the room relaxed as the stories unfolded. By the end of the night, everyone was excited: "Before tonight, we thought we were the only ones meeting as church in a home." "We didn't know whether or not our being church like this was valid." "We are so excited that there are others around who believe the way we do about being church in small groups." "How can we stay in touch to encourage one another?"

That group did not actually come together again in the same way, but after a while I knew something had to happen as a follow up to that significant gathering. I had kept in touch with most of the folks and sought to be encouraging and enthusiastic with each one. One day, while sitting at an old computer I barely knew how to use, I started a one-page newsletter. I called it 'OIKOS', the Greek word used in the Bible meaning 'household', such as we find in Romans 16:3-5. I had no particular vision, but just a simple desire to help those in that group to keep the bigger picture before them, and to gain inspiration and ideas from one another. So, from time to time, this little newsletter went out to those few folks and gradually to others who somehow heard about it and desired to be included.

THE VISION OF 'OIKOS' EXPANDS

In 1993, the Canberra Home Churches hosted the first National Home Church Conference. Large numbers of people came from all over Australia. As in that small Melbourne gathering a few years earlier, hearing and seeing something of the bigger picture encouraged people.

After this conference, the OIKOS newsletter started to go out to a wider group of people around the nation. The newsletter became a means of contact with house church people. Some began to donate towards the cost of publishing what had become a larger quarterly newsletter. It was, and indeed has remained, a simple photocopied publication, rather 'homespun' in appearance and very deliberately a newsletter and not a magazine. People found it encouraging and helpful in keeping them in touch with what God was doing with other groups around the nation, as well as providing some overseas house church news. Articles were kept short. Photos and cartoons were included and readers' requests regarding style and size were noted and incorporated where possible and helpful. Contributions for content have always been encouraged, including those from children.

A major turning point for this work came as the result of a phone call from David Wilson, principal of a major theological college in Melbourne.

He said that this newsletter was an important instrument in keeping house churches informed and connected. He encouraged me to have others around me for prayer and accountability and indicated his willingness to be a part of that. From that time, OIKOS has been a team ministry. As the house church movement has grown, so too has the more 'hands on' involvement of the OIKOS team. Regional teams are now forming around the country.

THE USE OF TECHNOLOGY

The Personal Touch

Right from the start of OIKOS, we have been available as a means of friendship towards house churches within the denominational churches, as well as independent groups. From the beginning, we have been careful never to tell groups what to do or to be. OIKOS has always sought to maintain the house church ethos in all we do. The sensitive use of developing technology allows for wide contact, but we also endeavor to maintain more personal ways of developing friendships around the country. While on the one hand, the use of email and the Internet provide the means for wide distribution of information, much of the work of OIKOS has focused on personal visitation of house churches and individual people who are seeking new ways of being church. We use old-fashioned letter writing and the telephone. It would be easy to lapse into impersonal ways by using only impersonal means of electronic communication. We have sought to guard against that happening as far as possible.

Cyberspace

The growth in technology in communications, including the Internet and email and mobile phones, is in place for such a time as this and for God's kingdom purposes. This can be used to the maximum benefit in networking house churches. OIKOS has been able to catch this wave to bring encouragement to house churches on cattle stations, in isolated townships, to busy marketplace church plants, and to Christians who, for all sorts of reasons, are feeling isolated.

Being able to produce better quality print media, including photos, and to send so much via email and the use of PDFs, has allowed communication to be more effective, efficient, and financially viable for greater numbers of people. Email has been the most common tool used for communicating with house church folks and for inquirers.

Talk technology, such as Voiceroom, via the Internet allows another level of communication. OIKOS team meetings bring interstate members together via the Internet monthly, as well as at other times for prayer. In the future, OIKOS is hoping to run 'live' seminars for people in remote areas.

The use of our web page has become a focus of the work of OIKOS. Through this medium, we provide information on events and activities of house churches, articles, resources, and a reading list. Subscribers to the newsletter also have access to a section of the web page. This includes a forum to provide a means of communication between subscribers. The forum is protected by a username and password. The forum is divided into 'rooms' indicating a virtual 'home' with different activities or interests to be discussed appropriate to each 'room'. For instance, the Front Porch allows for discussion of anything to do with welcoming new members. The Dining Room focuses on anything to do with the shared meal or communion. The Family Room deals with cross-generational ways of being church and anything to do with children and teens in house church. And so through the other 'rooms', various discussions can be streamed.

FACE-TO-FACE NETWORKING IS STILL VITAL

Regional Gatherings

While all this technology is exciting and is enabling so much communication, none of it can replace the value of face-to-face contact. OIKOS places a major emphasis on visiting house churches around the nation. Many kilometers are traveled to reach tiny gatherings of church to bring news of what God is doing in reforming his church in small groups just like theirs. Across our own nation, God is doing amazing things as more and more house churches are birthed. Groups are encouraged to hear such news. Descriptions of groups, ideas, resources, concerns, and questions are shared. Decentralization of much of the work of OIKOS is currently underway with the development of regional teams. This is enabling more personal contact and realistic assistance given to groups and inquirers. Seminars and celebrations seem to work best if these are held regionally at this time. For the last two years, informal gatherings of house church people over the Easter holiday period have been very effective in developing personal relationships and a deeper sense of connectedness amongst house churches in country areas.

National Conferences

During the 1990s, national house church conferences were organized bi-annually by Canberra and Sydney house churches. These were a massive challenge to organize for small numbers of house churches, and while they were encouraging and inspirational, the logistics have given way to pragmatism, and smaller regional gatherings have become the norm. However, national gatherings will take place in the future. Because many folks in house church only experience the 'small' of church, they are inspired by seeing, learning, and experiencing the bigger picture.

International Connections

With increasing numbers of house churches, the OIKOS team and some house churches encouraged and supported me to attend the National Home Church Conference in Denver (Colorado, USA) in 2005. House2House, a networking ministry based in Austin (Texas, USA) with Tony and Felicity Dale, hosted this gathering. This was a great opportunity not only for me to meet many people who are significantly involved in house church movements around the world, but also for the Australian house churches to experience a sense of connectedness with the worldwide movement. We knew that this move of God across Australia was truly in line with what God was doing across the world reforming his church, but to personally experience it added a deeper dimension.

While speaking with Tony Dale at that conference, I learned that he and Felicity were to visit Australia in 2006 to be involved in a medical conference. Tony offered to be available to speak with house churches. This was a wonderful opportunity for house churches to meet with them and to gain first hand something of the magnitude of what God was doing across the world. Local teams worked hard and efficiently to bring about these gatherings in four of our major cities. This was a wonderful impetus for the house church movement here. Advertising went out widely using all possible media. Many house churches came out from the fringes. In fact, we discovered whole networks we did not know existed. Many people came to the gatherings because they were hungry to find out alternative ways of being church. Others came not realizing the magnitude of what, in fact, they were a part. House churches that had sat with limited vision for years became ignited with a heart for the harvest outside their group. The feedback from these gatherings indicated a desire to stay in touch and to have follow up activities several times a year in their regions. OIKOS regional teams envisage many more of these gatherings in the future.

CONCLUSIONS

We need to have anointed ears that we may hear what the Lord of the church is saying to us as a nation, anointed eyes that we may perceive the way forward in which he is leading us, and anointed hearts to walk sensitively in obedience to the Lord Jesus Christ, the builder of the church. The house churches in Australia are aware that we live in the most exciting times of church history—and the best is yet to be. OIKOS is but one instrument of encouragement and connection for house churches across the nation.

STUDY QUESTIONS

1. What tools and methods does OIKOS use to connect house churches?
2. How is OIKOS seeking to remain a grassroots servant of the church?
3. What lessons can you apply to your city, region, or nation?

RECOMMENDED RESOURCES

BOOKS

- Atkerson, Steve (ed.) (2003), *Ekklesia: To the Roots of Biblical Church Life*, New Testament Restoration Foundation.
- Banks, Robert (1994), *Paul's Idea of Community: The Early House Churches in their Cultural Setting*, Hendrickson Publishers.
- Birkey, Del (1988), *The House Church: A Model for Renewing the Church*, Herald Press (to be rereleased in 2007).
- Broadbent, E.H. (1999), *The Pilgrim Church*, Gospel Folio Press.
- Bunton, Peter (2001), *Cell Groups and House Churches: What History Teaches Us*, House to House Publications.
- Driver, John (1999), *Radical Faith: An Alternative History of the Christian Church*, Pandora Press.
- Fitts, Robert (2001), *The Church in the House*, Preparing the Way Publishers.
- Garrison, David (2004), *Church Planting Movements*, Wigtake Resources.
- Gehring, Roger (2004), *House Church and Mission: The Importance of Household Structures in Early Christianity*, Hendrickson Publishers.
- Kreider, Larry (2001), *House Church Networks*, House-to-House Publications.
- Krupp, Nate (1988), *The Church Triumphant at the End of the Age: Characterized by Revival, Restoration, Unity, World Evangelization, and Persecution*, Preparing the Way Publishers.
- Simson, Wolfgang (1998), *Houses that Change the World*, Paternoster Publishing.
- Snyder, Howard (1996), *Radical Renewal: The Problem of Wineskins Today*, Touch Publications.
- Viola, Frank (2003), *Pagan Christianity: The Origins of Our Modern Church Practices*, Present Testimony Ministry.
- Viola, Frank (1998), *Rethinking the Wineskin: The Practice of the New Testament Church*, Present Testimony Ministry.
- Zdero, Rad (2004), *The Global House Church Movement*, William Carey Library.

WEBSITES

- HouseChurch.Ca (www.housechurch.ca, see 'Resources' section)
- House-2-House Magazine (www.house2house.com)

- The New Testament Restoration Foundation (www.ntrf.org)
- Robert Fitts Ministries (www.robertfitts.com)
- Home Fellowship Leaders (www.homefellowshipleaders.com)

VIDEOS

- *Against Great Odds* (1992) (29 minutes). Vision Video / Gateway Films, Box 540, Worcester, PA, USA, Tel: 1-800-523-0226, www.visionvideo.com. Documents the growth of Ethiopia's Kristos Church from 5,000 to 50,000 people using underground house churches during 10 years of Marxist oppression in the 1980s.
- *Church Planting Movements* (1999) (12 minutes). International Mission Board of the Southern Baptist Convention, Box 6767, Richmond, VA, USA 23230, 1-800-866-3621, www.imb.org/cpm. Documents church planting movements around the world today that use house churches and/or cell groups of 10-30 people. Accompanies the book by David Garrison of the same title.
- *When You Come Together: Simple Church Gatherings—What Do We Do?* (2006). This video explores the basic questions of what house churches are and how they work. Includes clips of house church meetings and interview segments with well-known advocates such as Wolfgang Simson, John White, Neil Cole, and others. Available from www.house2house.com.
- *Francis of Assisi* (1961). Feature length movie spanning the entire revival and renewal ministry of Francis. Drama.
- *Brother Sun, Sister Moon* (1973). Feature length movie about the early years following the conversion of Francis of Assisi. Drama.
- *Luther* (2003). Feature length movie about Martin Luther and the early years of the 16th century Protestant Reformation. Drama.

SUBJECT INDEX

Author Index

The list below provides a quick locator for the single or multiple contributions in this anthology of both historical and modern authors. The numbers following author name indicate Chapter/Page, etc.

ABOUT THE EDITOR

RAD ZDERO earned his Ph.D. degree in Mechanical Engineering from Queen's University (Kingston, ON, Canada) specializing in orthopaedic biomechanics. He is currently the director of a hospital-based orthopaedic research lab. He enjoys long walks, epic movies, books, poetry, short stories, music, coffee shops, and peaceful revolutions.

Rad has also participated in, led, and started alternative, grassroots, Christian communities called house churches and cell groups since 1985 in various contexts such as The Navigators, Campus Crusade for Christ, and in a traditional church. He is currently involved with the HouseChurch.Ca team, which is dedicated to encouraging the emergence of the worldwide house church phenomenon.

He is the author of *The Global House Church Movement* (2004), also published by William Carey Library, which has been translated into several languages. And his recent novel *Entopia: Revolution of the Ants* (2007) is an allegory whose tale of grassroots revolution unfolds inside the hierarchical and ordered world of an anthill.

Inquiries regarding potential translation projects of *Nexus: The World House Church Movement Reader* into non-English languages or requests for printing the English version of the book outside the USA and Canada should be directed to the editor.

ADDRESS
Rad Zdero
P.O. Box 39528
Lakeshore P.O.
Mississauga, ON
Canada   L5G-4S6

WEBSITE: www.housechurch.ca
EMAIL: rzdero@yahoo.ca

Also Published by
William Carey Library

*Biblical, historical, and practical insights to help you start
a house church network no matter where you live!
Guaranteed to challenge your understanding
of what church is really about!*

A primer that's perfect for …

- House churches and cell groups
- Pastors and ministry leaders
- Church planters and missionaries

… and others who believe that 'small groups' are the best
way to reach people and disciple them in Christ!

Product WCL342-1, Paperback, 164 pages

To Order:
*Tel: 1-800-647-7466 (Inside USA)
Tel: 1-706-554-1594 (Outside USA)
Secure Online Ordering at
www.missionbooks.org*

Also by Rad Zdero

In the allegorical tradition of John Bunyan's Pilgrim's Progress,
William Golding's Lord of the Flies, and
George Orwell's Animal Farm.

It is a world of hierarchy and order. And Gazer is but an ordinary
worker ant living in the ancient ant colony of Entgora. Yet, she's
also a dreamer. And she always has been. After a mishap during a
routine work expedition sends her plummeting to the ground,
snapping off one of her antennae, Gazer stumbles across the sacred
but secret mating ritual of a future Queen ant. The night before her
trial for this blasphemy and crime, she has a dream that changes the
course of her life and the lives of all antkind from that day on.
Along with her friends Tenspeed and Digdirt, Gazer finds herself
locked in a whirlwind of political and mystical intrigues, epic ant
wars and civil revolts, gender and class struggles, dreams and secret
societies, all culminating in a bittersweet end.

To Order "ENTOPIA: Revolution of the Ants"
Tel: 1-540-882-9062
Fax: 1-540-882-3719
Secure Online Ordering at
www.capstonefiction.com